Nehru

# Nehru
*A Political Life*

Judith M. Brown

Yale University Press
New Haven and London

For information about this and other Yale University Press publications, please contact:
U.S. Office: sales.press@yale.edu        yalebooks.com
Europe Office: sales@yaleup.co.uk        www.yalebooks.co.uk

Set in Columbus with The Sans by Northern Phototypesetting Co. Ltd, Bolton, UK
Printed in Great Britain by St Edmundsbury Press

Library of Congress Cataloging-in-Publication Data

Brown, Judith M. (Judith Margaret), 1944–
    Nehru: a political life / by Judith M. Brown.
      p. cm.
    ISBN 0-300-09279-2 (alk. paper)
    1. Nehru, Jawaharlal, 1889–1964. 2. Prime ministers—India—
Biography. 3. India—Politics and government—20th century. I. Title.
    DS481.N35B762 2003
    954.04′2′092—dc21                                    2003005807

A catalogue record for this book is available from the British Library

10 9 8 7 6 5 4 3 2 1

Frontispiece: Portrait of Jawaharlal Nehru by Fabian Bachrach, undated © Courtesy of the Nehru Memorial Museum & Library, New Delhi

CONIVGI ET FILIO
DILECTISSIMIS
MIHI
SAEPE ABSENTI
NVMQUAM IMMEMORI
INDIAM PATRIAM NATALEM NONNVMQVAM COLENTI
ET VENIAM ET AMOREM
LARGITIS

# Contents

# Illustrations

## PLATES

Unless otherwise stated all photographs are courtesy of the Nehru Memorial Museum & Library, New Delhi

## FIGURE

## MAPS

## TABLES

# Acknowledgements

A book such as this, which draws on years of earlier research as well as the study of recently available sources, rests on many debts of gratitude. My thanks must first go to those who have enabled me to consult original sources for the life and career of Jawaharlal Nehru. The location of the main sources is listed at the end of the volume but I would in particular wish to thank successive Directors of the Nehru Memorial Museum and Library in New Delhi and their staff, the Librarians of the India Office Library and Records in London, and the Librarian and staff of the Indian Institute Library in Oxford. The major source for this book is, as the reader will see, the huge collection of Jawaharlal Nehru's own papers. Without access to these, and particularly those from the years of Nehru's prime ministership, no substantially new account of his life would have been possible. Permission to use the pre-1947 papers had been kindly given to me by Nehru's heirs three decades ago; but I owe a major debt of gratitude to Mrs Sonia Gandhi for permission granted in 2000 to use the post-1947 papers almost in their entirety. They are quite simply one of the major resources for a historical understanding of the early and critical decades in India's independent history, as well as illuminating the mind and work of a man of singular integrity, vision and energy. I would also wish to thank James Billington, Librarian of the Library of Congress, Washington D.C., and the Director and staff of the Kluge Centre in that library for the privilege of a research visit in circumstances quite exceptionally conducive to scholarly endeavour. The University of Oxford's provision for sabbatical leave gave me the time to research and write, and I would like to thank the Modern History Faculty and the Beit Fund for financial support for research, and my colleagues in Commonwealth History for taking up the extra burdens which sabbatical leave inevitably places on a small group of teachers. Within the faculty Philippa Hicken and Stephanie Jenkins have also been of great assistance in different ways. While in India the staff of the British Council, particularly Sushma Bahl and Chandrika

Grover, have eased my passages to India in countless ways. Dr O. Kejariwal, present Director of the Nehru Memorial Museum and Library, has been quite exceptionally helpful in enabling my most recent research; and I remember with gratitude his predecessor, Professor Ravinder Kumar, with whom I had lengthy and illuminating discussions about Nehru just months before his unexpected death.

Yale University Press has again demonstrated to me its distinction and care as a publishing house; and I thank my editor, Robert Baldock, for encouraging me to write this book in the first place (as he did for my earlier work on Gandhi), for his advice, support and continuing understanding of the processes of writing history. I would also wish to thank Professor Wm. Roger Louis in Texas for being such a learned and supportive transatlantic colleague, and in particular for reading the manuscript. Sir Mark Tully, with his very special knowledge of and relationship to India, over many years, also read the manuscript, and I thank him for his time and encouragement. Both gave valuable advice, and have sustained me in believing that it has been of great importance to write for both an academic and a wider audience, to interpret the life of a man who was crucially influential in the making of a country which is of such significance in the modern world.

The dedication of the book to my husband and son indicates their significance in my life and the many untold ways in which their support and understanding have made it possible for me to pursue my profession and to write this book.

Judith M. Brown
Oxford

# Abbreviations

| | |
|---|---|
| AICC | All-India Congress Committee |
| BBC | British Broadcasting Company |
| CIA | Central Intelligence Agency (US) |
| CID | Criminal Investigation Department |
| CPI | Communist Party of India |
| CUP | Cambridge University Press |
| CWC | Congress Working Committee |
| CSP | Congress Socialist Party |
| *CWMG* | *Collected Works of Mahatma Gandhi* |
| DMK | Dravida Munnetra Kazhagam |
| IAS | Indian Administrative Service |
| ICS | Indian Civil Service |
| INA | Indian National Army |
| IOLR | India Office Library and Records |
| *LCM* | J. Nehru, *Letters to Chief Ministers* |
| MLA | Member of the Legislative Assembly |
| NAI | National Archives of India |
| NATO | North Atlantic Treaty Organisation |
| NEFA | North-East Frontier Agency |
| NMML | Nehru Memorial Museum and Library |
| OUP | Oxford University Press |
| PCC | Provincial Congress Committee |
| RSS | Rashtriya Swayamsevak Sangh |
| RTC | Round Table Conference |
| *SWJN(1)* | *Selected Works of Jawaharlal Nehru,* 1st series |
| *SWJN(2)* | *Selected Works of Jawaharlal Nehru,* 2nd series |
| *SWMN* | *Selected Works of Motilal Nehru* |

| | |
|---|---|
| *TOP* | *Constitutional Relations Between Britain And India. The Transfer of Power, 1942–7* |
| UN | United Nations |
| UP | United Provinces of Agra and Oudh/Uttar Pradesh |

# Glossary

| | |
|---|---|
| ashram | religious community |
| Azad (Kashmir) | the part of Kashmir controlled by Pakistan |
| bania | the third lowest caste grouping or *varna*: colloquially used to mean a trading or business person |
| Bapu | 'little father': affectionate name for M. K. Gandhi |
| charkha | hand spinning-wheel |
| crore | ten million |
| darshan | literally 'view'; viewing a holy man or object in order to gain merit |
| Gita (Bhagavad Gita) | one of the most popular sacred texts of Hinduism |
| Harijan | literally 'children of god'; name given by Gandhi to the Untouchables |
| hartal | strike; stoppage of work |
| -ji | title of respect added on to a name, e.g. Gandhiji, or to a title |
| Khalifah | world-wide leader of Muslims, the Sultan of Turkey |
| khadi | hand-spun cloth |
| Khilafat | movement for the protection of the Khalifah |
| Lok Sabha | lower house of the Indian Parliament in Delhi |
| Mahatma | 'Great Soul': honorific title for M. K. Gandhi |
| Maulana | title for Muslim learned man |
| Moulvi | title for Muslim learned man |
| Moharram | Muslim period of fasting and public mourning |
| panchayat | originally a caste or village council (from *panch*, Hindi for five); later used for officially constituted organs of local government |
| panchayati raj | 'rule by panchayats'; name given to new form of local government in the 1950s |
| Panchsheel | 'five principles' of peaceful coexistence agreed between India and China in 1954 |

| | |
|---|---|
| purdah | literally a curtain; used to mean the custom of veiling and secluding women |
| purdanashin | woman who is in purdah |
| raj/the raj | 'rule'; often used to denote British imperial rule |
| Rajya Sabha | upper house of the Indian Parliament in Delhi |
| Ram Rajya | the rule of Ram ( a Hindu god) |
| Rashtrapati | head of state |
| sanyasi | Hindu holy man; one who has retired from ordinary life to pursue religion |
| satyagraha | truth force; name used by Gandhi for non-violent civil disobedience |
| satyagrahi | one who practises satyagraha |
| Swami | respectful title for Hindu considered to be a holy person |
| swaraj | self-rule; home rule; independence |
| swadeshi | belonging to one's own country |
| tonga | light two-wheeled, horse-drawn carriage, often plying for hire |
| Talukdar | large landholder, particularly in UP |
| zamindar | landholder, often with a considerable holding |
| zamindari | land held by a *zamindar* |

# Introduction

Jawaharlal Nehru was one of Asia's most notable and important public figures in the twentieth century. His was a long life. He was born in 1889 when Queen Victoria was Empress of India, and died in 1964 after serving for nearly two decades as first Prime Minister of independent India. By this time Victoria's great great grand-daughter was on the British throne and head of a new multinational Commonwealth which included India, now a republic, alongside a growing number of nation states which had once been part of the British empire. Like many of his generation he saw dramatic and interlocking changes in domestic and international politics – two world wars, the Russian and Chinese revolutions, the emergence of the USA as a world power, the Cold War and the gradual decline of Britain. From his Indian perspective, one of the most significant changes was the erosion of the British and other western empires, generating a rapid phase of decolonisation and the emergence of newly independent states, including his own. He also witnessed major technological changes, which were to transform the lives and attitudes of multitudes of ordinary people. The coming of radio, film and rapid road and air travel, for example, was to link the world more intimately and to change a whole range of human activities and aspirations. New technologies of industrial and agricultural production began to transform economies and societies once fashioned by subsistence agriculture. Medical knowledge and techniques were to lessen the perils of disease, child-bearing and infancy, enabling rapid growth in population in countries such as India, where it had been limited by heavy burdens of sickness, want and mortality.

Most of Nehru's own life was dominated by politics. His was, in a profound sense, a political life. He first found a meaningful career in the politics of nationalism, under the patronage and guidance of Mahatma Gandhi. Building on this foundation, he became a major political leader in his own right in the intricate business of decolonisation following the Second World War; and in the final and most influential phase of his career he was India's first Prime Minister for nearly two decades, from independence in 1947 until his death. It was almost at the end of his life, in September 1962, that I was privileged to see him. As a teenager I was returning to England to study as an undergraduate at Cambridge, and was told that I should check in early for the flight. It transpired that the Prime Minister himself was travelling on the same scheduled Air-India flight to a Commonwealth Prime Ministers' meeting in London. I saw at first hand something of the awe and affection in which he was held by ordinary people, and I sensed I was seeing a person of profound historical significance as I watched from the back of the crowd in the airport the diminutive figure bidding a temporary farewell to his country. Now I have found myself studying his life, reading the huge quantity of letters, notes and speeches he wrote, as well as his major books, and seeking to interpret this man and his life to readers who will probably not remember him, and who will almost certainly never have seen him except through the medium of historical photographs or newsreels.

There have, of course, been many works on Nehru, including biographies and studies of particular aspects of his life and work.[1] However, some forty years after his death the time is ripe for a re-evaluation of his life in the light of fresh insights into Indian history and new trends in the writing of it, and because Nehru's place in India's domestic history is being questioned in quite different ways which would have been impossible while he was still the object of considerable and often uncritical adulation. The best biographical study still remains the three-volume work by the late Professor S. Gopal, published between 1973 and 1984. It drew on privileged access to Nehru's personal archive, and was authoritative in terms of its evidence as no other study could have been. However, it adopted a largely narrative rather than an analytical approach to the examination of the life; and its very size limited its audience. Later biographies, such as that by the prominent historian of India, Professor Stanley Wolpert, were hampered by the lack of access to the Nehru papers for the period after 1947, except those which had been published, and in consequence his book was primarily an account of the nationalist years, with only approximately sixty pages out of nearly five hundred being devoted to Nehru's years as Prime Minister. I am therefore profoundly grateful to Nehru's heirs, and Mrs Sonia Gandhi in particular, for having permitted me to work on the crucial papers for the years of the prime ministership, thus building on work done earlier on the papers of the younger Jawaharlal and his father, Motilal. With access to such a resource, as well as to other important material recently collected by the Nehru Memorial Museum and Library, it has been possible to examine Nehru's life afresh.

My approach is also somewhat different from other accounts of Nehru's life. In the first place, I hope to portray him in a broader context, as a man who belonged to a crucial generation in the history of Asia, and whose life thus illuminates the lives of many of his contemporaries. It shows the diversity and complexity of the major issues which confronted them in a time of profound and unusually rapid transition. Some of these issues were at root intellectual, though they had strong emotional connotations, and eventually fed into new forms of politics. How were Nehru and his contemporaries to understand the nature and meaning of the encounter between Asians, particularly those who like Indians were colonial subjects, and western people with their assumptions of superiority and modernity? Linked to this were important questions of culture and an appropriate sense of one's own identity. To what extent should Asians adopt the outward trappings of western public life and domesticity? More profoundly, should they patronise western educational institutions in Europe and at home, and should they internalise the values taught in them? What significance were they to give to their own cultural and religious traditions; and if necessary how and on what authority were they to reform them so that they could flourish and provide meaning in a changing environment? By the early twentieth century political issues increasingly subsumed many of these other areas of disquiet and questioning. Reflective and articulate contemporaries of Nehru were increasingly sceptical, as he was, of the right of representatives of western economic and political powers to influence even where they did not rule local societies and polities. New forms of nationalism began to probe the vulnerabilities of colonial regimes, to experiment with more radical forms of opposition, and to wrestle with the problems faced by the need to generate wider support for the demands and campaigns of nationalist politicians.

In time, with the departure of colonial rulers, hastened by the Second World War, this generation had to transform themselves into rulers and in turn to manage the polities they had inherited or created; they had to reflect on the meaning of the nation as a working identity; and they had to work with or transform existing modes of governance. This last had a profound impact on their capacity to engage with issues of major social and economic change. Most aspirant leaders of Asian nation states had made explicit promises of change in the lives of ordinary people as they challenged their colonial rulers. Everywhere there were implicit expecta-tions of relief from poverty and hunger, and of the provision by government of medical care, education and a rising standard of life. How could new governments deal with these problems without new administrative tools and techniques and new resources? The answers to such questions lay not only in domestic policies and politics, but in the interplay of states in a post-colonial world, and in partic-ular in the economic relations between them. Thus a further and critical aspect of the challenges to Nehru's generation when it came to power was the nature of international relations and the most appropriate foreign policy for safeguarding a new independence while also underpinning the economic reality of freedom in the lives of ordinary people who were becoming increasingly articulate and influen-tial members of their national polities.

This study of Nehru is not only designed to enable the reader to see through his life many of the issues facing his generation, and many of the influences at work in a historical period of rapid and momentous change. It also uses his life as a window into Indian politics and shows how his work and concerns, his ambitions and failures can help the analysis of some of the deeper forces operating within the Indian polity. Professional historians are properly sceptical of works on individuals which portray them as great shakers and movers of history. Most significant historical changes and developments are the result of long-term trends and influences rather than of individual ambitions and interventions. But at particular historical junctures individuals can be of considerable importance, because of their skills, their particular role in a political system, or at times through sheer chance. (Here Nehru's own longevity is an example, when compared with the death soon after independence of M. A. Jinnah in Pakistan, and its implications for the instability of Pakistan's political system as compared with India's.) Moreover, the way prominent individuals deal with major problems – or fail to deal with them – provides valuable historical insight not only into their own lives but also into their deeper and broader historical setting.

Consequently this study is structured in five major sections, each one of which deals with a distinctive phase in Nehru's life, which also coincides with a particular phase in the development of India's polity and politics. It begins with Nehru's formative years as he was brought up and educated under, and in a sense in cooperation with, the British raj, which then seemed invincible and immovable. At this point he imbibed and interiorised many of the values which were to mark him out for the rest of his life. It proceeds to his years of political apprenticeship under the leadership of Gandhi, when the Mahatma was experimenting with radical non-violent modes of mass opposition to the British raj; and then to the period when Nehru emerged as a major political leader in the tragic period of British withdrawal from the subcontinent, when nationalists found their goal of independence scarred by the partition of the subcontinent into India and Pakistan, the mass migrations and violence which accompanied it, and the assassination of Gandhi. Drawing on all his internal resources to confront these national and personal catastrophes, Nehru as Prime Minister continued the work of founding the new nation, providing it with a new republican constitution, redirecting its economy, and attempting to set the norms and conventions of a new secular and democratic politics. This is the substance of the penultimate section. The final section analyses the frustration of Nehru's vision of a new India and a new world order based on non-alignment and peaceful coexistence. It places the frustration of so much he had dreamed of and worked for in the context of deep-rooted aspects of India's society and politics, as well as relating it to the nature of the role Nehru had carved out for himself. It shows how, as he recognised many of the barriers to change, he seems to have drawn fresh inspiration from the insights of his political mentor, Gandhi, whose vision he had once decried as anti-modern and anti-scientific.

The focus of this book is primarily on Nehru's political life. However, the historian who seeks to understand the public man must also try to discern and empathise with some of the personal dimensions of his life, as the two are intertwined. For this task there are ample sources in Nehru's case, although his unpublished letters to family members and a few intimate friends remain closed. Nehru was an articulate observer of himself as well as of the political scene; and he divulged much about himself, if only in asides, in correspondence with a few trusted colleagues, friends and his daughter, as well as in the autobiography covering his earlier life. Moreover, observers both Indian and foreign were often drawn powerfully to him and did not hesitate to comment on his personality in their assessments of him.[2] Nehru's political career was rooted in a vision of a new India, which in turn gave him the intellectual and personal energy and commitment essential for such a long and demanding public life. Appreciating the origins and power of this vision is essential for an understanding of the man and his remarkable stamina often in the face of hardship, imprisonment, loneliness and frustration.

Similarly the personal relationships which helped to create and sustain Nehru, particularly in his earlier life, are of profound importance. His father, Motilal, and his great mentor, Gandhi, in different ways helped to create the mature man who was to be India's first Prime Minister and one of the principal architects of its political system and economy. In the later years the comparative personal isolation of the widowed Nehru was also to be important, even if in a more negative way, in the prime ministerial style and role he fashioned for himself, and in his inability to take time out – to give himself space to think about large issues – except when forced to by exhaustion. Moreover, his personal understanding of himself in relation to his country, his own definition of his role, was fundamental to his political life. It enabled him to make the transition from radical opponent of colonial rule to leadership of a new, mass democracy; and to sustain his resolve in the face of opposition and the ebbing of his physical strength as he aged.

It is my hope that this work is also timely in the sense that it will contribute to a wider understanding of India at a time when the subcontinent is undergoing changes and experiences of world significance. The final decade of the twentieth century tragically witnessed the assassination of Rajiv Gandhi, the last Prime Minister in the direct line of the so-called Nehru 'dynasty', as well as the emergence of an overtly Hindu form of Indian nationalism, and the dismantling of the economic system which originated under Nehru. It is therefore all the more important to examine the prime ministerial role he created, and the foundations of India's national polity which he helped to put into place. Further, India and her subcontinental neighbours are, at the start of the twenty-first century, of manifest international importance. India's growing population, its huge economic potential and its role as an exporter of people have had and are having a global impact;

while its strategic position as a nuclear power, in a region whose fragile polities have generated international instabilities on a frightening scale, makes its recent history profoundly important, for a public far wider than specialists and students of the subcontinent.

## Part 1

# An Imperial Heritage, 1889–1920

# Chapter 1

# India and the British Raj: Opportunity and Challenge

The foreign traveller to India at the turn of the twenty-first century encounters a world which is immediately recognisable, and in many respects similar to that in many other modern countries. There are bustling cities, highly educated citizens, modern communications and transport, large industries, familiar lifestyles and patterns of leisure. Only in rural areas does it become apparent that the new and cosmopolitan is juxtaposed with far older economic and cultural patterns and pre-existing modes of authority, with old and new interacting with each other.

By contrast, in the late nineteenth century, when Jawaharlal Nehru was born, India stood in a very different political and economic relationship with the wider world, and most of those who journeyed in either direction between the subcontinent and the countries of Europe or America found the other strange and confusing. British people, for all their long connection with India, going back to the seventeenth century, still struggled to make sense of the society they found in India. They saw in it both similarities with earlier phases of Europe's own history, and what they deemed to be 'essential' qualities which marked India out as different and often irrational by their own standards. Indians who made the westward journey were equally perplexed by the way of life and often disapproving of the values they encountered in the imperial metropolis. M. K. Gandhi (later 'Mahatma'), twenty years Nehru's senior, took refuge in his cabin on the voyage to Britain, uneasy with English food and table manners, and spent months adjusting to life as a law student in late nineteenth-century London. As he later remembered, 'Everything was strange – the people, their ways, and even their dwellings. I was a complete novice in the matter of English etiquette . . .' Moreover, what vegetarian food he could find was 'tasteless and insipid'.[1] A brief introduction to the India into which Nehru was born is thus essential for an understanding of his life and of the magnitude of the journey he was to travel in the seven decades of his life, as well as for an appreciation of the range and grandeur of his vision of a new India in the making.

## INDIA UNDER THE RAJ

The fundamental aspect of life on the subcontinent, which no one could ignore, was that India was part of Britain's worldwide and apparently invincible empire. Although British traders, soldiers and administrators had effectively controlled the country from the early nineteenth century, it was not until 1858, in response to the debacle of the Indian 'Mutiny' the previous year, that India was formally taken under Crown control. From then onwards the monarch's representative, the Viceroy, was the pinnacle of an increasingly regular and bureaucratic system of government in India itself, while in London a Secretary of State for India, always a cabinet member, was ultimately responsible to Parliament for Indian policy and affairs. The British recognised publicly that they had responsibilities to their Queen's Indian subjects – responsibilities of civil peace, good governance, law, and a modicum of welfare and education. Apart from debates on Indian issues and policies, Parliament also received official annual reports on Indian administration and public welfare somewhat quaintly called statements 'exhibiting the moral and material progress and condition of India'. But the British priority, even if it was seldom articulated, was to ensure that India performed major functions within Britain's worldwide imperial system and buttressed its world supremacy.

India was crucial to Britain and its world standing in a number of ways. Most obviously, the Indian Army, officered by expatriates, was an imperial fighting force which could be used across the world in pursuit of British interests at the expense of the Indian taxpayer. It was the single largest item of government expenditure, often running at well over 30 per cent of total, and followed by the expenses of revenue collection. It was deployed widely in the service of empire, from China, India itself, Persia, Africa, to the Middle East and the Western front in the First World War. India was also of considerable financial significance to Britain. It was Britain's principal bilateral trading partner, taking manufactured goods in return for raw materials, and exports to countries where Britain had trading deficits, thus helping to balance Britain's worldwide trading books. India was a major receiver of British investment, absorbing nearly £300 million of capital raised on the London stock market between 1865 and 1914, thus coming second only to Canada as a place for investment within the empire. Moreover, the management of Indian public finance also helped to sustain sterling as the world's major currency.

Further, for a significant and articulate group of British people India was a place for interesting and well-paid careers in the army, the Indian Civil Service, the police and other civilian services such as forestry, medicine and education. All the major churches in Britain also sent missionaries to the subcontinent; and the Indian taxpayer supported an Anglican ecclesiastical establishment. Few British people made India their permanent home. Apart from those who made their money in tea and coffee plantations, most soldiers, civil servants, teachers and missionaries were essentially temporary migrants, returning to Britain in retirement. Thus there was no displacement of an existing population as had occurred in Spanish America or in British colonies of settlement, and none of the settler mentality or vested interest which was to embitter imperial politics in parts of Africa. Although many rural Indians lived for years without ever seeing a European face, none could remain untouched by the strength of the raj, as it bore down on India through land settlement, taxation, civil administration, criminal and civil law, and the spread of cultural institutions ranging from the railway and the post office to the school and college.

Many British observers tended to create an image of Indian society from what is now perceived as an Orientalist perspective, emphasising what they saw as its essential differences from western societies, particularly the significance of religion, caste as a social institution, and attachment to land and the ancestral village. It seemed in their terminology backward, traditional and static. Later historians have disputed much of this imperial image of India, and shown how it not only fed imperial assumptions of superiority and authority, but at times influenced the ways Indians saw themselves and related to themselves and the raj. Nonetheless, Indian society in the late nineteenth century was very different from British society at the time, not least because of the small size of the British Isles and the impress of the industrial revolution on its peoples over nearly a century. India was after all a subcontinent in its own right, the size of Europe without Russia, and it took several days to travel by train from the north-western frontier down to the southern tip of Cape Cormorin, or from Bombay on the western coast to Calcutta on the east. Moreover, its population was vast by the standards of Britain or any other European country: a census taken two years after Nehru was born counted nearly 280 million Indians. Population was probably growing slowly but reasonably steadily, but it was not until the mid-twentieth century that the growth took off to precipitate the demographic challenge which confronted Nehru and his successors. Disease, poverty and famine still took a heavy toll, and in the first decade of Nehru's own childhood life expectancy for all Indians at birth was only just over twenty years. The vast majority lived and worked in the countryside. In 1891 there were only 1,999 towns (an urban area being one with a population of at least 5,000); and the urban population was 26.7 million, or 9.4 per cent of the total population.[2]

It is somewhat misleading to talk about Indian 'society', for there were many regional societies, each moulded by geography, demography, economic resources, language, religion and local culture. Despite these differences there were central and common features. Almost everywhere land was crucial to the shape of local society; access to land determined wealth, authority and to some extent status. The actual distribution of land varied from region to region, as a result of patterns pre-

*1. India under British rule: early twentieth century*

dating British rule, as well as of changing British policies of what was called land settlement, the fixing of rights in land in return for payment of land revenue, the major source of government income well into the twentieth century. In a few areas (including parts of Nehru's home region, the United Provinces of Agra and Oudh) there were large landowners, buttressed by British political support as a measure of local control; but in many others there was a substantial and independent peasantry, both owning and renting land. Everywhere rural society was complex and hierarchical, marked by a patchwork of rights and obligations, between Indians and each other and Indians and the state. However, there were disturbing trends, including the subdivision of land according to inheritance rules which made many

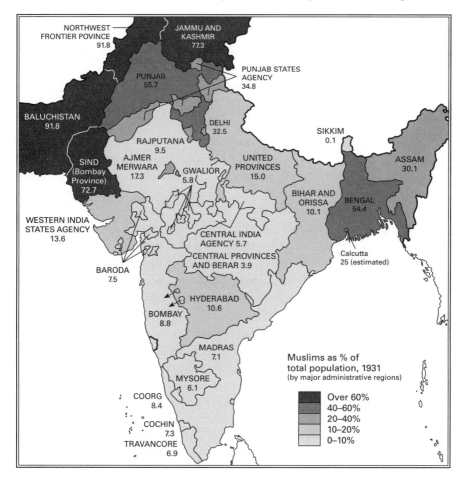

*2. Distribution of Muslims in pre-Partition India, c. 1931.* J. E. Schwartzberg (ed.), *A Historical Atlas of South Asia*, University of Chicago Press, Chicago and London, 1978, p. 94

plots too small for efficient agricultural use; high revenue demands which could lead to land loss; and the growth of a body of the rural poor, who had no resources except their family labour.

In every region there were at least some towns, many of them having existed for a long time. They performed vital political and socio-economic functions, as places of administration, education and religious devotion and as trading marts and sites of non-agricultural production. Nehru's home town, Allahabad, on the River Ganges, was an administrative and trading centre, a site of Hindu religious devotion, and the home of one of India's earliest modern universities, created in 1887 out of a college founded a decade earlier with the financial support of wealthy locals – landowners, lawyers and bankers. At the time of his birth the town's population was probably around 150,000 – a significant size but nowhere near that of the great coastal trading cities of Bombay, Calcutta and Madras.[3] Such urban worlds were deeply embedded in their local environment, sustaining strong links with the surrounding rural society through networks of kinship, patronage, provision of food and other raw materials, and trade.

Regional societies were also structured round and to an extent segmented by a number of social and cultural identities. Religion was one. Although Hindus were in a majority across the subcontinent, in some areas there were substantial Muslim populations, either just forming a majority, as in Bengal and Punjab, or constituting a significant and influential local minority, as in the United Provinces, or UP as it was commonly known. There were other, smaller religious minorities contributing to the subcontinent's religiously plural society, such as Christians, Sikhs and Parsis. For much of the time members of these religious groups lived in harmony alongside each other; they worked together, and at times worshipped in each other's holy places. But they tended socially to interact closely only with co-religionists, and in particular marriages were arranged within the community, thus forming kinship networks bounded by religion, and to an extent differentiated by cultural patterns. Within Hindu society caste was a particular type of social segmentation. The British tended to see caste as fundamental to Hindu society, immutably ranked in ritual order with Brahmins securely at the apex and those who were ritually unclean as Untouchables at the bottom. Such a view was implicit in the decennial censuses which in the late nineteenth century enumerated and ranked caste groups, and in the writings of British ethnographers, who were often also members of the Indian Civil Service. Modern scholarship has, by contrast, shown how caste has changed considerably over time, how the significance of ritual identity has altered in time and place, how castes have risen and fallen ritually in local societies, how new caste groupings have emerged in particular economic and cultural settings, and how ritual status was often no key to local economic power. Caste is thus no longer seen as an unchanging and fundamental organising principle of Hindu society, the key to social position and economic role.[4] Yet local caste kinship networks reinforced by marriage arranged within the caste were significant elements in regional societies and their hierarchies, and they could not be ignored, either by imperial governments or aspirant Indian politicians.

Despite imperial assumptions that Indian society was traditional and static, it had clearly provided for a good deal of movement and flexibility, both physically and in terms of group if not individual status. Before the nineteenth century there had been literally space for movement; the ratio of people to land was low and individuals and groups could move to new places to escape hardship or hostility. This gradually ceased to be the case as population grew. Moreover, the imperial rulers disliked and feared wandering groups who evaded taxation and seemed likely to generate disorder. Agriculturalists were increasingly settled by revenue obligations, and legislation defined many traditionally nomadic groups as criminal castes and tribes, to be restrained and reformed into cultivators. Nonetheless, socio-economic changes generated new forms of movement. Not only did people travel on pilgrimages or for trade, as they had done for centuries. Some rural people began to migrate to cities where there were employment opportunities, such as Bombay with its burgeoning textile industry and its opportunities for work in the mills. Increasingly they became permanent urban residents, bringing up their children as second generation urban men and women. Men newly educated in English began to take service with the new raj and to travel in its service, taking their close families with them. This was the origin of the Bengali communities in Punjab and UP, for example. Nehru's own family moved from Delhi to neigh-bouring UP, fleeing the disasters of 1857. Despite these opportunities the vast majority of Indians lived out their lives in or near the place where they had been born. Even at the start of the twentieth century only 3.3 per cent of Indians were counted in the census as living outside the province of their birth.

Of incalculable significance for Nehru and his generation was the impact of new technologies of communication, which were to change how Indians thought of themselves and how they related to each other and their rulers. The first rail-ways were built in the 1850s, and by the end of the century government and private enterprise had together built 25,000 miles of track. This combined with the laying of metalled roads began to draw India into a new political, social and economic unity. So, too, did the development of the telegraph and postal services. In the year of Nehru's birth there were 35,224 miles of telegraph line and cable and it was officially calculated that over 3 million telegrams were sent in that year. Post offices and pillar boxes were being built at a considerable rate and the number of letters, newspapers and parcels passing through the post office was about 305 million, 6.3 per cent up on the previous year.[5]

Simultaneously the technologies of cheap printing generated a growing output of English and vernacular publications, serving the intellectual needs of a growing reading public. They took the form of newspapers, journals, pamphlets, books. In 1889–90, for example, in Bengal alone there were thirty English papers and seventy-four vernacular newspapers. Nehru's home province saw a significant rise in publications in English, Urdu, Hindi and Arabic, and over a hundred newspa-pers were circulating locally:[6] and this was an area with lower literacy than Bengal, with a reputation for being far more backward in the development of a public sphere. Of course, by the standards of mass literacy at the end of the twentieth century the percentage of literates was low. At the start of the twentieth century only about 6 per cent of Indian men were literate, and far fewer could read English. Women's literacy was even lower. The government, nonetheless, realised that print was the medium for the spread of new ideas and identities. It required the registration of printing presses, newspapers and all published material, and did not hesitate to ban anything which could be construed as seditious. But officials were painfully aware that, for all the apparent might of the raj, print had taken off, even in the smallest market towns, and was instrumental in generating new attitudes and identities which they could not control. What was possibly of the most profound significance for the future of India, and certainly for the young Nehru's future, was the fact that English was becoming a common language across all the regions of India. No longer could ideas be contained within one language group, and at least among those elite groups with access to English education the idea of India as a shared public realm was taking a new and lively shape.

The technology of communications between India and the rest of the world also changed in the late nineteenth century. In particular the international telegraph and the opening of the Suez Canal in 1869 brought India and Britain closer to each other. This meant that international news could travel faster. It also enabled a few Indians who could afford it to travel to Britain and to send their sons there for education and further training. It also meant that more British people could travel to India easily and quickly, as visitors to friends and family, as journalists and tourists, as well as those bound for work. As a result a distinctive European society emerged as another element in the complex social formations of the subcontinent. The European presence was always tiny in terms of absolute numbers. Early in the twentieth century there were only about 157,000 Europeans in that part of India directly ruled by the British. Of these nearly a third were women. They developed a lifestyle which marked them out from Indian society, living in their own areas within towns, in distinctive bungalows with large gardens and protective walls. They socialised together in their houses, theatres and clubs, and took their holidays either at home in Europe or in hill stations built as cool retreats where they could temporarily forget the rigours of imperial service.

Imperial society was, like many migrant societies, old-fashioned compared with the society at home: it was rigidly upper middle class, hierarchical, and deeply conscious of the racial boundary which separated it from the rest of India. Social relations between Europeans and Indians were either non-existent or often fraught with misunderstanding, as the novelist E. M. Forster brilliantly portrayed in the early twentieth century. Nonetheless, European social conventions, familial relationships and patterns of domestic consumption provided a standard of modernity to which educated Indians had to respond – with subtle variations and combinations of acceptance and rejection and modification. Moreover, the racism, which was at times overt but never far beneath the surface, was deeply hurtful to Indians proud of their country and culture, particularly when they were equal in educational and economic status to the representatives of the ruling race. These problems of racial encounter were to generate powerful if unquantifiable aspects of the ideology and politics of nationalism, clearly visible in the lives of men and women who were contemporaries of Gandhi and Nehru.

The nature of the Indian economy, and the way the British influenced it and tied it to British interests, was another important theme in Indian critiques of colonialism. Indians accused Britain of draining wealth from India in the form of taxation and the cost of military and civil aspects of government; of 'de-industrialising' her economy, and failing to tackle poverty and famine. This is a complex subject, which has subsequently generated intense academic discussion, particularly in the light of independent India's subsequent economic problems and policies.[7] It is also a subject dogged by such questions as 'What if the British had not ruled India?' Nevertheless, some understanding of Indian economic life is essential because it provides the context for much of Nehru's thinking about public affairs and the British connection, and moulded the environment in which he and his contemporaries sought to construct a powerful nationalist opposition to the raj.

What is patent is that the British assumed that India would undergird Britain's economy and worldwide imperial power – hence the patterns of administration and defence developed in the nineteenth century at the expense of the Indian taxpayer. Moreover, the British, like virtually every government at the time including their own at home, assumed that the role of governments was very limited in relation to economic management. They did not have the economic tools and understandings to engage in development in the modern sense; and their image of India and its society encouraged them to look for explanations of economic ills in India's own climate and geography and her peoples' socioeconomic attitudes. Nonetheless, the very presence of the British rulers and the growing linkages between India and a world economy profoundly changed India's economy. This is not to suggest that India had earlier been an isolated, subsistence economy. Modern scholarship has suggested that there were important trading networks within India itself in earlier centuries, commercial links by sea with the Indian Ocean world from the Middle East to South East Asia, and domestic centres of large-scale if not industrial production. Moreover, to sustain this complex economic network there had emerged financial networks of banking and credit. Indeed, it was because of India's financial and economic sophistication that the earlier British traders of the East India Company were able to lodge themselves in the economic life of the subcontinent and eventually to finance much of their conquest. But the emergence of the British as rulers disrupted old centres of production and earlier commercial networks, and linked the Indian economy to the world in new ways, which in turn made India vulnerable to shifts in world prices as it increasingly became an exporter of raw materials.

At the end of the nineteenth century the Indian economy was still essentially rural and agricultural, as demographic figures have already suggested. Most workers were involved in agricultural pursuits, and agriculture produced around 70 per cent of the national income. Even by 1911 about three-quarters of the work-force was engaged in agriculture of various kinds, while just over 12 per cent were involved in industry, and 13 per cent in trade, commerce and other services.[8] But India's was not primarily a subsistence agriculture. Although many families still grew crops for their own consumption, much agricultural produce was destined for the market – either the domestic market of the local town or further afield, or for consumers outside India. The growing road and rail networks were in part designed to assist in transporting raw materials to their markets or to ports. In the final decades of the nineteenth century India was exporting to Britain alone £30,000,000 worth of raw goods annually, including cotton, indigo, rice, linseed and flax, jute, hides and tea. What effect this had on domestic consumption is debated. Although commercial crops certainly displaced basic food crops in some areas, it seems that agricultural production was probably continuing to meet the food requirements of the slowly rising population, except in the devastating years when famine still swept particular areas. Although famine was virtually an afflic-tion of the past by the early twentieth century, it was rapidly becoming clear after the First World War that India's sluggish agricultural sector could no longer sustain a rising population.

Just as Indian agriculture was only dynamic in certain areas at certain times, so the emergence of modern industry on the subcontinent was contained in a rela-tively small number of areas, particularly in Bombay Presidency and in Calcutta and its environs. The major push to modern industrialisation and its diversification and spread throughout the subcontinent only occurred in the twentieth century. At the time of Nehru's birth an initial development of large-scale factory enterprise was developing in three industries – jute, cotton and iron and steel. Cotton was the major product in western India, and in the Bombay area a major mill industry developed, owned by a cosmopolitan group including Indians and Europeans. By contrast, in eastern India industry was largely controlled by expatriates, who used the form of Managing Agency Houses as their business organisations, and through them spread their interests widely through the modern economy.[9] In the first decade of the twentieth century there were around 200 cotton mills in India, employing some 200,000 workers. Jute mills were rising to around 50 in number, employing between 150,000 and 200,000 people. Nonetheless, industry still only accounted for around 12 per cent of the work force and about 20 per cent of national income.

These figures suggest not only that many more Indians were living and working in new industrial settings, with implications for their expectations as well as lifestyles; but that opportunities were available for Indians to break free of a social and economic order tied to access to land. The labourers at the base of the new industrial order tended to be those who had migrated to relatively nearby urban areas as an escape from poverty and landlessness. In 1911, of the millhands employed in the Bombay cotton mills, only just under 10 per cent had been born in the city, while just over 63 per cent came from places between one and two hundred miles from the city.[10] At the level of ownership, despite the dominance of expatriates in the industry of eastern India, Indians with capital, credit and the right social networks could begin to embark on new economic ventures which were to be the foundations of the industrial dynasties of twentieth-century India. Many of these were already established in existing forms of commerce and seized on new opportunities in a strategy of modernization and diversification. One such was G. D. Birla, a member of the long-established Marwari commercial and kinship network, whose financial success was to bring him close to the nationalist movement, and to Gandhi and to Nehru himself.

The impress of the imperial rulers was most apparent on India's polity. As the East India Company transformed itself from a trading enterprise into a primarily political operation in the late eighteenth and early nineteenth centuries, so it demolished the regional polities which had grown up to replace the failing authority of the once-mighty Mughal empire based on Delhi. By the time India was taken under Crown control just decades before Nehru was born, government had become regularised and increasingly bureaucratised, and Indians had been excluded from the highest echelons of the army, police and civilian services. This was now quite clearly foreign dominion: and moreover, India was drawn together politically and administratively as never before.

After the 1857 Mutiny about one-third of the subcontinent remained under the rule of Indian princes. They were subordinate to the Crown and forced to accept at court a representative of that authority from the Indian Political Service, to watch, advise, and at times warn on matters of government and behaviour. The remaining areas of India were directly administered through a bureaucratic system which relied on the Indian Civil Service (ICS); from the middle of the century it was recruited by competitive examination, which virtually excluded Indians and made India an attractive source of careers for the British professional classes. Under the sovereign's representative the country was divided geographically into provinces (some the size of a small European country), each governed in roughly similar ways under a Governor or Lieutenant-Governor at the head of the province's cadre of ICS men. The Viceroy himself and the governors of the three senior provinces or Presidencies (Bengal, Bombay and Madras) were political appointments from Britain; but the other governors rose from the ICS ranks. It was a system which gave this administrative elite very considerable power and initiative in the districts which made up the provinces, though by the twentieth century district officers were complaining about excessive paperwork and control from provincial capitals. Those who through seniority or secondment manned the secretariats in the provincial and all-India capitals to a large extent determined policy towards Indian problems, through their control of information and their positions in the decision-making structures.

The ICS provided a secure salary and a reasonable pension on retirement to Britain. For those at the top of the service the financial rewards were very considerable. As late as the mid-1930s the Viceroy was paid more than the President of the USA, and the Governor of UP received almost twice the salary of the Governor of New York State or of a British cabinet minister. The Chief Secretary to the Government of Bihar received only slightly less than the Secretary to the Treasury in London.[11] Many of those who went into the service, often following in relatives' footsteps over several generations, had a genuine commitment to India and its peoples; but their paternalist attitudes, their comparatively affluent lifestyle, their cost to the Indian taxpayer and their foreignness all combined to alienate them from many of those of Nehru's generation.

Yet the number of expatriates involved in government in one way or other was always tiny compared with the Indian population and the size of the subcontinent. The ICS itself was never more than about 1,100 people, and at any one time some of them were on furlough or sick leave. The British therefore needed the cooperation of Indians to fill the lower ranks of government. Beneath the expatriate elites in the army, police and civil service were a multitude of Indians who were in the paid employment of the raj – the clerks and record-keepers who manned the civil offices, the rank and file of the police service, and the thousands of sepoys who made up the Indian Army. However, the events of 1857 shook the raj to its core. Although the military revolt and various simultaneous civil rebellions which made up the Mutiny were confined to a relatively small part of the north of India, the fact that British rule could unravel so quickly once the loyalty of paid servants of the government and the acquiescence of much of the populace were compromised made the British much more sensitive to Indian opinion. The events persuaded them to take new measures to listen to that opinion and to elicit the loyalty of those whom they deemed to be significant in local society.

Securing the remaining Indian princes in their territories and encouraging their loyalty to the person of the sovereign were of course aspects of this strategy. It replaced the growing absorption of princely areas under direct British control which had been the pattern in the first half of the nineteenth century. (Oudh, for example, in the United Provinces of Agra and Oudh, had been a sovereign territory in the lifetime of Nehru's grandfather.) The strategy also gave rise to some of the most grandiose of British attempts to align themselves to what they presumed to be a traditional India, and to demonstrate their raj in terms of elaborate and largely confected ceremonial.[12]

At a lowlier level in India's regional societies the British also followed a policy of binding to themselves people they thought to be natural leaders of society, those who could secure for the foreign rulers the loyalty of their clients and followers. These tended to be the larger landowners and others with established local authority and influence. They were offered posts as honorary magistrates, given honours at the sovereign's birthday and at new year, and given privileged access to the district officer. One of the clearest examples of this strategy of eliciting local collaboration from those who were considered local notables was in Nehru's home province. Here in Oudh a motley group known as Talukdars, whom the British had tried to dislodge from rural influence just before 1857 in favour of smaller peasant farmers, had turned out to be crucial in the swing of local opinion during the turmoil of the rebellion. In 1859 the British decided to put their trust in a local alliance with them, and re-established them in their estates. But they did more than that. Attempting to turn them into reliable landed gentry, they enforced on them rules of primogeniture, and assisted them when their estates fell into financial trouble. But by the early twentieth century it was becoming clear that this imperial strategy of collaboration was running into serious trouble and threatening to generate a popular and disturbing backlash against the raj as relations between these landlords and their tenants deteriorated. Nehru was to become one of the politicians whose careers flourished as he championed the cause of the tenants of this reinvented gentry group.[13]

The British as imperial rulers in India had always been pragmatic, and they had increasing need to be so as Indian society and public opinion began to change in the later nineteenth century, and as they become acutely aware of the financial fragility of their regime. Accordingly they began to extend their strategies of listening to notables and giving them a place in the imperial structure of governance, by incorporating a wider range of those they called native gentlemen. These were not solely those whose status rested on land or control of urban wealth. Western-style education in the English language developed from the early years of the century as a result of initiatives by government itself, by prominent Indians, and by Christian missionaries. By the last quarter of the century this process had produced a growing group of well-educated Indians, mostly from social groups with long traditions of administrative service, who were finding careers in the law, medicine, education and journalism. The Nehrus themselves were a prime example of this social trend. Such people had high aspirations for their families and for their country, and were anxious to make their mark in the changing polity. Not only were they essential for the functioning of the modern professions on the subcontinent. These were the authors and readers of the burgeoning English and vernacular publications which the British watched with suspicion; these were the people who could and did generate a new sort of public opinion in their provinces and across India by virtue of their command of English on matters as wide-ranging as literature, economics, religion, social reform and politics.

Despite their concerns that the English-educated were upstarts, not traditional leaders of men, policy-makers recognised they had need of them as allies and collaborators. They thus embarked slowly on processes of establishing consultative mechanisms which were eventually to change the nature of the Indian polity. This happened at various levels within the imperial state from the 1860s. At the local level the British set up Municipalities and District Boards to which Indians could be elected, and then, it was hoped, schooled in loyal politics and persuaded both to tax themselves and their compatriots to enable expenditure on roads, schools and drains, and to take some of the local administrative load off district officers. As the Government of India itself noted publicly in 1882 in relation to the constitution of Local Boards: 'as education advances, there is rapidly growing up all over the country an intelligent class of public spirited men, whom it is not only bad policy, but sheer waste of power, to fail to utilise.'[14] Higher up in the echelons of government, governors of provinces and the Viceroy himself were from 1861 given small consultative councils as a means of modifying older autocratic forms of politics, although all the Indian members of these were nominated until the last decade of the nineteenth century. These may have been small beginnings. But native gentlemen were fast discovering that the structures of imperial government were opening formal and informal routes by which they could influence policy and at least local administration, and providing opportunities for them to claim to speak for Indian interests of different sorts in new ways. The British had, in their attempt to buttress their raj, invited the development of new forms of political action and organisation, which would in turn necessitate further reform of the structures of government to give a more prominent role to Indians whose alliance and cooperation they sought.

## OPPORTUNITY AND CHALLENGE

The young Jawaharlal was born at a time when and in an environment where Indians were clearly experiencing unprecedented and often disturbing change. In many respects British rule offered them opportunities as well as profound challenges.

The material opportunities are perhaps the easiest to discern. Yet it must be remembered that these were open to comparatively few, and that for all those who seized on what the new could offer, there were others who felt excluded or who lost former positions of authority or access to livelihoods. Economically there were some real success stories under the British. These people were very diverse. Some were directly involved with the British and their institutions – military contractors, suppliers of goods to military cantonments or hill stations, shopkeepers, builders of houses, and landlords. Comparatively few British people were involved in routine commerce and the service sector which sustained modern life, and Indians performed all these functions. More removed from the physical presence and needs of British people were those who adapted their agriculture to international markets like the cotton growers of western India who capitalised on the disruption of cotton supplies at the time of the American civil war. Agricultural profits enabled the expansion of a prosperous peasantry in many places. And there were the new colonists of the canal colonies of the Punjab, offered newly irrigated land because they were thought to be sturdy farmers of proven skill; and the retired soldiers settled on land as a reward for their services and insurance against rural unrest. To the disquiet of the British, who believed that rural India was the real India and feared the disruptive tendencies of the urban interloper, there were also money-lenders who seized the opportunities offered. They used the spread of the cash economy and the rigid cash demand for land revenue to extend their influence in rural society and sometimes became rentiers and landlords in their own right on the proceeds. Operating on a far greater scale were those who built on family traditions of banking and commerce and became the first modern Indian industrialists, men of such different backgrounds as the Tatas, the Tagores or the Birlas.

The opportunities for new and profitable careers in modern professions were clearest among those who took up the new forms of western education for themselves and their children. The later half of the century saw a rapid expansion in English language higher education in India, on the model of London University with numerous local colleges providing the teaching and universities being the examining bodies. India's first three universities were founded in 1857, and other regional universities soon followed. Initially higher education had been most available in the Presidencies of Bengal, Bombay and Madras, and even in the last decade of the century these were the areas with the most colleges and pupils. Bengal for example had thirty-four colleges then, compared with only twelve in Nehru's home province, and almost five times the number of pupils in them.

Not surprisingly the pupils tended to come from families of some social standing and wealth, with traditions of literacy and public service. Few came from very wealthy landowning or commercial homes, and even fewer from low caste and rural families. This sort of education led to a whole range of modern careers, including government service, law, journalism, medicine, and teaching in secondary schools and universities. Even though the numbers were comparatively small in the context of the whole population, there was by the time of Nehru's birth considerable disquiet among the educated that the opportunities open to them were inadequate. The various local bars were, for example, increasingly overcrowded, and many aspirants to a legal career failed to make their way. In Bengal government officials and Indian observers alike were commenting on the melancholy sight of graduates unable to find even lowly legal or government employment. The young Gandhi in Bombay was himself in this position, despite his London training. He sought refuge in South Africa, where a Gujarati firm of traders needed a lawyer who spoke both English and Gujarati. It was not surprising that the educated criticised government for the regulations governing the Indian Civil Service entry examination, which made it so hard for Indians to prepare for and present themselves in the competition. By 1887 only a dozen Indians had entered the ICS through the open competition.

It was those most exposed to western values, assumptions and examples in daily life, principally through the new forms of education and contact with British people, who faced the deepest challenges at this time, as well as being poised to take advantage of some of the new occupational advantages. They heard the western criticisms of Indian society as backward, static and dominated by religious authority; and the missionary critiques of Hinduism and Islam. They saw or read about the lives western people were living, and the social and political problems with which they were engaging. They read the books their contemporaries were reading at school and university, and were equally influenced by new ideas about the desirable nature of the polity, right forms of government, and desirable social change. It then fell to them to interpret what these ideas might mean for their own lives in particular and for the wider and deeper world of India's own cultures and religious traditions.

The deepest and most intimately felt challenges were experienced in the broad realm of religion and social culture. India's major religious traditions, particularly Hinduism and Islam, became the site of intense and profound debate as a result of a range of external pressures generated by the British presence. Overt criticism of Indian religions and the possibility of alternative belief systems came from the activities of a wide range of western Christian missionaries, who had become increasingly important in India during the nineteenth century. Official critiques of Indians' belief and social arrangements often had implicit if not explicit ideological foundations in Christian belief or in western rationalist traditions. Moreover, Indian society was particularly vulnerable to western condemnation because so many aspects of it were rooted in religious belief and tradition. Sensitive and articulate Indians had to make painful decisions about their religious inheritance. Should they convert to forms of Christianity, reform their own traditions, stay with fierce defence of those traditions, or even abandon religion altogether and adopt secular lifestyles and standards?

Very few opted for a strategy of secularisation and relinquished beliefs and practices, though some increasingly viewed the modern workplace as an area where religious practices and attitudes rooted in religion (such as the observance of purity and pollution in personal relations) were inappropriate. Comparatively few chose to leave their natal religious tradition and convert to the religion of the imperial ruler. Those who joined the tiny but long-established Christian community in India in the nineteenth and twentieth centuries tended to come from the lowest ranks of Hindu society, and were those for whom Christianity could, in contrast, provide new meaning, status and lifestyles and often new resources of education, assistance and patronage. By 1911, in those areas of India directly ruled by the British, Christians formed just over 1 per cent of the population; but in some provinces mass movements of conversion among Untouchables had led to a dramatic increase in Christian numbers. In Nehru's home province the Christian population trebled in the two decades between 1891 and 1911, while in Delhi and Punjab the number quadrupled.[15]

Far more stayed within their own religious inheritance and from inside grappled with a wide range of issues relating to belief and practice. These included the sources of religious belief and worship, and the validity of tradition as opposed to scripture in discerning what should be retained and what changed or abandoned; the nature of scripture as a source of enlightenment and authority; the proper role of established religious functionaries of various kinds; and the appropriateness of different kinds of worship and devotion. Probably no other period in Indian history had seen such religious debate and turmoil. It was manifest in the growing number of publications on religion in English and in the vernacular languages, and in particular in the flowering of religious reform movements throughout the subcontinent and affecting all the major traditions.[16] Among the earliest Hindu reform movements was the Brahmo Samaj, founded by the Bengali Brahmin, Rammohun Roy, which preached theism and rejected idolatory. It developed into a discrete community, mainly in Bengal. Other movements flourished within mainstream Hinduism and spread far more widely. At the time of Nehru's birth two of the most influential were the Ramakrishna movement and the Arya Samaj. From the late nineteenth century these two were to spread the vision of a reformed and modern Hinduism throughout the world, and in particular among Indians who had migrated as indentured labourers to places as far as Natal or the Caribbean. In the Gangetic heartland of Nehru's UP and neighbouring Bihar there were by the last quarter of the century vibrant movements within the Islamic and Hindu milieus to sustain and revive orthodoxy as well as to reform and modernise.

Religious turmoil and debate were also evident in individual lives. Gandhi was an obvious case as he wrestled with the meaning of Hinduism for a western-educated Indian, challenging in the light of reason and conscience the role of Brahmins, the nature of scripture, ritual practices and social customs rooted in religion, and seeking after a pure and original Hinduism hopefully untainted by the accretions of erroneous traditions over time.[17] But he was not alone, and countless other individuals and families had to make significant decisions about their religious identifications and practices.

A further element in these complex processes was a redefinition of what constituted a religion and who belonged to what religious communities. Obviously internal Indian debates about orthodoxy, revival and reform fed new and clearer understandings of what it meant to be Hindu, Muslim or Sikh in a changing world, and helped to draw more definite boundaries between those who were inside the fold of the faithful and those who were outside. But British understandings of religion and of India, and their strategies of listening to those they felt spoke for important social groups, and of incorporating them into the formal institutions of the polity, also sharpened these processes. The British understood India to be in a sense inherently marked by religious difference, and coming from a theistic tradition with an emphasis on orthodoxy of creed as well as practice they assumed that such clear boundaries also separated Indian religions and their adherents from each other. Easy slippage across and through apparent boundaries of belief and worship, which undoubtedly still occurred in India, was really outside their comprehension. Their vision of Indian religion and its significance was written into the decennial census: from the later nineteenth century it asked questions about religious identification, and demanded that Indians define themselves as Hindu, Muslim, Sikh or Christian. Moreover, they gradually enshrined these categories in the new nominated and elected institutions of local self-government, reserving seats for religious groups, and eventually in the twentieth century in the provincial and central legislative councils. It was little wonder that Indian politicians and public men began to worry about the numbers of each community counted at the census, and seized the opportunity to speak for religious constituencies in the new arenas of public debate.

Debates on religious identity, authority and practice quickly incorporated discussions on wider issues of social practice, and generated movements of social reform. Indian society was particularly vulnerable to external and internal criticism at this juncture because so many social patterns and customs were rooted in religious tradition and sustained by religious authority. From the lifetime of Rammohun Roy onwards some of the bitterest and most prolonged public debates in India concerned social issues, and they engaged not only prominent publicists for orthodoxy and reform, but countless families among the newly educated elites of the subcontinent. Among Hindus issues relating to caste generated movements for caste reform in relation to marriage practices and education, but also led to ostracism of those who were considered to be adopting western standards to the detriment of caste tradition and standing. Many of those high caste Hindus who travelled to Britain for higher education and training faced fierce caste criticism and even outcasting for their challenge to orthodoxy. This happened in the case of both the Gandhi and Nehru families. The practice of Untouchability also provoked profound controversy, as reformers struggled to show that the practice was not only repugnant to modern ideals and degraded Hindu society in the world's eyes, but also contrary to Hindu teaching.

Muslims as well as Hindus became involved in controversies with each other and with their rulers over gender, and particularly over the treatment of women. The seclusion of women, patriarchal family forms and the lack of women's civil rights were aspects of Hindu and Muslim social patterns, though by no means uniform in either tradition. But the British criticised Indian society on the grounds of the treatment of women: women's place was seen as the touchstone of civilisation, and Indians' apparent failures in relation to women sustained imperial assumptions of superiority and authority. Indians responded with deep pride, concern and sometimes hurt. Some took the road of social reform, anxious that India should take its place as a modern, reformed society. They campaigned for legislation to ameliorate the lives of widows, to prevent child marriage, and to forward the cause of female education. Others resisted change, determined that the imperial ruler should not be allowed to touch such intimate aspects of their world as gender and familial relations.[18]

The challenges to Indians posed by social issues were also opportunities for creative dialogue with other religious and social traditions, and in many cases produced new visions of society, and new patterns of social life and relations, which drew on India's own traditions and on external inspiration. They were visible not just in great debates or in public institutions and movements, but in the daily life and manners of thousands of ordinary men and women. Newly educated men whom the professions made more mobile than their fathers had been were forced to reshape their family lives and relations. This, reinforcing the messages of western example and literature, gradually changed the nature of marriage and began to create ideals of romance and companionate marriage. In turn husbands increasingly dependent on the companionship and support of wives, and hoping in turn to arrange the marriage of their daughters to men of similarly professional families, took seriously issues of more modern education for their spouses and their daughters. Gandhi touchingly recorded how as a teenager he had read cheap reformist pamphlets which, among other things, lauded conjugal love, and how he had tried to teach his child bride to read – just years before the young Nehru was born.[19]

Decisions also had to be made about more everyday matters such as table manners and modes of eating, or the sorts of clothes one chose to wear. These were markers of what was presumed to be modern, the hallmarks of those who could relate to the rulers in their own cultural style. They were thus profoundly symbolic. It was no coincidence that they provoked huge soul-searching in individuals. Gandhi agonised about the right clothes for himself and his family when he was a lawyer in South Africa, and made the point of his new ideals on his return to India by choosing to wear only Indian dress and eschewing the modern dress of the Indian professional man. As one of his contemporaries noted with amazement in 1915, 'The odd thing is he was dressed quite like a *bania*: no one could mark the slightest difference.'[20] The Nehru family were to face a crisis of conscience five years later when Gandhi asked them and their compatriots to burn their foreign clothes and use only cloth made in India.

The presence of the British and the manner of their rule in India finally produced both challenges and opportunities in the realm of politics. They had opened up new roles for Indians within the new polity they had created – as collaborators of various kinds, and as representatives and spokesmen in the new consultative structures. Moreover this was just at the time when a common language and new communication techniques enabled Indians to converse across old regional and linguistic boundaries; and when Indians were themselves engaging with major questions of religious and cultural identity and integrity. Although for many educated Indians social problems were the priority, their responses soon generated new political debates and activities. They began to ask themselves why their country with its long traditions of civil governance, its wealth of political theory, and its skilled communities of professional men had succumbed to British rule. Was this a result of cultural and moral weakness, or of political and military disaster? Was it a providential occurrence designed to bring India into the modern world? In trying to find answers they began to use western political discourse and to think and talk in terms of an Indian nation. The meanings ascribed to the nation varied. Some referred to their regional linguistic and cultural group. Some visualised the whole subcontinent as a nation ground down by the foreign ruler, or alternatively as a nation being made by contact with the west. A prominent Bengali public figure and politician, Surendranath Banerjea, born in 1848, significantly called his autobiography *A Nation in Making*.

Others thought less in terms of an Indian whole than of particular communities and interest groups, as they took advantage of the new political opportunities offered by British rule. This tendency to forward the interests of the particular was encouraged by the British understanding of Indian society as composed of important interests which should be represented in the changing structure of governance and consultation. So, for example, caste groups used the census to try to improve their local standing by having it formally ratified in the official documentation of the raj. Religious groups likewise tried to ensure that people defined themselves in such a way that local census enumerators bolstered the numbers of their particular community, and adopted mechanisms to retrieve those who had converted to Christianity. Of major political consequence for the future was the tendency of those who sought election or nomination to seats in Municipalities and Boards reserved for religious minorities (and eventually in the provincial and central legislatures in the twentieth century) to present themselves as representatives of particular religious groups in need of special consideration and protection.

It was hardly surprising that just as issues of social and religious reform generated new and voluntary associations in support of their causes, so, too, did political questions. In mid-century men began to come together to discuss political matters, to engage with the raj, and to further their ideals and interests. They cooperated from very different backgrounds, from landowners to urban taxpayers, from provincial journalists to high-flying lawyers; and ranged over issues of common concern as disparate as taxation, the cost of government, the right to carry arms, control of the press, reform of the legislatures and the problems of Indian access to the Indian Civil Service. The political culmination of much mainly regional and local associational activity was the first and experimental meeting of an Indian National Congress in 1885.[21] It met annually thereafter and became the premier gathering of India's group of western-educated men who were aware of the political problems and potential of living under British rule. Until after the First World War it was a fluid organisation, with little in the way of an organisational base or financial security which would have permitted some permanent *modus operandi*. It was largely an annual Christmas vacation convention dominated by higher Hindu castes and lawyers who could take the time off and afford the train journey to its meetings. It was also dominated by delegates from those areas where the new forms of education were most available and where the modern professions were most developed. In the years 1885 to 1909 nearly 20,000 delegates in total attended its meetings, the largest single gathering being nearly 2,000 in Bombay in 1889, the year Nehru was born. His home province produced just over 3,000 of the total delegates in those years, a sign of the development of a new regional political awareness and organisation, even if it could not match the numbers coming from Bengal, Madras or Bombay.

Congress's interests represented those of the groups from which its members came. All had benefited from the presence of the British, and as a body it was studiously loyal to the raj. These were the least likely people to have revolutionary attitudes or to want to destroy the regime which had given them professional opportunity and political space. Their wish was to reform the imperial regime, to make it more amenable to educated public opinion, and to expand the influence available to Indians within it. Despite its inherent moderation, and its refusal to tackle socio-economic and religious issues which might have broken its fragile unity, Congress was nonetheless of great political significance. It was the only major all-India political organisation which claimed to speak for the whole country, and as such it received some grudging recognition as an significant political body from the imperial rulers. It thus had great importance for those who were debating issues of national identity, who had a vision of the revival and construction of a vibrant nation, and who recognised the potential of new styles of political action and organisation.

Nehru was born almost at the same time as Congress, in a period when Indians were engaging in new forms of politics and tackling new issues which were to take them into new relationships with each other and with their rulers. He was to be part of this process, just as he was heir to the other challenges and opportunities occasioned by the presence of the British raj. He would, in his own lifetime, have to make his own responses to them.

## Chapter 2

# The Young Nehru: Privilege and Promise

## THE FAMILY BACKGROUND

The Nehru family came originally from Kashmir, a mountainous area in the north of the subcontinent, of great natural beauty. Like many of their fellow Kashmiri Brahmins they migrated to the plains of northern India, in search of professional opportunities. Jawaharlal's own ancestors had journeyed south in the early eighteenth century, to take up service in Delhi under the Mughal emperor. Their home was beside a canal or *nahar*, which became a part of their family name, and eventually their western-style surname when Jawaharlal's father, Motilal, adopted the style used in British society. Motilal and his family were part of a tiny immigrant minority in north Indian society. This was to be important in several ways. It was to mean that Motilal and then Jawaharlal were not immersed in and limited by regional politics, as they might have been had they come from dominant local caste groups, used to wielding power and patronage. Both were to have primarily an all-India vision and standing in public life. Moreover, like many migrant groups, they were not only prepared for further physical movement, but sought social mobility in a changing environment.

Motilal was born in 1861 in Agra. Just four years earlier his family had fled from Delhi to avoid the bloodshed that occurred when the British reasserted their authority in the old Mughal capital and destroyed the remnants of the imperial court for ever, sending the last emperor into exile. His father, who had been a police officer, lost his job and almost all his possessions in the flight, and died just before his last son was born. Motilal was then brought up by one of his two older brothers, who, thanks to the help of a British principal of Agra College, went into the service of the small princely state of Khetri in Rajasthan, rising to become its chief minister. On the death of his employer, the Raja, he returned to UP and to Agra and joined his other brother there in the legal profession; eventually he moved to Allahabad when the High Court was transferred there. The two older brothers were the first in the Nehru family to learn English, and when the younger Motilal was receiving his early education at Khetri from the Raja's own Muslim tutor, he read only Arabic and Persian, as was typical among service families in the princely milieu of northern India. But back in UP he attended institutions offering western-style, English-medium education, eventually studying at Muir College, Allahabad. His academic record was undistinguished; indeed he spent time at the Taj Mahal rather than taking his final examinations, after thinking erroneously that he had done badly in the first paper! But it was clear that he was a young man of immense character and energy. This personal promise was amply fulfilled when he embarked on a legal career as a *vakil*, or native lawyer, initially in Cawnpore and from 1886 in Allahabad, the town which was to be his career base and family home.[1]

Motilal was a classic example of migrant upward mobility, as well as of someone who succeeded in seizing the new opportunities opened to Indians by the presence of the British raj. Although he never travelled to London to train for the Bar as his slightly younger contemporary, Gandhi, did, and as his son was to do, he became one of India's most outstanding lawyers, receiving permission to appear as an advocate in the Allahabad High Court and ultimately before the judicial committee of the Privy Council in Britain. Aspiring to a legal career, he took one of the few professional openings into the public world of the British raj where there was no major barrier to Indian success. He was a civil lawyer, specialising in Hindu inheritance law, and made his name and fortune partly in cases relating to inheritance of property belonging to the Talukdars and other large landowners of UP. His earnings were very significant indeed, and he invested them in property and stocks and shares, as well as in an increasingly affluent and westernised lifestyle.

Of property and money he had need, because the year after he moved to Allahabad the older brother who had been a father to him died in his forties. He left Motilal – then in his mid-twenties – as the head of an extended family of his brother's widow and seven children whom it was his responsibility to educate. He himself had no children at this stage. His first wife and their baby had died when Motilal was in his teens; and his second wife, Swarup Rani, had as yet no living child. The sign of his professional advancement and his growing professional success was his move from the crowded Indian part of Allahabad to the 'civil lines', that exclusive part of most Indian towns where Europeans had their domestic space and security in bungalows built in large gardens on wide streets. Here was an Indian professional and householder who was increasingly confident and successful in the public world of the raj, and more than able to hold his own socially with those who were to be his new neighbours.

Motilal Nehru came from a generation which had to find answers to many of the social and religious questions raised by India's new relationship with Britain and the western world, as well as respond to the material and political

# Nehru Family Tree

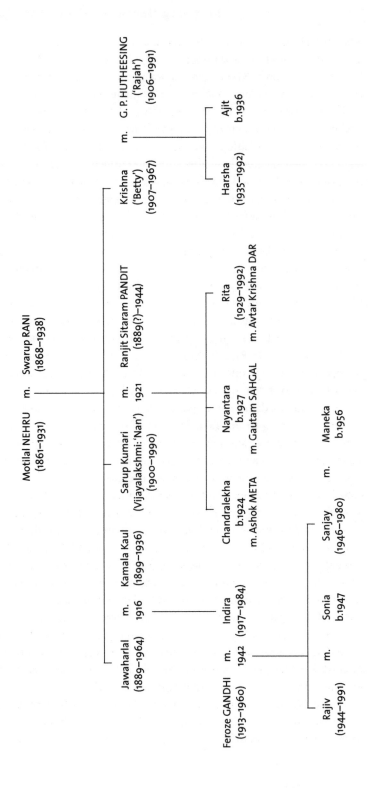

opportunities the raj provided. Allahabad was a town where some of these issues were at their sharpest. The responses he made moulded the environment in which his son was to be brought up, and provided some of the ideals which were to mark Jawaharlal for life. Motilal was of course a high caste Hindu, and immensely proud of his family. But in matters of belief he was a cheerful agnostic; while matters of religious ceremonial were left to the women of the family, particularly his wife. She was a deeply religious woman who managed the family's domestic rituals, as was customary, and would take her son to bathe in the sacred River Ganges, to visit the town's temples or to see particularly notable Hindu holy men. But as Jawaharlal later commented, religion 'seemed to be a woman's affair. Father and my older cousins treated the question humorously and refused to take it seriously.'[2] Motilal had no part in or sympathy with the Hindu revivalist movements which were making their mark in Allahabad at the time. Moreover, as the heir to the old courtly culture of the Mughal empire, he was as much a product of Islamic society and education as of high caste Hindu culture. Increasingly, too, he was at home in the company of British people, and they in turn relished his affable companionship, as well as appreciating his professional expertise as a lawyer and as a performer in court. This catholicity of cultural sympathy, and lack of religious conviction, fed into his broad political vision. But both father and son were later to be unable to comprehend the sharpening religious sensitivities and fears that were emerging among Muslims as well as Hindus, coming as they did from such a composite cultural tradition.

Motilal's attitude to caste was increasingly reformist. He married within his own caste, and arranged his son's marriage within it; though both his daughters married non-Kashmiris. But caste restrictions on what was coming to be seen as modern behaviour were abhorrent to him. He broke conventions about what food Brahmins could eat and who they could eat with, cheerfully enjoying meat, wine, whisky and cigars in his heterodox social interactions. (As a child, Jawaharlal knew whisky when he saw it, but when he first saw his father drink red wine he was horrified and ran to tell his mother that Motilal was drinking blood!) In the last year of the nineteenth century Motilal flew in the face of the caste's most conservative faction by travelling to Europe and then refusing on his return to undertake a ceremony of purification. He was aggressively contemptuous of those who still clung to traditional ways, and became the effective leader of the most socially advanced and modern section of his caste, anxious that they should take up all the secular opportunities open to them. Kashmiri Brahmins had never had a rigid tradition of seclusion of women; and Motilal disliked this practice, encouraging the women of his own family to gain a modern education and to take up roles in public life. Jawaharlal reminisced later in life that his father was no theorist: he did not think much about basic social and economic issues, but reacted very strongly against things that he thought represented social 'backwardness'. He ascribed this to his father's exposure to western ways of living and thinking, and also to his upbringing in the mixed Hindu–Muslim culture which had helped to produce the Kashmiri Brahmins.[3]

Concern for social reform as well as legal practice drew Motilal into the public and political life of Allahabad, though in these decades his main concern was with his legal career and the raising of his growing family. He attended some of the early sessions of the Congress; but his political attitudes were essentially moderate. He had no incentive to take any other stance. He was, after all, one of the success stories of India under the raj, he lived a comfortable life, and he admired the British and their ways. In his son's estimation, Motilal was a nationalist in a vague sense, but he felt that Indians 'had fallen low and almost deserved what they had got'. Moreover – and here there was a characteristic which his son amply inherited – he felt 'just a trace of contempt in his mind for the politicians who talked and talked without doing anything'.[4]

## THE SON AND HEIR

Jawaharlal was the first child born to Motilal and his second wife, and their only living son. Another baby boy born in 1905 lived only a month. They also had two daughters younger than Jawaharlal, Vijayalakshmi, known as 'Nan', born in 1900, and Krishna, nicknamed 'Betty', born in 1907. The three children joined the extended family of older cousins already under Motilal's care. It was Motilal who was the dominant figure in the household, his character, energy and career moulding its way of life, his laughter and his occasional fury echoing round the home. Undoubtedly he was the parent who most profoundly marked the son. Nehru was, nonetheless, deeply devoted to his self-effacing and much less westernised mother – his depth of feeling indicated when he refused to write anything at all about her for the Motilal birth centenary, suggesting that Vijayalakshmi should do this instead of him.

The year his first daughter was born, when Jawaharlal was ten, Motilal moved house again within Allahabad, buying a far bigger if more dilapidated mansion, 1 Church Road. He set about renovating it and importing furnishings and artefacts from Europe for its decoration, and it became one of the grandest houses in the elite area of European residence. The house and grounds were vast, and the double-storeyed mansion round an inner court provided enough room for the growing family, and for the two distinctive domestic styles the family now sustained – one western, where Motilal could entertain and the family men could socialise, and one Indian, where the more orthodox women members of the household could retain their eating and living habits. The house had electricity, which was most unusual at the time, and there was a riding ring for the children and a swimming pool. The young Nehru quickly learned to swim and loved it. His father could just struggle a length. Other Indian visitors often could not, and Jawaharlal remembered how they delighted in frightening these unfortunates. T. B. Sapru, rising lawyer and later prominent Moderate nationalist politician and Law Member of the Viceroy's Executive Council, was one such, who shouted if anyone attempted to move him from his position on the first step of the pool in fifteen inches of water![5] Not surprisingly a goodly army of servants was needed, and at a more intermediate level a Muslim controller of the household, a Eurasian housekeeper, an English governess for the two girls who stayed with them for sixteen years and became part of the family, and briefly an Irish-French tutor for the son. Such was Motilal's wealth and westernised lifestyle that it was even rumoured that he had his shirts laundered abroad: this was nonsense, but some of his formal suits were certainly tailored in London, including the full court dress he wore in 1911 at a royal durbar in Delhi, the invitation to which was a seal on his high repute in the eyes of the raj.

This was a world of material privilege beyond the dreams of most young Indian boys. It also gave Jawaharlal exposure to western styles of domesticity, to components of a modern lifestyle, such as his father's collection of motor cars, which normally only the wealthiest of Europeans could aspire to, and to the beginnings of an imaginative but western education with a European tutor. There were no religious or racial barriers to the social circle round Motilal. Most surprisingly for the time, foreigners were welcome not only living within the household, but as honoured guests. Among the latter was Sir Harcourt Butler, of the famous British political Butler family, an Indian Civil Service man who at the apogee of his Indian career was Governor of the United Provinces. The Nehru girls knew him as 'Uncle Harcourt'; and he and Motilal later acknowledged years of friendship and conviviality over the champagne bottle. However, the Nehrus were well aware of the strong streak of racism in British expatriate society, and when Motilal was asked by the Chief Judge of the High Court whether he would like to be put up for the exclusive Allahabad Club he declined, not willing to suffer the humiliation of being blackballed on racial grounds. Jawaharlal's older male cousins would frequently talk about British and Eurasian social slights to Indians, and the young boy began to resent such behaviour and the presence of alien rulers. However, he had no feeling against individual British people, and like his father rather admired them.[6]

Hardly surprisingly, Jawaharlal grew up feeling that such an unusual family setting was natural for him. He also imbibed from Motilal, as did all the children, a sense that the Nehru family was very special. Although Motilal was to a large extent a self-made man, he had enormous pride in his family, and he and they saw themselves as drawing high status from their place in Hindu society as well as from the processes of modernisation the family had undergone. But privilege also meant obligation, particularly in setting a social example to 'backward' Indian society around them, and in playing their rightful part in public life. It was clear throughout his later life that Jawaharlal had interiorised this complex sense of superiority, which drew on Indian ideas of status as well as British assumptions about modernity and appropriate social codes and styles. It was to mark him out from most of his Indian associates, and would attract criticism from them, but undoubtedly contributed to his commitment to play a major role in the transformation of India. But as his childhood ended, the sense of belonging to the Nehru family was also a burden to bear. In 1905 his father took him to England to begin his education at Harrow School, one of England's premier public schools on the north-western outskirts of London. As he travelled home to India Motilal wrote from Marseilles to his son saying that the painful separation they were all enduring was for Jawaharlal's own good. It would give him the foundation for his professional life and make a man of him – the man who would build the dynasty he, Motilal, had founded.[7]

Jawaharlal was to spend six years in England, with only a brief visit home to India in 1908. The impress of this experience never left him. The evidence of his time away from home comes in a long series of letters exchanged between father and son in English. His mother wrote to him weekly in Hindi when she was well enough. At Harrow he spent two years, 1905 to 1907, thrown into public school life at the deep end, as it were, with no preparation, and lodging in the holidays with English middle-class hosts, when he was not visiting Indian cousins. At first everything seemed very strange – from the timetable and the school conventions, to the fact that some of his uniform was secondhand. Most of all he missed his family. But he rapidly adapted to the new life. His academic progress was good, except in scripture and Latin composition, and at the end of his first term he come top of his form and won a prize. He also threw himself into sport and joined the cadet force, which gave him a rudimentary military training. Eventually when he left he admitted to feeling sad, and was surprised to find this was so, not having realised how attached he had become to the place. Later he wondered if his sadness was real, or whether he had just conformed to the school's traditions in order not to feel out of place.[8] His headmaster thoroughly approved of him and told his father that all the staff thought highly of his ability and industry. Then, with a typical public school turn of phrase – and praise – he commented that he was 'a thoroughly good fellow and ought to have a very bright future before him'.[9]

But what had Harrow given Nehru? He dismissed his school in a couple of pages in his *Autobiography*, but there were important and lasting legacies. Firstly – and quite outside the curriculum taught – there were aspects of the social experience which were in retrospect investments for later life. When he arrived he was used to western styles of behaviour from life at home, but public school taught him to relate to his British contemporaries as an equal and in ways they understood. He understood the nuances of interaction among the British professional classes, and this marked his relations with officials when he was a nationalist opponent, and eased his relations with Britain's rulers in the sensitive years after independence. (It is noteworthy that he never felt this ease of shared background and values with Americans.) Moreover, the school life gave him his first taste of loneliness and taught him how to cope with it. He felt desperately lonely when he was first left behind at Harrow and then again after his father's visit to him there, and 'homesickness' was compounded by a feeling that he was different from so many of the other boys there – not on grounds of race but more because he felt older and more mature than they in his tastes and interests. Harrow also gave him more obviously the foundation of a serious intellectual training. His academic aptitude and capacity for concentration and hard work were fostered here, and he developed attitudes and skills which were to be essential for his later political roles. He was learning to become an intellectual, a thinker who struggled with big issues and broad pictures – unlike his father. Moreover, he was laying down the foundations of that elegant literary style which was to mark his adult letters and more lengthy writings.

What is more difficult to discern is the extent to which Nehru interiorised the public school ethos of Harrow – that ethos which marked out the English gentleman and played a major role in forming the way the British perceived themselves as different from and superior to Indians. Indian contemporaries later complained that Nehru was too much a gentleman, and worse, an English gentleman. Certainly in his subsequent life he demonstrated values and characteristics that marked him out as a public school man. He was, for example, reticent about personal and emotional issues, except when confiding to his diary in prison. He loathed displays of 'emotionalism' and criticised a close Muslim friend for this fault, feeling that it 'cheapened' emotion. 'The teaching of the West has made me value restraint a great deal and I feel that we as a race are continually indulging in emotionalism and lessening our activity thereby.'[10] He also accepted and displayed in his own life a commitment to physical activity and discipline as one of the hallmarks of the serious-minded and disciplined person. Much of his concern in later years for the health of his daughter when she was an adolescent and then grew into a young woman was the lack of 'character' which was often displayed by illness. Harrow, like other major public schools, prepared its boys for adult careers in public and imperial service. Nehru shared in this ethos that a public role was to be expected, and also that privilege and position brought its obligations of probity and public conscience. It would be facile to think that Nehru simply accepted the values by which he was surrounded at school. Some had already been part of his Indian upbringing, not least in Motilal's sense that he and his family had obligations as well as opportunities in the wider public domain.

It was, indeed, a hope that Jawaharlal might enter the Indian Civil Service that made Motilal insist that his son should leave Harrow a year earlier than was normal, in order to complete university and have time to prepare for the ICS examination before he was over the age limit. His headmaster felt that this was too great a burden on the young man, and that another year at school would have brought out the best in him. But Motilal had his way, and his son agreed, not least because he felt he had outgrown Harrow, however good and essential the public school training might be. So, in the autumn of 1907 he went up to Trinity College, Cambridge, to read natural sciences, joining a college of great prestige. His father was acutely aware of the important connections forged in such a place, but was also sure that his son's school record would be the precursor of major university achievement, which in its turn would make the university and college proud to have him as one of their alumni.

Decades later this was to be the case. But at the time Jawaharlal made little mark on Cambridge. He worked at his science – chemistry, geology and botany – but not overenthusiastically. He took sport with some seriousness, coxing a college boat on the river, and taking regular riding lessons. He played some tennis, and also learned some ballroom dancing – at his father's insistence. Wider reading well outside his field of study broadened his intellectual horizons, as did the company of new and cosmopolitan friends, and the chance to go and listen to famous public figures who came to lecture at the university and its societies. He heard George Bernard Shaw, for example, and Roosevelt; and listened to many of the Indian politicians who came to speak to the Indian students' organization, the Majlis. Although he was increasingly interested in British and Indian politics, and wrote of them to his father, he was no political activist at this stage, and even found it hard to speak in the college debating society because he was inhibited by his shyness and diffidence. But on his own admission, work, sport and amusements took up most of his time, and he later warned his daughter, then at Oxford, against becoming insular and unaware as he had been.[11] His leisurely and enjoyable life owed not a little to his father's generosity. He had an allowance of £400 a year, which was almost half a professor's salary! Even so, he sometimes ran short of money. Early in 1908 he had to borrow money in order to pay his last term's college bill, and still outstanding was his landlady's account and some small bills in Cambridge, as well as his account with his London tailor. A cheque from Motilal saved the day.[12]

Nehru thought in later years that he had lived a somewhat shallow life at university. He and his friends burned the midnight oil, like most undergraduates, and talked grandly about life, politics and sex. But little was urgent and serious for them. This was the *fin de siècle*, the final years before world war destroyed the illusions of at least a generation and exposed the young to death and anguish. 'But the veil of the future hid this and we saw around us an assured and advancing order of things and this was pleasant for those who could afford it.'[13] Despite his evident conviviality, the young Nehru did not feel entirely at ease in Britain. He still felt a profound sense of inner loneliness, of being 'almost over-powered by the sense of my solitary condition'; and on his return to England in 1908 he was struck not only by the familiarity of the country but also by the constant reminders that he was a foreigner and an intruder.[14]

Yet at Cambridge there had been at least two major developments in his life. The first was his exposure to the serious study of science – a subject which had interested him since the days his tutor had set up a rudimentary laboratory for him in the grand family home. He was not, at university level, a particularly distinguished student, and gained a second-class honours degree. He himself suspected that he was near the bottom of the second class, and felt he had not deserved anything higher, no matter what his father might have hoped for. But it seems that his three years of study left him with a profound respect for what he was later to call the scientific attitude. For him this meant an attitude of mind which was the opposite of clinging to the past and of blind commitment to tradition. It implied the exercise of reason, an intellectual openness, particularly to possibilities of change, and a serious commitment to respect for evidence as the basis for rational thought and debate. It was also the hallmark of the modern man who seemed to have the fashioning of his world in his grasp. Perceptively he later wrote that he was 'influenced by my scientific studies in the university and had some of the assurance which science then possessed. For the science of the nineteenth and the early twentieth centuries, unlike that of to-day, was very sure of itself and the world.'[15] When he was back in India Jawaharlal would contrast a scientific attitude to that engendered by religion. But he records nothing about any religious experience or concern while he was in England, in stark contrast to the young Gandhi who, just a few years earlier in London, had begun on a journey of religious discovery partly because of the experience of living among Christians whose religion was a matter of deep faith rather than the badge of an imperial nation.

The second development was his growing interest in Indian politics and his increasingly radical attitudes. The younger Nehru had at school begun to think that his father was too moderate in his political views, and too inclined to trust the British. As his attitude sharpened he became increasingly critical of his father's political stance and this created tension between them. News of Indian politics came from the newspapers Motilal sent him, the debates among Indian students at Cambridge, and the visits of Indian politicians to the university. A growing rift in Congress circles between so-called Moderates and Extremists drew from Jawaharlal early in 1908 a sharp comment on the Moderates who might represent part of the country 'but they seem to think, or at any rate try to make others believe, that they are the "natural leaders" and representatives of the whole country'. He thought that soon there would be no Moderates left, and their assumptions were hastening their doom.[16] This was hard stuff for his father to swallow, as he had been one of the leading Moderate delegates at the Congress meeting in Surat at the end of 1907 when the rift had led to most unusual and indecorous physical assaults, and led to the police clearing the hall. His reaction to his son's youthful opinions was extreme disapproval, and a refusal to enter into any proper discussion on the subject.[17] The rift lasted some weeks and in the end Jawaharlal apologised for the offence he had unwittingly caused.

As Jawaharlal's Cambridge career came to an end he and his father faced the future for the son and heir of the Nehru family. The ICS was now dropped as a possible career destination. Motilal was delighted at his son's degree result, recognising that he could not have expected a first class, given the time spent away from his work, not least in company with his father in England and Europe on a recent visit. He now recommended the Bar because he had come to feel that Indians had no prospects in the ICS and were likely to be humiliated in it. (It is likely that his attitude had changed partly because one of his nephews had just failed the entrance examination. Jawaharlal's own middling academic record at university probably also contributed to this decision.) But the Bar in India by contrast could give the highest rank and position to Indians who deserved it. In a legal career he could, moreover, ensure his son's success, provided that Jawaharlal acquired 'thoroughness' in his chosen subjects. Again the pressure of parental expectation was heavy. Motilal wrote that he could see his son's future quite plainly: he would take his father's place in the profession and he himself could retire contented.[18] A further advantage of this change of plan was that the son and heir would at last come home, and work at home rather than being in a career which would demand frequent postings away. Writing his *Autobiography* as a prisoner in an imperial jail for his nationalist opposition to the raj, Jawaharlal meditated with a wry irony on the fact that he might so easily have become a part of the imperial establishment. Despite his own growing political radicalism he did not oppose the idea of becoming a cog in the raj's administrative machine; though such an idea would later 'have been repellent to me'.[19] Other members of the extended Nehru family did indeed join the ICS and went on to distinguished administrative careers. Indeed, this spread of elite educated families into both government and opposition helped to ensure the easy transition to independent government after 1947, and to prevent revolutionary change.

Jawaharlal and his father had seriously considered further study in Oxford, as preparation for the next stage of Jawaharlal's life. The son was anxious to broaden his intellectual horizons rather than concentrate immediately on law, and his brash comments on becoming 'a mere lawyer' again temporarily and rather naturally irritated his father. Cambridge was not a congenial prospect as he was now bored by the place and felt it was too full of Indians! He contemplated going to Oxford in the long vacation 'to interview the various heads of colleges' with a view to entrance, but was deterred by the possibility of an immediate rejection when they saw he was an Indian. Here again was evidence of a complex character, one sure of his own superiority in relation to his compatriots, confident in his own worth and status and prepared to approach eminent academics, yet also concerned at the prospect of racially motivated snubs.[20] So the choice was made to go to London, join the Inner Temple and study for the Bar.

Nehru stayed in London from 1910 to 1912. It was a time of legal training, social experiment, and to an extent social 'polishing'. During these two years he travelled extensively with friends and relatives in the British Isles and in Europe. But he also took up lodgings in the fashionable West End of London and developed very expensive habits in company of some old Harrovian friends. He commented in later years that this had been a 'soft and pointless existence', and that he had been aping the English 'man about town'. It did him no good except to raise his own opinion of himself.[21] His capacity to spend money and so get into debt horrified his father, who, though himself a big spender, earned by his own labours the money he spent. It led to the biggest rift between him and Jawaharlal that had yet occurred – far deeper than the comparatively minor disagreements over politics or the profession of law and the intellectual breadth required for it.

The requests for money started early in his London life, normally for £100 a time or more. In June 1911, for example, he admitted that he had been very extravagant and had run up some bills which were now the bane of his life, and asked for £150 to settle outstanding debts and enable him to leave his father in peace, in comparison with his 'incessant demands during the last few months'. Six months later he was again in debt, and admitted that he had no money sense and could not economise, however hard he tried. 'It is a jolly good thing that I am returning home soon, otherwise I might conceivably get into trouble.' The great row occurred in mid-1912, occasioned by the loss of £40 which Jawaharlal had lent to a friend. It was not returned and he had to pawn his watch and chain to extricate himself from his financial straits. Motilal wrote his son what can only be called a snorter of a rebuke (which he subsequently regretted), condemning his apparent lack of study, the company he kept, and his financial incompetence. He also demanded an account of his son's expenditure over the last six months. Jawaharlal responded with stunned surprise, particularly at the request for an account of his expenses: 'the very idea . . . is anathema and suggests of my being on ticket of leave'. He had never kept accounts and so could not do what his father required, and he was mortified that his father was questioning his veracity. He had just been called to the Bar, and intended now to return home with as little expenditure as possible. But yet again he asked for £100 or more to settle his debts as he was at his 'wits' ends and do not know what to do'.[22]

The father relented and eased his son's return; but such episodes show a side of the young Nehru which could easily have wrecked his future. Throughout his life he was to be comparatively cavalier about money, believing that other things were more important. But never again was he to behave in such a profligate manner. The influence of Motilal and then of Gandhi with his call to simplicity was certainly behind the transformation of this dangerously elegant and westernised young man.

The prospect of home-coming must have been accompanied by considerable anxiety for the only son, now in his early twenties but totally unused to the discipline of regular work. He knew only too well the high hopes his father had of him, and the psychological pressure was considerable. Motilal made no secret of his immense pride in his family and his son, and his intention to ease him into a successful legal career like his own. He wrote to his older brother after Jawaharlal had passed his final law examinations that he wanted to keep up his law practice in order to hand over at least some of it to him. 'The one object of my life after his return will be to push him on and if within the next four years he can manage to be independent of me I shall retire in peace and comfort . . .'[23]

Another issue looming on the horizon was that of marriage. It was inevitable that Motilal should follow custom and seek to arrange the marriage of his only son as soon as possible. This was the duty of a caring parent, particularly one whose only son was to carry on the family name and prestige. To leave the question until the son returned home in his twenties was to risk curtailing the range of appropriate girls to choose from, given that he would have to take into account the status of the family within the Kashmiri Brahmin community from which a bride could come, as well as such issues as looks, education and personal compatibility. He had himself been married for the first time in his teens, as was usual in his generation. The matter had already been discussed in some of the letters between the son and his parents. Even before he left Harrow the subject had been raised, and Jawaharlal did not demur at the prospect of an arranged marriage, clearly trusting his father's wisdom in the choice of a bride. But he did not want an engagement to happen suddenly without his knowledge, and Motilal assured him that this would not occur. By 1909 he was concerned that his parents were worrying unnecessarily about his marriage, and told his mother that there was no need for him to marry within the Kashmiri community, and indeed that he did not wish to. He was, in any event, not particularly eager to marry. As his return to India became imminent his anxiety became more pronounced, although he was prepared to allow his parents to go ahead with an arrangement. But he insisted that he should not marry a total stranger. This was the person with whom he would spend his whole life, and he wanted at least to like her. 'In my opinion, unless there is a degree of mutual understanding, marriage should not take place. I think it is unjust and cruel that a life should be wasted merely in producing children.'[24] Perhaps inevitably his association with young men of his own age from a different culture had influenced his view of marriage and of the place of the wife within the marital relationship, and so distanced him from his parents' generation.

If marriage was a problem in prospect, so also must have been the idea of returning home to his father's political environment. This had changed considerably since he left Allahabad as a school boy. In 1909 constitutional reform – the so-called Morley–Minto Reforms after the Secretary of State for India and the Viceroy of the day – had opened up new political opportunities for Indians in an extension of the existing imperial political strategy of listening to important sections of Indian society, and incorporating notables of various kinds into the imperial structure. What was intended was a constitution which would satisfy the legitimate aspirations of all Indians except those with the most 'advanced' or 'extreme' views. In the words of a Government of India despatch, 'We anticipate that the aristocratic elements in society and the moderate men, for whom at present there is no place in Indian politics, will range themselves on the side of the Government and will oppose any further shifting of the balance of power and any attempt to democratise Indian institutions.'[25] By the standards of later reforms the changes were limited. But they enlarged the provincial legislatures and did away with the majority of officials from the bureaucracy in them, allowing most of the non-official members to be elected rather than nominated. The Viceroy's Legislative Council was also enlarged, though it retained an official majority. Behind this strategy of reform lay an imperial vision of a society made up of various interest groups, religious, economic, or professional, and these were the groupings who were to be 'represented' in the new consultative structures through complex electoral arrangements rather than a territorial franchise. Congress initially responded with enthusiasm, but when the limitations of the reforms became clear it considered them 'a fairly liberal measure of constitutional reforms', but deeply regretted that the British had given separate electorates to Muslims.

Motilal shared these misgivings about the potential religious divisiveness of the reforms, and also their limited nature. Nonetheless, he was prepared to take up the opportunity offered to a man of his standing. He was elected to the new UP provincial legislature and his political work and horizons were thus expanded. Although he was quite prepared to be critical of government within the legislature, he remained essentially a moderate, one who was prepared to work within the imperial system. His official public standing was also enhanced by this new departure. An indication of this was the invitation to him and his wife to attend the 1911 Durbar in Delhi, at which the new King-Emperor, George V, and his Queen received the homage of their princely subjects in the presence of a vast assemblage of Indian notables. Motilal ordered formal court dress from London (through his son), and he and his wife and two small daughters travelled to Delhi from UP in the special train for the Lieutenant-Governor and his wife and the province's official and unofficial guests. Although they did not meet the royal couple, they had prominent places at the important functions. The message was clear. The Nehru family was now accepted in a sense as part of the imperial 'establishment'. How Jawaharlal would react to this on his return was unknown. His English education and social grooming would make him naturally at home in such surroundings; but his political views and his consciousness of the potential for discrimination on grounds of his race were likely to make him profoundly uneasy in this world of Indian allies of the raj.

## THE DISSATISFACTIONS OF HOME-COMING

The joys of home-coming and reunion with his family (including the youngest sister he did not recognise) in August 1912 were profound. His parents were immensely proud and relieved to have him home, and the older of his two sisters remembered how she adored her elegant elder brother, and how he would ride with her, and read and talk with her, though she was only twelve. Life at home was easy and there were no money worries, given his re-immersion in the family. But his major task was to establish himself as a young professional.

He settled into the legal world of Allahabad as his father's junior, helping him also with the complexities of his finances. He later remembered spending many hours preparing his father's income tax statements, and even then they were only an approximation. However, he was increasingly dissatisfied with the legal profession. Law only interested him to a certain extent and he could not give it his whole-hearted enthusiasm: as he later remembered, 'I carried on with it because there was nothing else to be done.'[26] As problematic as the profession itself was the social life which went with it. Although Jawaharlal was happy at home, he increasingly felt a misfit in the wider society of the town and its legal circles. His time in England had given him broader horizons, and the provincial society in which he now found himself was staid and boring, focused on the Bar Library and the club, where the same people met each other and discussed the same old topics, normally to do with the law. 'Decidedly the atmosphere was not intellectually stimulating and a sense of the utter insipidity of life grew upon me. There were not even worthwhile amusements or diversions.'[27] He felt that Indian English-speaking professionals had adopted the social style of imperial officials, stamped by the monotony of file-pushing during the working day and concern for their professional status while at leisure in their closed world, devoid of serious intellectual and cultural activity.

By contrast he continued his habits of wide reading, and underneath the somewhat aimless and dissatisfied exterior, serious social and political ideals were stirring. He was even attracted by the moderate and reformist Servants of Indian Society, whose well-educated recruits devoted themselves to the service of India for minimal financial reward, because they were committed and single-minded in their vocation. However, looking back a few years later he wrote to Motilal that ever since his return from England he had done too little reading and his intellectual life was in danger of atrophying. Life centred on the legal world, continuously in contact with the sordid side of human nature, lacking any organised intellectual activity, threatened to kill free thought and appreciation of art or beauty. 'We cling to our physical comfort, and a very second rate, bourgeois comfort at that. We do not even know how to live well or to enjoy ourselves. Few of us have any *joie de vivre* left. And so we live out our lives with little said or little done that beautifies existence for us or for others, or that will be remembered by anyone after we are dead and gone.'[28] Here for the first time, perhaps, we can hear the young man articulating some of the dissatisfactions of a privileged, western-orientated Indian at the debilitating cultural impact of living under imperial rule, as well as the personal response which was to drive him into later work of reconstructing India's polity and Indians' own attitude to themselves.

In his personal life Jawaharal was also having to make profound emotional adaptations, as he was soon to become a husband and a father. Some months before his return from London a cousin began in earnest the task of finding a suitable bride, and recommended to Motilal the thirteen-year-old daughter, Kamala Kaul, of a Delhi Kashmiri family as an appropriate bride and desirable acquisition for the Nehru family. Her father was a businessman, owner of a flour mill, and the family was, naturally, socially conservative and less western than the Nehrus. Kamala had been educated at home and spoke Hindi and Urdu only. The marriage would not take place until she was seventeen (and Jawaharlal was twenty-six) in February 1916. Meantime she came to Allahabad to live with relatives, and was entrusted to the Nehru girls' British governess for further education and socialisation in her new family's more modern ways. She was also allowed to get to know her future husband before the wedding, though the couple were always appropriately chaperoned. These sensitive departures from the traditions of their parents' generation were not only a response to Jawaharlal's own feelings, but a sign of changing ideals of marriage among the educated. The wedding took place in Delhi amidst considerable splendour and celebrations lasting for a week, not unnaturally, as marriages were occasions where family status was displayed, and familial connections strengthened. The couple returned to Allahabad, where they had their own apartment within the family home, a degree of privacy rare for newly-weds. In November of the following year their first and only surviving child was born, a daughter, Indira. (Kamala was subsequently to have a son prematurely in 1924 who lived only two days, and a further pregnancy in 1928 which ended after three months with a miscarriage.)

One cannot know in any detail the dynamics of this relationship. Years later Jawaharlal acknowledged the toll politics took of his capacity to sustain deep and intimate family relations. But Kamala, nonetheless, attracted him deeply. Writing years later after her death to Gandhi, in a rare confession of emotion, he told the austere Mahatma and advocate of celibacy within marriage how very much in love with her he was throughout the marriage, how her touch would thrill him, and how there was always a magic in their relationship. There were irritations and quarrels, and he was always a profoundly lonely person, but only Kamala could ever pierce the shell of loneliness.[29] For her part Kamala found the ebullient and western style of the Nehrus, with its stream of guests, a difficult contrast with her own home, and despite the love of her parents-in-law there seem to have been strains in her relations with the sister-in-law who was almost her own age and devoted to her brother. She began to suffer from headaches, which Motilal robustly put down to hysteria. But there was no doubt that after the baby's birth she was frail and tired easily, and from about 1919 had a persistently raised temperature.[30] To what extent she felt pressure at having given birth to a girl rather than a son and heir of the family name is unknown, though her background would have underlined the importance of a son early in the marriage. A further dimension of her unease within the family must have been the fact that her husband was still financially dependent on his father, rather than having achieved the independence which Motilal had hoped for in 1912.

Father and son had a potentially turbulent relationship, given that both of them had highly developed opinions of their own, a capacity for outspokenness, and considerable tempers when roused. In these early years after Jawaharlal's return politics were often a trigger for disagreement. In his own words, 'political questions were not peaceful subjects for discussion, and references to them, which were frequent, immediately produced a tense atmosphere.'[31] Motilal, for all his own ambivalence towards aspects of the British raj, was gravely worried at his son's evident hostility to foreign rule, and his condemnation of what he called the politics of talking rather than action. But though Jawaharlal wanted action it was not clear what this might be, and he was not attracted to the politics of violence or of terrorism which had emerged among a tiny group of young men in Bengal in the early years of the century. At this juncture all his own tendency to a more extreme sort of politics amounted to was a more aggressive attitude to foreign rule to satisfy both individual and national honour.

However, both father and son were soon to be swept up in the sea-changes in Indian politics which resulted from the impact of the First World War. The war itself was very far away from the provincial world of Allahabad, even though the Indian Army played an important role in many theatres of conflict. But India felt its impact in terms of war loans, higher taxation, price rises, shortages of goods, and tough recruiting campaigns. Jawaharlal remembered that though there was no outspoken disloyalty among Indians, there was little sympathy for the British, and many of them watched with mixed feelings, including some desire to see the humbling of the foreign ruler. In the world of high politics, the war generated a concerted Indian political demand that Britain should state its goal in relation to India and should embark on more constitutional reform. If this was a conflict fought in part for the rights of small nations, and if Indian soldiers were giving their lives for the allied cause, then India's own national aspirations should receive recognition.

The main manifestations of this political radicalisation were the launching of two Home Rule Leagues, by a western Indian leader, B. G. Tilak, and Annie Besant, the maverick Irish theosophist leader whose headquarters were outside Madras, and the coming together of the Congress and the Muslim League in a joint demand for far greater Indian participation in the processes of government. Of these the Congress–League cooperation was the most dangerous from the perspective of a raj, for the raj worked on the assumption that India was not a nation but an agglomeration of distinctive groups who could not cooperate, and therefore needed the British to provide both peace and a measure of unity on the subcontinent. The new agreement brought together on the one side the major and mainly Hindu party claiming to speak for India's people; and on the other the small Muslim group which had emerged in the first decade of the century, and with constitutional reform in prospect had supported the idea of separate electorates to mark and protect the status of Muslims as a distinctive group in Indian society.[32]

Under the pressure of war the British recognised that they must offer their more moderate political friends a constitutional package which would convince them to remain loyal buttresses of British rule. They moved slowly towards a declaration in 1917 by the then Secretary of State for India, Edwin Montagu, that their goal for India was the increasing association of Indians in every branch of government and the gradual development of self-governing institutions so that India could one day achieve responsible government within the empire. Montagu came to India in the cold weather at the end of the year, and with Lord Chelmsford, the Viceroy, toured the subcontinent, taking soundings of political opinion of all shades. Among the UP politicians Montagu saw was Motilal, on 27 November. The interview was good-tempered and it seemed that Motilal and his colleagues would be content if India could achieve responsible government in twenty years. But Montagu was realistic in his assessment that Motilal was not a major all-India leader, and that such moderation could easily be swept aside by a more radical agitation.[33]

The upshot of all this deliberation, their formal report and subsequent parliamentary discussion were the Montagu–Chelmsford Reforms of 1919. These provided for major change in the Indian political scene. The central and provincial legislatures were alike enlarged and freed from an official majority. The Government of India retained control of certain strategic subjects such as foreign affairs, military matters and criminal law; while a wide swathe of other matters were made 'provincial subjects'. In the provinces a system known as 'dyarchy' was instituted: under this some key topics such as policing and land revenue were reserved for control by the governor and his executive council, while other topics were transferred to Indian ministers responsible to the provincial legislature. So power over a considerable area of daily life was handed over to elected Indians, including agriculture, education and local self-government. Aspirant politicians now had a far larger prize to play for in public life. Moreover the pathway to power in the new councils was election in a transformed political environment, for the franchise was enlarged and overhauled, and about one-tenth of the adult male population received the vote. However, the British were still determined to retain control of political life. This was clear from those subjects still controlled by Delhi, and in the provincial capitals by the governors and the civil service. It was also evident in the details of the franchise, where rural areas received more representation than urban areas, thus inviting the political dominance of rural notables rather than educated urban men; and in the continuation of a communal franchise for religious groups and the reservation of seats for them. Here was no vision of an Indian nation receiving its rightful representation, but rather the continuing perception of a subcontinent composed of interests of different kinds, each of which needing special representation through which to protect itself.

The Nehrus were caught up in these changes. Father and son were alike horrified by the internment of Annie Besant for her political actions: they joined her Home Rule League and withdrew from cooperation in a government initiative to give young educated Indians some rudimentary military training in an Indian defence force. Jawaharlal had already sent in his application for this, perhaps remembering that Indians were excluded from the Officers' Training Corps in Cambridge in his day. Jawaharlal wrote a tough letter to a local paper, condemning the internment as official high-handedness, and suggesting that the time had come to withdraw cooperation from the government if it did not withdraw its action. 'Ours have been the politics of cowards and opium-eaters long enough and it is time we thought and acted like live men and women' who placed the honour of their country above the likely reaction of their rulers.[34] Meantime Motilal was drifting away from his former Moderate allies, partly because of their refusal to stand up to the British about the limitations of the proposed reforms, and partly because now the Congress–League alliance suggested to him that there was a real prospect of more radical action. In mid-1918 he broke with his old friends politically and in the special session of Congress held to consider the reforms he spoke on the main issue, on the side of those who said that the reforms were an inadequate fulfilment of the pledge of 1917.

Despite the appearance of a new political radicalism in Congress and in the Nehrus' stance, Indian politicians who demanded greater political reform were in a cleft stick. The British set the parameters of what was acceptable politics, stopping actions of which they disapproved by censorship and their powers of imprisonment. Indians had effectively to play by the rules of this political game, where their rulers were both players and umpires. The alternative was a resort to violent action, which to most of them was profoundly distasteful and seemed obviously to lead nowhere but prison and possibly the gallows. Jawaharlal like his father was caught in this dilemma, not least because both of them were enmeshed in and sustained by the professional life which the British raj enabled, and to an extent shared the values of their rulers. The younger man was increasingly disturbed by the world of privilege he had inherited, privilege which came without power to make a major contribution to the life of his country. Sometime early in 1919 he wrote a part of a review of Bertrand Russell's *Roads to Freedom*, published in 1918. Here he wrestled with the meaning of freedom, political and social. The reforms then on the anvil promised some sort of representative institutions and 'a toy responsible government'; but the experience of western countries suggested that even full responsible government would not solve the country's multiple social and economic problems. Democracy in the west had proved a delusion, as it was 'manipulated by the unholy alliance of capital, property, militarism, and an overgrown bureaucracy . . . assisted by a capitalist press'. Indians must think in advance about what form of politics and governance would serve their people best when eventually they had travelled the long road to responsible government. Maybe the genius of the Indian people would lead to some form of communism, of a politics of concern for the whole community, rather than majority rule.[35] Here were the seeds of a new and far-ranging vision of the transformation of India and its public life, but as yet no prospect of a means to its enactment.

## Chapter 3

# The Turning Point

The years 1919–20 were a turning point in the life of Jawaharlal Nehru and of his whole family. By the end of 1920 they had voluntarily abandoned the prestigious lifestyle enabled by Motilal's success in the law courts of the raj. Father and son had taken up a stance of outright hostility to government. Moreover, Jawaharlal had given up the attempt to establish himself as a lawyer and, thanks to his father's generosity,[1] was able to pursue what he now saw as his path forward in public life. Most particularly, he had met the man who, alongside his father, was to have the most profound influence on his life – Mohandas Karamchand Gandhi, who became popularly known as Mahatma (Great Soul) or Bapu (the diminutive of the Hindustani word for Father).

## GANDHI'S EMERGENCE IN INDIAN POLITICS

It is important to step briefly aside from the disappointments and ambiguities of Jawaharlal's life back in India in his late twenties, in order to look at the man who would transform him so deeply. Gandhi was to have a profound influence on the lives of many individuals who were wrestling with issues created by the presence of the British raj. He was also to help to generate a phase of turbulence and realignments in all-India politics in 1919–20, which made the fisticuffs of the 1907 session of Congress look superficial and unimportant by comparison. For his presence not only broke up old political alignments and loyalties: he also offered his compatriots a new political strategy and a radical vision of India's present predicament and possible future.[2] From the Nehrus' perspective here also was a man who, despite the privilege brought by a western education, had turned his back on much that was essential to their lifestyle and prestige, and to their sense of their public position and role. How were they to respond to this novel and unsettling presence in Indian public life?

Gandhi came of a family of trading caste in western India, and his father had risen high in the service of a small princely state. The early death of his father had led to his own departure for London to train as a barrister, in the hope that he would be able to sustain the extended family on his return. But he was a very different character from Motilal, eight years his senior. He was painfully shy and unsure of himself, and had neither the drive nor the connections to succeed in law in India. Failure led him to South Africa in 1893, in the temporary service of an Indian firm with a law case on its hands. He stayed for almost twenty years, raising there his family of four sons, establishing himself as a lawyer and representative of the Indian community, and eventually becoming a political activist and journalist.

The cause which had claimed him and made him stay in South Africa was the treatment of the Indian population by the white settler communities in Natal and Transvaal. South African Indians were a mixed group: most were indentured labourers, brought to work in the mines and plantations; their children who in time became free citizens; and an elite group known as 'Arabs', free and sometimes temporary migrants who came for trade, mostly from Muslim families in Gujarat, Gandhi's home region. Indians came from different areas of the subcontinent, spoke different languages, and included Hindus, Muslims and Christians. Few of them were experienced in politics, and it was to Gandhi that some of them turned when varieties of racial discrimination seemed to threaten their existence in the country, in the hope that his legal knowledge and command of English would enable them to deal with the settler governments. Gandhi took up the cause, determined that his compatriots should receive their rights as British citizens within the empire, as equal subjects of the Queen-Empress. The challenges of the situation transformed him, and turned him into the disquieting yet compelling figure who would eventually confront the Nehru family and turn it upside down.

The young lawyer initially chose to adopt western dress and to live in a recognisably western style, much as the Nehrus had done. For him the motivation was to gain political credence as an Indian representative. In time he veered to a life of far greater simplicity and eventually abandoned his bourgeois family home to found a community called Phoenix on the outskirts of Durban, where he, his family and political associates could live simply by their own labour and produce their newspaper, *Indian Opinion*. This move owed much to Gandhi's chance reading of John Ruskin's *Unto This Last*, pressed into his hand for the long train journey from Johannesburg to Durban by a Jewish friend. The outward changes were symbolic of a gradual but radical internal transformation, which turned a thriving professional and family man into a celibate who abandoned worldly achievement and threw all his energy into public service as the road to the discovery of the divine within him. Although he was brought up a Hindu and remained so all his life, his religious vision was deepened and enlarged by encounters in England and South Africa with adherents of other faiths who introduced him to their scriptures and helped to convince him that God was not to be found in any one religious tradition exclusively. He sensed that Hinduism, Islam, and Christianity, the three traditions he came to know best, all enabled a search for God and a partial vision of the divine. But for him true religion was essentially a pilgrimage, a continuous searching after a Truth which lay at the heart of all things. His life now displayed a stripping away of inessentials which hindered this pilgrimage, and a cutting of the familial and emotional bonds which sustain normal domestic life.[3]

Gandhi's religious vision encompassed the whole of life, and thrust him into public and political work. As he later wrote, 'To see the universal and all-pervading Spirit of Truth face to face one must be able to love the meanest of creation as oneself. And a man who aspires after that cannot afford to keep out of any field of life.' This was what had drawn him into politics; and 'those who say that religion has nothing to do with politics do not know what religion means'.[4] Gandhi's inner vision sustained him in the deepening struggle with the South African authorities. It also led him to the method of conducting a struggle and managing conflict, whether in private or in public, which was to become his hallmark – non-violent resistance, or *satyagraha*, truth force, as he came to call it. For him this was not only a practical *modus operandi*. It was also highly moral, because it respected the opponent's integrity, and endeavoured to change the situation by one's own suffering rather than violence, which was for him the negation of the search for truth. In any situation it was important to choose only moral methods, as means and ends were indistinguishable, and only good means would lead to good ends. The reverse was equally true.

Gandhi's religious vision also forced him to confront the fact of British imperialism in India, and the reasons for it. His one extended political tract, *Hind Swaraj* (Indian Home Rule), written in 1909 in a spirit of great urgency, examined the plight of India and how Indians might deal with this.[5] For him India's predicament was not foreign rule *per se*: it was not primarily political but moral. Western influences, and particularly the values of modern materialism bred in industrial society and imported into India by the British but often internalised by western-educated Indians, had helped to erode India's own civilisation. The remedy was not political home rule, for this would only leave India in a similar state except with Indian rulers. A moral revolution was needed, which would be manifest in a renewal of the values of Indian civilisation and in the nature of relations among Indians themselves. Only then would they be truly free and able to order their own lives. However, contemporary Indian politicians were not offering their compatriots any road to real 'swaraj', despite their debates on home rule or self-government. The tiny minority who advocated violence were using immoral means, while the more moderate were engaging in a politics of petitions which was derogatory to Indian status – and they were not anyway tackling the root of the problem. The path to swaraj was therefore non-violence, that holding fast to truth, armed with the strength of a disciplined life, with which he was experimenting in South Africa. Indians should repent and mourn, knowing that British rule was their own fault, and they should also take steps to change their lives. Those who had become party to modern ways and values should abandon them, even to the extent that lawyers should give up their profession and doctors should give up western medicine: while all should give up the use of imported, industrial products, use things made in India and relearn the art of hand-making cloth.

It was hardly surprising that Indian politicians found Gandhi strange and threatening, however much they admired his long struggle for Indians in South Africa. His vision of swaraj was indeed the reverse of almost everything they had gained under the raj – in their education, their careers, and in the presumed material benefits of modern living. Further, they aspired to create a modern, independent state in India, in effect to inherit and reform the raj, rather than to engage in political revolution and radical socio-economic change of the sort he seemed to envisage. In his personal life he also seemed strange. He had taken to dressing like a poor Indian rather than a westernised lawyer; and his home in Ahmedabad, an industrial city in Gujarat, was an ashram, on the lines of a Hindu religious community round a spiritual teacher, but in this case dedicated to the simple life and the search for truth, in order to train men and women for the service of the nation in the ways he deemed essential. His wife and close family stayed with him, but this was a community where new forms of social relationship were to be created, breaking older conventions of caste, status and gender. Prayer, celibacy and hard physical work were its hallmarks. A more profound contrast with the opulent Nehru household in Allahabad could hardly have been imagined.

Gandhi does not seem to have envisaged for himself a political career in India, and had initially hoped to join the Servants of India Society (whose single-minded commitment to service so attracted Jawaharlal). But he withdrew his application when he realised that his priorities were very different from those of its members, and that they found his views anarchical, in the words of one of its senior members.[6] However, he found himself gradually drawn into public life in a series of situations where he and other people began to feel that his mode of non-violent resistance to perceived wrong might be practical and productive. So in 1917 he found himself confronting planters and local government in the Champaran district of Bihar on issues relating to the cultivation of indigo, and in 1918 in Gujarat leading protests in Kaira district against the land revenue demand, and in Ahmedabad on the pay of workers in the cotton mills. These were the occasions which brought him to the notice of Jawaharlal and the young people of his generation. He had actually met Gandhi at the Congress meeting in Lucknow in 1916, but Gandhi played no part in national politics at this stage, and Nehru and his contemporaries felt he was 'very distant and different and unpolitical'. But his subsequent local campaigns made them realise that he was prepared to use his methods of non-violence in India, too, and that they might prove successful.[7] These campaigns also alerted the government to recognition that they had a new sort of political activist on their hands, one whom it would be difficult to handle because of his growing public repute, as well as his steely internal resolve on what he saw as moral issues. As a young ICS man in Champaran had reported, 'We may look on Mr Gandhi as an idealist, a fanatic or a revolutionary according to our particular opinions.' But to the village people he seemed like a saviour and they credited him with extraordinary powers. He moved among them, asking them to tell him about their problems, and as a consequence was 'daily transfiguring the imaginations of masses of ignorant men with visions of an early millennium'.[8]

The continuing impact of the world war on Indian public life provided the occasion for Gandhi's dramatic emergence into all-India politics. The war generated issues which Gandhi saw as wrongs – moral affronts to Indian sensibilities. They also showed up the weakness of current Indian political strategies, whether of constitutionalism or of violent opposition to the raj; and caused many, including the Nehrus, to look afresh at the curious stranger who had returned from South Africa with a novel political strategy as well as an idiosyncratic vision of India's present and future.

The first of these issues was the British strategy of retaining emergency powers to deal with terrorism after the end of the war and the lapse of the Defence of India Act. The so-called Rowlatt legislation, named after the chairman of the committee appointed to enquire into 'revolutionary conspiracies' and their control, caused an outcry. The Secretary of State for India, who had invested so much time and energy in constitutional reform, sanctioned the legislation with great reluctance, finding it repugnant and telling the Viceroy privately that he 'loathed' the suggestion of preserving the Defence of India Act in peacetime.[9] Every Indian member of the Viceroy's Legislative Council opposed the proposed law but the Viceroy and his officials nonetheless felt they should push it through with the official majority. (In the end its provisions, which lasted for three years, were never used.) All Indian politicians saw this as an affront to themselves and their country. What was the use of the proposed constitutional reforms if they could only be had at such a cost – potentially repressive controls pushed through a legislature in the face of Indian opinion? The Indian press expressed outrage, but feelings ran even deeper, to be voiced on the streets among the illiterate.[10]

Gandhi (of course a trained lawyer) felt that the proposed bills were 'devilish' and began to contemplate for the first time non-violent resistance to the government as a result. He threw himself into a campaign against the proposals and with the help of members of the Home Rule League in the Bombay Presidency he created an organisation devoted to satyagraha should the bills be passed. Direct action was to take the form of a day on which all business stopped and Indians should devote themselves to fasting and prayer. Following that, civil disobedience was to take the form of distributing banned books, including Gandhi's own *Hind Swaraj*. The strategy generated an unprecedented response in urban areas across the country, disturbing both the government and a wide range of Indian politicians who feared the results of civil disobedience, even if they detested the Rowlatt legislation. Worst of all, it led to outbreaks of violence in some areas, including Gandhi's home Gujarat, and in Punjab. Appalled, he called off the campaign, confessing to a 'Himalayan miscalculation' in suggesting civil disobedience to people not yet prepared for it by a disciplined life of following after truth.[11]

Gandhi had now embarked on a new phase of his life from which he could not pull back. His moral sensibilities had been aroused. Moreover the violence which broke out in Punjab precipitated events which were to have a powerful influence on his own life and thinking and on that of many of his contemporaries. The civil authorities in the Punjabi city of Amritsar lost control and the army was called in to restore order. In this process the infamous shooting at Jallianwalla Bagh occurred. In this walled enclosure, troops under General Dyer dispersed a crowd of some 10,000 with gunfire, leaving nearly 400 dead. Subsequent official enquiries led to official condemnation of Dyer, and his dismissal from the army. But the damage had been done. Indians were disgusted not only at the official violence but also at the racial attitudes it betrayed, which were compounded by vocal support for Dyer in England. The official enquiry was seen as a whitewash. By the middle of 1920 Gandhi had concluded that Indians would have to withdraw their cooperation from government as a protest against this official violence, encompassing the original shooting and the apparent condoning of violence by the imperial regime. He wrote publicly in July that he felt that the representatives of the empire in India had no regard for Indian wishes, and counted Indian honour as of little consequence. Despite his earlier loyalty and his hope that the Montagu–Chelmsford Reforms would mark the start of a new era in Indian politics, he now could 'no longer retain affection for a government so evilly manned as it is now-a-days'.[12]

Gandhi's movement to outright hostility to the raj, and his decision to invite India to take the way of satyagraha, was also caused by another longer term problem arising out of the war. The Government of India had felt considerable concern for the sensitivities of its large Muslim minority when the Sultan of Turkey, as worldwide Khalifah of Muslims, was ranged on the side of Britain's opponents. Although nothing came of these fears during the war, in the months during which a peace treaty was being discussed a movement in support of the Khalifah built up among some Indian Muslims, claiming that he should be permitted to retain such political power as would enable him to perform his functions as worldly protector of Islam and its holy places. Gandhi was drawn into this because of his insistence that Muslims should be perceived as equal partners in a new India – a concern he had expressed when he wrote *Hind Swaraj*. He had also worked closely with Indian Muslims in South Africa, and was anxious to achieve a similar position in India. Moreover, he hoped that this would be an issue on which he could demonstrate the efficacy of satyagraha. After the publication of peace terms in May 1920 he began to advocate non-cooperation with the government as a way of securing what he perceived as justice, but also of avoiding violence on such an emotive issue. The young Nehru remembered later how concerned even some Muslims were at the implications of what Gandhi was suggesting. 'He was humble but also clear-cut and hard as a diamond, pleasant and soft-spoken but inflexible and terribly earnest. His eyes were mild and deep, yet out of them blazed a fierce energy and determination.' Gandhi warned his listeners that non-cooperation would involve a great struggle, and that if they were to succeed they would have to subject themselves to the strictest non-violence and discipline. He would have to be in a real sense a dictator of the movement, until they felt they had no more need of him.[13]

## GANDHI'S IMPACT ON THE NEHRUS

The Nehru family was rapidly swept up into the turbulence caused by Gandhi and his new political style. Jawaharlal was immediately inspired by his opposition to the Rowlatt legislation, and invigorated by the sense that in satyagraha there was a mode of direct action which could break the existing political mould and put serious pressure on the raj. His father was firmly opposed to the idea, feeling that voluntary jail-going would do nothing to move the government. Moreover he hated the idea of any of his family going to jail. Both men were aware that Gandhi's politics would involve a complete overturning of their lives, and each tried to avoid hurting the other. But Jawaharlal paced around at night, wrestling with the sense that he had no option but to join Gandhi. Gandhi eventually came to the Nehru home at Motilal's request and the two men had long talks together without the son present. Gandhi eventually advised Jawaharlal against taking any action which would upset his father. Some years later Jawaharlal looked back on this time and his sense of being torn apart, and wrote to Gandhi's secretary, Mahadev Desai, 'I shall never forget the advice that Bapu gave me in those far off days of the Satyagraha Sabha when the conflict in my mind was almost too great for me to bear. His healing words lessened my difficulties and I had some peace.'[14]

Nonetheless, in Jawaharlal's own mind the die was cast. He believed that non-cooperation was the only political way forward, as a strategy which enabled them to challenge the raj when the older political modes which had been shown to be ineffective by the British insistence on pushing through the Rowlatt legislation and in the face of attitudes such as that which inspired Dyer at Jallianwalla Bagh. He wrote to a local newspaper in September 1920: 'I am an ardent believer in noncooperation with all that it implies and I am firmly convinced that noncooperation and no other course will bring us victory.'[15] Jawaharlal's transformation into an active and radical politician did not go unnoticed by the government and soon the Criminal Investigation Department (CID) was on his tracks. In May 1920 he was asked to give an undertaking that while he was in the Himalayan hill station of Mussoorie with his wife and mother (who were both ill) and his sisters, he would have no dealings with representatives from Afghanistan who were currently staying at the same hotel in order to discuss peace terms with the government. He refused and left for the plains, while his father registered his anger with his old friend and drinking companion, Sir Harcourt Butler.[16]

By contrast with his son, Motilal still hoped that Indians could use the Montagu–Chelmsford Reforms, whatever their limitations. As president of the 1919 meeting of Congress he urged his compatriots to use the power which had been given to them but at the same time to continue to press for what was their due.[17] However, the issue of the Punjab was drawing him into close contact with Gandhi, because both were members of the Congress committee of enquiry into events in the province in 1919. He was impressed by Gandhi, the lawyer, in this context, and was furious at the tone of the official responses to events in the Punjab. He told Jawaharlal that his blood was boiling over and that they should now 'raise a veritable hell for the rascals'.[18] Even so, he was worried about the way Gandhi's politics were developing through 1920; and in June he still believed that non-cooperation in the sense of boycott of the new legislatures would be inadvisable, and that he should prepare for the elections because he felt Congress would not bind itself to such a boycott.[19] Even in July he had not resolved the question in his own mind, and told his son that though he sympathised with the principle of non-cooperation he did not see what form it should take in practice. He still tended to feel that the best strategy of opposition would be to get elected and then either to refuse to sit in the legislature or to obstruct its business.[20]

Gandhi had launched non-cooperation on 1 August 1920 as a protest on both the Punjab and Khilafat issues. But its viability as an all-India strategy, uniting Muslims and Hindus in a programme of opposition which would effectively move the raj, depended on the formal reaction of Congress at a special session scheduled for early September in Calcutta. The session displayed many of the ambiguities of Indian nationalist politics at the time. Although the Congress had in 1916 demanded self-government at an early date, it was still not an organised party with a clear ideology. Locally it was often little more than a plate on a lawyer's door except when it came to choosing delegates for the annual session: even then there was no regular system of election or of numbers of delegates according to population. Interested parties could, and did, send delegates in large numbers for specific meetings. Moreover, prominent provincial politicians subscribed to no party line; they often voted with an eye both to all-India issues and to the more complex political worlds they inhabited in relation to their local positions of influence and the way continental alliances might buttress such positions. However, Congress was, for all its amorphous quality, a valuable resource in the multiple interlocking political systems which made up Indian political life. Individuals and groups of allies with ideals or interests at stake could rarely afford to ignore it by this time.

At Calcutta in September Gandhi offered his strategy of non-cooperation to a gathering which included seasoned political activists with far more experience than he had. Many of them were hostile to this new idea and its potential threat to their orderly political world, inhabited by people like themselves. However, gradually the Subjects Committee, which produced the resolutions for the open session, began to swing in his favour. His proposal was carried after prolonged discussion by a majority of twelve – 144 voting for it, and 132 against. In the open session the majority for Gandhi was around 1,000, though half the registered delegates did not vote, probably because there was no alternative proposal which permitted them to register outright opposition to the idea of non-cooperation. Not surprisingly there was an outcry at this result, and considerable heart-searching as to how this could have happened. It seems clear that many of Gandhi's supporters, particularly in the open session, came from areas and communities which had previously had little influence in Congress sessions. Among them were Muslims supporting the Khilafat cause and voting to swing the Congress into non-cooperation on this issue. Of the provinces whose delegates sided most strongly with Gandhi were UP, Bihar, Punjab and Bombay (which included Gujarat). UP was home to some of the most articulate Khilafat leaders, while the other areas had all received Gandhi's particular attention or were the sites of his local satyagraha campaigns. However, this victory for Gandhi was not the result of any wholesale conversion to his views, or even commitment to the idea and practice of satyagraha. Many of those who eventually voted for his programme did so because they recognised the weight of opinion in its favour and feared for their own positions if they flew in the face of it. Gandhi's apparent dominance was thus the result of multiple and diverse decisions to experiment with a new political strategy in particular circumstances. The success of his programme in operation was in no way guaranteed by the votes at Calcutta.[21]

The days of the Calcutta Congress were Motilal's personal turning point. He had arrived in Calcutta apparently determined to oppose Gandhi's programme, but ended supporting Gandhi in the Subjects Committee. Jawaharlal portrayed his father as coming through a time of grappling with the personal implications for himself of aligning with Gandhi, as well as weighing the worth of Gandhi's strategy in the context of the sense of national humiliation following the Punjab tragedy and its political aftermath, and then coming to a final and considered decision. However, other considerations almost certainly played a part. One was the certainty that if he continued to oppose Gandhi he would split his family. Another was the clear evidence that in his own province political opinion was flowing in favour of non-cooperation, and that he would lose local credibility if he continued to oppose it. Just days before the Congress the UP Provincial Congress Committee (PCC) had resolved in favour of non-cooperation, and at the session 259 as opposed to 28 of provincial delegates voted for it.

Motilal's stance as a major figure behind Gandhi thrust him into the forefront of the new style of politics, and he became part of the three-man committee appointed to work out the details of non-cooperation, alongside Gandhi. In this new role he threw himself behind a radical programme which included the boycott of official titles and of government functions; the gradual withdrawal of pupils from government schools and colleges; gradual withdrawal of lawyers from the courts and the foundation of national arbitration courts; boycott of the new councils to which elections were about to be held for the first time; and progress towards *swadeshi*, using goods made in India, buttressed by the practice of hand-spinning and weaving. It is remarkable that it was Motilal who suggested that social boycott should be imposed on people who did not accept the decision of the new arbitration courts.[22]

Motilal was nothing if not thorough – a quality he had once commended to his son. In his own life he immediately set about following Gandhi's programme. He resigned his membership of the existing UP legislature and announced that he would not stand for election in the reformed legislature. He wound up his legal practice, and he began the process of dismantling the elaborate lifestyle he had created for himself and his family. Foreign clothes were disposed of or burnt, the wine cellar was done away with, and from now only one kitchen provided for the family's simpler needs. Father and son had found a new unity of purpose and style, and both adopted the sartorial symbolism of hand-made Indian dress and what became known as a Gandhi cap. Their political and social world had been turned upside down by the Mahatma and his radical intervention in public life.

For Jawaharlal 1920 had proved even more significant than adopting a stance of outright opposition to the British and of embracing a novel political strategy. The very core of his understanding of India and of the meaning of politics was also changed by his first experience of the life of the rural poor. When he left the hill station where the womenfolk of the family were staying, rather than give the undertaking the government required, he returned to the searing summer heat of the UP plains. A group of peasants had come in from the countryside to Allahabad to seek help from more modern political activists in their campaign to resist exactions from and ejectment by the Talukdars, their landlords, the trusted allies of the UP government. Nehru knew nothing about this movement, and before these persistent rustics forced him to come to see something of their problems, he had never really gone into the UP countryside before. Nor was he used to having to walk for hours in the sun, where there were no motorable roads. He took some pride in his physical stamina and in the unusual rich tan he had acquired in these days, as in the fact that he gave his 'escort' of police, CID men and an ICS man a bad time by forcing them to walk such distances in the countryside.[23]

Nehru now saw for the first time something of the depth of rural poverty to be found in parts of India, and in particular the gross imbalances of power in Indian rural life and politics, in places where there were substantial landowners backed up by the imperial regime. Only now did be begin to see India in terms of such men and women as those who confronted him with their poverty and their hope of the help he might give them. He felt shame and sadness at the petty politics of the city he had left behind him, and a different image of India 'seemed to rise before me, naked, starving, crushed and utterly miserable'. From then onwards he never lost sight of them in his mental picture of India.[24] The casually intellectual parlour socialism he had toyed with in Cambridge paled before this human evidence, forcing the young and privileged city man to think far more deeply about the social and economic order in India and its relationship to politics. It also made him more receptive to Gandhi's concern for the poor, and his vision of a radical transformation of Indian society. At a more practical level, the UP peasants forced Nehru to overcome his shyness at public speaking, particularly in Hindustani. He discovered to his surprise that he lost his inhibition in such company and evolved a conversational style, talking to them directly as individuals rather than attempting to play the role of orator. So the provincial government unwittingly gave Nehru the opportunity to develop his own political style, so different from that of his father and much more suited to the arena of mass politics, where great ideological issues were transformed into issues deeply felt by ordinary people. It had also forced him to expand his vision of the meaning of freedom for Indians outside the elite circle in which he had been brought up.

The emergence of Gandhi into all-India politics as a result of the government's post-war policies had had a dramatic effect on the lives of all the Nehrus. This was to become even clearer in the subsequent decade when politics ravaged their domestic peace, and led father and son to prison. He had offered them a mode of political action which seemed to resolve the dilemma in which they had increasingly found themselves – of being boxed in by a regime which set the parameters of accepted politics but would not move when it considered that its security and essential interests were being threatened. Now, in non-violent non-cooperation they had a strategy which was overtly moral (in comparison with violence), but also potentially destructive of the raj's stability, given the extent to which it relied on Indian cooperation. Outwardly they had, in response to the Mahatma, committed themselves to non-violent withdrawal of cooperation from a regime which relied heavily on Indian allies like themselves for its daily functioning. They had also abandoned the trappings of a lifestyle created by association with the raj.

However, there remained profound differences between them and Gandhi. He was groping for ways in which to transform India's society, economy and polity and lead Indians away from much that imperial rule had enabled in India; and he drew deeply on Indian traditions in this attempt. The Nehrus, though their commitment as nationalists was as great as Gandhi's, had a vision of India which was essentially born of contact with western ways of thinking, and more profoundly marked by them. They wished in pursuit of this vision to overturn the raj, but without abandoning many of the values and changes which they thought a new India would do well to retain and adapt from its experience of living under an imperial regime. Such differing responses to India's situation lay at the heart of many of the debates which were to emerge in the politics of nationalism, they were to cause a series of deep and painful disagreements between Gandhi and Jawaharlal, even though the younger man was essentially the Mahatma's political protégé and further bound to him by deepening emotional ties.

## Part 2

# The Ambiguities of Mass Nationalism, 1920–1939

# Chapter 4

# The Making of a Politician

## THE INTER-WAR YEARS: PERSPECTIVES

Between 1920 and 1939 Jawaharlal Nehru emerged as one of India's foremost nationalist politicians, first as an apprentice under the guidance of Gandhi, then as a close friend and ally, despite their often profound differences of opinion and style. These were also years of deep personal change for Nehru. His politics lead to the total destruction of ordered family life. He also suffered the death of both parents, of a baby son and then of his wife; and he was left to bring up his only daughter, Indira, who was barely out of adolescence when her mother died in 1936. At two stages, in the early 1920s and early 1930s, he also spent considerable time in jail for his participation in Gandhi's movements of satyagraha. This was a totally novel experience for him and for people of his social status, requiring personal adjustments of a radical kind. It also gave him time to read and reflect on his life and politics, and eventually to begin to write seriously and at length. His *Autobiography* was the fruit of his jail term ending in 1935. Concluding it he wrote of the ghosts of dead yesterdays with their poignant memories who seemed to ask if it had been worthwhile. His answer was unhesitating. If he had the time over again he might have changed his personal life, or improved on some things he had done, but his major decisions in public affairs would remain. 'Indeed, I could not vary them, for they were stronger than myself, and a force beyond my control drove me to them.'[1]

Nehru indeed experienced a vocation to the politics of opposition to the raj as a result of Gandhi's unexpected emergence into all-India politics. However, the politics of nationalism were complex, and far less clear-cut than he later assumed them to be. Most articulate political activists after the 1914–18 war would have considered themselves to be nationalists, in the sense that they looked eventually to self-government for India. But the timescale for such a development was debatable, as was the precise nature of self-government. Many would, for example, have had as their goal Dominion status like that enjoyed by existing Dominions within the British empire, such as Canada or Australia. It is important to remember that this was several decades before the processes of decolonisation which marked the years after the Second World War, and nobody of Motilal's or Jawaharlal's generations had yet witnessed the voluntary withdrawal of a European imperial power from either Asia or Africa.

Moreover, the politics of nationalism in India was deeply intertwined with local and regional politics, and these affected decisions made on pan-Indian policy and strategy. In the inter-war years the interests and sensibilities of a far larger swathe of the population became interlocked with all-India politics. Sometimes this occurred through the politics of active opposition to the raj, particularly when Gandhi's satyagraha movements connected with existing local political struggles, or tapped into popular discontents. More continuously, new connections between what had often been separate political worlds were being forged through the processes of constitutional politics and governance, as constitutional reforms in 1919 and 1935 enlarged the franchise and demanded that aspirant leaders and representatives made new linkages with their potential supporters. In the longer term, as India's formal political system evolved, laying down the structural basis for India's eventual independent constitution, the modes of operating within it became part of a far broader Indian political culture which was eventually to sustain its democracy. However, in the shorter term these new processes of connecting all-India and more local politics threw up ambiguities of interest and actual or potential divisions – not surprising, given India's great size and diversity. As Indians took increasing control of their local and provincial affairs, and as the prospect of a self-governing India became a practical reality, so the idea and vision of a new India became both more powerful and more disputed.

These years consequently witnessed increasing political controversy and turbulence, as Indians interacted with each other as well as with the raj. A number of major issues demanded attention, and were to surface and resurface during Nehru's own experience in this phase of his career. They were particularly acute within and in relation to the Congress because Congress was the largest Indian political organisation at the time, and so in a sense activists made their responses and decisions in response to it, not only from within but also as peripheral observers or as opponents. It was also because Congress was itself such a loose organisation with multiple connections to local political worlds that these issues surfaced within its own ranks.

The underlying question was that of ideology. What was the nature of the India activists sought? Was it defined in cultural, religious or political terms; and was it an inclusive or exclusive vision, rooted in the cultural pluralism of the subcontinent or in the self-perception of a particular group? Consequent in part on the answer to this was the further question of political strategy. Was the goal to be achieved through careful use of the new structures and institutions of politics which enabled Indians to participate in government to a far greater extent and thus to put pressure on the raj in new ways? Or was a new India to be sought through the violent direct action of a few, or through its opposite, the non-violent Gandhian politics of passion and piety involving disciplined mass campaigns of opposition to the existing government? Congress in particular, as the self-professed and major figurehead speaking for the nation, had to address the problem of organisation. In the changing political environment all types of considered political action which involved larger numbers of people, whether as participants in oppositional campaigns or as voters, needed better organisation than had ever been achieved before 1920. This meant money, new structures of authority and discipline, and particularly the making of ties which would ensure that Congress as an all-India body could expect loyalty from its local members and supporters, and could control their actions to some degree. Finally, these issues taken together demanded the development of many new kinds of political leadership – people who could forge connections between the different strands and arenas of Indian politics by their command of ideology and rhetoric, their capacity to visualise a new India in idioms explicable and attractive to a far wider and non-elite audience, their work to strengthen political organisations and organise broad movements, and their ability to engage with the British and the world from which they came. These were issues with which Nehru had to struggle, now and even after India's attainment of political independence. They also gave him the opportunity to become a major player in all-India politics.

## THE POLITICAL APPRENTICE, 1920–1926

Nehru's initial political apprenticeship took place within the non-cooperation movement of 1920–2, and his first prolonged encounter with Gandhi and his politics. The initial acceptance of this new strategy, at the deeply contested Calcutta special session of Congress, was confirmed at the party's Nagpur gathering in December 1920. Despite rumblings of opposition to non-cooperation from experienced politicians of very different persuasions, Gandhi prevailed, benefiting from support among the rank and file of delegates and from critical revisions of attitude by some key leaders who calculated that it would be better for their local positions if they sided with the rising star. Such considerations seemed likely to deter any remaining opponents from launching any alternative party or strategy in the immediate future.[2] They were in serious disarray, and as one of them noted gloomily, working with Gandhi seemed the best option, particularly as there was considerable provincial flexibility within the overarching programme. 'The time is ripe for us all now, reserving the right to ourselves to express our differences amongst ourselves whenever a proper occasion arrives, to close up our ranks and offer a united front to the government under the guidance of the only man – Mahatma Gandhi – who can be somewhat of a leader to us, under the present circumstances.'[3]

In the subsequent year the campaign spread throughout India, leading to a broad range of manifestations, from return of titles from those honoured by the raj, to boycott of schools and colleges and the opening of 'national' educational institutions, withdrawal of lawyers from courts and the creation of arbitration courts, to campaigns against the use of foreign cloth, and temperance movements. Nowhere did it make government impossible, just as the abstention of many candidates and voters from the elections in November 1920 did not prevent the working of the new constitution. (Only in six cases out of 637 seats was an election impossible because there were no candidates; the turnout varied wildly from 50 per cent to as low as 4.4 per cent of the electorate.) However it showed dramatically the potential of a new kind of mass politics in the name of a national demand. More worryingly – both to the government and the leaders of the new movement – it demonstrated that where an all-India strategy dovetailed with local discontent or became the vehicle for local and sectional demands, that strategy might race out of control of an all-India leadership and, at worst, lead to violence against property and people. Some of the worst instances occurred where non-cooperation tapped into long-standing peasant discontents, as in Malabar in south-western India or in the Nehrus' own UP. In the latter Gandhi even had to issue stern instructions to peasants against violence and intimidation.[4]

Nehru flung himself into the movement, speaking at meetings, writing to the press, and involving himself both with the provincial Congress and the UP peasant movement. This was his apprenticeship within the politics of mass activism. Looking back he could see how 'abnormal' he had been, as a result. To his daughter, who had then been only a small child, he admitted, 'I had a flame-like quality, a fire within me which burned and consumed me and drove me relentlessly forward; it made me almost oblivious of all other matters, even of intimate personal relations. I was in fact wholly unfit as a close companion of anyone except in that one sphere of thought and action which had enslaved me.'[5] He and his colleagues felt a kind of intoxication, and a huge sense of excitement and enthusiasm, at working for the new movement: the old sense of oppression and frustration had gone, and they felt they were working to change the face of India, with a considerable glow of moral superiority. For Nehru himself there was also the initiation into a new kind of relationship with India's rural population. He later wrote perceptively of himself: 'I experienced the thrill of mass-feeling, the power of influencing the mass. I began to understand a little the psychology of the crowd, the difference between the city masses and the peasantry, and I felt at home in the dust and discomfort, the pushing and jostling of large gatherings, though their want of discipline often irritated me.'[6]

In retrospect he could see how the enthusiasm of the time prevented them from coming to grips with important issues. There was no clear thinking about the goal of the movement, and no definition of the meaning of swaraj; and the absence of a clear goal or ideology meant that any popular movement was likely to disintegrate. Gandhi himself was vague on the meaning of swaraj, and seemed to give assurances both to the privileged and the poor. His stress 'was never on the intellectual approach to a problem but on character and piety'.[7] Nehru's own views were also less than clear at this stage. Speaking as president of a local conference in mid-1920 he defined swaraj partly in political terms and partly in cultural terms of a new vision of India. Swaraj was for all Indians – rich and poor, and people of every religious affiliation. This unity was to be made real through a political system of panchayats, or local councils, whose members were under the control of those for whom they worked.[8] He hated the system of government through which the British ruled India, but insisted that he did not feel ill-will towards them as a people or as individuals, except perhaps momentarily. Again, with considerable self-perception, he admitted to Gandhi that he still admired the British greatly 'and in many things I feel even now that an Englishman can understand me better than the average Indian'.[9]

Gandhi clearly had a profound influence on the younger man, as a political mentor and a source of inspiration. In company with him, old frustrations gave place to a sense of courage, of being free from fear and of being able to deal with the imperial ruler. Moreover, Nehru found the technique of satyagraha increasingly attractive, as suiting Indian conditions and traditions, although he never gave the doctrine of non-violence his absolute allegiance. It seemed to him that it was sound practical politics as well as good ethics, and that following it would increase Indian self-respect. But even at this early stage he recognised that there were fundamental differences of opinion between him and the Mahatma. The younger man and most of his colleagues did not share Gandhi's hostility to modern civilisation and its economic underpinnings, and were critical of his lifestyle. 'Often we discussed his fads and peculiarities among ourselves and said, half-humorously, that when Swaraj came these fads must not be encouraged.'[10]

At the same time Nehru was increasingly worried about the religious aspects of the non-cooperation movement, which stemmed not only from Gandhi's manner and rhetoric, but also from the influence of Muslim religious leaders in support of the Khilafat cause. All this led to a revivalist atmosphere, particularly among a broader public, and Nehru disliked what he saw as the exploitation of the people by so-called men of religion. 'I did not like it at all. Much that Moulvies and Maulanas and Swamis and the like said in their public addresses seemed to me most unfortunate. Their history and sociology and economics appeared to me all wrong, and the religious twist that was given to everything prevented all clear thinking.' Even some of Gandhi's own phrases jarred on him, like the frequent reference to a coming golden age, *ram rajya*, the rule of the Hindu god, Ram.[11] Nonetheless, more than at any time since his early boyhood (when he had come under the influence of Theosophy through his tutor), he came somewhat nearer to a religious frame of mind as a result of Gandhi's influence.

In later middle age Nehru looked back to the way Gandhi had trained him and others like him as if they were soldiers, with great discipline and strictness. He drove them mercilessly, so that prison was a rest.[12] His own first experience of prison (and his father's) came late in 1921. He was released in March 1922 and then re-imprisoned in May, emerging finally at the end of January 1923. During his trial in May for picketing to prevent the sale of foreign cloth in Allahabad he said he went to prison willingly and joyfully. To serve in India's battle for freedom was a great honour, and he thanked the British for giving him this opportunity: to serve under Gandhi made people like him doubly fortunate. Later he added in a letter to Motilal that his sense of good fortune was even more personal because he felt that both his parents had given him high ideals and had added to his strength and spirit.[13] Despite this brave talk, prison was a daunting prospect physically for a man like him, brought up in comfort, but perhaps even more daunting psychologically because prison was assumed to be a place for criminals and the dregs of society. Gandhi gave him sound advice, drawn from his own experience of prison in South Africa. He should try to distance himself from the outer world, for he could do nothing about it or even know accurately what was happening, and he would only vex himself uselessly. Instead, he should take up some serious study and also some demanding manual labour, particularly the *charkha*, or spinning-wheel.[14]

The British authorities made sure that important political prisoners were kept apart from ordinary criminals, and had somewhat more favoured treatment. Even so, life was extremely spartan, although prisoners were allowed to receive food from outside, and also spare clothes, bedding and books. Nehru managed to keep reasonably healthy in prison, and his weight varied only slightly between 114 and 121 pounds, which was reasonable for his comparatively short stature. (His slight physique had suited him to coxing rather than rowing at Cambridge.) He took care to take plenty of exercise – running where possible, playing volley-ball if there were enough political prisoners for a game, drawing water from a well, and doing German breathing exercises. He also spun regularly, often for between two and four hours daily, and as a good member of the Gandhian movement, he kept a record of this. Between 16 August and 28 September 1922 he had spun for 92 hours and 25 minutes, and had produced 9,394 yards of cotton thread.[15]

He had clearly taken to heart Gandhi's advice on how to survive and manage jail life, because he also attempted to study Urdu (a language conversationally close to Hindi but written in the Arabic script, and widely spoken among educated Muslims as well as men such as his father in UP). He also returned to his fundamentally intellectual approach to life, and read voraciously. He had with him in jail at one time or another over 130 books and periodicals, mostly in English but a few in Hindi. They included books on Indian and European history and modern politics, Gibbon's *Decline and Fall*, large volumes of English poetry (including Wordsworth, Shelley, Byron and Tennyson), several Shakespeare plays, essays by Tolstoy, works by Ruskin, and even the Harrow Association Record. He read over fifty items, mostly poetry, politics and history. At one stage the English superintendent of the Lucknow prison seemed to get irritated at the sight of so much reading. He told Nehru that he had finished his general reading at the age of twelve; Nehru privately thought that this had probably saved him from troublesome ideas and helped him rise eventually to be UP Inspector-General of Prisons! Nehru attempted to read some Einstein, but found the mathematics too hard for him. In notebooks he copied out passages which were particularly meaningful to him, and also made sizeable summaries of the books he had read. Among the portions copied out were some which obviously threw light for him on the Indian situation. There were verses redolent of a romantic European nationalism. The raj and the challenge of non-cooperation must surely have been in his mind when he copied out from Romain Rolland's *Fourteenth of July*, 'When order is injustice, disorder is the beginning of justice.' More immediate were large parts of Oscar Wilde's *The Ballad of Reading Gaol*. A note of humour occurred with a quotation taken from the *New Statesman* of 12 August 1922:

> If men be judged wise by their beards and their girth
> Then goats were the wisest of creatures on earth.

Feeding and stimulating the mind was comparatively easy, given Nehru's access to books. More difficult was the task of emotional adjustment to the constraints of prison and the absence of loved ones. He had shared the first brief imprisonment with his father, but the second sentence he shared with others who were not close to him personally although he knew them from their common cause. They included Gandhi's secretary, Mahadev Desai, one of his sons, Devdas Gandhi, and another Allahabad politician whom he had known since they were boys, Purshottam Das Tandon. (Three decades later he was to contend with Tandon in a bitter struggle for the leadership of the Congress.) One of the worst trials for Jawaharlal was the utter lack of privacy. They bathed and washed their clothes in public, took exercise together, and talked in their limited group until they 'had largely exhausted each other's capacity for intelligent conversation'. It was like the dullest aspects of family life, hugely magnified, with few of the graces and compensations of a family: 'And all this among people of all kinds and tastes. It was a great nervous strain for all of us, and often I yearned for solitude.'[16]

He would try to escape into the open part of their prison enclosure, and take consolation from watching the grandeur of the passing monsoon clouds. He missed the sounds of normal life, like dogs barking or women talking. Understandably he worried about his wife and news of her ill-health; and he was concerned that their daughter seemed to be difficult to deal with, and paid no heed to any kind of study. However, he received reasonably regular visits from his family, including his mother, wife, daughter and sisters. At one point these were weekly, though latterly interviews were only permitted once a month, and for a short period he and others refused all interviews as a protest against the way the prison authorities treated the visitors and searched them. He also wrote and received some personal letters, though these were subject to censorship and could be held up in transit. He was allowed to write and receive a fortnightly letter, and these were mostly to and from his father and Kamala. Despite the stresses and privations he managed to find an emotional equilibrium in prison. He assured his father that he had adapted well to the strange life, and indeed, he was thankful to have been given time to read, and a chance to break out of the small-minded life and politics of Allahabad to which he had returned from England. 'Ever since my return . . . I have done little reading and I shudder to think what I was gradually becoming before politics & N.C.O. [non-cooperation] snatched me away from the doom that befalls many of us. Freedom in many of its aspects is denied us but the freedom and the glory of thought is ours and none can deprive us of it.' Fate had intervened and taken him out of the rut and placed him on the mountainside. 'We may not reach the top yet awhile but the glory of wider vision is ours.'[17]

Nonetheless, both Nehrus felt ill at ease with aspects of Gandhi's politics. Motilal made it plain to his son that he could not follow Gandhi's 'politico-religious philosophy' beyond a certain point; and he told Gandhi outright that his own religion was his country and he would serve it to the utmost according to his lights – when he agreed with him it was on political, economic and sometimes moral grounds, but not 'on the identical grounds upon which you rely . . .'[18] Jawaharlal's disquiet was more anguished, particularly in February 1922, when Gandhi suspended civil disobedience following a major outbreak of violence, when a crowd of village people set light to a police station in Chauri Chaura, UP, burning alive the twenty-two police inside it. Jawaharlal deplored the incident; but Gandhi's response seemed to throw in doubt the viability of the non-violent method of opposing the raj. For Jawaharlal and many of those who had gone to prison for their participation in the movement, non-violence was a policy, a method promising results, and not a dogma or creed. If sporadic acts of violence meant that the campaign was always liable to be called off, how could it succeed? He and other prisoners managed to get word to Gandhi, who was still at liberty, of their extreme distress; and Gandhi replied in a letter which was read out to Jawaharlal by his sister, Vijayalakshmi, during a visit to him. For Gandhi this violent incident was the last straw, coming on top of news that participants in non-cooperation were becoming 'aggressive, defiant and threatening'. The movement had to return to its non-violent moorings, and the cause could only prosper by this apparent retreat.[19]

The gulf between Gandhi and Jawaharlal on the issue of non-violence remained. For Gandhi it was a creed, and a total commitment to a mode of functioning which he felt worked a moral and practical change in those who adhered to it. Therefore any departure from it was morally wrong and would vitiate the desired end. For Nehru and many other Congress members it remained a method among many possible methods, and one they had chosen not because of a theological position, but as the result of calculation that in these particular circumstances it would be effective. However, he learnt one major lesson from this traumatic episode. The movement was disintegrating for lack of organisation and discipline, whatever its apparent power and popular support. Any future movement would have to be preceded by work to remedy these weaknesses. There would have to be better organisation, and clear principles and ideals. So possibly the decision in 1922 was the right one, although 'the manner of doing it left much to be desired and brought about a certain demoralisation'.[20]

Jawaharlal, the activist in non-cooperation and then the prisoner, had begun to glimpse some of the profound ambiguities in a nationalist movement which tried to achieve popular support. He had seen fundamental problems emerge over woolly or non-existent ideology, weak organisation, a strategy that had apparently failed them, and a leadership which, though deeply attractive and apparently in touch with the Indian people as no previous politician had been, seemed erratic and at times incomprehensible. However, his dilemmas were even starker when he emerged from prison and was forced into action. In attempting to resolve the problems which confronted him he experienced another part of his political apprenticeship. For the first time he had experience of working within political institutions on a routine basis – within the Congress Party, and within local government. This was to be as important as his more dramatic immersion in the politics of confrontation and mass action, a humdrum investment of time and energy which would pay considerable dividends in his later career.

Jawaharlal left prison to find Congress a house divided against itself in the wake of Gandhi's response to Chauri Chaura and his imprisonment soon after. Congress had in 1922 appointed a committee to enquire into civil disobedience: it included Motilal. As the members toured each province they found mixed opinions, but considerable consensus that the Gandhian programme had not worked, and that there must be changes, including possibly a return to using the provisions of the new constitution.[21] The committee was itself divided, and this was plain from its published report, which Motilal himself drafted. Although members agreed that the country was not yet ready for civil disobedience, and that aspects of non-cooperation should continue (even if somewhat toned down), they disagreed on the crucial question of council entry. Motilal was among those who thought that they should enter the councils and obstruct them from within. If they declined to fight the next elections they would be shut out for the next three years, and nobody could tell what might happen during that time.[22] He was joined, among others, by a prominent Muslim, Hakim Ajmal Khan, who felt that entering the councils and proving the reform scheme useless was the only viable strategy, as he doubted whether Congress members throughout the country would really put their backs into the 'constructive programme' advocated by Gandhi, which included the practice of swadeshi, *khadi* (homespun cloth), temperance, communal unity, and opposition to untouchability. 'The constructive programme is the basis of all our actions and therefore we should have recommended only [it] . . . but I cannot shut my eyes that excluding a few Provinces, in others we are not only [not] making any progress but on the other hand we are going certainly backwards.'[23]

When the Congress meeting at the end of 1922 declined to shift policy on council entry, Motilal was one of the leaders who formed a new Swaraj Party determined to adopt a new approach. Their goal remained swaraj, but more immediately the speedy attainment of dominion status. To this end they intended to contest elections to the central assembly and the provincial legislatures, to obstruct their work and make government through the councils impossible. Looking back, Motilal insisted that he took this leading part out of conviction that non-cooperation had practically ceased to exist, and that the imminent elections were 'a splendid opportunity for reviving it in a new form which would capture the imagination of the country'.[24] Congress then split into those who wished to change the strategy and those who were 'no-changers'. The controversy became even more acute when Gandhi emerged from prison in 1924, leading to considerable tension between Motilal, now leader of the Swarajists in the Central Legislative Assembly, and the Mahatma. Eventually a compromise was achieved, and the Swarajists carried on as effectively the political wing of Congress, while Gandhi committed himself to 'constructive' work. Gandhi still attracted considerable personal regard, and the government recognised that it could not write him off politically: nonetheless, his strategy of opposition had for the time being failed.[25]

Jawaharlal was confused and disturbed by the collapse of the strategy into which he had flung himself, and felt humiliated by the divisions within Congress. His inclination was to oppose the constitutional route of elections and council entry, but he recognised that there was in reality no other political programme before the country. He clung to the ideal of non-cooperation and non-violence, and the goal of complete independence. But even he began to have doubts about parts of Gandhi's programme. He said publicly that he almost wished that Congress had not accepted non-cooperation at Calcutta in 1920, thus leaving a small band of disciplined adherents of Gandhi to pursue direct action, instead of which they had been overwhelmed and paralysed by the weight of numbers.[26] For him the dilemmas and ambiguities of mass nationalism were all too apparent.

Moreover, they created renewed political tensions between father and son. It was perhaps not surprising that Gandhi told Motilal in 1924 that he thought Jawaharlal was one of loneliest young men he knew in India.[27]

He found some relief from the confusion and conflict in his life by working within the Congress organisation, first as secretary of the Provincial Congress Committee (PCC) in his home province, and then for the all-India body. One of Gandhi's more lasting influences on the Congress was to remodel its constitution at the end of 1920, so that it could sustain constant political activity throughout the year through the All-India Congress Committee (AICC) and the much smaller Congress Working Committee (CWC). The party was also divided into linguistic provinces, each with its own PCC as the directing core of Congress work locally. Delegates were to attend annual meetings only in proportion to the province's population, thus making Congress more representative of the whole country than it had been in the earlier days when attendance was more haphazard, and meetings could be 'packed'. Jawaharlal was one of the AICC's general secretaries from May 1923 until December 1925, during which time he came to know the organisation well, and to recognise its many problems and persistent frailties. Nonetheless, from the outset he felt a misfit in the heart of Congress; and he recognised that many members of the CWC distrusted him and disliked his presence as secretary.[28] Despite his close connection with Gandhi he inhabited a middle ground in Congress, firmly aligned with neither his father's group nor the 'no-changers'. He was seen as too young and too self-opinionated, and he had no firm local power base on which to build an all-India presence.

One of the main problems he encountered in Congress was lack of money. His own PCC had only Rs 20 in the bank early in 1924, and the AICC was hardly in a better state. Money was to be a persistent problem for the party throughout the years until independence, despite the fact that Gandhi was adept at raising cash for special causes, particularly aspects of his own social work. Nehru was also aware that handling public money was likely to generate suspicion and dissatisfaction, and that Congress practice had been very slack. (Currently there was also controversy about sizeable sums alleged to have been embezzled from money collected for the Khilafat movement.) He tried to insist that Congress should have clear and regular rules about the management of public funds, and asked even senior Congress members for accounts for their personal expenditure and for funds entrusted to them. As secretary he encountered deep rifts within provincial organisations; and he also had to try to disentangle irregularities within Congress in relation to local membership and the lists of delegates to Congress sessions. It was evident that despite the intentions of Gandhi, the organisation was still inadequate to sustain a major campaign, or to guarantee loyalty to an all-India policy.

In his role as Congress secretary Jawaharlal was also brought face to face for the first time with deepening suspicions and controversies between Hindus and

Muslims. For example, in September 1924 he spent three days in two places in UP, trying to discover what had happened during trouble between Muslims and Hindus during the solemn Muslim observance of Moharram. He found the whole experience deeply dispiriting: local people seemed to have been themselves responsible, and his attempts to discover what had really happened were vitiated by 'a considerable amount of hard lying on both sides'.[29] A month later he was writing lengthy reports directly to Gandhi on disturbances in Allahabad between Muslims and Hindus. He noted that each community honestly felt that the other was in the wrong, accused the other of premeditation and planning, and was entirely ignorant of the other's viewpoint or losses.

Outbreaks of violence in the name of religion were one of the manifestations of local politics in northern India in the wake of the collapse of non-cooperation and the ending of the Khilafat movement, when the Turks abolished the Khalifah's position in 1924. In UP alone between 1923 and 1927 there were eighty-eight incidents classified as 'communal riots', which left eighty-one people killed and over 2,300 injured. Sporadic violence sparked by religious antagonism was nothing new in areas where Muslims and Hindus lived in close proximity. But what was now occurring was new in depth and spread. Both at local level and in the realm of articulate politics Hindus and Muslims seemed to be drifting apart from each other in mutual suspicion and antagonism. The Muslim League began to meet separately from Congress from December 1924, and Muslim membership of Congress slumped – to 3.6 per cent in 1923 compared with nearly 11 per cent in 1921. Moreover, specifically Hindu political groups began to emerge as Congress began to disintegrate as an encompassing movement with a viable programme.

These manifestations have often been referred to as 'communalism', by contemporaries and by later commentators. This shorthand masks deep complexities. For these developments were not only diverse, they also did not involve complete and united communities. Hindus and Muslims alike differed in socio-economic and political position according to their region and locality, and their developing political identities stemmed from these positions as much as from any overarching sense of being Muslim or being Hindu. Perhaps no other issue has aroused such historical debate and fierce controversy, in the light of the subsequent partition of the subcontinent. Historians still have no final and conclusive answers as to why apparently religious disunities should have become so critical in many arenas of politics in the early twentieth century, why religious identities rather than other social or economic senses of belonging should have become particularly contentious in a time of change. The numerous religious reformist movements which had emerged in the nineteenth century had clearly heightened religious sensibilities and sharpened boundaries around religious communities. These continued into the twentieth century and gave rise to movements to convert new adherents and to rescue those who were deemed to have fallen away or been lured to another religious allegiance. As people involved in such movements turned to politics they were often primarily concerned with the strengthening and reform of their own community's local place in society and the polity. This in turn affected their relationship with the Congress Party.

The structures of public and political life were also changing at this stage, as the British began to devolve power into Indian hands in local government institutions and then through the constitutional reforms of 1909 and 1919. Given their vision of Indian society, and mindful of the need to retain the loyalty of significant groups of allies, the British confirmed religious differences as having political significance by giving religious minorities special seats and electorates, just as they did for landlords and other important socio-economic groups. Once belonging to a religious minority provided a political platform for electioneering, it was hardly surprising that aspirant politicians used the rhetoric of religion to appeal to voters. Simultaneously the Khilafat movement in alliance with Gandhi's particular rhetoric and programme made religion a popular political idiom, as Jawaharlal had commented with distaste. Once religious idioms had penetrated both high politics and popular awareness, outbreaks of communal violence were more likely; and a cycle of violence, retaliation and recrimination developed which political leaders could not control. Even Gandhi was tempted to despair by the late 1920s, when his various strategies for achieving unity – his personal example, journalism, a fast, and the Unity Conference in the autumn of 1924 – seemed to have failed.

Jawaharlal was horrified at what he saw. For him ignorance and bigotry were overwhelming what to him was a primary value, the ability to think rationally. True religion was being degraded and used as a cover for other things. He pleaded with his colleagues from UP even in 1923:

> We seem to have drifted back to a state of affairs which prevailed in Europe during the dark ages when to think rationally was considered an evil. I think it is time for persons who wish to regard religion as something good and sacred, and the exercise of rational thought as essential for human progress, to protest with all their might against all kinds of bigotry and superstition.[30]

A year later in preparation for the Unity Conference organised in Delhi (and chaired by his father) he wrote of the way intolerance was poisoning national and civic life, how passion and prejudice were apparently displacing sanity and reason. The only solution he could see was religious tolerance, which would permit every person to hold and practise his or her faith, and indeed to change faith freely.[31]

At the time he does not seem to have attempted to delve at all deeply into the reasons for this deterioration in relations between Hindus, Muslims and Sikhs. Looking back on the period over a decade later he had modified his earlier response and had begun to understand what he called communalism in socio-economic and political terms, rather than as a simple function of the moral and intellectual weakness which bred bigotry and intolerance. By the time he wrote his *Autobiography* he argued that communalism was the work of political reactionaries within every community, who chose to use the cloak of religion to pursue their own material ends, and who thus played along with a government which, for its own reasons, was content to create and use divisions among its subjects.[32] However, even this more sophisticated analysis underestimated the complexity both of British attitudes towards Indian religious identities, and the diverse political and cultural stances which he bundled together under the label of communalism.

Unexpected relief from the political problems generated by the collapse of Gandhi's movement of non-cooperation came to Jawaharlal in the shape of urban administration. All political groups within Congress agreed on the need to use the elected institutions of local self-government, and the 1922 Congress Civil Disobedience Enquiry Committee had specifically recommended that non-cooperators should enter these bodies and use them to facilitate the constructive programme. Soon after his release from prison in 1923 Jawaharlal was elected to the Allahabad Municipal Board, and surprisingly found himself chosen to be its chairman, as the figure who would receive most support in a complex local political situation.[33]

He dreaded this new role because of his ignorance of municipal work and his other political preoccupations, and he told UP Congressmen that they must not forget that their goal remained swaraj. 'Let us be careful that we do not forget this or else our capturing the municipalities will become a curse to us rather than a blessing.' It was to be a persistent theme of his politics throughout the 1920s and 1930s that constitutional action was a snare for protagonists of a mass nationalism aiming for independence; for it would side-track them and generate divisions and tendencies to think most about the material rewards of office. For the moment he still thought that his main role was that of secretary of the UP PCC and only undertook the chairmanship of the municipality in order to hasten swaraj. He still preferred 'not to wander in the shady alleys and lands of constitutional activity. My mentality is revolutionary. I believe in revolution and in direct action and in battle.' But he had learned the lesson of the previous year: 'I know also that revolutions require training and discipline, that direct action requires soldiers. Therefore, we must organise and instil discipline amongst our workers.'[34] However, within six months he had discovered that he liked municipal work and that it had begun to interest him seriously. His attitude had changed because he now felt that the board had the power to make life somewhat better for Allahabad's inhabitants.[35]

Among the issues he took up for the town's residents were the poor state of the roads, and matters of public health such as infant mortality, the disposal of rubbish and the purity of the water supply. He also tangled with the long-standing question of the town's prostitutes, displaying both moral sensibility and social awareness that this was a result in part of women's low status and lack of alternative employment in Indian society. Yet he was painfully aware of the structural and cultural problems which prevented boards such as this from delivering an effective service to the residents. Many members of the board and its committees lacked commitment to serious work for the town, and were more absent from than present at deliberations. People, including board members, looked on the board as a source of patronage. 'There is evidently an impression amongst some people that the Board is a charitable organisation meant to supply soft jobs to the needy and the deserving, an asylum for the halt and the lame who have failed in the battle of life and who now seek shelter under the hospitable roof of the municipality.'[36] He pleaded with his fellow members not to perpetuate this attitude, and to foster an employment policy which only recruited competent people.

Even more fundamentally he recognised that there was just not enough money to pursue the urban improvements necessary for the town, and its poorer parts in particular; and he soon found that suggestions for increased taxation raised opposition, particularly among the privileged who lived in the civil lines (where his own home was). For the first time he also experienced at first hand the frustration of working within a government marked by authoritarian and bureaucratic attitudes and habits which was almost impossible to shift out of its existing ruts. He may have made comparatively little difference to the citizens of Allahabad by the time he resigned the chair after two years, but he had won respect even from officials as an able and fair chairman. He had also encountered many aspects of government which were to inform his own attitudes later in life. It was thus an important aspect of his political apprenticeship, as well as an episode which gave him considerable personal interest and fulfilment.

However, the three years after his release from prison were a time of personal stress and anxiety. He was ill for some weeks in the autumn of 1923, having contracted typhoid fever probably in prison in Nabha state, where he had been temporarily detained after he had gone there to witness a Sikh demonstration. His pride in his health, nurtured by his English education, took a severe blow, as he experienced prolonged weakness after the crisis of the fever was over. But the enforced leisure gave him time to think, and a sort of detachment which was almost like a spiritual experience. More prolonged was a nagging worry about money. He had virtually no income of his own once he had given up his legal practice. Although he and Kamala had considerably simplified their lives, as had other members of the family, for example by wearing khadi clothes and travelling third-class on the railway, they were still financially dependent on Motilal, and this made Jawaharlal uncomfortable. Paid work would have taken him away from his political work in Congress and the Municipality, and he increasingly disliked the idea of returning to law; he was also averse to the idea of an appointment in a large industrial firm, though several made him generous offers. But Motilal refused to allow his son to draw even a small salary from Congress; and the financial issue festered in Jawaharlal's mind, disturbing his mental peace.

Jawaharlal's concern over his financial dependence on his father was deepened by the growing need to provide expensive medical treatment for his wife. Kamala had been frail since the birth of their daughter in 1917, and her married life had been seriously disrupted by the family's politics. In November 1924 she gave birth prematurely to a son who died after two days. One can only surmise at the grief both parents felt; and this would have been compounded in the Indian social context by the knowledge that the boy would have been the Nehru heir, so deeply valued by parents and grandparents.[37] From then onwards Kamala seemed to grow weaker: she had problems with her lungs and a persistent low fever. Late in 1925 she was in hospital in Lucknow for several months. The family consulted a prominent British doctor in Allahabad, Professor C. A. Sprawson, and also several Indian doctors. It seemed very likely that the problem was tuberculosis. By the end of 1925 it was agreed that Jawaharlal should take her to Switzerland for treatment.[38]

Nehru's apprenticeship to many aspects of Indian politics had been tumultuous. By the mid-1920s he was well on in his thirties and was no longer a young man, though he was seen by his seniors as representing a younger generation of Congressmen. Yet he was still perplexed about the course of Indian politics and of his own career, not least because the leader to whom he had commited himself with such enthusiasm in 1919 had increasingly withdrawn from active politics to pursue a campaign of social reconstruction. The prospect of a visit to Europe was a welcome respite from the many unanswered questions which his experiences had raised in his mind. He later recorded, 'My mind was befogged, and no clear path was visible; and I thought that, perhaps, if I was far from India I could see things in better perspective and lighten up the dark corners of my mind.'[39] With the prospect of departure in mind, he wrote cryptically to a close woman friend of the family about his ambivalence towards both Europe and India. 'On the whole perhaps it is as well that I am going but I doubt if I shall be very happy there. India is so like a woman – she attracts and repels.'[40]

# Chapter 5

# A Radical Bound, 1926–1931

Jawaharlal and his immediate family spent nearly two years in Europe, from March 1926 until December 1927. This was the start of a phase in his life when he became recognised by Indians and by the imperial government as an all-India figure and leader in his own right.[1] He also emerged as an intellectual and political radical, with a clear goal of independence from the British combined with major socio-economic change for India. By temperament and belief he pronounced himself to be a man who delighted in revolutionary action. This was a considerable shift for the former earnest young chair of the Allahabad municipality, whose under-standing of swaraj had been, at best, inchoate. However, he was to find himself on his return to India a radical bound – constrained by Gandhi's presence and patronage, by the nature of Congress itself, by divisions in Indian society, and eventually by the British raj, as it imprisoned him twice more for engaging in civil disobedience. In personal terms his world also changed considerably. By the end of 1931, as a man in his early forties, he was no longer in the context of his family the treasured son and representative of the younger generation. Motilal died early in 1931 and Jawaharlal was left with great responsibilities for his mother, his ailing wife and his growing daughter. The loss was only partially compensated for by a developing relationship with Indira, and a deepening concern for and mutuality with Kamala, as she increasingly shared some of his political activities.

## IN EUROPE

The Nehrus lived first in Geneva and then in the mountain resort of Montana, as Kamala received different sorts of treatment for what was now firmly diagnosed as tuberculosis. Treatment was expensive, and Motilal was deeply concerned that his son might be economising on living expenses, so he sent them funds willingly.[2] Jawaharlal found he had considerably underestimated the expenses they would incur, and once again he was entirely dependent on his father's generosity as the months progressed. Early in their visit they were briefly accompanied by the older of Nehru's two sisters and her husband, and later by his youngest sister and then by Motilal himself. But for a while the little family of three had their first real time together alone. Kamala experienced married life outside the constraints of the large Nehru family for the first time, and Jawaharlal began to form a real relationship with his small daughter as they enjoyed leisure time together. Eventually she went away to boarding school in the mountains, in part because he was worried lest she should fall victim to the same disease as her mother. In the school holidays she would return to her parents, and father and daughter skied together as he continued to concern himself with her physical welfare. Kamala made slow progress, but by the spring of 1927 she seemed far healthier than she had been for years, although Jawaharlal told Gandhi that he feared she would always need special care to prevent further relapses.[3]

For his part Jawaharlal enjoyed the total change from India, and the physical and mental relaxation Switzerland afforded. He attended a wide range of lectures and special courses in Geneva, and then in the Alps delighted in winter sports. He also wrote occasional articles on India for local publication, such as one for *The Review of Nations* in January 1927, entitled 'The psychology of Indian nationalism'.[4] He met a wide range of Europeans who visited Geneva in particular as the home of the League of Nations and the International Labour Office; and he noted the changes in Europe since his carefree days there before the war. A deepening radicalism emerged in his comments on socio-economic issues, such as his reaction to the breaking of the National Strike in England in 1926. Later in his stay in Europe he briefly visited England and in a mining area was shocked by the fear among the strikers and the impact on their families.

However, his immersion in left-wing politics came with the chance to represent the Indian National Congress at a Congress in Brussels in February 1927 against Colonial Oppression and Imperialism. Here he encountered a wide range of European communists and socialists, and also representatives of countries which had felt or were feeling the impact of European imperialism – in Latin America, Africa, the Middle East, South East Asia and China. This experience gave him insight into the weaknesses and divisions of the European labour movements (and would colour his view of the British Labour Party and its attitude to India), and drew his sympathies towards communism, not in any sense of doctrinal commitment but more generally for its commitment to major socio-economic change, and its absence of ties to imperialism. But he later commented wryly that 'Communists often irritated me by their dictatorial ways, their aggressive and rather vulgar methods, their habit of denouncing everybody who did not agree with them. This reaction was no doubt due, as they would say, to my own *bourgeois* education and up-bringing.'[5]

As important as this leftward shift in sympathy was Jawaharlal's new sense that India's own struggle with the British was part of an international problem. He began to articulate his belief in a symbiotic link between imperialism and international capitalism, clearly visible in the case of India. Each reinforced the other, and both had to be confronted. A further dimension of Nehru's wider international vision was his developing interest in China, where the Nationalist revolution was endeavouring to unite the country and remove foreign influence. He urged the AICC back in India to realise the significance of this – for the Chinese were not just engaged in a struggle for independence, but in a challenge to the whole capitalist system which sustained imperialism. He had spent a long time talking with the Chinese delegates to the meeting in Brussels, and he advocated ways in which Indian and Chinese nationalists could begin to cooperate.[6] Some weeks later he wrote a note for an Indian audience on the Chinese revolution being a phenomenon of world importance: its influence would mark both Asia and Europe, but most particularly India. He hoped that the current 'pious hope and empty sympathy' in India for China would develop into practical help such as sending a trained ambulance corps. 'China is holding out her hand of comradeship to India. It is for us to grasp it and to renew our ancient and honourable association and thereby ensure the freedom and progress of both these great countries, which have so much in common.'[7] This sense of affinity with China as another great Asian country and nation in the making, sharing interests with India, was to remain over decades in Nehru's mind, and would eventually lead to one of the most profound misunderstandings of his prime ministership.

Nehru found the Brussels experience exhausting. While sending his report on the congress back to the Working Committee he noted that he had 'not had a good night's sleep or hardly a decent meal' since he arrived over a week earlier.[8] Despite his commitment to the proceedings and the League against Imperialism which emerged from them, he had no illusions about the League in relation to India. He frankly told Gandhi that its members would only help India if it suited their own interests. But he felt that India for its own sake should cultivate such external contacts. 'I am afraid we are terribly narrow in our outlook and the sooner we get rid of this narrowness the better. Our salvation can of course come only from the internal strength that we may evolve but one of the methods of evolving such strength should be study of other people and their ideas.'[9]

Nehru's personal education about other people and their ideas was furthered by a brief visit to Moscow in November 1927, after his father had come from India. They were invited for celebrations of the tenth anniversary of the Russian revolution, and were in three short days taken to a show at the Bolshoi Theatre, to a cinema for films on the revolution, to a central peasants' house, a prison and the Ministry of Education, and invited to a banquet and numerous meetings. He also saw Lenin's embalmed body in the Kremlin. To his sister, Vijayalakshmi, he wrote how 'topsy-turvy' it all felt, particularly addressing everyone as Comrade. 'It seems alright in theory but in practice it takes some getting used to.' He was left full of admiration for the immense amount the new system had accomplished so quickly, and clearly considered the implications for India's own future. 'We are always complaining of the poor human material we have in India; yet in Russia it is or was no better.'[10]

Later he published a whole series of articles on Russia for the Indian newspaper, *The Hindu*, and they were collected and published in book form in 1928.[11] They showed his immense intellectual curiosity, as well as the wide range of reading he had done on the theory and practice of communism. He argued at the end that India had nothing to fear from Russia: such fear was the by-product of British imperialism, and Indians must not be party to it. He tried to get across to his compatriots the enormity of the problems the new Russian state had set itself to resolve – tasks which India would in turn have to face, including the use and ownership of land, questions of minorities, education, women and marriage laws. Here evidently was an example of state initiative to expedite profound socio-economic change, which provided an alternative inspiration to that of moral revolution offered by Gandhi. Of course this was just before major shifts in Soviet policy which presaged violence by the state against its own citizens, and also the abandonment of any support for anti-imperial nationalist movements in other parts of the world, which came to be seen as imperial collaborators rather than part of a longer and necessary historical process of social and political change. Evidence of these would in turn influence Nehru's attitude to Soviet Russia. But for the moment the brief Russian experience was a landmark in his personal development.

Jawaharlal did not, of course, forget Indian politics, despite his domestic and political preoccupations in Europe. He received regular news from his father in particular. Motilal showed increasing despair at the rifts which had opened up among those who purported to be nationalists, the signs of abject reversion to collaboration with the raj, and the evidence of growing communal antagonism. In April 1927 he wrote to his son:

> Indian politics were low enough when you left India a year ago but even you who know your country & your people so well can have no idea of the almost universal rot which has since set in. I don't think there is one man among the old or the new sort of Congressmen who will not go into a fainting fit on hearing the words complete independence for India.[12]

It was the news of the deterioration of relations between people of different religious communities that most upset Jawaharlal. He wrote to Syed Mahmud, a UP Muslim who was close to him and to Kamala, expressing his anguish. It was driving him to think that religion as currently practised in India would kill the country, just as it had already stifled originality of thought. The only future course he could see was to attempt to secularise the intelligentsia and to proceed on secular lines in politics.[13] He felt relieved to be out of the petty squabbles of Indian politics, where divisions seemed so bitter and pointless, and where most politicians, whatever name they gave themselves, were fundamentally moderate, steered clear of the idea of independence, and avoided big issues like the future of the princely states, foreign policy, the army and defence. He told the Congress president, 'I am afraid this very tame and constitutional and legal and proper and reasonable activity raises no enthusiasm in me.'[14]

One particular issue took up a considerable amount of his attention, the need for Congress to begin thinking about an eventual foreign policy for a free India. He had urged the Working Committee to recognise the importance of wider world issues when he reported back on his experiences at Brussels. Later in the year he wrote an extended note on the question of foreign policy – perhaps one of the first signs of his deep interest in this question which was to lead him to be in a sense the foreign affairs expert of the Congress before independence, and to combine the External Affairs portfolio with the premiership after 1947.[15] For him the first priority was complete freedom from Britain, including control of finance, military forces and foreign relations. Moreover, India could not remain within the British Commonwealth because Britain stood for so much that India opposed, while India did not share the ties of sentiment or economic interest that tied the white Dominions to the mother country.

India would of course have to have efficient and modern defence forces. Here he was not only realistic about the developing technology of warfare, but scathing about British discussions on the Indianisation of the officer corps of the Indian Army. 'By the time the present government of India gets to work and produces a few toy Indian officers, smartly dressed and well up in all the rules of parade, they will be about as useful to us as the ancient warriors with bows and arrows.' However, he felt that India was in little danger of attack or invasion, and should cultivate a policy of friendly relations with countries in Asia, the Middle East and Europe, including Russia, even if it did not itself choose the socialist path. With considerable perspicacity he saw that India would have to adopt some attitude towards the many Indians resident outside their homeland; and in particular must encourage them to cooperate with their hosts and win their position there by 'friendship and service'. Finally, as there was a serious possibility of another world war, India must make it plain that it would not be dragged into it with Britain without its consent, and that if it was then Indians would not help in the war in any way. As early as 1927 he was clearly laying down some of the principles which would mark his attempt to shape Indian foreign policy over twenty years later.

Nehru's European interlude had been intellectually productive, and restorative of mind and body. Despite his reservations about Indian politics, he soon longed to be back in the fray. In December 1926 he wrote of getting restive and wishing to 'hurl myself into the whirlpool of Indian politics. The suppressed energy of some months wants an outlet.' His combative temperament was reasserting itself and he longed to have a go at so many of those who practised politics in India.[16] His goal for India was complete swaraj, and in relation to Indian society that meant a freedom which would benefit the majority of Indian people, rather than one which enabled a few Indians to get richer or to achieve high office. What worried him was the possibility that some in Congress or among the Swarajists would try to pull them back from such a goal.[17] His outlook was now far wider than it had been when he left India in 1926, and his vision was more radical. Nationalism alone seemed a narrow and inadequate creed. Political freedom was an essential first step, but it had to be accompanied by social freedom, a more socialistic structure of society and more socialist state policy.

## THE CONSTRAINTS OF INDIAN POLITICS

On his return from Europe at the end of 1927 Jawaharlal had hoped to immerse himself in village life, to experiment with rural organisation and to educate himself by getting into the mind of the Indian villager. But once more he was swept up into Congress politics, and again became Congress Secretary. He plunged into the December meeting of Congress with a range of resolutions reflecting his recent experiences in Europe, including one calling for independence. To his surprise, this was adopted by the CWC and the open session of Congress. But he – and the government – recognised that this did not mean any serious radicalisation of Congress policy. Clearly the fact that Motilal was still in Europe was an important element in the absence of stiff opposition to this resolution, as was the fact that Gandhi was still holding somewhat aloof from Congress politics.[18]

The passage of this resolution precipitated a major confrontation between Jawaharlal and Gandhi, which showed just how far the younger man had moved since the days of non-cooperation. Gandhi initiated the exchange in January 1928 with a letter telling him that he should have taken time to think on his return to India, possibly remembering his own year of silence on public issues on his return from South Africa a decade earlier. 'I feel that you love me too well to resent what I am about to write. In any case I love you too well to restrain my pen when I feel I must write.' Jawaharlal was going too fast and his resolutions in Congress encouraged 'mischief-makers and hooligans'. Even if he had changed his views in Europe and no longer believed solely in non-violence he must realise that any strategy needed disciplined instruments and exponents to be effective. Jawaharlal replied with a sense of amazement at the tone of Gandhi's letter, and in effect reprimanded Gandhi for criticising accepted Congress policy when he was a member of the CWC. He then poured out his anguish about Gandhi's 'leadership' (or rather lack of it) since the collapse of non-cooperation, and his insistence on the importance of khadi as the supreme strategy. He had felt earlier that Gandhi was one who could lead India to freedom, and had admired him intensely, despite his many ideological differences with him. These were particularly his condemnation of the West, his hostility to industrial society, his failure to understand what Jawaharlal saw as the inevitable conflict between capital and labour under a capitalist system, and his refusal to attack the fundamental causes of poverty in India, including the zamindari system of landholding and capitalist exploitation of workers and consumers. But now he was bewildered by Gandhi's apparent inaction, and full of 'mental agitation', not least because for him the demand for independence was more important than almost anything else.[19]

Gandhi replied at length, relieved that at last the differences between them were out in the open. He now gave Nehru full freedom from any allegiance to himself, and said that he must carry on 'open warfare' against him and his views if he felt it was right. 'The differences between you and me appear to me to be so vast and radical that there seems to be no meeting-ground between us. I can't conceal from you my grief that I should lose a comrade so valiant, so faithful, so able and so honest as you have always been.'[20] Nehru was horrified at the thought of any public confrontation and drew back from an open break with his mentor. He wrote movingly of their complex relationship.

> Is any assurance from me necessary that nothing that can ever happen can alter or lessen my deep regard and affection for you? That regard and affection is certainly personal, but it is something more. No one has moved me and inspired me more than you and I can never forget your exceeding kindness to me. There can be no question of our personal relations suffering. But even in the wider sphere am I not your child in politics, though perhaps a truant and errant child?[21]

This episode demonstrated the new relationship between Gandhi and the younger man. Even though Jawaharlal was now far more radical intellectually, had a more sharply defined understanding of India's interlocking political and socio-economic problems as a key part of Britain's worldwide empire, and was no longer swept along in the emotional enthusiasm of 1920–1, he remained committed to working with Gandhi towards a new India. For him this was not merely out of personal affection, but because of a deep sense that Gandhi above all had the ability to touch a wider swathe of the population than any other politician, and that independence would only come through the work of Congress in alliance with Gandhi. Radical movements outside Congress had no lasting effect, as he was soon to discover in the failure of his Independence for India League, and in the divisions and weakness of the Indian trade union movement, with which he became associated. But Congress without Gandhi was prone to excessive moderation and timidity, and would always reflect the interests of the comparatively privileged. Only Gandhi, for all his ideological peculiarities and apparent inconsistencies, could weld the disparate camps in Congress together, and with his curious amalgam of political astuteness and moral revivalism, generate a more popular politics of opposition to the raj.

Gandhi, meantime, was deeply fond of the younger man, and admired his intellectual ability and his courage in standing up for his principles, compared with so much of the uncritical adulation and even fawning that went on in the circles around the Mahatma. He also recognised that he represented in a sense a younger generation who needed to be recruited into Congress as an organisation and as a movement of popular opposition. Each needed the other, and they became locked in a symbiotic relationship. From this Jawaharlal gained a privileged place in the Congress organisation and a major voice in its decision-making. But the price was a constraint on his radicalism: his mind might still be free, but in action he would have to give priority to Congress unity and Gandhi's strategic direction. In consequence he would continue to be plagued by intellectual doubts and personal crises, and he would feel profound ambiguity in his relations with the more radical politicians, such as the Bengali Subhas Bose, who would in a sense have been his natural political allies.

The realities of politics soon further constrained Jawaharlal. In 1928 he became bleakly aware that most politicians did not share his priorities. This was demonstrated in the aftermath of the appointment by the British government of the Statutory Commission, the so-called Simon Commission, to enquire into the workings of India's 1919 constitution. A Conservative government had appointed it earlier than required by the terms of the 1919 reforms for fear that a more radical government might use it to push for further reform. Having by its constitution only representatives of the Lords and Commons on it, it was inevitably 'all white' – a fact which led to immense hostility in India, a boycott of its consultations by many Indian politicians, and numerous processions carrying black flags and bidding Sir John Simon and his colleagues to go home. Jawaharlal threw himself into the organisation of this opposition, and was beaten by the police in the course of a demonstration in Lucknow. He managed to restrain himself from responding with violence, but was deeply shaken by his first real experience of physical violence and what seemed to him the hatred of the European police sergeants who did most of the beating.[22]

However, the politicians' formal political response to the challenge of the Simon Commission was the construction of an alternative constitution by an all-parties conference. Motilal had returned from Europe in the spring of 1928 and became deeply involved in this endeavour, eventually drawing up the final report with his old friend, Sir T. B. Sapru. The negotiations leading up to the so-called Nehru

Report and to its final terms showed the younger Nehru that most politicians still set their sights on Dominion status rather than complete independence, and were not prepared to contemplate major socio-economic change at the expense of the privileged. Moreover, it was clear that divisions between Hindus and Muslims were deepening with the prospect of major devolution of power to Indian hands, and that there were powerful Hindu forces working on the fringes of Congress to prevent a communal agreement. Clearly few shared his own commitment to a secular stance in politics. However, rather than break up the work of the conference and of his father, supported by Gandhi, Jawaharlal and his colleague, S. C. Bose, preferred merely to dissociate themselves from any diminution of the goal of independence and then to attempt to work for independence in the country at large. Nehru offered to resign from the post of Congress Secretary, so wide did he think the gulf was between him and its leaders, but his offer was refused.[23]

Indian politics were making him feel his age, and he felt he had lost some of his earlier zest for life. He was also increasingly frustrated at the social conservatism of so many Congressmen, and recognised how they distrusted him because he spoke about socialism. He was also wearied by what he saw as the lack of good and competent people in politics. He told a close friend that it was difficult to organise all-India political work because provinces wanted to choose their own paths; but above everything else there was 'the extraordinary difficulty of finding really competent men to do any work. The result is that almost everything has to be done by oneself and that is no way of carrying on any work.'[24] This sense of superiority and special competence was a characteristic of both father and son. Some while later he wrote to his father that worry was a waste of energy, but 'one cannot help it at times, when one comes into contact with persons whom I have described as having a perpetual hartal of the mind. You do not suffer fools gladly, and unhappily there are a fair number of this breed about. They are even more aggravating than knaves.'[25] This was one of the earliest manifestations of an attitude that was to generate hostility and irritation in Congress circles. Moreover, when Jawaharlal's sense of being indispensable was carried into his premiership it led to a tendency to gross overwork and an inability to delegate in government.

The numerous divisions within Congress and the possibility that it might break up over the issue of accepting the Nehru Report provided the occasion for Gandhi to return to active participation in Congress, and late in 1928 to achieve a compromise which preserved Congress unity.[26] His proposal was that Congress should endorse the Nehru Report, but that if the government had not accepted it by the end of 1930 Congress would revive non-cooperation. Despite the fact that this did not overturn the goal of independence adopted by Congress in 1927, Jawaharlal and Bose indicated that even this compromise was unacceptable to them. Gandhi was insistent that Congress must retain its unity if it was to offer effective resistance to the raj, and that honourable compromise was therefore needed. He finally, after intensive private discussions, moved the resolution that Congress would revive non-cooperation if the government had not accepted the Nehru Report by the end of 1929. Jawaharlal was highly ambivalent at this juncture, torn between his radical goal and his awareness of the importance of his relations with Gandhi, and of Gandhi's role in Congress. He did not attend the crucial discussions in the Subjects Committee and half-heartedly opposed Gandhi in the open Congress session.

The prospect of confrontation with the government did not remove the constraints on Nehru. It seemed to increase his dilemmas. The first was the extreme weakness of the Congress as an organisation which might have to sustain a renewed programme of non-cooperation. Congress finances were in disarray and in some provinces not even the PCC was operative, while in most areas there was no organisation beneath the PCC. During 1929 Gandhi, in conjunction with Jawaharlal as a Congress Secretary, investigated this sorry state of affairs. Even in UP any work in the villages had collapsed and the organisation had virtually disappeared.[27] All-India figures suggested that membership was patchy, and statistics unreliable. It boded ill for a mass and disciplined movement of non-cooperation. Even those Congressmen who were core activists in that they functioned as Congress members within the legislatures were not amenable to all-India discipline. When the Viceroy, Lord Irwin, postponed the elections scheduled for late 1929 until after publication of the Simon Report, the CWC called on all Congress legislators to abstain from attendance in the councils and to concentrate on Congress work in the country. Such was the outcry by those who wished to continue with legislative work, often for good reasons,[28] that eventually at Gandhi's suggestion the matter was shelved until the end of the year.

Nehru recognised that he could not extricate himself from the myriad political roles he now seemed to be performing; but he was horrified when Gandhi suggested in July that he should become Congress President. He felt that he represented nobody but himself, and that he lacked flair for generating a supportive group.[29] He hoped that Gandhi would preside, as did a majority of Congress provinces; but the Mahatma refused and at his insistence Jawaharlal was elected. He felt grave misgivings, and a sense of humiliation at having emerged as President, not through the front door or even a side door, but 'suddenly by a trap-door', and, as he remembered, he 'stole away with a heavy heart'.[30] Worse was to follow. He had agreed to become President in the hope of soon fighting the government on a clear issue, but events soon overwhelmed even that prospect.

A Labour government had come to power in London in June and it supported the Viceroy, Lord Irwin, in endeavouring to find some way out of the apparently imminent conflict. The Government of India had already taken steps to prepare to deal quickly with any revival of non-cooperation, but it also responded to evidence that there were many politicians, including Liberals outside Congress and even prominent Congressmen such as Motilal, who still wished to come to an agreement with the government on the basis of Dominion status for India. The result was a viceregal declaration on 31 October 1929 that the British government wished him to state clearly that it assumed that the natural outcome of the reform process already in motion was India's attainment of Dominion status. This was coupled with an invitation to Indians from British and princely India to confer in London at a Round Table Conference on India's future. Irwin hoped that this would rally a wide range of Indian politicians, including more moderate Congress members, but he was sure that whatever the response 'we shall rally enough support to introduce into the ranks and policy of opponents a good deal of difficulty'.[31]

Among the people for whom this initiative caused some of the most difficulty was Jawaharlal himself, the president-elect of Congress. In discussions which rapidly took place between the CWC and prominent Liberals on 1–2 November in Delhi, it was agreed that they hoped to cooperate with the government provided that certain issues were resolved.[32] Jawaharlal had been pressed very hard by Gandhi to adhere to Congress discipline and accept this compromise, but within days Jawaharlal told Gandhi of his sense of personal disintegration and confusion. He felt they had fallen into a government trap, and as for himself he was an interloper who had had to suppress himself rather than upset the gathering. He therefore resigned from the Congress secretaryship and said he felt he could not be president.[33] Gandhi and Motilal both weighed in to prevent an open rift. As the weeks progressed it became increasingly obvious that the agreement reached in Delhi was crumbling. This was not least because the government could not give Congress the assurances it had requested on critical issues such as a general amnesty for political prisoners, or that the proposed conference would actually frame a Dominion constitution and that Congress would have predominant representation at it. Moreover, Gandhi had moved towards conciliating Jawaharlal and reintegrating him into the Congress core through a CWC meeting which resolved that the Delhi agreement would run out at the forthcoming Congress session. For him the unity of Congress and the reincorporation of Jawaharlal and those he represented within the national party were ultimately more important than a working alliance with the Liberals, particularly as it was evident that a strategy of cooperation in a London conference would make Congress seem to be only one Indian voice among many.

Jawaharlal now urged the country to prepare for struggle, speaking as President of the All-India Trade Union Congress at the end of November, and then as President at the Congress session held at Lahore.[34] The Congress session accepted Gandhi's resolution on independence and civil disobedience, despite the articulate presence of some who wished to avoid a break with government. But even this did not resolve the dilemmas of actual confrontation. As Jawaharlal remembered, they had no well thought out programme of disobedience, although they were uplifted by the ideal of independence, particularly the celebration of an 'Independence Day' in January 1930. Moreover, there was the unresolved problem of what would happen if violence broke out, which had caused him such anguish early in 1922. Gandhi gave them the impression that he now felt that sporadic acts of violence would not lead to the abandonment of civil disobedience, provided that violence had not become part of the movement as a whole, and at least this he found reassuring. Further, the Mahatma determined to start civil disobedience on an issue which was the least likely to precipitate violence, and the most likely to create unity within Congress and across the social and religious divisions which still threatened any viable campaign of opposition to government. After prolonged thought and discussion with the CWC, Gandhi proposed that only those who believed in non-violence as an article of faith rather than as an expedient policy should initiate civil disobedience, and that the issue on which they should disobey the law was the government's salt monopoly. He himself began the new movement with his famous 240-mile march from his ashram in Ahmedabad to the coast at Dandi, where on 6 April he ceremoniously picked up a lump of mud and salt. Across the country people undertook token acts of defiance by making salt.

## A RADICAL IN PRISON

Jawaharlal was arrested on 14 April, tried on the same day under the Salt Act, and imprisoned in Naini jail, Allahabad. The whole family had attended the trial, and Motilal was permitted to see where his son would be confined. Once in prison Jawaharlal was alone in a circular enclosure surrounded by a 14-foot wall. In the middle of this was a small building; he inhabited half of it as his cell and had his own bathroom. But to begin with there were no curtains and he had little privacy. 'Even when I am sitting in my room I can be gazed at through the bars from various angles. Rather disconcerting. One feels as if one was in a cage and always being watched.'[35]

The physical constraints the government now placed on him were perhaps less stressful than those he had experienced at the hands of his compatriots on his return to India. He settled back into a routine of prison life which was restful compared with the previous months of hectic activity. He normally rose at 4.00 a.m., rested in the middle of the day and went to bed at 9.00 p.m. His day was occupied with reading, writing, weaving and spinning; and he took at least an hour's exercise, walking or running within the barrack. He noted that he was sleeping a lot in the middle of the day and having a comparatively easy time compared with those who were outside and engaged in civil disobedience. 'But I wish I could have a fling outside also. This dull lotus-eating existence with walls surrounding you and warders always guarding you is not very cheerful.'[36] He was permitted only six books at a time, which caused complications about multi-volumed works, but the prison superintendent allowed him to keep others in his own office. Nehru noted ironically, 'Evidently the gentlemen who make these rules are not in the habit of keeping company with books.'[37] Nonetheless he read about forty books during his sentence, including a considerable number in French, and in English several Shakespeare plays, two volumes of Churchill's *World Crisis 1916–18*, the two volumes of Spengler's *Decline of the West*, and a book about the Kuomintang and the Chinese revolution. He was permitted some regular letters and interviews, which he looked forward to greatly and for which he prepared himself by wearing his cleanest clothes and shaving with a new razor blade. He was thus able to keep in touch with his family, and he delighted in the news that his womenfolk, including Kamala and his mother, were participating in the movement outside by picketing foreign cloth shops. Despite the comparative privilege of his own conditions, he was depressed by the whole atmosphere of the prison. 'The way jail is run in India is not unlike the British Govt. of India. There is great efficiency in the apparatus of govt. – which goes to strengthen the hold of the govt. on this country – and little or no care of the human material of the country.'[38]

Early in July his tranquillity was broken by the arrival of his father and Syed Mahmud, who joined him and the other prisoner who had arrived in May. Now there was considerable congestion, and father and son shared a cell and a bathroom; when it rained and they could not be outside there was virtually nowhere to sit because their cell contained their luggage and cooking supplies and utensils. Eventually the prison authorities built a new verandah to solve the problem. The younger men did their best to ensure the comfort of the older man, who was in poor health, and all benefited from the special food which was sent in by the family.

Politics now pursued them inside the prison – in a series of visits which showed how eager the government was to balance its firm action against civil disobedience with assurances that would assuage more moderate politicians even if did not lure Congress back into negotiation and discussion. Jawaharlal was in no mood to return to the agonies of late 1929. He noted in his diary at the end of May that he hoped the conflict would continue to the bitter end. 'Nothing more unfortunate than a premature compromise could take place.' He had no time for the so-called moderates outside Congress who seemed to 'behave like old women – weeping & howling and feeling terribly oppressed about everything! . . . If they have not got gumption enough to do anything why do they not shut up?'[39] However, the Viceroy, Lord Irwin, agreed to permit an attempt at mediation between the government and the Congress leadership by two moderates, M. R. Jayakar, and the Nehrus' old Allahabad friend, Sir T. B. Sapru, who had viewed their swimming pool with such suspicion in Jawaharlal's boyhood. Irwin hoped that even if nothing came of it in the form of Congress cooperation, at least it would persuade non-Congressmen to cooperate in the forthcoming Round Table Conference.[40]

The mediators knew that some staunch Congress supporters and other moderates wished for a compromise, and that a prominent group of Bombay businessmen did as well, and in late July they took this evidence to Gandhi, who was by now himself in prison outside Poona in the Bombay Presidency. He felt he could not do anything without consultation with the Nehrus, and that Jawaharlal's must be the final voice (as Congress President *in absentia*). He was not, however, entirely opposed to a deal. Jayakar and Sapru had a much tougher reception when they talked to the Nehrus in Naini jail. Jawaharlal had no wish to go back on their existing stand and feared any false move, himself delighting in the present conflict and feeling prouder of India's peoples than he had ever been. He was again worried by talk of peace, and felt that it would only divert attention from the true situation. Interestingly, Kamala had written to him of her own agitation at the thought of peace moves, and said there should be no peace except on the basis of full swaraj. He was clearly delighted by the way she had taken up political responsibilities after his arrest, although some people were apparently worried at the thought of her taking up a formal role in Congress and muttered about 'petticoat government'.[41]

Irwin gave permission for the Nehrus to travel by special train to Bombay to see Gandhi in mid-August. They stayed a week in Yeravda jail with him. (Their return was delayed by a rapid deterioration in Motilal's health. He was an asthmatic of long standing but was now clearly in very poor health, and in Yeravda he developed a high fever and began to spit blood.) The outcome of these talks, which included several other Congress leaders who by this time had also been imprisoned with Gandhi, was only a stiff response, laying down stipulations which would clearly be unacceptable to the government (such as the right of India to secede from the empire and the formation of a national government with powers to control economic policy and defence) as the precondition for an end to civil disobedience. The mediators then shuttled again between the Viceroy, the Nehrus back in prison in Allahabad and Gandhi in Yeravda, but in early September it was clear that their attempt at mediation had collapsed, and that Gandhi had come to share the Nehrus' views, in comparison with his initial stance. It was evidence of the singular importance of Jawaharlal in his strategic thinking.

Motilal was discharged from prison on 8 September after only ten weeks, as his health was now rapidly worsening, and his own and government doctors recognised that nothing could be done for him in prison. He went to the UP hill station of Mussoorie in the hope of some improvement, and Jawaharlal was left behind to complete virtually his whole term. He eventually left prison on 11 October and immediately indicated in a public statement that he hoped 'to do my little bit to hasten the dissolution of the British Empire and take part in its final obsequies'.[42] He and Kamala went almost immediately to see Motilal, and with their daughter and three small nieces they were able to have a tragically brief family interlude. Jawaharlal played with the children in their new-found tranquillity, and was relieved that his father seemed to be regaining his strength. It was to be their last time together before his fatal illness a few months later. In the few hours Jawaharlal had been able to devote to politics in Allahabad on his release he had spoken publicly of his refusal to retract anything he had said at the Lahore Congress, and declared that all Indians should now consider themselves rebels. Resuming his presidential role, he urged all PCCs to continue with the programme of civil disobedience to the Salt Act, and boycott of foreign cloth, British goods and liquor. He was also party to a UP PCC decision to sanction a no-tax campaign among those liable for land revenue payment, partly in response to the very real economic difficulties agriculturalists were suffering as a result of the world economic depression, but also as an attempt to inject new vitality into a civil disobedience movement which was losing momentum. It came as no surprise when he was rearrested on 19 October and returned to Naini prison, only eight days after he had left it. He refused to defend himself at his trial, but used the occasion to make a defiant statement that there could be no compromise with British imperialism and that he had no other profession or business than to fight it and drive it out of India.

This term of imprisonment lasted until 26 January.[43] He returned to his usual round of exercise and reading, mostly literature and politics; and now the presence of his brother-in-law, Ranjit Pandit (Vijayalakshmi's husband), brought additional pleasure with his gift for gardening even in the confines of a prison barrack. Although Nehru professed that prison life taught detachment, he was clearly unable to practise this most Gandhian of virtues. He was deeply troubled at the news that in several jails political prisoners were being flogged for apparent offences against jail discipline, and he and his immediate colleagues in Naini went on a voluntary three-day fast in protest. News of the London Round Table Conference on constitutional advance was also dispiriting as it became clear that so many shades of Indian politicians were now prepared to collaborate with the British in the pursuit of a further devolution of power. He was even more concerned by a visit from his father in January. Motilal was evidently very ill, despite weeks of treatment in Calcutta, and for the first time Jawaharal felt a real chill of fear that his father might not live. Motilal had always laughed at the idea of death, and now his son found it hard to contemplate a life apart from this powerful and rich personality and his great warmth of affection.

Jawaharlal also used this prison term to collect his thoughts on matters which were in his view critical for the Congress.[44] One was the need to have an economic programme of relevance to ordinary people if Congress was seeking to become a mass movement. They would have to tackle issues of capital and labour and of landholding, and he envisaged an eventual and radical policy which would change the current landholding system throughout the country. But he recognised that the time might not yet be ripe for that, not least because so many Congressmen still feared to antagonise those with powerful vested interests, particularly the landed. Congress did not desire class war, but eventually it would have to make hard decisions, and the leadership must be prepared in advance for that; when the choice came they would have to back those he called the 'vital groups' – the ordinary people in the countryside – even at the cost of alienating the larger landholders. Eventually large estates would have to be broken up and compensation paid, and their goal would be a society of peasant proprietors.

Another urgent matter was that of maintaining the momentum of their movement, and of constantly remembering that their goal was a radical change in the national political structure. They should recognise that all revolutionary movements had to go on being dynamic, and should draw strength from below by inspiring the masses with the belief that change would better their economic conditions. Consequently the very base of the movement had to be well organised, and people at the base had to be given initiative and a sense of responsibility. Some might say that it was better to concentrate on constructive work outside prison; but this, in his view, was a foolish and dangerous line of reasoning. Constructive work often meant not doing any dangerous work, and they must remember that theirs was a movement out to conquer power by revolutionary means, and was built on defiance.

Here was a man staking out his basic views on the struggle for independence and the future shape of India. Events and institutions constrained his ability to pursue these goals, but the bitter experiences of political life since his return from Europe had only sharpened his perception of the issues which really mattered to him. He had also laid bare some of the profound dilemmas of mass nationalism in the Indian context.

## THE CONSTRAINTS OF PEACE

Early in 1931 Jawaharlal had to face two of the greatest crises of his life: the death of his father on 6 February; and the subsequent agreement made between Gandhi and Lord Irwin, the so-called Gandhi–Irwin Pact, almost exactly a month later on 5 March. These crises were interlocked and each reinforced the pain of the other: they heralded a phase in his life (until his next imprisonment late in December) which he described as 'one of the most painful episodes in my life'.[45]

The backdrop to these events was the end of the Round Table Conference in London, at which the British government achieved an unprecedented degree of

Indian support for further constitutional reform. From its perspective the most important aspect of this was the support of the representatives of Indian princes for an eventual federation of British and princely India which would be a Dominion within the British empire. The prospect of a loyal and conservative princely bloc in any future central government reassured them and enabled them to embark on much more far-reaching constitutional change than they had ever contemplated before, or than the ill-fated Simon Commission had felt able to suggest. The Viceroy, supported by the Secretary of State for India, Wedgwood Benn, immediately began to search for ways to achieve peace with Congress, for now the stakes were infinitely higher than they had been in mid-1930 when the attempted mediation with the jailed Congress leadership broke down. Irwin thought that this was the best chance for a political solution that was likely to come for five or ten years. It was also a means of lessening the strain which civil disobedience had imposed on the government services at a time when the government was vulnerable to political attack which drew on the very real agrarian distress resulting from the depression.[46] After further discussion with his governors and his council in India, Irwin released unconditionally all members of the CWC to enable them to respond to the new situation.

Gandhi went from prison to Bombay and thence to Allahabad for discussions with the CWC. Jawaharlal was too distraught by his father's condition to play a major part in them. Motilal knew that he was dying, took little interest in the meetings and told Gandhi that he now knew he would not see swaraj, though he felt it would soon come. Old friends came quietly in to see him, knowing it was near the end. When the meetings were finished the family took him to Lucknow where there were better medical facilities than at Allahabad. But there Motilal died, with his wife and son beside his bed. Jawaharlal noted a sense of peace in place of his father's struggles of the last ten days, and, without realising its significance, was relieved, but his mother with her greater experience of life and death knew that Motilal was gone. They took his body home, wrapped in the new national flag, and after ceremonies at their home he was cremated on the banks of the Ganges in the presence of a vast crowd. As reality began to dawn on Jawaharlal he experienced a deepening sense of loss and a bitter loneliness. It was somewhat softened by the messages of sympathy which began to flow in for him and his mother, including one from Lord and Lady Irwin. But the main source of comfort was Gandhi, whose 'wonderfully soothing and healing presence . . . helped my mother and all of us to face that crisis in our lives'.[47]

There was no time for private mourning because Nehru was caught up in Congress discussions about the appropriate response to the new political situation. For his part he had indicated to his father before his release that he was deeply worried at the thought that the CWC might do anything to suggest that Congress was weakening on its objective or 'coquetting with compromise'.[48] However,

Gandhi knew that there were strong pressures building up within and outside Congress for him to attempt to achieve some sort of settlement with the government, not least from the moderate Hindu politicians who had just returned from London and did not wish to see their conference labours wrecked by Congress intransigence. They manoeuvred Gandhi into contact with the Viceroy, and the two men began a series of meetings in Delhi. V. S. S. Sastri wrote to a close friend and fellow Liberal in mid-February of their work to bring together the Hindu Mahatma and the devout Anglican Viceroy, 'This afternoon "the two uncrucified Christs" meet. Sapru, Jakayar and I have prepared each for the other! . . . If they hit it off, then serious negotiations will begin.'[49]

The two men did indeed 'hit it off', each recognising the other's sincerity in a deeply problematic situation in which each of them was subject to contradictory pressures. For Gandhi such meetings had the bonus of giving him as Congress spokesman a unique status in Indian eyes, thereby boosting Congress claims to be representative of India in a special way, and it appealed to his belief that a satyagrahi must always be willing to talk with an opponent and be prepared for honourable compromise. He stayed at the Delhi home of a prominent Muslim Congressman, with the whole Working Committee. He kept them in close touch with the conversations, which covered the objective of a future constitutional conference at which Congress would be represented, and the concessions government was prepared to make in return for the cessation of civil disobedience. Nehru was increasingly concerned at the trend of the negotiations and at the end of February was anticipating a return to jail. As he told his sister, 'This is all to the good. Only I should like a few days in Allahabad to set our house in order.'[50] Within days he was also making his views plain – at Gandhi's request: he told the CWC he thought the terms indicated insurmountable barriers to any cessation of civil disobedience or Congress participation in the proposed conference.[51]

Despite this, Gandhi pressed ahead and on 5 March a settlement was reached. Congress would send representation to London to discuss a new federal constitution which would give Indians responsibility for their own government, subject to certain safeguards, and would call off civil disobedience: government would meantime, among other things, release civil disobedience prisoners and withdraw the Ordinances making Congress and other bodies illegal organizations. Moreover, people could make salt for themselves in areas which naturally produced salt, and peaceful picketing of foreign cloth and liquor shops could continue.

Jawaharlal had kept close to Gandhi during these days of discussions, and the death of Motilal made their relationship deeper and more intimate. Often he accompanied Gandhi on his morning walks in Delhi, when they ranged over many topics including Gandhi's vision of Congress after independence as an unpolitical pressure group. But the news of the Gandhi–Irwin Pact appalled him, and he made no secret of his misery to Gandhi. He felt that Gandhi had been party to a diminution of the goal of independence and briefly contemplated dissociating himself from it. Moreover, in his mind there was the question whether the decisions would have gone a different way had Motilal still been alive. Finally, with great mental conflict and physical distress, he agreed to accept it. So yet again the younger radical was bound by his connections with Gandhi and the realities of the political situation, which would have made it virtually impossible to renew the struggle. But the episode took its toll on him and he suffered what he called 'a little breakdown in health'. It was hardly surprising. He had been unwell in jail, and the pressures of prison, his father's death and now the Pact were just too much for him.

He recovered sufficiently to attend the Congress session at Karachi in the last week of March. It was evident there that he was not alone in his hostility to the terms Gandhi had agreed with Irwin. Black flags greeted Gandhi at the station on his arrival, and later Nehru had himself to defend Gandhi against a physical assault by some of these opponents. But within the sessions themselves those who, like him and his close colleague Bose, disliked the Pact declined to attempt to split the Congress on the issue, knowing that that would further strengthen the government's hands.[52] Gandhi contrived an ingenious resolution which both declared Congress's goal still to be swaraj and agreed that Congress representatives should go to London to work for this end but could accept whatever adjustments were in India's interests. Jayakar commented, 'His formula . . . is very clever, and I believe the Congress will swallow it.'[53] Congress did indeed swallow it, and Nehru himself moved the resolution.

However, for Nehru the Karachi session also marked a real advance on the socioeconomic front. Gandhi had encouraged him to think widely about the broader implications of swaraj as they walked together in Delhi in the early mornings while the Pact was being formulated. Now they collaborated on a resolution on fundamental rights, to indicate that political freedom must mean economic freedom for 'the starving millions'. It was passed in Congress and Nehru made little of it in his *Autobiography*. But it was to be of considerable consequence for it laid down a blueprint for the rights Indians would enjoy under a swaraj government. These included rights of association, speech and conscience and the practice of religion; and equal citizenship regardless of gender or social status. It also indicated the provisions such a government would take to ensure a more egalitarian society – including a reduction in land revenue and rent, progressive taxation on agricultural income, inheritance tax, the right to form unions, social protection for industrial workers, control of usury, state control of key industries and mineral resources, free primary education and, out of deference to Gandhian principles, abolition of the salt duty, prohibition, and the exclusion of foreign cloth and yarn from India.[54] At least some observers thought this was the price Gandhi had to pay for Nehru's continued allegiance; but that interpretation did less than justice to their complex relationship where each learnt from and depended on the other.

Nehru's emotional and physical weakness at this point were hardly surprising. As the head of the family he was now having to cope with business matters following Motilal's death, as well as his political work and his own emotions. His doctors suggested he needed a real rest, and so he and Kamala therefore decided to take a month's holiday in Ceylon with their daughter. They were away for seven weeks in all, including some time in southern India on their return journey. Nehru was captivated by the loveliness of Ceylon, and soon husband and wife were beginning to feel the benefits of the rest. Kamala needed it as much as he did, having suffered a further miscarriage in 1928 followed by appendicitis, and then the renewed disruption of their domestic life in 1930, culminating in her own imprisonment in 1931. Their marriage now entered a new level of closeness as they rediscovered each other on this, their first and last real holiday together.[55] Nehru had always found Kamala physically enchanting, but now there was a deeper intimacy between them, created possibly by his agonising loneliness after his father's death, but also by her new sharing in his political life. She deeply regretted her own lack of education and what she saw as her own wasted life as a result. She had begun to interest herself in women's education in the 1920s, pleading powerfully, for example, with their friend Syed Mahmud to end purdah – female seclusion – in his own family and to educate his daughters. In her view India would never be free without the education of Indian women.[56] She continued this campaign in Hyderabad on their return from Ceylon, addressing a small group of women in purdah. Nehru recorded how some weeks later a husband of one of the group wrote to Kamala in agitation that since her visit his wife had been behaving oddly, and failing to be submissive! Nehru was now undoubtedly very proud of his wife for her involvement in public affairs.

However this was to be only a brief interlude of happiness and relaxation. Once back in Allahabad he was sucked into Congress work, yet again being one of its secretaries, in charge of general administration. Gandhi left for the Second Round Table Conference in London, as the sole representative of Congress, at the end of August; but the intervening months had been fraught with difficulties and at several points it had seemed that there would be a breakdown of the settlement he had reached with Irwin.[57] Nehru was still profoundly sceptical of the possible outcome of the conference, and just two days after Gandhi had boarded ship for England he made it plain to all PCCs that they had to be prepared to renew civil disobedience either on his return or beforehand, if local situations warranted it, and that they must now take steps to strengthen their local organisations.[58] He kept in touch with Gandhi, sending him details of CWC meetings, which provided his brief for the conference.

Among the issues which clearly perturbed him were the claims by some Muslims for separate electorates, and for major powers in any federation to reside with the provinces – a strategy which would protect Muslims where they were local majorities, but which would weaken the central government. Congress had proposed in a CWC resolution in early July to protect minorities through the provision of fundamental rights, adult suffrage and the reservation of seats for minorities who formed less than one quarter of the population of any province. It did not, however, agree to separate electorates. Moreover, as Nehru understood the CWC, it was clear that any future central government of India must be provided with strength through the provisions of federation and that any claim for sovereignty by the provinces should be stoutly resisted.[59] This insistence was natural, given the functions of government presumed by Congress in the resolution on fundamental rights at Karachi. For Nehru personally a socialist government was *de facto* a strong government; and the example of Russia in 1927 cannot have been far from his mind. He marvelled at Gandhi's patience in the face of 'communal demands', particularly the insistence by M. A. Jinnah on a package for Muslims which included separate electorates, and wrote privately to Gandhi of Jinnah speaking 'unmitigated nonsense'. However he was concerned that Gandhi's dealings with such Muslim members of the conference was too 'sugary'. In public in India he was far from sugary, and declared robustly that for him there was no such thing as a communal problem because it did not affect the masses. Communal questions merely concerned those who wanted the spoils of office, because it gave them power and patronage. What he wanted was something much more radical – a 'socialist republic'; but in the meantime he felt the best arrangement for the country and for the minorities was a system of joint electorates. (He did admit that if a majority of Muslims insisted on separate electorates he would not stand in their way.)[60]

Nehru thought the constraints of the Conference would have been purgatory to him. But in India he was becoming enmeshed in the serious problems of UP agriculturalists. The UP government had gone a considerable way towards attempting to mitigate the problems as a result of the fall in prices caused by the depression in the market for agricultural products, and had given remissions in both rent and revenue. Nehru now took the leading role, in Gandhi's absence, of negotiating with the provincial and central governments on this matter, convinced that insufficient remissions had been made and that agriculturalists were being ejected from their holdings in large numbers and subjected to other forms of harassment. By the end of October Nehru was asking for permission from the CWC to start civil disobedience at least in Allahabad district – in the form of non-payment of rent and revenue. The CWC delegated responsibility for such a decision to Vallabhbhai Patel, and he in turn tried to avoid the descent into conflict before Gandhi's return to India. But Nehru pressed on, and the PCC permitted Allahabad and four other districts to proceed to civil disobedience. The Delhi and UP governments were convinced that Nehru deliberately wanted to break up the Delhi settlement, and force Gandhi's hand on his return. Nehru stoutly denied this later, and said it was the local government's actions which forced the issue.[61] Whatever his precise role, he was clearly a profound influence in the PCC's deliberations; and in the face of cultivators' manifest problems he would have found it hard to draw back, given his commitment to making Congress a mass organisation through the support of genuinely popular issues. The UP government armed itself with emergency powers to deal with the new situation, and Nehru was himself arrested as he prepared to travel to Bombay to meet Gandhi on his return from England. Once more he returned to prison, a radical bound by imperial restraints.

The Nehru who went back to prison at the end of 1931 was very different from the man who had returned from Europe four years earlier. The demands and stresses of the intervening years had pushed him to the very edge of his physical and emotional limits, and he had visibly aged – to the extent that on their holiday in the south the tiny and fragile Kamala had been mistaken for his daughter. Moreover, despite his obvious public repute and increasing popularity, he had discovered that his own compatriots and their political structures, as much as government policy, prevented significant advance towards the more radical polit- ical and socio-economic goals he envisaged for India.

Some of his frustrations arose from his own ambiguous political position. Although he came from UP he was not really a provincial politician with roots and support deep in local social and political structures. He was to a considerable extent an outsider whose role was more an all-India one by virtue of his relationship with Gandhi and his proven work as a secretary for the Congress organisation, for he had failed to organise or sustain any more radical group outside Congress through which he might have realistically worked towards his goals. But both these foundations of his increasingly acknowledged position as an all-India figure were also serious constraints on him. He recognised that there was no hope of independence, or of major change in India's socio-economic order, without the cooperation of both Gandhi and Congress. But Gandhi was an excep- tional and bewildering mentor who, though he could attract widespread support, thought in terms of moral transformation rather than concrete political, social or economic plans: and Nehru was deeply concerned to maintain the unity of Congress if at all possible. Congress, for its part, was still not a reliable party with a sound organisation and a clear ideology. It accommodated within itself people of many different interests and senses of identity. Nehru was ill at ease with those who spoke in a far more Hindu idiom about the nation; and was open that his socio-economic views, for example on relations between landlords and tenants, were not shared by a Congress which had the landed within its ranks and wished to prevent conflict between landlords and tenants. He would only act within the limitations set by Congress, but he insisted that it was his right to attempt to convert Congress and the country at large to his viewpoint.[62]

In grappling with the problems of his own personal position, and the limitations on his freedom to manoeuvre, he also began to understand and articulate the problems of achieving a genuinely mass nationalism. For him the struggle for swaraj demanded a mass movement rather than the elite politics of his father's generation. But this implied the pursuit of goals which would appeal to ordinary Indians, particularly their economic problems; a new form of leadership which enabled organisation and participation 'from the bottom up'; and serious consideration of strategies of opposition which would drive the movement on and sustain the morale of its adherents. This put him at odds with many within and outside the Congress who feared such outcomes, among them moderates who feared revolutionary political change and the possibility of mass turbulence, and those who appealed to community rather than socio-economic status as the criterion of political identity and aspiration. His radicalism opened his eyes to profound problems some politicians would have preferred to ignore in their pursuit of power and place. But it also made him incapable of understanding the real fears of India's minorities at the prospect of the devolution of power to Indian hands where Hindus were a large majority, fears which were in part behind what he denounced as communal strategies for the preservation and strengthening of minority status. The constraints which bound Nehru in these often unhappy years were, in retrospect, evidence of the profound ambiguities of mass nationalism on the subcontinent.

# Chapter 6

# Whither India?

From his imprisonment at the end of 1931 until his release in September 1935 to fly to Europe to be beside Kamala, who was now gravely ill, Nehru spent most of his time in jail. He had a few brief months of liberty between August 1933 and February 1934. For him this was a phase of immense inner turmoil, with a re-assessment of himself in relation to those who were closest to him, and of anguish over India's present and future. It was also a time of intellectual creativity, when it became clear that the man who professed that he delighted most in action, who had studied science at university, was also a very considerable man of letters. He completed a second series of letters to his growing daughter, which were published as *Glimpses of World History* in 1935; he wrote a series of articles late in 1933 which were gathered together under the title *Whither India?* and at breath-taking speed between June 1934 and February 1935 he wrote his autobiography, which was published in London in April 1936 and received considerable public attention.[1]

Although these literary endeavours were all written in particular circumstances, in part to satisfy the author's own intellectual and emotional needs, they proved eventually to be a significant source of income. This was to be important as the family finances were in disarray after Motilal's death. Their domestic expenses had been somewhat reduced in 1930 when they moved out of the vast home where Nehru had grown up and begun his married life, following Motilal's decision to hand the building over to Congress and to build himself a smaller house in the grounds. Nonetheless, without his income they were in considerable straits, particularly as there was substantial outstanding tax of about Rs 20,000 left to pay after his death. (Although Nehru had begun to pay this, once he was in prison he refused to cooperate, and the government attached some of his stocks and shares to settle the bill, though it did not touch the family home.) What was left of the family's invested wealth had to support family members including Jawaharlal, his mother, wife and daughter and his youngest sister, who did not marry until 1933.

Their expenses included medical bills for Kamala and his mother, and eventually travel to Europe for Kamala, Indira and Jawaharlal, as well as Indira's education (which cost Rs 100 a month while she was in a small private boarding school in Bombay). Nehru himself had no salary at this stage, and declined offers of subvention. They even had to sell Kamala's jewellery in 1933 to improve their immediate financial situation, though this gave Nehru considerable pleasure and relief from the burden of unnecessary possessions.

Nehru's personal turmoil was to a significant extent a result of the political situation in India, even though prison walls insulated him for so long from personal involvement in politics. A brief note on this political backdrop is therefore essential in order to comprehend how the questions Whither India? and Whither Jawaharlal? confronted and oppressed him. The Government of India pursued a dual policy towards India. On the one hand it pressed ahead with preparations for constitutional reform, promised at the end of the first Round Table Conference in 1931. The upshot was the Government of India Act of 1935, which gave the provinces of British India autonomy, and promised major reform at the centre once the princes had settled on terms for entry into an all-India federation. On the other hand, it determined to squash the civil disobedience campaign which was renewed on Gandhi's return to India at the end of 1931. The upshot was a swift crackdown on the Congress leadership, organisation and funds. Gandhi was himself imprisoned within days of his return, despite his wish to talk to the new Viceroy, Lord Willingdon. Between January 1932 and April 1933 nearly 75,000 people had been convicted in relation to civil disobedience, including nearly 4,000 women.[2] The peak number of political prisoners was reached in April 1932 when roughly 32,500 were in jail.

This alone would not have perturbed Nehru, for he delighted in conflict and loathed anything that smacked of peace or truce with an imperial government. However, the force of government action and the lure of politics within a reformed constitution combined to break up the civil disobedience movement and to convince many politicians, within as well as outside Congress, that Gandhian politics were no longer viable or productive. The pattern of the early 1920s became visible again, as Congressmen, who had adopted satyagraha as a strategy for the time being, cast about for alternatives which would enable them to deal not only with the British but with their fellow Indians.

Gandhi, for his part, retained his idiosyncratic understanding of swaraj as moral revolution, and began to concentrate on the problem of India's outcastes, the Untouchables of Hindu society, whom he named *Harijans* or children of God. His own failure to reach any compromise with representatives of India's minorities at the second Round Table Conference in London in the autumn of 1931 led the British to announce in 1932 a 'Communal Award' of reserved seats and separate electorates for minorities, including Untouchables, to drive on the reform process. Gandhi objected profoundly to separate electorates for Untouchables, believing that this would further divide Hindu society. He was also aware that the Indian nation, which he had claimed uniquely to represent, had already displayed its disunity through the demands of Muslims for special representation. As he was in prison, the only strategy of protest he could adopt was that of the fast – designed, he claimed, to sting the consciences of caste Hindus into reform of their attitudes and practices. It is also likely that he hoped it would ultimately lead to his release and to renewed contact with the government. The upshot was a hastily gathered conference of Hindus and representatives of Untouchables in Bombay, and – thanks to those indefatigable mediators, Jayakar and Sapru – a compromise was reached which Gandhi approved of from his prison outside Poona, as he grew markedly weaker.[3] Thereafter Gandhi concentrated his energies on work to ameliorate the conditions of Untouchables, and was given special facilities for this inside prison. He increasingly ceased to be a serious political leader, and eventually, sensitive to the mood of Congressmen who wanted to return to some form of productive politics and to escape the impasse into which conflict with the government had led them, he advised the end of civil disobedience in 1934, and announced that he would 'retire' from Congress.

## COPING WITH PRISON

Against this background Nehru had to cope with another long sojourn in prison. (In this phase he experienced a number of jails, but all of them in UP so he could see family members, apart from a brief spell in prison in Bengal in early 1934. During the last months of his sentence in 1934–5 he was in Almora jail in the UP hills so he could be nearer to Kamala who was in a sanatorium in Bhowali.) He was, as always, self-aware. He told his sister, Vijayalakshmi, that he was an old hand at jail, having had ten years experience of it. (In fact he had spent just over five years in prison by mid-1935, although his sentences totalled ten and a half years.) On the whole he felt it taught one what things were of true value – home, children, friends – and if one could handle it then it did one good. If not, of course, the result was physical and mental breakdown. For himself 'a certain calmness, a peace of the mind comes, and a power to detach oneself a little from the passing show and watch it almost as an outsider. And a feeling of satisfaction, of confidence in oneself, the joy of having overcome one fear, one obstacle, and to that extent having brought life in control.'[4] He reassured his daughter that he was not 'the pining sort' and flourished in the face of adversity. 'When any action or work faces me I concentrate on it and try to do my best. When action is denied me I shut that drawer of my mind and open some other.'[5] Here were perhaps echoes of Gandhi's teaching of the importance of the immediate moment and the possible action, which he would sum up in the words of one of his favourite Christian hymns, 'one step enough for me'.

However, Nehru's jail diaries for these years[6] show that he was not always as calm and detached as he liked to portray himself. Indeed these were years of considerable mental distress. He noted in March 1932 that he had not been able to settle down in jail as he had in the past, and was subject to considerable mood swings, although the *charkha* brought him some peace of mind. In mid-1934 he admitted that jail was telling on his nerves and that he had never before felt quite so helpless. There were several reasons for his inner turmoil. One was his grief for his father. Politics had permitted him no time to mourn the loss of the one person who could begin to understand him through his love and intellect, despite their difference of views; but now he had emotional space and he thought much about Motilal and missed him deeply. Being in jail again only brought back the memories of their time together in prison, and now he felt a profound emptiness. He also worried about Kamala and her declining health. The old illness had gripped her once more, and Nehru, who had so recently lost his father, began to fear that his wife was also slipping away. For a few days in August 1934 he was released to be with her in Allahabad when she seemed to deteriorate markedly. Thereafter he was allowed out regularly to see her, and when she was moved to Bhowali he was taken to Almora jail nearby.

To compound this personal distress there was also the news from the wider world – of the government's policy, the unpredictable actions of Gandhi and the fear that he would kill himself fasting, and of the political responses of both the Congress and the moderates on its fringes. He reacted with anger and bewilderment. In November 1932 he confided to his diary that he felt tired and stale, with thoughts of his wife's illness and his daughter far away at school, 'and all the world going awry, and knaves and scoundrels in the seats of authority shouting and haranguing and threatening, and good men silent, and fools, oh! So many of them everywhere!'[7] In February 1933 he fumed inwardly at the Indians who cooperated in the final Round Table Conference in London. 'I get very angry at the scandalous and shameful way the Liberals and others have agreed to the monstrous abortions which are the outcome of the R.T.C. . . . these Liberals and other Round Tablers! What morons they are – or is it merely that they are a lot of old women?'[8] Here was the famous Nehru anger and sense of superiority, which he had shared with Motilal, but which in prison had no outlet and only helped to disturb and disorientate him. His sense of oppression and depression was deepened by his own poor health, which was unusual for him and made him annoyed with himself. Furthermore, for some months he refused interviews with family members, because of what he interpreted as an insult to his mother during an interview with her imprisoned son-in-law, Ranjit Pandit.

The conditions in which Nehru was kept varied from prison to prison. What he seems to have hated most were the places where he was housed in a barrack and locked up at night, and the lack of privacy. In March 1932 he was aware that he was making life difficult for his three fellow prisoners, one of whom was the UP

Congressman, G. B. Pant, whom he felt to be 'very decent & we get on well together in spite of many differences'. But he found it a 'sore trial' to live with people in a barrack.

> Always together – no privacy – and the same persons from morning to evening – day after day – time without end! It is terrible at times and one is tempted to prefer solitary confinement even. This close association in a barrack has most of the disadvantages of married life with none of its advantages. How people get on each other's nerves and how every little failing of another seems to grow and grow on one till it becomes almost intolerable.[9]

As in a previous prison term he felt like an animal in a zoo when the prison superintendent at Dehra Dun brought some British officers of a Gurkha regiment to look at him.[10]

As in the past, Nehru kept himself comparatively fit and composed by walking long distances wherever there was room. He calculated that in Alipur jail early in 1934 he walked six miles a day! He also used the *charkha* for spinning, and increasingly took a new interest in gardening, particularly in Almora. He wrote in his diary of the amount of time he spent thinking about his plants, and it is evident that he also took considerable interest in animals, wild and domesticated, that penetrated the prison. To his daughter he confided, 'Latterly I have felt drawn more and more towards nature – to plants and animals. Maybe it is a relief and an escape from human folly, human cowardice and human knavery!'[11]

However, his greatest solace was reading. In a press interview during his brief period of liberty in 1933 he said that he had read much politics, economics and science in the past months. 'Solid reading is a necessity in prison; without it the mind stagnates and rots. Novels for a relaxation occasionally, yes, but one must have something more substantial on which to concentrate.'[12] One of his main aims had been to study contemporary problems and to see how these might affect India. In his subsequent incarceration, between 15 February 1934 and 15 September 1935 he read 188 books, averaging between 15 and 20 a month. Many of them were history and politics, including one on the second Soviet five-year development plan. But he also read contemporary plays, a few great classics such as Tolstoy's *War and Peace*, a variety of lighter literature, including some P. G. Wodehouse and Lewis Carroll's *Alice Through the Looking Glass*, a major modern Indian novel, Mulk Raj Anand's *Untouchable*, and a book called *Keeping Fit at Forty*![13] Some of these were from the library of whichever jail he happened to be in; but most were sent or brought to him by friends and family. His intellectual concerns and passions ran deep, and he confessed he could not understand those who did not share them. He wrote to his younger sister,

Even apart from my personal obsession, I find the world today an absorbing and fascinating place to life in. We live in an age of mighty changes and terrible conflicts, when hope and despair fight for mastery in each thinking mind. A person who is not affected by these events and who has no desire to take part in them, is hardly a live person intellectually.[14]

In contrast to his previous times in prison, Nehru also wrote. Completing his 'Letters to Indu' – his letters to his daughter, Indira – 'have helped me wonderfully in getting through the last fifteen months in prison', he recorded in mid-1933.[15] In 1934–5 he wrote one of his major works, the *Autobiography*. As he said in the Preface, his objective was primarily to occupy himself in prison, but also to review events in India to enable him to think clearly about them. He was trying to understand his own mental development, not to write a history of recent events. Moreover, he claimed to have written with an Indian audience in mind, although the book was first published in London.[16] It was an extraordinarily interesting and powerful book, deeply honest about his own limitations, and at the same time frank about his criticisms of so many others in political life, including Gandhi. Moreover, despite his evident hostility to British imperialism it was not a bitter book, and he showed that magnanimity towards British people which was to be so important in the construction of new relations between Britain and India after 1947. Here was a strong and critical mind at work, thinking deeply about India's place in the world and its participation in broad trends in world history.

The book also showed him coming to grips with many of the religious, moral, social and political issues which faced his generation – as he ranged from political strategies to the economic problems of the peasantry, to questions of religious belief and identity. Perhaps above all it showed that he thought of himself as having primarily a political life, as a man obsessed with the idea of freedom and renewal for his country. In the Epilogue he wrote that the years he had tried to record had given him the rich gift of looking on life as an adventure of absorbing interest, in which there was so much to learn and so much to do. He felt he was continually growing up, and this gave zest to all he did. But he also admitted that he felt he was a curious blend of East and West, and therefore out of place everywhere and at home nowhere. This dual inheritance gave him a feeling of 'spiritual loneliness not only in public activities but in life itself. I am a stranger and alien in the West. I cannot be of it. But in my own country also, sometimes, I have an exile's feeling.'[17] In retrospect the quotation from *The Talmud* which he placed at the head of the Epilogue seems prescient: 'We are enjoined to labour; but it is not granted to us to complete our labours.'

## FAMILY RELATIONS

Prison made Nehru value his family relationships more deeply, as he had confided in his sister, Vijayalakshmi. Events also made him more sensitive to his wife and daughter, particularly Kamala's growing frailty and apparent isolation within the family home in her husband's absence, and Indira's advance through adolescence. But even with them he was reticent on personal matters. As he reminded a close family friend, 'You ought to know me sufficiently to realise that I never discuss them unless the other party takes the initiative. I would not do so even with Kamala or Indu. Such has been my training.'[18]

Nehru and his teenage daughter wrote to each other regularly while he was in prison.[19] They addressed each other in terms of close endearment, and Indira often – and interestingly – referred to herself as his 'Indu-boy'. Much of their correspondence dealt with everyday matters of school and prison life, Kamala's health and news of relatives. But increasingly he wrote to her as a young woman in the making, about her education and her future. Looking to the time when she had left school he hoped that she would spend time at both English and continental universities, and that eventually she would take up work which was worthwhile and contributed something to the larger society. He compared this to his old profession as a lawyer, which he said he disliked intensely and considered antisocial for it did not create anything or add anything to the good things of the world. (His criticism of lawyers had clear echoes of Gandhi's earlier denunciation of Indian lawyers in *Hind Swaraj*.) Nehru arranged for Indira to leave school in Bombay and in mid-1934 to go to Rabindranath Tagore's renowned educational establishment at Shantiniketan in Bengal. But he chided her at the idea that she might live apart from the ordinary pupils where conditions of boarding, and particularly food, would not be up to her accustomed standards! That seemed to him vulgar and snobbish, and she should not put barriers between herself and other students. He reminded her of the conditions he had put up with at Harrow – always feeling hungry and having to wait on older boys![20] He also worried about her health, felt she was too introspective for her age, and wanted her to avoid acquiring an invalid's mentality, which he felt was so common in India, in comparison with his own robust and critical attitude to those who fell ill.[21]

It was a tragic irony that someone who on his own admission had such an 'intolerant and aggressive' attitude to ill-health should have had such a profoundly sick wife. He admitted that her illnesses irritated him, despite his deep concern for her and fear for the outcome. When she left for Bhowali he gave her as a symbol of his love for her lines from 'To One in Paradise' by Edgar Allan Poe. The privacy of his prison diary allowed him to record the depth of their relationship during the months when she was in Bhowali and he was permitted regular visits. They had some of the most profound conversations they had ever shared early in 1935, and seemed to resolve many of the tensions in their past relationship. Nehru marvelled at how much they meant to each other. He began to count the days to his next visit and longed for release more than he had ever done, to be with her even if she were an invalid.

However, there was still a gulf between them, largely caused by Kamala's increasing religious devotion. Over the past three years she had become close to the Ramakrishna Mission in Calcutta and became a lay devotee. Nehru disliked this sort of religion and considered it more 'a type of hysteria' than a genuine search for God. His male pride was also piqued as he sensed he meant less to her. Now in February she announced that 'she wanted to realise God and give her thoughts to this, and as a preparation for this our relations should undergo some change. Apparently I was not to come in the way of God.'[22] Nehru was devastated: not only was he an isolated and unhappy figure in politics, but now even his marital life seemed to be ending. They parted next day after he had tried to tell her how he felt. But it evidently wounded him even more than he could express, for some nights later, as the anniversary of the death of his father dawned, he dreamed that his wife also left him.

On subsequent visits they talked companionably but Nehru felt deeply disturbed at his mood swings as he thought of her. 'How much she means to me and yet how little she fits in or tries to fit in with my ideas. That is really the irritating part, that she does not try, and so she drifts apart.'[23] Most unusually for him, he appears to have found some relief in a heart-to-heart talk on one of these visits with Kamala's cousin, Dr Madan Atal, about 'personal matters'.[24] It was Atal who eventually accompanied her and Indira to Europe in May for further treatment, leaving Nehru alone in prison, not knowing what the future might hold for his married life. Nonetheless, he wrote gently to her when she was away, urging her when she was well to develop attitudes and habits of independence, and not to depend on him. 'I am a traveller, limping along in the dark night. Why should I drag others into this darkness, however near or beloved they may be; why should they suffer the travails of the journey? I have no right to do so.' Later he tried to explain to her in a lengthy letter why he felt so lonely, how so few people shared his thoughts and principles, and how during the year it had begun to dawn on him that he would have to travel alone on his mental journey.[25]

## RELATIONS WITH GANDHI

Nehru also had to reassess his relationship with that other figure with whom he had the closest emotional and political bonds, Gandhi. The agonising process this involved raised for him the interlocking questions of Whither India? and Whither Jawaharlal? There was no doubt that Nehru became emotionally closer than ever to Gandhi in the aftermath of his father's death. Gandhi reciprocated, and as his secretary and close associate, Mahadev Desai, wrote to Jawaharlal on board the ship taking them to Britain in August 1931, 'He seemed so moved as he talked about you as we left the shores of India. If Papa doted on you, there is now Bapu to dote on you. I cannot tell you the depth of his affection for you and the last event in our lives has made it deeper, if possible.'[26] Gandhi, however, still perplexed Nehru deeply, and his actions during this period plunged their relationship into several crises.

The first of these was the Poona fast of September 1932 against separate electorates for Untouchables. Nehru in jail recorded two days of inner turmoil, when he was consumed with anguish that he might not see Gandhi again. He was also annoyed that Gandhi seemed so willing to throw away his life on what Nehru considered 'a side issue', and to act in a way which might jeopardise their whole movement. He also found the technique of the fast problematic – as did many other Indians. 'And I felt angry with Bapu at his religious and sentimental approach to a political question. Was he entitled to coerce people in this way? What would happen to this country if the practice spread? And his frequent references to God . . . were most irritating. What a terrible example to set!'[27] He wept in his confusion and worry, but eventually regained some composure, helped by a kind telegram from Gandhi, and the sense that Gandhi often had the knack of doing the right thing, even if he from his perspective could not justify it. To Gandhi he wired support and relief that a settlement seemed likely, but added, 'Danger your methods being exploited by others but how can I presume advise magician.'[28] Indira wrote to tell her father all about the fast, and was clearly very moved by it. But though Nehru supported Gandhi on the Untouchables issue eventually, he told his sister somewhat later that he was 'not terribly excited over this question'.[29]

Within months, in May 1933, Gandhi was again fasting on the much broader issue of Untouchability itself. Before the fast began he wrote to Nehru to explain why he felt this to be essential for him, for to him Untouchability was the worst thing in the world and could not be defeated by mere intellectual effort. Nehru replied from prison that he was utterly lost and did not know what to say, as religion was unfamiliar ground to him. He agreed that Untouchability was very bad, but certainly not the worst thing in the world. Then he poured out to his mentor how he had made life so much richer and fuller for him over the last fifteen years as they had worked together, yet now in a lonely world Gandhi seemed to be wanting to make it even lonelier.[30] Although he was profoundly relieved that Gandhi lived, he reverted privately to his earlier critique of Gandhi's methods, feeling that this was sheer revivalism, and that such moral rhetoric did not encourage clear thinking, while probably even Gandhi himself had no clear objective. How different this was from Communist dialectics, he mused, and how he felt drawn more to that, while 'more and more I realise the gulf between Bapu & me and I begin to doubt if this way of faith is the right way to train a nation. It may pay for a short while, but in the long run?'[31] Further he could not understand why Gandhi let himself be surrounded by 'the pillars and the beneficiaries' of the current socio-economic order, who might talk about dear 'Bapu' but would never take risks. He wanted to break from such people completely and to place the ideal of a radically new India before everybody, but Gandhi would persist with compromise and 'sweet reasonableness'. For himself he sensed that a stiff battle would come between his loyalty to Gandhi and his ideals, so for the time being the best place for him was probably jail. As the weeks unfolded and Gandhi effectively presided over the running down of civil disobedience, and even sought an interview with the Viceroy, Nehru became convinced that there could no longer be further political cooperation between him and Gandhi.[32]

At the end of August 1933 Nehru was released from prison, and the time had come to act on these convictions and to confront Gandhi. He travelled to Poona in early September, where Gandhi was recovering from yet another fast. (He had been released lest he die in prison during the three-week fast in May, but on re-arrest he had fasted again for the facilities in prison to carry on his work against Untouchability, and as he rapidly deteriorated the government released him yet again rather than have a martyr's death on their hands.) The two men talked at length, not having seen each other for over two years, when Gandhi boarded ship for the voyage to London. They ranged over their outlook on life, politics and economics, and recognised amicably that they had different points of view and temperament, yet they also had many things in common. Nehru seems to have been reassured that they shared sufficient fundamentals to continue their cooperation. They exchanged letters, which were then published.[33] Nehru's main concern was with recognition that the national objective meant complete independence, and that this meant also alleviating the condition of the masses, which in turn would mean the 'devesting' of vested interests including the raj itself, the princes and landowners. Gandhi agreed with much of what Nehru said, although he himself preferred to concentrate on right means rather than keep reiterating goals, and he reminded Nehru of the significance of the constructive programme. Nehru also issued a public statement which indicated that despite differences of approach, he had no intention of challenging Gandhi's methods, which he still thought were right for India, and that for such methods Gandhi's leadership was essential.

To observers it was clear that both men recognised their need of each other and were striving to prevent any break, which would weaken themselves and the national movement. Nehru himself confirmed this in a later letter to Subhas Bose.[34] Gandhi, for his part, later told Nehru that he was not at all disturbed by him, and indeed that he would be 'in a wilderness without you in the Congress'. He also took pains to soothe relations between Nehru and other Congressmen, urging them to tolerate his moods and outbursts.[35]

Yet Nehru's reassessment of his relationship with Gandhi was not over. Back in jail in 1934 he learned that Gandhi had finally called off the civil disobedience movement early in April. He was devastated and wrote in his diary that this marked the end of an epoch in the freedom struggle and in his own life. After fifteen years he would have to go his own way. How could he work with Bapu, he mused, when he functioned in such an inexplicable way and left people in the lurch?[36] Recording the time in his autobiography, he entitled the chapter 'Desolation', reflecting his own incomprehension at Gandhi's arguments, and what seemed to him the poverty of the programme of nation-building which Gandhi had suggested in place of civil disobedience. With pain he recognised that his allegiance to Gandhi seemed to have snapped, despite the many times he had tried to be loyal to him for the greater cause of national freedom. He then elaborated on all the aspects of Gandhi's leadership he found troubling – his religious idiom, his lack of a clear objective, his concentration on means rather than ends, his hostility to modern life, his praise of poverty, suffering and the simple life, and his glorification of celibacy. By contrast Nehru felt that India's problems were not so much moral as systemic; and that no permanent solution could be found in reliance on such methods as self-reform and khadi. Only a change of system, and the establishment of a socialist order would be effective, though quite how and with what degree of compulsion was still unclear.[37]

In a brief period when he was let out of prison to be with Kamala in August 1934 he poured much of this frustration into a letter to Gandhi, where he admitted that he now felt absolutely alone. Gandhi replied in soothing fashion, assuring him that he had not lost a comrade in him, that he was still the same as when they first met, and that he still had the same passion for independence. But he urged on him a greater tolerance for the members of the CWC, for they were, after all, their colleagues. He now asked Nehru for 'construction' after the 'explosion'. But before Nehru could turn his mind to this he returned to prison.[38]

## WHITHER INDIA?

During the period of liberty at the end of 1933, when he was committed to working with Gandhi after their Poona discussions, Nehru nonetheless tried to elaborate his ideas and to encourage clear thinking as the civil disobedience movement petered out. He wrote in a private letter in September that he found it 'quite amazing how extraordinarily vague are the ideas of many of our closest colleagues in regard to our objective. Perhaps that is inevitable for nationalism hides a host of differences under a cover of anti-feeling against the imperialist oppressor.' But he was intent on encouraging clearer thinking, even though this would result in further socio-economic cleavages and apparent disunity.[39]

The result was a series of press articles of 9–11 October, which were later reprinted in pamphlet form with additional material in which he answered criticisms, entitled *Whither India?*[40] He wrote that he was trying to take his readers back to first principles, and away from the more trivial political questions which seemed currently to command attention. Their goal was independence, but that raised the question of freedom for whom? Consequently they had to grapple with the conflicting interests which were to an extent masked by nationalism, and accept that freedom was much more than paper constitutions, and involved serious redistribution of wealth to end class privilege. Setting India's own struggle for freedom in the context of world economic and political movements, he wrote powerfully of the realities of mass nationalism.

> Is our aim human welfare or the preservation of class privileges and the vested interests of pampered groups? The question must be answered clearly and unequivocally by each one of us. There is no room for quibbling when the fate of nations and millions of human beings is at stake. The day for palace intrigues and parlour politics and pacts and compromises passes when the masses enter politics. Their manners are not those of the drawing room; we never took the trouble to teach them any manners. Their school is the school of events and suffering is their teacher. They learn their politics from great movements which bring out the true nature of individuals and classes, and the civil disobedience movement has taught the Indian masses many a lesson which they will never forget.

Given this commitment, the real question before India, in his view, was one of fundamental change of regime – politically, socially and economically. 'Whither India? Surely to the great human goal of social and economic equality, to the ending of all exploitation of nation by nation and class by class, to national freedom within the framework of an international cooperative socialist world federation.' When questioned about the means to such a goal he replied that it was essential first to be clear about the goal. In a further reflection obviously on Gandhi's priorities, he said he did not believe that preaching and philanthropy were adequate means – rather, some element of coercion was probably inevitable. Indeed, their non-violent mass movements had been powerful weapons of exercising pressure. He himself would greatly prefer non-violence as a method, but it was no creed for him, and he would prefer freedom with violence rather than subjection with non-violence. He also made it clear that he envisaged progressive industrialisation for India, though he accepted that khadi was appropriate at the present time for political and socio-economic reasons. When queried on the issue of civil disobedience he responded categorically that any withdrawal of civil disobedience would be a betrayal of their cause as it would encourage compromise with imperialism.

Although prison insulated Nehru to a considerable extent from having to grapple with the mundane questions of where this vision of India's future led him as an individual, he did, at least during his months of liberty, have to clarify where he stood within Indian politics and in relation to its different political groups. His discussions with Gandhi made it plain how difficult were his relations with Congress, despite the key role he had played within its organisation over the past years. He did not contemplate withdrawing from it, as Gandhi periodically did to concentrate on his ashrams and his constructive work. Nehru had no such alternative base of operations or strategy for change: moreover, he felt he could attempt to influence views within it, and he did not wish to leave such an influential organisation in the hands of people with a more reactionary outlook. He had been privileged to work within it for the best years of his life, and he would stick with it as long as he felt that it was the most effective radical organisation in the country and the institution through which to work best for change in the mass mentality. 'So long as I feel that, I shall gladly and most willingly work with this great organisation, which has done so much for the country, even though it may not go far enough from my point of view.'[41]

Yet he often felt desperately isolated and out of place, particularly in 1934 as the CWC struggled with the issue of post-civil disobedience strategy. When it resolved in June that class war was contrary to the creed of non-violence Nehru swore at his diary: 'To hell with the Working Committee – passing pious and fatuous resolutions on subjects it does not understand – or perhaps understands too well!'[42] In 1935 in prison he railed privately at the timidity of Congress and the lack of able people in it. In the months of liberty he had made public not only his more radical views than most Congressmen, but also his contempt for those whose views differed from his own. In January 1934, for example he had criticised social and village uplift work as 'safe and pious activity' which could be 'left to old ladies', in contrast to his work for freedom and a new deal for the Indian masses. Very rapidly he had to apologise in public for this as a slur on old ladies and to explain that he did not mean to run down village work.[43] When Nehru returned to prison, Sapru wrote of his sadness that such a fine intellect and character should moulder in jail. But Nehru seemed to him to be totally out of tune with everything around him. 'Unfortunately . . . Jawahar Lal has made himself impossible. Recently I saw something of his temper . . . It is absolutely uncontrollable. He is honest, desperately honest, but he lives in a world of his own, he hates the British and the present system equally and my fear is that even if you could bring about a settlement between him and the British he would continue to be at war with the present social system.'[44]

Nehru's personal dilemmas about his future were the more poignant because of the emergence in mid-1934 of a small Congress Socialist Party in response to the collapse of civil disobedience. The Congress Socialists' aim was to stay within

Congress, but to work to reinvigorate it, to rid it of its defeatist attitude and to draw in both industrial and agricultural labour. Their programme included a planned economy by the state, the elimination of princes and landlords, and the creation of cooperatives for production, credit and distribution. They also criticised Gandhi's concentration on moral change, his apparent failure to confront major socio-economic issues, and his insistence on non-violence. Many of those who were within this new group were people with whom Nehru felt a natural political affiliation; and their programme echoed many of the criticisms he had made of Congress and Gandhi in the privacy of his prison diary and in his exchanges with Gandhi.[45]

Nehru was of course in prison at this juncture, but the previous year when he was at liberty he had been involved in considerable discussions with many of those involved in this departure. Although he made it clear that he would like to see Congress move towards a more socialist programme, he felt that their efforts must be integrated within the mainstream of Congress nationalism. Otherwise they would leave Congress to people with more reactionary inclinations, and would risk becoming an ineffective bunch of parlour socialists who spoke much and did little.[46] Writing in 1934–5 he acknowledged that he shared many of the intellectual conflicts of those who became members of the CSP, but he was riled by their tendency to academic discussion, which he thought was a refuge for inaction. 'It was a little irritating to find people, who did little themselves, criticise others who had shouldered the burden in the heat and dust of the fray, as reactionaries. These parlour Socialists are especially hard on Gandhiji as the arch-reactionary . . . But the little fact remains that this "reactionary" knows India, understands India, almost is peasant India, and has shaken up India as no so-called revolutionary has done.'[47] There was considerable criticism of Nehru from those who hoped he would use his unique position in Congress to free it from Gandhi's influence. Subhas Bose wrote strongly in his autobiographical work about Nehru's failure during his time of freedom, despite his prestige and intellectual capacity, to take hard decisions and give Congress the sort of lead which would have rescued it from its confusion. Privately he wrote, 'Nehru's ideas are more in our favour. But in action, he gives full support to Gandhi. His head pulls one way and his heart in another direction. His heart is with Gandhi.'[48] He misunderstood Nehru. Not only was his affection with Gandhi. His mind told him that isolation from Congress would prevent him pursuing the ideal of radical mass nationalism.

This ideal also lay behind Nehru's public attacks on what he saw as reactionary communalism in the months of liberty in 1933. He had not wished to concentrate on this question while the priority was to pursue civil disobedience. But in the comparative lull in the struggle in 1933 he 'felt compelled to come out strongly' on the issue, as there was no longer any danger of diverting effort from the conflict.[49] His earlier views had not changed, and now he condemned both those who claimed to speak for all Hindus through the Hindu Mahasabha, and those in the Muslim All Parties Conference and the Muslim League who insisted that they represented all India's Muslims. Both groups of self-styled leaders, he insisted, represented not the vast bulk of Hindus or Muslims, but 'the rich upper class groups and the struggle for communal advantages is really an attempt of these groups to take as big a share of power and privilege for themselves as possible'.[50] He admitted that friends were warning him against antagonising many people by his stance. But he felt he could not remain 'a silent witness' to such attempts to weaken the struggle for freedom, even if his outspokenness was politically dangerous.

> I must say frankly what I have in mind. That is not perhaps the way of politi-
> cians for in politics people are very careful of what they say and do not say
> lest they offend some group or individual and lose support. But I am not a
> politician by choice; forces stronger than me have driven me to this field and,
> it may be, that I have yet to learn the ways of politicians.[51]

The remedy for communal fears which he advocated was that of a Constituent Assembly, elected on the widest franchise, which would draw up a new constitution. He was even prepared for separate electorates to such an assembly to assuage minority fears. If in such an assembly Muslim representatives still pressed for apparently communal demands for protection, then he would urge that these should be accepted. 'Much as I dislike communalism I realise that it does not disappear by suppression but by a removal of fear, or by a diversion of interest. We should therefore remove this fear complex and make the Muslim masses realise that they can have any protection that they really desire.' His hope was that through this strategy of an assembly the 'masses' would bypass those who claimed to speak for them, whose true motivation was to safeguard as much as possible for themselves and, in alliance with the British, prevent any radical socio-economic change. By contrast, in an assembly, Indians would confront the real issues facing India, principally economic ones, and communalism would fade into the background. 'It has been a hothouse growth nurtured in the heated atmosphere of conference rooms and so-called All Parties Conferences. It will not find a solution in that artificial environment, but it will wilt and die in the fresh air and the sunlight.'[52]

Nehru, the idealist who claimed that he was a reluctant politician, by the closing months of 1935 had spent nearly four years of painful personal and political reassessment. Prison and political developments outside his jail walls, particularly the collapse of civil disobedience and the seemingly erratic and unproductive nature of Gandhi's leadership, had caused him possibly greater personal anguish in relation to public matters than he had ever experienced before. Further, two of his closest personal relationships had proved deeply problematic. This phase in his life was about to come to a close in tragic circumstances. He would have served his full prison term in February 1936. But on 2 September 1935 a telegram from the Beidenwaler sanatorium where Kamala was staying indicated that her condition was critical. The government released him to join her, imposing no restrictions on what he could do in Europe, and trusting to his sense of honour not to use the time before he left India to make political speeches. His diary shows the depth of his emotions. On 28 August he had noted, 'She is slipping away and the thought of it is unbearable, hellish.' Then on 2 September came the telegram which was like a 'thunderbolt'. 'So this is the end . . . I felt broken up all day . . . I tried to occupy myself with arranging my books and papers.'[53]

# Chapter 7

# Isolation

The years from Nehru's hasty departure to Europe to the outbreak of the Second World War were a time of isolation for him. This was obvious enough in his private life. But it is also clear that he felt he was a misfit in Indian political life, particularly in Congress – ironically, as this was a phase when he had come into his own as a public figure in India, and as an acknowledged representative of Indian nationalism abroad, and when he displayed frenetic energy in political affairs, and was active at the very heart of Congress. This chapter explores the dimensions and implications of this isolation (rather than attempting to provide a detailed history of Congress affairs during this period).[1] It examines how an apparent misfit had emerged as one of the major players in, and leaders of, the politics of nationalism, and shows how Nehru's experience throws light on significant changes in Indian politics, and in particular the increasingly ambiguous status of Congress as the representative of an Indian nation and of mass nationalism.

## THE LONELINESS OF MIDDLE AGE

Nehru flew to Europe in September 1935, reaching his wife's bedside in Germany within five days of his release from prison. This in itself was remarkable as commercial flights between Europe and India had only just started, and most people still travelled by sea. Planes had to refuel constantly during such a long journey; Nehru travelled from Delhi to Jodhpur and Karachi, to Baghdad, Cairo and Alexandria. Then a seaplane took him to Brindisi, and from there he went by train. During the four-hour stopover in Jodhpur, he enjoyed having a really good hot bath in an English-style bath provided by the hotel where the passengers rested. The contrast with the facilities of Almora jail was evidently striking! But when he reached Badenweiler in the Black Forest the full impact of Kamala's illness hit him. She seemed to rally a little with his company, and twice a day he walked from his pension to the sanatorium to sit with her, to talk of the past and occasionally of the future, and to read aloud to her. In the loneliness of those weeks he thought much about their marriage and problems in human relationships.

When she seemed to regain a little strength he went briefly twice to England. He had already seen in Germany that Europe had changed markedly since his last visit, and later noted how he deliberately patronised Jewish shops, and was irritated at the Nazi appropriation of the Indian symbol of good fortune, the swastika. He went to London, Oxford, Cambridge and Birmingham, to see friends and also to re-educate himself in the contemporary western scene, though inevitably he was treated as in a sense representative of Indian aspirations. He was even met by a man from Scotland Yard who had been deputed to look after him by the Home Office, and found him to be courteous and helpful, in contrast to the CID in India. He met Indian students, small groups of Christian and left-wing sympathisers, and a wide range of English people, but avoided anyone responsible for British policy in India. As he told one English woman who was deeply sympathetic to Gandhi and India, he could not stomach the idea of meetings with people implicated in the policy of oppression which was suffocating India. He remembered Motilal saying that the raj was the greatest terrorist organisation in India, and he hated terrorism in all its forms, but at the moment 'the most monstrous thing is a powerful and organised government trying to crush the spirit of a nation and to break its finest children in an endeavour to protect its own vested interests as well as those of its reactionary hangers-on'. This was to him a crime against human dignity which no nation could tolerate.[2] Nonetheless, he carried away with him a sense that whatever the imperialist views of politicians of all shades, many others in England felt a true good will towards India and shared his socialist ideals.

Kamala was moved to Lausanne in Switzerland in February 1936, and Indira was able to visit regularly from school. She was with both her parents when the end came. Kamala seemed somehow to detach herself from her surroundings, and told Jawaharlal that she felt someone was calling her, or that she saw someone enter the room. She died early on 28 February, and was cremated two days later at Lausanne crematorium. Father and daughter spent several days together at Montreux, and then Indira returned to school and Nehru flew to India, carrying an urn containing his wife's ashes. The impact on Nehru and his teenage daughter, who had adored her mother and endured so much with her, was profound. Nehru later remembered that these were black days and his mind seemed not to function properly; something inside him had broken. In 1941, in a letter to Gandhi discussing the problems of Indira's impending marriage, he hinted at his devastation at the loss of Kamala, the only woman who ever had really shared something of his lonely personal life, the one he had really loved, despite the ups and downs of their relationship and the fact that he was 'the worst possible husband for any woman' because of his public commitments.[3]

The homecoming was a bleak one. Some time later he wrote to Indira of his solitary presence in the family home in Allahabad, feeding himself and working alone. He would go into his daughter's room and feel her presence there, and not wish to disturb anything from the way she had left it.[4] The effective end of family life, as he had known it, was in part the result of Kamala's death. She was no longer there. But more than that, Nehru threw himself into his political work and particularly into travel throughout India to help him adjust to her absence and to mask his loneliness. 'I feel terribly lonely often enough,' he told Indira, 'and seek an escape in intensive activity and work. That is a poor way of escape and yet it serves its purpose.'[5] In January 1938 death struck again, and Nehru's mother and her widowed sister who had lived with them died of strokes within hours of each other. Nehru spent the final hours watching beside his unconscious mother, as he had done with his father and wife, all in the same short span of seven years. Mercifully both his sisters and their children were visiting at the time. Writing to Indira of these events he told her not to grieve 'for she died at the right time and as she should have done. For years now she was almost a wraith, weary of life. Death must have been a release to her.'[6]

Nehru's remaining close relatives were now dispersed. Both his sisters were married with their own homes. Indira was away in Europe, at school first in Switzerland and then at Badminton in western England, and finally (after a holiday at home and in Burma, Malaya and Singapore with her father) studying at Somerville College, Oxford, from October 1937. As much as possible Nehru tried to keep her abreast with family and political news, and to take an interest in her work and health. It seems it was her health which perturbed him most. He had long thought that good health was largely a psychological matter; but now he suspected that she had inherited weak resistance to infection and disease from Kamala, and urged her to 'take yourself in hand scientifically' to get rid of minor ailments and build up her resistance. He reminded her of his own good health, despite his work load and time in prison, which he attributed to a simple and disciplined life, following three rules of health – exercise, good sleep and simple food.[7] In this admonition his public school training echoed Gandhi's insistence on simplicity of life, and the connection between a person's spiritual and physical state. Nehru's fears for his daughter were not without foundation, and in the autumn of 1939 she suffered a severe attack of pleurisy, which took her first to an English hospital and then to a sanatorium at Leysin in Switzerland, of which Gandhi himself approved for its natural healing methods, including exposure to sun. She stayed for nearly a year. By this time she was a young woman in her early twenties, and also deeply in love with a young man who had been associated with the family and its politics for some years, Feroze Gandhi. However, her letters to her father did not disclose the depth of this relationship, and father and daughter seem at this stage to have drifted apart emotionally, compared with their easy affection of her teenage years. Even he had noted and commented on this in 1937 after their holiday together, when they had talked of their daily activities but nothing deeper. He felt the gap between their generations and could not bridge it, and thought it was best they were so often apart, as this would enable her to grow up outside his shadow. Later he would write that he felt they had grown progressively more ignorant of each other, despite their mutual love, and that she was now a stranger to him.[8]

However, in the later 1930s Nehru formed other relationships which did something to mitigate the loneliness which followed the ending of his previous family life, though they did not give him daily companionship. One of these was with V. K. Krishna Menon, a maverick Indian in London, slightly younger than Nehru himself, whom he first met properly on one of his London visits in 1935. Krishna Menon came from southern India, and worked in London organising the India League, which was associated with the Labour left wing. They began to correspond very frankly on Indian politics, and Nehru soon came to value his friendship and intellectual stimulus. He was one of the few people whom Nehru considered to be his intellectual equal, as well as sharing his radical sympathies; and as he was outside the circle of Congress politicians in India, he was a safe confidante and sounding-board.

Another friendship, carried on by correspondence, was with Frances Gunther, wife of the American journalist and author John Gunther. She herself wrote an article entitled 'Nehru, Hope of India' for *Life*, the American magazine, during the war. Nehru first met her in Bombay in January 1938 and they began a friendship which sustained him in the gruelling years which were to follow. He would write deeply revealing letters which covered all manner of philosophical, political, personal and intellectual topics. She wrote back, sent telegrams and presents, and helped to sustain his mood. 'How delightful you are as a friend, so full of surprises, of welcome gifts, and just the right messages sent at the right moment!' he wrote in February 1940, saying how much he had enjoyed James Thurber's *The Last Flower*, which she had sent him – as had Gandhi![9] Like Krishna Menon, Frances Gunther was a safe recipient for frank confidences, and it seems that the distance between them and the medium of the written word enabled him somewhat to overcome his emotional reticence, while the fact that she was a woman enabled him to write in ways he would probably not have written to a man.

Nehru's other close friend and correspondent in these years was Padmaja Naidu, daughter of the notable poet and Congress member, Sarojini Naidu, from Hyderabad. She was the same age as his sister, Vijayalakshmi, and friend of the whole family, including his daughter. It was inevitable that people gossiped about a comparatively young widower, who was remarkably attractive as well as being a notable public figure; and his name was linked with several women as potential brides. Nehru noted this with some humour. However, it was unlikely that he would ever have consented to marry again, given his sense of being a hopeless husband because of his total commitment to political life, and his concern for his daughter's feelings, as she had been deeply devoted to and protective of her mother in the often fraught atmosphere of the extended Nehru family home. However, he and Padmaja, known to the family as 'Beebee', became more intimate in the late 1930s. The letters which remain from the period 1936–8 show not only his deep affection and at times passion for her, but how he was able to confide in her in a time of loneliness. But he recognised again (as he had with Kamala and Indira) his ignorance of what was passing in other people's minds, and his own capacity for causing profound emotional distress. He also understood that there was a limit to the extent to which he could give himself emotionally to any other person, however much solace he found in their company and friendship. He wrote with some self-knowledge in 1938:

> I know well how true it was when you said that I never give anyone what I receive. It was not perhaps the whole truth but it was certainly the truth. I am too self-centred, too individualistic to give much, the bars of my temperament keep me prisoner. And so I can never enter the gates of the earthly paradise which open only to those who can give unreservedly.[10]

## POLITICAL ISOLATION

In this letter Nehru also noted how his sense of going through life unattached could be a virtue in public affairs. But increasingly he saw himself as a misfit in Indian politics, despite his busy political life, his position in the heart of Congress, and his growing public acclaim. He wrote again in 1938 to Padmaja Naidu that he felt 'a misfit in the political scene. I carry on through sheer habit and habit is strong enough to carry me through with a measure of success. But I have lost my self-assurance.' A year later he told Krishna Menon that he had lost all 'pep and feel devitalised, and my interest in life itself seems to be fading away Most of the things that I value and for which I have worked seem to be going to pieces, and it is not surprising that I should also disintegrate in the process.'[11] He began to abandon his earlier hope that Indira would play a part in public life and in the building of a new India, because of the 'heartache and the crushing of the spirit that this involves'. Although he knew that there was no escape from such a vocation for himself, he felt a sense of withdrawal; and, surprisingly, began to think there was some merit in the Hindu idea of becoming a *sanyasi*, withdrawn from domestic obligations after a certain stage in life.[12] Attempting to understand what lay behind Nehru's bleak sense of himself within his political world suggests why an isolated Nehru was paradoxically such a central figure in Congress, and also illuminates one of the shifts in Indian politics at this time – the ebbing of militant and radical mass nationalism as major constitutional change offered new avenues for political influence and advancement.

Nehru returned early in 1936 to a Congress party which was deeply divided on ideological grounds between those who tended to gather round Gandhi and were known as the 'Old Guard' and those who had a more radical, socialist ideal of India. The former tended to be able to dominate and manage the central institutions of Congress, but the latter were a force to be reckoned with because they had considerable support in organisations of agriculturalists outside Congress. The party was also in turmoil over the question of whether to use the new and much enlarged opportunities for political influence under the 1935 Government of India Act. Even some of those who had no left-wing sympathies resented the group around Gandhi and the 'holier than thou' attitude they tended to adopt. One such, Bhulabhai Desai from Bombay, muttered into his diary about the supercilious attitude of the Gandhians towards legislative work, and their need to remember that satyagraha was an apparent failure. 'I think the superior caste must be met openly for they get all the work out of us, they get sacrifice out of us and they get money out of us and yet they pretend this superior attitude.'[13] But by early 1936 it was clear that almost all the provincial groups within Congress (except for Bengal and Punjab where Hindus were a minority) were wanting to contest the forthcoming elections on a much enlarged franchise and, where they succeeded, to take office in the newly autonomous provincial governments. They reckoned that if they did not accept office Congress would lose out on the best means for consolidating its position and would leave the field open to other groups.[14] Nehru was personally hostile to this strategy, but had allowed himself to be elected as Congress President for 1936 at the request of Gandhi, and reassured by the conciliatory feelers from men such as Rajendra Prasad. Accepting that he was something of a bridge between the Old Guard and the more radical, he agreed to be used by them in this role in order to further his own goal, which was to unite the forces of anti-imperialism within Congress, and to bring together experience and idealism.[15]

However, on his return it quickly became evident that this put him in an extremely painful position, and only Gandhi's mediatory role was able to keep him from resigning office and to ensure the cooperation of the Old Guard with him. At the Lucknow session of Congress in April 1936 Nehru's presidential speech made plain some of the issues of controversy.[16] He ranged widely over the history of Congress struggle, the broader forces of capitalism, imperialism and fascism, which he saw ranged against nationalism and socialism in the wider world, and the problems facing India. He stated that his own creed was socialism, though he would not force the issue in Congress and would gladly work with all those whose goal was independence. Although he agreed they should contest the forthcoming general elections in order to carry the Congress message throughout India, he strongly opposed the strategy of accepting office, 'the old sterile creed of reformism' which would undermine national self-respect and divert them from the big issues facing them. He argued that it was dangerous to accept responsibility without power, and that under the 1935 Act ministers would be hedged in by safeguards, reserved powers and mortgaged funds – indeed all the devices by which the raj wished to keep essential powers to itself.

What also concerned him deeply was the growing divorce, as he put it, between the Congress organisation and the masses. Congress would have to address this, and it should devote itself to putting its own house in order, sweeping away the defeatist mentality which was creeping in, and building up its organisations with mass affiliations. Nehru may have taken pleasure in this unusually intellectual and wide-ranging oration; but observers were clear that the Congress as a whole was well under the influence of Gandhi's allies, while the presidential speech was essentially 'thrown into the waste paper basket', in the satisfied words of one of Gandhi's closest business associates.[17] The question of Congress's links with the masses and possible representation for peasants' and workers' organisations was diverted into a committee, a resolution partly drafted by Nehru on a radical programme for the countryside was watered down, and the issue of accepting office was shelved until after the elections.

In the following weeks Nehru as President found himself locked in a series of conflicts with his colleagues in the heart of Congress, from which only Gandhi was able to rescue him. A CWC meeting on 27–8 April became deadlocked on the issue of Congress relations with the masses, which crystallised round the proposal to have enquiries into the problems of labour and agrarian society, mainly by people who did not belong to the CWC (that is, the more radical). Nehru suggested that he should resign the presidency in view of the profound differences of opinion between him and the rest. As the meeting was held at Wardha, near Gandhi's new ashram, the warring colleagues turned to the Mahatma for help. Handwritten minutes of the meeting, mostly by Nehru himself, noted laconically, 'There was a general desire to avoid a crisis and Gandhiji was invited to participate in the discussion and generally to give the benefit of his advice to the members. He heard the views of the members on the situation & his advice was that the Committee should pull together. This advice was accepted and the Committee proceeded with its business.'[18] The upshot was just a labour subcommittee, of which only one member was a socialist.

In May and June further and even more bruising conflict erupted over the composition of the CWC. Eventually all the Gandhians on the CWC resigned, and were only persuaded to withdraw their resignations by the personal intervention of Gandhi himself.[19] Nehru thanked Gandhi for 'smoothing over matters and in helping to avoid a crisis', but confessed that he felt exhausted and troubled by his relations with the CWC and felt it might be time for him to stop trying to work within Congress, as he had done since his return. Gandhi in turn urged Nehru not to precipitate a crisis in Congress, but to think calmly, keep a sense of humour, and treat his CWC colleagues with more tolerance. He seemed to him now 'a care-worn, irritable man', who had lost his usual sense of humour. Nehru himself admitted to another colleague that he was under huge strain, and this made him aggressive and often intemperate.[20] It is interesting that when this crisis was at its height Nehru tried to take his mind off it by reading parts of Vera Brittain's *Testament of Youth*. Congress, in its own way as constricting and frustrating as prison, sent him back to his beloved books and the inner life of the mind.

He obviously tried to take Gandhi's advice, and at a CWC meeting in August Vallabhbhai Patel, one of those who had resigned from the committee and felt most humiliated by Nehru's criticisms, told Gandhi's secretary, Mahadev Desai, that they had 'found not the slightest difficult in cooperating with him and adjusting ourselves to his views on certain points'.[21] Some time later Nehru explained to S. C. Bose that through this tumultuous time his priority had been to avoid a split in Congress, which would have pushed out the Gandhians, for this would have injured the interests of the country and the socialist cause. Gandhi's own concern was to sustain Nehru in the presidency because he felt this was the best way to steer him towards eventual power.[22] He was by this time publicly proclaiming that Nehru was his heir, and felt that Nehru with his many gifts and total commitment to India rather than to any sectional cause or personal concern was the one who could be relied upon to achieve the greatest unity in a Congress dedicated to a transformation in the lives of ordinary Indians.

To a considerable extent the election campaign in the second half of 1936 and early 1937 gave Nehru an outlet for his energies, and liberated him from the stifling atmosphere of conflict in the CWC. He told an English friend, 'It is an exhausting business and yet I find a strange relief in it from the politics of commit-tees and individuals. I seem to feel a little nearer to reality and I suppose the enthu-siasm and the crowds cheer me up.'[23] He travelled like a hurricane, with a hectic schedule, using every conceivable form of transport from plane, train and car to elephant, camel, horse, bicycle, and varieties of river boats. He addressed vast crowds and virtually wore himself out. His longest waking day in the campaign was twenty-three hours, during which he had covered 415 miles. Rather than engage in electioneering for particular candidates he used the occasions to reach a mass audience with the Congress message of independence and what this might mean for ordinary Indians. He had himself drafted the Congress manifesto, which spoke of rejecting the 1935 constitution and pursuing an independence which would mean major economic and social rights for all, on the lines laid down at Karachi in 1931. It also insisted (as he had repeatedly) that the communal problem was not a genuinely religious problem, and did not affect ordinary people as it had nothing to do with the major problems of poverty and unemployment.[24]

The huge public response Nehru received during his election tours seems to have influenced him profoundly. He began to see how powerful he might become, given this public adulation, and how he could make connections with people from all walks of life and all religious communities in ways other politicians could not. He published an anonymous article, 'The Rashtrapati' (a Sanskrit word meaning Head of State), in October 1937, in which he described his electioneering, his capacity to attract people, and the dangers this might hold for India. He wrote of himself, 'he is bound up with the present in India, and probably the future, and he has the power in him to do great good to India or great injury.' He also noted the potential in himself for dictatorship:

> vast popularity, a strong will directed to a well-defined purpose, energy, pride, organizational capacity, ability, hardness, and, with all his love of the crowd, an intolerance of others and a certain contempt for the weak and the inefficient. His flashes of temper are well known and even when they are controlled, the curling of the lips betrays him. His over-mastering desire to get things done, to sweep away what he dislikes and build anew, will hardly brook for long the slow processes of democracy.

He wrote it partly for fun one evening, and as a 'low-down trick . . . to watch people's reactions', and got Padmaja Naidu to send a typed copy to *The Modern Review*. Nonetheless, it portrayed aspects of his personality as well as his popularity, which were to become even more prominent with time, and which contributed to his strengths and weaknesses as Prime Minister.[25]

Congress did spectacularly well in the elections, winning 716 out of 1,585 seats, and achieving clear majorities in five provinces – Madras, Bihar, Orissa, Central Provinces and United Provinces. Now came the critical moment when it had to decide whether to use this new-found power through electoral politics to take office, a decision it had so far postponed to mask the different opinions within it. The Congress leadership in the CWC was itself divided: the majority felt there was no viable alternative strategy which would continue to attract public support, and supported Gandhi's idea of office acceptance if certain conditions were agreed by government, while Nehru and two others opposed the idea altogether. At provincial level it was clear that most Congressmen wanted to take office. After prolonged negotiations with government the CWC agreed that Congress members could now proceed to form provincial governments. They did so in seven provinces, including Nehru's own UP.

The one ominous sign was Congress's failure to attract Muslim support in the elections, except on the North-West Frontier, where a local movement among the Muslim Pathans had been strongly allied with Gandhian non-violent methods and with Congress for some years.[26] Overall 482 seats in the provincial legislatures were reserved for Muslims: Congress could only manage to contest 59, and won 26 of them, that being just 5.4 per cent of all Muslim seats. Congress clearly did not represent Indian Muslims, despite its claims to speak for all Indians. Even in UP where the educated Muslim minority had so much in common with their Hindu counterparts and had often collaborated in politics, cooperation broke down ostensibly over the possible participation in the new provincial government of two representatives of the Muslim League, one of whom had been a Congress member, while the other had been prominent in the Khilafat movement. Behind this breakdown lay both the hostility of the League leader, Jinnah, towards any local settlement with Congress, and also the fears of the Congress that League participation in the provincial government might lead to disunity within it and a dilution of its programme, particularly in relation to reform of land ownership. They consequently set conditions which would have meant the winding up of the UP League and the inclusion of Muslim members of the new legislature in Congress, subjected to Congress party discipline. Nehru was not personally involved in these negotiations, and felt very uncomfortable with the idea of bargaining over seats. But he and important Congressmen felt it was worth attempting to find an accommodation, if it meant that Congress in UP could effectively absorb the League, for he felt that this would have been immensely important throughout India. 'This would mean a free field for our work without communal troubles [and] would knock over the British Government which relied so much on these troubles.'[27]

Nehru agreed to continue for a second year as Congress President, even though his health had broken down after the elections, forcing him to take a holiday with his daughter in Burma and the Far East. Thereafter he continued to shoulder a huge burden of work for the party. But his immersion in party affairs only increased his sense of isolation from his colleagues and their priorities, and his disquiet over the party as a whole. He was in fact caught up in one of the great sea-changes of Indian politics in the first half of the twentieth century, and his personal distress reflected the wider forces at work. Congress, which had once led a loose coalition of hostilities to imperial rule, now found itself the provincial government in large parts of India. It had come to power, not by the sort of mass appeal and organisation Nehru had advocated, but by the ballot box. The franchise was still limited by property ownership, but had given the vote to about 30 million Indians, most of them men. In order to win the election it had in effect made complex patterns of alliance with men of some substance and dominance in each locality, as well as appealing to voters through its party machine and reservoir of volunteers, which was far more professional than anything other parties could deploy. In response to this many who had once belonged to minority parties or who had been independents in the legislatures now hastened to join Congress and receive its ticket for the elections.

Moreover, as Congress succeeded, and became the effective local government, so many more people joined its ranks as ordinary members, hoping to further their interests through it and through connection with the party's Members of the Legislative Assembly (MLAs). All-India membership rose from just under half a million in 1935–6 to over four and a half million in 1938–9. Many of these new Congressmen came from rural rather than urban backgrounds, and belonged to locally dominant agricultural castes, with considerable interests in land. As Congress became the party of power, so its priorities shifted, and it increasingly represented the interests of its members and those who had voted it into office, rather than the vast mass of those who were still disenfranchised.[28] Furthermore, Congress in each province began to have its own regional priorities and interests, and to become less amenable to all-India discipline on policy issues, just as Motilal Nehru had found in the 1920s when Swarajist party identity and discipline had foundered on the rocks of provincialism. Even more disquieting, the experience of government drew Congress ministers into the realities of ruling and away from the ideal of a transformation of governance, distressing alike the Mahatma who hoped for a moral revolution, and Nehru who feared the lure of office and the corroding effects of association with the imperial regime.

Nehru wrestled with many of these problems in the months following the elections. He recognised the need for internal organisational discipline if Congress was to remain a national party, motivated by an ideal, following a common policy and goal, and he spoke out against 'bogus membership', fictional Congress members whose alleged support would have contributed to internal factional fighting; against disputes within the Congress at every level; and against 'self-seekers' who joined the Congress, sensing it was now a route to power. He lamented to Gandhi in April 1938 that Congress was being torn by internal group and personal conflicts, and that they were descending to 'Tammany Hall' politics, and 'to the level of ordinary politicians who have no principles to stand by and whose work is governed by a day to day opportunism'.[29] He also saw the problems generated because Congress had become in so many provinces the local government. In his view Congress ministers were having to spend too much time on the minutiae of governance, on trying to work with and through the imperial governmental services, and within the financial constraints imposed on them under the constitution. Consequently they often could not tackle really big social and economic problems, and yet were criticised by their own supporters for their role. Moreover, party members seemed to think that they could interfere in the work of ministers, generating conflict between Congress as a party and Congress as government – an issue which recurred after independence. On the other hand, ministers seemed to be too prone to follow in the footsteps of their imperial predecessors and use the coercive apparatus of the state, particularly to curb labour unrest.

In retrospect Nehru said he felt that the experiment with office was a necessary one and he was generous towards those who had become ministers; but he was profoundly relieved when Congress ministries resigned in protest at India being brought into the war in 1939 without its consent. He wrote in the press of Congress now being freed from the 'trammels of office and from the bondage of the Act of 1935'. Privately he wrote to his friend, Syed Mahmud, 'I can assure you with all earnestness that I am exceedingly pleased that the Congress Governments have resigned. I am pleased from every possible point of view and for the last six months or more I had been wanting them to resign.'[30]

The problems generated by Congress's political success sickened Nehru, who delighted in clear ideals and definite programmes rather than the messy compromises inherent in the politics of government. He could see that Congress was losing sight of the need to have a truly mass base as it luxuriated in the votes it had gathered and the numbers of new adherents. He continued to campaign for a deeper rootedness in the vast numbers of Indians outside the scope of the franchise. The idea of a Congress 'functional franchise' for peasant and labour groups, which he had supported early in 1936, had effectively petered out with the election triumph. But the problem of attracting Muslims into Congress remained, and this continued to occupy Nehru's thoughts and energies.

On the one hand he continued to argue that communal demands had nothing to do with ordinary people, and also to dispute the claims of Jinnah that the Muslim League represented all Indian Muslims. In one sense he was right, because the League had done poorly in the recent elections. It had won just over 20 per cent of the seats reserved for Muslims in the legislatures (109 out of 482), and had gathered just under 5 per cent of the Muslim vote. However, the great electoral success of the Congress and its capture of governmental power perturbed many Muslims, who began to fear that their minority status boded ill for them politically and culturally. The man who became the major spokesman for an all-India Muslim 'cause' was the former Congress member and later independent, M. A. Jinnah. His earlier goal of claiming reserved seats and separate electorates for Muslims, and more Muslim provinces, had been largely achieved with the 1935 Act. But in the Hindu majority provinces this had only placed power in the hands of the Congress, and in the Muslim majority provinces of Bengal, Punjab and the new Sind power was in the hands of Muslims who were often split among themselves and prepared to engage in cross-community alignments in pursuit of provincial priorities. In the North-West Frontier Province, with its huge Muslim majority, Muslims aligned with Congress had come to power.

It was little wonder that Jinnah now concentrated on building up the League as a vehicle for Muslim political demand, and to stress the significance of religious identity as the critical marker of political identity. (Quite what Jinnah's ultimate goal was remains obscure. Certainly it was not at this stage a separate homeland for Indian Muslims as a presumed nation defined by religion, but it was probably to demonstrate Muslim strength across the subcontinent as a preparatory safeguard of Muslim interests in anticipation of further devolution of power to Indians at the centre.) Congress was, in Jinnah's rhetoric, a Hindu party, which had no right to speak for Muslims. Nehru, with his forthright criticism of all kinds of religious appeals in politics, whether Muslim or Hindu, became one of the major targets of his criticism. Consequently Nehru spent considerable energy in trying to refute Jinnah's accusations against himself and Congress, and early in 1938 engaged in an acrimonious but fruitless correspondence with him.[31] When Bose as the new Congress President in 1938 held talks with Jinnah, and the latter insisted that only the League was the authoritative and representative organisation of Indian Muslims, Nehru, then in London, condemned this as an unacceptable basis for negotiations with the League, and as an 'absurd and preposterous' claim.[32]

Nehru's other strategy, which reflected his determination that Congress should not abandon the idea of a mass base as well as his concern that communal claims should not hijack the idea of India and Indianness, was to forge ahead during his time as Congress President with making 'mass contacts' among Muslims. In March 1937 in the aftermath of the elections he urged PCCs to make a special effort to enrol Muslims and to establish committees to do this and to maintain contacts with Muslims.[33] This campaign, under the immediate management of an AICC department headed by an energetic and left-wing Muslim, K. M. Ashraf, had some success in enrolling Muslim primary members of Congress, and had appealed to both Muslim intellectuals and some *ulema*, those learned in Muslim law who provided the local voice of Islam. However it failed to make much headway in rural areas among the peasantry; and early in 1939 the movement collapsed. It had been Nehru's brainchild, but many other Congressmen disliked it for a variety of reasons, and eventually Congress scrapped the strategy. Nehru found himself once more isolated by the very nature of Congress, in particular its current priority of forming provincial governments, and the presence within it of those whose ideal of a new India was a far more Hindu one than his own.

Possibly the most stark demonstration of Nehru's uncomfortable position in Congress, and the most personally painful for him, was the breakdown in relations between Gandhi and his group of senior Congress members and the radical Bengali, Subhas Bose, who succeeded Nehru as Congress President. Actual and aspirant all-India leaderships in Congress had always faced huge problems of internal control and discipline within the party when it was engaging in constitutional rather than agitational politics. The fruits of constitutional power and who had access to them often caused profound division. The late 1930s became another example, when local issues, and the emergence of dissident groups within Congress, threatened the party's unity. In 1938–9 discontent crystallised round the figure of S. C. Bose. The Gandhians had managed to contain dissent at all-India level in 1938, and had striven to prevent dissident and more radical Congress members from building up alternative power bases in peasant movements and in agitational movements against the princely states. But Bose issued an unprecedented challenge by insisting on standing a second time for the Congress presidency against the wishes of the so-called Old Guard, who had their own candidate. In this successful bid he was supported by the votes of local groups who for a variety of reasons wanted to register hostility to current Congress policy or to the particular Congress leadership in their province.

Nehru, having refused to stand a third time for the Congress presidency, now declined to make a public choice between Bose and the CWC candidate. After Bose's triumph, the Gandhians refused to cooperate with him and twelve members of the CWC resigned. Nehru refused to resign, and wrote an anguished letter to Bose, pleading with him to try to understand his colleagues, though he admitted he could see no way out of the present 'unhappy tangle'. For himself he hated the way that provincial rivalries in Congress now seemed to be being 'transferred or extended to the all-India plane'.[34] Soon after he wrote an impassioned series of articles in the press entitled 'Where are we?', in which he discussed the history of Congress and his own role in it since his return to India early in 1936. He pleaded for unity in the pursuit of their common cause. 'For the organisation is greater than the individuals of whom it consists, and the principles we stand for are more important than personalities.' Moreover, they must remember that it was essential to bear in mind the dominance of Gandhi in the nationalist movement, and in public esteem, even if he held no office in Congress. 'In any policy that might be framed he cannot be ignored. In any national struggle his full association and guidance are essential. India cannot do without him.'[35]

As he later told Krishna Menon, writing these articles was a type of therapy in an intolerable situation. He apologised for confiding the depth of his mental anguish, but it was a relief to him, and there 'is hardly anyone here to whom I can speak with frankness about myself'.[36] No compromise proved possible between Bose and the Gandhians, and eventually Bose resigned the presidency. The weeks of deadlock had hurt Nehru profoundly, but he had remained aloof, feeling there was nothing he could do.[37] He subsequently declined a place on the new CWC. He felt helpless, caught between two groups he thought were both in the wrong, and wanted to retain 'a certain integrity of mind and dignity in action'. What hurt him most was the sense that Indians were themselves breaking up the unity of the nationalist movement, at a time of profound international crisis. None of the older leadership seemed aware of the world situation, while even Bose seemed to be not only out of date in his leftist rhetoric, but also becoming a symbol for many who were bitterly hostile to Congress.[38]

The divisions in Congress in 1938–9 and the bitterness these engendered among people who had been colleagues and friends demonstrated the complexities of Indian politics as it developed in response to British policy, and the many interests, ideologies and opportunist alliances which lay just beneath the claims of Congress to speak for an Indian nation. Nehru was caught in these turbulent currents, increasingly isolated and perturbed at the departure from his ideal of a mass, radical nationalist movement, and often in revolt even against Gandhi, his oldest friend and mentor.[39] However the Bose episode showed in retrospect why he was so important to the Old Guard, and why Gandhi viewed him as his heir, despite their differences of opinion and their often fraught relationship. His vision of India might have been more radical than that of the Gandhians, and couched in a political rhetoric alien to them. But he was utterly reliable when it came to the need for Congress unity under Gandhi's leadership, even at the cost of his own friendships and opinions. Moreover, he had qualities and skills which made him increasingly valuable to Congress as it became a party of government, with the potential for an all-India governmental role if the federal part of the 1935 Act were to come into being.

There were two aspects of Nehru's activity at this difficult phase in his life which seem to have given him some satisfaction and fulfilment. Both added to the unusual portfolio of skills he brought to Congress in subsequent years. In 1937-9 he travelled abroad quite extensively, in a real sense becoming known internationally as a representative of India, and simultaneously learning himself about the complexities of international politics, and about the position of Indians overseas. In 1937 he went to Burma, Malaya and Singapore on holiday to recover from the immense workload he had carried during the elections. Then in mid-1938 he went to Europe, in part because he felt so out of place in Indian politics. He wanted to refresh his tired and puzzled mind, and he could get no rest or even much of a change in India. He hoped to study something of what was happening in Europe, and also wanted to see his daughter where they could get some privacy together. Krishna Menon, his new friend, was to be largely in charge of the programme. During this time he wrote a series of semi-private letters about his activities to the President of Congress, the CWC and Gandhi.[40] During a brief stopover in Egypt on the way to Europe he met leaders of the Wafd Party and they spoke of the problems of nationalist movements. He also went briefly to Paris and to Spain, in the grip of civil war, where he was taken to see the International Brigade.

Once in England Nehru had a busy round of meetings with the press and with a wide range of politicians, meeting as many people with interest and influence in Indian policy as possible, including Lord Linlithgow, the Viceroy who was on leave, the Earl of Zetland, Lord Halifax (who as Lord Irwin had been Viceroy during the talks and pact with Gandhi which had so distressed Nehru in 1931), Lord Lothian, Clement Attlee, and Sir Stafford Cripps. He gave press interviews and spoke informally at meetings, and was generally entertained and fêted. Indeed, he so wore himself out that he had to take a brief holiday in France. In all he felt it had been worthwhile for the publicity he had been able to give to the Indian cause. He sensed a real change in attitudes towards India, no doubt in part because of the impending international crisis, and even Conservatives were thinking seriously about independence.

Equally important, the visit raised Nehru's own public profile as a significant Indian leader, who was at home in the British political scene as much as (or perhaps even more than) in the circle of Congress leaders around Gandhi. This was to mark Nehru out from all the other Congress leaders of his vintage. Moreover, being in Europe at the time of the Munich agreement, and visiting Czechoslovakia, gave him, among Congressmen, a unique sense of the dangers of fascism and distrust of the intentions of the British government, while it sharpened his existing interest in a wide range of international issues.

In 1939 he travelled abroad again, to Ceylon at the behest of the AICC to enquire into problems relating to Indian labour; and then to China. The Ceylon visit did nothing to resolve the issue of the 10,000 Indian estate labourers whom the government was threatening to discharge and send home. But it alerted Nehru to the complex problems of Indians abroad, and convinced him that such Indians must not align themselves with 'reactionary elements', but must 'help in every way the freedom movement in the country of their adoption and make it clear that they are not there to exploit the people'. Given that basic stance, they should stand up for their rights.[41] His China visit was cut short by the outbreak of war in Europe. What little he saw only confirmed his earlier vision of two great Asian countries facing similar problems, and a period of painful change; and he noted the need for greater cultural and political contacts between them.[42]

Apart from his foreign visits, and the contacts and insights these gave him, Nehru's main source of interest, even enjoyment, in public life in the late 1930s was his involvement in the new work of a National Planning Committee set up by Bose as Congress President. Nehru became the Committee's chairman, and it absorbed an increasing amount of his time and energy.[43] He told his daughter of his enormous interest in the whole issue, the way he was having in middle age to learn about new topics, and the novel experience of presiding over a committee consisting of a very mixed bunch of ministers, scientists, professors, economists and businessmen. Gandhi, not surprisingly with his priorities of the small-scale and of revived village life, thought the committee was a waste of effort and did not understand it.[44]

The only previous time when Nehru had really tried to get to grips with economic issues was in 1931 in connection with agrarian distress in UP. Now he began to see that planning for India's future involved agricultural and industrial policy, a range of connected issues such as transport, power, conservation of natural resources and the pressure of population, as well as wider and more profound social issues. He returned to the 1931 Karachi Congress's resolution on fundamental rights as one of the key guides on the social goal of all future policy, and argued that any national planning must make its primary objective an adequate standard of living for all Indians. At the present time this meant the development of cottage industries on a large scale, but he insisted that there was no conflict between this and the rapid development of large-scale machine-based industry. The latter was also fundamental to real political and economic freedom, and to raising standards of life. The evils of industrialisation could and should be avoided through planning an equitable scheme of distribution. Recognising some of the failures of Soviet planning (however much he admired the attempt), he argued for a coordinated approach of progress on multiple fronts over a ten-year period. In this the role of the state would evidently be crucial, and not only in formulating and implementing plans, and in raising the necessary finance. Defence industries, public utilities and other key industries would have to be in state control. However, he recognised that such a change in the role of the state and in public socio-economic orientation would have to be achieved with discretion and a realistic awareness of the importance of the existing 'middle classes'. The last thing which India needed was a 'premature conflict on class lines [which] would lead to a break-up and possibly to prolonged inability to build anything'. (The example of contemporary China was patently in his mind.)[45]

Nehru had effectively taken refuge in these personally interesting and constructive activities, and distanced himself from the politics of Congress and of its governments, as a result of his sense of political isolation and frustration. He had seen clearly that government policies of constitutional reform, adopted to stabilise the British raj and ensure India's role within the empire, had created political opportunities which Congressmen had embraced with enthusiasm. Moreover, if ongoing negotiations between government and the princes were to succeed, then a pan-Indian federation with Dominion status seemed the likely outcome. Not surprisingly, he was bowed down by the ambiguities of a party which professed to claim independence, but seemed to have lost its way in the complex paths of government, and to have abandoned any attempt to appeal to those millions of Indians who were still outside the effective political nation. His personal sense of loneliness reflected the gulf between his vision of a new India and a vibrant mass nationalism and the realities of a Congress entangled in government and increasingly alienating substantial minority groups. However, in September 1939 the outbreak of war shattered emerging patterns of politics and engulfed his own political life.

## Part 3

# The Tragedies of an Imperial Ending, 1939–1948

# Chapter 8

# The Experience of War, 1939–1945

The Second World War changed the face of Indian politics in ways which no one could have foreseen in 1939. In the short term it precipitated a breakdown in constitutional cooperation between Congress and the British raj, sending Congress reluctantly back into civil disobedience, and the Congress leadership into jail. This in turn enabled other political groups, particularly the Muslim League, to entrench themselves in public life as legitimate representatives of large sections of India's peoples. In the longer term war shattered British policy of devolving power to Indians in a controlled way over a considerable period of time, firstly within the provinces of British India, and then within a new all-India federation including the princely states, in such a manner as to ensure India's continuing financial and strategic role within the empire. Soon after the outbreak of war the Viceroy suspended negotiations with the Indian princes on their accession to a federation. By 1942 under pressure of war the British government had declared that India would be free at the end of the conflict to decide its own future, even if that meant severing ties with the Empire-Commonwealth, and that no province would be forced into the new Indian state, thus opening the way to locally dominant minorities to opt out, or at least to use the provision as a powerful bargaining tool.

For Nehru personally the experience of war was predominantly that of imprisonment, from 31 October 1940 to 4 December 1941, and then for the longest sentence served in his life, from 9 August 1942 to 15 June 1945. However, war was the context for the start of the second part of his political life, when the nationalist, so often at odds with his fellow Congressmen and his mentor, emerged as one of Congress's core leadership, and then as India's major leader on the domestic and international stage.

## CONGRESS AND THE DILEMMAS OF WAR

Although the war ultimately weakened Britain as an international power and undermined its ability to retain control of India, in the immediate circumstances the raj appeared much stronger. Driven now by the huge value of India in the war effort, the British cabinet was determined that the raj should use its considerable reserve powers to control public life, even at the expense of a long-term erosion of imperial rule. The immediate British stance was to offer no substantial constitutional change or governmental practice to elicit Indian cooperation, and to make preparations to combat any further reversion to civil disobedience.[1]

As Congress struggled to respond to the new situation Nehru emerged as one of the small group of leaders who determined Congress policy. His grasp of international affairs, his experience of the party organisation and his skill at drafting resolutions and letters in precise English were all important to the CWC. As significant was the fact that Gandhi felt himself to be less and less able actively to lead Congress, and thought that only Nehru had the drive to take his place.[2] But for Nehru and his colleagues, responding to the war and government refusal to make any substantial movement of concession or conciliation was deeply problematic. The ideological and practical issues involved created differences between them, and posed problems of viable strategy. Should the Congress support a war which was obviously against fascism, given its public commitments to the processes of democracy? Would any such support and cooperation with the British be conditional on concessions within India? If they were to resort to civil disobedience, which had served them well in previous periods of impasse with the raj, how could they do this without incurring the sort of official response which had so demoralised the movement in 1932–3? Moreover, would civil disobedience further alienate Muslim groups and strengthen the Muslim League? Added to this was the ideological issue of non-violence, and the deep disquiet of Gandhi and those closest to him about any possible Indian involvement in armed defence of India.

Nehru was the primary drafter of the first CWC statement which indicated sympathy for the war but insisted that only a free India could throw its weight into the war; and he was made the chairman of a subcommittee to deal with the war emergency, alongside two other members, A. K. Azad and Vallabhbhai Patel.[3] He elaborated the Congress position in a private letter, which is worth quoting in view of the subsequent controversies of 1942 over Indian control of defence in any wartime settlement. Congress 'demands a clear declaration of India's independent status and India's right to frame her own constitution through a constituent assembly. Further . . . this must be applied in the present to the largest possible extent, both in the governance of India and in the control of war so far as India is concerned. This inevitably means India's control of her defence policy.'[4] Although he personally did not wish to precipitate a conflict with the raj, an interview on 3 October with the Viceroy, Lord Linlithgow, gave him little grounds for hope. He was proved correct when Linlithgow merely reiterated that the goal of British policy was Dominion status, and offered consultation with all political interests when the war ended. The Congress interpreted this as the divergence of paths between them and the government, and resolved that the Congress ministries should resign. Nehru himself believed that conflict with the government was inevitable, but not in the immediate future. Linlithgow's continued discussions with Congress and League leaders proved abortive, and by early 1940 Nehru was convinced that there was no chance of a settlement with the government. He wrote to Gandhi that personally he felt 'sure that there is no real chance of a settlement, although the British Government would no doubt like it. But they are very far from agreeing to what is our minimum. The British Government today is more reactionary and imperialist than it has even been . . .'[5] (Nehru was of course not aware of the discussions within the British cabinet at this time, but these demonstrated the strength of Churchill, who had bitterly opposed the 1935 Government of India Act, and Sir John Simon, whose proposals for India had been swept aside in 1930. Churchill was to become even more significant when he became Prime Minister in 1940 on the departure of Chamberlain.)

Nehru's personal letters to Indira at this time suggest that he was out of sympathy with the 'listless and argumentative folk of the cities', and more invigorated by his contacts with village people. But he had began to wonder if all his political work was worthwhile. 'But my mind is elsewhere and my heart still further away. Doubts creep into my mind if all this is worthwhile or not. Still I go on as most of us do.' He confessed that he sometimes longed to retire for a while from what seemed like pointless activity, to read and write.[6]

Nehru's state of mind reflected the stalemate with the government, but probably also his anger and distress at the way British policy seemed to have given leverage to the Muslim League and to Jinnah in particular. Immediately on the outbreak of war the League's working committee claimed that no declaration about constitutional advance should be made, nor any new constitution framed, without the consent of the League, for only the League represented Indian Muslims. This was unacceptable to Nehru and most Congressmen, given the presence within their party of some prominent Muslim sympathisers, the evidence of limited electoral support for the League, as well as Congress's own commitment to permitting the country's minorities a major role in the formation of a new constitution, particularly via a constituent assembly. The gulf yawned wider when Jinnah asked Muslims to celebrate 22 December 1939 as a 'Day of Deliverance' from the 'tyranny, oppression and injustice' of the Congress ministries. Nehru was particularly unable to empathise with minority fears or to understand them except in terms of a leadership's pursuit of vested interests, given his socio-economic understanding of the underpinnings of political behaviour. His very background, coming from a province where educated Hindus and Muslims shared so much in culture and language, also moulded his hostility to Jinnah and the League, as did his friendship with Muslims within Congress, such as the new President, Maulana A. K. Azad, for whom he had a deepening respect.[7] If such a devout and learned Muslim was at ease at the heart of Congress, who was the westernised Jinnah to claim to be a guardian of Indian Muslim interests? It was hardly surprising that Nehru withdrew from planned talks with Jinnah on hearing of the 'Day of Deliverance'. The most profound difference between them was Jinnah's claim that the League was the sole authoritative and representative organisation of Indian Muslims. Nehru agreed that Congress did not represent all Indians, but argued that equally the League did not represent all Muslims. However, Congress opened its doors to all who subscribed to its ideals, whatever their religion, while the League was only open to Muslims. Congress could not give up its national basis and open door without 'putting an end to its existence'.[8]

In March 1940 at the League session at Lahore Jinnah went even further, claiming that Muslims were a distinct nation, requiring a homeland and a state; and the meeting adopted what later became known as the Pakistan resolution, though that word did not appear in it. The claim was for Indian Muslims to have independent states where they were a majority. Nehru believed this idea to be 'fantastic'.[9] Nehru was not alone in his response to the claim, and many Muslims condemned it as absurd, while in the very majority Muslim areas which were to receive such 'independence' there was as yet comparatively little support for the League. Nonetheless, it showed how the war had helped to change the dynamics of Indian politics, entrenching new groupings and shifting the terms in which Indians could now make claims of the raj.

Almost simultaneously with the League's meeting, Congress met at Ramgarh in Bihar in late March, and began to move towards civil disobedience as a way of taking a decisive stance after months of inaction. No timetable was set, but local Congress committees were urged to prepare themselves for renewed satyagraha. As before in 1929–30, the leadership, and Gandhi in particular, faced the question of how to launch an inclusive and viable movement. Nehru was convinced that preparation for renewed conflict was the right move. It would strengthen Congress at a point when India was fundamentally threatened by 'internal adventurism and conflict', but it also stopped short of outright opposition to the British at a time of dire danger in Europe.[10] Briefly the Congress leadership grappled with the problems of non-violence and what might be their stance if it came to having to defend India itself against invasion, given Gandhi's total commitment to non-violence.[11] However, the possibility of any cooperation with the British in defence of India passed in August when the Viceroy only offered further Indian membership of his Executive Council and of a War Advisory Committee. Dominion status remained the goal, and it was stated that power would in any case not be transferred to a government whose legitimacy was denied by large and powerful elements in public life. This was a profound public challenge to Congress's standing as the party of an inclusive nationalism and it had no option but to respond decisively. Moreover, it was likely to receive the support of a wide spectrum of Hindu political opinion which had increasingly swung against the government during the previous six months.[12] Gandhi and the CWC quickly mended fences, after their brief disagreement on the ideal of non-violence, and Gandhi planned a carefully staged campaign of 'individual' civil disobedience, rather than a mass and potentially divisive campaign which would invite government retribution. The issue would be the moral one of freedom to speak against the war – just as the issue in 1930 had been disobedience on the moral and inclusive issue of salt.

Nehru determined to give Gandhi his full support, though Gandhi recognised that this was a great strain to him. Evidence of the discussions among members of the CWC in mid-October indicates that Nehru and Azad were both at odds with Gandhi on his plan, and that Nehru was despairing at their endless talking and longed for decisive action. He was even prepared to take his own line of resistance to the government if need be.[13] Eventually he was the second person chosen by Gandhi to defy the government. However, he was arrested on 30 October, before he could protest ceremonially, on charges relating to previous speeches, and subsequently sentenced by a district judge to four years imprisonment as a deterrent to others – a sentence of such severity that it caused much public disquiet, and surprised the governments in London and Delhi as well as the Governor of UP.

## PRISON

Most of this prison sentence was passed back in his old 'home', the jail at Dehra Dun, in the UP foothills, apart from the first few days in Gorakhpur and several weeks in Lucknow in the spring of 1941.[14] Nehru noted with some amusement that the transfer from Gorakhpur to Dehra Dun was done in utmost secrecy in a special railway saloon with the shutters up, as if he were a *purdanashin,* a woman in purdah. These precautions against the gathering of large crowds suggested the degree of significance the government now accorded him. Although the prison term generated its share of conflict with the jail authorities about the number and kinds of letters he could receive, he noted that he was in general treated with unusual courtesy by the jail staff, the British Superintendent of the prison and the Indian Muslim District Magistrate. 'I suppose a powerful inducement for treating me well is the belief that some time or other the Congress will be top dog and I might have influence and power.'[15]

As usual Nehru tried to keep his body and mind in good order. Again he took to gardening, immediately turning part of the prison yard into a flower garden with the help of the authorities and fellow prisoners allotted to help him dig. Although he prided himself on his fitness he was ashamed at how quickly digging tired him, while the non-political prisoners seemed capable of sustained manual labour. He wondered if it was lack of practice or whether age was taking its toll, as he was now fifty-one. The height of Dehra Dun and the cool winter season permitted the planting of seeds of a wide variety of English garden flowers, including sweet peas, hollyhocks, nasturtiums, candytuft, lupins, stocks and dianthus. The prison gardener amused him with his rendering of English names, calling a hollyhock 'Ali Haq'! Nehru's other regular physical labour was spinning. By the end of nine months he had spun 112,500 yards of yarn.

To keep active intellectually Nehru of course read widely. It is intriguing that he read Hitler's *Mein Kampf* in full for the first time. He had read excerpts when Hitler came to power in Germany in 1933 and had disliked it, and had been struck by 'an element of vulgarity about him' – 'vulgar' being one of the deepest grounds of criticism he used of people in public life. Now he sensed the power behind the book, and understood better both the man and how he had been able to effect such change in Germany. Nehru also took up more writing of his own, including a postscript to his *Autobiography*, prompted in part by news of the success of the American edition of the work. How deeply Nehru was a natural author is clear from his record of how ideas for a new work began to play around in his mind, and how he then began to devise a shape and structure for the work. He told Gandhi that he felt at peace, and in no other prison phase had experienced such inner calm. However, within months he was admitting to feeling stale and depressed – partly because of the war and the political situation in India, but also because of his daughter.[16]

Indira had insisted on leaving her Swiss sanatorium and at the end of 1940 had managed to travel to England via France, Spain and Portugal. In blitz-torn London she rejoined the man she was now determined to marry, Feroze Gandhi, and in March they sailed together on a troopship in convoy to India. Her return confronted her father with the problem of her marriage. He probably knew little of his daughter's deepening relationship with Feroze while they were both in Europe, given Indira's reticence with him and the difficulties in communications over the past months, and he was concerned at her seeming immaturity. There was little he could now do in prison, and he felt deeply that jail prevented him from coming closer to her at this critical time when they seemed to be almost strangers to each other. A long letter from him to Indira on 9 July 1941 hints at some of the strain in their relationship. Although he indicated that he would not stand in the way of her desired marriage, he did ask her to discuss it with her close relatives, including her aunts and her maternal grandmother, and of course with Gandhi. Significantly he wrote of Gandhi, 'Bapu . . . has been very intimately associated not only in public life but in private life with mummie and me. Also, apart from his other activities, he is one of the wisest men I know. He understands and appreciates the other's viewpoint and his advice is always valuable, even if we cannot always follow it.'[17]

He clearly felt uneasy at Indira's choice, for Feroze was a man who lacked the cultivated background and interests of the Nehru family, had no university education or indeed any profession. The fact that he was a Parsi was probably not a primary cause for concern, as Nehru's sisters had both married outside the Kashmiri Brahmin circle. Nehru warned Indira that he knew nothing about Feroze's family or circle, and that therefore it was very important that she went delicately about the business of discussing the marriage with her own family. 'Give them time and opportunity to adjust themselves. Avoid also breaking as far as possible with old contacts and ways. You do not know what the new ones will be like and you might well be landed high and dry.' For all his socio-economic radicalism, and his personal religious agnosticism, Nehru understood well the pressures of Indian society and perceptively wished to ensure his daughter's future, however much she herself may have failed to reflect on the realities of Indian life as a result of her long time abroad. Eventually both he and Gandhi agreed to the marriage, but the couple in turn agreed to postpone their wedding until Nehru was at liberty.

External political affairs contributed also to Nehru's lack of tranquillity in prison. The individual civil disobedience movement was in Gandhi's eyes thoroughly satisfactory, as groups of Congressmen in carefully chosen waves disobeyed the law and went to prison, and he saw no reason to alter the programme.[18] It was not a mass movement; but it was not designed to be. It was, rather, a symbolic exercise designed to ensure Congress solidarity, and to demonstrate opposition to the raj within the peculiar constraints of the war. But the movement began to ebb from May 1941, and there were signs of disquiet, disillusion and some defections in Congress ranks, as there had been in 1933, when civil disobedience had seemed increasingly a political dead end.

Nehru generally agreed with Gandhi's policy but was uneasy that the movement seemed to be less and less dynamic. As often before he felt that the Congress members who were at liberty were not thinking clearly or expounding the Congress position in public, and there seemed to be a general malaise, a feeling that not enough was being done, and yet no clear notion of what should be done. Further, he felt the Congress organisation was falling apart or being rent apart by internecine intrigues. In this situation only Gandhi seemed to be rock-like. But Nehru was worried that even he was deflecting people from the real issues. 'So far as present action is concerned I have very little fault to find with Bapu's technique. Where he has erred, I think, is the unnecessary emphasis on certain personal aspects of nonviolence. The result has been to direct many people's attention to this question when they should be made to think of one fundamental question only – India's independence and the removal of British control completely.'[19]

Late in the year there were rumours that he and other Congressmen might be released early. At first he shunned the idea, because he wanted to finish the writing he was doing inside prison, and because he saw no obvious outlet for his energy outside. But soon he began to think that in the prevailing confusion, where there seemed to be only slogans and jargon which had lost all meaning, he might have a role to play, and he wanted to get outside again. The Government of India had indeed been considering releases since the end of July, when the Viceroy's Executive Council had been expanded to include six new Indian members. It was this reconstructed council which decided to go ahead with a programme of releases, and Nehru found himself at liberty early in December.

## THE LOST OPPORTUNITY

However, Nehru quickly recognised that freedom only confronted him again with the dilemmas generated by the war which had so distressed him in late 1940. Congress was still essentially boxed in by the deepening crisis of the war and the government's stance, while Gandhi's policy seemed to be leading Congress nowhere but internal stasis. As Nehru travelled to a meeting of the CWC in Bardoli, Gujarat, he told Padmaja Naidu that life was so difficult that the dull jail routine seemed simpler and preferable: 'already I have a feeling of suffocation and distress, for we are going to have a hard time there, and whatever happens, it is hardly likely to be too pleasant and agreeable to any of us'.[20] His own opinion was that Congress must persist in resolute opposition to the British, based on a disciplined Congress under Gandhi's leadership, but he worried that the theoretical question of non-violence and India's own defence seemed to be intruding on their discussions and deflecting them from the major issues at stake.[21]

The CWC meeting did indeed prove difficult as Gandhi seemed increasingly to be concerned with the ideal of non-violence, and to be turning from active opposition to government towards an emphasis on the creation of swaraj through an elaborated programme of constructive work, which he presented to his colleagues. Eventually he resolved the problem for Congress by formally withdrawing from Congress leadership and reserving civil disobedience to himself and those who like him opposed all war. The crucial resolution on the political situation was drafted by Nehru, and reiterated the party's stance in September 1940 that only a free India could cooperate in the war: 'a subject India [cannot] offer voluntary or willing help to an arrogant imperialism which is indistinguishable from fascist authoritarianism'.[22] A subsequent meeting of the AICC ratified this, on Gandhi's own urging, though he disapproved of it, for his primary concern was to maintain Congress unity even if he felt he had to be at one remove from its policy. The Governor of UP noted with acidity that history had repeated itself and once again

Gandhi had managed to weld the Congress together 'with his usual cunning'.[23]

For his own part Nehru was certain that there could be no compromise with the government, even though civil disobedience had ended; and he warned Rajagoplachariar, a Madras Congress leader who had led the movement within the party for a reversion to parliamentary politics, that there would be 'nothing more dangerous than our being saddled with responsibility without complete power. Complete power is inconceivable in the present and partial power will make our position worse.'[24] Nehru's own position in Congress was at this stage considerably enhanced, as Gandhi had said at the AICC meeting that Nehru was his 'heir'. There was of course nothing formal to 'inherit', but Gandhi was clearly determined to use the weight of his own personal influence to establish Nehru as the central Congress figure in the event of his own death. Moreover, he had exhorted those closest to him ideologically not to split Congress on the doctrine of non-violence, thereby neutralising some of the Old Guard who had found Nehru such an unpalatable colleague in 1936. The Delhi and UP governments were clear that Nehru was one of the most important Congressmen with whom they had now to cope. The Viceroy thought him obsessed with hatred for the British, and 'blind to the harm he is doing to his own countrymen', but was anxious to treat him in such a way as not to bolster his standing even further.[25]

Nehru's immediate concern, however, was with his daughter's impending marriage, now brought nearer by his unexpectedly early release. When news of the engagement began to circulate in public there was very considerable hostility to such a union across religious boundaries. Gandhi consequently made known his support publicly, and Nehru himself issued a press statement to the effect that he had long felt that in questions of marriage only the couple concerned could make such a momentous decision, while parents should advise and then accept their children's wishes. In this case he willingly accepted the marriage, as did Gandhi and his own and Kamala's families. He concluded by indicating that he was not in favour of the elaborate celebrations which often marked Indian marriages, particularly at the present time of national and international crisis. Preparations went ahead and, in consultation with Gandhi and a Sanskrit scholar in Delhi, Nehru took care over the details of a simple religious ceremony which would be fitting for a Hindu and a Parsi, and would not give rise to even further criticism from conservative Hindus. The marriage took place in Allahabad at the family home in late March, and Indira then moved with her husband to their own rented house nearby. The wedding had been a conscious demonstration of new social attitudes, and also of Gandhi's vision of national reconstruction, because of the simplicity of the ceremony and the following dinner, and the fact that Indira wore in place of the usual elaborate silk sari one made of yarn her father had spun in jail. The strain in their relationship, which had been so obvious on her return to India, now eased, and by the middle of 1943 he was deriving joy and comfort from the new relationship which seemed to be developing with his married daughter as she matured and reached out to him, now as a friend.[26]

Even at his daughter's wedding Nehru could not escape the political life, and many of the core Congress leadership were present and used the time to discuss the issue now confronting them – their response to a mission by Sir Stafford Cripps, now a member of the British cabinet, who had come with a fresh initiative to seek Indian cooperation in the war effort. The Cripps mission was to be a turning point in relations between India and Britain, for the cabinet was now prepared to offer India the right to total independence after the war, in anticipation of immediate cooperation by the Government of India in pursuit of war. Moreover, it also made plain that any province could opt out of a post-war constitution to create an alternative state, thus giving further leverage to the Muslim League in particular in constitution-making. However, in the short term the mission was a disastrous failure, leaving a legacy of bitterness between Congress and the British, and sending Congress once more down the sterile path of civil disobedience during the war.

The mission in March–April 1942 remains one of the most disputed episodes in Britain's imperial ending in India.[27] However, the details belong as much to British political history as they do to Indo-British relations. They show how Churchill's government, strengthened by more left-wing members such as Cripps and Attlee who had considerable understanding of Indian problems, was moved to make a deeply significant offer to attract Congress cooperation in the war as military danger in Asia deepened with the fall of Singapore and Rangoon, and under pressure from Britain's American allies as well as moderate Indian political opinion. Yet the prospect of Cripps successfully negotiating the entry of Congress into a quasi-cabinet type government triggered a Linlithgow–Churchill axis of opposition. A Viceroy bitterly distrustful of the Congress leadership and lacking political finesse joined forces with a Prime Minister who had no wish to see Indian independence, and for whom the mission was primarily a device to deflect American criticism. Cripps, acting in good faith and with a deep commitment to India's independent future, was basically stopped in his tracks by this alliance just as it seemed some agreement might be reached after the intervention of a special envoy of the American President, F. D. Roosevelt.

Nehru's experience of war had shown how Congress was boxed in by the ramifications of the international conflict; and by the time of Cripps's arrival in India the Congress leaders had found no policy to help it break out of this impasse. The cabinet's need to reassure political opinion in America, the British labour movement and among moderate Indians opened a brief opportunity for Congress to escape from its predicament. Nehru and Azad, as Congress President, were the dominant figures in the Congress response to Cripps's offer, but Nehru's role was particularly important because he knew Cripps from encounters in England in

1938 and later in India, had corresponded with him and shared his socialist sympathies. If anybody could bring Congress and the raj into a fruitful alliance it would have seemed that these two could. Nehru was evidently tired and unwell when he met Cripps, and he seemed deeply worried about what might happen if India did not cooperate in its own defence now that war had reached its own borders. Moreover, as Azad later remembered, Nehru was also concerned that India should help China resist Japan, and this disposed him to respond positively to the Cripps offer. It was evident to his close colleagues that he was deeply stressed by the negotiations, even muttering about them in his sleep.

However, the proposals Cripps had brought did not satisfy the CWC: the future arrangements seemed to encourage disunity and also ignored the people within the princely states, while for the present there seemed to be no suggestion of radical change in government which would give Indians genuine responsibility over their own affairs, including defence. As the negotiations progressed Nehru received a personal appeal from Cripps to throw his weight into using a chance which would not recur. He responded by saying that he was overwhelmed by the implications of a possible breakdown and still hoped for a positive outcome. However, he did not think he could carry enough of his colleagues with him to accept the offer, and this was 'a tragedy for all of us'.[28] The sticking points were the interlocking ones of the degree to which an Indian within the government would have responsibility for defence, and whether the Viceroy would treat his ministerial colleagues as a cabinet; and eventually it became clear that Churchill's government had no intention of permitting such a radical change in the practice of government during the war. In a letter drafted by Nehru (echoing much that he had said in previous years), Azad told Cripps that the picture of the proposed government was so like the existing one that Congress could not fit into it: 'we cannot undertake responsibilities when we are not given the freedom and power to shoulder them effectively and when an old environment continues which hampers the national effort'.[29]

Nehru was deeply distressed by the breakdown, and critical of Cripps for apparently misleading them on the key issues of defence and a 'national government', and for the statements he made subsequently. All this indicated that a man from whom he had had such hopes now appeared to be an archetypal member of the British cabinet dealing with a troublesome group of colonial people. Later Nehru accepted that Churchill was most to blame, but Cripps's personal failure had contributed greatly to Indian bitterness because so much had been expected of him.[30] As Nehru had recognised during the fraught days of negotiation, it was a tragedy that this unique moment of opportunity had passed.

Once again Congress was plunged into agonies of indecision, and for Nehru there was the added twist of personal pain when he sensed that he was drifting apart from Gandhi on what Indian reaction should be to any Japanese invasion.

For Nehru it was utterly impossible to render any assistance to the Japanese and he said at the CWC meeting in late April that he feared that Gandhi's approach would make them into 'passive partners of the Axis powers'.[31] Azad as Congress President steered the CWC to accept a draft resolution by Nehru which advocated total non-cooperation with the Japanese if they were to invade. In subsequent weeks Nehru's concerns over Gandhi's position lessened, as it became clear to him that Gandhi's growing determination to launch a further campaign of civil disobedience in support of a demand for total British withdrawal from India did not involve withdrawal of Allied troops or any change which would give advantage to an aggressor. Where he had previously held back from any mass campaign which might precipitate violence, now Gandhi appeared to think that even if anarchy ensued this would be preferable to the present situation.[32]

Eventually Gandhi and Nehru together worked out drafts of a CWC resolution calling in July for British withdrawal from India, and failing that indicating that Congress would embark on a further non-violent struggle led by Gandhi. Even in mid-July there still seems from Nehru's conversations with a member of the US mission in Delhi to have been a very slender hope on his part that some sort of deal might still be worked out with the British. But in late July he told a close colleague that although he had been 'worried and distracted beyond measure' over the past nine weeks he had now become convinced that there was no way out of their current predicament except through a renewed movement. 'The risk is there. I hate anarchy and chaos but somehow in my bones I feel some terrible shake-up is necessary for our country.'[33] He was also deeply worried, as he had been during the Cripps negotiations, about not taking any step which would harm China in its struggle against Japan.

The CWC and AICC took the plunge early in August, with what became known as the Quit India resolution, drafted by Nehru, calling on the British to withdraw, and leading the party to a mass struggle 'for the vindication of India's inalienable right to freedom and independence'. Nehru was in good spirits now some definite action was clear. But an opportunity had been lost by the British and the Congress. The result was even greater bitterness in Indo-British relations and the condemnation of Congress to the political wilderness until the end of the war.

## THE LONG INCARCERATION

The Government of India, backed by the cabinet in London, had made elaborate preparations to deal with any renewal of civil disobedience. British determination to neutralise the Congress leadership was sharpened by the extreme danger from the Japanese in Asia. As the Secretary of State for India noted to Churchill, 'We are dealing with men who are now definitely our enemies, inclined to believe in the victory of Japan, and anyhow determined to make the most mischief they can. To appease them or delay in striking at them can only discourage the army and all other loyal elements. I don't believe the effect in America would be serious: anyhow, nothing like as serious as the effect of hesitation and weakness.'[34] The historical record suggests that this was a tragic misunderstanding of the real anguish and the dilemmas experienced by prominent Congressmen, particularly Nehru, at this juncture. But it shows why the British were determined to hit hard when Congress accepted the 'Quit India' resolution.

Consequently within hours the whole CWC was arrested in Bombay, early on 9 August, and taken swiftly to the prisons decided for them – Gandhi to the Aga Khan's palace outside Poona, and others including Nehru to Ahmednagar Fort, a Mughal fort where tight security could be guaranteed. The Congress organisation was declared unlawful, and its funds and offices were seized. As the cabinet minuted, this action was to be publicly justified as being taken in defence not just of British interests but of all the wartime Allies, as Congress action was just the start of a far wider scheme to undermine India's cooperation in the war effort. Rather to the surprise of the Governor of Bombay, the elaborate preparations for the imprisonment of the leaders remained a secret. From the government's perspective the only trouble in the whole operation was that G. B. Pant was so angry at being woken early that he refused to get up and so did not catch the special train laid on; and that Nehru and another CWC member jumped out of one of the train windows at an unscheduled stop where a crowd had gathered who were being controlled by the police with what Nehru thought was excessive force. It took several policemen to control him, and he expressed himself forcibly about the British raj and the police before returning to the train.

So Nehru began his longest incarceration – of nearly three years. It was spent largely in Ahmednagar, but briefly at the end also in Bareilly and Almora jails in UP. He later said that Ahmednagar was the best jail he had ever been kept in, for the rooms were large enough, and there was electric light. However, the food was poor, largely because of the bad cooking, as only a prisoner was permitted to be cook, and no prisoners had prior experience. He attributed his thinness in 1945 to this. (Surprisingly J. B. Kripalani turned out to be good at making cakes out of very inadequate ingredients!) The colleagues lived an orderly life, mainly because Azad could not tolerate the slightest lack of punctuality over meal-times. Outside meal-times they each kept their own timetable. For his part Nehru got up around 5.00 a.m., did some breathing exercises and running, watered his plants and had his bath. After breakfast at 7.30 he would do some solid reading. In the afternoon he would again read something lighter or the papers, and do two hours of language (Hindi and Urdu) study with Syed Mahmud. In the late afternoon he played badminton, watered the garden again, and generally socialised before a further bath and dinner. They would also talk together after their meal until Azad retired, and Nehru himself would be in bed around 10.30.[35]

Because of the unaccustomed company in prison Nehru could not devote as much time as he normally did in prison to serious reading and writing. However, he continued to read widely – for example taking comfort in Plato's account of Socrates' trial and last days. He also used the enforced leisure to write another of his most important books, *The Discovery of India*, in five months between April and September 1944. He dedicated it to his fellow prisoners and thanked them for their endless talks which had helped to clarify his mind on aspects of Indian history and culture, and to make the lengthy sentence more tolerable. It covered a thousand handwritten pages, demonstrating not only Nehru's energy and delight in literary production, but also his wide-ranging intellectual vision. The early part dealt with his own life from Kamala's final illness, but then he wandered through India's history, concluding with detailed chapters on the nationalist movement and with the Indian political experience of the Second World War. It is a reflective, subtle and mature book, very different in tone and intention from the *Autobiography*, and indicates many of the personal and public issues with which Nehru had wrestled over the years, from problems of personal relations, to questions of religion and science, to the essential nature of India and Indianness, and the future of India's polity and culture. In many ways it lacks the urgency and freshness of the *Autobiography* and reads in a far more didactic way. It also emphasises the role of culture in historical change rather than socio-economic forces. One of its most significant themes – significant intellectually and for an understanding of Nehru's vision of India after independence – is his realisation that 'India' had emerged over time with a richness rooted in layer upon layer of cultural influences and changes, which would in turn give it the strength to continue adapting to the challenges of the modern world. Here was no static nation, but one which would grow by creative change.

Nehru's public writings and speeches often reflect his private confidences to friends, and there is a fascinating connection here between the new book and the intimate letter to Gandhi in mid-1941 when he had surprisingly poured out his heart on matters of personal intimacy. He admitted that this highly westernised Indian was becoming far more comfortable with his Indian roots and heritage. 'India grows upon me more and more and I am ever discovering something new in her. It is a voyage of discovery which has no end. And yet people call me, because of my ways and outlook, a European and an Englishman. They are right in a way and yet only superficially so.' He believed 'intensely' in India though he was often disgusted by his own sort, the middle classes, whose 'vulgarity and weaknesses and limited outlook appal me. Always they seem to be willing to sell their immortal selves for a dirty mess of pottage.'[36] Now in 1944 he wrote in a vein almost redolent of Gandhi himself when he looked forward to a new India, drawing on her past and yet learning from others.

> To-day [India] swings between a blind adherence to her old customs and a slavish imitation of foreign ways. In neither of these can she find relief or life or growth. It is obvious that she has to come out of her shell and take full part in the life and activities of the modern age. It should be equally obvious that there can be no real cultural or spiritual growth based on imitation. Such imitation can only be confined to a small number which cuts itself off from the masses and the springs of national life. True culture derives its inspiration from every corner of the world but it is home-grown and has to be based on the wide mass of the people.[37]

Alongside such long-term musings Nehru kept himself sane and alert by practical activity, including the passion for gardening which prison permitted. He enjoyed the business of tending flowers and watching their development as well as their mature beauty. 'I love to play about with the soft warm earth. I think there is a certain psychic satisfaction about the earth, and we, who have cut ourselves away from it, miss this very essential thing; if I read or write all day, there is something that I lack, and this contact with the earth goes some way to supply it . . .'[38] During this sentence in Ahmednagar no family visits were permitted and Nehru admitted that letters from friends kept him sane. He was particularly grateful for the kindness of an Englishman, his near contemporary, Edward Thompson, former Methodist missionary and academic who now devoted himself to interpreting India to Britain, for sending him stimulating books as well as letters. 'I often think of him and of the bond of friendship that ties us. Such bonds have helped me greatly to keep sane and sober, and not to allow "black thinking", as they call it very appropriately in the language of prison, to find a home in my mind.'[39] Nehru was well aware of the damage prison could do to the mind and psyche, quite apart from the body. He strove consciously to guard against this and believed that in contrast jail had given him a greater appreciation of life and of things those outside would take for granted.

However, during this incarceration he found living in close proximity to his Congress colleagues a challenge. They all got along reasonably well most of the time, but the stress of prison and the news from outside sometimes created tensions and induced depression and anger, though Nehru tried to restrain his famous temper. He found himself increasingly respectful of the good qualities of his colleagues, and particularly appreciative of Azad, for despite their huge difference in background and outlook Nehru recognised his erudition and profound combination of the old and new, and came to value his opinion and advice on public and private matters. Stresses among the colleagues also opened up when they discussed affairs outside their prison, as in late 1943, when Azad raised the whole issue of whether Congress should suspend the Quit India movement. Nehru noted that some of their company considered any criticism of Gandhi to be *lèse-majesté*, while Kripalani and Patel disliked Nehru's pretensions to authoritative knowledge on international affairs. Nehru for his part found Pant the easiest to talk to as he had a good mind and a grasp of modern problems. But he felt afresh how out of place he was in the CWC, though events had conspired to keep him there.[40] In 1945 the group engaged in further discussions, about the relationship of communists and socialists to the Congress, and then about the fraught events within Congress in mid-1942 after the breakdown of the Cripps mission. The latter subject produced what Nehru called 'a burst-up', and relations between him and Vallabhbhai Patel and Kripalani became very strained after all three had lost their tempers.[41]

Given the stresses inherent in jail life as well as news from outside, it was not surprising that Nehru was subject to considerable mood swings and to deep distress which manifested itself in nightmares and his moaning and shouting in his sleep, which often disturbed his colleagues. (This was an old habit which Kamala had noted, and which had recurred during the Cripps Mission.) Nehru noted that the nightmares involved a sense of oppression, of being cornered and not being able to move or even shout out in warning. News from outside had indicated that the government had hit the civil disobedience movement hard, and soon it petered out, though in certain places such as Bihar it had temporarily been perhaps the greatest challenge to British rule since the 1857 Mutiny.[42] As violence had erupted at the hands of people on the fringes of Congress, Gandhi faced immense problems in trying to prove that Congress was not responsible for the violence, and then after his release on health grounds, in planning for the future. Nehru in prison heard of Gandhi's three-week fast on the issue of non-violence in mid-1943; and then in 1944 of his attempt to get in touch with the new Viceroy, Lord Wavell, with the suggestion that he was prepared to advise the CWC to call off civil disobedience and cooperate in the war effort if a declaration of Indian independence were made. He heard too of Gandhi's abortive talks with Jinnah. Nehru was plunged into despair: he felt stifled and could not even breathe properly. He reviewed in his mind all the occasions of conflict and misunderstanding between Gandhi and himself since his return to India in 1936, and now felt that Gandhi was grovelling before the Viceroy and Jinnah. He could not see what he could do if he were released, and noted, 'I feel I must break with this woolly thinking and undignified action – which really means breaking with Gandhi.'[43] Prison saved him from having to make any dramatic response, and he kept himself busy with other things, trying not to become disturbed by what was happening or even to participate in discussions on the events among his colleagues.

Nehru relied on letters to keep in touch with his close family as no interviews were permitted in Ahmednagar. He wrote regularly to Indira and waited eagerly for the birth of her first child. In the last month of the pregnancy he wrote to her of the mystery of individuality, and how facing birth and death brought one to peer into 'the dark unknown'.[44] When the little grandson was born he heard the news by telephone, and Pant provided some special tea-time confection. He also concerned himself over his two married sisters, particularly the growing rift between the two of them, which caused him to ponder on the roots of their estrangement in the disruptions of their family life in 1919–20, and his younger sister's sense of losing out. Ironically just a year earlier Krishna had herself published an article, 'My brother – Jawahar', in which she recounted their child-hood, and how greatly she had loved but feared him, for he had a terrible temper. Despite his great qualities of kindness and gentleness, his weakness, in her eyes, was his insistence that everybody should do things well and efficiently: he was a hard taskmaster who became annoyed with people who were not quick to learn or act.[45]

In 1944 Nehru was further distressed by the sudden death of his brother-in-law Ranjit, Vijayalakshmi's husband, and then by the financial complications which ensued because he died intestate. Under Hindu law in such cases the widow and daughters inherited none of the joint family property, though if there had been a son he would have inherited a considerable amount. Nehru was determined to care financially for his sister and her three daughters, and sent Vijayalakshmi money from jail. The situation was partially resolved after a court case which became something of a *cause célèbre*, and was much discussed in the press and by women's organisations. But it made him reflect on the nature of Hindu law and also on the mentality of people who could think this treatment of women was just.[46]

Even before these financial complications developed, Nehru had drafted his own will. What prompted him was mainly his concern that Indira should be without any doubt his heir. Her marriage was not strictly legal because of the different religion of husband and wife and he wished there to be no legal compli-cations in the event of his sudden death. Moreover, he wished to ensure that his body was cremated without religious ritual and that his ashes should be partly thrown into the Ganges and partly from a plane over Indian soil. But there was also the knowledge and sense that he was himself ageing, while those who were senior to him in the nationalist movement were passing away. While in prison he began to wonder whether even his generation had the energy to make the changes which India so sorely needed, and whether they would have the time to do so, even if they saw Indian freedom. He read admiring references to him in the Amer-ican press, but in mid-1943 he wondered if he had any big role to play in the future. 'Vanity says yes. And reason says no: You are too squeamish, idealistic, proud, unbending and aloof, and in any event totally unfitted for the political game. You do not represent India or the average Indian; you cannot walk in step with the West. It is your fate to fall between the two.' As he confided in Indira, 'age as it comes inexorably and relentlessly after a certain period of one's life is no welcome visitor. The sense of the work to do, so little done, and ever less and less time to do it, oppresses.'[47]

For Nehru the experience of war had been deeply negative. It had led him into conflict with his closest colleagues, torn him apart with his conflicting ideological convictions, and eventually brought him to long periods of incarceration whose only productive result appeared to be a new book. For the Congress it had proved a time of irresolvable constraints, and the Gandhian way of civil disobedience had led yet again into the wilderness. Not only had the government suppressed their movement; it had also carried on governing either through governors' emergency powers or through elected governments composed of more willing Indian collaborators, including the Muslim League. Yet much Indian opinion was now resolutely opposed to the raj, and likely to support Congress once the war ended, even though the British had effectively put political change on hold for the war's duration.

Well before war ended, Lord Wavell, formerly Commander-in-Chief but Viceroy since late 1943, recognised that some initiative was necessary to break the political deadlock. Even before he took up office he was planning a political initiative to resolve the current impasse, aware of the frustrations of a broad spectrum of Indian opinion. But he faced opposition from a cabinet dominated by Churchill, who in his estimation 'hates India and everything to do with it'. He found discussions with the cabinet subcommittee on India depressing. 'I do not believe', he wrote in his journal, that 'these men face their fences honestly, they profess anxiety to give India self-government but will take no risk to make it possible.'[48] By mid-1944 he was convinced the raj would find itself in a very dangerous position if it made no move before or just at the end of war in Europe, and in this he was supported by all his provincial governors. He told Churchill forthrightly that a proper settlement in India was essential for Britain and the Commonwealth, yet India's problems seemed to be treated by London with 'neglect. Even sometimes with hostility and contempt.' He urged him to recognise that the raj could not continue indefinitely and not even for long, and that if India was to remain a willing member of the Commonwealth then some imaginative and constructive move had to made without delay.[49] After months of negotiation he was permitted to make a major political move and to invite Indian politicians to enter a reconstructed Executive Council, much on the lines Cripps had earlier proposed. It was to confront this proposal that Nehru and the Congress leadership were released in June 1945.

# Chapter 9

# The Experience of Independence, 1945–1948

Early in his last and longest imprisonment Nehru had wondered if he would ever have the opportunity to play a major role in the making of a new India. 'What of the big things and brave ventures which have filled my mind these many years? Shall I be capable of them when the time comes? Or will the time itself come for me to play an effective part in moulding events? To some extent . . . I have made a difference to events in India in the past. But I hunger for constructive work on a vast scale.'[1] On his release in 1945 the time had indeed come for this man of vision and singular skills, who was now in his mid-fifties. As the ageing Gandhi threw himself increasingly into the work of combating violence and played less of a guiding role in Congress, Nehru was one of a small core group who represented the party in negotiations for independence, which the British had promised in 1942. He was re-elected Congress President in mid-1946, and from that position became the Vice-President of the Interim Government which preceded independence, and eventually independent India's first Prime Minister. However, for him the coming of independence was an experience of tragedy as much as celebration. He witnessed the partition of his homeland, the horrific killings which preceded and accompanied it, and the violence which locked India and the new state of Pakistan in conflict over the former princely state of Kashmir, draining for defence money which both countries sorely needed for development. He also experienced the more personal devastation of Gandhi's assassination in January 1948.

To the historian this complex phase in Nehru's political life is also a window on to some of the most difficult problems which accompanied the ending of European empires in the mid-twentieth century. It demonstrates the crucial issues of who and what constitutes a nation, and the often disputed nature of nationalism and national identity in colonial situations. It also displays the complexities of decolonisation in plural societies where distinctive identities have often been sharpened by the colonial presence. It must be remembered, too, that this was the first time any European state had voluntarily in peacetime handed authority over to former colonial subjects, with immense implications for those who inherited power and had to learn the arts and crafts of government in relation to their own peoples and the wider world of international relations. Nehru and his generation on the subcontinent were among the first to experience the realities of such a transfer of power, to have to transform themselves from opponents of an imperial regime to legitimate practitioners of government, and, more problematically, to become managers of an inherited regime, in the absence of any revolution which might have overthrown the system they had opposed.

## SEEKING AN IMPERIAL ENDING

The months between the release of the CWC and the entry of Congressmen into an Interim Government in September 1946 were a time of immensely complex and often frustrating negotiations, aimed at bringing the raj to a peaceful end. These were now conducted between three major players, the British, Congress and the Muslim League. The British were already committed to giving Indians choice over their own future. New impetus was given to this policy by the end of Churchill's regime in London, and the formation of Clement Attlee's Labour government in July 1945. British priorities were now to liquidate the raj and leave in its place if possible a united India which would be a willing partner in the Commonwealth. To British politicians it was evident that India no longer had its earlier commercial and financial significance for Britain. Trading links had lessened in the 1930s, and much British capital had been repatriated since the heyday of British overseas investment at the start of the century. Moreover, India was now a creditor of the UK, as payment for much of its war contribution had piled up what were known as the sterling balances in London. Although Gandhian civil disobedience had never threatened the stability of the raj, except temporarily in tiny pockets, the Viceroy and his governors now felt they could not contemplate having to combat any possible renewal of civil disobedience, because the bulk of the Hindu population saw Congress as the natural government of India, while Indians were themselves in charge of large parts of government.

It is noteworthy that at the apex of government by 1947 over half the ICS was Indian, and though its members were scrupulously loyal they could not be expected willingly to help crush a popular movement often led by their friends and relatives. Only a significant reinforcement by British civil and military manpower could have guaranteed British rule for long, and this was unlikely to have been acceptable to a parliament whose priorities were post-war reconstruction of Britain and the demobilisation of British troops. Until early 1947 the cabinet did not think in terms of a set timetable for independence, but Wavell exhorted his political masters to recognise that the governmental machine was fast weakening and that they must face the need to have a 'breakdown plan'. On the last night of 1946 he confided to his diary, 'while the British are still legally and morally responsible for what happens in India, we have lost nearly all power to control events; we are simply running on the momentum of our previous prestige'.[2]

The main Indian players in the negotiations of 1945–6 were the Congress and the Muslim League. Congress wanted independence as quickly as possible. Given its previous commitments to the articulation and protection of minority rights in any new state, it recognised it would have to negotiate with those who spoke for those minorities, particularly Indian Muslims. But it abhorred the prospect of partitioning the subcontinent, although this was effectively on the political agenda following the League's demands in 1940, the terms of the Cripps declaration of 1942, and talks between Gandhi and Jinnah in 1944. However, as Congress also hoped for an India with a strong central government capable of tackling India's major social and economic problems, as well as ensuring India's independence of any great powers, the prospect of a loose federation with a weak centre was also unpalatable. The Muslim League was by this time in a far stronger position than it had been before the war to claim legitimately that it spoke for Indian Muslims – on the evidence of votes cast for it in elections in 1946 (see below), and given that Muslim leaderships in provinces where Muslims were a majority were now, with the exception of the Frontier, in alliance with it.

Jinnah's claim was for a separate homeland for what he and many other Muslims now perceived as the Muslim nation. But precisely what he meant by a homeland was unclear, probably deliberately so, particularly in view of the fact that Muslims were scattered throughout India and only concentrated in two major areas of the north and east, which were not contiguous. He probably still thought of 'Pakistan' as a bargaining device to achieve for Muslims a secure position as a nation in their own homelands within a loose subcontinental and multinational federation.[3] At this stage none of the other minorities were large enough or suffi-ciently organised to enter into serious negotiations about the ending of empire; while the future of the Indian princes was effectively put on hold by the three major parties to the discussions.[4]

The first stage in the post-war discussions was a conference at Simla convened by the Viceroy with a view to reconstructing his Executive Council so that it was entirely Indian except for himself and the Commander-in-Chief. Its long-term role would be to enable India to move towards a new constitution. Azad, the Congress President, insisted that Nehru should come to Simla to be available for consulta-tion, even though he was not an official Congress representative. He had an immense public reception. One can only speculate on the state of mind of someone who had spent years in prison, denied normal social company, now finding himself the object of popular enthusiasm, and having to grapple with unprecedented political complexities. He admitted to his sister that he found the whole experience a strain. He also wrote to Indira of the impossibility of sleep on the night journey to Simla because of the crowds at the stations, and of his having to appear on the balcony of the house where he was staying with Azad to give *darshan* – a sight of himself – to the public. He had not lost his sense of humour, and commented that the house was government property, and though he could bring himself to use soap embossed with 'Viceregal Lodge', he found it quite impossible to use Viceregal writing-paper![5] Wavell had two lengthy and wide-ranging conversations with Nehru and found him pleasant and interesting, and more politically 'practical' than when he had met him during the Cripps mission. Lady Wavell and their staff all liked him. It was a mark of his magnanimity, and of his upbringing, that during these difficult months he showed little bitterness and no discourtesy towards the British officials with whom he now had to work in close proximity.

The CWC had given Azad instructions for the conference in the hope of cooperating in Wavell's initiative; and Nehru later commented that Congress had sincerely wanted to make the conference a success. However, the instructions insisted that the Muslim League should not nominate all the Muslim members of the proposed government, but that nominations for all the seats should be made by all groups at the conference. This was consistent with the long-standing insistence by Congress that it was a national rather than a communal organisation.[6] It eventually submitted its own list of names, including three Leaguers among the suggested non-Congressmen, but when Wavell accepted a slate which included one non-League Muslim Jinnah insisted that all Muslim members of the government should be Leaguers, and that they should have a virtual veto within the government on topics where Muslims had objections. So the conference collapsed. In Wavell's words, 'The root cause of the failure was Jinnah's intransigence and obstinacy. But it represents a real fear on the part of the Muslims, including those who do not support Jinnah, of Congress domination, which they regard as equivalent to a Hindu Raj.'[7] Nehru himself acknowledged that many Muslims were indeed fearful of Hindu domination, though he felt this was unwarranted, despite the fact that some Hindus were 'out for complete Hindu domination'.[8] However, he felt that elements within the raj had used the communal division to sabotage the conference, though he believed Wavell personally had wanted the conference to succeed.

Nehru was not at ease in this form of politics. It stifled him, whereas temperament and conviction urged him to be up and doing. He told a group of students in Calcutta that he did not consider himself to be a politician. Politics irritated him and he only participated in politics at present because it had an element of idealism in it – that of freedom for India and of ending poverty by rapid economic advance. 'It is a politics of revolutionary changes.' This did not mean violent revolution but fundamental change in the conditions of life for ordinary people.[9] It was hardly surprising that he should feel frustrated at the apparent impasse, despite the declared British policy of giving India freedom. The Governor of Bengal thought that Nehru and Patel were the 'firebrands of the outfit [Congress] and are suffering from suppressed frustration, indignation and a rather hysterical impetuosity particularly on Nehru's part'.[10] Both men found some outlet in the elections to the central and provincial assemblies, which were spread out during the cold weather of 1945–6. Nehru drafted both the AICC resolution in late September that Congress should campaign on the issue of complete independence, and also the manifesto for the central assembly election with an eye to foreign readers and also to promote the image of Congress as a party with a broad vision as opposed to the League with its demand solely for Pakistan. Congress stood for independence and for equal rights and opportunities for every citizen. This meant the removal of inequalities and special help for the backward, and also unity and tolerance among communities. The constitution should be federal and should give considerable autonomy to its constituent units. However, after freedom, the most urgent problem was 'the curse of poverty' and how to raise the living standards of the masses.[11]

Despite this idealism, many of those who clamoured for the Congress ticket obviously had more material intentions, given that Congress seemed set to be a major player in any central and local governments. Even the eminently realistic Patel found the selection of candidates 'a bad business', and noted that it was 'a sad thing to see the mad competition for going into the Councils'.[12] However the election results clarified the standing of those who claimed to negotiate for India. In the central assembly the League won all the Muslim seats and the Congress 91 per cent of the rest. In the provincial elections the League won 439 out of 494 seats reserved for Muslims, while Congress won a majority of the rest and formed provincial governments in eight provinces. Congress was now clearly the accepted party of the Hindu majority, but only on the Frontier did it still command the loyalty of Muslims, thus giving the League far greater legitimacy as the voice of Indian Muslims.

As the elections unfolded Nehru wrestled with the question of how to weld India's different communities into an independent nation state. This was urgent now, not just because of the League's growing status and Jinnah's ability to block political initiatives. Violence also seemed frighteningly near the surface of public life. He was now back in regular correspondence with Cripps, and told him that he felt any partition of the country would have to be accompanied by joint institutions for defence, communications and foreign affairs, for Pakistan by itself could never be truly independent. Even Muslims who supported the idea had not thought out its true consequences. Moreover any partition would involve the partition of Bengal and Punjab with their areas of Hindu and Sikh majorities, and this

Jinnah was currently rejecting. The only solution was Congress's idea of a federation of autonomous units with a minimum list of compulsory common subjects. The way to such independence had to be through a constituent assembly, not by any outside imposition. For his part he hoped there would be no more conflict with the British for this would be a terrible waste of national energy and would leave a bad legacy. 'I have spent enough of my life in conflict and during the years that remain to me I want to build and not to destroy.' Only independence could open the way to such constructive effort.[13]

Nehru was not only perturbed about the future. He was also exhausted by the election campaign, and Patel urged him to look after his health in view of the heavy responsibilities which he would soon have to shoulder. Moreover, 'The three Big Guns are coming from England and we will require all the freshness of your mind to deal with the huge and intricate problems that will face us when they come.'[14] Here Patel was referring to the three members of a Cabinet Mission to India, one of whom was Cripps himself, who came to tackle the problem of the machinery for Indian determination of independence. The Big Guns, or in Wavell's phrase, 'the three Magi', came at the end of March and left three months later, after a gruelling and dispiriting round of negotiations which did little to resolve the fundamental issue of the shape of any new state or states on the subcontinent.[15]

Nehru was one of the main Congress negotiators in this period, as well as being the major drafter of all Congress statements. However, he was by no means the dominant voice in Congress discussions, for Azad was still President, Patel was a major force to be reckoned with, and Gandhi had re-emerged to be a significant element in Congress discussions. Wavell thought Patel, the recognised 'tough' of the CWC, to be the most forceful of them; but he could not help liking Nehru, thought him sincere, intelligent and personally courageous, but – interestingly – lacking the political courage to stand up to Gandhi.[16] Wavell also had profound reservations about the strategies pursued by the three cabinet members, and by their closeness to the Congress 'camp'. Nehru himself appears to have been deeply worried by the proceedings. He felt that though his colleagues knew their minds on fundamentals they had not thought out constitutional arrangements, and tended to get side-tracked by details, and to be too absorbed by the communal issue. Moreover, he felt there was no real change in the British outlook, not least among the officials surrounding the Viceroy and Mission members.[17]

The Mission, having failed to achieve common ground by negotiation with Indian politicians, proceeded to construct its own plan for the long-term and immediate future, which it hoped would ensure the transfer of power to one successor state, but would assuage the fears of the Muslim minority in particular. On 16 May it suggested a three-tier federal government for India with a central government at the top exercising power on a limited number of essential common subjects such as defence and foreign affairs; provinces at the bottom exercising residual powers; and area groups in the middle which provinces were free to form to deal with topics of their choice. A Constituent Assembly, elected by existing provincial legislators, would work out the details, and an entirely Indian Interim Government should be formed immediately.

Congress and the League both accepted the long-term plan though each had its reservations. Congress was deeply anxious that 'grouping' should not be compulsory, in order to protect, for example, non-League Muslims on the Frontier or Hindus who might in places such as Assam and West Bengal be forced into a League-dominated Muslim 'group'. The League, according to Jinnah, only accepted the plan because it seemed a step towards the goal of Pakistan. Ultimately it withdrew its acceptance, citing as reasons government breach of faith to the League over the proposed Interim Government, and Congress intransigence over the fundamentals of the Mission Plan. This second accusation has given rise to criticisms that Nehru was largely responsible for the League reversal of policy, primarily as a result of several speeches in July, at the AICC and then in Bombay, when he argued, correctly, that the Constituent Assembly was the sovereign body in deciding India's future shape, and that in all likelihood the three sections in it would not accept 'grouping'. Nehru was primarily addressing opponents of the Mission Plan within Congress, particularly from Socialists, and urging them to accept it, rather than demonstrating any wish to wreck the Plan and the Constituent Assembly. His remarks may have sounded intemperate or been politically inopportune from the perspective of relations with the League, as Gandhi and Patel both recognised, but they demonstrated the difficulty even within Congress of attracting support for a compromise deal on the future shape of India.[18]

Nehru's statements were now more important because in July he was elected Congress President. He had said privately that he did not want this office as it would bind him down and prevent him functioning effectively. But he was Gandhi's nominee, and in deference to this the other three who had been proposed by PCCs withdrew their candidatures. Once again Gandhi clearly felt Nehru would be a bridge between long-serving members of the CWC and the new people Nehru had brought in, including several with left-wing sympathies as well as Rajagopalachariar, who for several years had been out of sympathy with Congress policy.[19] Once in office he started to work to revitalise and discipline the Congress Party, as he was profoundly disturbed by its weakness and its factional divisions. It was clearly in no position to act as the party representing the Indian nation. He was determined that Congress should visibly be a broad and inclusive party rather than a sectional or communal party, both at local level and in the CWC. This was essential in this interim phase before a new government was set up and as elections to the Constituent Assembly were in progress, and he exhorted Congress provincial office-holders to spread this message, particularly its commitment to Muslims. As so often before, he seemed unable to pace himself, such was his sense of political urgency – and indeed of his own significance; and Gandhi had to chide him for overworking and risking a nervous breakdown.[20]

Although Nehru's primary concern in the year after his release was the search for an imperial ending, he had wider interests and experiences which were to be significant in the coming months. One was the role of India in Asia and the position of Indians abroad, particularly those who had been caught up in the war in Asia. At the behest of Congress he spent a hectic eight days in Malaya in March 1946, but before that visited Singapore at the request of the Supreme Allied Commander, Lord Mountbatten, who had been instrumental in smoothing the path for his visit, conscious that he was likely to be free India's first Prime Minister, and believing him to be a man of sincerity and culture.[21] Nehru thus met the Mountbattens for the first time, his first encounter with Edwina being when she was knocked to the floor by a rush of Indian soldiers who had come to see him. At Mountbatten's request he did not give any public recognition to the INA, the so-called Indian National Army which had collaborated with the Japanese; and the main thrust of his public rhetoric was that a free India would be a pivot of a new structure of freedom in Asia, as it had once been the pivot of imperialism. He spoke of a united, renascent Asia and of India playing a new role in the Indian Ocean region.

A further concern of Nehru's at this time, and again evidence of the meaning of freedom in his mind, was his anxiety over the future of the princely states. He was President of the All-India States' Peoples' Conference, a post he had first held in the late 1930s when Congress recognised the potential for rebellious groups in the states to destabilise Congress itself. Now he saw that the issue of freedom within the states was increasingly urgent and inseparable from independence for British India, even though communal issues dominated discussions about the future. This took him in June 1946 to Kashmir, where the Hindu Maharaja had imprisoned Sheikh Abdullah, the non-League Muslim leader of a broadly based party demanding political reform. The prospect of princely action against such an important Congressman as Nehru was highly embarrassing to Wavell and to the rest of the Congress leadership. He was arrested as he crossed the border and detained for two days until the CWC required him to return. Privately he admitted that this expedition cheered him up and the detention permitted him to catch up on lost sleep. Moreover he felt he had put his head out of the net in which he was inexorably entangled in Delhi during the Cabinet Mission, which had given him 'a sense of being tied hand and foot and strangled'.[22] He would need all this energy and refreshment, for within weeks he had become the Vice-President in the newly constructed government heralded by the Cabinet Mission Plan, but against a backdrop of appalling communal violence in eastern India.

## NEHRU AS MINISTER

Wavell and the cabinet were determined to retain the political initiative even though the Cabinet Mission Plan seemed doomed. On the cabinet's insistence, Wavell pressed ahead with negotiations for an Interim Government, even though Jinnah refused to permit League members to participate. He told a governors' meeting that forming an Interim Government with Congress was the only course open to them, given Congress authority in the country and the erosion of British power in an increasingly unstable situation.[23] Recognising that this was an 'opportunist policy' and no long-term strategy, he urged the London government to recognise the severity of the situation and to discuss meaningfully a 'breakdown plan'. Congress, too, was increasingly rattled by the dangers of widespread labour disorder as well as communal violence, and Patel particularly seems to have been insistent that Congress take power at the centre to deal with these problems.[24] On 10 August Nehru told Wavell he would be prepared to form a government, and after abortive negotiations with Jinnah for League cooperation, the Interim Government was sworn in on 2 September, with Nehru as its Vice-President.

So Nehru embarked on his first experience of high office. His only previous experience in government had been briefly as chair of the Allahabad Municipality in the 1920s. He could hardly have taken office at a more difficult moment, for now the post-war industrial unrest was compounded by communal violence on an unprecedented scale. The League, having rejected the Cabinet Mission Plan, proceeded to a day of 'Direct Action' in Calcutta on 16 August, which triggered what became known as the Great Calcutta Killing. Here and in East Bengal Hindus were initially the victims, but they soon took to revenge, and when violence spread to Bihar, Muslims were in turn the main targets. In Calcutta in that one August week about 4,000 were killed, probably up to 15,000 wounded and many thousands made homeless. The Governor of Bengal told Wavell that mobs behaved in bestial fashion, and that it was as bad as anything he had seen as a Guardsman on the Somme. Nehru was equally appalled.[25]

Given Nehru's temperament, it was hardly surprising that he was soon overworking to the point of breakdown. Within weeks he was writing to Padmaja Naidu that his life had changed so much that he really had no personal life left. Over 300 letters came daily to his home, apart from the office correspondence; and everything seemed 'a burden and a ceaseless strain'. The communal violence taxed him not just with its ferocity, but also because when he went to Bihar and Bengal in person Congressmen were hostile to the Interim Government for not preventing it: he now had to recognise, in Wavell's words, 'that Governments are seldom generally popular' – and this was a far cry from the adulation to which he was accustomed.[26]

Nehru had no obvious role models for his unique position as an imperial appointee working towards independence. As far as possible he attempted to behave as a democratically elected Prime Minister within a cabinet which had joint responsibility for its decisions, but he insisted that it should be a strong and active government, despite its interim nature. At the outset he held daily meetings of all the ministers, which he considered to be the real cabinet meetings, and they discussed everything which then came up at the formal meetings with the Viceroy presiding. Despite the preliminary discussions and decision-making the formal meetings were treated seriously. Wavell was impressed by the seriousness and moderation of Nehru and his colleagues once they were in government, and he increasingly liked Nehru as a man though he confessed to distrusting his 'political aims and his judgment'.[27] An experienced Indian member of the ICS became his Principal Private Secretary, and this must have eased the transition from opposition to government for him, and also provided him with insider knowledge of the workings of government. However, the smooth running of the new government was disrupted when League members entered government and refused to cooperate with these conventions. Wavell had persisted in negotiating their entry, given the dangerous situation in the country, but public pronouncements of at least two League members suggested that they intended to use their new position to continue the campaign for Pakistan. From this perspective it was not surprising that they declined to recognise Nehru's position as a quasi-Prime Minister, and refused to attend his informal meetings prior to the official gatherings. The government came to function effectively as two blocs, with the two sets of members rarely meeting or discussing things except in the Viceroy's presence.

This 'very unreal coalition'[28] generated friction between Nehru and the League members and between Nehru and the Viceroy, and on several occasions Nehru was on the point of resigning. Nehru privately thought Wavell was encouraging the Muslim League in violence, and told him directly that he seemed to be encouraging its members to function as a separate bloc in government.[29] A whole range of other irritants disturbed their relationship, particularly the role of British governors in the Muslim majority areas of Sind, Bengal and the Frontier. Nehru declined Wavell's advice to refrain from a visit to the Frontier in October (advice which almost certainly was repeated within the Congress). He was met with considerable and sometimes violent opposition, organised by the League; but he insisted that the real problem was the outmoded political system on the Frontier and the hostility of officials to Congress and its allies. Wavell commented that the visit was a 'dangerous and foolhardy escapade', and that Nehru was out of his political depth in the particular situation of the Frontier.[30]

However, Nehru, holding the External Affairs and Commonwealth Relations portfolios, also took steps to elaborate the future lines of India's foreign policy, and to begin to set up a foreign service. Some of his initiatives generated tension with the British, particularly his use of Krishna Menon as a personal envoy to the USSR. But he proved he could work well with those already holding administrative positions in his response to advice from the British ICS man who was currently Joint Secretary in the External Affairs Department on the expansion of the Foreign Service. It was also significant that he wrote to a senior Indian ICS man, G. S. Bajpai, who had been Agent-General for India in the USA, saying that although he disliked the ICS 'outlook' on virtually everything, he hoped that he would be available for his country in the new situation as India needed men of ability.[31] The most public demonstration of his vision of the international role of a free India came in an Asian Relations Conference in Delhi, in March 1947, where he spoke of India playing a major role in an Asian setting as a force for peace in the new era marked by the end of imperialism.[32]

The backdrop to Nehru's work was the disturbing fact that the mechanisms for attaining freedom seemed deadlocked. The Constituent Assembly, duly elected, had not yet met because of League refusal to accept the long-term plan of the Cabinet Mission. Consequently Attlee's government convened a small conference in London of Congress, League and Sikh representatives to try to kick-start the process. Nehru eventually accepted his invitation, after a personal intervention from Attlee on 27 November, though Patel declined, fearing that such a meeting would only put pressure on Congress to make more concessions to the League. So Nehru paid a flying visit to London in early December. (He marvelled at the speed of air travel – twenty-four hours actual flying time between London and New Delhi – and had lunch at Buckingham Palace as well as sittings with the sculptor Jacob Epstein, but most of his time was taken up with meetings.) But the conference yielded no agreement between Congress and the League on the vexed question of 'grouping'. The British government hoped to edge the processes a little further with a statement that grouping was – initially – a fundamental part of the plan: they hoped this would bring the League into the Assembly, while assuaging the Congress with a commitment that a Federal Court should decide on disputed matters of interpretation over the processes of constitution-making.[33] However, the final outcome of this phase, played out in India rather than London, only hardened the deadlock on making a new constitution. Congress eventually accepted the government statement, but insisted that individual provinces (thinking of Assam and the Frontier) had a right to absent themselves from the group processes. Not surprisingly the League declined to participate in the Constituent Assembly.

Nehru in London did his best to be constructive, but he was profoundly worried that the League had no real intention of cooperating in the constitution-making processes. In view of the subsequent Congress acceptance of a partition of India it is significant that he said at a formal meeting which included the Viceroy and the Secretary of State that Congress wanted League cooperation 'because nothing could be done socially or politically if the co-operation of large groups was lacking. The Muslim league was not interested in social or political advance and lost nothing by not co-operating.'[34] He was thinking to the future and the type of government which could achieve those broader goals to which he personally as well as Congress were committed. Moreover, he was constrained by the fact that he spoke for a Congress in which there were numerous opinions, some of which were strongly opposed to what seemed like further concessions to the League. The sharp discussions back in India within Congress showed that Gandhi was adamant that the Assamese, for example, should not be left at the mercy of a Muslim majority vote in their potential 'group', while others were equally hostile to any apparent climb-down, including the left-wingers Nehru had so carefully engineered into the CWC to make it more inclusive. Congress's official reaction to the government initiative demonstrated these internal pressures as well as Nehru's ambiguous position, despite his prominence and role.[35]

Far more important for Nehru's own formation as a potential Prime Minister was the way the outbreaks of communal violence in India in late 1946 forced him to recognise what his compatriots could do to each other, and made him question his own understanding of what it meant to be an Indian. He told his closest friends and colleagues after a visit to Bihar in November that he was appalled by the brutality of Hindu mobs who had set on their Muslim neighbours and massacred them – and these were ordinary peasants whom he so liked, and who shouted the name of Gandhi. 'To think that the simple, unsophisticated, rather likable Bihar peasant can go completely mad *en masse* upsets all my sense of values.'[36] Struggling to make sense of something he had always assumed was the product of vested interests, he still searched for the influence of some outside hand – Hindu Sabha agitators, black marketeers, landlords – reluctant to believe that ordinary Indians could behave in such a way as a result of religious identification.[37] As the new year dawned he felt desperately lonely and adrift in uncharted seas, and thought that they were living in a perpetual state of crisis, with no grip on the situation. He made urgent appeals to Gandhi to leave his work in eastern India and come to Delhi. Tellingly, he acknowledged, 'I know that we must learn to rely upon ourselves and not run to you for help on every occasion. But we have got into this bad habit and we do often feel that if you had been easier of access our difficulties would have been less.'[38]

At this time of crisis he was thrown into an even greater sense of turmoil by Gandhi's own personal strategy to inject non-violence into an appalling situation, and to prove his own moral strength and purity and thus commitment to non-violence. This involved sharing a bed with his grand-niece, Manu, who was in her late teens. Although it was understandable in terms of Hindu understandings of the power generated by sexual abstinence, it caused concern in Congress circles, and even gossip among foreign journalists. Nehru told Gandhi he was greatly troubled by all this, and profoundly disliked people talking about such issues. It injured their cause and might set an unfortunate example. He wrote of it to Gandhi because the Mahatma had himself raised it with him, but, true to his personal reticence on emotional issues, he said, 'I feel a little out of my depth and I hate discussing personal and private matters. You will I hope forgive me.'[39]

Nehru was not alone in perceiving that India was in a state of crisis. Attlee had told the cabinet at the end of the abortive London talks that he felt the Indian leaders had no will to find an agreement, and that although there was a real risk of civil war they seemed not to recognise the consequences of a collapse in ordered government.[40] The cabinet had for some time been at odds with the Viceroy. They thought him politically inept and also unduly pessimistic about the possibility of achieving a political settlement with the Indian politicians; they also considered unworkable his plan of last resort, which was for the British to make a staged withdrawal. By December 1946 Attlee had determined to replace him and was casting about for a successor. Within weeks it was clear that the government needed not only a new Viceroy but also a new policy initiative, given the refusal of the League to come into the Constituent Assembly, and the subsequent assertion by Nehru and other non-League members of the Interim Government that the League members could no longer continue in it. In early February Wavell was given a month's notice. (Wavell had been expecting his dismissal, but though his public response was one of utmost rectitude, he wrote in his diary on 4 February that it was 'not very courteously done'.)[41] Shortly afterwards it was announced that the new Viceroy would be Lord Mountbatten, recently Supreme Allied Commander for South-East Asia, who had visited India on several occasions and had met Nehru in Singapore. Further, the government announced that it would transfer power to Indian hands not later than June 1948, and hoped it could do so in a manner acceptable to a fully representative Constituent Assembly: failing this it would have to devolve power to whatever successor states seemed feasible, even to existing provinces.[42]

Nehru personally felt that this was a courageous move which would have far-reaching consequences. Moreover, from his perspective the arrival of Mountbatten opened up new possibilities. The change of Viceroy heralded at least two further significant changes. It was clear from the outset that the new Viceroy wanted to work very rapidly towards independence and had the full backing of London. He brought a new energy and verve to a deadlocked situation, in contrast to his exhausted predecessor. Becoming the last Viceroy of India responsible for a peaceful transmission of power was a challenge at which he greatly desired to succeed. Moreover, he represented a younger generation (born in 1900 he was eleven years younger than Nehru) and had an informal and open style of dealing with Indians which was far removed from the protocols of imperial India. He and Lady Mountbatten made a point of entertaining Indians at dinner, luncheon, and at garden parties, and had a rule that at social events no fewer than half the guests must be Indian. Never before had so many Indian names appeared in the Visitors' Book of Viceroy's House, he reported; and he threatened to send home any British person heard expressing racist sentiments.[43]

Among the Indian leaders it was Nehru with whom Mountbatten achieved the greatest rapport. Despite the decade's difference in age there were similarities in their temperaments – both delighted in being public figures wielding significant influence, both were to an extent 'showmen', acutely aware of their public image. Mountbatten found Nehru civilised and intelligent, and better company than any of the other leaders, though he formed an admiration for the more dour and pragmatic Patel, and recognised the extreme importance of treating Gandhi with good-humoured respect, even though he now exerted much less influence in Congress decisions. He was convinced that Nehru was the most important Congressman with whom he had to deal, and set himself to manage this relationship, despite difficult moments and occasions when he felt he had to restrain Nehru's temper or impetuosity. Moreover, he recognised the immense strain under which Nehru was working at this time. A telling moment came in June when Nehru made a speech at an AICC meeting which denigrated the British members of the ICS, and the Governor of Punjab complained to the Viceroy. Mountbatten replied that he had political and psychological difficulties with Nehru, but his goodwill was essential in the critical transition period. 'He is appallingly over-worked, is liable to lose his temper and generally shows many signs of extreme strain. I shall mention this speech to him at the right moment, but I am sure you appreciate that I cannot hope to achieve very much.'[44] Mountbatten's under-standing of Nehru and his position within Congress was also helped by his contacts with Krishna Menon, Nehru's confidante who was outside the circle of Congress leaders but was a conduit of information. Nehru was convinced that Mountbatten was able, intelligent and had a strong sense of urgency – unlike Wavell. Friendship blossomed as the two men recognised their need of each other. For Nehru Mountbatten was an ally rather than a competitor, a person outside the Congress circle who could to an extent be trusted. When independence came just months later Nehru wrote Mountbatten a graceful letter of thanks and appreciation for that friendship, and the support the viceregal couple had given him.[45]

It is significant that Nehru included the Vicereine in his gracious tribute. Edwina Mountbatten was a complex and fascinating woman, whose youth had been marked by extreme wealth, privilege within the heart of British society, and a highly colourful social life. However, the war had liberated within her hidden talents for hard work, sound administration, and the use of her manifold social connections for compassionate work, through the Red Cross and the St John Ambulance Brigade. By the time her husband was appointed Viceroy, she was an international figure in her own right, intelligent and glamorous, and determined to make Mountbatten's posting a success. She threw herself into the task of making Indians socially welcome in viceregal circles, and herself made a range of close Indian friends, as well as pursuing her professional interest in medical work, and playing the grand role of consort on ceremonial occasions. Among the Indians with whom she naturally felt at ease were Nehru and his sister Vijayalakshmi.

However, it was not until after independence, probably in the spring of 1948, that she and Nehru found, to their surprise, that their personal relationship had deepened and blossomed. Edwina had had other close men friends in the course of her tempestuous marriage. Mountbatten had struggled to understand and accommodate himself to them; but with Nehru he had no problem as he was in his own collegial way as deeply attached to Nehru as was his wife. There has been much speculation about Nehru's relationship with Edwina. The extent to which it was in any way physical, however, pales into insignificance beside the fact that two lonely and complex individuals, both driven personalities, found in each other in middle life a source of inspiration, fun, solace and strength, even though their meetings were few once the Mountbattens had left India. They corresponded regularly, in the early years of their friendship weekly and then fortnightly. Nehru would regularly spend weekends at their Hampshire home, Broadlands, whenever he was in England, and Edwina would visit Delhi when she could. In terms of his political life Nehru found in his relationship with Edwina one of the rare people he could trust entirely and with whom he could exchange his thoughts. His friendship with the husband and wife also gave him an easy entrée into the world of the British 'establishment', confirming the advantages given to him by his education in England.[46]

Nehru was central to the events which unfolded in the five months following the arrival of the new Viceroy, and the decisions which shaped the nature of the states which succeeded British rule in India in August 1947. Even before Mountbatten's arrival it was clear that Congress leaders had indeed grasped the dire urgency of the situation, particularly as communal violence spread to Punjab, and in several provinces ordered government seemed precarious. On 8 March the CWC accepted that Punjab (and by implication Bengal) might have to be partitioned as the way of achieving a solution which would involve the least compulsion. Nehru told Gandhi, who was deeply concerned at any suggestion that they were recognising the 'two nation theory', that there was no option in the current situation.[47] The new Viceroy was also rapidly convinced that any solution avoiding some sort of partition was impossible. He had exhaustive discussions with the political leaders and his own hand-picked team of staff, and began to evolve a plan for a transfer of power according to radical self-determination, the choice of each province, or parts of provinces where this was necessary. This would be accompanied by a rapid devolution of power which could be achieved quickly if it occurred at least initially within the Commonwealth, to one, or probably two successor

Dominions. He believed that Jinnah would accept it and that he had the support of Congress, for Congress leaders had accepted the tactical idea of Dominion status as a mechanism for a quick transfer of power, in the expectation this would be dominionhood for a central government, to be followed by provincial choices, and of course subsequent freedom for successor states to withdraw from the Commonwealth.

However, when Nehru was his house guest at Simla Mountbatten showed him the revise of his plan which was just in from London, and Nehru was horrified at what he saw. To him it seemed a blueprint for the 'Balkanisation' of India, a complete departure from what he had assumed to be a slight variation of the Cabinet Mission Plan, and quite different from what he had gathered was the thrust of the draft plan going to London.[48] The evidence of the previous weeks, when the Viceroy and Indian politicians were all handling huge problems under great pressure, without precedents to guide them, and often through intermediaries, suggests that there had been no deliberate misleading but assumptions about the other's intentions which were not clarified; and these were compounded by the intervention of London which reinforced the potential within the plan for multiple independent successor states rather than one or possibly two.[49]

Nehru's explosive response to the news from London and his subsequent discussions with Mountbatten led the Viceroy back to London for consultation and eventually to a plan for devolution of power to two successor Dominions only. With this he returned to India and placed it before the major Indian politicians on 2 June. They took away copies of the plan to show their colleagues, and at a meeting the next day all agreed, though all parties had their reservations which they had privately expressed to Mountbatten. He decided not to let them speak at the second meeting for fear of losing this fragile agreement, but acknowledged that there were these disagreements, while asking for their assent to the plan. When this was given he handed round a document outlining the administrative consequences if partition and transfer of power were to happen rapidly, by 15 August at the latest. While they were all in a state of shock he ended the meeting as quickly as possible.[50] He subsequently broadcast to India, as did the major leaders. Nehru's broadcast acknowledged that this was not the way they had hoped freedom would come. It was surrounded with violence and marked by division, and he had no joy in commending the proposals to his compatriots. But this was a historic opportunity for a new beginning and he urged them to bury bitterness and recrimination and to look to the future.[51]

For Mountbatten this was something of a personal triumph because he had appeared to achieve the peaceful ending of the raj by agreement between Britain and India's major political groups, and to have forced the politicians to recognise that swift action had to be taken to prevent the collapse of civil order and government. For Jinnah the proposed mechanisms for provincial choice about their proposed Dominion allegiance threatened what he had decried as a 'moth-eaten Pakistan'; and bound him to an idea and strategy of separate Muslim nationhood which he almost certainly had hoped would yield up not a poor and geographically bizarre two-part nation state but Muslim blocs secure within a loose federation. For Congress the plan meant the end of an ideal of one Indian nation state, and the rebuttal of its insistence that independence should precede any partition, but on the other hand it gave it the prospect of a strong state with the potential for major socio-economic change, and acknowledged the legitimacy of the Constituent Assembly as the constitution-making body for much of India. There was really little doubt that the AICC would follow the lead given by Nehru, Patel and Kripalani as Congress President at its mid-June meeting, when they argued that this was in effect the best of a bad job, the only way of dealing with harsh reality and the drift towards anarchy. Even Gandhi, profoundly saddened, supported the core leadership.

The weeks leading up to independence in mid-August were Nehru's final ones as a minister within an imperial regime. The realities of partition and independence only gradually began to dawn on him and other politicians as Mountbatten drove them on to confront a huge range of necessary choices and tasks – the provincial choices about joining India or Pakistan, the setting up of a Boundary Commission to deal with the partition of Punjab and Bengal, the division of the assets of British India, including the army, the question of who should be Governor-General of each of the new Dominions, control of escalating violence and the creation of a special Boundary Force to try to deal with violence in the Punjab, and the future of the Indian princes. It can hardly be stressed too much that there was no precedent to guide those involved in these processes of the transfer of political power and the division of a former colonial state; and both administrators and politicians had to deal pragmatically with the issues as they pressed in on them – all in the blazing heat of a Delhi summer.

Nehru was not a member of the Partition Council which oversaw much of the detail of the division: Patel and Rajendra Prasad were the Congress members who took this role. But as a leading Congressman and minister Nehru was deeply involved in a wide range of practical issues – including the withdrawal of British troops, the future of the Gurkhas in the future British and Indian armies, the invitation to Mountbatten to stay on as Governor-General of India (though Jinnah opted to take that role in Pakistan for himself), and the future of princely India. The latter problem was immensely important to him, since he had long wished to integrate the princely states into a more egalitarian and democratic India, and now Congress recognised that if they could not make a deal with the princes before independence there was a danger of yet further 'Balkanisation' of the subcontinent as British paramountcy lapsed. Several major states within India were indeed investigating the possibility of becoming separate Dominions at the end of the raj.

Nehru was deeply suspicious that the existing Political Department, which handled relations with the states, was abetting such moves towards further disintegration of India, and pressed successfully for the creation of a new States Department, which would deal with the princes and provide continuity at the change of regime. This new department began work early in July under the control of Vallabhbhai Patel – and this was a considerable relief to Mountbatten who felt that Patel was 'essentially a realist and very sensible', whereas the more volatile Nehru might have wrecked the chances of a deal with the princes.[52] As it turned out, Patel, with very considerable assistance from Mountbatten's personal pressure on the princes, was able to achieve agreements with all but three princes via limited accession to either India or Pakistan on three essential matters – defence, foreign affairs and communications.

Nehru understandably was working immensely hard, and he was already displaying characteristics which would inhibit his efficiency as Prime Minister. As Krishna Menon told Mountbatten, he was overworking to the point of breakdown, deploying relays of shorthand typists day and night, and attending to every little item rather than dealing only with the big problems.[53] Mountbatten subsequently found his senior Indian minister often so fraught with overwork, stress and sleeplessness that he could not control his temper.[54] Not surprisingly meetings of the Interim Government could be extremely tense, and, overwhelmed by issues of huge magnitude, the routine business of government virtually ground to a halt. The worst tension was only relieved when the central government was divided after the passing of the legislation in London which would lead to the creation of two Dominions, and parallel ministerial groups were reconstructed for each. Nehru also had to plan his own new government, an exercise which worried the Viceroy in his final days in office, as he felt that Nehru was too reliant on older Congress allies and was losing out on the chance to recruit younger talent for the huge tasks ahead. Some new names did appear, but the core of the cabinet were well-tried Congress members, including Vallabhbhai Patel as Deputy Prime Minister. Despite their differences of temperament and style, and their clashes in the past, both Nehru and Patel recognised that their skills complemented each other's. Patel placed his service and loyalty at Nehru's disposal with the sentence, 'Our combination is unbreakable and therein lies our strength.'[55]

However, ideological challenges more demanding than administrative ones perturbed Nehru, causing him to question the whole nature of the India which was coming into being. He was aware that many Hindus blamed Congress for the impending partition, and he felt increasingly out of touch with the prevailing sentiments and sense of self-identification among so many of them.[56] For him partition meant that it was all the more urgent that Indians should not fall back on to a narrow Hindu sense of national identity, but continue to uphold an ideal of an inclusive, composite nationalism. In a correspondence with Rajendra Prasad about demands for a ban on cow slaughter he said how distressed he was by the evidence of Hindu revivalism which represented 'the narrowest communalism. It is the exact replica of the narrow Muslim communalism which we have tried to combat for so long. I fear that this narrow sectarian outlook will do grave injury not only to nationalism as such but also to the high ideals for which Indian and Hindu culture has stood . . . We are facing a crisis of the spirit in India today . . .'[57]

## THE TRAGEDIES OF AN IMPERIAL ENDING

India's independence occurred formally at midnight between 14 and 15 August, to prevent it falling technically on an 'inauspicious' day for Hindus. This occasion evoked from Nehru one of his greatest speeches in the Constituent Assembly that 'at the midnight hour' India would awake to life and freedom.

> Long years ago we made a tryst with destiny, and now the time comes when we shall redeem our pledge, not wholly or in full measure, but very substantially . . . A moment comes, which comes but rarely in history, when we step out from the old to the new, when an age ends, and when the soul of a nation, long suppressed, finds utterance. It is fitting that at this solemn moment we take the pledge of dedication to the service of India and her people and to the still larger cause of humanity.[58]

The following day was full of pageantry and electric excitement, with huge crowds participating in the capital's celebrations: probably nobody, either British or Indian, had ever witnessed anything like it before. Of all the Congress leaders only Gandhi did not participate, but 'celebrated' what was for him the tragedy of partition by fasting in Calcutta.

Nehru, too, soon found that what should have been the personal and national triumph of an imperial ending turned to tragedy. Within hours of partition, the Punjab erupted into flames and violence. This was one of the provinces which was to be divided under the terms of the boundary award made known after independence because it had a small Muslim majority which had opted that one part should join Pakistan; but this meant that immediately thousands of Muslims and Hindus found themselves on the assumed wrong side of the new international border. Moreover, Punjab was home to the small but significant and cohesive Sikh community who felt that Congress and the League had ignored their interests, the more so when the areas where they were predominant were partitioned. The warning signs had been there in the preceding months, but no one anticipated the scale of the migrations and massacres which now took place, both in Punjab and to a lesser extent in Bengal.[59] No one community was the victim or the aggressor: Hindus, Muslims and Sikhs were all implicated and all suffered. Probably over a million died, often in circumstances of utmost and calculated brutality. Around 15 million people over time were uprooted and fled across the new borders, leaving all their possessions and land behind them, while thousands of women were systematically raped and abducted in profoundly symbolic assertions of community identity and humiliation of the opponent through violation of the female person and body.

This plunged the new government of India into crisis, and Nehru and Patel with Mountbatten's cooperation set up an emergency committee chaired by the now Dominion Governor-General. It had to deal with a host of urgent problems which ranged from burying the dead, to arranging for the transport and settlement of refugees, to organizing the harvest in deserted Punjab villages. Violence had spread to Delhi, where there was a significant Muslim population, particularly in the old city. At the end of September Mountbatten told his daughter Patricia that he had never been through anything like it. 'The War, the Viceroyalty were jokes, for we have been dealing with life and death in our own city.'[60] Nehru ignored his personal safety and when he could leave his office desk, went out and about trying to quell the turbulence and to comfort the distressed. He admitted that they were all initially taken by surprise at the scale of the violence, and he was deeply affected by what he saw, turning to Mountbatten to unburden himself of his feelings of helplessness and sickness.[61] To Rajendra Prasad he was equally forthright, confessing that the violence had shaken him greatly and was even shaking his faith in his own people. 'I could not conceive of the gross brutality and sadistic cruelty that people have indulged in ... open murder committed in the most brutal way stalks everywhere and we hesitate to say much about it lest we may lose our hold on the people. I must confess that I have no stomach for this leadership. Unless we keep to some standards, freedom has little meaning, and certainly India will not become the great nation we have dreamt of for so long.'[62]

He did not hesitate to spell out in public as well as private what this meant for the identity of India, and the profound dangers in visualising India as for Hindus only, following the communal nationalism espoused by the Muslim League. In a top-secret note for the cabinet on the disturbances and future policy towards Muslims he spelt out the implications. Were they to aim at or encourage trends which would progressively eliminate Muslims from India, or were they to 'consolidate, make secure and absorb as full citizens the Muslims who remain in India? That, again, involves our conception of India; is it going to be, as it has been in a large measure, a kind of composite state where there is complete cultural freedom for various groups ... or do we wish to make it, as certain elements appear to desire, definitely a Hindu or a non-Muslim state?'[63] The 'nightmarish' quality of life, as he explained to an Indian diplomat abroad, and the experience of violence in the name of religion convinced him that the very foundations of India had been shaken and that they would have to rebuild the

1. With his parents, 1894

2. At Harrow

3. At Cambridge

4. With his father, Motilal, 1918

5. With his wife, Kamala, and their daughter, Indira, 1918

6. With Indira, Feroze and Rajiv, at Anand Bhavan, Allahabad, 1945

7. With his two grandsons, Rajiv and Sanjay, at Palam airport, New Delhi, 6 October 1949

8. Nehru and Gandhi, 6 July 1946

9. With Edwina Mountbatten, on the ramparts of the Red Fort, Delhi, 16 August 1947

10. With Winston Churchill in London, October 1948

11. Commonwealth Prime Ministers' conference, 21 April 1949, London

12. With Mao Tse Tung, Beijing, 21 October 1954

13. With 'Ike' and Mamie Eisenhower, 16 December 1956

14. With Chou en-Lai, New Delhi, 1 January 1957

15. With Indira Gandhi, President John F. and Mrs Kennedy, Washington, 1961

16. In London addressing a meeting in Trafalgar Square, 17 July 1938

17. At his desk, 28 February 1958

18. Nehru's funeral cortege passing the Lok Sabha (Parliament) building, New Delhi, 28 May 1964

19a and b. Front and (*facing page*) back of Teen Murti Bhavan, Nehru's official New Delhi residence

20. Bust by Jacob Epstein, located in the entrance to the Nehru Memorial Library,
New Delhi

foundations of their national life and identity. 'If the roots dry up, how long will the leaves and flowers continue?'[64]

Simultaneously another crisis seemed to Nehru to strike at the heart of the new India, and to imbue the experience of independence with acute danger. This was the future of the princely state of Kashmir. Within weeks of independence it was evident that Kashmir was the major problem facing Nehru's government, after the restoration of relative order in the areas torn apart by communal violence. The Hindu Maharaja had not yet chosen whether to accede to India or Pakistan; and he still held in prison Sheikh Abdullah, the leader of the state political party known as the National Conference, which had widespread support in the state, and had been in close alliance with Congress. Moreover under pressure of events in the Punjab, violence was beginning to occur in the area of Poonch within the state, where members of the Muslim majority were in virtual rebellion, while in the Jammu region, with its significant Hindu minority, violence against Muslims was being organised almost certainly with the Maharaja's connivance, and fuelled by Punjabi Hindu and Sikh refugees and the actions of one of India's most militant Hindu organisations, the Rashtriya Swayamsevak Sangh, the RSS. In early October Pathan tribesmen began to infiltrate from across the Pakistan border, with the tacit support and logistical help of Pakistan. The complexity of this situation should remind us that Kashmir's demography and internal politics were always central elements in what became the 'problem' of Kashmir, and that it was never solely one of Indo-Pakistan relations. Moreover, those internal politics were not static, and Nehru's government (and those of his successors) always had to consider the dynamics of Kashmiri society and politics in their calculations, as well as the ways in which these were influenced by movements and ideologies emanating from both India and Pakistan.

Kashmir was of vital importance to Nehru for a number of reasons. For personal reasons he loved Kashmir, particularly the beautiful valley, and considered it as the Nehru homeland. As he told Edwina Mountbatten, Kashmir affected him in 'a peculiar way; it is a kind of mild intoxication – like music sometimes or the company of a beloved person'.[65] Further, Kashmir represented to him many of the problems of India's undemocratic princely states; and he was convinced that in order to achieve any stability in a turbulent situation the Maharaja would have to come to terms with popular opinion in his state, and this meant an alliance with Sheikh Abdullah and the National Conference.[66] In the immediate circumstances of Partition Kashmir had taken on an even greater significance in his thinking. It was one of the few key routes to the north, and bordered Afghanistan, Russia and China, and therefore strategically it was essential for India that it did not fall into unfriendly hands or collapse in disorder.[67] Moreover, as Pakistan was confessedly a Muslim state, India's claim to be a secular state for a nation composed of many religions, in his words a 'composite nationality', was in a sense proven by the accession of Kashmir to India and the free choice of Muslims to stay within India. He wrote privately in November that Kashmir was undoubtedly going to be a drain on India's resources but it was an example of communal unity and cooperation. 'This has had a healthy effect in India and any weakening in Kashmir by us would create a far more difficult communal situation in India.'[68]

Events reached a climax in late October when the terrified Maharaja fled from his capital, Srinagar, in the face of the tribal advance, and appealed for India's help. This India was prepared to give if Kashmir was part of India, and the ruler signed the Instrument of Accession, flown to him by the indefatigable V. P. Menon, the ICS man who was Patel's right-hand man in dealing with the princes. In making this decision the Cabinet Defence Committee also insisted that the Maharaja should invite Sheikh Abdullah to form an interim government, and committed itself to giving the Kashmiris themselves the opportunity to express a final opinion on the ruler's accession to India, though 'any reference to the people can only take place when law and order have been fully established'.[69] Forthwith Indian troops were airlifted to Srinagar and secured the city. Jinnah was prepared immediately to send in the Pakistan army, but drew back once he realised that Britain would withdraw all its remaining army officers in India and Pakistan if war formally broke out between the two Dominions.[70]

Although Nehru was by no means the most 'hawkish' of his cabinet, he told T. B. Sapru, his father's old colleague, how it would have been 'unbearable agony for me to remain a silent witness to the sack and ruin of Kashmir'. He felt they had rescued Kashmir from collapse and from forced accession to Pakistan. He also hoped that as people from all communities were engaged in the defence of Kashmir it would help the communal situation in India, for, as he told Attlee, if the raiders had 'reached and sacked Srinagar this would have had very far-reaching consequences over [the] communal situation all over India'.[71] However, he was well aware of the precarious nature of Hindu–Muslim relations at least in Jammu, and urged Patel to try to prevent Hindu communal organizations fomenting further trouble there and to be sensitive about the community of the Indian troops operating there, lest any handle should be given to Pakistani propaganda.[72]

Mountbatten meantime worked anxiously to try to achieve a resolution of this conflict, which promised to be so damaging to the two Dominions, but Jinnah and his Prime Minister insisted that the Maharaja's accession to India was illegitimate, and would not countenance any withdrawal of the invaders while Indian troops remained; while Nehru insisted that a referendum, under United Nations auspices, could be held only when peace and order had been established.[73] There was, in fact, strong feeling in the National Conference against such a referendum; and Nehru understood and to an extent shared this feeling. However he recognised the importance of world opinion, and particularly opinion within the UN, and did not wish to harm India's cause by any apparent backing down on a public commitment. But he gave Abdullah the assurance that in existing circumstances any refer-endum was an academic question and out of the question for months.[74] Mount-batten meantime was casting round for ways of controlling a situation which seemed to threaten outright war between India and Pakistan; he even suggested that Attlee might fly out to meet the two prime ministers. Eventually he persuaded Nehru to refer the whole dispute to the UN, though the terms he envisaged of such a reference were unclear. His main hope was that the UN could in some way help to stop the fighting. Nehru and his cabinet felt passionately that they were the aggrieved party and therefore could not make a joint reference to the UN with people they perceived of as aggressors, and as Pakistan denied complicity India could not ask the UN to arbitrate between India and a bunch of invaders with no formal standing as a state. Consequently India made reference to the UN on New Year's Day, asking the body to note Pakistan's assistance to the raiders and to insist that it should refrain, though India retained the right of military self-defence.[75]

In the light of subsequent events the wisdom of Mountbatten's strong advice to Nehru to involve the UN is questionable. It internationalised the whole problem, eventually involving Kashmir in the international politics of the Cold War, and provided a platform where both India and Pakistan could parade their views, thus hardening positions and militating against more discreet diplomacy, until the issue came to be seen as critical for the identity of both states, though in different ways. However, at the time it must have seemed, at least to Mountbatten, a device to stave off war, at a time when the UN seemed to embody a new international idealism and the Commonwealth was still primarily an embodiment of the old empire and therefore not acceptable as a potential mediator between its two newest members.

For Nehru the experience of independence was marked by a final, crushing tragedy, the assassination of Gandhi late in January 1948. Although Gandhi had played virtually no role in the negotiations immediately preceding independence, he had hurried to Delhi to help in the extreme circumstances which engulfed the city soon afterwards. He was in a number of ways an important and stabilising presence outside the new government but acting on its key members. As so often before, his was a mediatory role. In mid-January (without confiding even in Nehru) he embarked on yet another fast for communal amity, but he incorporated into its rationale the vexed question of the payment to Pakistan of the agreed share of the cash balances with the Reserve Bank of India at partition. A balance of Rs 55 crores (about £30 million at exchange rates then) was still outstanding, and India had withheld this sum in view of the conflict over Kashmir. Mountbatten had been unable to persuade the cabinet to release the money, but when Gandhi began to fast, and after Nehru and Patel had been to see Gandhi, the cabinet capit-ulated. Nehru accepted that this was a U-turn, but insisted that it was a gesture of goodwill which should lessen tension with Pakistan just after India's reference of the Kashmir issue to the UN. He also hoped that it would strengthen India's standing and claims in the international arena.[76]

Gandhi was also the one person who could potentially deal with the friction which was building up between Nehru and Patel, his Deputy Prime Minister. This had reached such a pitch by the end of December that it was even the subject of public gossip. Ever since their entry into the politics of nationalism in Gandhi's orbit at the close of the First World War they had both been significant Congress figures, though Patel was always more rooted in the politics of his home region, Gujarat, and was much more adept at managing the party. They had very different temperaments, and Nehru's more flamboyant style and self-possessed cosmopolitanism had often jarred on the older Patel. Moreover, the one was conservative on socio-economic issues, while the other was a self-confessed socialist. Patel's attachment to Gandhi was also strengthened by his sense of the vital importance of Hindu culture in the making of the new India, compared with Nehru's assertion that Hinduism was holding India back from becoming a modern nation. This now led them to have very different sensitivities towards Hindu refugees from partition, and the place of Muslims in India. Gandhi had mediated between Nehru and Patel, among other members of the Old Guard, in the past, and now they both turned to him when tension reached breaking point.

On top of existing sources of friction there was the crucial issue of Nehru's role and style as Prime Minister, in particular his intervention in matters properly belonging to particular ministries. To Patel, Nehru's understanding of this new role was leading him perilously towards virtual dictatorship, in opposition to both democratic and cabinet government. Nehru felt that in order to play a coordinating and supervising role he had to have freedom to act when and how he chose.[77] To Mountbatten it was evident that in this difficult and unprecedented situation, where both men were learning the ropes of central government, both had on occasions 'trespassed' on each other's official territory, but he bluntly told Nehru that even Winston Churchill in the heyday of his power would not have dared to ride so roughshod over his ministers as Nehru seemed to be doing. He warned him that feeling in the cabinet over his high-handedness and interference was far deeper than he knew, even among his most devoted and apparently uncomplaining colleagues.[78] Gandhi spoke individually to Patel, Nehru and Mountbatten, and arranged to see them altogether on 31 January: but the meeting was not to be.

Gandhi was staying at Birla House in New Delhi as a guest of his wealthy supporter and admirer, G. D. Birla. Each day he held a prayer meeting which all could attend, and though there were police guards in view of the strong feeling among some Hindus about partition, he had refused the pleas of Patel, as Home Minister, to let the police search those who came, for he believed that the divine Rama was the only sure protection. On 30 January as he was walking to the prayers in the early evening a young Hindu man jostled to the front of those assembled and shot him three times at point-blank range. Gandhi slumped to the floor, dying, with the name of Ram on his lips. His body was taken inside and laid quietly to rest, supported by sobbing women devotees, while his male colleagues from the government and the party arrived and stood silently in stunned grief. Mountbatten came as soon as he heard the news, and the press attaché who accompanied him found the occasion one of the most moving and emotionally charged he had ever experienced. Beside the grief there was a sense of victory – that the strength of Gandhi's ideals, evident in the great devotion now displayed, would 'prove too strong for the assassin's bullets and the ideas they represented'.[79] Mountbatten brought Nehru and Patel together in a dramatic embrace, after telling them that Gandhi's dearest wish was to reconcile them.

Nehru looked inexpressibly sad and careworn, and cannot have been unaware of the possible danger to himself. But he steeled himself with utmost discipline to make arrangements for the cremation the next day, according to Gandhi's wishes, and for the body to be placed on a table outside so that the great crowds which gathered could file past for a final *darshan* and pay their last respects throughout the night. He and Patel both broadcast to the nation within hours. With no time for preparation, Nehru's way with words caught the moment as he spoke of the light which had gone out from their lives, leaving darkness everywhere. Yet that light had not gone out for it would continue to illumine India, the world would see it and it would give comfort to many hearts. 'For that light represented something more than the immediate present; it represented the living, eternal truths, reminding us of the right path, drawing us from error, taking this ancient country to freedom.' Indians would have to root out the poison which had spread among them and had ended Gandhi's life; they should hold together with dignity and without violence, for 'in his death he has reminded us of the big things of life, the living truth, and if we remember that, then it will be well with us and well with India'.[80] The following day he accompanied the body in procession to the banks of the Jumna River, outside the old city, among crowds as vast as those who had celebrated freedom a few months before, and witnessed the harsh reality of a cremation on an open fire, consuming the remains of the man who had been closer to him than any other except his father.

Nehru had lost a mentor and patron, one who had given him a vision of the politics of passionate idealism, had ushered him into the nationalist movement, and had managed his often turbulent relations with other leaders in the Congress Party. They had disagreed on a whole range of issues, some of them profound, and they had differed greatly in style. Yet Nehru had remained loyal to Gandhi, believing that he was essential to the unity of the national movement and its appeal beyond the educated and urban. While Gandhi, for his part, had nurtured Nehru as his successor in leadership, convinced of his integrity, and his commitment to the country above any personal gain, and sure that despite their differences of opinion they shared a determination that independence would mean more than political freedom, and would lead to changes in the lives of those at the base of society. Moreover, between them there had grown a bond of affection which sustained them both. Now the younger man, who was himself now, at nearly sixty, well on in middle age, faced a dangerous and uncertain future without the one to whom he was accustomed to turn for advice and help, and without the influence of the person who had helped to keep Congress colleagues working together, in however uneasy an alliance. For him the experience of independence had become one of exhaustion, sickness to the point of despair at violence among those who should have been brothers, and now the heartache of grief.[81] Yet there was no time for private mourning or for rest, as the magnitude of the issues India faced summoned all his energies and his vision of what might be built to replace the India of the British raj.

## Part 4

# Founding a Nation, 1948–1956

# Chapter 10

# Imagining the Nation

After the death of Gandhi, Nehru became the key figure in the processes of founding the newly independent Indian nation and creating a nation state to replace the British raj. At home and abroad he became recognised as the architect of the new India, and he saw his own life as now totally political and dedicated to this goal. Half a century later historians and political commentators view the enterprise of resurgent nationalism and the building of nation states, in India and elsewhere, with considerable intellectual reservations, and a sharpened awareness of the deep ambiguities and conflicts which have been the result both in relations between nation states and in the socio-economic and political interactions within states claiming to represent new nations. However, later observers need to make a leap of imagination to grasp something of the immense enthusiasm and sense of heroic destiny with which many of Nehru's contemporaries approached these issues after the Second World War, when it seemed that the decline of European empires would lead to a new world order, and also to the creation of post-colonial states which would serve the needs of their people as alien rulers had not done. These optimistic visionaries and activists included not only Asians and Africans, most closely touched by the processes of decolonisation, but also sympathisers in the western world.

Yet nations are profoundly complex historical phenomena, however clear their identities and pedigrees may seem to their protagonists. Historically they have emerged in the modern world in very different historical contexts which have worked to convince groups of people that they belong together at some deep level and share a unique bond, one that takes political precedence over other loyalties. In practice nations have sometimes been created out of long historical continuities of shared experience, or out of combinations of revolutionary or anti-imperial struggles that marked more abrupt breaks with the past. All assume that a nation state is their political fulfilment.

*3. Independent India before the reorganisation of the states (also shows Pakistan and the cease-fire line in Kashmir)*

However, processes of nation-building do not stop at this moment of political fruition. Nations have to go on being constantly re-created in the experience of those who compose them, particularly in the context of decolonisation, when the common enemy against which nationalists defined themselves, the former imperial power, has been removed. This work of re-creation has a number of key aspects, and if one or more is lacking the national group can split apart or its sense of commonality may weaken, while the state can come to represent and serve the interests of a small segment of the so-called national community. There is, fundamentally, the work of imagining the nation, of establishing it in the hearts and minds of its members with a rhetoric of identity and belonging, and of endowing it with symbols which display the meaning and nature of the national community and have deep emotional resonance. More prosaic is the task of structuring the nation and giving it political shape. Political institutions have to be created or adapted from the past to provide for decision-making according to the expectations of those who consider themselves as belonging, and the norms which flow from their shared sense of identity, and to link state and society in new and more responsive ways. Moreover, there is often an urgent need to work to forge an expanded understanding and reality of shared nationhood, particularly where large swathes of the population or critical segments of it have effectively been excluded from the initial processes of nation-building. Proving the value of national belonging is a continuous process, for as the years pass and new generations inherit the nation, there needs to be a reforging of shared identity, often in the context of rapid socio-economic change. Finally, where there is an abrupt political break with the past, the new nation has to be installed in the international order and has to fashion the guiding principles of its international persona.

The Nehru who came to political maturity as Gandhi's apprentice and colleague was a nationalist visionary as well as activist. But he was also an intellectual, who was increasingly widely read in the history and politics of his times, not least because of the leisure enforced on him in prison. After his early financial excesses in Cambridge and London his only serious expenditure above the running costs of the family was on books. He understood many of these issues of nation-building not only in relation to India, but in broader theoretical and historical terms. He also recognised that India as a nation in 1947–8 had a deeply ambiguous inheritance. He had realised since the early 1920s that the nationalist movement had often been deeply irrelevant to and detached from large sections of Indian society, however hard he tried to press Congress towards a commitment to a mass movement, with all the implications for new styles of leadership, new strategies and new goals. In his view even Gandhi, despite his passion for a swaraj, which implied moral and socio-economic transformations, had often, for the purposes of unity, masked some of the fundamental cleavages of interest and ideology which a new India would have to address. The nature of the Indian nation was now, ironically, even more at issue, in the particular circumstances of independence. The common opponent, the British, against which Congress had identified the Indian nation, and in opposition to which it had just managed to cover over its own internal divisions, was now gone. Moreover, the manner of the imperial ending had generated violence in the name of religion, which now so embittered relations between Indians, and between India and a Pakistan which defined itself in religious terms, that the definition of being Indian was a critical and reopened question.

Nehru also recognised that although India had done comparatively well out of the division of the subcontinent, in terms of territory, population and resources, the very fact of continuity with the preceding regime would be a barrier to creating structures and styles of governance which were national rather than imperial. How could the inherited structures and norms of government, evolved to meet imperial needs but which had become so deeply embedded in Indians' own practice, now be geared to serving new needs and pursuing new goals?

Given this very considerable intellectual grasp of the dilemmas facing India, Nehru consciously set himself and his government to the immense tasks of creating a new nation and its means of self-articulation and reconstruction. As he said in 1954 in a speech ranging over many aspects of national reconstruction, 'Almost all of our activities are aimed at laying the foundation of a new India.'[1] For himself this was a punishing role because he became not only Prime Minister and Minister for External Affairs, but Chair of the Planning Commission and for some years President of Congress. But he felt they were all essential if he was to fulfil his vocation of making a real difference to his country, of engaging with the task of creation to which he had for so long aspired and which he had feared time and age might have snatched from his grasp. This section therefore looks at four major aspects of the work of nation-making that he set himself, in order to understand his early years as Prime Minister and through them a critical phase in the history of modern India.[2]

## IMAGINING THE NATION

Western imperialism in the nineteenth and early twentieth centuries was the context for some of the most articulate and elaborated imaginings of the self and the other, both by imperial rulers and their subjects. India was a particularly fertile ground for such intellectual and emotional constructions, given the length of British rule on the subcontinent and the resulting interactions of different and deeply rooted cultures. British images of India and Indians emerged in the nineteenth century which justified British rule, while Indians in turn constructed their own images of themselves and their rulers, drawing both on their own cultural traditions and the norms associated with western education.[3]

Nehru was more articulate than most of his contemporaries about his own 'discovery' of India, as his book of that name shows. He recognised that his India was the result of a personal intellectual and emotional journey of exploration. He brought with him on that journey a mixture of intellectual baggage, including his western liberal training, superimposed on his father's own understanding of India's current weaknesses, a historical sensitivity to India's historical diversity and cultural depth, exposure to Gandhi's imagery of a spiritual and rural civilisation superior to anything that passed for civilisation in the modern western world, and a reflective sense of the power of socio-economic forces that stemmed from his sympathy with Marxist understandings of historical change. Nehru did not feel that there was any essential difference between India (and Asia as a whole) and the modern West; but he felt that Indian civilisation had for a time lost its creativity and its ability to respond to change, partly as a result of its religious and social formations, and that this had left it open to western imperialism, which was, by contrast, built on social and economic dynamism. But in his view now was the time when India could seize that rare historical chance, to which he had alluded at the midnight hour of independence. He set himself to spread the vision of a resurgent India, drawing on its own cultural roots as well as on many resources originating from outside India, which would fashion a new state and a new social order, and would become a force for peace and equality in the wider world.

At the heart of Nehru's vision of India was the conviction that it was a composite nation, born of a civilisation which over centuries had drawn from and assimilated the many religious and cultural traditions present on the subcontinent. It therefore followed that the nation state must be secular, not aligned with or identified with any particular religion, but providing for religious and cultural freedom for the many different groups within it. On this there could be no compromise. As he urged Chief Ministers in 1950, in one of his regular letters which he used to address major issues, 'There can be no half-way house and no sitting on the fence ... There can be no compromise on this issue, for any compromise can only mean a surrender of our principles and a betrayal of the cause of India's freedom.'[4] It was vital to hold on to this principle in the wake of the tensions between Hindus and Muslims which still threatened northern India in the wake of partition, and in view of the fact that Pakistan had founded its national identity on religion. But for Nehru theocratic notions of the state were not only destructive to India in particular but also to any nation which espoused them, for theocracy was outmoded and had no place in the modern world.[5] The stark contrast and choice he thus posed between theocracy and a secular state, between the modern world and a presumed outdated world, seemed to many a false one. He was soon to find himself at odds with many of his compatriots and indeed his colleagues in Congress who, while recognising India's diversity, felt that community and cultural identity were still profoundly important and an essential part of national identity. They feared that Nehru's insistence on a secular state denigrated these older loyalties and values and threatened to undermine the nation they had struggled for.

A sense of embracing the modern world was an essential aspect of Nehru's idea of India. This did not just mean abandoning such ideas as theocracy. It meant being prepared to embrace change, after reflection and rational discussion, and determining to take charge of change and use it for the good of the whole, in the fields of politics, society and the economy. Such a stance was, in his view, rooted in a basically scientific attitude to life. He was unabashed in his belief in and commitment to social and economic progress as essential to the new India, and argued that this in turn meant weakening old attitudes of acceptance, and creating political, economic, social and legal structures which would facilitate change.[6] Over the months and years which followed independence he elaborated what he meant by progress – in large part it was real change in the daily lives of ordinary people, without which there could be no genuine freedom. This did not mean subscribing to any particular 'ism' or socio-political theory, but dealing with urgent but wide-ranging problems. Writing on the seventh anniversary of independence he argued: 'The building up of new India has always seemed to me not merely a question of improving agriculture, industry, etc., important as that is. The social, economic and the community aspect of it is equally important.' There could be no economic advance without breaking down 'restrictive social customs', including caste divisions and barriers to women's full participation in national life. This in turn fed back into a new understanding of the meaning of being Indian. 'In fact, we cannot build up the unity of India unless there is this emotional awareness of not only political, but economic and social equality. When we talk about a secular State, this does not simply mean some negative idea, but a positive approach on the basis of equality of opportunity for everyone, man or woman, of any religion or caste, in every part of India.'[7]

Even before independence Nehru had spoken of the 'vast measures of social change which we envisage' and argued that Congress sought power in order to build a government which had legitimacy to pursue this goal.[8] Only a democratic national government, freely chosen by the adult population, could have such legitimacy, and could do for Indians what imperial rulers had had neither the motivation nor the power to attempt. Although authoritarian and dictatorial regimes could attempt to address poverty and inequality, he felt that by contrast only a democratic government could involve people in the processes of change and make them partners in the benefits and obligations involved in the work of the state, thus liberating popular energy as well as support.[9] Nehru had a horror of what he called 'narrow nationalism', and its potential for encouraging divisions at home and abroad, and he envisaged for India the development of a mature and tolerant sense of the nation, which would not only lead to unity and creative change at home, but would also extend beyond India to work for an international order also based on equality and committed to peaceful cooperation.[10]

How did Nehru attempt to spread his vision of the new India? One way was in his personal interpretation of his own role in Indian public life. He insisted that he was temperamentally unsuited for politics and a Prime Minister accidentally because of the force of circumstances rather than his own choice.[11] But he evidently felt that after Gandhi's death he was in a unique way called to embody as well as expound the values on which the new India should be based. He would build on his sense of being the 'Rashtrapati' (see above p. 128) and use it to new purpose.

Soon after Gandhi's assassination, Patel (as Home Minister and responsible for security) and Mountbatten (in his last months in India as Governor-General) took to the cabinet the proposal, which originated from Mountbatten, that Nehru should move from his modest New Delhi home on York Road to a new official residence, the former house of the Commander-in-Chief, built twenty years earlier as part of the grand imperial design of the new capital city. It was large and imposing, set in spacious gardens, and was considered potentially more secure as well as more befitting to Nehru's new role. Nehru himself disliked the idea of taking over a residence so redolent of imperial rule, but felt he had no option in the face of cabinet opinion. He moved into what now became known as Teen Murti House early in August 1948, assisted by Indira, who became his official hostess and eventually moved in with her two small sons, Rajiv and Sanjay, leaving her husband in Lucknow. The government's own hospitality organisation looked after the house and paid for official guests and entertainment, but Nehru paid the expenses of his own family and personal guests. He declined to take the entertainment allowance granted to all cabinet ministers, in view of the amount spent officially on his housing.[12]

Despite the imposing nature of his new residence, Nehru determined to live as simply as possible, almost certainly remembering Gandhi's insistence that Congressmen who came to provincial or national power should behave like servants of the people, rather than like their imperial predecessors. He continued to dress in Indian fashion (except initially when he went abroad and wore a western-style suit) and the family and their guests ate simply together. He had a modest staff, including one personal servant who had worked for the family in Allahabad, and a personal assistant, M. O. Mathai, who had independent means and worked for Nehru without salary. In Nehru's papers there is evidence of his anxiety about the money spent on the house, and its power costs, particularly at a time when Delhi was suffering a power crisis. He insisted, for example, in 1956, that air-conditioning should be taken out of his own bedroom, and that Teen Murti House should have a separate electricity meter (and he also enquired into the monthly electric bills for the President and some of his ministers!). He extended this concern for economy to his own travels within India, and asked for simple Indian food and no elaborate preparations for his visits.

He was also horrified at the level of security provided on his travels and its cost. After a security scare early in 1955 when a man with a knife got on to the running board of his car, Nehru was told by G. B. Pant, now Home Minister, that his wishes would not be consulted over security. Nehru commented to his sister that this was all 'rather silly' – obviously there was an element of risk but that was inevitable, and by contrast 'the Maginot line outlook is bad and dangerous'. His subsequent note on new security arrangements was acerbic, if not somewhat arrogant. It was also obvious that he felt constrained, even caged, by the presence of security personnel, and noted that he did not wish a security officer on the upper floor of his house, given that it was guarded downstairs and outside: 'I should at least be left in peace in my room on the upper floor.'[13] Moreover, he insisted on allowing members of the public to gather on the front lawn of the house, and on granting interviews to virtually everyone who asked for one. This was an essential part of his approach to the public, as he told a protesting Chief Minister. He had learned it from Gandhi and would not give it up.[14] His whole lifestyle was in a sense iconic of the new nation and also of the new relationship between government and people, in contrast to the contrived display of the imperial regime and British concern for social separation and security as a small group of foreigners. It was also evident that, although Nehru was no Gandhian and did not object to possessions as such, he was determined that the new rulers should be seen to be treating the country's scarce resources as trustees rather than making money out of office. He refused all monetary gifts and presents in kind of significant value, giving money presented to him to public purposes and charity, and sending gifts to museums.[15]

Nehru had never been a good manager of money, and indeed latterly somewhat cavalier about it, knowing that he could earn if necessary by his writing. Now as Prime Minister he received a regular salary, though at one stage he discreetly took a cut in this in a time of national financial crisis. But it is evident that he also earned a considerable amount from his royalties, and Mathai managed his tax affairs with good sense and efficiency. This cushioned the family financially, but also gave Nehru a comfortable and somewhat un-Gandhian base from which to take the high moral ground about standards in public life.[16] However, there is no evidence that he spent at all lavishly, except perhaps on books, and when abroad on presents for the close family, including toys for his grandsons. He also gave regularly to charity and to political causes.

Nehru sought to spread his vision of a new India by means other than his personal lifestyle. He also adopted a pedagogic role, exhorting and teaching Indians. Indeed, his condemnation of behaviour he considered unbecoming in the new nation was such that he sounded almost imperial in his criticisms of his compatriots. His tone was often one of exasperated paternalism. A top secret note circulating in the United States State Department in 1950 in fact called Nehru's attitude towards the mass of his compatriots 'Brahmanic'. 'He is their leader, their teacher, their critic; they look to him for guidance, not he to them. He does not tolerate their opposition.' Perhaps simplistically, and without recognising the consciously educational task he had set himself, it interpreted his attitude as deriving from his caste status, 'reinforced by his education in the aristocratic tradition of the English public school and university thirty-odd years ago'.[17]

Some of Nehru's most powerful criticism was launched against what he called 'disruptive tendencies' which threatened India's precarious unity, whether this was in the name of community, caste or region. He lambasted public demonstrations on a whole range of issues as childish, immature, and signs of a second- or third-rate nation. More narrowly he criticised those who indulged in 'vulgar' behaviour, particularly conspicuous consumption, when many of their compatriots were still desperately poor. The 'cocktail habit' in the capital received scorching criticism, as did the 'wasteful and vulgar illuminations of weddings' and other social occasions. Mindful of the need to inculcate modern, scientific patterns of thinking as integral to national identity, he also criticised those who still clung to astrology as a guide to public affairs – for example, on the date for the inauguration of the new Republic in January 1950, or over rumours that there would be war with Pakistan on a particular date in September 1951. He told a public meeting in Delhi on the latter issue that it was absurd to fall into astrologers' clutches and get into a panic unnecessarily. 'What I cannot tolerate is foolishness. What do we wish to make of our country? Do we want to make it a nation of brave people or a nation of sheep who would run helter skelter on the advice of astrologers? What is all this?'[18] Three years later he insisted that the UP government should remove astrological predictions from one of its annual information publications.[19]

It was not surprising that the assumption of such a schoolmasterly and superior tone should have riled people, even among his colleagues and friends. In 1953 one of his Chief Ministers took him to task for his public and personal denunciation in the AICC of a member who criticised an important measure of social reform, calling Nehru intolerant and undemocratic. Nehru was unrepentant, insisting that it was his duty to give the sort of lead he had.[20] Even an old UP colleague and member of the cabinet had warned him frankly in 1952 of the dangers of his style of leadership. Too much hero-worship of Nehru was potentially destructive of democracy, but also Nehru was prone to be supercilious and critical, and to say things which made people feel small. 'I very often feel nervous when you talk of pigmies and giants, of experts and ignoramuses.'[21]

The most dramatic assertion by Nehru of his own idea of India, his sense that he uniquely had the right vision of the nation and his determination to impose this on his Congress colleagues occurred in 1950–1 in a series of events which echoed the late 1930s when Gandhi and the Old Guard had ousted Subhas Chandra Bose from the Congress presidency by refusing to work with him. In the months before and immediately after independence Nehru had felt out of sympathy with many Hindus in Congress and in the Constituent Assembly, asserting that they were as much communalists as were those who claimed separate national status for Muslims. He was also deeply worried about those organisations which worked overtly for a Hindu vision of the new India, such as the Hindu Mahasabha and the RSS. Gandhi's death swung the tide of popular and political opinion and some of these were temporarily banned. However, from mid-1949 Hindu 'communalism' was again one of Nehru's most profound concerns: 'I have viewed with dismay and sorrow the narrow and communal outlook that has progressively grown in this country and which shows itself in a variety of ways. I shall cease to be Prime Minister the moment I realise that this outlook has come to stay and that I cannot do my duty as I conceive it.'[22] Or again, in early 1950 he told Chief Ministers (in relation to the actions of the Mahasabha): 'my mind is clear in this matter and, so long as I am Prime Minister, I shall not allow communalism to shape our policy, nor am I prepared to tolerate barbarous and uncivilised behaviour.'[23]

For Nehru any claim that India was or should be fundamentally a Hindu nation was an affront to his historical sense of India being a composite nation: he also saw it as profoundly dangerous in a situation when partition and its aftermath had disturbed public opinion and left large groups of refugees distraught and dispossessed. The rhetoric of communalism also offended him culturally and socially, and his response echoed former imperial critiques of Indian behaviour, when he told a senior Congressman that he felt the situation was almost as bad as immediately after partition, and that speeches by 'Hindu communal leaders are practically incitements to murder. Worse than this, the grossest vulgarity is indulged in and the basest passions of the mob pandered to.'[24] It was his sense of the danger of such attitudes spreading within Congress which led him into further confrontation with Patel and then with P. D. Tandon, an old UP colleague and childhood acquaintance, when he stood for the Congress presidency in 1950.

In March 1950 it was clear that Nehru felt there were fundamental differences between Patel and himself on whether the new India should be at heart Hindu or secular, though Patel asserted that all he wished to do was to serve and strengthen Nehru in his last years, as he had promised Gandhi.[25] (Patel was in fact a sick man and he died in mid-December 1950.) A crisis was averted as Patel backed Nehru very strongly in dealing with a dangerous situation in Bengal as a result of the flood of refugees in both directions, by reaching a pact with his opposite number, the Pakistani Prime Minister, Liaquat Ali Khan, which bound both countries to safeguard their minorities. Patel's personal intervention in arguing for Congress support for the pact in Bengal drew congratulations from Mountbatten, who recognised how much this support for moderation must have cost him.[26]

However, within months Patel's ally, Tandon, stood for the Congress presidency. Nehru viewed this as a personal challenge to his own idea of India, as he felt that Tandon had already been party to the corruption of the UP Congress. To an old UP ally he voiced his hurt and anger. 'Our province pains me most, partly because of personal association, partly because of my pride in it. Congress work has completely gone to pieces and our friend, Purushottam Das Tandon, goes about talking about Hindu culture and telling Muslims to adopt it.' What this 'Hindu culture' was he did not know, for he felt that all that was best about Hindu culture was being 'violated' by such protagonists as Tandon.[27] He refused to stand for the Congress presidency himself, and made it plain to Tandon, to Patel and, more guardedly, to the public that he felt that Tandon represented a shift in

Congress away from the idea of India as a nation where people of all religions were welcome.[28] However at the end of August the ballot went Tandon's way, and he gained 1,306 votes, about 250 more than the seasoned Congressman, J. Kripalani, who had been put up to oppose him. There followed a full year of acute controversy within Congress.[29] Nehru's strategy was to work (albeit reluctantly) with Tandon in his Working Committee, but meantime to ensure that Congress publicly stood by its policies on key issues, including the question of whether the new India was to be secular, or whether they were to espouse a narrow form of nationalism, inimical to their minorities. He also tried to maintain the unity of Congress, which seemed to be perilously endangered.

However, as the crisis continued into 1951 control of the party became even more crucial for opposing groups, as the first general election was imminent. It became further complicated by the question of relations between the Congress Party and the Congress government. Ultimately Nehru resigned from the CWC and explained to Tandon that he felt that Congress was 'rapidly drifting away from its moorings and more and more the wrong kind of people, or rather people who have the wrong kind of ideas, are gaining influence in it. The public appeal of the Congress is getting less and less. It may, and probably will, win the elections. But, in the process, it may also lose its soul.' As he explained to the Bengali Congress leader, B. C. Roy, who attempted to mediate, the twin issues of the 'narrowing', communal outlook of many Congressmen and the issue of party control, via the President and the CWC, over the government, were behind this, and he was utterly clear in his own mind that this was the right decision.[30] Eventually Tandon stepped down, and in September 1951 the AICC elected Nehru as Congress President by 294 votes to 4.

Nehru had established himself as indispensable in the party organisation, and had confirmed the pre-eminent role of the prime minister over the Congress president in matters of policy and government. But from his own perspective perhaps the greatest gain from this whole painful period of turmoil was the platform it gave him to publicise his vision of India and to extract an affirmation by Congress that it shared his vision rather than Tandon's. In retrospect one can question whether men such as Patel and Tandon and those like them were communalist in quite the stark way Nehru (and some of his closest allies) portrayed. Both of them were more at home in vernacular politics, operating in a different style and a different idiom from Nehru, who was happiest speaking English and deploying concepts and terms from western politics, including that of secularism. Both of them were also acutely aware of the fear and resentment among refugee groups and sought to assuage this; while Nehru, committed as he was to the vision of an Indian nation encompassing all religious groups, and disliking the intrusion of religion into politics in any way, was blind to the very real fears of many Hindus. Even Kripalani, who had stood against Tandon in 1950, had to warn Nehru of this,

telling him bluntly that many Hindus felt that they were not getting a fair deal
from the government, and believed that it was behaving like the British before it,
rallying the minorities to its side.[31]

In playing this pedagogic role Nehru sounded at times like Gandhi and at times
like his British predecessors. He combined some of the tone and content of
imperial criticism of Indians for sectional loyalties and communal identities, which
militated against a sense of national identity, with Gandhi's high moral tone about
religious unity and tolerance and his preparedness to walk away from the
Congress organisation if it would not accept his ideals. It was a lonely role, and
took a heavy emotional toll. It was not surprising that at times Nehru felt so
exhausted and imprisoned by the problems which beset his government and the
complexities of internal Congress politics that he experienced extreme self-doubt
and contemplated resigning the prime ministership. One such episode occurred in
March 1950, when the refugee crisis in Bengal was acute and many of his
Congress colleagues seemed hostile to government policy. He felt trapped behind
his desk, and wanted to be up and doing; and the memory of Gandhi's very
personal intervention in Bengal in the crisis of 1946 also made him wonder
whether he, too, might not make a difference working as a private individual in
the disturbed areas of Kashmir and Bengal. Eventually he decided to stay where
he was, encouraged by the pact with Pakistan, and a sense that he owed it to the
people who had entrusted him with high office, and also to the memory of
Gandhi.

Another dip in his confidence occurred in the autumn of 1954 when he told
Chief Ministers and senior Congressmen that he was feeling stale and uncreative
and was wondering if he should step down from high office for at least a while.
He was also aware that people were asking the irritating question 'After Nehru,
what?' and he felt this was bad for him and for India. Birla in the USA even read
about this in the *New York Herald Tribune* and told M. O. Mathai that he thought
Nehru was wearing himself out on small matters and should learn to delegate in
order to maintain his health and activity – because he was essential to the stability
of India. Krishna Menon, also in the US, pleaded with Nehru to remember how
crucial he was to India's role in world affairs. Nehru left for China soon afterwards
and was clearly given a new lease of life by his international role.[32]

Apart from his personal example and teaching, there were other media through
which Nehru endeavoured to encourage his compatriots to imagine and make real
a new India. Of major importance were the great set-piece statements of national
purpose, in the creation of which he was heavily involved. The greatest of these
was the statement of India's founding principles enshrined in the constitution,
which was hammered out in the Constituent Assembly from its halting beginnings
until its adoption of the new republican constitution on 26 November 1949. His
major individual contribution to this process in fact occurred before independence,

when he drafted and then moved in the Assembly a resolution laying down its objectives.[33] These included the declaration of India as an independent republic in which all power and authority were derived from the people. In the new India everyone should be guaranteed social, economic and political justice, equality of status and opportunity, and freedom of thought, religion and association. More-over safeguards would be provided for minorities, backward and tribal areas, and those at the base of society. In the subsequent discussions and drafting of the new constitution Nehru, Patel, Rajendra Prasad and A. K. Azad were the most influ-ential of the small group who effectively steered the deliberations. Nehru himself chaired three of the most important of the Assembly's subcommittees – those dealing with the princely states and the constitution and subjects of the future Union government.[34]

When the constitution was completed it not only provided for the way in which the country would be governed, it also laid down the fundamental principles on which the nation was founded and according to which government would func-tion. Nehru's vision of India (and his 1946 draft of objectives) were clearly embodied in this seminal document of national identity. The people through the constitution pledged themselves to constitute a republic and secure for its citizens justice, liberty, equality and fraternity. This was elaborated in the section on funda-mental rights and the directive principles of state policy. The former were to be justiciable, and included rights to equality and to various freedoms, including culture and religion; while the latter were not enforceable in a court of law but bade the state to promote the people's welfare through the formation of a social order based on social, economic and political justice. Whatever the subsequent failures to live up to these ideals and sentiments, this was a formidable statement of national intent, designed to declare publicly the nature of the new national community which should replace the India of the raj.

Once the new constitution was in place India embarked on another major national enterprise, that of general elections for the first time on an adult suffrage for all men and women aged twenty-one and over. Nehru seized this opportunity to present to all Indians his vision of their nation, and he drafted the Congress election manifesto, which was published in the press after its adoption by the AICC.[35] It was a discursive document, as much about ultimate goals as immediate policies, and reiterated the theme that political freedom had to be translated into economic and social freedom through careful economic planning, welfare and labour legislation, improved education and public health, and special care for the most underprivileged, including the lowest castes and women. It also reiterated that as India was a secular state, all citizens had the same duties, rights, privileges and obligations, and the state itself had a particular duty to protect the right of minorities and enable them to play a full part in the economic and public life of the country.

Nehru personally played a very significant role in the electoral processes, both in choosing and vetting over 4,000 candidates and in demanding electioneering tours, for he was now, in late 1951, Congress President after the ousting of Tandon. He admitted to finding the business of organising the election and choosing candidates 'heart-breaking'.[36] He was distressed by the quality of candidates, their motivations, and the internal Congress politicking in the choice of names. It all seemed a far cry from his image of a party dedicated to building a new nation, as aspirant candidates scrambled for nomination in the hope of power, as powerful politicians pushed their cronies, and as people metaphorically threw mud at each other. To his well-trusted Chief Minister of UP, G. B. Pant, he confessed that the 'election business is making me lose my faith in Indian humanity or, at any rate in a large part of it. I could never have imagined that many of our people could have sunk quite so low as they have done.'[37]

Although this aspect of the electoral process almost made him doubt the value of democracy, he found his personal electioneering exhilarating. For about ten weeks he lived a nomadic life, constantly on the move, covering over 25,000 miles by air, car, train and boat. He addressed vast crowds; and by the end he thought he had addressed about 35 million people. He loved the personal contact with ordinary people this involved, and despite the physical demands on him, probably found it a great liberation to get out of Delhi. But above all for him it was a chance to spread the vision of a new India on the march, and the vital role of Congress in the regeneration of India.[38] Moreover the sight of millions of voters, many of them illiterate and women who had never previously played a public role, now peacefully using the ballot box was a display of the new nation at work, and one of which he was justifiably proud. Nearly 81 million votes were cast in around 132,600 polling stations, the turnout being about 46 per cent. (For electoral data see Appendix.) In 1952 this was a particularly dramatic assertion of India as a democratic nation. No other Asian or African part of the British empire had yet gained its freedom, and here was India proving itself to be the world's largest democracy, despite earlier imperial assumptions that India was unfit or unready for democracy, or that democracy could never take root in Indian culture and society.

Nehru was deeply aware of the significance of symbols and icons in the imagining and construction of India. Nobody who had worked closely with Gandhi could have failed to see how the Mahatma used his own life, body and clothing as a powerful symbol of a moral politics and of service to a new nation, particularly the poor, or forgotten his insistence on the spinning-wheel as a mark of unity across class and caste, and his castigation of dirt in public places as a sign of national weakness. India, like all other nations, began to adopt its own symbols to distinguish it from its status as part of the British empire. It had a new national anthem, and a new flag; it renamed many of its roads after luminaries of the nationalist movement or translated them into the vernacular; statues of viceroys and governors were put out to grass and replaced by ones of Congress leaders. Nehru argued powerfully for the symbolism in some of these decisions.[39]

He did not stop there. During these early years after independence, he continued to address a wide range of symbolic issues, some big and some apparently petty. But for him these were all part of the work of imagining the nation. He made suggestions for the appropriate dress of government servants, both those working in India and diplomats abroad on formal occasions, and even advised on the decor of Indian embassies abroad. He watched the behaviour of government servants, particularly those under his control in the Ministry of External Affairs, insisting that they should act in ways becoming to the new India. For example, in 1955 he banned a Foreign Service officer from importing a Cadillac into India and selling it at considerable profit. Nehru noted that times were changing and even he as Prime Minister felt out of place in a big car and preferred his Hindustan – the precursor of the Ambassador which was still the less than streamlined mainstay of the Indian motor trade until nearly the last decade of the century.[40] Weeks later he urged his Home Minister to clean up Delhi and even to ban cows from the city, and in Gandhian tones told him of 'the sins and lapses of our senior officers and others in regard to uncleanliness, etc.'. The greatest sinner of all was A. V. Pai, the Home Secretary of the Government of India. 'But if the Home Secretary himself collects cow-dung in heaps, what is one to do? . . . It is bad enough for the refugees to invade us and interfere with this [civic] cleanliness. But surely our officers and others should behave.'[41] Government corporations also came in for criticism for behaviour unfitting in the new India, and liable to reflect badly on the nation. Air-India began advertising its new service to Sydney with Koala bears, and the phrase that 'if you are good, we'll let you take a pretty hostess for a ride – Koala-like'. Nehru was sent this by the father of an Air-India hostess, and immediately told his Communications Minister to deal with Air-India as this was vulgar, improper and likely to have a bad effect on the national government.[42]

Symbols which aroused religious sensitivity were more difficult to handle. Temperance had been a strong element in the nationalist movement, since it enabled both opposition to the government's excise revenue and the display of behaviour conducive to social climbing among many Hindus. Gandhi had, of course, frowned on alcohol for religious and moral reasons. Nehru was realistic about prohibition after 1947 and argued that provincial governments should be very careful about giving up sources of revenue when India had such major social problems demanding government investment. He argued robustly that people were more important, and that it was worse to permit people to live in conditions which were a disgrace to the nation than to fail to adhere to the principle of prohibition. (He also suspected that prohibition did not actually lead to a decline in consumption because people merely made and drank illicit liquor.)[43] However he felt that attitudes towards alcohol were deeply symbolic in view of India's cultural traditions and her current poverty, and in 1955 in preparation for a visit to Russia he insisted that at no party given by him would alcohol be served, even if this upset his Russian guests. When he went to China the Chinese were told in advance that he did not drink and that the Indian embassy did not serve alcohol.[44]

Much more important to him were places of religious sensitivity, the handling of which were symbolic of India's commitment to public secularism and a care for all religious groups within the nation. He was deeply concerned about the placing of Hindu images in a mosque built on the site some Hindus believed was the birthplace of their deity, Ram, in Ayodhya late in 1949, and at the failure of the UP government to do anything about it, although relations between Hindus and Muslims were strained, and this was clearly an important test of the new secular state. His own failure to deal with this issue laid up one of the most profound challenges to Indian civil peace and to the idea of India at the end of the century. However, at this stage Nehru was not sure of his dominance in Congress and presumably did not wish to provoke a conflict with Pant, the Chief Minister, who assured him that he could deal with the matter locally.[45]

Another symbolic issue precipitated in 1951 a serious difference of opinion between Nehru and Rajendra Prasad, who had become the first President of the new Indian Republic in 1950. Prasad had decided to attend the opening ceremony of a Hindu temple at Somnath in Saurashtra, western India, which had recently been rebuilt, and felt there was no impropriety in doing this as the invitation had come from the local prince, who chaired the board of trustees, and because the temple had been built with private subscriptions. Nehru did not press the point, but was deeply concerned that the President should seem to be associated with a 'revivalist' affair, and that the local government should be setting aside considerable sums for the ceremony at a time of acute economic crisis when Nehru's government was preaching austerity and economy. He was acutely aware of the potentially negative symbolism if the national government was thought to be associated with the celebration of the opening of a new temple.[46]

Nehru also seized on positive symbols of the new India, exhorting his compatriots to see their significance. He was immensely proud of India's investment in hydroelectricity, flood control and irrigation, and for him some of the big new dams were powerful icons of modernity and the harnessing of science to the cause of building up the nation. (It was only later that people were to realise the human and ecological cost of some of these projects, as well as the potential significance of smaller water conservation and irrigation schemes.) Nehru hailed the Damodar Valley Scheme in early 1948 as 'the most notable piece of legislation that has ever been passed in this country'; and hoped that it would transform the economy of the countryside in parts of Bengal and Bihar in the same way as the Tennessee Valley Scheme in America, on which it had been modelled. Some weeks later he inaugurated the construction of Hirkaud Dam in Orissa, and was filled with a

great sense of enthusiasm and adventure as to what this might mean for the transformation of an area prone to flooding and erosion.[47]

The building of new provincial capital cities was also symbolic of a nation
building its own future, and embracing and managing change. He told his Chief
Ministers that he had laid the foundation stone of Bhubaneswar, the new capital
of Orissa, and how it was planned to serve the people who would inhabit it by
making it a city of self-contained neighbourhoods, while in the centre the public
buildings would be built round a memorial pillar symbolising Gandhi's life and
teaching.[48] The most dramatic new city, Le Corbusier's Chandigarh, was by
contrast conceived of as a city of government. It was to be the capital of Indian
Punjab, replacing Lahore, which was now in Pakistan, and Nehru saw it as a place
that symbolised India's new freedom, a break with the bonds of the past and an
expression of the nation's faith in the future.[49] In using new cities as symbols of
the new national community Nehru was in a long line of rulers of India who had
built their capitals to symbolise the nature of their rule, culminating with the
British and their construction of New Delhi only two decades before the end of
their raj.

But bricks and mortar were not the only way to symbolise the new nation. For
Nehru perhaps one of the most important living symbols of India's new beginning
was its women and the way they were treated. Gender issues and what become
known as 'the women issue' had for decades been at the heart of British and
Indian self-identification, with each group using the status of women as deeply
symbolic of their own civilisation. It was for this reason that social reform had
been such an emotive question among Indians for at least a century before independence. Women's symbolic representation of the nation as well as their biolog-
ical role as carriers of family and ethnic purity and honour also underlay the
horrific treatment of many women during the Partition violence. Rape, abduction
and forcible marriage were all means of stamping the mark of the opponent on the
victim, and dishonouring and violating the identity of the opponent, as they have
been in many other ethnic conflicts. The same reasoning was present in those who
killed their own women rather than let them be forcibly 'polluted' by men of other
communities, and in the state-sponsored attempts in the following years to rescue
women abducted from their families, ignoring the possible wishes of the women
as individuals at the prospect of 'rescue'. Nehru supported this work, known as
'recovery', and criticised those who were reluctant to receive their women back.[50]
He was ashamed at the scale of violence towards women by all communities, and
although the recovery programme embodied a patriarchal attitude of the state
towards women, he was also convinced that women would have to play a new role
in that state and in the broader making of the new India.

For Nehru the treatment of women was the touchstone of advance towards a
desirable modernity, and before independence he had argued that the nation's

progress depended on the position of its women. Now he threw his authority behind strategies which would make women powerful symbols of India's new nationhood, as well as contributors to national reconstruction. Women were immediately enfranchised under the new constitution. He insisted that women should be admitted to the Foreign Service and to the Indian Administrative Service (IAS) which replaced the ICS, and the 1951 Congress election manifesto, which he had drafted, committed the party to the removal of social disabilities on women so that they could play a full part in the re-creation of the country. 'Women are more responsible even than men for the next generation, and unless they are enabled to participate fully in all national activities, the progress of the nation suffers.'[51] He worried that not enough women would be elected to the new parliament, and when only nineteen were elected to the lower house of Parliament, the Lok Sabha, and fourteen to the upper house, he told Chief Ministers that this was not just a matter of injustice but of harming the future of the country. 'I am quite sure that our real and basic growth will only come when women have a full chance to play their part in public life . . . the future of India will probably depend ultimately more upon the women than the men.'[52] It was for the same mixture of symbolic and instrumental reasons that he also engaged in the often unpopular cause of reforming Hindu law, to give women a new legal status, arguing during the election campaign that a country could be judged by the status of its women.

Nehru as Prime Minister had by the mid-1950s expended a huge amount of energy on visualising a new nation and spreading his vision of what India should be like. His work to this end stretched from the way he managed his own life and household to major issues of national policy, and to apparently tiny issues which he felt symbolised the task ahead. By taking so much on himself, and attending to so many details, he tended to wear himself out and blunt his creativity, and those who valued his presence at the heart of India's national life and government warned him of the dangers of overwork.[53] Friends also warned him that his failure to delegate was damaging to the political system, since it stunted the creativity of others and held back the progress of younger politicians. Deep within him he almost certainly recognised this, but he was driven by the sense of having a special and vital role to play in making the nation. It was perhaps understandable that this volatile and energetic person, driven by a sense of his personal responsibility, should have swung between a style which could be hectoring and ruthless to periods of agonising self-doubt. Although he had longed to play a major part in the building up of a new India, within a few years of experiencing the reality of that role he was looking back with nostalgia to the days of the nationalist struggle and claiming that this was the most significant period of his life when he found the most fulfilment.[54]

# Chapter 11

# Structuring the Nation

This chapter is concerned with another aspect of Nehru's work in the complex processes of founding a nation – namely, providing it with political structures appropriate for its perceived nature and goals. Nationalist discourse had for decades argued that the colonial state in India was structured and operated for the benefit of the British rulers and their worldwide empire; and that independence would give Indians their own state, which would in contrast manage political power on behalf of the people and use it to do for them what imperialists could or would not do. Now the nationalist leadership faced the problem of fulfilling such commitments. This meant devising means so that power could be used for new ends – either by creating new political structures, or by working with the imperial inheritance and attempting to bend old structures to serve new purposes. It also meant attempting to link the state and its officials more closely to society, in contrast to the perceived isolation of imperial administrators and their lack of sympathy with Indian aspirations. It would almost certainly also mean reconstituting internal political boundaries and replacing those that had sustained imperial rule by constructing constituent units of the nation which more closely reflected popular aspirations and loyalties.

Nehru was deeply involved in such processes of structuring the nation, and not just because he was Prime Minister. Unlike Gandhi, who believed passionately that if swaraj was to mean more than political independence it would have to be grounded in a total moral transformation, Nehru was committed with equal conviction to making freedom a reality for all Indians through the exercise of state power.[1] He was not essentially a party politician, but was profoundly interested in political power because he felt that it was the only way to change India's society and transform its economy. It was partly for this reason that he had always been deeply suspicious of any move by Congress to take responsibility within the colonial state without real power. However, in the particular circumstances of independence another set of pressures impinged on his attitude towards structuring the nation. He had been horrified at the potential in 1946–7 for the 'Balkanisation' of India as the British withdrew, and now the unity of the country was one of his primary concerns. Moreover, the violence which surrounded Partition not only sickened him but convinced him that Indian society could easily disintegrate unless the state retained the capacity for firm government. Industrial unrest and subsequently Communist-inspired rural protest movements, as well as communal tension in the wake of Partition, confirmed his belief that only a strong nation state could hold the nation together and combat the forces of division which he saw as threatening the new India. Later observers need to appreciate the sense of multiple crises threatening India, which Nehru and some of his colleagues shared, as they tried to discern and create the most appropriate political structures for the nation.

## CREATING NATIONAL POLITICAL STRUCTURES

India's core political structures were established through the new constitution which came into effect in January 1950. However, much of it was not new. It drew very heavily on the 1935 Government of India Act, taking from it about 250 articles, and it was no surprise that the way government was structured and functioned bore such a family likeness to the imperial regime which had preceded it, despite its proclamation of new national goals and principles. India became a democratic federal state, with power divided between the central government in Delhi and the governments of the states which made up the Indian Union.[2] In Delhi the head of state is the President, but real executive power lies with the Prime Minister, chosen because he or she commands a majority in the lower house of Parliament as in the British system of government. Parliament itself is composed of the Lok Sabha, the lower house, whose members are elected, and the much smaller Rajya Sabha, or upper house, whose elected members are supplemented by some nominated by the President for their special expertise. In the states, structures of government in part mirror those in Delhi. There are state legislatures, to which members are elected (often simultaneously with national elections), and a Chief Minister operates like the Union Prime Minister, having secured command of a majority in the state legislature. Like Nehru in Delhi most Chief Ministers in these early years were the local leaders of the state Congress parties. However, the Governor of the state is appointed by Delhi rather than elected as the Indian President is, and though state governors play a ceremonial role similar to that of the President in the all-India polity, they are also the eyes and ears of the central government and act as its agents, in uneasy relationship to the elected Chief Ministers.

India's federation according to the constitution gives a dominant role to the centre. Power is divided according to three lists between the centre and the states – powers exercised by the Union, those by the states, and those which are concurrent. The centre deals with issues of national importance such as defence, foreign affairs, national finance and income tax, while the states have charge of local government, industry, agriculture, health and welfare, education, public order and land revenue. Concurrent powers include social and economic planning, and civil and criminal law. The centre's greater powers are confirmed by its greater access to revenue resources, and by the capacity of the centre to direct states to comply with central legislation, and in certain cases to take over government by a mechanism known as 'President's Rule'. It can also create new states and change state boundaries. Thus, the new national political structure reflected closely the imperial one, where ultimate power lay in Delhi with the Viceroy, despite devolution of power to the provinces. But now the rationale was not sustaining an imperial regime but holding together the new nation and enabling its elected rulers to pursue the national good as defined in the constitution.

However, from the perspective of Delhi and a reforming Prime Minister, there were uncomfortable limits to central power and influence. The states had authority over many of the problems that Nehru saw as critical to genuine change on the subcontinent, such as industrialisation, agriculture and education. As he discovered, states' failures of governance or indeed opposition could block central policies of change and visions of progress. Furthermore, electoral and party politics required cooperation between central and state politicians, and this in turn meant that any prime minister and central government would have to develop accommodative rather than combative relationships with their colleagues in state governments. A senior American academic and consultant on public administration, Paul Appleby, reporting in 1953, noted the irony that Delhi was dependent on theoretically subordinate states for the successful pursuit of programmes deemed essential for the new nation. At least one of Nehru's senior diplomats and intellectuals agreed with him and argued bluntly to Nehru that the centre did not have power commensurate with its responsibilities and intentions. Despite the centre's financial leverage and political authority, the major states were becoming more independent in areas reserved to them. 'The great states have in fact become satrapies, a tendency which cannot be avoided when outstanding political leaders have control of local government and of the political machinery of the State over long periods.'[3]

Politics and emerging practice determined the way the constitution worked in the matter of centre–state relations. In the same way the role of Prime Minister was effectively moulded by Nehru through his own patterns of political behaviour.[4] The formal political structures give the Prime Minister immense potential power in his powers of advice to the President, particularly in the choice of ministers, governors and holders of high judicial office, and in his reading of political situations which might require the exercise of President's Rule. He is the head and the lynchpin of government on a daily basis, assisted by ministers of his own choosing. Nehru, by virtue of his energy and ability, and his huge public repute within and beyond the Congress Party, used the potential available to him, dominating the cabinet and the Lok Sabha. Of course he had no predecessors on whom to model himself, and no precedents from within the Indian political system, and to an extent he made his own job. Given his commitment to economic reform and his role in the new Planning Commission (see below), his control over foreign affairs by virtue of being his own Minister for External Relations, and his sense of vocation to make profound changes in India, he worked like a human dynamo, and little in government escaped his notice and concern. It is debatable whether such a dominant, almost viceregal understanding of the prime ministerial role was dysfunctional for the Indian political system in the longer term, preventing serious delegation of authority to colleagues and encouragement to younger men to rise in governmental experience, and standing in the way of genuine cabinet government. But in the short term Nehru used his position within the new national structures of deliberation and governance to push forward a twin strategy of national consolidation and change.

One of the key issues in providing the new India with national structures was that of the nature of the administration. The Indian Civil Service, once called the 'steel frame' of empire, had been the focus of much nationalist opposition, because its members were responsible for carrying out imperial policy and were the most obvious and critical interface between the raj and its Indian subjects. Nehru was one of its sternest critics, and in the later 1930s was saying that it would have to go before India could create a new order, and that the spirit of authoritarianism could not coexist with freedom. He also felt that most ICS men, whether English or Indian, were not competent to do serious and specialist work outside their established administrative rut.[5] However, by the time he was working in the Interim Government his attitude had mellowed. He set his face against any general witch-hunt of members of the ICS after the experiences of the Quit India movement of 1942, and he was prepared to draw into the service of the new India any civil servants who were happy to adjust to the new situation and work for the new nation state. However, it was Patel as Home Minister after 1947 who argued most forcefully the critical need for a strong all-India service, with high morale, protected from the sort of political interference which would hinder administrative efficiency. It was Patel's influence and insistence which not only produced constitutional guarantees for those Indians recruited into the civil and police services under the raj, but also secured for their successors in new all-India police and administrative services (the IAS) independence from political interference, at least in the early decades of independence.[6]

Independent India was thus rapidly equipped with a civil service which had the same all-India status as its imperial predecessor, which recruited well-educated young people from families of considerable wealth and status, and which trained and moulded them to understand their role in ways which were very similar to those experienced by their predecessors, both English and Indian, in the ICS. The continuity and cooperation of Indian members in the ICS and the members of the new service in a period of considerable turmoil was important in giving India administrative stability, despite the departure of British administrators (and some Muslims to Pakistan) in 1947. Even Nehru recognised their significance, and privately admitted that they were almost the only effective tools on which the new nation could rely. By mid-1950 he was saying that the experience of the years since independence had convinced him that in dealing with communal tension the attitude of the local ICS/IAS official was crucial. In a tone redolent of his imperial predecessors he argued that 'where the men in charge are sound and competent and have clear ideas, there has been no trouble'.[7]

Although continuity in governance served India well in a time of acute civil stress, the civil service and its ethos, which India inherited from the raj, was a fundamentally conservative one, designed to deliver stability and an adequate flow of revenue. Its members were not modernising technocrats, but generalists who were expected to turn their hands to any governmental role. Moreover, as an educated elite with a guaranteed place in government, they were prone to see themselves, as their predecessors had done, as Platonic Guardians, with privileged knowledge, rather than as colleagues and enablers of the mass of citizens. Soon Nehru and a range of other observers of the Indian scene were commenting on the undesirable aspects of continuity in governmental styles and attitudes between the raj and the nation state. As early as 1950 Nehru noted that the civil servants and the police were tending to behave in authoritarian ways unbefitting to a democracy, and 'to revert to the days of British rule, when they looked upon the public as some kind of an enemy or opponent which had to be put down'. This was profoundly dangerous as it would alienate the national government from its own people, on whom it relied in the last resort for its existence and ability to function.[8] A UP Minister was even more forceful, telling Nehru in 1951 that the nature of government would have to change if they were seriously to engage with radical transformation. 'We inherited an administrative machinery which is not suited to present conditions. Individual exceptions apart, members of the Civil Services are strong repositories of conservatism. We have slipped into office routines which compel us to seek and rely upon their advice to a large extent. We have perpetuated the old type of Public Service Commission with the result that the new recruit to the services will be an almost exact replica of . . . his predecessors in office.'[9]

Others in and outside government pointed to the need for administrative reform, and to the way old attitudes and administrative procedures stultified efforts to effect genuine change. One particularly stern critic was T. T. Krishnamachari, who was Nehru's Minister of Commerce and Industry from 1953 to 1956 and particularly felt the brunt of administrative inertia in a ministry meant to be at the forefront of change.[10] Another was the American academic expert on public administration, Paul Appleby, whose advice was invited by the Government of India. He reported trenchantly in January 1953 on desirable ways of changing the outlook and methods of the administration. Nehru agreed that they had been far too hesitant in dealing with administrative reform, and that it was essential if India was to work for a welfare state.[11]

However, little practical was done, despite discussions in cabinet and the many papers on issues of administrative reform. In part this was because those in administrative posts were adept at fending off radical reform by mandarin practices of delay and deflection. It was also because of Nehru's own stance. He could see only too well the broad picture of the problem, but he was incapable of pushing through reform, partly because of the power of vested interests, but also because he was too busy and also temperamentally disinclined to work on the hard detail which would have been involved. Someone of Patel's standing and organisational grasp would have been required to deal effectively with such a deeply rooted and complex range of problems, which affected not only structures but attitudes and procedures. Nehru became deeply frustrated by the agonising slowness of government, his inability to achieve and implement swift decisions, and at the incapacity of structures of governance to manage policies of much-needed change. In 1954, for example, he was appalled to discover that neither the centre nor the states had been able to use to the full money allocated under the current Five Year Plan. The administrative machinery was responsible for this failure, but all Nehru could do was to comment that the machinery was designed for other purposes and that 'this has to be remedied'.[12]

Although Nehru failed to transform the structures of government he and his colleagues had inherited from the British, he did oversee the creation of two new structures specifically designed to address the new issues of economic development, which he saw as vital if the nation was to achieve the goals it had set itself at independence. One was the Planning Commission, created in 1950, when it was clear that government would have to take some major steps to solve the country's escalating economic problems, despite opposition from more conservative members of government and party, including Patel.[13] Nehru became its chairman, adding to his huge portfolio of offices and interests, but continuing the personal interest and enthusiasm which he had developed in the late 1930s. The role of the Planning Commission was advisory, but some Ministers and their colleagues began to feel it was interfering in their preserves and acting as a 'super-cabinet'. This Nehru stoutly denied.[14] To him the Commission was of great importance as a mechanism for wide-ranging thinking over the broad field of Indian development and for coordination of policy. But even he became worried that it was developing many of the attributes of a government department and was becoming engrossed in the details of administration. He began to feel 'quite out of it and quite unable to follow the trend of the Planning Commission's activities. I know that I cannot spare much time. But the result really is that I have to catch up later and spend more time and yet not understand what has happened . . .'[15]

Nehru's debilitating experience of attempting to press old administrative structures to fulfil new national purposes of social and economic change increasingly disposed him to rethink the value and strategy of self-help from below, rather than reform from above. This had been central to Gandhi's thinking, and remained a significant strand in political discussion after his death. Nehru now in the early 1950s began to argue that overcentralization was destructive, and initiatives and action by the people themselves would liberate new energy and commitment to change. In 1952 the Planning Commission initiated a small number of Community Development projects, and on this was built a National Extension programme in 1953, which aimed to provide village-level infrastructure for intensive agricultural development and the necessary social changes to sustain and enable it. As Nehru wrote to his Chief Ministers in September 1953, 'I attach the greatest importance to the new national extension scheme. It has in it the seeds of a great revolutionary change in India. If we can succeed that way, we can really change the face of India peacefully . . .'[16]

In September 1956 a new Ministry of Community Development was constituted, signalling the importance Nehru placed on strategies for involving village workers and ordinary citizens in the building of a new India. It could almost have been Gandhi speaking when Nehru said that their basic task was to strengthen and reform human beings. In this enterprise the task of community development schemes was 'to bring the message of hope to the masses of our people, to teach them self-reliance and confidence in themselves and the way to realise our objectives through hard and cooperative effort'.[17] He had recognised that the nation needed not only new governmental structures in order to pursue its proclaimed goals, but also ones which were founded on a new relationship between society and government, between citizens and officials. Their effectiveness, however, he could not guarantee, in the face of India's great diversity, deeply rooted patterns of social and political influence in local life, and the paucity of resources and responsibility allowed to them.[18]

## RECONSTITUTING POLITICAL BOUNDARIES AND COMMUNITIES

In India, as in many other territories that were once part of European empires, internal boundaries often reflected imperial patterns of conquest or strategies to elicit local collaboration, rather than being in any sense natural boundaries, defining local communities. The processes of decolonisation have thus often involved some reconstitution of administrative boundaries to reflect more closely local aspirations or a local sense of identity. In India the most urgent of these problems was the continuation of enclaves of authority other than that of the national government, particularly the areas under foreign control, and the princely states.

France and Portugal both had small areas of imperial dominion, mainly coastal enclaves, possession of which pre-dated British rule over the subcontinent and reflected the time when several European powers had political and trading interests in India. Independence from Britain did not change their status, and one of the most symbolically important aspects of structuring the nation was to bring them under the control of the national government. The issue of the French possessions was resolved peacefully in late 1954, after Nehru had shown considerable understanding of the domestic pressures on the French government, and had muted demands in India which might have jeopardised the diplomatic process. Moreover, French language and culture were given special protection after Pondicherry, for example, was incorporated into India.

The position in relation to the Portuguese territories, particularly Goa, was far more difficult. Portugal, under Salazar, was still committed to imperialism and unwilling to consider any transfer of its possessions to India; and Portugal's NATO allies, including Britain, appeared unwilling to bring pressure to bear, much to Nehru's disgust.[19] India had closed its delegation in Lisbon in 1953, but Nehru recognised that there was little more his government could do, committed as they were to a peaceful resolution of the problem rather than the use of force. Indeed, he sought to defuse a crisis in 1954–5 caused when Goanese exiles and Indian left-wing sympathisers in Bombay launched a non-violent agitation in pursuit of the 'liberation' of Goa. He was determined that his government would not be pushed into undesirable actions by local activists; and eventually when a number of *satyagrahis* were killed Nehru stopped the movement and sealed the border. Once again the issue had reached what was for Nehru a worrying stalemate. But he was determined that India should not use force, partly for ideological reasons, but partly as a matter of tactics, for non-violence would enhance India's international repute and show up the Portuguese as living in 'a medieval climate of mind'.[20]

The princely states were a further problem left over from India's imperial past, for they had very different political structures from those which had evolved in British India. The national government now faced the problem of integrating them into the nation state, following the emergency accessions Patel had worked to achieve with Mountbatten. Most urgent were those states where there had been no accession, or where accession had generated conflict. These stretched Nehru's diplomatic ability to deal with his fellow countrymen to its limit, and made him reluctantly recognise that at times non-violence might not be in the best interests of the nation state, particularly if its territorial integrity was at stake.

Hyderabad in southern India was one of the largest of the former princely states, whose income and expenditure in 1947–8 was roughly equal to that of Belgium. It could therefore have been a viable independent state in its own right, but it was landlocked by Indian territory, which meant that its independence would be a threat to the territorial integrity of India. Moreover, a majority Hindu population was ruled over by a Muslim Nizam, and this made it yet more sensitive a problem in the context of India's own communal tensions. Its fate would also have had a profound impact on the parallel problem of Kashmir, and India's relations with Pakistan. The Nizam had reached only a standstill agreement with India in 1947, and it was evident that he was arming himself with legal advice as well as weapons in order to achieve independence, or even accession to Pakistan. Nehru assured his Chief Ministers in March 1948 that he had no wish to force a full accession on Hyderabad, and it was for the people of the state to decide; but neither could India permit Hyderabad to continue as 'an autocratic feudal state while the rest of India becomes democratic'. In private he confessed he felt that those who wielded power in Hyderabad were 'a lot of bigoted fools and I fear they will do much mischief'.[21]

The situation rapidly escalated out of control on the ground as Muslim militants began to turn on the population with the connivance of the state, at the same time as a Communist-inspired peasant movement began to 'liberate' villages from their landlords and redistribute land to the peasants. Public opinion in India was in favour of decisive action; and by late August Nehru noted semi-humorously that there was a general impression in India that he was the only one standing in the way of action. (He was not: Mountbatten tried to find a peaceful outcome until his departure from India in June 1948.) But Nehru had become convinced that it was impossible to solve the Hyderabad problem except by military action.[22] On 7 September he addressed the Constituent Assembly, explaining that free and democratic India could no longer tolerate the presence of an enclave of autocratic rule within it, nor could it permit such violence to continue in the geographical heart of India. Hyderabad was in an organic interrelationship with the power which ruled India as a whole, despite the lapse of British paramountcy, and both had mutual obligations towards each other.[23] Within days the army had moved into Hyderabad, and the Nizam acceded to the Indian Union.

There was considerable international unease at this exercise of force, not least in Britain, where Attlee had to work hard to mute Conservative criticisms of Nehru and his government's treatment of a former princely ally of the British raj.[24] For his part Nehru was pleased at the smoothness of the operation, and relieved at the calming effect it appeared to have on relations between Hindus and Muslims throughout the country, writing of being 'relieved of a nightmare' in this respect. However, his concern with the integrity of the nation state was central to his understanding of the problem Hyderabad had posed. 'Once for all we have solved the problem of the paramount authority of the Central Government in India all over India. Of course we do not want any paramountcy in the old sense of the word but it is clear that no dissident element is going to be permitted to challenge the Central Government.'[25]

Kashmir proved an ongoing challenge of a dual kind to Nehru's government, and to the integrity of the nation state. There was the international aspect of the situation, as India and Pakistan disputed the status of the territory in the wake of India's reference of the issue to the Security Council of the United Nations. But perhaps even more challenging was the internal problem of governance, as Nehru's government in Delhi strove to find political allies in a state riven by internal tensions who could command a degree of loyalty and guarantee the state's adherence to India.

The international dimension of the Kashmir issue and its long-term effects on Indo-Pakistan relations is well known. It has generated huge controversy about the role of Indian, Pakistani, British and other UN participants in the unfolding of the conflict, from the initial outbreak between India and the invaders backed by Pakistan and eventually assisted by Pakistan troops; to the cease-fire brokered at the end of 1948 by the UN; and the subsequent failure of mediation between the two neighbours, despite Nehru's initial agreement to a Kashmiri plebiscite on the state's future.[26] From the perspective of India's own national structures, however, the international stalemate on Kashmir had created a *de facto* solution. The cease-fire line became in effect an international border and in India it was becoming accepted that this border should be the basis of the long-term solution of the conflict with Pakistan. Rajendra Prasad, as President of India, told Nehru in 1953 that he felt Kashmir should be divided along the existing line without a plebiscite – on the grounds that it was not at all clear that Kashmiris would choose India if a plebiscite involved the whole state, and that even in the event of a pro-Indian choice, India would be faced with a turbulent and hostile population in what was known as Azad or Free Kashmir. Nehru, too, was coming round to the view that any solution to be reached with Pakistan would be best achieved on the basis of the status quo.[27] He was sceptical of the role of the UN in effecting any solution, not least because he felt that Britain and the USA were playing a pro-Pakistan role. Moreover, he became convinced that appropriate conditions did not obtain for a plebiscite, given the presence of Pakistani troops in Azad Kashmir, and then in 1954 the military alliance between Pakistan and the USA, which appeared to place further force at Pakistan's disposal and encourage aggressive postures on Kashmir.

Although the *de facto* border in Kashmir was stable by the early 1950s, Kashmir's place within the Indian Union was deeply problematic. For Nehru the willing presence of predominantly Muslim Kashmir within India was an icon of India's composite nationality and the secular nature of the state, as well as being of strategic importance. He put this forcibly to his old friend, Stafford Cripps, who had pleaded with him late in 1948 to try to achieve a settlement on the issue with Pakistan.

> If Kashmir went, the position of the Muslims in India would become more difficult. In fact there would be a tendency of people to accept a purely communal Hindu viewpoint. That would mean an upheaval of the greatest magnitude in India. And I am quite convinced that it would be complete ruin of Kashmir if it went over to Pakistan. A barbarous lot of people would over- whelm some of the most cultured and intellectual people of India. But the real question to consider is how far the settlement in Kashmir would affect the rest of India.[28]

To achieve a stable Kashmir within the Indian Union proved even more difficult in terms of its internal politics and their interaction with the rest of India than the case of Hyderabad. Initially Nehru and his government put their trust in an alliance with Sheikh Abdullah and his National Conference party, which seemed to have widespread popular support, as the basis for reconstructing the polity of the former princely state. Nehru and Abdullah were old friends and allies, and Congress had supported him in his conflict with the Maharajah before independ- ence. However it soon became apparent that Hindu elements in the state were hostile to Abdullah and his policies. Hindus predominated in the Jammu region of the state (as opposed to the Valley of Kashmir itself) and they were alienated by the narrowly Muslim-Valley basis of Abdullah's government, and by his radical policies which hurt their interests as landlords and traders. Thus class and community reinforced each other, and this discontent was a fertile ground for the destabilising intervention of Hindu communal organisations from within India. These included the Jan Sangh, which demanded full integration of Kashmir within the Indian Union and an end to its special constitutional status. The situation was enflamed when the leader of the Jan Sangh, S. P. Mookerjee, died in custody in Kashmir after defying a ban on his entry into the state. Within India at Jan Sangh and Hindu Mahasabha meetings there were violent slogans against Abdullah – and against Nehru, too – as murderers. Perhaps not surprisingly, such Hindu reactions reinforced Abdullah's fears for Kashmir's unique status, and his tendency to play with notions of Kashmiri independence.

Nehru found his whole policy towards Kashmir's internal politics crumbling before his eyes. Despite an agreement with Abdullah in 1952 on principles governing internal relations between India and Kashmir, he found his ally refusing to implement them, while the issue provoked widespread Hindu opposition in the state and within the rest of India. Further, the National Conference was no longer solidly behind Abdullah. With great disquiet he accepted an internal coup within the Conference, which brought to power Bakshi Ghulam Mohammed, a strong supporter of Kashmiri integration within India, and left Abdullah in prison.[29]

Nehru did not find the new premier congenial to deal with, but recognised that he would now have to depend on an alliance with him to stabilise the position within Kashmir and to bring the state securely within the structures of the Union. His new alliance strategy paid off and by stages, culminating in 1956, Kashmir was integrated into the Indian Union, and Nehru abandoned his earlier commitment to a plebiscite. In reply to a complaint from Pakistan, Nehru insisted that Kashmir's position as an integral part of the Union was the culmination of developments over the past six years, and must now be considered as final.[30]

The integration of the other princely states into the Indian Union and the redrawing of internal boundaries to incorporate them within the structures of the nation state happened much more rapidly and peacefully. It was largely the work of the old allies, Patel and V. P. Menon, who had collaborated so effectively in the hectic weeks before independence to gain limited accessions from the princes, rather than of Nehru as Prime Minister. Within two years all the princely states had been integrated in some way into the national political structure – either through merger with existing provinces (which became states of the Union under the new constitution), or through merger into new unions of small princely states, as in Rajasthan, or, in a few cases such as Hyderabad, as distinctive entities with their old boundaries.[31] Simultaneously the princes were 'persuaded' to begin the path to democracy and to conform to the pattern of division of powers between the centre and the states which would be written into the new constitution.

Many of them, however, retained considerable wealth and power and some deployed their resources to continue with careers in politics. Until 1956, when there was a further reorganisation of India's state boundaries (see below), the larger rulers were given significant positions in the democratic order by becoming the equivalent of governors of their old states or unions of them. In 1956, when they were effectively sacked, Nehru and his Home Minister wrote to thank them for their services and to express the hope that they would continue to assist and advise in the new states. But Nehru also inserted a hortatory paragraph in his letter about the virtue of equality in the new India, reminding them: 'The highest privilege that any of us in this country can have is that of a citizen of India with equal rights and obligations with others.'[32] He was also deeply concerned about the generous pensions which had been guaranteed to them in 1950, and had said so at the time. In 1953 and 1954 he revisited the issue and urged them to see that these were out of all proportion to the living standards of their compatriots and invited them to set aside some of their pensions for national purposes. Not surprisingly, many of them were very angry at what they saw as a reneging on the promises given to them by Patel, others prevaricated, some promised a small amount and others failed to reply.[33]

Nehru was evidently concerned about the former princes and hoped they would play a useful role in the new India. He could be extremely abrasive when he thought they were clinging to a status which was at odds with the new India, as in the case of the Nawab of Bhopal, who refused to supply the government with information about his foreign assets.[34] But there is evidence of his humanity as well as his prime ministerial concern. He wrote to the Nizam of Hyderabad in 1956 about the Nizam's senior son, whose behaviour he considered scandalous, since he had got into debt in spite of a huge monthly allowance of Rs 50,000. He felt he should not be given a position of responsibility. However, the Nizam's grandson was a very different young man, who had been educated in England and was now very apprehensive about an arranged marriage to someone who did not share his education. Nehru, with some diffidence, urged the Nizam to permit him to choose his own bride who fitted with his own educational background, and also hoped that he would avoid the temptations money could bring and play a useful role in India.[35] Almost certainly he was remembering his own experiences over four decades earlier, in relation both to money and to marriage.

India's linguistic diversity also generated sensitive questions about the appropriate boundaries of the states which composed the Indian Union. This forced Nehru, much against his will, to address the reorganisation of the states at a time when he felt that India had far more urgent problems to tackle. This was not a new problem, and under the British there had been a number of movements of protest and linguistic affirmation, particularly where linguistic groups felt that they were being subordinated to speakers of another Indian vernacular. Such subordination was experienced not just in cultural terms but in the more material matter of employment where people felt disadvantaged if they did not speak the majority or official vernacular of the provinces where they lived. Congress itself had restructured its own organisation on linguistic lines rather than always following the provincial boundaries of the raj, and had recognised, as far back as the Nehru Report of 1928, that this was a genuine problem which would have to be faced in independent India. Within months of independence Nehru and his government had to engage with it.[36]

In November 1947 Nehru tried to stave off an immediate demand for reorganisation of state boundaries with the stern warning that there were far more urgent problems for the country. 'First things must come first and the first thing is the security and stability of India. Before we can undertake any major schemes we must have a strong state and a smoothly running governmental machinery . . . If India is enfeebled, all her component elements grow weak.'[37] In subsequent months he was clearly irritated at agitation on what he saw as a minor issue compared with India's major problems, and also deeply concerned that any consideration of the matter would open the floodgates of demand throughout India, wherever political and linguistic boundaries did not coincide. The issue was temporarily managed through the appointment by the Constituent Assembly of a committee chaired by S. K. Dar, a prominent UP judge, to consider the creation of four new states, bearing in mind not only language but financial, economic and administrative consequences for the states concerned and for their neighbours. It reported in December 1948 and advised against the creation of new provinces for ten years.

It was soon evident that the issue would not go away, and Congress used the mechanism of an AICC committee, consisting of Nehru, Patel and Pattabhi Sitaramayya, to throw its weight behind the Dar Committee's report. Nehru drafted the AICC committee's report and it showed all the hallmarks of his thinking. India had other major problems following independence and partition, and this meant that Congress must look at its old policy towards linguistic provinces in a new light. 'The first consideration must be the security, unity and economic prosperity of India and every separatist disruptive tendency should be rigorously discouraged.' However, if public opinion was insistent, then a democratic government would have to consider each case on its merits. But 'taking a broad and practical view' they felt the time was not yet opportune for the formation of new provinces. 'It would unmistakably retard the process of consolidation of our gains, dislocate our administrative, economic and financial structure, let loose, while we are still in a formative stage, forces of disruption and disintegration, and seriously interfere with the progressive solution of our economic and political difficulties.'[38] Congress accepted this report and then Nehru's Cabinet also approved it, agreeing that there should be no changes in provincial boundaries until at least the new constitution had come into force. As Nehru reported to his Chief Ministers, disrupting India's growing equilibrium would be a serious risk, and inevitable arguments about new provinces would generate 'deplorable and upsetting' passions.[39]

Nehru's response to the issue of provincial reorganisation primarily on linguistic grounds displayed some of the key aspects of his thinking – his passion for the stability and unity of India, his fear that 'fissiparous tendencies' of caste, community and language would tear India apart, his somewhat Olympian critique of those for whom the vernacular languages were a burning issue, and his insistence that the central government should play a decisive guiding role in structuring the new India. But he was also a democrat, and – somewhat grudgingly – a political realist. Although he managed to stave off the problem when India was in the initial and critical process of stabilising its polity after independence and partition, he subsequently recognised that opposition to linguistic demands would threaten the unity of India more than consolidating it.

The turning point was a protest movement among Telugu-speakers in southern India, who claimed a separate state where they would not be dominated by Tamil-speakers, as they felt they were within the state of Madras. It was a claim with a long history, and one Nehru felt was more legitimate than most. When an old Gandhian worker fasted to death in late 1952 in support of an Andhra state Nehru's government recognised that it would have to yield on this issue; and in October 1953 an Andhra state was created. But this, as Nehru had feared, only

4. *India after the reorganisation of the states in 1956 (including later changes)*

opened the floodgates of demand. To manage it he announced the appointment of a commission to examine the reorganisation of the states. It is noteworthy that he still maintained that any restructuring should not be solely on linguistic grounds. As he wrote privately to his Home Minister, 'we ought to give up talking about linguistic provinces and refer to this question as the redistribution of States, wherever found necessary. The factors to be considered in such redistribution are: cultural (including linguistic), geographical, economic, financial and those relating to security and defence. An overriding consideration is the unity of India as well as the economic development of the country as a whole.'[40] The committee reported in 1955 and rejected the theory of 'one language one state', though it accepted that linguistic homogeneity was conducive to administrative efficiency. Its overall thrust was to recommend the redrawing of state boundaries to conform with major linguistic regions, and a States Reorganization Act was passed in Delhi in November 1956.

With the exception of the future of Bombay, which was bitterly disputed by Marathi- and Gujarati-speakers right up to 1960, and the demand for a Punjabi-speaking state where language also carried the religious aspirations of Sikhs for political status and autonomy frustrated in 1947, the issue of 'linguistic states' was now resolved. Local political and administrative structures of the new Indian polity were now in place, reflecting popular aspiration rather than imperial practice. Nehru had learned the hard way that a prime minister who saw himself as a Platonic Guardian could become damagingly embroiled in local politics over which he had no control and little leverage. But despite the disputes and at times violent turmoil, the resolution of this issue also demonstrated that Indian national identity could coexist with, and indeed be built on, other senses of belonging which, if given recognition in the polity, could strengthen and deepen commitment to the Indian nation. Despite his grave misgivings and initial opposition, he and his government, by bowing to democratic pressure, had made the formal structures of state administration and decision-making conform more closely to the shape and nature of Indian society.

## THE ROLE OF THE CONGRESS PARTY

Structuring the nation also involved the Congress Party as the one large-scale India-wide political organisation at independence. For decades there had been controversy over its nature and role. Was it a band of devoted servants of the nation working for moral revolution, as Gandhi had hoped? Was it a revolutionary mass movement against imperialism, as the young Nehru had envisaged? Was it a party organised to gain political power, as many of its members presumed? The truth was that it incorporated elements of all these visions, and some dominated at different times. But since the reforms of 1935 it had become more obviously, and uneasily, both a vehicle of anti-imperial struggle and a means of attaining power over provincial administration, with a view ultimately to inheriting the raj. Congressmen had tasted the fruits of power and learned new skills for attaining and retaining it through elections and through controlling party structures. They brought with them established expectations and political practices as they achieved swaraj. These dominated thinking about the future role of Congress once the British had gone, and only Gandhi seriously articulated just before his death the vision of Congress as an association of servants of the people, rather than as a political party.[41]

Gandhi's vision of Congress in a free India reflected his understanding that genuine social change flowed from individual belief and action, from the base of society upwards. Nehru, of course, viewed the dynamics of change differently, and believed that the state had the major role to play, through the processes of administration and politics, and through educating its citizens. In this Congress had a significant role to play.[42] The importance he attached to Congress was clear from the lengths to which he was prepared to go to prevent Tandon from controlling it before the first general election, and his determination to control it by being President or handing on the presidency to those he could trust. In defeating Tandon he was asserting not only that Congress stood for a composite India, but also that the party would be subservient to the government in the routine running of the country, although it had a part to play in the discussion of broad policy outlines.

Although Nehru's pronouncements about the role of Congress were vague, and partly reflected his temperamental distaste for party politics, he hoped that it would perform a number of functions. In the first place, the democratic political system required some mechanisms of political organisation and articulation, and he could see no point in dissolving the Congress and turning it into an apolitical body for social work as Gandhi had suggested. 'If we dissolve the Congress, we shall have to organise a new party for shouldering political responsibilities. The same Congressmen will have to function more or less in the same manner but under a new name.'[43] Somebody, after all, had to go on winning votes, and it was clear that Congress was very good at this. Further he sensed that the strength and legitimacy of his own government depended on the strength and prestige of the Congress and the degree to which it represented public opinion.[44]

He also spoke of Congress having a historic and ongoing mission, which no other party or group could fulfil, of working to fashion the new India, to solve its many problems, and perhaps above all to help to maintain its unity. He spoke of Congress as serving the nation, but quite what that would mean in practice in the new political situation was unclear, particularly when this idea with its Gandhian echoes was divorced from Gandhi's plan of constructive work.

> It is vital that it should function, not only at election times, . . . seeking to serve the cause of the people and to render the work of our Parliament, legislatures, local bodies and Panchayats [village councils], part of the life of our people. This does not mean intervention in the affairs of the local administration or coming in the way of the organs of government, local, state or national. Our party organisation must be something more than a party and must win confidence and respect by patient and self-sacrificing service, and thus live in the hearts of our people.[45]

Behind this somewhat flowery exhortation he seems to have been feeling his way towards the concept that Congress was a countrywide mediating structure, bringing the state and the people closer together, acting as the government's eyes and ears but also helping convince citizens that the government belonged to them in a new way – in sharp contrast to the imperial government which was perceived as remote and often minatory.

Nehru's vision of Congress was unrealistic, given the mixed and often mundane motives which increasingly drew people into its ranks now that it was the party of power, and given his diffuse understanding of its potential role. He was, therefore, in the years after independence, increasingly frustrated by its nature, and by the characteristics of its members and their behaviour. His letters and speeches became almost despondent in tone, as he pointed out what he saw as the deterioration of Congress. Whether there really had been deterioration is questionable in the light of Nehru's own experiences within Congress before independence. But harking back to the great days of the nationalist movement and of Gandhi's insistence on discipline, unity and moral fervour was probably a sign of his increasing age as well as being a technique to cement national unity by the use of powerful symbols and memories. He inveighed against the weakness of the Congress organisation, the indiscipline which pervaded its ranks, causing members to criticise their colleagues in public, including those who were in office in their name. He bewailed the fact that so many state Congress organisations seemed to be riven by such factional divisions that they inhibited Congress work. As early as 1949 he was deeply anxious about 'the cracking up' of the Congress, its disorganisation, and the emerging feuds within it.[46] The Bengal Congress organisation seemed in a state of 'complete collapse', and its members 'utterly inept and narrow-minded and stupid': they were so divided that they could not even cooperate to contest an election in south Calcutta. Congress in Punjab ran Bengal 'pretty close'. By 1953 he was complaining that the UP Congress was probably now the worst in India.[47] In 1954 he was writing to the Chief Minister of Bihar, noting seven major problems with the state Congress, including 'lack of functioning of the Congress organisation', unsatisfactory candidates for local elections, opposition by some Congressmen for Congress candidates, voting on caste lines, and Muslim alienation from the party and the local government.[48]

Inevitably as Prime Minister leading a Congress government, and as Congress President from 1951 to 1954, he became embroiled in the domestic politics of the Congress organisation, particularly where these impinged on the Congress's local repute, its ability to win elections and its capacity to form stable governments in the states. Wherever possible he would mediate or exhort, for after all many of those concerned were old colleagues. Working with him to maintain Congress unity and keep state Congress organisations and governments in line were colleagues in the CWC and in the Congress Parliamentary Board. But on rare occasions he would use party and state instruments of discipline. The most drastic example was in Punjab in 1951 when intra-Congress feuding had generated such instability in the state government that Nehru and the Parliamentary Board forced the Chief Minister, Dr Bhargava, to resign, and the President, on Nehru's advice, invoked President's Rule for the first time in the country's history. After Nehru handed over the party presidency to the trusted U. N. Dhebar from Saurashtra, one of the new President's main concerns was to sort out the problem of party organisation, and to rebuild it through a strategy of decentralisation. As Nehru himself admitted, he had not had the time to deal adequately with internal Congress issues of organisation.[49]

Despite the problems Nehru encountered in the Congress in these early years of independence, and his dire warnings about its weaknesses, the party did perform important structuring functions for the new nation. In the first place, it enabled the new democratic system to work. It won elections in an inhospitable context of mass illiteracy and poor mass communications; and it sustained stable governments in the states and at the centre – a task of immense value when the fate of other newly independent democracies is compared with India's. Nehru recognised this, and spent considerable time not only in helping the party win elections, but also in relating to the party in the central Parliament, through an efficient Whip system, and by his own appearances and speeches in the Lok Sabha.

Congress also functioned as an integrating mechanism by virtue of its ideological openness, welcoming many shades of opinions with its ranks to the extent that it was not only the dominant party within the polity but almost within itself an ideological party system. The only groups excluded from Congress were those Nehru believed to be guilty of attitudes and actions which threatened to divide and destabilise the country, particularly Communists and those who overtly defined India in Hindu terms, or those who excluded themselves, such as a small band of Socialists.[50] Nehru was perplexed by the disaffection of the latter, recognising that he needed their ideological convictions in the struggle for a more equal India, but discussions on their re-entry into Congress in 1953 were abortive. Congress, by its social openness and flexibility at state level, put down roots in every part of India, welcoming into its ranks virtually all those with a stake in public life who saw it as a vehicle for influence and power. Its chameleon-like adaptability to local social configurations of power was reflected and confirmed by its choice of candidates to fight elections for particular seats.[51] However, this growing rootedness, particularly in India's still largely agrarian society, threatened to compromise the capacity of Congress to support Nehru in his vision of radical socio-economic change as a necessary element in forging a new nation on long-term foundations.

By the mid-1950s Nehru and his colleagues in the Congress Party and in government had done a very significant amount of work in providing the new nation with a state and political structure which not only managed the mundane processes of the transfer of power from imperial hands, but also began the far more difficult task of using power for new ends. This was all done in a time of considerable domestic turmoil and external pressure, and provided the backbone of vital political stability, combining the considerable use of state power with a degree of flexibility in response to democratic demands. However, Nehru's vision of the central role of the state in founding and forging the nation was fraught with dilemmas and ambiguities. It presupposed that the state would have the material resources to deliver on its promises, and to satisfy the most basic aspirations of citizens, raised by the rhetoric of Congress itself as the major voice of anti-imperial nationalism. Further, many of the crucial structures of the nation state were little different from those created by the imperial rulers for their own ends; and it was therefore questionable whether they could be reshaped and redirected to serve new purposes. Inheriting the raj without social or political revolution was certainly an aid to stability in the immediate aftermath of the end of imperial rule, but in the longer term it brought its own dilemmas.

Finally, emphasis on the state's dominant role in creating the new India put Nehru himself in an unusually prominent position, particularly given his unique popularity in the country and the sense within the party, and thus in government circles, that to challenge him was unpatriotic and in personal terms politically destructive (as it had been for Tandon). Two decades earlier he had recognised within himself the psychological potential to embrace a position which amounted to a popular dictatorship. Now his personal commitment to democracy, the power of the states in the Indian polity, the entrenching of locally dominant groups within Congress itself, and the sheer weight of the bureaucratic system of government militated against the possibility of such a role. But even as he deliberately nurtured Parliament, toured the country, spoke at length to vast crowds, and kept in regular touch with his Chief Ministers through the party and through his series of discursive, pedagogical letters on national matters, he seems clearly to have seen himself as in a unique way the one who knew what the new India should be like, the one on whom the burden of national reconstruction rested most heavily. He responded to this sense of vocation with all his intellectual and physical strength, his personal loneliness and isolation freeing him to make his country his priority, much as Gandhi's freely chosen rejection of normal social ties had been designed to do. Whether such a highly personalised national leadership, and his view of the role of Prime Minister, was desirable or functional in the longer term remained an open question as India struggled with fundamental socio-economic issues in the 1950s.

# Chapter 12

# Forging the Nation

Nehru and Gandhi had disagreed profoundly in their vision of the India to be constructed after independence. But of one thing they were both convinced – that swaraj must mean more than political independence, and must be seen to bring real change in the lives of ordinary people, particularly the most disadvantaged. Gandhi, of course, came to this conclusion as a result of his religious conviction that, for the individual, service of the poorest was the way to discover the divine, and that true self-rule depended on a new sense of moral community rather than on political arrangements. Nehru's approach was secular and political. He argued that freedom would only be genuine if people were released from the bondage of poverty and of ascribed social status, and given new life chances and choices. He also recognised that the nation had to go on being forged, that is, created in the lived experience of Indian people, particularly those who had had little part in the initial processes of nation-building, or who in the peculiar circumstances of Indian independence felt threatened and potentially excluded. He used the metaphor of the journey the nation had before it, indicating that he recognised that forging the nation was a long-term process of moulding attitudes and also of giving many disparate and previously disadvantaged groups a stake in the nation.

Nehru's painful awareness that nationalist opposition to the raj had never become a truly mass movement, and his doubts about the Congress commitment to radical change, made the challenge of forging the nation one of the most important he set himself. It was a process which offered him considerable personal fulfilment. Not only was the prospect of using the tools of the state to plan and achieve a new socio-economic order intellectually exciting. He also had a sense of the historic significance of the task before the country, that India was trying to achieve change on a scale never before attempted by a democratic political system.

## MAKING CITIZENSHIP A REALITY

Nehru recognised that in independent India national citizenship was a fragile and disputed concept. In the climate of fear and violence which accompanied independence and Partition, there were minority groups for whom being Indian was now deeply problematic, particularly as the raj had gone, and with it the political safeguards for minorities entrenched in communal electorates. It was by no means clear that the constitution, with its assurances of equal citizenship and fundamental rights, would give minorities adequate protection and mechanisms for the articulation of their fears and interests. Nehru, sensing this, felt that the Hindu majority had a particular duty towards Indian minorities, who needed to be encouraged to 'believe that they are as good citizens of India as anyone else'. He wrote in 1948 to his Chief Ministers of the need to 'produce the sense of absolute security in the minds of the . . . minorities. The majority always owes a duty of this kind to minorities.'[1]

Indian Muslims had the most obvious dilemmas of national belonging in the new situation. Despite the creation of Pakistan out of the former Muslim majority areas to the north-west and north-east of the subcontinent, and the migrations which followed Partition, Muslims were still India's largest minority – around 35–6 million people – scattered throughout the subcontinent, but found particularly in Kashmir and the Gangetic plain, and forming between 10 and 11 per cent of the population. In the first census decade, 1951–61, their numbers increased, in percentage terms slightly more than the Hindu increase. (India had the third largest Muslim population of any country in the world, and after Bangladesh broke away from Pakistan in 1971 had the second largest, with Indonesia having the largest.) As before Partition, Indian Muslims formed no single community and were socio-economically and linguistically diverse as well as differing in their local status. However, in the north, where they had been a significant and well-educated minority, many of their natural leaders and spokesmen had gone to Pakistan. The threat of violence against Muslims in the wake of Partition was worst in Delhi and the north, but throughout India they were deeply traumatised by the circumstances of independence, and fearful of Hindu neighbours, whose spokesmen talked of Muslims as covert sympathisers with Pakistan and of their having to 'prove' their loyalty to India.[2] Such accusations were threatening but not surprising, given the rhetoric of the Muslim League that Muslims were a separate nation, and the violence experienced by many Hindu and Sikh families who fled from Pakistan.

Nehru was deeply sensitive to Muslim fears and ambiguities. He acknowledged in mid-1948 to one of the major Muslim princes who had acceded to India that there was a 'painful tussle of the spirit' occurring among Muslims, and that Muslims would have to develop new attitudes to become part of the new India. Nehru wanted to help them in this process of adjustment, though he recognised that many Hindus did not and 'would rather do without the Muslims. I think that would be a fatal disaster from the point of view of India and I wish therefore to resist it.' Two years later he was still criticising the tendency to demand a particular loyalty to India from its Muslims. 'Loyalty is not produced to order or by fear. It comes as a natural growth from circumstances which make loyalty not only a sentiment which appeals to one but also profitable in the long run. We have to produce conditions which lead to this sentiment being produced. In any event, criticism and cavilling at minorities does not help.'[3]

Among the 'conditions' which he recognised as critical for Muslims to have a sense of security and belonging were material ones, as well as the psychological one of attitudes among non-Muslims. He tried to point these out to senior members of the government wherever a Muslim sense of belonging was clearly being affected. The face of Gandhi, gentle but reproachful at what was happening to Muslims, haunted him when he heard of the difficulties experienced by Indian Muslims who wished to sell property and were caught up in the provisions of legislation relating to evacuee property (which was only repealed in 1956).[4] He watched with dismay the declining numbers of Muslims in the public services, including the police. In 1952 when the UP government limited Muslim recruitment to the services to 14 per cent he pointed out to the Chief Minister how unfair this was in areas of the state where Muslims were a far greater percentage of the population. This not only denied India the services of talented young men, but also generated a sense of 'unfairness and frustration'. Nearly two years later he addressed all his Chief Ministers, asking for data on minority recruitment to the services because from what he could see the doors to both all-India and state services were largely closed to minorities of all kinds. This was not in keeping with the letter or spirit of the constitution, and would generate frustration and despair for the future among large numbers of Indians, which would in turn have far-reaching political and social consequences. When he did receive the replies he was deeply disturbed. Muslims in particular were under-represented in the services, and this compounded their other sources of disquiet, including the decline of Urdu, the vernacular most associated with Muslims. Even more disquieting to him than what was actually occurring was the fact that so many of the Hindu majority did not seem to think that this was a problem. By implication he clearly felt many of his closest colleagues in government to be guilty of this.[5] Muslim fears for the future of Urdu, particularly in UP and the new state of Madhya Pradesh (MP), suggested to him that despite constitutional guarantees, Muslims felt they were being cut off from their cultural roots, and he chided the Madhya Pradesh government on this issue, as well as writing to Chief Ministers generally about it.[6]

It was becoming clear that Nehru as Prime Minister might talk about issues he felt to be critical to the emotional and psychological integration of India, and the deepening and expansion of a sense of belonging to the nation as full citizens among minorities, but in practice the fate of the minorities rested not on the Prime Minister as visionary, nor even on the provisions of the constitution, but on the attitudes and practices of state governments, and by extension, those on whom they relied for electoral support. In a democracy the nation could only be forged to a limited extent from the top down; and in the circumstances of India's federation the government of the state rather than the Union was the most important determinant of practice. As Nehru also recognised, the Congress, which he hoped would be an integrating and transforming mechanism within India, was itself part of the problem in respect of the minorities. The failure of Congress to recruit Muslims, for example, into the party and allow them to rise in the organisation meant that it, too, compounded the problem and deprived him of a resource with which to tackle it on the ground.

In relation to Indian Christians Nehru experienced similar frustration of his hopes, primarily by the state governments. Christians were India's second largest and fastest growing religious minority. In the decade 1951–61 the increase in the Christian population was just over 27 per cent, and by 1961 they numbered well over 10 million. Like Muslims, they were diverse in origins and status, and scattered through the country. However, many of them were the result of mass movements of conversion from among the lowest and most disadvantaged sections of society, particularly from among Untouchables and tribal groups. Their position in independent India was therefore doubly problematic, combining socio-economic deprivation with fear of being a minority associated by belief with the former rulers.

Before independence Nehru had publicly stated in a Roman Catholic newspaper published in London that Indian Christians had no need to fear for their religious freedom in the new India; they were an integral part of India with a long tradition of belonging on the subcontinent, and were 'one of the many enriching elements in the country's cultural and spiritual life'.[7] As in the case of Muslims, Nehru also became perturbed that Christians were feeling apprehensive about their place in India and their future, particularly when his Christian cabinet colleague, Rajkumari Amrit Kaur, drew attention to the issue. He exhorted his Chief Ministers to remember that India was a composite country, and that attempts by the majority to impose itself on minorities could lead to internal conflicts as destructive as external attack. 'The basic problem for us today in India is to build up a united India in the real and inner sense of the word, that is, a psychological integration of our people.'[8]

One of the key issues in relation to Christians was the presence of foreign missionaries from many countries and of different Christian denominations, who came not only to assist local congregations (where there were still comparatively few indigenous leaders and ministers) but to continue to work to spread their faith. In some places such as the north-eastern frontier areas they were considered a security problem, but in others, such as Madhya Pradesh, local governments were driven by a commitment to a Hindu vision of India to actions which were interpreted by Christians (and by Nehru) as harassment. Nehru personally found missionaries' proselytising work distasteful, though he felt it was unlikely to come to much; but he admired their social work among the disadvantaged which he felt shamed Hindus. However, in the early 1950s he found himself embroiled in a controversy about foreign missionaries which threatened his vision of forging a composite Indian nation, and seemed likely to exacerbate Indian Christian fears and to undermine India's reputation abroad. Moreover, he feared particularly that, in as much as Indian Catholic Christians felt alienated from India, this would set opinion among the Goans against India, and might deprive his government of significant help from the Indian Catholic hierarchy and the Vatican on the Goa issue.[9] Nehru was determined to deal with the missionary question as a political and social one, not as a religious one, and to take as his guidelines national security, the need not to take employment from Indians, and the undesirability of having increasing numbers of foreigners in the country. (He seems to have been particularly perturbed at the large numbers of Americans and the likelihood that they would preach an American way of life while preaching Christianity.) But he insisted that any policy should take as a basic principle that Christianity was a long-established Indian religion, and Indian Christians were protected under the constitution.[10]

Nehru's broad understanding of the issue and its international ramifications, as well as its impact on the Christian experience of Indian identity, was not shared by many in state governments, and even some of his closest colleagues in Delhi. He had to remonstrate even with the President, Rajendra Prasad, for appearing to associate himself with anti-missionary feeling. The President was head of a secular state, whatever his personal views, and if he appeared not to treat all religions equally then this would create 'apprehensions' in the minds of many Indian citizens.[11]

Late in 1954 a new policy was established, which did not disturb existing missionaries provided that they were sponsored by Indian churches, but discouraged new missions and also prevented missionaries from Commonwealth countries entering freely, as they had before. This policy gave state governments considerable freedom in the matter of recognising missions and permitting missionaries to return after leave, as well as in their general attitude to Christian minorities. Nehru consequently found, as he had on the issue of treatment of Muslims, that he was at the mercy of the state governments over the treatment of Indian Christians and of foreign missionaries. Madhya Pradesh seemed the most problematic in this respect, partly because of the activities of local Hindu organizations, but also because of a state government enquiry into missionary work which Christians found intimidating. Nehru found himself having to field embarrassing complaints from important Catholic bishops; but what really worried him was the fear of local Indian Christians that they would not be treated fairly in their own country.[12] He admitted to the Congress President that he had tried unsuccessfully to urge the Chief Minister, R. S. Shukla, to curb anti-Christian behaviour in the state, and he hoped Congress might intervene instead. This also proved impossible as no local Congress members seemed able to stand up to the Chief Minister.[13]

Linked to the issue of the reality of Indian citizenship for Christians was the future of India's tribal communities. These very different groups were mostly found in more remote and isolated parts of the country, and they had their own culture and economic life which marked them out from Hindu society. For decades there had been friction when tribal people felt themselves threatened by settled Hindu social groups, agriculturalists and traders, who seemed to threaten their way of life. For their part many Hindus saw them as primitive people outside the bounds of accepted civilised behaviour, who should be incorporated into the mainstream and transformed into modern Indians. A further dimension of the issue was the conversion of significant numbers of tribal groups to Christianity in recent decades, particularly in the north-east of India, where some groups, particularly some of the Naga tribe, were now campaigning for secession from India.

Nehru's response to tribal questions was twofold. Firstly, any demands for secession were out of court. Even before independence in 1947 he had assured the Nagas that Congress policy was that although their territory would have to be part of India, they would have as much autonomy as possible. But, as the secessionist Naga leader, A. Z. Phizo, was told in 1951 in a letter drafted by Nehru, 'The government of India ... cannot recognise any attempt by any section of the people of India to claim an independent status.' Nehru reiterated this in person to Phizo, when he agreed to meet him in Delhi in March 1952.[14] When the campaign continued and turned violent, Nehru's government felt it had no choice but to take the military option of suppression of a movement which threatened the integrity of India, and the security of the border. It was a sad reflection on the reality of the nation that within several years of independence Indian troops were being deployed against their fellow citizens.

However, Nehru was deeply uneasy at this treatment of vulnerable tribal people, to whom the constitution gave special protection and the promise of special types of administration suited to their culture and history as groups outside regular district administration. He believed that tribal groups had their distinctive cultures, and that it would be destructive to try to absorb them culturally or administratively in a hurry. On the other hand, it was wrong to preserve them as if they were museum specimens. The best way to deal with them would be to interfere as little as possible with them, protecting their customs and lands, but they should be given access to those social resources such as transport, schools and medicine which would gradually integrate them as full citizens of India.[15] Late in 1952 he went himself to tour the North-East Frontier Agency (NEFA), and this confirmed his sense of the need for a specially sensitive policy towards tribal people, both culturally and administratively. Tribal people would benefit India, adding to its richness and strength, just as contact with the rest of India would ultimately benefit them.[16] Soon afterwards he asked a most unusual Englishman, former Oxford don and missionary, and amateur anthropologist, Verrier Elwin, to be his special adviser on tribal issues. This was an attempt to circumvent those administrators who had little sensitivity to the nature and value of tribal cultures and institutions, and Elwin set about enthusing a generation of Indian Frontier Administration Officers with his passion and vision for Indian tribal communities.[17]

However, Nehru soon saw that the attitude of the state governments was a powerful disincentive to the process of forging the nation in the minds of tribal peoples. NEFA was kept under the direct control of the Ministry of External Affairs, but the neighbouring Assam government seemed to maintain a hard line that tribals (and the Nagas in particular) would have to be dealt with firmly and integrated into what it assumed to be civilised society and full state administration. By early 1955 Nehru was writing sadly of the failure of his government's tribal policy in the north east, and that even among those Nagas who had not taken up arms there was now an attitude of non-cooperation, and more widely among the tribes a demand for a separate state. There were strong feelings of frustration and fear that they might be compelled to submit to the Assam government. He pleaded with his Chief Minister to be realistic, to try to win the people by friendship and to recognise that they must have a measure of autonomy. 'We cannot have a discontented population near our frontier or, indeed, anywhere, in the country. We have to make them feel they are parts of India, not only politically but emotionally and otherwise, and that their future is tied up with India's.' Indian independence would have little meaning for these people 'unless they are sharers in it and unless they feel that they can manage their own affairs'.[18] As the Naga problem dragged on into the second decade of India's independence it was evident that for some tribal groups there was still little sense that the nation was one in which they had either an emotional or political stake.

Tackling the fears and needs of recognisable minorities was not the only aspect of making belonging to the new India a lived and desirable reality. Nehru also saw that those who had suffered some of the most profound inequalities in society, by virtue of their ascribed status, needed to be given the substance of freedom. Those at the base of Hindu society were some of the poorest Indians, as well as being discriminated against on grounds of permanent ritual impurity. Nehru had long argued – as in *The Discovery of India* – that caste was a social force which had weakened India. He returned to this theme in the 1950s as he tried to spread his vision of a strong, resurgent India. Moreover, in his view caste was incompatible with democracy. 'Let me tell you that so long as the caste system continues to exist in this country, democracy and people's rule have absolutely no meaning . . . How can the concept of equality and of equal opportunities for all exist side by side with the caste system which divides people into compartments and leads to suppression of one section of society by others?'[19] Yet he recognised that state action could not do away with the system itself, and that any attempt to do so, by compelling people to marry outside their caste group, for example, would be a violation of personal freedom.[20] Only education and economic progress would ultimately erode the system.

However, that most gross and degrading manifestation, the treatment of the lowest in society as untouchable, could be prohibited by the state. Congress had committed itself to this under Gandhi's leadership before 1947, and in the late 1930s some provincial governments had begun to take legislative action against the practice. The new constitution then declared in Article 17 that Untouchability was abolished and any observance of it would be made a punishable offence. In 1955 Parliament in Delhi proceeded to use its exclusive right to legislate in this matter and passed the Untouchability (Offences) Act. The Supreme Court subsequently struck down challenges to the Act, but it remained to be seen whether legislation made any actual difference in the lives of those formerly perceived of as Untouchable. Recognising the limitation of legislation as a mechanism for social change, Nehru's government also provided special funds for welfare programmes for the Untouchables, and scholarships, as well as reserved quotas in government employment. Most notable of all as an indication of the new nation's commitment to integrating Untouchables into the polity in a new way was the retention of reserved seats for them in the Lok Sabha and the state legislatures (for ten years in the first instance), just when religious minorities lost the special political provisions granted to them by the British. These changes marked a major declaration by the nation's representatives about the importance of forging a new national identity in society and polity, and a serious investment in change. We shall return to practice in a later chapter, where intentions will be measured against experience, and where we shall see how far popular attitudes supported or undermined the intentions of the nation's leaders and legislators.

The role of women had also been a deeply contested issue in discussions about the Indian nation before independence, and the constitution took a clear stand that women were to be equal citizens in the new nation state, enfranchised and possessed of the Fundamental Rights laid down for all Indians. For Nehru the equal treatment of women, and a new role for them in society and politics was a vital part of forging the new nation. He had argued that the treatment of women was the touchstone of the new nation, the sign of its maturity and modernity. He also believed that women were a powerful agent for social change by virtue of their status in the family. Moreover, his own experience of how Hindu inheritance laws had threatened to leave his own widowed sister almost destitute had been a powerful reminder of the discriminatory force of Hindu law and of conservative male Hindu thinking, even among the educated and westernised. Consequently he committed himself and his government to the passage of a package of reforms of Hindu personal law, known as the Hindu Code Bill.[21]

Nehru had no reason to expect a campaign of opposition to these reforms. A government committee, chaired by an eminent Indian lawyer, had been considering the nature of acceptable legislation since the early 1940s, and the Constituent Assembly had accepted the notion of fundamental rights for all citizens without demur. Now in 1948 Nehru was confronted by a barrage of opposition in the Assembly (which was also the all-India legislature as well as the constitution-making body until after the first general elections under the new constitution). Many shades of Hindu opinion joined forces to oppose it, criticising particular aspects of it, such as insistence on monogamy, registration of marriages and equal property rights for women. Some, moreover, felt that any legislative interference with Hindu law was an assault on the religious foundations of society. Clearly the Assembly was content to accept broad principles of equality on the one hand, but, on the other, when it came to translating equality into practice within the domain of the Hindu family, ideological and vested interests in male dominance and the rights of male inheritance to protect the assets of the Hindu joint family were of paramount importance.

Even more disquieting to Nehru was the fact that close colleagues within Congress and government shared such views and contributed to the collapse of the legislation. Rajendra Prasad, as President, took a stand against the Code in July 1948, arguing that the Constituent Assembly was not competent to discuss this issue, which should first be put to the electorate in the campaign before the first elections. He also insisted that the Congress Party had never been given a chance to discuss it properly. K. N. Katju, Governor of West Bengal and later Home Minister, agreed with him, writing robustly, 'In my opinion any drastic change in the structure of Hindu society will cause great resentment and great discontent, and this is not the time to multiply or accentuate differences.'[22]

In subsequent months the campaign of opposition and delay, assisted by the openly conservative attitude of the Deputy Speaker, sickened Nehru: but, realistically, he searched around for devices to enable even part of it to pass into law, and decided to divide the bill and press ahead with the part relating to marriage and divorce. Once more the President launched into the fray and threatened to use his power to refuse assent if the bill went through the Assembly, arguing that the proposals were revolutionary and that the Assembly did not have competence to pass it, given that it had not been directly elected. This would have precipitated a constitutional crisis, because Nehru and his legal advisers argued that the President could not refuse assent against the advice of his ministers.[23] Eventually Nehru decided to defuse the crisis and the bill was dropped temporarily. His Law Minister, Dr Ambedkar, resigned, bitterly disappointed in his Prime Minister and in the Assembly. But Nehru was insistent that this was not the end of the matter and that India would have to advance 'on all fronts – political, economic and social'. There could be no keeping society apart from change and concentrating only on political and economic reform, for social conservatism would hold back the country's progress.'[24]

Nehru had placed in his draft of the Congress election manifesto (which was finally adopted just weeks after the dropping of the reform measure in the Assembly) a paragraph dealing with the need to remove disabilities which prevented women from playing their full part in the country's life, and in the family and local community. So when Congress was elected to power for the first time on a universal adult franchise it had a significant mandate on the issue, which Prasad could no longer deny, and also a large majority (364 out of 489 seats) in the Lok Sabha. Moreover, Nehru had directed the Law Ministry to divide the Hindu Code Bill into suitable parts, to work on these in the light of criticism and to circulate the drafts to state governments for their views. Such careful ground-work and some softening on controversial issues meant that the separate bills covering marriage, succession, guardianship, adoption and maintenance eventually passed into law between 1954 and 1956. Nehru considered these Acts to be the greatest real advance of his career; and as each was passed he commented to his Chief Ministers on their significance – confrontation of conservative forces in society and a commitment to social progress alongside economic and political progress. He admitted that they were not socially revolutionary, but they were of deep symbolic and practical significance. 'They have broken the barrier of ages and cleared the way somewhat for our womenfolk to progress.'[25] Although Nehru drew satisfaction from his achievement on an issue critical to him and his commit-ment to go on forging the nation, and drawing its disadvantaged into the national polity, the experience had demonstrated the limits to his ability to enthuse even his close colleagues with his vision of India and to use state power to work social transformation. Women's experience was subsequently to suggest that even legis-lation was a poor tool with which to achieve real change in ordinary lives.

## DEALING WITH STRUCTURAL INEQUALITY

In tackling Untouchability and the status of women, Nehru had dealt with status ascribed to distinctive groups by caste and gender. However, he and many of his colleagues recognised that there were also profound inequalities caused by socio-economic structures which prevented access to resources that were crucial for real change in Indian society. Among these resources were land and education. The former was the foundation of most wealth and power in Indian society as well as the key to subsistence for the very poorest in the countryside. The latter was the entry to new occupations as well as the prelude to profound shifts in attitudes, as Nehru and those as privileged as himself had experienced for themselves and their families. Providing land and education to all citizens was a huge task, but Nehru was determined to make a start as part of the process of giving far more Indians a stake in India's polity and economy.

Patterns of landholding in India were regionally diverse and complex. At the base of rural society were the many who owned minute parcels of land or none at all, while at the top in some regions were landowners who controlled thousands of acres, much of it actually worked by tenants. In the middle were substantial farming groups who owned some land, rented some, and made a reasonable living from land, feeding their families and producing for the market. The generation of Congress leaders who came to power in the late 1940s had experienced the agricultural crisis of the 1930s. Then the collapse in world prices of primary goods had led to profound disruptions in credit supplies and labour markets in rural India, and generated deep tensions in rural relationships, particularly between landlords and tenants, and agriculturalists and suppliers of credit. They drew the lesson that large landlords, or *zamindars*, were a major barrier to profitable peasant farming, and even in the late 1930s before Congress governments withdrew cooperation from the raj, several had begun to plan the abolition of *zamindari*. Coming from UP, which was one of the areas with a significant groups of *zamindars*, Nehru had been committed to *zamindari* abolition since the 1920s, though he recognised that his views were more radical than those of many Congress members.

However, as with the Hindu Code Bill, Nehru found that reformist legislation was problematic in its initial stages, let alone in implementation. *Zamindari* abolition was a state matter, but in a candid letter to Rajendra Prasad he admitted that the government and the Congress Party should have tackled the issue centrally and provided a detailed and feasible policy for states to adopt.[26] He was anxious that Chief Ministers should consult with Delhi on their intended measures, not least because the federal centre did not have adequate funds to make large loans to states to finance schemes of acquisition of landlord holdings. At one stage the whole project was on the verge of collapse when legal opinion indicated that compensation would have to paid in actual cash.[27] In Bihar a further crisis threatened *zamindari* abolition across the country. The state's abolition Act of 1950 was challenged in the courts, and the Patna High Court declared that it contravened Article 14 of the constitution, which assured all persons of equality before the law and protection under the law. Nehru was appalled at this legal barrier to the solution of what he saw as one of the most important problems facing his government. 'Having for long proclaimed as a major point in our policy the abolition of the zamindari system and having repeatedly made attempts to do so and raised expectations high, we just cannot, either on moral or practical grounds or even on the basis of legal difficulty, stop this process or delay it.'[28] The UP's abolition Act, passed in January 1951, was similarly challenged in and stalled by the courts. In June 1951, therefore, Parliament in Delhi amended the Constitution and removed all *zamindari* abolition acts from the purview of the courts. Nehru was greatly relieved and urged all states to proceed swiftly towards abolition, for it was not only a symbolic issue but was also the precondition for achieving a more just landed system.[29]

However, where detailed case studies have been done on the working of these Acts, they suggest that abolition was far from radical in practice. In UP, for example, the Act as it eventually took shape only sought to undermine 'land-lordism', not to produce a revolution in rural society or a major redistribution of land. It confirmed in their holdings all who 'cultivated' land, meaning those who managed and financed farming as well as those who personally cultivated land. Consequently a wide group of protected agriculturalists emerged, some of whom had been small *zamindars* in the past. Their presence in the local Congress, along-side substantial tenant farmers, had helped to mould the state government's strategy on land reform, and as one Congress minister later admitted, Congress policy had been designed to ensure political stability in the countryside and to produce a substantial group of independent landowning peasants as a bulwark against political extremism.[30] In neighbouring Bihar *zamindari* abolition similarly proved to be no revolutionary panacea to rural inequalities. The state government did not have the administrative competence to implement it fully. Former *zamindars* were well advised and knew in advance the provisions of the forthcoming abolition legislation, and they were in many cases able to circumvent the intentions of the measure and retain for themselves significant landholdings. One in Muzaffarpur district, for example, managed to retain 500 acres.[31]

Evidence from just these two cases indicates the dichotomy between the original vision behind the policy of abolition and the practice in rural society – and the gulf between Nehru's vision and the numbers in his own party who had ideological and vested interests in protecting inequalities in rural society, even when they were prepared to do away with some of the most egregious manifestations of unequal access to and control of land. For Nehru this was just the start, and he soon began to raise more radical issues such as the placing of upper limits or ceilings on landholdings, the redistribution of land and the formation of rural cooperatives of different kinds, though he realised that this would be a very complex problem with many regional variations.[32] The Delhi government, through the mechanism of planning (see below) began to urge this as national policy, and in the Second Five Year Plan (1956) made suggestions for the enactment of the policy. The planners believed that the creation of a hard-working and prosperous peasantry would lead to increased output and purchasing power, and also promote social justice. Opponents disputed this, and argued that there was not enough land to redistribute in this way, that ceilings might lead to a reduction in food production by fragmenting viable holdings, and that the whole process of attempting to impose ceilings might lead to economic disruption and social tension. Ceiling legislation was anyway a state matter, and few states passed laws on this until the 1960s. Bihar was again a case in point, where a proposed bill of 1955 was shelved because of deep divisions within the ruling Congress party on the issue.[33] Once again the working of the federal constitution and the functioning of a democracy in which the Congress was dominant foiled Nehru's hopes, despite his apparent power at the centre and within his own party.

Another source of structural inequality in India was the absence of a free educational system. This meant that education at all levels was available only to those whose families could pay. In practice the poor, and girls in particular, were denied access to the experience which could transform both attitudes and life chances. Recognition of this was behind Gandhi's scheme of Basic Education, which envisaged an end to the predominantly literary educational system imported from Britain, and a concentration on the practical skills needed by ordinary people. It would be financed by the students' own labour, and therefore would do away with dependence on state finance. Nehru shared Gandhi's understanding of the long-term significance of education, liked his scheme, and was increasingly disillusioned with what India had in the way of an educational system. By 1952 he was arguing that their system of literary education was almost doing more harm than good, that it needed a radical overhaul, and that it was no good just saying it was constitutionally a subject for the states and that they had no money to invest in education. India desperately needed trained and disciplined people for its future progress.[34] Universities in particular perturbed him, with their exhibitions of student indiscipline and involvement in party politics, and their production of graduates who did not have the technical skills to help their country. His lamentations persisted in subsequent years, as he regularly pronounced on the need to break out of the present scheme of education, and at its base to adopt the Gandhian approach. This culminated in his resolution on Basic Education at the Avadi session of Congress in January 1955, which called on the state governments to implement a policy of educational reform and the provision of Basic Education at primary and secondary level within ten years. As he told the party gathering, he was saddened at the sight of India's uneducated children; what would their country be tomorrow if its children were denied education?[35]

The provision of free mass education was part of the rhetoric of the new India's national identity. The Directive Principles of the constitution had proclaimed that the state should endeavour to provide free and compulsory education to all children up to the age of fourteen within ten years of the constitution coming into force. (The 'state' here specifically included central and state governments.) The need was clearly great. At independence literacy stood at only 14 per cent of the population, and this average masked some much lower figures for girls and for some areas: in three large states, Madhya Pradesh, Rajasthan and UP, under 11 per cent of the population was literate. In the six to eleven age group only one in three children throughout India were enrolled in school, and in the group aged eleven to fourteen only one child out of eleven was enrolled. (The proportion with access to secondary and higher education was even tinier.) Even within this small group receiving education, girls were profoundly disadvantaged – for example thirty-six girls enrolled in the age group six to eleven for every hundred boys, and twenty-two for every hundred boys aged eleven to fourteen.

But midway through the decade in which radical changes in provision of mass education up to the age of fourteen were supposed to occur, little progress had taken place. This was perhaps not surprising. Education clearly had a low priority in the government's planned expenditure, and allocations to education actually dropped from 8.7 per cent of total outlay in the First Five Year Plan to 6.7 per cent in the Second Plan, despite the Directive Principles of the constitution. Nehru himself had so much work on his desk that other matters took up his attention, and successive Education Ministers did not have the authority he might have wielded to push the states forward on a matter which was primarily their responsibility. In the states, education, particularly at primary level for ordinary children, was not glamorous or politically significant for local governments, and it would have taken a massive injection of cash to transform provision, or a radical restructuring on Gandhian lines to avoid the need for state funding and to circumvent the existing educational bureaucracy. Neither initiative was forthcoming. Most politicians could afford to educate their children and had themselves profited from the existing system; while state governments did not have the funds to make major investments in social provision. Consequently one pathway to long-term change in attitudes, and access to a resource which changes lives, was still closed off to millions of Indian citizens, despite Nehru's understanding of the significance of such a failure to the longer-term forging of the nation.[36]

## MANAGING THE ECONOMY

Many of the deepest problems in independent India, and the barriers to forging the nation in reality, were at root or in part economic. Where poverty was acute and endemic people had little stake in the new nation, and little chance to remake their own lives and contribute to the whole; while governments had inadequate revenues to spend on social investment. For Nehru the proper management of the economy was central to his vision of forging the nation in the years after independence. He even said in 1955, 'I am fed up of politics. My entire life has been spent in politics and even now I have to give most of my time to it. But I do not want to waste my time in either politics or international affairs. My mind is full of our economic problems and the need to make economic progress, to make the people better off, and so on ... the real problem before us is the economic progress of India.'[37]

Increasing national wealth, particularly by encouraging industrialisation, was of primary importance to him for a number of reasons. In his view, it would lift people out of poverty and, by an ongoing process of 'trickle down', would ameliorate deep-rooted inequalities. It would also generate revenue so that governments could invest in communications, welfare and social construction, as well as in necessary defence. It would also make the nation state self-reliant, and independent of international sources of aid or vital goods which might undermine its hard-won independence. Furthermore, he thought it would also provide employment and goods for India's growing population.

This last issue was to prove particularly problematic. India's population had begun to grow slowly but steadily after the 1914–18 war. In 1951, the first census in independent India counted a population of 361.1 million, an increase of over 13 per cent during the previous decade (see table below). By 1961 the population was 439.2 million, an increase of over 21 per cent during the decade. The rate of growth continued to increase and by 1971 the population was 547 million. This was mainly due to the availability of antibiotics and comparatively simple advances in health care, which cut infant and maternal mortality, and meant that more infants were surviving, and that women of child-bearing age were living longer. Life expectancy for women was just over 31 at independence (and just over 32 for men), but by 1962 that figure had risen to just over 46 for women and 47 for men. But in a society where the vast majority were illiterate, where there was little provision for primary health care, and where children and particularly sons were a major source of family stability and care in old age, there was little knowledge of birth control and little incentive to practise it. The growth of population caught planners in India by surprise when the 1961 Census revealed the true rate of growth. But at least in the early years of his prime ministership Nehru did not think population was an urgent problem in India. He did not think India was over-

**Population increase in India, 1941–1971**

| Year | Population (millions) | % increase over previous decade |
|------|----------------------|---------------------------------|
| 1941 | 318.7 | 14.2 |
| 1951 | 361.1 | 13.3 |
| 1961 | 439.2 | 21.5 |
| 1971 | 547.0 | 24.7 |

populated or that the growth rate was uncomfortably high: what was needed was higher per capita production and proper distribution of resources.[38]

Nehru had envisaged managing the economy through processes of planning for a decade before independence, and had revelled in the prospect, despite Gandhi's disapproval and complete lack of appreciation of the enterprise. (This was hardly surprising, given Gandhi's distrust of state power, and his vision of a village-based society where people lived simply with what they could grow and make in their own environment.) Now Nehru drew immense intellectual stimulation from the task ahead, and exuded an almost messianic zeal for the planning process. When each successive plan was on the anvil he would write to his Chief Ministers outlining the proposals and their long-term significance for India. In December 1952, nearly two years into the First Five Year Plan, when Parliament in Delhi had given it final approval, he underlined to them the states' responsibilities and explained how he saw the Plan as fundamental to forging the nation.

> Behind the Plan lies the conception of India's unity and of a mighty co-operative effort of all the people of India. That should always be stressed and the inter-relation of one part of India with another pointed out. If we adopt this approach, we shall be dealing with the major disease or weakness of India, i.e., the fissiparous tendencies and parochial outlook that often confront us in this country. The more we think of this balanced picture of the whole of India . . . the less we are likely to go astray in the crooked paths of provincialism, communalism, casteism and all other disruptive and disintegrating tendencies.

He revelled in the vision of an India which had again become dynamic, poised to deal with its economic and social ills as it had dealt with alien political rule, with government and people working together in a 'mighty enterprise'. 'We have, therefore, to take this up in all earnestness and try to infuse in our work something of the spirit of a missionary for a cause.'[39]

A few months later he was writing again to them of the 'mighty adventure' on which they had embarked, which was historic in its significance. 'To build up this country and to solve the problems of poverty and unemployment in a democratic way on this scale is something that has not been done elsewhere. The magnitude of the task and the difficulties we have to overcome may sometimes oppress us, but, at the same time, they should fill us with the enthusiasm that great undertakings bring with them.'[40] As the Second Plan was being drawn up he wrote of his great excitement at something which was 'not a matter of dry figures or statistics . . . but rather a living, moving process affecting hundreds of millions of our countrymen.' India had a unique chance to effect major change in a democratic way on a scale never done before. He had often before spoken of India finding a socialist path towards a fairer economy and society in its own way, taking a flexible rather than doctrinaire approach which suited India's particular circumstances; and now he urged his key political allies in state governments to see that there was no conflict between socialism and democracy – but rather a conflict between democracy and an economic structure which did *not* lead to 'economic democracy'. Again he voiced the sense of a historic enterprise where India had no clear precedents and had to discover its path for itself.[41]

Nehru drew his intellectual inspiration for a planned economy from many different sources, moulding them into an approach which was eclectic rather than doctrinaire. In his student days he had been exposed to the gradualist approach to socio-economic reform of leading British socialist writers, George Bernard Shaw, R. H. Tawney and Sidney and Beatrice Webb. His visit to Soviet Russia in 1927 and his subsequent reading had opened his eyes to the potential of state planning to energise a backward economy and tackle inequality. In the immediate aftermath of the Second World War he was also impressed by British efforts to build a democratic welfare state out of the rubble of conflict. But he was not alone in believing that only the state had the resources and authority to plan and manage major strategies of socio-economic reform. This was part of a broad international intellectual consensus in mid-century, particularly where the task in hand was post-war reconstruction or the management of new national economies in the aftermath of imperial rule. In India itself there was considerable support for this, even from big business, which recognised the role of the state in providing essential infrastructure for economic change and industrialisation.[42]

However, some opposition came both from the left and the right in the Indian political spectrum – with the former complaining that Nehru's government was too willing to accommodate private enterprise in its Plans and had abandoned true socialism; while the latter feared that such an exercise of state control would undermine democracy and individual liberty, and weaken Indian society. Into this latter category fell two old Congress stalwarts, Vallabhbhai Patel and C. Rajagopalachariar, and the Finance Minister, John Matthai, who resigned in June 1950 with considerable bitterness.[43] But it was not until well over a decade after Nehru's death that Indian voices began to denounce the whole strategy of development behind the Five Year Plans, as India became infamous for sluggish growth rates (the so-called 'Hindu rate of growth'), excessive government controls which bred corruption and bottlenecks and earned the scathing title 'licence-permit raj', poor management of state enterprises, and a massive population increase which outstripped the capacity of the state to invest in social goods such as health, housing and education.

Serious planned management of India's economy did not begin immediately after independence, since the government was struggling to deal with the prolonged impact of the war on the economy.[44] Moreover, there were serious differences within the Congress leadership itself, which prevented any radical moves. The government's 1948 Industrial Policy Resolution looked towards a mixed economy in which private capital was to play an important role, and government would own only strategic industries. No mention was made of nationalisation to achieve social justice, though Nehru in his speech to Parliament spoke of the need to end 'the vast gap between human beings', which he felt in this day and age no one of sensitivity could tolerate. (Reverting to one of his most serious forms of criticism he denounced socio-economic disparities as 'so vulgar, and vulgarity is the worst thing that a country or individual should support'.)[45] Moreover, when the Planning Commission was set up in 1950 its goals were watered down in CWC discussions, on the insistence of Patel, to link it with the Directive Principles in the constitution rather than with the elimination of exploitation and inequality, the profit motive in economic activity and social organisation, and 'the anti-social concentration of wealth and means of production'.[46]

The First Five Year Plan (1951–6) was a modest enterprise, consisting partly of pre-existing projects. The largest outlay was on irrigation and power (28.1 per cent), followed by transport and communications (23.6 per cent), with 15 per cent on agriculture and community development projects, and only 7.6 per cent on industry and mining. (This included 1.3 per cent on village and small industries – an indication of the relegation of the Gandhian vision of development.) Education, health, housing and other social welfare schemes were allocated 22.6 per cent of the outlay.[47] The role of the state in leading development and strengthening its range of controls over the economy was explicit, but the role of the private sector was seen as complementary and valuable.

It was only in the formulation of the Second Plan (1956–61) that Nehru's own vision became critical and planning the driving force in the Indian economy. By this time Patel was dead and Nehru had asserted his dominance over Congress policy-making. In the Planning Commission he had gathered round him a powerful and small group of politicians, civil servants and specialists who shared his vision of planning for development which would create a more egalitarian society rather than just delivering economic growth. Among the members were Tarlok Singh, an ICS officer who played a major drafting role in Plan documents and was an expert on rural matters;[48] V. T. Krishnamachari, a lawyer, ICS officer and experienced administrator, who was appointed a deputy chairman; Gulzarilal Nanda, another deputy chairman who was a seasoned Congress member and trade union organiser; and Professor P. C. Mahalanobis, a physicist and statistical expert. The last was considered to be the chief architect of the Second Plan once he had convinced Nehru of the benefits of a strategy which drew heavily on the Soviet model. Nehru and his small cohort not only dominated decision-making in Delhi on economic issues. They also exercised major influence over the states through their strong corporate vision and expertise, and the financial leverage of the central government over the states.

The preparation of the Second Plan coincided not only with Nehru's dominance in Congress deliberations, but also his determination to steer both party and government away from its initial caution to a clear commitment to what he called a socialist pattern or picture of society, where the principal means of production were under social ownership and control, for the benefit of society as a whole. As 1954 turned into 1955 he obtained a commitment to this end from the Lok Sabha and then from the Congress Party at its session in January 1955 at Avadi.[49] Writing to PCC presidents in March he noted that some people had taken fright at what they considered to be a revolutionary change in policy. He insisted that he hoped to achieve change peacefully and to deal with conflicts of interest by cooperation if possible, but that the objective was clear, and everything had to be judged by 'the yardstick of the good it does to the masses of our people'. He invoked Gandhi, the most important icon of the nation: 'the test is always the good of the masses of our people. This combination of firm adherence to principle and objective, and yet a friendly approach even to those who differ and whose interests clash with that objective, is the way that Gandhiji taught us. It is in keeping with the genius of India.'[50] He took pains in speeches to a wide range of groups to spell out that a 'socialist pattern' or 'Socialism' was not some doctrinaire commitment, but at heart the determination to provide ordinary people with what he called the six basic necessities of life – food, clothes, housing, health care, education and employment. These were an essential goal in the nation's ongoing struggle to fashion itself anew economically and socially, just as it had done politically.

This was to be the goal the planners now set themselves, and they sought to achieve rapid economic growth, expansion of employment and a reduction in economic inequality. The strategy was to increase public spending significantly, to emphasise capital goods production and industrialisation (to replace imports) dominated by the public sector, though private enterprise was still permitted – and indeed vital – outside what were seen as strategic industries, which included transport and utilities. Accordingly resources given to agriculture declined, while the percentage of Plan outlay devoted to industry more than doubled compared with the first Plan. Expenditure on social services also declined as a percentage, including that devoted to education. Alongside a vision of economic progress led by industrialisation was the planners' recognition that the Indian economy also needed major changes in the use of land if the nation was to be fed, capital was to be released for investment, and labour was to become available for industrial work. But land reform had already proved an arduous and disputed project; and the states now had considerable flexibility over strategies and timetables for the imposition of land ceilings and the development of cooperative farming. The weakness of Indian agriculture was eventually to prove a profound flaw in the whole planning process, and it demonstrated that even at the height of his influence in the polity and the party Nehru could only partially push through policies he considered central to the forging of the nation.

By the later 1950s the shape of Nehru's model of planned management of the economy was firmly in place. Its effects would take time to demonstrate, but the results of the first five years of tentative planning had been reasonably encouraging. Between 1951 and 1956 the annual rate of investment averaged 6 per cent of national income, and national income itself rose by 18 per cent. Agricultural production grew modestly, increasing by 4.32 per cent between 1952 and 1956, while industrial production surged ahead, growing by 10.51 per cent in the same period. This progress was as much due to external conditions as to planning, particularly good monsoons in the early 1950s, the revival of international trade, and India's ability to draw on the sterling balances built up in London as a result of its contribution to war expenditure. Nonetheless, it produced a sense that India was economically on its feet again, and the national government was tackling problems with a vision and vigour the imperial government had not possessed. It also encouraged Nehru and his planning advisers to advance more ambitiously towards a national reconstruction interpreted in social as well as economic terms.

Nehru's experiences of attempting to forge the nation as a reality for many who had been barely touched by the idea of the nation in earlier decades had shown how complex was the task he had set himself. It had to prevail in an India composed of many often competing interests, and where the nature of the administrative tools at his disposal and the working of the federal constitution could effectively block his policies and erode the stated principles by which the nation state had chosen to define itself. Nehru was indisputably a political visionary, in his own way as fired and sustained by his commitment to forging a new India as Gandhi had been. In the mid-1950s he was also at the height of his public repute and influence within the Indian polity. But even he had begun to learn the hard way that vision could not easily be translated into reality. Interests and structures worked against him. But there was also an inadequacy deep within himself. He could so often see the nature of the problem but could not see how to solve it – hence his increasingly frustrated and somewhat hectoring tone on issues where he felt at a loss. As he often admitted, he was not at heart a politician or an administrator, as, for example, Patel had been. (It was no coincidence that Mountbatten had been so relieved that Patel had taken over the problem of the Indian princes in 1947, with his political skills of ruthlessness, compromise and a way of working within and through entrenched administrative and party structures.) Nehru was the visionary and cosmopolitan intellectual, who could see the broad picture and expound the significance of issues facing India in sweeping historical terms. He was less at home with the details of government, and increasingly did not have the time to master the mountains of paper that crossed his desk daily, despite his frenetic expenditure of emotional and physical energy. In retrospect, and despite the enormous respect and affection in which Nehru was held by so many Indians, and indeed by those who served him in government,[51] his experience suggests that a different style of prime ministership, delegating power to colleagues with different skills to complement his own, might have been more effective, and laid down a pattern for the future which did not depend so much on his own person.

## Chapter 13

# Creating an International Identity

One of the key tasks in founding the new Indian nation after independence was to give India an international identity and standing, which meant fashioning both a coherent foreign policy and a foreign service to conduct the nation state's relations with the outside world. This was a task which Nehru relished. He was the most cosmopolitan and well-travelled of his Congress colleagues in 1947. As a result of his visits to Europe in 1927 and 1935–6, and his wide reading on world history and politics, he had developed a profound interest in foreign affairs and a sense of India's place in worldwide historical developments. Consequently he had become effectively the major Congress authority on future foreign policy, given too the comparative inexperience of his colleagues in this field, and the ideological vacuum left because Gandhi took little interest in foreign policy issues, preferring to concentrate on moral revolution within India. It was thus understandable that he decided to retain for himself the External Affairs Ministry as well as being Prime Minister, even though this was to prove unwise, given the immense workload the two offices generated. Furthermore, he derived considerable personal refreshment from his foreign visits in this dual capacity. Following a visit to Britain in 1953 for the coronation of the new Queen Elizabeth (when he processed down the aisle of Westminster Abbey in the small group of Commonwealth Prime Ministers) and a Commonwealth Prime Ministers' Conference, he spoke of the mental refreshment such visits gave him despite the pressure of work.[1]

Obviously he was most relaxed on his visits to Britain: it had been home to him as a schoolboy and student, and it enabled him to spend time with close friends, including the Mountbattens, whom he visited at their country home, Broadlands in Hampshire, at weekends. He also enjoyed shopping in London for presents for Indira and his two young grandsons – touchingly one of the rare luxuries of relaxation he permitted himself, and a reminder of his deep family commitment, as well as his empathy with children, despite the almost total dedication of his life to politics.

As Minister for External Affairs Nehru himself set and articulated the broad outlines of India's foreign policy, emphasising their significance for the new nation in his set-piece speeches on foreign issues to the Lok Sabha, and in his letters to Chief Ministers. Few if any of his colleagues in the party, in government or in Parliament were genuine interlocutors of his vision of India's place in the international world, or influenced his thinking on foreign policy and defence. After the death of Patel in December 1950 there was almost complete deference to his views within government circles, and he effectively dominated India's foreign affairs for nearly two decades, gathering round himself a loyal band of those who shared his vision. This domination was to have serious effects within the governmental process, because it prevented the development of independent and critical expertise among civil servants, and among other politicians and parliamentarians in this area, and gave undue influence to people who were close to Nehru but often lacked experience and judgement.[2] Among these was pre-eminently Krishna Menon, the Indian he had met in London and whom he had come to use as a sounding-board when he felt isolated within the Congress Party.

## SETTING THE GUIDELINES OF POLICY

Before independence Nehru had spoken about a free India working for world peace and the end of imperialism, and of the need for a new Asian unity including China. In the turbulent months after independence he recognised that they had not had the time to formulate coherent policies. In late December 1947 he acknowledged to Parliament that India's foreign policy was still 'rather vague, rather inchoate', but that it would be fashioned according to what was most advantageous to India.[3] By the end of 1948 the main themes of policy were becoming clearer. India would, first and foremost, pursue an independent policy as befitted a newly independent state. (This now seems self-evident, but was in fact a live issue because in the early years of India's independence the Soviet Union assumed that India would continue to follow British policies.) Its fundamental goals would be to pursue world peace, and to combat racism and imperialism. Nearer to home, India would play a leading role in the revival of Asia in world affairs and in seeking to readjust India's relations with Europe; though this did not mean attempting to create an Asian bloc of nations. Most significantly, India would refuse to align itself with either of the two world blocs being built up in the aftermath of the Second World War, as America squared up to the Soviet Union and what it saw as the challenge of world communism. This was not neutrality but a stance of non-alignment, leaving India free to judge issues on their merits and in relation to India's interests.[4] Nehru was, however, under no illusion about the potential difficulty of maintaining such a stance, particularly given India's need to stabilise and reconstruct its economy in the immediate aftermath of independence, as he told the distinguished American journalist and author, Marquis Childs.[5]

But what were India's interests? From the perspective of Nehru's desk in the External Affairs Ministry in New Delhi these were largely dictated by India's geographical position, and its domestic politics. In the first place, there was the basic question of India's security. Its northern borders were the only ones through which invasion could take place by land, and this necessitated both the mainten-ance of a modern army and the desirability of friendly relations with Pakistan, Russia and China. (Kashmir was of course partly a strategic issue for India as well as one of national territorial and ideological integrity.) However, standing at the intersection of Asia and the Middle East, with strong ties through traditions of democracy and the English language with Britain and America, India was also seen by Nehru as a world power in its own right, in terms of influence though not of military might. As a major stable independent power in Asia, India had a partic-ular role to play in leading and interpreting Asia, and specifically South East Asia to the wider world, and in trying to incorporate Asia into a world community in a new way. This was in a sense India's geographical and historical destiny in a world where imperialism was a waning force and Asian countries needed to find a way of relating as equals to the richer powers of the western world. India's large Muslim population also made it sensitive to issues affecting Muslim interests, particularly in the Middle East.

Moreover, as a democratic state valuing liberty and equality, yet committed to state intervention in the social and economic order, India was uniquely placed to see virtues in the ideologies of both emerging Cold War blocs, but equally able to see the weaknesses and misinterpretations, if not vices, of both as they faced each other and sought to fashion the wider world in their own image, tied in by mili-tary and economic arrangements of aid. Indeed, by 1956 Nehru had concluded that the Cold War was far less about ideology than about two large nations wishing to exercise world power. However, India also needed foreign aid, partic-ularly as the Second Five Year Plan was on the drawing board, and this, too, suggested a very material interest in friendly relations with all potential donors of money and expertise. Nehru was deeply concerned at the thought of India becoming permanently tied to any bloc through aid, and perturbed at the distorting cultural influences which went with aid, particularly American aid. Interest therefore reinforced a policy of pragmatic responses to foreign issues and a stance of non-alignment.[6]

Idealism, pragmatism and self-interest were thus intertwined in Nehru's judge-ment of world forces and their impact on India. But unlike many other countries, India's foreign policy, as enunciated by him, was often couched in idealistic and moral terms, particularly with reference to India's own struggle for freedom from imperialism, its non-violent strategies, and Gandhi's ideological influence.

Although this rhetorical style to an extent boosted India's image and Nehru's personal standing, it also provided hostages to fortune when India seemed to fail to live up to its enunciated ideals.

## IMPLEMENTING FOREIGN POLICY

This is not the place for an exhaustive account of Indian foreign relations under Nehru's government. The purpose here, in probing a key aspect of Nehru's political life, is to indicate his personal influence in the field of foreign relations, both on the domestic scene and abroad, and to highlight the policy themes which, under his guidance, created India's new international identity. These were central to the making of the nation, but lasted long after the initial phase of giving India a distinctive international personality.

### THE MECHANISMS OF FOREIGN RELATIONS

As Minister for External Affairs, Nehru had first to preside over the creation of mechanisms to enable India to conduct diplomacy and determine policy. India had had no foreign service while under British rule but as early as 1946 the imperial External Affairs Department (with Nehru as its Minister in the Interim Government) had begun to plan for a new single diplomatic cadre. Recruits were drawn from a variety of sources – underlining the mundane problems, often ignored by historians, which new nation states have in adjusting from colonial rule to independent governance and the difficulties in building up expertise in diplomacy and intelligence. Some officers were borrowed from existing central services such as the ICS. Around a hundred recruits came from the defence forces: they had served during the war and had subsequently been interviewed by a special selection board. Others came via direct applications or more informal routes, but were interviewed by a special recruitment board under the Secretary-General for External Affairs, G. S. Bajpai, one of India's few ICS officials with serious foreign expertise, gained from his six years preceding independence as India's agent-general in Washington. Not surprisingly, there were initially difficulties over seniority among such a motley bunch of people.[7]

Given India's lack of diplomatic expertise in the early years of nation-building, the country was initially represented only in countries considered to be central to Indian interests, and Nehru decided to draw on an assortment of trusted friends and relatives for key diplomatic assignments. He counted as his four best diplomats[8] individuals with no experience of diplomacy, only one of whom had any proven administrative expertise. Two were academics, K. M. Panikkar, a historian who had also served in Indian princely states, and S. Radhakrishnan, a former Professor of Philosophy at Calcutta University who from 1935 had held the Chair of Eastern Religions at Oxford. The other two were the older of his sisters, Vijayalakshmi Pandit, and his eccentric friend from London, Krishna Menon.

Of these, Menon was the most problematic and embarrassing, and in a very real sense would become Nehru's nemesis in 1962, when China invaded India in circumstances where Menon as Minister of Defence had helped to leave India unprepared for self-defence. Menon had no experience of Indian politics, having lived for nearly two decades in London, working as Secretary of the India League. But Nehru began to involve him in informal diplomacy in the months before independence, and then in 1947 made him the Indian High Commissioner in London. From London he went to America to the Indian delegation to the UN, and in 1956 became a Minister without Portfolio and then Defence Minister. Menon was undoubtedly intellectually able, and devoted to what he saw as India's cause, and to Nehru personally. But he was psychologically unstable, very difficult to work with, incapable of delegating, self-willed and self-opinionated and thus liable to disastrous misjudgements. Nehru recognised many of his defects.[9] In the spring of 1951 Menon was clearly in the throes of a major nervous breakdown, caused in part by his overwork, and Nehru did his best to force him to take sick leave, in October virtually ordering him to take six months off. Menon contrived medical opinion to the effect that he had recovered and eventually served out his appointment.[10] When he subsequently went to the UN his relationship with his superior, Vijayalakshmi, was so bad that UN gossip-mongers would ask why Indians could not get on together when they seemed so good at suggesting solutions to world problems.[11]

Even more damaging to India, and to Nehru personally as an international figure, was Menon's tendency to strident public outbursts and hectoring tone in the UN towards the western powers, which did much to alienate American opinion in particular. President Kennedy even had to tell Nehru in person in 1961 of the intensity of American feeling against Menon, and an acerbic pen portrait of him in the *New York Times* noted that he had a talent for 'making a few devoted friends and many devoted enemies'.[12] Nehru's support of Menon, despite so much evidence that he was often a liability to his country, indicates not only his talent for personal loyalty, but also his isolation at the apex of India's political world, where few were his intellectual companions, as Menon was, and even fewer were prepared to confront him with possibly unpleasant truths.

Nehru also threw himself into the work of personally representing his country. He embraced the new possibilities of rapid air travel to visit foreign countries, to attend conferences, and to meet foreign heads of state. Among the most important and regular of his foreign visits were those he made to Britain for meetings of Commonwealth Heads of Government, where he became a senior and articulate figure, and in a sense the representative of the former colonies and dependencies which joined the Commonwealth as independent states as the British adjusted to the processes of decolonisation. (The remarkable and ultimately transformative effect on the Commonwealth of India's continued membership as a republic is discussed later in this chapter.) He fitted easily into the British establishment, the path paved by his long-standing relationships with prominent politicians and his close friendships with 'Dickie' and Edwina Mountbatten. The latter lasted until Edwina's death in 1960 and his own in 1964. He had the sense of humour to recognise the remarkable transformation in his standing for one who had so lately been a resident of an imperial prison. As he wrote to Indira in October 1948, he 'rather enjoyed' his stay in England, particularly his two weekends at Broadlands. He could not help but respond in kind to the welcome and friendship he found. 'Perhaps also my vanity was tickled for there was praise enough. I am told I made a hit, from Buckingham Palace downwards.' Even his old foe, Winston Churchill, went out of his way to be friendly. Nehru sensed that India itself was also being regarded far more highly and reported to his daughter that an article in the *Economist* had been entitled 'India – the new Great Power'. 'So I basked in all this praise and adulation. But at the same time I felt rather uncomfortable and somewhat out of place and counterfeit.'[13] Perhaps he remembered descriptions of Gandhi's visit to London in 1931, and his mentor's iconic simplicity of dress and life as he stayed in an East End Settlement to distinguish himself from other Indian delegates who were content with the posh hotels provided for them.

This was one of the last letters Nehru would write about his travels to Indira, because from 1949 she began to accompany him, acting in effect as his consort, just as at home she had adopted the role of his hostess. Sometimes she brought her two sons, as in July 1956 when they all visited West Germany. By this time she was internationally recognised as official companion, confidante and hostess, and a pen portrait in the *New York Times* that year on the eve of her arrival in America with her father referred to her as the 'First Lady' of India. It provided readers with key biographical details, mentioning her growing political status in Congress, and concluded that she was 'a strange mixture'. She took after her father in facial appearance, in her sophisticated mind, and in 'sudden bursts of temper'; yet she was also a fragile-looking and attractive woman who 'set the fashions in India with her simple yet elegant saris'.[14]

Nehru visited the USA several times in his life, and in these formative years of India's international standing he went in 1949 and 1956. He went to China in 1954, to Russia and Eastern Europe in 1955, and in 1956 paid brief visits (on a trip primarily to London for a Commonwealth Prime Ministers' Conference) to Syria, Lebanon, Egypt, West Germany, France, Yugoslavia and Ireland. This unrelenting travel demonstrated his physical energy and his huge intellectual curiosity, as well as his personal commitment to an international role, though he did not find all these visits naturally easy. His 1949 visit to America, for example, was culturally fraught, as his sister remembered. He found American hospitality ostentatious. (He probably referred to it as vulgar in his own mind.) And he was 'too British' and embarrassed to ask outright for aid, and this annoyed a meeting of bankers who had come to meet him, prepared to offer help.[15] Americans for their part found him culturally confusing. Before his visit a Central Intelligence Agency profile had called him a man of broad vision and integrity, but suggested that his character was 'weakened by emotionalism which at times destroys his sense of values. He is gracious as well as brilliant, but volatile and quick-tempered.'[16] Many in or close to power tended to think that he had a sense of superiority to all things American, born of the 'snobbism of a wealthy Brahmin' combined with the intellectual snobbery of 'the ivied halls', in the words of Marquis Childs. The Secretary of State, Dean Acheson, himself not a little condescending towards Nehru, found his visitor prickly and difficult, and deeply resented being addressed as if he were a public meeting, as Queen Victoria had said of Gladstone.[17]

Nehru often turned his travels into educative opportunities for people at home, writing detailed notes about them for distribution to his colleagues, and to his less travelled Chief Ministers of the Indian states. Two notes on his summer 1955 tour ran to twenty-eight typed foolscap pages, dealing with social and economic issues as well as world politics. A year later another lengthy note was sent to Chief Ministers on his month abroad.[18] Nehru carried on his personal diplomacy in Delhi, receiving a stream of distinguished visitors of all kinds, including foreign heads of state. Chou En-lai visited from China in mid-1954 (and again in late 1956), so did Colonel Nasser on his way home to Egypt from the Bandung Conference, and Amir Faisal, the Crown Prince and Prime Minister of Saudi Arabia. Bulganin and Khrushchev came from the Soviet Union late in 1955. The latter were the equivalent of box office hits. According to one observer, they looked like pilgrims from another planet with floppy felt hats and trousers so wide they could have been used as sails! Huge crowds turned out to see them, and Nehru greatly enjoyed their visit, and sensed it was a personal triumph for himself as a diplomat as well as a prime minister.[19] As with his own travels, Nehru would often describe these visits and the contents of discussions in his regular letters to Chief Ministers. He wanted not only to educate them, but to ensure that they would support his foreign policy at a time when India seemed to be called upon to play a significant international role but when there was some 'unintelligent criticism', as he put it, at home.[20]

However, Nehru's role as his own foreign minister had its drawbacks. He obviously could not give as much time to the ministry as a full-time minister could have done, unencumbered by the other commitments which Nehru also shouldered as Prime Minister. M. O. Mathai, as Nehru's confidential personal assistant, was best positioned to see some of these problems, and when N. R. Pillai, Secretary-

General in the Ministry of External Affairs, was thought likely to move to the governorship of the World Bank, Mathai noted for Nehru directly, 'PM needs more and more competent assistance as years go by and I cannot . . . think of any person who can replace Pillai.' Pillai was senior and effective in dealing with foreign diplomats and therefore relieved his chief of some of the burden of interviews with them. Over a year later in September 1956 Mathai again noted that Nehru had neither time nor the inclination to manage the ministry effectively, with disastrous effects.[21] There was considerable evidence of administrative slackness in the Ministry. Late in 1954 Vijayalakshmi Pandit still owed a debt of over Rs 12,000 incurred nearly two years previously, and officials in the Ministry of External Affairs were belaboured by their colleagues in the Finance Ministry who thought they should have the courage to present the bills to her. R. K. Nehru, the Foreign Secretary, detailing the problem, wanted to talk to Nehru about the issue, as he worried at what might leak out if anybody who saw the file talked about it; he felt it was symptomatic of administrative weakness in the ministry.[22]

Nehru himself became anguished at the lack of security ('feeble to the point of absurdity') in his ministry, following a loss of secret documents. He referred to it as effectively an 'administrative collapse', instituted a security review, and castigated his officials for their lack of responsibility, 'loose talk' to outsiders, for tearing up, rather than burning, secret papers and putting them in waste paper baskets, from where they could be retrieved and pasted together, and for circulating telegrams to such large numbers of people.[23] However, he never gave up his dual role as Prime Minister and Minister for External Affairs, despite the burden on him, and the evidence of its administrative drawbacks.

### THE COMMONWEALTH CONNECTION

One of the first and greatest foreign policy decisions which Nehru and his government had to make was whether India should leave the Commonwealth once it became a republic. Ironically a decision which did not figure on his ideological list of foreign policy goals, and was achieved pragmatically and administratively to protect the interests of India and Britain, turned out to be one of Nehru's major legacies to his country and to the world in the field of international relations, when other more trumpeted ideals such as non-alignment had become irrelevant. The Commonwealth which developed in the second half of the twentieth century as a multinational association of states which had once been part of the British empire was an unprecedented cultural and political phenomenon, and a far cry from the tight group of old Dominions which had formed its core in the 1940s. It was India's continued membership when it became a republic which broke the old mould and provided the example as well as the mechanisms for the expansion of the Commonwealth to include people of diverse ethnicities and creeds, and states with differing constitutional arrangements, bound together by mutual ideals and interests, rather than by political dominion or formal constitutional connections.[24] Before 1947 Nehru had been forthright that he could not see any future for a free India in the Commonwealth. This was hardly surprising, given the composition of the Commonwealth and the dominant role of Britain within it at this time. Even in April 1947 he was stating categorically to a colleague that India would have to leave the Commonwealth at independence.[25] However, he and his colleagues were persuaded that as a temporary measure dominionhood within the Commonwealth was a convenient mechanism for affecting a swift transfer of power to Indian hands before India's republican constitution was completely worked out. Although Nehru was evidently anxious for close relations with the Commonwealth on a longer-term basis, he did not see how this could be achieved with India as a republic, and he was not prepared to rock the political boat in India when so many people were already feeling sore because Congress had reluctantly accepted the principle of Partition.[26]

However, there were others in India who were anxious to resolve this constitutional conundrum, including Baldev Singh, Defence Minister in the Interim Government, the indefatigable old Moderate mediators, M. R. Jayakar and T. B. Sapru, and the formidable Vallabhbhai Patel himself, despite his concerns about what he saw as British Tory machinations in relation to Hyderabad and British attitudes on Kashmir.[27] In Britain itself Krishna Menon as Indian High Commissioner found willing allies in Attlee's government who were anxious to contrive a formula which would permit India as a republic to stay within the Commonwealth. A friendly India within the Commonwealth suited Britain's own interests, particularly its political and strategic concerns in South East Asia, where it saw India as a vital ally in combating the spread of communism from the north and east. The opposite, an India outside the Commonwealth in a sensitive region, and the difficulties which would arise if Pakistan and Ceylon stayed within the Commonwealth and India did not, concentrated the British official mind.

Attlee himself started the ball rolling in earnest with a long private and personal letter to 'My dear Nehru' on 11 March 1948. In this he suggested that the Commonwealth had reached a new stage in its pragmatic development, bound together as they were less by constitutional formulations than by adherence to 'certain absolute values, faith in democratic institutions, belief in the rule of law and acceptance of the need for toleration. All these things make up together a "way of life" which with many local differences yet give a general sense of community.' Apart from these intangibles the only link was common allegiance to the Crown, and he asked Nehru whether there was any real objection to India remaining in the Commonwealth because of that common allegiance. He urged Nehru to think of the benefits of a head of state above section or community, and to see how Commonwealth membership might promote Indian unity and help it to take a 'right and natural' leading part in Asia, and in world terms how an expanded Commonwealth would contribute to unity in place of fragmentation. Carefully playing the themes which Nehru held dear he argued for the Commonwealth as a unique experiment in which members had complete freedom along with association, and the possibility of varying their precise relationship to the whole or the other parts because there was no formal constitution.[28] Nehru felt he could not give a definitive answer immediately but indicated that he hoped India's relations with the Commonwealth would be close and intimate, though at the moment he was not clear in his own mind how to ensure this. He told Krishna Menon privately at the same time that there was no possibility of India continuing as a Dominion.[29]

However, there followed intensive negotiations to try to evolve some formula which would permit a republican India to stay within the Commonwealth. By the time Nehru came to London for his first Commonwealth Prime Ministers' Conference in October 1948 it was evident that he, too, was very keen on finding a mechanism for continued Commonwealth membership, and though this did not figure on the formal agenda, he had informal talks with the Prime Minister and with his close friends, the Mountbattens and Cripps, in the privacy of Broadlands weekends. As politicians and jurists struggled with the problem in Britain and India, while consulting the existing members of the Commonwealth, it was clear that finding a formula was no easy task. The stumbling block was the nature of the Crown in relation to the members. For Australia and New Zealand, in particular, allegiance to the Crown was vital: to India it was a denial of independence. However, Nehru, despite his recurrent anxieties on the issue, began preparing the way for India's continued membership of a changed Commonwealth, arguing the case in the Congress Party and to Chief Ministers. To the latter he argued that there were solid advantages to India and to the cause of world peace in remaining within the Commonwealth, and that it would not prejudice India's independence of policy or mean lining up with any power bloc.[30]

The consummation of so much effort came in a conference in London of Commonwealth Prime Ministers in late April 1949, called specifically to review relations between Commonwealth countries.[31] India's delegation consisted of Nehru, Krishna Menon as India's High Commissioner in London, and Sir G. S. Bajpai, who had been responsible for the formula which eventually produced agreement. As the London Declaration subsequently put it, India would remain a welcome member of the Commonwealth because, even though becoming a republic, it wished to remain a member and accepted the King as the 'symbol of the free association of its independent member nations and as such the head of the Commonwealth'. The UK, Canada, Australia, New Zealand, South Africa, India, Pakistan and Ceylon (by now independent also) thus declared that they remained united as free and equal members of the Commonwealth, cooperating freely in the pursuit of peace, liberty and progress. Nehru's own major contributions in the formal meetings were on the opening day when he laid out the background to India's hope to remain within the Commonwealth without altering the relationship of the Dominions to the Crown, and his suggestions as to a way forward now, which included India's acceptance of the King as a symbol of the free association of Commonwealth countries; and in the final meeting when he talked of Commonwealth cooperation not just for mutual defence but for peace, which meant tackling underlying problems of social deprivation, for these were the root of movements hostile to democracy. He also spoke of India's attraction to democratic ideals and the way its own institutions were largely modelled on British ones.

Many others with Nehru were central to the evolution of this formula, but it is right to say that if he had not been convinced of the desirability of continued Commonwealth membership, had not worked for it and been prepared to 'sell it' back in India in the Congress Party and Parliament, then it is likely that India would have followed Ireland as a republic and out of the Commonwealth. Vallabhbhai Patel was generous in his acknowledgement of Nehru's contribution to the prolonged and delicate negotiations which had achieved such a successful outcome. As it was, Nehru had to field considerable hostility from the left wing in Indian politics. Even an old colleague like J. P. Narayan felt strongly that Nehru was going back on all they had stood for over many years, and believed that Commonwealth membership would tie India to Britain and commit it to one of the two power blocs.[32]

Nehru was, however, delighted with the outcome and with the friendly way in which it was achieved. He told Indira that he felt the gracious way it was done was the Gandhian way, and that India had given up nothing that mattered and had gained much. 'The objection can only be on sentimental grounds and that too on false sentiment and hangovers from the past.' (He also reported that Churchill had insisted they had a meal together and had admitted that 'after much painful thought he had changed his opinion about India', and had been 'deeply moved by the recent decisions and more especially by my magnanimity'.) Nehru sensed it was a historic decision which would have far-reaching consequences, as he told Canada's retired Prime Minister, W. L. MacKenzie King.[33] However, behind the warmth and idealistic rhetoric there were solid reasons for all parties to wish to remain in a Commonwealth association. For India these were diverse, but they included easy access to the sterling balances which were vital to India's economic plans, mutual trading interests, access to defence supplies when the army had for so long been tied to British equipment, the hope of ameliorating conditions for Indians living in Commonwealth countries, and belief that the Commonwealth connection would help India in its relations with Pakistan. In a dangerous world

India could not afford to be isolated, and the Commonwealth connection guarded against this, while not tying India into either the Soviet or the American bloc.

Nehru used the Commonwealth as a forum in which to expound his views on world affairs. As early as the October 1948 Conference of Commonwealth Prime Ministers he was using it to promote his vision of a new Asia, its problems and increasing significance. Several times he reverted to the crucial issue of improved living standards and economic development: only these were a sure defence against communism, for communism thrived on deprivation. Thus Commonwealth defence must include positive policies to promote peace through development as well as military preparedness. He also voiced the fear that America was allying with reactionary regimes, and this in turn would play into Communist hands: moreover America seemed to be using the same strategies of world power as the Communist bloc, particularly the acquisition of bases for defence and aggression.[34]

In January 1950 at the meetings of Commonwealth Foreign Ministers in Colombo, Nehru was clearly growing in stature as a Commonwealth leader with a particular expertise on Asian affairs. Later that year the British High Commissioner in New Delhi sounded him out for Attlee about his possible attendance at a Commonwealth Prime Ministers' Conference which was important for discussions of Commonwealth defence, and Nehru was given to understand that Attlee thought Nehru's presence was vital 'because of what I had come to represent in the Commonwealth and in Asia'.[35] At the subsequent conference in London in January 1951 Nehru was a major participant, particularly on Asian affairs, and he urged his colleagues to recognise the significance of China and not fall into line with the USA and attempt to isolate China.[36] At subsequent meetings Nehru was again anxious to 'interpret' China to his Commonwealth colleagues, and determined to use the Commonwealth forum to preserve world peace. He did not regret the decision taken in 1949, and for example in his letters to Chief Ministers regularly defended the Commonwealth connection as giving India advantages and also making for world peace. Even in the bleak days of the Suez crisis in 1956 he argued against India leaving the Commonwealth, for this would be a step of angry reaction rather than wisdom, whereas it was obvious that the Commonwealth did not stand in the way of India pursuing its own policies.[37]

Although the Commonwealth gave Nehru an international position and helped to incorporate India into the international community, it did not, as he had hoped, resolve the tensions which built up in many Commonwealth countries over the role of Indian migrants and their relations with local groups striving for political and economic freedoms. Nehru urged Indians to behave with decorum in their host countries and to work with local people, but he had little success in resolving problems confronting Indians in Ceylon or in parts of Africa.

## WORKING FOR WORLD PEACE

One of the great themes of foreign policy which Nehru emphasised, and in which he undoubtedly believed passionately, was the pursuit of world peace. In this he drew on the spirit of Gandhi's vision of India and his own socialist commitments to the brotherhood and equality of men, as well as on his growing understanding of the horrors of war if new weapons of mass destruction were unleashed. In 1951 he seemed to an American journalist, with whom he had a lengthy talk, to be haunted by the fear of a third world war 'which would bring barbarism, wiping out any semblance of civilisation; tribalism and militarism would hold whatever remained out of the general chaos'.[38] Nehru emphasised the need for peace, and India's own wish to live in peace with all nations, in countless speeches at home and abroad.

Moreover, he attempted to interpret people to each other when misunderstanding threatened to have dire consequences, as for example during his 1949 visit to America when he tried to make President Truman understand what he thought was happening in China, or when he expounded Asian problems and ideas in Commonwealth conferences. A striking example occurred in 1953 when he wrote a secret and personal note to Churchill on world affairs at Churchill's suggestion, when he was in London for the new Queen's coronation and a Commonwealth Prime Ministers' Conference. In it he expounded his understanding of key issues such as politics in Egypt, the upsurge of political consciousness in Asia and Africa, the urgency of questions relating to land ownership in Africa and Asia and the significance of racial discrimination.[39] He sometimes tried direct mediation between opponents, as before the Suez crisis of 1956; or instructed his ambassadors to perform a mediatory role, as in the case of his ambassador to the Soviet Union, K. P. S. Menon, who shuttled between Moscow and Budapest during the Hungarian crisis. Nehru's support for the Commonwealth was in part because he felt it could be an institution through which to work for peace and mutual understanding. But the principal institution through which he hoped for a more peaceful world order was the infant United Nations.

Speaking to the UN General Assembly in November 1948 he pledged India's commitment to the principles and purposes of the UN Charter, and talked about throwing aside the many fears which generate conflict, invoking the teachings of Gandhi, which he hoped could be exported from the Indian situation as a means of dealing with the world's problems.[40] In subsequent years he had his misgivings about the UN and the way great power politics came to operate within it, for example on the issue of Kashmir. But he supported it constantly as a vehicle for peace. In the early 1950s he argued forcefully for the acceptance of the People's Republic of China into the UN, against American opposition, on the grounds that once the Communist government was firmly in control it could not be ignored, and ostracism would only increase Chinese bitterness; whereas if China were incorporated into the UN it might well become a force for world peace, and the UN would more properly represent the world community.[41] He also threw India's weight behind the UN in its attempt to deal with the repatriation of prisoners after the Korean War by agreeing that India should take up the thankless task of chairing the commission for repatriation and that Indian troops should be in charge of the process.

## NON-ALIGNMENT

Nehru's most significant strategy for the prevention of war in the 1950s was the policy of non-alignment, which for him had profound ideological significance as well as being a realistic and pragmatic way of protecting India's interests in the Cold War situation. Looking back from the perspective of the end of Nehru's century and the ending of a world order demarcated by blocs ranged against each other in fear and hostility, it is perhaps difficult to recognise quite what an innovative and visionary stance India took under Nehru. It would have been far easier to shelter under the protective umbrella of one or other alliance structure, but Nehru was determined that India would refuse to be constrained into such a mould, would stake a claim for a moral stance which might serve and unite many Asian and African countries seeking a genuine independence of policy, and would work for peace by preventing the building up of antagonistic power blocs.

Despite this commitment to non-alignment, Nehru's initial leanings were towards the United States, a country with which India shared ties of language and democratic governance, and from which it hoped for considerable aid, both for food and for investment in development. At this early stage the Soviet government hardly took the new Indian regime seriously, believing it still to be tied to British policy by neo-imperial strings. By contrast Nehru was seen in America in educated and official circles as a major Asian figure, and, as in British official eyes, central to hopes of containing the spread of communism in Asia. As the *New York Times* indicated in a leading article entitled 'Our Stake in India', the US administration was concerned to use India as a bulwark against communism, and also saw its potential as a market, if its economic problems could be overcome. China appeared to have been 'lost' to the West, but India was 'in safe hands'.[42] Accordingly the paper reported Nehru's visit in great detail. Here was someone with whom American governments felt they could – and indeed had to – deal.

However it soon became apparent that this was not as easy as it seemed. As the Secretary of State, Dean Acheson, reflected after the 1949 visit, Nehru was hugely important. 'He was so important to India and India's survival so important to all of us, that if he did not exist – as Voltaire said of God – he would have had to be invented.' But he proved to be one of the most difficult people with whom

Acheson had ever had to deal.[43] The persistence of European imperialism in Asia, the question of Communist China's international status, and Kashmir all caused tension. When he left he seemed irritated, despite his manifest welcome, and indeed felt that the American administration was asking of him more than he could give; while his hosts felt he was not facing reality and would not for long be able to sit on the fence in an increasingly bipolar world.[44] Within a year a top secret report in the Department of State was commenting that Nehru clearly distrusted America and probably disliked it as well. The author attributed this in part to his socialism, his hostility to American support of western powers that still had colonies, his aggravation that large-scale US aid was not forthcoming, and particularly the fact that he was assumed to be a frustrated revolutionary and still at core an aristocrat despite his professions of commitment to democracy.[45]

In 1951 the problem of food aid caused considerable misunderstanding and contention between the two administrations. Nehru had believed that America recognised that India wanted to pursue an independent foreign policy, yet was still prepared to assist with a long-term food credit. But when the Indian food situation worsened and formal approach was made to the State Department for 2 million tons of food grains on easy terms, the project became mired in US Congress procedures, and the bill which eventually emerged had what seemed like 'strings' attached to aid, including American supervision of the distribution system. Here both cultural differences of approach and, as Nehru recognised, Indian lack of diplomatic experience in dealing with American politicians and their institutions led to real misunderstandings.[46]

Relations between India and America further deteriorated over America's role in Korea and on the issue of Kashmir, and what seemed to Nehru to be American support for Pakistan in the UN. By 1951 the *New York Times* was describing Nehru as a 'lost leader', a great disappointment who had once seemed a champion of a free, democratic and anti-Communist Asia but had now 'turned aside from his responsibilities, proclaimed India's disinterestedness, and tried to set up an independent third force India, suspended in mid-air between the two decisive movements of our time' – Communism as personified by the Soviet Union and Democracy, whose champion was the USA.[47] Nehru of course did not see himself in this light. For him the idea that America was the only champion of democracy was a nonsense, for India was pursuing the difficult path of democracy *and* large-scale development, thus tackling at the roots the living conditions which provided the environment for the spread of Communist rebellions and revolutions throughout Asia. Moreover, he felt that the two power blocs which were emerging in the early 1950s were more to do with Soviet and American power politics than ideology.

Relations with America dipped dramatically when it seemed to Nehru that America was bringing the Cold War right into the South Asian subcontinent, by entering into a military pact with Pakistan in 1954. Nehru placed before Parliament in Delhi an exchange of letters between him and President Eisenhower in February 1954, in which Eisenhower assured Nehru that the assistance given to Pakistan would not be turned against India, and committed America to further substantial economic and technical aid to India. Nehru stood by his policy of non-alignment which he said was 'based on our desire to help in the furtherance of peace and freedom', and told Parliament that he believed that America's new stance would make tension even greater between India and Pakistan, not least in the matter of Kashmir. All talk of demilitarisation in Kashmir as a prelude to a plebiscite was now thrown into disarray because 'large additional forces are being thrust from outside in[to] Pakistan and put at the disposal of Pakistan.'[48] He made plain to his Chief Ministers his distaste for America's whole foreign policy and reading of the world situation, and its increasingly conservative support for what seemed like reactionary regimes in opposition to the Communist bloc, 'McCarthyism' abroad as well as at home. India subsequently refused to permit American planes carrying French troops to fly across India, arguing that that would be a breach of its policy of non-alignment.

Voices in America were hostile, and they also taunted India for accepting developmental aid from America while objecting to military aid to Pakistan. Nehru admitted that he was worried about accepting any aid from America, and would have preferred not to; but he calculated that refusal now to accept it would only add further to what he admitted was 'ill will' between the two countries.[49] It would of course have hurt India's development plans disastrously, for despite the poor relations between the two countries, America was by the mid-1950s India's largest foreign supplier of aid, and by the end of the decade was giving far more to India than to Pakistan, nearly $348 million compared to nearly $209 million in 1960–1.

Nehru's commitment to non-alignment made India's relations with America problematic. But it also kept India from any close relations with the Soviet Union. The Soviet scepticism as to the reality of India's independence in foreign policy was only gradually overcome, but from 1952 Russia supported India in the UN on resolutions relating to Kashmir. Nehru, however, refused any suggestions of treaties of friendship or agreements not to engage in actions directed against the other. Nonetheless, Indo-Soviet relations entered a new era, which led to the exchange of visits between the leaders in 1955, and to the grant of considerable Soviet economic aid to India, particularly in the form of assistance with the technology of industrial development. Nehru also obtained during the visit of Bulganin and Khrushchev the assurance that the Soviet Union would not intervene in India's internal affairs by assisting the Indian Communist Party – a problem which had contributed to Nehru's perception of India's own Communists as anti-national as well as prone to violent agitation which was disruptive just at the point when India needed internal unity and strength in the wake of Partition.

This confirmed his own reading of the post-Stalin regime in Russia which he expounded after his visit in the summer of 1955. He saw the leadership now as far less doctrinaire, far more pragmatic as it grappled with the Soviet Union's domestic and foreign problems, in contrast with communists elsewhere who were of a 'purely agitational variety with fixed and inflexible grooves of thought based on a theory which had ceased to have much application in the Soviet Union' – that is a theory of international communism and permanent revolution 'till the entire world became Communist'. He envisaged a future where local Communist Parties in different countries would act on their own authority in relation to local conditions, and the Soviet Union (and indeed China) would concentrate on their own internal development rather than world revolution, and 'will not seek to impose themselves either politically or economically upon others'.[50] These were countries with whose leaders he now felt he could cooperate where it was useful without compromising non-alignment. For their part the Soviet leaders saw the usefulness of the non-aligned leader to them in a fast-changing world where Asian and African states were becoming increasingly important.

The most dramatic public demonstration of the policy of non-alignment was the Bandung Conference held in late April 1955, which had emerged from meetings of the Prime Ministers of Burma, Ceylon, India, Indonesia and Pakistan the previous year. Invitations to Bandung were sent to nearly thirty independent governments in Asia and Africa, and the objective was to promote understanding and goodwill among them, to discuss domestic issues of common interest and to look at their international position and their possible contribution to world peace.[51] Nehru saw this as a historic showcase for the countries of Asia and Africa, and he was determined that all the forward planning should be efficient to enable it to run smoothly. He worried that if arrangements did not come up to standard this would harm Indonesia's reputation, and the conference could disintegrate and slip out of the control of India and the other organisers. His manoeuvres behind the scenes displayed his competence in the world of international conferences – insisting on a proper agenda, organisation, rules of procedure and so forth, obviously drawing on the UN example, as well as his own experience of Commonwealth conferences. He also demonstrated his fear that the Indonesian government was not up to the task; and in almost imperial tones was determined to keep the joint conference secretariat up to the mark. He even intervened in the domestic arrangements for delegates, insisting that they should receive ample room rather than being 'herded up like cattle'; and that above all there must be 'adequate provision of bath rooms and lavatories' – something which 'is usually forgotten in Indonesia'. As he told the Indian ambassador to Indonesia, these might be considered trivial matters, but 'these trivial matters upset people and frayed tempers are no good when we consider important problems.'[52] (The faithful Mathai determined to go with Nehru, partly to keep an eye on his chief's privacy and creature comforts. Another key Indian was the ubiquitous Krishna Menon, who was the main Indian drafter of the conference communiqués.)

There were obvious divisions of opinion and allegiance in the conference, and Nehru noted secretly that India and Burma took an independent line, normally followed by Indonesia and Egypt, but Turkey, Pakistan, Iraq, Lebanon and Iran were the most aggressive and in favour of American policies, supported quietly by Thailand and the Philippines. The Egyptian Prime Minister proved important in achieving compromises. The delegate who attracted most attention was Chou En-lai, the Chinese Prime Minister, because he was such an unknown quantity. He presented himself as able, moderate and cooperative in the conference work, assuring delegates that China desired no expansion or internal subversion in any country. On reflection Nehru felt that quite apart from the final communiqué (which established ten principles for developing friendship and cooperation among nations but included the right to self-defence in accordance with the principles of the UN Charter), the conference had generated a common feeling among participants, had had a psychological impact on world opinion, and had certainly enabled him to get the measure of some of the leaders there through personal contact.[53]

Nehru was a quiet and humorous observer of people, and he painted a number of pen portraits of delegates for Edwina Mountbatten, from two 'hefty and giantly persons' from Gold Coast, towering above their Indonesian colleagues, to those who were 'permanent performers of the UN' who 'functioned with all due pomposity'.[54] Nehru's own contribution was obviously a major one, and there was some feeling among delegates that he was attempting to play too dominant a role. He spoke several times, mainly on the need for Asian and African countries to take a positive stance to secure world peace – which of course in his eyes meant adhering to a policy of non-alignment and peaceful coexistence; but he also engaged in some sharp exchanges, as when he criticised the Prime Minister of Ceylon for referring to Soviet 'imperialism' in Eastern Europe – for as he said, these countries were independent and recognised as such by the UN.[55] Although Nehru felt the conference had been of substantial benefit in various ways, he was aware that the states there represented no united group or movement, and that only careful management and drafting had maintained a minimal unity among them in 1955. It was for fear of publicly exhibiting differences among participants at Bandung that he and others decided that no subsequent meeting would be desirable.[56]

The greatest challenge to Nehru's commitment to non-alignment came late the following year when the crises of the Anglo-French invasion of the Suez Canal and the Soviet invasion of Hungary occurred simultaneously late in 1956. Taken together these episodes of Indian diplomatic endeavour showed not only the difficulties of pursuing a policy of non-alignment without generating considerable hostility at home and abroad for Nehru personally and for his policy. The phase also showed up the weaknesses of Indian intelligence and diplomacy at a time when it had not yet had a decade since independence to build up expertise in these fields. Moreover, from the perspective of Nehru's own desk the juxtaposition of the two crises demonstrated the huge weight of work which fell on him because he had no Foreign Minister with whom to share the load. This was, of course, also the time when the Lok Sabha was dealing with the domestic question of states reorganisation and discussing the Second Five Year Plan.[57]

Nehru's significance as the senior non-aligned world figure was clear from the outset in relation to the crisis which developed after Nasser's nationalisation of the Suez Canal. Not only was he in constant contact with Nasser, sharing intelligence and giving advice. He was also used by the western powers as a mediator, for he had a good working relationship with Nasser and had recently met him on the way home from a visit to Europe, as well as having easy access to London and Washington. But India had its own interests in achieving a peaceful settlement over the canal. This was a critical question of sovereignty and the reality of the independence of a state which had once been under imperial control, and therefore of great significance to Nehru both as a leader of another newly independent state and also as an articulate champion of the need to end imperialism worldwide. But as Nehru told the Lok Sabha and his Chief Ministers in September 1956, the peaceful and proper functioning of the canal was vital to India's economic interests; and if India's imports and exports were disrupted it would play havoc with its own estimates and planning.[58] There was also a Muslim angle to the Indian stance, and G. B. Pant as Home Minister did not lose the opportunity to point to the stand India took in support of Egypt, compared with Pakistan's stance in support of the USA, France and Egypt.[59]

Nehru was determined to work to avoid the risk of a war, and to that end tried to achieve a negotiated settlement, supporting Egypt on the merits of the case but also hoping to avoid any humiliation of Britain and France. Despite his support for Egypt he was not willing to accede to Egypt's request for military supplies, because he felt this would undermine India's policy of supporting peace, and in alienating the UK and other western governments would destroy India's capacity to play a mediatory role. He himself did not stir out of Delhi, but stayed at the heart of India's intelligence gathering and diplomatic strategy, keeping in touch with President Eisenhower and Dulles, the American Secretary of State, and the Prime Minister and Foreign Secretary in London, directly and via the British High Commission in Delhi; but he sent Krishna Menon on an early form of shuttle diplomacy between Cairo, London and the United States. As late as mid-September Nehru still hoped that the work he and Menon had put into a plan for a settlement, in their different but complementary ways, would achieve a peace, and in Labour and Liberal circles in England there was strong appreciation of

Nehru's stand and role, as well as of Menon's diplomacy, and a hope that their work had made the Tory 'hotheads' pause in their 'suicidal course'.[60]

It was little wonder that Nehru was shocked, angered and resentful at the Anglo-French intervention in Egypt at the end of the month, and he made his attitude plain in messages to the British and American governments and to the Secretary-General of the United Nations, and to his colleagues in the governments represented at Bandung. This was naked aggression, a reversion to colonialism, a violation of the UN Charter, and could not be tolerated.[61] American hostility to the Anglo-French move eventually led to a cease-fire and the end of the crisis. A spin-off of this was increasing warmth in relations between Delhi and Washington. Eisenhower sent a message to Nehru, thanking him for the way their two countries had been able to work together and later asked for his continued help in resolving the situation without any widening of military reaction. A month later, in December, Nehru visited Washington and New York. On this visit relations with the President were much more cordial, and Eisenhower and Nehru had prolonged private talks which evidently led to considerable mutual understanding on foreign affairs. Nehru seemed happy and relaxed in a situation where there was a new appreciation of his non-aligned position, and less of an insistence that any country must be in one ideological camp or the other. (Dulles was in fact kept apart from the discussions between Nehru and the President, because his ideological stance was such an irritant to Nehru.) Nehru himself admitted that he now saw that American policy towards non-aligned nations was far more flexible than he had previously thought.[62]

Suez undoubtedly raised Nehru's profile as a world leader, despite the failure of his attempts to enable a peaceful settlement, but it also led to considerable hostility in India to his decision that, despite Britain's apparent reversion to colonialism, India should stay within the Commonwealth. Far more damaging to his repute, both in India and abroad, was the way he dealt with the crisis in Hungary, where Soviet troops invaded, simultaneously with the Anglo-French intervention in Egypt, to crush a revolt against the nation's subservience to the Soviet system. Nehru was in a difficult position. He had far less information about what was going on within the eastern bloc in the early autumn of 1956 than he had about events in relation to the Suez Canal, and what little he did know came mainly from the Indian embassies in Russia and Yugoslavia. When the crisis broke intelligence was further hampered by the illness of the Indian ambassador to Moscow (who was also accredited to Budapest), and the impossibility of getting news directly from K. A. Rahman, the First Secretary and a relatively junior diplomat, who was the most senior Indian representative in Budapest itself. Normal communications had been disrupted, and Rahman could not send secret telegrams because he had no safe in which to keep ciphers. The only news he could get out was by cryptic telephone calls. When the American government enquired if India would join a proposal to refer the situation to the UN Nehru's government used their lack of direct knowledge as an argument for not agreeing and warned the US of the dangers of any intervention even by the UN at this stage.[63]

Nehru was in an embarrassing and difficult situation, quite apart from his lack of intelligence. He needed to keep Russia in play on the side of Egypt in relation to the Suez crisis if possible; and, moreover, he believed that there was a new and more flexible stance in the Soviet leadership which he had discerned in 1955. Further, he had no personal potential for mediation or discreet intervention as he had in the tangled diplomatic relationships around the Suez crisis by virtue of his standing in the Commonwealth and in the non-aligned countries. It was Suez which primarily commanded his attention and absorbed his energy. By the beginning of November Nehru was beginning to receive requests from Hungarians via his own diplomats to intervene on their behalf; and his most senior civil servant in the Ministry in Delhi, N. R. Pillai, was nudging him towards a reconsideration of events in Hungary 'with a view to deciding our attitude in the light of the principles we have been advocating'. Further, there was pressure from politicians outside government in India such as J. P. Narayan, who argued that he must speak out on Hungary or he would be guilty of abetting a 'new Imperialism more dangerous than [the] old because it masquerades as revolutionary'. Even the Indian ambassador in Washington warned him of the serious concern in America that India seemed to be silent on Hungary but had denounced western imperialism in Egypt. If his chief did not follow the same principle in relation to Hungary he would weaken UN authority against aggression in Egypt.[64]

Nehru asked his ambassador in Moscow on 2 November to make an informal approach to the Soviet authorities and tell them of Indian concern and sympathy for people seeking national freedom, but wanted no formal protest because he could not see how he could intervene effectively. But the next day he made it plain to his ambassador that any further conflict between the Russians and the Hungarians would be most unfortunate, not least because it would divert attention from Suez.[65] In person in a speech in Delhi on 5 November Nehru began to sound some public criticisms of Moscow's role, though he still refused to condemn the Soviet Union until he had precise information on what was happening. Eisenhower personally requested Nehru, on the same day, to help make the Hungarian problem known to the world, and Nehru replied that he was greatly troubled and that armed intervention in any country by another was highly objectionable.[66]

However, Nehru's emerging position was further and gravely embarrassed by Krishna Menon, who was now a minister in Nehru's cabinet but spoke on his own authority in the UN on 8 and 9 November, justifying India's abstention from voting on a motion condemning the Soviet use of force, by insisting that it was an internal matter for Hungary. Subsequent telegrams which passed between him and

Nehru displayed Nehru's acute embarrassment at this stance, just when he himself was coming round to public criticism of the Soviet action for suppressing what he now accepted was a nationalist uprising. He told Menon of the feeling in Congress on the Hungarian issue that India had not made its attitude as clear as it should have done.[67] Not only was he beleaguered at home. Astoundingly even the wife of India's permanent representative at the UN wrote to her prime minister an anguished letter without her husband's knowledge, saying how difficult it was to justify India's public stance and how India had been put in the wrong to an extraordinary degree. Clearly in her eyes the culprit was Menon and she pleaded with Nehru to say something decisive.[68]

Before he could have received this letter Nehru had already made decisive statements in the Lok Sabha. On 16 November he stated that India believed that Soviet troops should be withdrawn and that Hungarians should be permitted to decide their own future; and on 19 November he accepted that the Hungarian uprising was largely a popular nationalist revolt, reiterating that foreign forces should leave. The BBC correspondent in Delhi reported on the impact of the speech and the fact that for the first time Nehru had spoken out against Russian 'imperialism'. But he noted how difficult even his supporters had found it to justify his policy during the last few weeks when he seemed to have been adopting a double standard in response to Suez and Hungary.[69] Nehru subsequently used all his weight to attempt to press the Soviet Union to permit the UN Secretary-General and UN observers to visit Hungary, much to the Soviet government's anger, and both the Soviet leaders sought to get at Nehru where it would hurt most – by saying that Hungary was as close to the Soviet Union as Kashmir was to India.[70]

The juxtaposition of Suez and the Hungarian uprising had placed Nehru in an unenviable position and had almost overwhelmed him, as the BBC correspondent reported bluntly. He really needed a strong Minister for External Affairs who could have shared the burden with him and questioned the assumptions with which Nehru approached the interlocking problems. He had finally retrieved his position somewhat, and reaffirmed India's position of non-alignment and support for the right of national sovereignty. But his own reputation had taken a battering at home and abroad. Even at the end of November Nehru's sister, who was by now High Commissioner in London but also accredited to Ireland, told her brother she wanted to go to Ireland to explain the Indian stand on Hungary as she was being inundated with letters on the issue from there.[71] The weaknesses of Indian diplomatic activity abroad were also glaringly apparent, particularly the lack of intelligence in relation to the eastern bloc, and in Nehru's dependence on Krishna Menon, unreliable and stridently articulate, who had begun to damage India's reputation profoundly, and threatened to damage Nehru personally by his high profile outbursts.

ISSUES OF SECURITY

Nearer to home, on the country's northern borders, Nehru faced issues of India's own security, which interlocked with his reading of the world international situation and his determination that India should have a strong, independent and moral international persona. Of particular significance were India's relations with the neighbouring Soviet Union, Pakistan and China. During the early 1950s relations with the USSR reached a new warmth, and though Nehru would not sign any treaty of friendship or 'no-war' with the Soviet Union, he was confident that no threat to India's integrity would come from that quarter. Russia took on a quite different appearance to him than the face it had shown to his imperial predecessors, who had been obsessed by fears of Russian invasion or infiltration through the unstable tribal territories to the north of India. Now Russia was a more predictable and reliable partner in aid and trade, even if at times such as the Hungarian crisis, relations could still be uneasy.

In relation to Pakistan the acute tensions which had followed Partition and war in Kashmir had eased somewhat. At the time of independence many Indians had felt that Pakistan would eventually be reabsorbed into India, and certainly in the early months after Partition Nehru himself did not think that Pakistan could survive, because of the communal upheavals and the new state's lack of money and trained personnel.[72] However, within a year he was convinced that Pakistan was there to stay, that any reunion with India was inadvisable because it would only rekindle all the tensions they had felt before Partition, and that India and Pakistan should endeavour to live in peace as neighbours. Indeed, a stable and friendly Pakistan was in India's own interests. As Nehru told his Chief Ministers in 1952, the reverse would spell disaster: 'we cannot live for ever in terms of hostility with Pakistan. If we thought of doing so, then we have to give up all ideas of development and progress. Two countries like India and Pakistan are so intimately connected that continued hostility between them is likely to ruin both and invite foreign interference. We may do a great deal of injury to Pakistan and might defeat it in war. But both countries will in effect be ruined if that extreme step had to be taken.'[73] This was a prescient and tragic observation from the perspective of the half century following his death.

Despite the stalemate over the issue of Kashmir, it looked in 1953 as if a new understanding between the two governments might be emerging, following a change of regime in Pakistan. Nehru responded in kind to the message of friendship from the new Premier of Pakistan, Mohammed Ali, and in the summer of 1953 the two men met several times, in London at a Commonwealth Prime Ministers' Conference, and then in Karachi and Delhi. They discussed a whole range of issues left over from Partition, and Nehru was obviously delighted with the warm reception he received from government and people when he visited Karachi, believing that there really was now a will in Pakistan to achieve settlements of outstanding matters, including Kashmir.[74] Unfortunately internal events in Kashmir and the arrest of Sheikh Abdullah could hardly have provided a worse background for the subsequent meeting in August in Delhi (see chapter 11 above). Nonetheless, they got down to serious discussions on the nature of a plebiscite, and made progress on other issues such as evacuee property and small exchanges of territory on their eastern borders.[75] However, no further progress on Kashmir, the ultimate stumbling block to better relations between the two neighbours, could be achieved, given the establishment of a Kashmiri government hostile even to the idea of a plebiscite, and then, early in the following year the US–Pakistan military pact. This in Nehru's eyes brought the Cold War into the subcontinent, increased the Pakistani potential for military aggression, and prevented India and Pakistan from solving their problems by themselves, as had seemed more possible following his meetings with the Pakistan Prime Minister.[76] Nonetheless, India's strategic security was to a considerable extent safeguarded by the stable 'line of control' in Kashmir, and the knowledge that any overt Pakistani violation of it would be immediately condemned by the international community.

Far more problematic in terms of Nehru's own time in office was his vision of China and the cordial relations he attempted to achieve with it during the early 1950s. He had been interested in China since the 1920s, and increasingly convinced that the two great subcontinents shared many of the same problems and could learn from each other and work closely together to create a new Asian identity and role in the changing world. The need to support China had also been a key element in his attitude to Congress's possible support for the Allied war effort. However, in 1948 he watched the collapse of Chiang Kai-shek's government, and despite his close relations with the former nationalist ruler and his wife, he accepted that India should now cultivate relations with the new regime and use its influence to integrate China into the world international community. As he noted tersely late in 1948, 'Following a tottering government is not a good policy.' He was personally sorry for Chiang Kai-Shek and his wife but felt that his government could not possibly support such a politically bankrupt regime.[77] India eventually recognised the People's Republic at the end of 1949.

The new China was an unknown quantity to virtually all players on the diplomatic scene during the early years of its existence. Nehru had to rely on the doubtful intelligence provided by his ambassador, K. M. Panikkar (whose amateurishness and apparent acceptance of the Chinese government's views perturbed the experienced G. S. Bajpai), and his own understanding of the likely impact of the emergence of this new Communist power. From the outset he believed it would follow an independent policy rather than being a hanger-on of the Soviet Union, and that it would retain China's essentially Asian characteristics as it worked out the meaning of communism for its own people – just as Nehru argued that India had to work out the meaning of socialism for its peoples rather than following any rigid ideological line. He proposed an essentially friendly Indian stance, and he told the Burmese Prime Minister that he felt that there was little danger of any Chinese aggression across the Indian border. A few months later he told Panikkar that he attached great importance to Indo-Chinese friendship. 'I think the future of Asia and to some extent the world depends upon this.'[78] Consequently he was bewildered at the Chinese invasion of Tibet late in 1950, and China's hostility to India's diplomatic nudge towards a peaceful settlement of the problem. Nehru accepted that Tibet was a legitimate area of Chinese suzerainty, but hoped that it would be allowed its autonomy. Any other stance would profoundly damage China's standing in the eyes of the world, just when India had been working, at the expense of its own popularity, for China's inclusion in the UN.[79]

Even within the Congress Party there was concern at Nehru's failure to make tougher representations to China on Tibet. Nehru's old colleague and Deputy Prime Minister, Vallabhbhai Patel, weighed in with a scorching attack on Nehru's understanding of China. He had just been reading the correspondence between the ministry and Panikkar on the issue of Tibet and concluded that Panikkar had been duped by the Chinese government, which must have been planning the attack on Tibet during the period it had been convincing Panikkar of its peaceful intentions. He considered the attack 'little short of perfidy', and the Chinese response to India as that of a potential enemy. He now urged Nehru to recognise that China had expanded almost to India's own gates, and that now India's northern and north-eastern frontiers were at serious risk. He believed that communists made imperialists like any others and that Chinese irredentism and imperialism were more dangerous than western imperialisms because they carried a dangerous cloak of ideology, concealing racial, national and historical claims. He also had visions of Chinese communists supplying and assisting India's own, thus endangering India's internal security. He urged Nehru to instigate a serious military and intelligence appreciation of the Chinese threat to India and to begin long-term steps to increase India's military readiness, to improve communications with frontier areas, to strengthen administration in the frontier regions and to consider policy in relation to the McMahon line, which had settled India's north-eastern frontier in 1914.[80]

Nehru did not reply directly to Patel, but sent him a lengthy note he had prepared on policy towards China and Tibet. In this he discounted the idea of a major attack on India by China, and insisted that the major enemy was still Pakistan. Moreover, serious defence against China was impossible. 'If we really feared an attack and had to make full provision for it this would cast an intolerable burden on us, financial and otherwise, and it would weaken our general defence position. There are limits beyond which we cannot go at least for some years, and a spreading out of our army in distant frontiers would be bad from every military or strategic point of view.'[81] Within weeks of this exchange Patel died from a major stroke. There was nobody left of his stature and authority who could challenge the Prime Minister's view.

Nehru persisted in believing that China posed no security threat to India, and tried hard to understand the Chinese attitude as being a product of its history and culture; his aim was to break down China's isolation and xenophobia and create a more balanced and cooperative mentality within its government. However, he was determined that the border with Tibet should be seen as fixed and definite, and on this there could be no compromise.[82] Nonetheless, he did not press for any binding definition of the frontier, in large part because of his reliance on Panikkar, who argued that this was unnecessary. In retrospect this was clearly a serious miscalculation, and one which might well not have occurred had colleagues of Patel's standing had some role in the making of foreign policy. Nehru's hopes of a more stable relationship with China appeared to have been achieved in 1954 when the two countries reached a treaty in regard to Tibet. India gave up certain residual rights in Tibet, but achieved what to Nehru was to be the cornerstone of future Indo-Chinese relations, the so-called Five Principles – *panchsheel* – mutual respect for each other's territorial integrity and sovereignty, mutual non-aggression, mutual non-interference in each other's internal affairs, equality and mutual benefit, and peaceful coexistence. For him this was an immensely valuable safeguard of India's security on its China border, and he hoped that it would be a set of principles on which an area of 'collective peace' – as opposed to collective security – could be established, first of all in Asia.[83]

Following this the Chinese Prime Minister visited Delhi on his way back from the peace conference on Indo-China in Geneva, stopping for intensive talks, through interpreters, between 25 and 27 June.[84] Nehru considered this a historic event, and felt that the atmosphere was friendly, and that Chou was anxious for cooperation and friendship with India. His encounter with Chou, the skilled and emollient diplomatist, lulled Nehru's anxieties over the border, and he willingly accepted an invitation to visit China. The return visit occurred in October.[85] Nehru met Chairman Mao and his principal colleagues, and their talks covered a wide range of topics. Evidently he found Chou the man with whom it was easiest to do business, and he raised with him the question of the border and the fact that some Chinese maps showed as Chinese territory which belonged to India. Diplomatically Nehru said he was not worried on the issue, though many people were saying that they denoted aggressive intentions on the part of the Chinese. As far as India was concerned there was no doubt about the boundaries. Chou said these were merely old maps as they had not had time to produce new ones. Nehru left, confirmed in the impression that China's government and people were intent on peace and concentration on their own domestic problems of development in the next decade or so. He was hugely impressed by China and its people, who seemed disciplined, unified, organised and hard-working – an implicit contrast with the many domestic problems of division he faced at home. There was a certain drabness in their clothing, but a sense of discipline and efficiency, and there was no sign of real poverty, though he admitted he had not seen much of village life except one cooperative farm.[86]

Soon after this visit Nehru noted in January 1955 for the Minister of Defence Organisation that he could see no foreseeable danger on the north-eastern border. However, later in the year he began to initiate a new consideration of the need to develop communications with the frontier, not least for purposes of defence.[87] Then in the summer of 1955, and again in 1956, there were disquieting signs of Chinese incursions over the border, which necessitated formal protest to China. By October 1956 the Ministry of External Affairs was recommending serious military reconnaissance of disputed areas with a view to establishing border police posts.[88] Clearly Nehru's great hopes of providing for India's security through mutual understanding with China on the five principles guiding their relations were insufficient on the ground to meet India's security needs. His vision of China as a crucial and willing partner in the search for peace in Asia and the world blinded him to evidence that the Chinese government might have other priorities.

By the end of 1956 Nehru's conduct of India's foreign relations had created for his country a distinctive, independent international identity. India was seen as an important Asian country located by geography at a significant and sensitive juncture of several areas, by choice within the Commonwealth network of international relationships, and by ideology a major player in a group of non-aligned nations. The country had a foreign policy which was pragmatic and ideological, and which drew both admiration and hostility, depending on the perspective of the viewer. Whether that policy served India's more mundane needs was not entirely clear. It was certainly capable of attracting foreign aid, even from countries with whom its relations could be periodically cool, but there was considerable doubt about the robustness of its security arrangements on its land borders.

Nehru's own image and international role had undoubtedly advanced greatly since independence, in part because of his conduct of India's foreign affairs. Once known solely as a major nationalist leader, he was now seen as a well-travelled and well-connected Asian figure, a spokesman for Asian aspirations, and more broadly as a moderating voice for a more peaceful world order. By virtue of his standing at the juncture of different regions and his membership of different formal and informal groupings he was considered a useful mediator, and was called upon to interpret people of very different attitudes and policies to each other. The governments of the Soviet Union and the United States saw and used him in this role. But nowhere was his new standing clearer than in his relations with governments and politicians of different hues in the United Kingdom. Churchill had solicited his views on world affairs at the time of the coronation in 1953, while in 1955 Eden at the Foreign Office in London sought Nehru's good offices in trying to discover Chinese intentions in relation to a dangerous confrontation building up in the Formosa Straits. As Churchill came to the end of his time as Prime Minister he wrote to Nehru of the great pleasure he felt that their personal relations had been so agreeable 'after all that has happened' in relations between India and Britain, and urged him to think of the phrase 'The Light of Asia'. 'It seems to me that you might be able to do what no other human being could in giving India the lead, at least in the realm of thought, throughout Asia, with the freedom and dignity of the individual as the ideal rather than the Communist Party drill book.' Or again he wrote of Nehru's 'leading and constructive' contribution in Commonwealth Prime Ministers' Conferences, and his heavy burden of responsibility in shaping the destiny of millions of Indians and of 'playing your outstanding part in world affairs'.[89] There might have been an element of flattery from this other Old Harrovian and great master of words, but they signified that Nehru's political life had developed a new dimension, and that he had become an important world figure as he laid the foundations of his country's new national identity in international relations and affairs.

Part 5

Frustration of Vision,
1957–1964

# Chapter 14

# The Realities of Democratic Leadership

From the time of Gandhi's assassination until the mid-1950s, Nehru had thrown himself with all his prodigious energies into tackling issues which confronted the new nation state in the aftermath of imperial rule. These were probably the most creative years of his political life. Understanding very well the complexities of the task before him and his country, he tried to help his countrymen visualise and imagine a new Indian nation, and he was central to the creation of the nation state's structures of public life and governance. He encouraged civilised and democratic norms of public action, and worked to generate a continuous process of forging the nation in the minds and experiences of the many who had previously been, or felt, excluded from it. On him primarily also fell the work of creating a new international identity for India. For later observers his life is thus a window into a crucial phase in India's recent past, marked in large part by idealism in the search for a new political and socio-economic order; and the development of a remarkably stable democratic polity followed the traumas and instabilities which had marked the end of British rule on the subcontinent.

This last part of the study turns to the final phase of Nehru's life. It examines the years when his own increasing age and eventual decline in health became apparent, and looks at the frustration of his vision of independent India. As his sense of frustration deepened, with an awareness of so much work yet to do, so did his re-evaluation of Gandhi's ideals and their relevance to the present moment. Nehru's speeches and writings indicate that after Gandhi's death the image and memory of the Mahatma was still a constant and precious presence in his life, a reference point to which he often personally returned, and one to which he often made public allusion. He recognised that Gandhi had left no blueprint for modern India; but his principles were significant guidelines. As Nehru said in 1954,

I am more than ever convinced that the fundamental principles set by Mahatma Gandhi before the country are the only answer to our problems.

Only by following that path can we serve our country and the world. It is by no means a path for the weak or for the cowardly. Mahatma Gandhi talked in soft tones but his non-violence was not of the weak; it was born of an inner strength and courage and discipline. We must generate that strength once again.

Now that strength was needed for the building of a new India, by creating a new unity and by attracting the cooperation of ordinary Indians as opposed to attempting to achieve change from the top down.[1]

However, the seemingly insurmountable difficulties he encountered in pursuing this vision of a new India also illuminate a new phase in India's national experience. A decade after independence old leaders, schooled in Gandhian nationalism and the discipline of prison, were leaving the political scene, and the process of creating new systems, institutions and connections gave way to a more routine practice of government and politics. Furthermore, deep-rooted interests and connections resurfaced through the country's socio-economic and political institutions and often blocked visions of radical change. Long-standing economic problems also proved deeply resistant, despite the ending of the imperial regime and the inauguration of new policies designed to create greater wealth and equity. These trends raise questions about Nehru's own position, and the reality of his influence, despite his unique image as the country's undisputed leader at home and abroad. Moreover, in this phase of his own and the nation's life, as his increasing frailty became manifest, the political system had to face the first major succession in the national leadership since independence – a time of critical importance for the nature and stability of the polity, as almost every former colony or imperial dependency discovered, when a new leadership had to achieve legitimacy without the benefit of having led a successful anti-colonial movement.

## THE AGEING PRIME MINISTER

By the later 1950s Nehru was approaching seventy. Throughout his long life he had kept in good health, not least because he took care of himself, considering physical illness to be often a sign of mental weakness and indiscipline. He ate and drank sparingly, though he was no Gandhian ascetic, and he took exercise whenever possible, practising yoga in his later years. The deeply attractive young man who had been nicknamed the 'Glaxo baby' in Congress circles – a reference to Glaxo powdered milk advertisements – was now in late middle age still a magnetic presence. In the words of a notable American journalist, he was 'the photographer's darling', with an immensely expressive face, and in his three-quarter-length, high-buttoned coat (which gave the name to the Nehru style of jacket) and starched white Gandhi cap 'an austere, arresting figure'.[2]

Observers had noted his tendency to overwork ever since he was the senior Indian minister in the Interim Government of 1946–7, and he seldom had adequate sleep. By 1956 friends and colleagues were showing serious concern about his health and stamina. Sri Prakasa, a long-standing associate and now senior colleague in government, wrote to him in February that year, after Nehru had been running a temperature and was unable to attend a dinner, 'Along with all your friends, I too am very deeply concerned at the obvious fact that even you are getting older, and certainly are not as strong as you used to be. I do wish you would go slow and give your body some rest.'[3]

By the early months of 1958 Nehru recognised that he needed rest. He admitted to feeling mentally tired and stale, and deriving little pleasure from his work. External events had contributed to this, as well as his age and workload. He was deeply grieved by the death in February of the great Congress Muslim, Maulana Azad, whom he had come to know so well and to appreciate while they were in prison together during the war. Moreover one of his close and trusted colleagues, T. T. Krishnamachari, then Finance Minister, had just been forced to resign because of a scandal over some of the nationalised Life Insurance Corporation's investments which a public enquiry found to be imprudent and improper. (This issue was raised in Parliament by Feroze Gandhi and was symptomatic of his increasingly strained relations with his wife and father-in-law. He moved out of Teen Murti house completely in 1958.) Consequently Nehru approached the Congress Parliamentary Party at the end of April with the idea that he might be temporarily relieved of the premiership.

Not surprisingly, the party's response was a total refusal; and when the international community got wind of the notion, both Eisenhower and Khrushchev expressed their concern that his influence might be removed from the international scene.[4] Indira Gandhi, however, thought that her father should carry through his idea. Her advice was to 'Let them try to manage by themselves, otherwise they will only drag you down with their own rottenness. If you are outside, it may at least reassure the general public that you are not responsible for all the wrongdoing.'[5] Deeply loyal to her father, she shared his somewhat Olympian view of the vast majority in politics and public life. Subsequently Nehru dropped the idea of a sabbatical despite his daughter's views, and took two short holidays in May and June in the Himalayas, one in Manali, in the Kulu Valley, and the other trekking at a much higher altitude, despite medical advice. He gained some rest from these interludes in the hills, although he was never out of touch with Delhi, and continued to work.

Within a year Nehru was admitting that he found it difficult to keep pace with the urgent demands of both domestic and international affairs. He refused invitations to meals and declined to speak on the radio for the Minister of Food and Agriculture, on the grounds that he was very tired. In July 1959 he went on a brief holiday to Mashobra in the hills near Simla. He kept indoors except for morning and evening strolls, and refused to see people, finding his main relaxation in reading. Even there he was ill and a fever kept him in bed for three days. He could hardly speak, and subsequently had to cancel visits to Kashmir and South India.[6] By 1960–1 the decline in his vitality was clear both to him and to his closest colleagues. Sri Prakasa again noted, this time to the President, that the strain of work was too much for Nehru with the advancing years, and he thought that his recent 'grievous bereavement' must have been affecting him badly, though he did not allow this to interfere with his work. (He must have been referring to the sudden and unexpected death of Edwina Mountbatten in February 1960, which removed the deepest and most supportive personal relationship which had sustained Nehru since independence.) Nehru also accepted that he was over-whelmed with work, could not keep pace with correspondence, was avoiding all invitations to meals because they tired him, and was trying to conserve such energy as he still possessed.[7]

However, in the spring of 1962 illness caught up with him in the form of a viral infection in the urinary tract which laid him low in bed for most of April, and led to a continuing kidney problem. He found this a considerable shock. His long-standing Bengali Congress colleague, Dr B. C. Roy, explained his problem to him and urged him to take more rest, to delegate and do only what he alone could do (even at the risk of appearing uncooperative), and to give up making long speeches to crowds. Nehru agreed to try to follow this advice and began to rest regularly for over an hour each afternoon and to go to bed early, by 11.00 p.m. But he admitted that he had difficulty in discerning what was important.[8] He hated the public talk about his health, and the constant concern shown for him, but accepted that he now had to take care of himself. He wrote to his Chief Ministers in some irritation, echoing what he had said years earlier to Indira when she had seemed in constant ill-health, about the need to keep fit and not to complain about one's ailments, as people so often did in India.[9]

There was other evidence of his failing powers. There were often long gaps in his letters to his Chief Ministers in these final years. He also travelled abroad somewhat less, and when he did he could appear unresponsive and rather passive, as in his relations with President Kennedy when he visited America in November 1961. He visited California for two days, where stars and executives from the film industry gave him a pre-birthday party, and where he also visited Disneyland. His watchful and ever-present daughter commented that she was delighted to see her father having such fun in Disneyland – a reflection of the anxiety she found at the unremitting grind to which he still subjected himself in his seventies.[10]

Nehru's problems did not stem solely from the natural advance of the years. He had never been able to delegate successfully, and had built up a vast and unsus-tainable role for himself since independence, while missing the opportunity to train and nurture a younger generation of politicians who could eventually share the burden of government. Moreover, he had few close friends or confidantes with whom he could share his concerns. He tended only to be really frank and open with those removed from India's political system who would not gossip and could not challenge his position. Friends in Britain and America fulfilled an important function as recipients of his frustrations and fears. The most significant of these had been Edwina Mountbatten, in a relationship conducted through a regular correspondence and fleeting visits, by him to Broadlands, and by her to Delhi, normally as she passed through on her travels in the service of the St John Ambulance Brigade. Both were frenetic workers in their later years, driven by a sense of obligation and of their own capacity to play a particular and important public role, and both were to die in harness. Edwina's unexpected death in Jesselton, Borneo, early in 1960, when she was still in her late fifties and over a decade younger than Nehru, removed one constant source of strength and understanding in his later years. As a mark of his deep affection for her and of India's appreciation of the role she had played in the dark days of 1947–8, he sent an Indian frigate to escort her body when it was buried at sea off the south coast of Britain. It was a gesture which deeply touched Lord Mountbatten, and which he knew his wife would have greatly appreciated.

Within India Nehru depended on the support of a few people in different ways. The faithful 'Mac' Mathai had been his door-keeper and personal assistant, living in the Prime Minister's house virtually as part of the family, and totally dedicated to facilitating Nehru's work. However, it is evident from his own papers that he was building for himself a totally unconstitutional position of influence, as he filtered correspondence and managed visitors. Not surprisingly he became disliked and feared. As he received no salary, and had no 'boss' except the Prime Minister, who depended so heavily on him, it was difficult for anyone to question his position. However, early in 1959 charges of corruption were made against him in Parliament – again orchestrated by Feroze Gandhi. When he offered to resign, Nehru accepted his resignation. The Cabinet Secretary was asked to conduct an enquiry, since Nehru was concerned that anyone so near to himself should be above suspicion. Mathai was exonerated (though the Cabinet Secretary later said this was to protect Nehru's reputation) but not re-employed, thus removing from Nehru's side someone who had undoubtedly helped him manage his immense workload as well as ensuring that his travels within India and abroad were as smooth and comfortable as possible.[11]

Indira was increasingly at her father's side, her marriage having disintegrated well before her husband's death in September 1960. But, despite her increasing role in politics in her own right, she was far more of a social support to Nehru than a political confidante, and he was slightly surprised by her new-found aptitude for politics, rather than preparing her for any future role. When she was elected Congress President in 1959 he had no hand in it, the prime movers being the departing president, U. Dhebar, and G. B. Pant; and Nehru was somewhat dubious about its wisdom.[12] His political confidantes were few – Krishna Menon, now in the cabinet, one of the closest, particularly on foreign affairs, and one who attracted increasingly bitter hostility; a small circle of senior state leaders such as B. C. Roy for Bengal, Morarji Desai for Bombay or K. Kamaraj for Madras, whose significance in Nehru's understanding of states affairs caused criticism in Congress; and Pant on home affairs. The Vice-President, who became President in 1962, philosopher and former diplomat S. Radhakrishnan, increasingly became a source of personal and public advice. But as one of Nehru's earliest biographers put it succinctly in 1959, 'With the possible exception of Krishna Menon, Nehru no longer has close Indian friends.'[13]

Despite his essential loneliness and increasing weariness, Nehru refused to countenance retirement. People in many walks of life in India, as well as people abroad, were openly discussing the question of who or what would come after him, and he was profoundly irritated by it. He told T. T. Krishnamachari in July 1962 how he had responded to the deputy manager of the Punjab National Bank in Delhi, who had written suggesting that, given the talk of succession, Nehru should devolve his burden on to a team of assistants under his guidance. He had no intention of retiring, did not need a team of assistants when he had a cabinet, and found the gossip pointless. Some weeks later he told a Punjabi politician that he proposed to go on as long as there was any strength left in him. 'Naturally I get somewhat depressed occasionally. But even that becomes a reason for working and not for escaping from work.'[14]

How then did Nehru view his work, and how did he manage his anxiety and frustration? He acknowledged that he felt enmeshed by his responsibilities. To an American journalist he noted, 'Circumstances having thrust my office upon me, they have also made me a prisoner to a large extent. I find it increasingly difficult to leave this work even for a while.' Nonetheless he felt that 'the best way to serve the various bigger causes I have at heart is to try to function as adequately as I can in India'.[15] He had explained his philosophy of work to Krishna Menon as the Hungarian crisis unfolded and it was clear that the Soviet Union intended to hold on to Hungary, regardless of cost: 'None of us can control events. All we can do is to try our best and avoid any step which might aggravate [the] situation. At the same time we do not improve a situation by saying or doing something which we cannot easily justify and we have to adhere to our broad principles.' But in the midst of turmoil and perplexity he took some comfort from the maxim of the Gita (as Gandhi had done before him) 'that we should do our duty to the best of our ability and try to stick to the right path without worrying too much about the consequences'.[16]

The cultivation of detachment and awareness of the limitations of any individual's endeavours gave him some peace of mind. But he was clearly distressed in these years by international conflict and the threat of weapons of mass destruction, and dispirited by events in India itself. Despite nearly a decade of independence and all the work he had put in to encourage a new sense of national unity and vision, he felt haunted by the fear that 'we are succumbing to our old and corroding disease of lack of unity, disruptive tendencies and narrowness of outlook. The larger vision that inspired us and gave us strength seems to fade away and we spend our energies in petty controversies and conflicts. Not even the internal and external crises, not even the atomic and hydrogen bombs . . . seem to shake us up and pull us out of this rather parochial outlook and complacency . . .'[17] Subsequent letters to his Chief Ministers reiterated his disquiet at what he saw as the many divisive tendencies within India, and Indians' tendencies to think in terms of the small regional, caste or religious group rather than of the nation as a whole.

He also despaired at evidence of what he deemed ignorance and inertia, and the hold of old customs. In November 1957, for example, he read in the papers that a mad monkey was abroad in Lucknow, but that the District Magistrate did not dare have it destroyed for fear of hurting religious sentiment. (One of the most popular manifestations of the divine in Hinduism is Hanuman, the monkey god.) Nehru's reaction was brisk and scathing.

> If we are to function in this way in this country, then there is not much good our talking about planning and progress . . . I think it is little short of scandalous that such a question even should arise in the mind of a District Magistrate when a mad monkey is going about biting hundreds of people. We have to decide whether India is going to be a fit country for human-beings to live in or for monkeys or for other animals to take possession of.[18]

In these years when, despite all his personal efforts and the creation of a new nation state articulating new goals, so many of India's old social problems persisted, Nehru seems to have returned to the inspiration of his friend and mentor, and asked himself afresh what Gandhi's ideals might mean for India a decade after his death. He was oppressed with the possibilities of conflict – on an international scale as a result of the Cold War, within societies because of class differences, and specifically within India because of all the subnational identities such as caste, language and region. To cope with such situations of conflict he returned to Gandhi's insistence on the right means as the priority, for means and ends were fundamentally connected, good means producing good ends, and vice versa. He had 'come to the conclusion that it is more important to adopt the right way, to pursue the right means, than even to have the right objectives, important as that is. No method and no way which is bound up with the creation of hatred and conflict and which bases itself on violence, can ever yield right results, however good the motives, however good the objective.'[19]

Even more interesting was the way Gandhian ideals seemed to be modifying Nehru's belief in the power of the modern state and its structures to achieve fundamental change. Increasingly he argued the importance of self-reliance and self-help, and this was behind his commitment to community-based developmental work and to the cooperative movement in many aspects of rural life. When even voluntary organisations began begging for government assistance, he said that as a matter of fact government did not have the resources, but far more deeply, such dependence on government sapped the roots of self-reliance. The processes of government also depressed him. The very idea of committees and commissions of enquiry filled him with fear, given their interminable activities and few results except for fat reports![20] Like Gandhi before him he argued for greater simplicity in official functions and in the lifestyle of ministers, including a reduction in security measures, partly for the sake of economy, partly because 'showiness' was unbecoming in a national government, and partly to lessen the inconvenience to the general public. Even in tiny things Gandhi seemed to speak again through him. As he neared seventy he pounced on the fact that rubbish littered his secretariat floor, and when told that a sweeper would clear up, he suggested that each official should have a rubbish bin and that nothing should ever be thrown directly on the floor![21] With age he had lost none of his personal fastidiousness, nor his attention to detail.

## THE REALITIES OF DEMOCRATIC LEADERSHIP

However, in the late 1950s Nehru had to face the realities and constraints of democratic political leadership, as Gandhi had never done. Nehru had the reputation of having immense power and influence: some even accused him of dictatorship. Radhakrishnan as Vice-President and rather nearer the centre of politics, saw otherwise, and complained that Nehru was too democratic and not strong enough to push his ideas through.[22] Nehru himself had long recognised the limitations and discomforts of his position as a democratic prime minister. In June 1950 a journalist in Rangoon had asked him why, if he was a follower of Gandhi, he had used force in Hyderabad. He replied that Gandhi had been a prophet who could stick to his vision, regardless of the practical results. But a democratic leader (like himself) had to function through others and persuade others to accept his viewpoint, and was therefore bound to accept compromise. The issue for him was thus not to get into a maze of compromises but to remember the importance of principles. 'If he forgets that principle and lives only with compromises and opportunism then he has slipped and there is nothing left but the normal career of the politician.'[23] But the need to compromise, and to recognise political reality, pressed upon him more acutely as the years passed.

One of the major issues confronting the democratic polity was the nature and degree of its unity once the imperial government had been removed and with it the common enemy against which Indians had defined their own shared identity. Questions relating to the treatment of minorities of various kinds, and the nature of regional identities, had commanded Nehru's attention immediately after independence, and in many instances these remained. Communal relations, for example, were still capable of producing tension and at times serious violence, particularly in Bihar, UP and Madhya Pradesh. They were not on the scale of the horrors of 1947–8, but between 1954 and 1960 over 300 lives were claimed, and instances of violence seemed to be on the increase in the early 1960s. Nehru urged vigilance, and in 1961 the law was strengthened to punish and disenfranchise people convicted of fomenting enmity between different groups on grounds of religion, race or language. But Nehru's vision of a composite nationhood, where minorities were an essential and significant aspect of India's rich and complex identity, was frustrated. The place of religious minorities has remained a major question in the Indian polity, as a deeply disputed aspect of the fundamental nature of what it means to be an Indian, and as an urgent political problem capable of generating public violence outside the control of political leaders, and also increasingly of providing a populist platform for politicians.

Another of the most pressing sets of problems were those presented by India's linguistic diversity. Language was both a marker of distinctive regional cultures in India, and a crucial gateway to education and to employment in government. Nehru had unwillingly recognised in the early 1950s that he would have to accept the reality of strong linguistic movements undergirding the demand for the reshaping of the old provincial boundaries (see chapter 11), and that both he and the Delhi government would have to recognise the legitimacy of these regional identities as part of, and potential building blocs of, a broader Indian national sense of belonging. However, the 1956 States Reorganization Act had left unresolved the issue of Bombay, where Gujarati and Marathi speakers disputed the future of Bombay City in any division of the old Bombay Presidency. As local politics polarised along language lines, and Congress was severely weakened locally (as demonstrated in the 1957 general election[24]), Nehru's government bowed to reality and in 1960 the Presidency was divided into Gujarat and Maharashtra, with the former Presidency capital going to Maharashtra. As it was now clear that linguistic boundaries were still an open question, some Sikhs in the Punjab took up with renewed vigour the idea of a Punjabi-speaking state. But, under the leadership of the militant Akali Dali, this was essentially a movement for a Sikh majority state as opposed to a communally composite state of Hindus and Sikhs, and Nehru and his government resolutely refused to countenance any partition, despite the adoption by some of the Sikh activists of tactics of non-cooperation and fasting. Any further demarcation of political boundaries within India on communal grounds was essentially non-negotiable.[25]

In Nehru's later years the issue of Hindi as the national language became the most troublesome of linguistic issues. It raised major questions about the role of English as a language of communication within India and with the wider world, and the sensitivities of southerners. The languages in the south of India belonged to a different language family from the northern vernaculars with their Sanskritic roots, and southerners feared any imposition of Hindi upon them, particularly as a condition of government employment. When the constitution was formulated a compromise was reached which recognised the major regional languages as national languages which would be officially used in their own areas, while Hindi was given the status both of a national language in the area where Hindi was spoken on a daily basis, and of the country's official language. However for fifteen years English was to be retained as the official language of the Union and of communication between the states. Nehru was central to this multilingual solution. He disliked the trend towards a presumed purification and Sanskritisation of Hindi, which was linked, in his view, to a bigoted and narrow Hindu vision of India. He saw Hindi as a good working tool of communication throughout India, acting as a 'sister language' and functioning beside regional languages.[26]

However by the mid-1950s he was clearly aware of the strength of southern feeling about the future status of Hindi and recognised that the encouragement of Hindi throughout India would need great tact, while English would still play an important role. As the fifteen-year deadline drew closer there was overt hostility in the south to discontinuing the use of English as the country's official language, and Nehru spent much energy in trying to assuage southern fears. His principles on the issue were that no decision could be imposed by a majority on a minority, and that nothing should be done to put non-Hindi speakers at a disadvantage in government employment. He was in favour of English remaining a language of higher education and external contact, but not as the long-term all-India language, as this would be humiliating; but there should be no hurry about this and no strict deadlines.[27] Nehru found agitations on language issues distasteful and immature, and he was aghast when President Radhakrishnan (a Telugu-speaker from the south) was interrupted in Parliament for making his annual address in English rather than Hindi, feeling that this was not only an affront to parliamentary procedure but also foolish, in that it would hurt Hindi.[28] However, to calm fears which were potentially disruptive, as well as to underline the positive benefits of English as a scientific and international language, he backed a 1963 Official Languages Act which provided that English could continue to be used in addition to Hindi for all official purposes of the Union and in Parliament.

The problem of achieving a real national unity in the context of India's many diversities was also clear in Delhi's concerns over tribal groups, where outstanding problems remained into the final stages of Nehru's premiership (see above, chapter 12). He had been deeply concerned at the vision of Indian troops suppressing their tribal compatriots in north-eastern India, but his government would not countenance any secessionist movement, least of all in such a sensitive area for border security. However, it encouraged dealings by the Assam government with Naga leaders who were not committed to violent methods or the idea of independence; and in 1960 Delhi agreed to the formation of a new state within the Indian Union, Nagaland, which came into being three years later. Although Nehru recognised that force might still be needed to deal with those who did not accept this agreement, as a democratic leader he now felt much easier in his mind. Naga people now had freedom and dignity to live in 'the larger family of India'; he felt that his government had acted on democratic principles and as he admitted in 1960, 'My conscience is at ease now.'[29] Although democratic strategies of accommodation had drawn the sting of the worst tribal challenge to India's physical integrity, the long-term future of tribal peoples was still a profound cultural and socio-economic issue, to which there was no single or easy solution. Where tribal issues did not create problems for the state, there were few Congress politicians who considered them seriously, and the rhetoric of democratic pluralism took second place to an erosion of tribal life by processes of so-called development and the spread of education.

Much of Nehru's time was taken up with more prosaic aspects of working the democratic political system. Here again he often found his vision of democratic practice frustrated or distorted, and himself personally involved in uneasy and unwelcome compromise. To understand his disquiet, and sometimes revulsion, at the practice of democracy as it developed in India, it is worth asking what sort of democrat Nehru actually was. He was obviously committed to the structure and principles of the constitution, and had believed for decades that the government should be chosen by the people and should act in their interests – for this was the stuff of nationalist discourse. However he was not a natural party politician, a wheeler and dealer, a fixer or a manager. In practice he disliked the mechanisms by which votes were gained, group interests were assuaged and parties were organised; and it was with great reluctance that he accepted that Indian society and its different forms of connection, through caste, community, patronage and faction, had a role to play in anchoring democratic political forms and practice firmly in popular practice and imagination. His attitude was more patrician, even patriarchal, and he saw democracy far more in terms of a selfless and visionary leadership educating and encouraging willing voters and supporters. He was personally far happier talking to large crowds of admiring rural folk, presenting his vision of an India on the march, than cajoling groups of politicians representing various interests, or dealing with the daily problems of the Congress party. In this respect he was more like Gandhi, or even his imperial predecessors, with their own but very different visions of what India needed, and how it should be reformed, and their shared distaste for politicians.

The most obvious manifestation of India's new democratic life was the holding of three general elections in Nehru's lifetime – in 1952, 1957 and 1962 (see appendix). The magnitude of the electoral operation needs to be recognised: the electorate rose to well over 200 million by 1962, when there were over 238,000 voting stations, and a turnout of 55.1 per cent. In each Congress was the dominant party in the states and at the federal centre, and three times Nehru was effectively returned to office by the popular vote, as it was unthinkable that any other Congressman would challenge him for leadership of the parliamentary party in Delhi. In these elections Congress won between 45 per cent and 47.8 per cent of the votes cast in the elections to the Lok Sabha, and secured massive majorities – between 360 and 370 seats in a house of just under 500, or well over 70 per cent.[30] Congress obviously had the advantage of its nationalist past, both in terms of repute and rhetoric, and also its nationwide organisation, which had made it increasingly a desirable vehicle for candidates intent on power, and voters who wished to get things done. For its part Congress was open and flexible, ideologically and socially, welcoming virtually all who wished to operate within its ranks. By contrast, the few opposition parties were weak and divided and could not capitalise on the fact that fewer than half the electorate actually voted for Congress.

Nehru's name, and his association with Gandhi, were clearly able to exercise considerable electoral pull. But after the first election his active role in electioneering and in the selection of candidates declined. In the preparation for the 1962 election he admitted that he had had little to do with the selection of candidates and was too busy to attend the meetings of the Central Election Committee or to follow its work. Moreover, as he confided to T. T. Krishnamachari, 'Apart from not having the time for it, it bores me exceedingly.'[31] During the elections themselves he was ill. Despite the Congress success, and the obvious stability of the democratic polity, from the perspective of Nehru's desk all was not well with Indian democracy. In May 1957 he reflected that the picture of India 'as it emerged during these general elections . . . is not a pleasing one, and it has brought out, as democracy often does, both strength and the failings of our people, and indeed of ourselves'. Just at a time when India needed 'national cohesion and integrity of purpose' it was clear that Indians still had narrow and parochial outlooks and were prepared to sacrifice ideals for expedience. 'We have seen in these elections casteism often triumphant, communalism throwing its weight about, and in some places violence. We have seen in fact a certain immaturity in our public life as well as a certain lack of integrity.'[32]

He returned to this theme in 1962, claiming that the elections had so often turned on caste and communal lines, and on other narrow issues, when politicians of all parties were guilty of trying to gain advantage. Congress members seemed to have lost their old way of speaking to the masses about ideals, and also their 'moral fibre' which had been part of their mass appeal; though he thought the people generally were 'sound' and had a good deal of common sense.[33] Here Nehru was certainly right about the sophisticated realism of the electorate. But in his condemnation of Congress members he was hankering after an image which was more a myth than political reality. During the later years of the raj, when Congress honed the strategies of electioneering, it had learned to tap into local issues and loyalties under the overarching banner of nationalism, and its success then, as now, lay precisely in its capacity to draw on what Nehru considered narrow, parochial and sectional loyalties in order to build for itself a nationwide appeal.

Despite his reservations about politicians and their electoral behaviour, Nehru continued to nurture the practice of democracy in the arena of Parliament, treating its sessions with utmost seriousness, and encouraging appropriate practice. America's ambassador to Delhi in 1961 noted how he visited Nehru in his parliamentary office, where he usually worked when Parliament was sitting, as this was part of his determination to inculcate parliamentary practice in his lifetime: the visitor commented that the central Parliament functioned as efficiently and equably as the US Senate, though in the state capitals 'they throw things in their moments of truth'.[34] Glimpses of this personal commitment in action in even the smallest ways can be found in Nehru's papers – as when he noted in 1957 that one of the Congress Whips should educate a Scheduled Caste woman (the formal name for Untouchables), newly elected as an MP, in how she should behave in her new role. He also interested himself in the money she needed to set up house in her member's accommodation, and agreed to talk to her about the loan she had taken out to cover her election expenses of Rs 1,200. When India was facing China's invasion in late 1962 he found time to send a message to a Whips' conference in Bombay, reminding them of the many vital roles they played in establishing effective and decorous parliamentary behaviour.[35]

The Congress party was central to the establishment of democratic norms and practice in India, its value being demonstrated retrospectively by comparison with neighbouring Pakistan and other former imperial dependencies where democratic forms of politics and government were swiftly eroded or replaced after independence. It not only provided mechanisms to work and sustain the institutions provided through the constitution. It also enabled the federal system to work in its formative years, since Congressmen formed governments both in Delhi and in the state capitals, and conflict between the two was rare. Party mechanisms were used to ensure considerable conformity of policy between the centre and the states and to smooth out potential conflicts. The Union government needed the states' cooperation for the implementation of policy, while cooperative relations with Delhi, and with Nehru in particular, in turn gave Congress party bosses in the states considerable status and influence. However, the very success of Congress in becoming the dominant party, and virtually a party system within itself, generated its own internal problems, and it was a highly competitive, factionalised organisation which was difficult to manage. One old and devoted friend, formerly a close associate of Gandhi, even told Nehru bluntly in 1961 that she believed 'that power has corrupted the Congress party as a whole. Internecine strife, the struggle for linguistic divisions and all the other ills, including communalism and a fall in standards of morality and integrity, are surely evidence of such corruption.'[36]

Nehru had been deeply concerned about the nature of Congress since independence (see chapter 11). Managing it had been a significant part of his work, particularly in the years when he was party president. But in the final years of his life he became less involved in hands-on management of the party; although he was of course one of the core central party leadership and on most of its major committees. He was too busy with other things, often found party affairs depressing, and was at times unable to get to grips with the complexities of local Congress politics. In 1960 he struggled to find time to read a series of communications on Orissa party affairs, and when he had done so commented to the Congress President that he was quite unable to understand what had happened. 'I am completely at sea and do not know what to do about these matters.'[37] He relied increasingly on the four presidents who succeeded him, U. Dhebar, his daughter, Indira, and then Sanjiva Reddy and D. Sanjivayya, to do the routine work within the party, but it was clear that they held office only with his blessing and support. Some even described the role of the party President as 'a glorified office boy of the Congress central government headed by the Prime Minister'.[38]

Nehru's interventions in local Congress affairs personally, rather than through the President, tended to be only where he knew a region well, or on issues which he thought were vital. For example, in 1959, following communal disturbances in Bhopal, he suggested to the Chief Minister, an old colleague from the Delhi government, that Sadiq Ali, General-Secretary of the AICC, should investigate the role of the police, despite the Chief Minister's hostility to an enquiry. Nehru thought it was vital that in such situations Congress should be seen to be active and independent, rather than always accepting what government asserted.[39] Or again, much of his concern was with Congress in his own UP, where the state Congress party was rent by factionalism after Pant had left to join the Delhi government. After the 1957 elections he wrote to the Chief Minister of his fears that Muslims were drifting away from Congress, of the internal strife within the party, and that it had practically no organisation. His exhortations and even a personal visit in 1959 could do nothing to resolve the faction fighting which tore the party apart and attained public notoriety.[40]

Knowing his limited capacity to influence local Congress affairs, and indeed the undesirability of the Prime Minister becoming mired in local and factional conflicts, Nehru tended to intervene more generally with broader exhortations and pronouncements about the nature of the party and its weaknesses in the context of Indian democracy. In the 1957 elections to the Lok Sabha, Congress had raised its percentage of votes and its number of seats; but in the simultaneous elections to the state assemblies it had put up fewer candidates, and its number of seats fell by over 200, although its share of the votes rose by just over 2 per cent.[41] Nehru's analysis was that Congress had lost touch with great swathes of the population, particularly the educated, and that it now relied on a rural vote which was an unstable base, riven increasingly by class and caste loyalties. In many places it no longer had a genuine and permanent organisation, and it was plagued by splits. If it did not wake up and shake off its complacency, it would wither away. As he wrote to the Chief Minister of UP, 'We are now up against the full flood of democracy and the props that held us in the past are no longer supporting us. Perhaps the real explanation is that we have lost the crusading spirit that made us great.' He and Dhebar, the President of the party, agreed that there was something fundamentally wrong with the party organisation; and Dhebar noted that he thought the real problem was that the party had become the stepping stone to success in power politics, whereas voters wanted good service in social matters and good developmental government from Congress.[42]

This was of course the nub of the problem. Congress's problems stemmed in large part from its dominant role in the political system and its very success in recruiting disparate groups who saw its value for the forwarding of their careers and their interests. The openness of its doors meant that it would in turn reflect many of the divisions within the society in which it operated. Nehru also recognised that there seemed to be a lack of ideological conviction among Congress members, what he called a 'hiatus of mind'. The reasons for this in part went back into Congress's pre-independence history, as he well knew from his own experiences as a younger man often at odds with the party and its leadership. But those in the central organs of the party never seemed to have the time to talk about large issues such as land reform and cooperation, because they were taken up with 'daily difficulties'.[43]

Little, if anything, was done to address these problems, and in 1962 Congress performed even less well in both the Lok Sabha and state assembly elections, dropping its numbers of seats won and percentage of votes polled in Delhi and the states. Nehru continued to feel acutely the problems of working with the democratic tools at his disposal. In 1963 in a message to the Mysore PCC he noted how India was under threat from external aggression, and within its borders from a lack of unity and integrity. Congress had a vital role to play in strengthening the country, but this could only be done if it worked with a new unity of its own in place of its many internal squabbles, with discipline and enthusiasm, and with the spirit of sacrifice which had made it so great in the past.[44] Here again was the comparison with Congress present and a presumed Congress past, a hankering after a nationalist myth of the great days of struggle, and a vision of Congress as a band of disciplined workers. It reflected Nehru's reluctance to recognise and become enmeshed in the inevitable realities of political leadership within a vibrant democratic system which was increasingly rooted in Indian society with its manifold interests and identities. However, one particular episode showed him most forcefully the problems inherent in relying on Congress for the functioning of the democratic system, and the compromises he could be forced to make as leader of an all-India party that was built on powerful state parties with their distinctive regional interests. That was the Congress response to the establishment of a communist government in the state of Kerala as a result of the 1957 elections.

Kerala had been formed as a Malyalam-speaking state out of parts of former British and princely India in the process of states' reorganisation in 1956, so the 1957 election was the first in the state as whole. However, even before then the central Congress leadership was aware of the party's frailty in the area, and that the Communist Party of India (CPI) was gaining electoral support as well as organisational strength. When Nehru asked the Chief Minister of Hyderabad to go to Kerala as Governor he tried to refuse, and indicated that Kerala was 'the most difficult place now' and likely to be the most politically unstable state after the general elections.[45] The region's reputation was grounded in political reality: there had been six ministries in eight years, and as the *Hindustan Times* noted, there were more ex-Chief Ministers there than in any other state, and every third politician had at one time been a minister![46] Electoral politics revolved in part round socio-economic issues, and in part round community issues, because, most unusually, the region's population was composed of four major communities, low-caste Ezhavas, Christians, Nairs and Muslims. In 1957 the Communist Party came to power in the state legislature, winning 60 out of the 126 available seats, on just over 35 per cent of the vote, or 41 per cent counting the independents the party backed. Congress polled just under 38 per cent of the votes, but won only 43 seats. Thus for the first time a legitimately elected Communist government came to power in one of India's states, and the federal arrangements in the constitution had to function without the benefit of the shared party allegiance and organisation in the state and in Delhi.

Nehru accepted this as an appropriate democratic outcome of a properly held election, and clearly attempted to find ways of working with the Kerala government, despite his hostility to Indian Communists in the early years of independence, when he thought they were theorists ignorant of Indian conditions, and dedicated to destructive strategies at a time when all Indians should be uniting to ensure stability in the new nation. However, it was evident that some of his colleagues in the Delhi government, including Pant as Home Minister, and the Kerala Congressmen were far less minded to work with the unprecedented political situation. The actions of the new Kerala government, under the experienced and highly respected E. M. S. Namboodiripad, suggested that it intended to pursue radical policies, particularly in relation to land and tenants' and workers' rights, which Congress had never dared to envisage, despite its rhetoric. Further, it passed an Act which would have given government new controls over private educational institutions that accepted government funding, and thereby alienated the powerful Christian lobby, for whom schools were a vital aspect of community work and consolidation. By the spring of 1959 it was evident that a powerful anti-government coalition had built up, and that the Kerala PCC, under its new President, R. Sankar, was joining forces with its campaign to oust the Communist government. The main point of controversy was the Education Act, and the motley group of anti-government allies began a strategy of civil disobedience in early June, which led to thousands of arrests and several deaths as a result of firing by the police.

At this stage both Nehru and Indira, now Congress President, were anxious about the deteriorating situation and attempted to restrain local Congress members from becoming entangled in violent and undemocratic action. Nehru for his part admitted that there was now a very considerable upsurge of feeling against the local government, and urged it to consider why this was, in order to resolve the problems.[47] Father and daughter both publicly insisted that the local Congress was not attempting to oust the state ministry by unconstitutional means but were merely opposing particular aspects of its policies. Moreover, Nehru privately told the leader of the joint campaign that he feared it would lead to violence and to methods opposed to democracy, and that he could not countenance this while claiming to stand for democracy. Further the central government could not tolerate violent, undemocratic behaviour. To the Governor he wrote on the same day that he was deeply worried about events in Kerala and felt the local Congress was rapidly drifting in the wrong direction. To try to bring down a local government by such means as picketing schools and Collectors' offices was to store up trouble in other states, and the Delhi government might have to help the state government to maintain order. Moreover, agrarian reform legislation should be allowed through as it was in accordance with Congress policy, and it would look bad if Congress in opposition blocked it.

He also wrote a tough letter to the President of the Kerala PCC, as Prime Minister and as a long-time Congress member, in a similar vein. To him it seemed that local Congress members, however difficult their situation, were abandoning democratic practice and Congress principles. Principles were more important than strong feelings, and it was most undesirable for Congress members to associate with communal parties in this way. Indira added her own weight in a private letter to the local party president, insisting that the local Congress members were going far further than had been agreed, and that their actions were undemocratic. This was her reply to his ominous statement in a letter he had written to her, arguing that local Congress members could not stand aside from a popular movement, and that if they were asked to suspend their action, things would run out of control to the detriment of Congress, and (deploying Nehru's democratic fears against the central leadership) to the detriment of the 'democratic-minded' and innocent in the state.[48]

Evidence of the grave perturbation felt in central Congress circles at the crisis into which their local colleagues seemed to be dragging the party was the visit to Kerala by the former President, Dhebar, and by Sadiq Ali, General Secretary. Nehru himself flew down at the end of June to see the situation for himself and to attempt to find some resolution. He reported to Sri Prakasa, now Governor of Bombay, while on this visit, that the whole business was 'very complicated and distressing. I am afraid that after two days of it I see no clear way out of it.'[49] He had prolonged conversations with members of the government, with the local Congress leadership, and with over sixty prominent local people. At one stage he became so tired that little constructive could be done. As he left for Delhi he told journalists at the airport that he had made some suggestions but had issued no directives to either the ministry or the local Congress; but he thought an election was the obvious way to deal with an apparently popular upsurge against the government.[50] (Given his age, the pressure of this crisis and the exertion involved in this flying visit of several days, it is little wonder that he became exhausted and within a couple of weeks had had to take a rest in the hills.)

Nehru was caught in a cleft stick. If he condoned local party activists' opposition to the Kerala government he undermined his own commitment to democracy; yet there were many voices in politics and in the press urging him to take action because the Kerala government itself was acting contrary to democratic standards. If he gave in to Kerala Congress members he risked the political integrity of the Congress as a party committed to democracy, but if he opposed their behaviour with more than words he risked breaking up the party. A crisis meeting of the Central Parliamentary Board was held on 26–9 June in Delhi immediately on his return.[51] Nehru of course attended, even though he was not a member, and his voice and Dhebar's dominated the discussions. The consensus was that an election was the only satisfactory and democratic way of resolving the deadlock, and that the Kerala PCC should prepare a 'charge sheet' to be delivered to the President of the Republic (after consultation with the Parliamentary Board), requesting him to hold fresh elections in the state. Nehru was asked to draft the statement to this effect. Kerala Congress leaders were called in on the final day and after considerable discussion Nehru's draft was accepted.

At the same time a secret note of instructions was given to the Kerala PCC, insisting that it must accept the broad policy laid down in Delhi and try to persuade its local allies to accept it. First, they must demand new elections; and if the state government refused (as was likely) then they must proceed to the strategy of a charge sheet which should go to the President with a plea for elections and an enquiry. Picketing should be eased off, there should be no wholesale non-cooperation with the government, no abusive language or behaviour, Congress members should be prepared to talk with the local government and must do nothing outside the scope of this plan without the express sanction of the Parliamentary Board.[52] Nehru followed this with a confidential letter to the Chief Minister, saying how distressed he was at the almost hysterical atmosphere in Kerala, and urging that an election was the only democratic way of dealing with this extraordinary situation.[53]

The crisis had effectively prostrated Nehru; but even while he was on holiday he continued to work for a way out other than central intervention. He corresponded at length with the Chief Minister and eventually saw him for several hours in his hill retreat on 11 July, when he agreed to discuss Nehru's idea of a fresh election with his CPI colleagues.[54] Meantime news came in to him of a deteriorating situation on the ground, via private letters and the press: the agitation continued unabated, and the local government was arresting and imprisoning thousands of protestors. There were also growing demands for central intervention, and some hostility to Nehru himself and his apparent inaction. One newspaper from the Punjab pointed out the danger for democracy of thinking that Nehru was infallible. It argued that part of the reason for this tendency was Nehru's distance from the people, despite his belief that he knew India. 'It is because he is no "ordinary" person that the common man thinks Mr Nehru usually to be right.'[55]

While Nehru was recuperating in the hills political discussions in Delhi suggested that his colleagues in government were seriously contemplating the imposition of President's Rule, while the Kerala PCC presented the President of India with the fifty-page memorandum which asked for central intervention and fresh elections. Some form of central intervention seemed even more likely in mid-July when the Communists in Kerala turned down the compromise idea of a mid-term election. Namboodiripad told Nehru that if they gave way on this it would be a dangerous precedent for any non-Congress government in a state, and that he and his colleagues felt that Congress in Delhi either could not or would not restrain local Congress members.[56] Nehru was horrified when he heard that the local PCC seemed to be backing a policy of non-production of food, in an escalation of the pressure on the state government, and urged Indira and the Kerala Congress President to stand out against this. But as he recognised, and told Namboodiripad, the central party had no influence on non-Congress organisations involved, and only limited influence with the local party members.[57] Eventually on 30 July the cabinet after a lengthy meeting decided to recommend that the President impose President's Rule on the state. As Nehru told the Governor, the cabinet was most reluctant to take this step, but it felt it was better than allowing the situation to deteriorate still further. He recognised that this was not a good precedent and went against all the conventions they wished to establish in India. With considerable candour he accepted that the opposition in Kerala did not have clean hands, was often communal in orientation, and that he wished the Kerala Congress had not got itself mixed up with unsavoury allies who would certainly give it a hard time in the future. Moreover, he admitted that his own colleagues in party and government in Delhi were to blame for what they had *not* done over the months of escalating crisis.[58] (The sequel to this episode was a mid-term election in 1960, when Congress and its allies defeated the Communists, who won only 26 out of the 108 seats they contested, but polled just over 39 per cent of the votes. Congress alone won 63 seats, but polled only just over 34 per cent of the votes.)

Much controversy has surrounded this episode, particularly over Nehru's own role and his inability to control events, even within his own party; over the degree to which Congressmen in Delhi and Kerala ever really intended working with a Communist state government according to the constitution; and over whether Indira Gandhi as Congress President played a major role in swaying her father towards central intervention. Contemporary evidence does indeed suggest that Nehru could not control events within his own party in the states – but then that had long been the case, and he had lived with his frustrations at the nature of the Congress in contrast to his vision of what it should be. But he still retained the primary initiative in Delhi both in the party and in government, despite his age and temporary illness in the middle of July. What the episode showed were the intolerable constraints on him as a democratic leader who had to rely on a party which was founded not on ideology but to a large extent on being the gateway to office and its fruits; electoral success bred further loyalty to the party, but, conversely, defeat threatened to erode local support from those who were now prepared to look elsewhere for means of getting back into power. Even at the best of times Congress had trouble controlling and disciplining its local components. It was to an extent at the mercy of its local senior party members who, as Kerala showed, could embroil the party in Delhi in major political compromises which the central Congress felt forced to adopt in preference to risking the break-up of the party and imperilling its all-India identity and appeal.

In this instance, too, a determined local opposition confronted an equally determined state government: it was not in the interests of either to compromise with the other, and nor was it in the interests of Kerala Congress members to compromise with the party's High Command, unlike the earlier days of the Congress when compromise through Gandhi's carefully crafted agreements was vital for the Congress's local and national standing. The resulting erosion of public order placed Nehru, the central party and the Union government in a no-win situation: there were voluble demands for immediate action within and outside their ranks, but action or inaction were equally likely to tarnish the Prime Minister's reputation.

The question of Goa, still a Portuguese colony, further demonstrated to Nehru the painful realities of democratic leadership, and the need to compromise in politics. Although he had never been committed to non-violence in Gandhi's absolute way, he believed that in the particular circumstances of British rule non-violent methods had forced the British to withdraw. But now his renewed reflections on the meaning and relevance of Gandhian principles to contemporary India and its problems led him to contemplate in some depth the issue of non-violence in the contemporary world and on its practicalities for India.[59] He had concluded that India could not do without armed forces to protect it against internal disorder (as in the Naga hills) and against potential external aggression, particularly from Pakistan. Indeed, Parliament and people would not tolerate any government which left India weak and defenceless. But what perplexed him most was the issue of Goa. 'The most important and immediate question for India is that of Goa and how to deal with it without resort to arms.' He did not want to have to resort to violent means to dislodge Portuguese rule, both from principle, but also because such action would have a bad effect on world opinion and would jeopardise India's international influence. Moreover, he recognised that satyagraha had little chance because the Portuguese did not respond to it as the British had done, because they felt themselves to be standard-bearers of a glorious Christian civilisation, and were determined to retain this symbol of their past imperial power.

At this stage he was still prepared to wait to find a solution to the problem, though he recognised that this meant that India really had no policy on the issue. Gradually the tide of world opinion seemed to be flowing India's way. In 1960 the UN had passed a resolution demanding the end of imperialism, and by 1961 opinion was clearly hostile to continued Portuguese imperialism in Africa, and Portugal was condemned in the UN for not complying with its obligations under the UN Charter. In particular several leaders of African countries in the non-aligned movement made it plain that they felt Nehru was being soft on Portugal on the Goa issue, just when he should be more assertive, given the Angolan rebellion against Portuguese rule in mid-summer.[60] It was also clear that in India there was increasing frustration at apparent government inaction over the remnants of European imperialism on the subcontinent well over a decade after independence, and both left and right were attacking Nehru for hesitation on border and security issues, just months away from another general election.[61] The situation deteriorated further as a result of Portuguese attacks on Indian shipping and Indian police posts, and as the Portuguese regime increasingly proved unable to guarantee order within the colony.

By December the situation seemed critical. The American and British governments, and the Secretary-General of the UN, U Thant, attempted to persuade

Nehru to delay any armed action. But he explained forcibly to all three why India could no longer hold back from armed intervention.[62] To Britain's Harold Macmillan he argued (perhaps remembering Kerala) that sometimes leaders had to choose the lesser of two evils, and in this case armed action, though he detested the idea, was preferable to the outbreak of 'unauthorised violence'. Further, there were limits to what a democratic leader could do when confronted with widespread and resentful public opinion on an issue. The Ministry of Defence, now headed by Krishna Menon, seems to have had no qualms about direct action; though it seems unrealistic to assert, as Mountbatten later did, that Menon 'bounced' Nehru into military action.[63] Nehru may have hesitated on precise timing, but by now he recognised that more acceptable forms of pressure had failed, and that as a democratic leader he had to be responsive to popular opinion, just as he had been, for example, on the issue of redrawing state boundaries.

On 17 December Indian troops entered Goa, under the command of the lieutenant-general who had led the police action in Hyderabad in 1948, J. N. Chaudhuri; and in twenty-six hours they had asserted Indian authority. The Governor-General of Goa defied his masters in Lisbon and surrendered without a fight. There was virtually no opposition in India to this move. But in Britain, Europe and the US there was profound regret and criticism of Nehru in person as well as of the decision to use force. In the UN Security Council, America and Britain, with France and Turkey, proposed a resolution calling for an immediate cease-fire, but this was vetoed by the Soviet Union and three other countries (the United Arab Republic, Ceylon and Liberia). The Portuguese surrender overtook Security Council discussions, but Nehru was left in no doubt about the force of international condemnation. Dean Rusk, US Secretary of State, told the Indian ambassador, B. K. Nehru, plainly of American deep regrets at the action; and a long-term American supporter of India, Adlai Stevenson, said in the Security Council that he felt this could be the beginning of the death of the UN, reminding the gathering that the League of Nations had died when it no longer resisted the use of aggressive force.[64]

Into this hostile atmosphere stepped Krishna Menon, who arrived in America three days after the invasion of Goa. He insisted at a news conference that the Indian action was not aggression and that India had not violated anyone's sovereignty by its action; and the conference almost broke up when he publicly lost his temper with a reporter from UPI Movietone News who asked him what the Goan action was if it was not aggression. The two men ultimately shook hands, but it was another instance of Menon's irascibility, and his insensitivity to his environment, despite the fact that very recently he had been obliged, at Nehru's request, to call on President Kennedy to attempt to allay Kennedy's irritation with him.[65]

Nehru personally was accused in the American press of doing irreparable damage to India's good name and to the principles of international morality; of abandoning his ideals and of using Goa for domestic reasons; and of assuming the moral leadership of the world while denying a plebiscite to Kashmir's people and 'liberating' the Goans who had not said they wished to be liberated.[66] He was pained and surprised at this outburst of anger against him and his policy on Goa, but he declined to engage in the controversy. By contrast he was obviously deeply pleased by the understanding response of the Cardinal Archbishop of Bombay, himself a Goan, and explained to him how he felt there had been no escape from this step. Any backing away would have caused bitter resentment in India and possible chaos in Goa, with thousands of Indians and Goans entering the colony, and this would have involved India in force against its own citizens or standing by and watching its citizens shot by the Portuguese. He assured him that the Goans' culture and religious freedom would be safeguarded.[67]

He reiterated this argument of 'no choice' in a forceful letter to President Kennedy, launching a fierce attack on Portuguese imperialism and referring to the anger this had generated in India, and reminding the President, who of course was a Catholic, of the support of the Cardinal Archbishop and other members of the Catholic hierarchy in Goa itself. He ended by saying that he could cope with personal attacks on himself, but he hoped that this episode would not affect India's relations with the USA.[68] Once more the realities of leadership in a democracy, particularly for one who constantly spoke in terms of ideals and principles, was painfully clear to Nehru, causing him considerable personal conflict. Unlike his prophetic mentor, he could not walk away from the realities of politics, but had to exercise his leadership within the constraints it imposed upon him.

In the first phase of Nehru's prime ministership he had been in his element, combining his love of active campaigning with his intellectual power to conceptualise issues and trends. He had thrown his energy into laying the foundations of the new nation state, and articulating principles which should guide the country. He had deployed his considerable political skills, his powers of oratory, and his status as Gandhi's heir in the work of creating a new India. But as India's democracy developed its own particular patterns, and the era of primary national construction gave place to routines of government and politics, Nehru became more troubled and less assured. Age was inevitably catching up on him, with its limitations on his energies and his abilities to learn new political skills; and he became increasingly frustrated at the constraints on him as a leader within India's particular political context. The tools with which he had to work seemed to him blunt and unresponsive; while his allies in the Congress often seemed to be acting in ways which negated his vision and increasingly tarnished his own reputation. The demands of politics confronted the principled intellectual within Nehru's complex personality, causing hesitation, tension and often distress. Perhaps not surprisingly, advancing years encouraged deeper reflection, and he revisited the values Gandhi had taught in the two critical decades of his dominance in Indian political life. He recognised that Gandhi's role had been very different from his own – a prophetic role less trammelled by political necessity and the demands of governance, one in which Gandhi had sometimes walked away from politics as Nehru felt he could not do, imprisoned by a sense of obligation born of his long connection with Congress and his somewhat patrician sense of knowing what India really needed. For him, therefore, Gandhi could provide no practical blueprint for politics and government. However, he had articulated values which he thought should be the mark of an independent India, and many of these sustained the ageing Nehru as abiding aspirations while he battled with the realities of democratic leadership.

# Chapter 15

# A New India?

While Nehru was in prison in 1942 he had wondered if he would ever have the time and energy to address the huge tasks he had contemplated for so many years, and he confided to his diary that he hungered for 'constructive work on a vast scale'.[1] His vision of a new India to be created after independence was more radical and far-reaching than that of most of his Congress colleagues, stretching beyond political independence to include fundamental reform of society and reconstruction of the economy. By the 1950s he was talking with huge enthusiasm of India's grand project, which had no historical precedent – delivering a new socio-economic order by democratic means. There were two main policy prongs to his strategy for change, a series of economic plans to lift the economy into sustained growth, and legislation to tackle some obvious social inequities (see above, chapter 12). This chapter explores the degree to which his vision was implemented or frustrated. Obviously this is not the place for a detailed examination of changes in India's economy or society under Nehru; and indeed many of the effects of the policies he put in place were played out in the years following his death. But in his own lifetime there was evidence enough of the profound problems inherent in his policies, and these contributed to his sense of a vision frustrated, and immense tasks yet to be done. It was symptomatic of his frame of mind towards the end of his life that he kept on his desk lines of the poet, Robert Frost, which he had copied out.

> The woods are lovely, dark and deep,
> But I have promises to keep,
> And miles to go before I sleep,
> And miles to go before I sleep.

## THE MAGNITUDE OF THE PROBLEM

By the year of Nehru's death the face of India was in many ways different from the India which had achieved independence in 1947. Even to the superficial observer there was evidence of change, which reflected the new spending priorities of the independent government. Major changes in communications had brought the country together in new ways, enabling new social, economic and political interactions. There were over 50,000 more post offices, thousands more telephone exchanges and millions more telephone connections. A vibrant vernacular and English press was still the major source of mass communications, but radio coverage was growing. Over 2 million radio licences were issued in 1961 compared with just over a quarter of a million in 1947, though in 1961 only just under 0.5 per cent of the population and 2.3 per cent of all families possessed a radio. At the same time the road, railway and air networks expanded. Nehru's government had stressed the need to generate more power as the precondition for major economic change, and symbolic of this was the construction of a number of major dams. In 1950–1, 4.2 billion volts was generated annually, but this had risen to 33 billion in 1965–6. Agricultural and industrial production both increased: in the years 1950 to 1965 agricultural output increased by 5.16 per cent and industrial output by 7.7 per cent. Among the industrial success stories were steel and cement: the production of steel increased fourfold between 1950–1 and 1965–6, and cement almost fivefold.[2] There was also investment in social infrastructure, including schools, hospitals and primary medical centres on a scale far greater than before independence. For example, between 1951 and 1966 the number of mother and child welfare centres rose from 1,700 to 10,000, and hospitals and dispensaries from 8,600 to 14,600.[3]

However, investment in social and economic change was increasingly swallowed up by the rapid increase in the population. Nehru and his planners seem only gradually to have recognised that the goalposts were effectively moving. Earlier in his prime ministership Nehru had believed that India did not have a population problem, but by 1959 he was arguing that progress towards self-sustaining economic growth would have to be rapid if they aspired to cross the barriers of poverty and underdevelopment. 'To move forward slowly means that we never catch up as our progress is countered by the growth of population.' Two years later as the census material was being collated, he was warned that population figures were far higher than those on which the Third Plan had been based: further, the rate of growth was quickening alarmingly.[4] When the 1961 census was published the figures made plain the magnitude of the problem and its likely impact on all planning. In 1951 the population had been 361.1 million; in 1961 it was 439.2 million. This represented a growth rate of 21.5 per cent during the decade, or an annual growth rate of nearly 2 per cent, which was considerably higher than the figure of 1.4 per cent the planners in the mid-1950s had used for their work. Life expectancy at birth had risen during the decade from 32 to 42 for men and from 31.5 to 40.5 for women. India still remained a predominantly rural country, with under 20 per cent of its population living in urban areas, but still the rise in the urban population during the decade was considerable (18.5 million) and by 1961 over 80 million Indians were town and city dwellers.[5]

Population policy was limited and hesitant during the 1950s, geared towards providing more family planning clinics. A Central Family Planning Board was set up in 1956 and by the end of the decade all the states also had one. It was not until the Third Plan, which came into operation in 1961, that it was recognised that a central feature of planning must include the stabilisation of the population. At this stage the approach was still to provide access to contraception through clinics; but from 1963 it was accepted that a much wider policy of publicity was necessary, and even greater investment. The allocation of money in the Third Plan had been over five times that allocated in the Second Plan, and it was to rise again in the Fourth Plan, after Nehru's death.

Of course population growth is not in all circumstances detrimental to economic growth.[6] But in the particular circumstances of India in the mid-twentieth century population increase of this magnitude placed an intolerable burden on social resources such as schools, hospitals and housing, added to the large numbers of unemployed, and strained the food supply so that India could not feed its own citizens without recourse to food aid from abroad, particularly wheat from the USA, Canada and Australia. Even with foodgrain imports rising to over 6 million tonnes in the final year of Nehru's life, demand outpaced what was available. Or again, in terms of unemployment, for the total duration of the first three plans additions to the labour force outnumbered the additional employment created, and by the end of the Third Plan probably as many as 10 million were unemployed. Statistics for literacy tell the same story. Although literacy rates rose from 16.6 per cent in 1951 to 24 per cent in 1961, the actual number of illiterate persons also rose – by over 30 million in the same decade.[7] Given the population increase it is understandable how socio-economic change was visible alongside persistent and increasing inequalities and deprivation in Nehru's India, and how well-intentioned planning so often failed to get to grips with fundamental social and economic problems.

## THE FRUSTRATIONS OF POLICY AND PLANNING

By the later 1950s Nehru's strategy of planning was firmly in place, and he was surrounded by a small group of dedicated enthusiasts who shared his vision of the future and the economic strategies necessary to reach it. At the heart of this state experiment in the democratic delivery of a new socio-economic order was the Planning Commission, with its commitment to industrialisation based on import substitution, and to state investment in and control of heavy and strategic industry as the leading force in economic change. It was not until just after Nehru died that it became palpably clear that the strategy was not working. Rates of growth in agriculture and industry slowed considerably, targets of investment and production were not reached, there was no mass eradication of poverty, and government could not raise enough in taxation to invest in the wide range of social goods which would have transformed the lives of millions. But even before he died it was clear that the strategy was being frustrated by long-term problems, as well as being compounded by the need to treble defence spending, to meet the danger from the Chinese (see next chapter).

Among these problems was the actual financing of the plans. By the late 1950s the sterling balances, accumulated in London during the war and available to pay for imports in the early years of independence, had been used up. Moreover India's competitiveness as an exporter of raw materials and its share of world markets declined in the later 1950s, just as the prices of essential imports (food, steel, iron and capital equipment) increased. This led to a severe balance of payment crisis in the winter of 1956–7. By mid-1957 the foreign exchange position was 'pretty alarming', as T. T. Krishnamachari, now Finance Minister, told his Prime Minister and the cabinet: and if immediate steps were not taken the economy could grind to a halt and India would lose its international creditworthiness. Nehru confirmed the crisis in discussion with the cabinet, accepting that they clearly could not fulfil the Second Plan, but must at least implement the industrial core of it.[8] Consequently non-essential imports were drastically curtailed and plan outlays were scaled down. However, as Krishnamachari later admitted to Nehru in a frank assessment, some of the problems lay in the very planning itself. Foreign exchange costs had been underestimated and no allowance had been made for defence; nor had the Planning Commission and the Ministry of Finance and other ministries affected really discussed this issue or taken steps to control foreign expenditure.[9] At the same time the food situation was also deeply worrying, and in August Krishnamachari was telling Nehru that he did 'not think we, as a Government, have any comprehensive idea of the extent and nature of the problem in this regard'.[10]

It was not surprising that India became increasingly dependent on external aid both for food and for plan financing. Late in 1957 an aid agreement was signed with the USSR, which tied aid to major industrial projects; and the following year an Aid-India Consortium was created by Canada, Britain, the USA, West Germany and the World Bank. Aid as a percentage of total plan outlay more than trebled in the course of the Second Plan compared with the First. By 1960–1 America was the largest single donor to India, providing nearly 348 million dollars. This was

despite Nehru's own deep-rooted concerns about compromising India's fundamental independence in domestic and international affairs by overdependence on
aid – a concern shared by the Congress President, Dhebar, who wrote Nehru a
secret letter at the height of the foreign exchange crisis, pointing out the dangers
of a situation where they appeared to be becoming dependent on aid just for
survival.[11]

The frustration of planning did not lie solely in foreign exchange shortages. It
was increasingly clear that government-run industries tended to be deeply inefficient – in ironic contrast to private industries permitted in non-key sectors. Here
the problem of skilled management was paramount. Indian administrators were
trained as generalists rather than specialists, as their imperial predecessors had
been before them, and they did not have the knowledge and skills necessary to
run major industries, of setting clear goals, improving efficiency and closely moni-
toring progress. For example, in 1962 the outspoken T. T. Krishnamachari, no
longer Finance Minister but again in the cabinet, told Nehru about the baffling
problems of maintaining supplies of coal to the railway industry because of
networks of divided authority and the obstructive attitude of railway officials. He
painted a picture 'vitiated by a very inefficient system of transport, unintelligent,
unorganised and positively obstructive. The remarks that fell from the Railway
officials in the overview I had with them were such as would not be tolerated even
from a dictator. Presumably this attitude is excusable and it is intended to cover an
acute state of inefficiency.'[12] As he had earlier pointed out to Nehru, sheer lack of
administrative competence ran through the governmental machine in its attempt
to manage the economy, and the financial indiscipline of over half the state
governments was a cause of grave concern.[13]

There was the further problem of the state of agriculture. A flourishing
agricultural sector was vital to the whole planning process, in order to feed the
population and provide vital jobs, to create consumer demand, and to free up
savings which could be reinvested in major economic change. To create such a
sector provided much of the argument behind attempts since independence to do
away with various kinds of 'intermediaries' and to provide smaller farmers with
viable plots of land and sources of credit either as family operators or as members
of cooperatives. However, the abolition of *zamindari* and the halting progress of
ceiling legislation limiting landholdings had done little to transform the face
of rural society and of agricultural production by the later 1950s. What increase
in foodgrain output did occur was almost all the result of greater use of labour
or increase in the cultivation of unirrigated land. There was no major structural
change in the rural economy until the so-called Green Revolution which began
over a decade later and transformed parts of Indian agriculture with new high-
yielding forms of wheat and rice, which in turn reduced the need for food aid
and created commercial profits which could be invested in new agricultural

technology. Only then were the agricultural sector's constraints on overall economic advance in part removed.

Nehru and his planners were in the late 1950s confronted with evidence of fundamental constraints which frustrated their hopes and forced them to scale down their goals. But as they began to prepare the Third Plan, which would run from 1961, they did not deviate from their strategy of concentrating primarily upon industry. As Nehru told Nasser in mid-1959, real development could only be achieved by rapid industrialisation. The Second Plan had invested 19 per cent of its total on agriculture compared with 34 per cent in industry and power: the Third invested 18 per cent in agriculture and 36 per cent in industry and power.[14] (These are of course percentages to show the balance of investment: in actual terms the amounts increased very markedly.) The *Hindustan Times* was deeply critical at the outcome of an AICC planning seminar in May–June 1959 held at Ootacamund in South India, the hill station known in imperial times as 'Snooty Ooty'. It commented that it all sounded very depressing and nobody would think about what had gone wrong, and why nearly eight years of planning had not generated anything like the rate of progress hoped for. A few days earlier it had run a leader entitled 'The Questions Mr Nehru will not answer', in which it lambasted the leadership for taking refuge in big ideas without paying adequate attention to implementation of policies – whether on the question of cooperatives or the management of government enterprises, which seemed to lack a sense of purpose and direction.[15]

Nehru, however, had been thinking deeply about the problems which beset the economy, and it was evident that in mid-decade he was increasingly anxious that problems with agricultural production were endangering the whole economic strategy as well as leading to the painful recognition that ten years after independence the country could not feed itself. He wrote to his Chief Ministers about the debilitating slowness of actual reform of landholding, the lack of urgency in the states over food production, and the leisurely old routines of the state Agricultural Departments, which needed thoroughly shaking up. For him increased food production was utterly vital – without it all their plans would founder – and he desperately tried to inject into his senior state colleagues his own sense of urgency.[16] By early 1959 he was writing, with the Third Plan in mind, that India had to advance on two fronts simultaneously, food and agriculture, 'which is of the first importance', and heavy industry.[17] As he surveyed the agricultural situation he began to place increasing emphasis on the importance of implementing land ceiling legislation and of forming rural cooperatives. Early in 1959 a meeting of Congress at Nagpur resolved on an agricultural policy which reflected his views – including the swift establishment of rural cooperatives, first for credit, marketing and distribution, and ultimately for farming itself, although farmers would retain their proprietary rights. At this meeting it was also accepted that the goal of planning was the creation of a democratic and socialist society. The AICC at its May–June planning seminar carried forward this discussion, endorsing the need for cooperatives as well as the expansion both of the public sector and of control and regulation of large production units still in private hands, as it wrestled with the meaning of a democratic socialist society in the context of having to mobilise far greater resources for the Third Plan.

Discussion of the impending plan indicated the constraints on Nehru personally in the field of economic policy – just as the almost simultaneous issue of Kerala and President's Rule displayed the ambiguities of his role as a democratic leader. The juxtaposition of these issues in mid-1959, just months before he reached his seventieth birthday, must have made him wonder just how much influence he really had in Indian politics; and the tone of his reaction to criticism of his economic policies was surprised and even somewhat petulant.[18] Firstly, it was clear that even within the Congress Party there was opposition to his cautious radicalism. Even though the party preserved the appearance of unity on its socio-economic plans and goals at Nagpur and Ootacamund with convenient rhetoric, there was considerable hostility to Nehru's views within it. The leadership of the UP state Congress party, for example, was vocal in opposition to ceilings on landholdings, one of the chief opponents being UP's Minister for Revenue and Finance. (Subsequently when the state party found reluctantly that it had to accept national policy it paid no attention to the formulation of the law and left it entirely to senior administrators in the state.) Chief Ministers, mindful of their constituencies, which included many substantial independent farmers, succeeded in preventing the implementation of radical reform in rural institutions and relations.

The innate conservatism of the party in rural matters, which had so concerned the young Nehru, now resurfaced as a major constraint on the ability of his government to pursue policies it thought necessary to achieve both economic growth and a more equal society. Sri Prakasa had warned his old friend of this in 1957, when he argued that they were trying to achieve too much too quickly in the field of socio-economic change. People would not challenge Nehru while he was alive but he feared a backlash when Nehru was no longer there with his huge reservoir of respect and affection.[19] Now, after the Ooty seminar, even the President of India, old Congressman Rajendra Prasad, wrote Nehru a critical letter covering issues of unemployment, education and food, where he thought far too little was being done, and warning against social legislation relating to land distribution and cooperative farming. At least one newspaper pointedly said that the nation should be grateful to Prasad for his letter, as he was one of the few elder statesmen left in Congress who could advise and if necessary remonstrate with Nehru. Nehru wrote an emollient reply, assuring him that the government was considering all these problems, and that there would be no compulsion on the matter of cooperatives.[20]

External opposition was even louder. In the spring of 1959 a new opposition party came into being, the Swatantra Party, dedicated to free enterprise and opposing government control over the economy through planning control of key industries and agrarian reform.[21] It swept up into its ranks dissident Congressmen who were alarmed at the way Nehru was leading the party and government, while its main base was a coalition of big business and rural notables, including land-lords and aristocrats. At the same time there were foreign voices from aid donors, expressing concern at the ambitious public sector programme, and urging India to tackle its food crisis as a priority.

Of these sources of opposition probably the most dangerous and insidious was that within the heart of Congress, for Congressmen in key positions in the states were well placed to undermine whatever plans came down from Delhi, given that they were not only anxious to trade on the prestige of Nehru and the Congress as India's major political party, but equally concerned to protect their own interests, those of the substantial rural elements who were increasingly the core of the party, and those of their supporters at the polls. Some understanding of the weakness of government in pushing through reforms on the ground throughout India, given the nature and size of its own administrative machine, persuaded Nehru and his government to embark in 1958 on an experiment with rural democracy, instituting a somewhat Gandhian system of *panchayati raj*, or rule by village councils. These were not the old village or caste panchayats, which had decided small-scale issues of ritual and social control, but three tiers of new elected institutions designed to aid the development process from the bottom upwards by incorporating local people and getting round the established bureaucracy with all its cultural assumptions and weaknesses in fostering real change. As Nehru insisted in 1963, he was a strong advocate of the twin projects of community development and panchayati raj, in the hope that they would liberate and energise ordinary Indians, where state enterprise was such a frail tool for genuine radical revolution. The key objective was 'developing the human factor and . . . vitalizing and modernizing the man who works in the field. It is this aspect which must be emphasized and our work should concentrate on this.'[22] Decades after his death village democracy was indeed to engage some of the most deprived and to give them a new voice within the polity. But in the early years those who benefited most from them tended to be those already wielding power in rural communities, while the development officers who were supposed to work with the local institutions often behaved suspiciously like the very established bureaucrats whom the policy-makers had sought to circumvent.

Despite all his efforts at reasoned intellectual argument, political persuasion and some structural innovation, Nehru was faced towards the end of his life, even before the Chinese invasion of 1962 and its disastrous implications for planning, with evidence that many of his colleagues did not share his goals and that the pace of change was inadequate to transform India's economy and society in the way he had wished. He confided this to T. T. Krishnamachari, and the latter warned him that available statistics were already showing that midway through the Third Plan targets were again not being met and the plan was going awry.[23] In retrospect it seems clear that Nehru's model of planned economic transformation was flawed in the context of India's democratic polity, and given the resources at the government's disposal. On top of this was the weakness of the tools with which major change was attempted, and Nehru's own incapacity as a leader to energise change within the bureaucratic system. He could see where there was a problem, but he often could not see how to resolve it, and in particular how to achieve serious implementation of policy. Consequently, as he aged, he often resorted to rhetoric rather than action, thus generating hostility which often quietly worked through the system to frustrate his vision. After he was dead it became dramatically obvious that his policy of planned economic transformation, however idealistic – particularly in the context of his time – had only worked to constrain economic growth and burden the economy with the weight of government control.

## THE FRUSTRATIONS OF LEGISLATIVE REFORM

The second prong of Nehru's strategy for radical socio-economic change was legislation to end practices and relationships which enforced glaring inequalities in society. Achieving the passage of such legislation had itself often been difficult – for example, in the case of reform of Hindu women's status through the Lok Sabha, or with state laws to abolish *zamindari*. It was perhaps not surprising that implementation of such laws proved even harder.

Take first the issue of redistribution of land through the abolition of large landlords and placing limits on the holdings permitted to individuals, so-called ceiling legislation. Although laws to abolish *zamindari* were passed by the mid-1950s in all states, ceiling legislation was still haltingly coming into place in the early 1960s. However, on the ground it was clear that landlords had not been abolished. In the mid-1950s about 20 per cent of all cultivated land was still rented out, though this figure declined to just over 12 per cent by 1962. Tenants tended to work very small plots of 2.5 acres or less. Tenancy agreements were often not cash-based, but took the form of share-cropping, and often tenants had little protection in law because of the absence of documentary evidence of rights in and on land. For this reason it was easy to evict them and take once-rented land into 'personal cultivation', which was permitted under ceiling legislation, or to mask evictions as voluntary surrenders, again permitted without infringing ceiling legislation. Consequently old power relationships within rural society were not undermined, and the complexity of rural relations and practices made ceilings a nightmare to implement and (just as in the case of the abolition of *zamindari*) an easy field for landlords to exploit, as the Planning Commission itself recognised in 1961.[24] By 1961–2 the dimensions of rural inequality in relation to landholding were clear. The vast majority of landowning households (over 81 per cent) owned just 31.5 per cent of cultivated land, most of it in plots of one to three hectares. By contrast the remaining landholding households (nearly 19 per cent) owned over 68 per cent of cultivated land, in holdings over three hectares. The very largest holdings of over twenty hectares constituted just over 11 per cent of cultivated land, and were in the hands of under 1 per cent of landholding households.[25]

A study of Bihar, a state where there had been considerable *zamindari*, has shown the disillusion at the base of rural society with the working of the Acts intended to transform rural society. The precise effects of the reforming legislation varied from district to district, but rarely did those at the very base of rural society benefit significantly. The gains tended to go to groups of middling farmers who gained greater status and power, or to the former landlords themselves. To take a single example, which is telling politically and economically – in one village in Muzaffarpur district there had been one single *zamindar* with an exclusive inter-mediary right over all the land in his village, about 600 acres. In the mid-1950s he was a Congress member of the Bihar state legislature and a prominent member of the local Congress party. He managed to retain 500 acres of contiguous land and his so-called village residence, which was in fact the house of his estate manager, and by the mid-1950s was using his land for commercial farming of tobacco and sugar. His former tenants had not done well. They had tiny plots (the average being 1.65 acres fragmented into non-contiguous plots), twelve had been evicted and were now landless and had to work for the *zamindar* as waged labour. Many of those who now owned land paid rents to the state which were higher than the ones they had paid to the *zamindar*. None of the ex-tenants had achieved economic independence of their former landlord and even those who had some land had to work for him as waged labour to make ends meet, for daily wages which had dropped since the abolition of *zamindari*. As one village elder grimly stated, 'Our condition is one of not having enough in our bellies to have the strength to be concerned about our position. Lower wages for labor, higher rent for land – these make little difference. We are already poor.'[26] Clearly 'develop-ment' had passed them by. None of the villagers could afford brick houses, and they ate two meals daily, mostly of poor quality rice. Their village had no school and no electricity, they had little regular contact with the wider world, and no community development work had touched their lives.

By 1961 the Planning Commission itself recognised that ceiling legislation was a frail tool for radical reform of rural relations and unlikely to liberate any appre-ciable surplus for distribution.[27] This meant that one means of dealing with the economic deprivation of the Untouchables as well as other landless groups was closed off. The Untouchables' position of extreme deprivation was both economic and ritual. Ritual impurity reinforced lack of access to education and land and to work other than the most demeaning kind, trapping them in poverty and degradation. The 1955 abolition of Untouchability by law was intended to deal with the ritual aspect of their status, giving them equality of status with other citizens of the Union under the provisions of the constitution. However, in reality the law was rarely used to challenge the practice of Untouchability, convictions were few and penalties risible.[28] For example the highest number of cases in any year reaching the state courts was just under 700 in 1956. Thereafter the number dropped and by the last three years of Nehru's life it was running at between 371 and 393 – for the whole of India. Simultaneously the number of convictions in such cases declined – from nearly 43 per cent in the first three years after the legal abolition to just over 31 per cent in 1960–3.

As with legislation to abolish landlords and impose ceilings on landholding, the powerful and privileged were able to hire skilled lawyers who exploited numerous loopholes in the legislation to avoid conviction. Untouchables could seldom afford good lawyers, even if they were given state legal aid, witnesses were understandably reluctant to come forward, and often police and magistrates not only shared the prejudices of the accused but were reluctant to alienate those who were powerful in local society. Penalties in the few convictions secured might only be a few rupees, which were no deterrent to the more powerful in society who were determined to stick to old ways and ignore the law. It was perhaps not surprising that Untouchability remained a fact of Indian social life, particularly in rural areas, right through the twentieth century.

Reform by law and the constitution of the status of Hindu women was similarly limited. Perhaps the most successful aspect was the incorporation of women as enfranchised citizens into the polity. In the 1962 elections nearly 47 per cent of female voters cast their vote, compared with a total turnout of nearly 55 per cent. Just over 15 per cent fewer women than men voted. Far fewer women actually participated in political institutions. In 1962, of the few women who stood for the Lok Sabha, only just over half were successful. Between 1952 and the early 1970s only 212 women had served in the central legislature – 129 in the Lok Sabha and 83 in the Rajya Sabha.[29]

The impact of laws intended to give women equality in such matters as marriage, divorce and inheritance was even more restricted.[30] As with the law abolishing Untouchability, so in relation to the reforming laws of the mid-1950s few women were in any position to use the law to protect themselves, given their low levels of education and lack of access to money and advice independently of their husbands and families. Dowry, despite its legal abolition, persisted and seemed to be on the increase, when a National Committee on the Status of Women made its enquiries a decade after Nehru's death. Educated people also seemed to be expecting higher dowries. This practice brought with it acute financial problems for a bride's family, and distress for the bride herself in cases where her marital family felt the dowry to be inadequate and exposed her to extreme unhappiness, if not actual physical harm. The committee noted that this practice was not in accordance with the goal of a socialist society and needed to be combated in a variety of ways, including enforcement of the legislation prohibiting it.[31]

A whole range of socio-economic indicators showed how women were still in many ways denied the reality of equality in Indian society. In the first decades of independence the ratio of women to men declined markedly, from 946 women to every thousand men in 1951, to 941 in 1961, to 930 in 1971. This reflected a lack of medical care and higher female mortality. Even by 1971 females at birth could expect to live two years less than a male. (Towards the end of the century, when sex testing of foetuses made selective abortion of unwanted females easier, this demographic scandal prompted anxious enquiry into the 'missing millions' of Indian women and the description of women as an 'endangered sex'.) Girls were still married very young and often under the legal age, although the mean age of marriage had risen significantly for women since the start of the century. In 1901–11 the mean age of marriage for men had been 20.2 for men and 13.2 for girls: by 1951–61 the mean age for men was 19.8 and 15.4 for girls. Urban males as well as females tended to marry at a later age than rural young people, so the all-India figure masks an even lower age for rural girls.

Although some women were becoming high achievers in the more modern sectors of the world of work, as doctors, teachers, civil servants and other professionals, the majority of women, particularly in the countryside, had little access to education and were declining as a proportion of the paid labour force. Female literacy was indeed rising, but was still far lower than male literacy. In 1951 just under 8 per cent of women were literate, and by 1961 that figure had risen to almost 13 per cent. The figures for male literacy were just under 25 per cent in 1951 and almost 34.5 per cent in 1961. Given the rising population the percentage rise in literacy does not tell the full story. Actual numbers of illiterates were also rising – in the case of women from nearly 162 million in 1950–1 to over 185 million in 1961. At every stage in the school system girls' enrolment was lower than boys', with the gap widening the higher the stage in school. A National Committee on Women's Education in 1958–9 was so perturbed by the widening gender gap in education that they recommended a special programme to close the gap. Its results were only temporary and by the later 1960s the growth rate in female enrolment in school was declining markedly. Furthermore, the drop-out rate for girls was higher than for boys in primary school – by about ten percentage points.[32]

The fate of legislative and constitutional provisions intended to achieve a more equal society suggests a number of common reasons why law proved a limited tool for social engineering, and indicates the deeper reasons why Nehru's visions of a more egalitarian national community were frustrated. Nehru recognised many of these problems, but his response to this conundrum, as to so many things, was rhetorical rather than practical. He told the Associated Chambers of Commerce of India in 1957 that one of the things which pleased him most in the first decade of independence was the series of legal changes in women's status, for these were truly revolutionary and were the prelude to and touchstone of change in the rest of society. Admitting that the law was frequently broken, he commented, 'Well, something will have to be done about it.'[33]

The fundamental reason for the failure of law as a means of radical change was the fact that the laws on sensitive socio-economic matters which were central to the exercise of power in society and also within the family tended to be out of step with prevailing and deep-rooted attitudes and values. They passed, often with difficulty, through legislatures, but that did not indicate support for them in practice by those outside the legislative chambers, or even within them, as was shown by the case of the Congress legislator from Bihar who contrived to pursue his own interest in the face of legislation on land reform backed by his own party. Again and again it was clear that those who were in a position of authority or had the influence to encourage the actual implementation of reforming laws failed to do so. Magistrates and police often frustrated the use of the law prohibiting Untouchability out of deference to local caste Hindus with local influence. Male family members, lawyers and magistrates often worked to frustrate laws on women's rights which would have endangered what they perceived as family interests, particularly in matters of inheritance.

Against entrenched social prejudice the legal and administrative structures of the state would have had to be strong, well financed, and actively intrusive to achieve change in practice. They had none of these characteristics. Lack of political will was translated into minimal administrative commitment and investment. There was no central enforcement apparatus in relation to the 1955 Untouchability Offences Act, nor any central agency which systematically gathered information about problems relating to the Act and its enforcement. Enforcement lay with the states, and it was clear that their priorities often lay elsewhere when money was scarce. In Bombay, for example, prohibition was seen as a far more worthy cause for state intervention than the removal of Untouchability. Administrative frailty also helped to undermine the implementation of land reform. Extra staff were rarely employed to supervise land reform, and no change was made in the keeping of land records, which were essential for real change in rural relations. Village record keepers on paltry salaries had every interest in staying on the right side of substantial local landholders. A study of the fate of ceiling legislation in UP showed that at the Board of Revenue only seven officers were assigned to the programme of change, and only five clerks had responsibility for maintaining the records of ceilings. In the districts no official were exclusively assigned to oversee implementation and very few were given even temporary duties in relation to the programme and its records.[34]

Moreover, there was no party commitment to supplementing the activities of government officials. A strongly organised cadre party might have been able to overcome the failings of the state's administrative structure, but Congress was not this sort of party, and, moreover, many of its members tended to have vested interests in the rural status quo. Dhebar as Congress President wrote tellingly to Nehru in 1957 of the problem of landless labourers in the Punjab, who were mainly Untouchables and who had been evicted from land. The state's bureaucracy was doing nothing about this problem, but neither was the party machinery. He was thinking of trying to have a small group from the members of the AICC who might awaken the party organisation to this matter.[35]

Another deep-seated reason for the frustration of reform by legislation was the lack of mass education (see above, chapter 12). Education for all, and particularly for the deprived and despised, would have helped to generate new attitudes within society at large, and would have encouraged the disadvantaged to see that change was possible in their lives and those of their children. It would have helped to empower the disadvantaged, enabling them to do something about their situation, either by choosing new jobs or by grasping the levers offered by the law and the franchise. Although literacy rates were rising under Nehru's government, those who needed it most were still the least likely to have access to it. Literacy rates for women as compared with men have already been cited; for example, in 1961 nearly 13 per cent of women were literate compared to almost 35 per cent of men. However, in rural areas both men and women were less likely to be literate, the figure for men being just under 30 per cent and for women 8.5 per cent. Not surprisingly, Untouchables, who were largely rural people, had particularly low rates. Among those officially recognised as the most deprived, and taking men and women together (which of course masks a pathetic rate for women) only 10 per cent of Scheduled Castes were literate in 1961, and only 8 per cent of Scheduled Tribes. Just being literate was of course no indication of possessing the levels of education adequate to lift a person out of poverty. In 1961 only 10 per cent of the male population had primary or basic junior education, and only just over 3 per cent had attained the level of matriculation or above. (The figures for women were 3.8 per cent and 0.6 per cent respectively.)

Nehru was increasingly aware of the problem. In January 1958 he wrote a special letter to his Chief Ministers, beside the regular fortnightly letters, particularly urging them to think creatively about primary education, even to the extent of concentrating on paying teachers rather than putting up buildings. Pupils could be taught outside for most of the year and could take their holidays in the monsoon. Teachers and schools should be given plots of land, to raise their status and remuneration. He exhorted them to see that the slow pace of educational change was totally inadequate for modern needs. An educated citizenry was essential if they were to solve their country's problems. He returned to the subject a few weeks later, urging Chief Ministers to see the importance of the well-trained and well-paid teacher rather than buildings; his tone indicated extreme frustration: 'I feel that in this matter I have not succeeded in convincing others and I go on crying in a wilderness of disbelief.'[36] At the end of 1958 he put the importance of education even more bluntly.

> In the final analysis, the greatest and most revolutionary factor in bringing about political, economic and social change is education. I am not sure in my mind if everyone realizes this, but I have come to this definite conclusion We cannot go far in industrialisation or better agriculture or indeed better anything except on the base of such widespread education. Of course, education by itself is not enough, and we have to keep pace with our other schemes of development. But, without education, there is no real development.'[37]

The President of the Republic added his voice to the concern about the state of education in his critical letter of 7 June 1959 to the Prime Minister, in which he dealt with a range of outstanding policy problems. As a result the Secretary for Education in Delhi wrote to all state Education Ministers, Secretaries and Directors of Education, drawing their attention to the President's concerns and urging them to press ahead with educational reform, tackling in particular the problem of the low status and efficiency of teachers.[38]

However, exhortation was not enough to change political and financial reality. It was not only that education was a subject for the states and therefore not under the immediate control of central government. As India lurched towards a financial crisis in its planning in the late 1950s, and then was forced to spend more on defence in the early 1960s, education became even less of a priority for government spending, whatever the Prime Minister or President might say. The Directive Principle of the constitution which laid down that all children should receive free primary education to the age of fourteen by 1961 was nowhere near fulfilment by 1961. In the first five primary grades (bringing children to the age of nine or ten) enrolment was just over 62 per cent of the age group – 82.6 per cent for boys and 41.4 per cent for girls. In the next two grades the enrolment was far smaller – 22.5 per cent overall, with about 33 per cent of boys and 11 per cent of girls. Between 1950–1 and 1960–1 government expenditure on education had more than trebled, though it ran persistently below the level of expenditure on defence, or on administration, police and justice.[39] But this was totally inadequate, given the needs of the growing population, if Nehru's vision was to be fulfilled.

During the 1950s aspirations to change Indian society and to energise the economy were widespread in India, as was the sense that it was the duty of government to plan and enable change. This was itself a major shift in public attitudes. But Nehru's encompassing vision of socio-economic transformation within a democratic framework was deeply frustrated. The very processes of democracy themselves worked to inhibit radical change, particularly where they reflected and even entrenched deep-rooted social conservatism. Moreover, by the end of the decade it was clear that opposition to his policies was building both within and outside the Congress. Criticism came from different perspectives. Some felt he was attempting to drive India too fast along the path of change, while many with established interests felt he was threatening private enterprise and giving the state far too great a role in socio-economic issues. Their voices were to be heard inside Congress and in the new Swatantra Party. Others on the left wing of Indian politics felt his government was doing too little, was ignoring issues of implementation in favour of grand socialist rhetoric, and was basically in hock to vested interests. A tiny group turned their backs on state initiative and tried more Gandhian ways of working for change at the grass roots.[40] The most powerful criticisms of Nehru's economic policies in particular only became widespread several decades after his death, when the impact of government controls and planning on the economy became apparent. His model of change is seen from a later perspective to have been deeply flawed, as was its implementation.

However, Nehru has to be put into his historical context and seen as a man of his time and place, with limited examples and options open to him. In the mid-twentieth century he had no other example of radical change on such a vast scale to look to, except the Soviet model. (Little was known about the working of the Chinese economy at the time.) Eschewing compulsion on the scale of the Soviet experiment, and the violence which went with it, he looked also to the experiments with rebuilding the economy in Britain after the war in a democratic environment, and tried to combine elements of the two – persuasion and rational argument within an open political system, with planning and government control and initiative.

Nonetheless there were issues he failed to tackle which proved to be important in other places where radical socio-economic change was later attempted, and as a result Indian economic growth was inhibited for decades to come. One was the failure to educate India's citizens and provide them with skills which would have lifted both individuals and the economy itself into a new phase of change. Another was the comparatively small significance accorded to small-scale enterprises, which might have provided vital jobs when unemployment was a major social problem. Yet another was the nature of the administration, still cast in an imperial mould and suitable for the maintenance of order and stability, but not for the management of major socio-economic change. Above all there was the problem of controlling the increase in population, which was not really seen as a problem until the evidence was provided by the second decennial census after independence, but which threatened to overwhelm the attempts to end poverty and invest in a range of desirable social goods in order to transform social relations and the lives of ordinary people. Nehru began to see the significance of some of these issues towards the end of his life, and to recognise their impact on his model of change, although he never doubted the appropriateness of the model for his country. At times his response was frustrated and even petulant criticism of his colleagues and compatriots. At others it was a renewed appreciation of Gandhi's concerns for the poor and underprivileged, and his insistence on working from the grass roots upwards, relying on the efforts of individuals and small communities to help themselves, rather than depending on the structures of the modern state and the actions of a bureaucracy inherited from the raj.

# Chapter 16

# The Erosion of Authority

Nehru's position at the apex of India's political system gave the impression that he was a leader of considerable power, as did his recognition abroad as a world figure, who was influential through his connections and his articulation of non-alignment for a group of diverse countries in the context of the Cold War. His authority within India was, in practice, limited by many aspects of the situation in which he worked and strove to implement his vision of a new India. The structures and practice of democratic politics, the nature of the administration, finance, and his own compatriots with their mixed abilities and diverse attitudes on what he saw as key issues, all worked to constrain his ability to achieve change. Often opposition to him personally was muted, or was deflected on to his allies, since his public image remained that of an irreplaceable national leader and Gandhi's heir, and few would risk challenging him openly. However, at the end of the 1950s more overt criticism of his role and his policies was becoming clear – from opposition parties, within Congress, and even from the President of India.

What really precipitated a serious erosion of his authority was his policy towards China and the invasion of India by Chinese troops in October–November 1962. For the first time in the nation's life India faced a critical threat to its physical integrity, which it could not meet, of a sort vastly more dangerous and humiliating than the sputtering conflict with Pakistan over the status of Kashmir. This unexpected war with China signalled the frustration of a crucial aspect of Nehru's international vision, and the collapse of the keystone of his vision of a new Asia and ultimately of a more peaceful world order. Not surprisingly it had a profound impact on him as a person, and on his public image at home and abroad. It also necessitated much greater expenditure on defence and damaged the state's ability to pursue the policies of socio-economic change on which his prime ministership had been built.

## THE FAILURE OF NEHRU'S CHINA POLICY

Deep at the heart of Nehru's policy towards China was his belief that China, as the other major country in Asia with an equally deeply rooted civilisation, was India's natural friend and ally in the construction of the post-colonial world and the emergence of Asia as a strong influence in the international order. Most of his personal diplomatic dealings had been with Chou En-Lai, whom he found reasonable and easy to deal with, and this had worked to confirm his deep and long-standing ideological commitment to friendship with China. The Five Principles of peaceful co-existence – *panchsheel* – agreed with China in 1954, were also for him the blueprint for a more peaceful world in which India could lead the way. He therefore did not see China as in any sense a threat to India. For example, in a long note on India and non-violence and how to deal with Goa without resort to arms, sent early in 1957 to the Gandhian, Vinoba Bhave, Nehru calculated that India was not at risk from any great power, and that the only military threat was Pakistan now that it was in alliance with the USA, and that its domestic politics had concentrated power in a few hands, particularly the army.[1] Furthermore, Nehru backed away from confronting issues of clarifying India's long borders with China, apparently convinced that these were sufficiently clear and would be respected by the Chinese, even though in many places they had not been demarcated on the ground.[2]

The overriding importance of Nehru's own understanding of China (and thus subsequently the responsibility he bore historically for the failure of India's policy towards its neighbour) lay in his personal dominance of foreign policy-making. Very few people outside the Ministry of External Affairs interacted with him over foreign policy, and neither the cabinet nor Parliament had a major role in the formation of policy. Parliament was, in fact, initially kept in the dark about the deterioration of relations with China. Within the ministry officials tended to go along with their chief, and were reluctant to give him serious, critical advice. The few people with the knowledge or position to challenge him received short shrift or were ignored. Vallabhbhai Patel's very early warnings in 1950 were not answered. Four years later Nehru's government brushed aside warnings from one of its most senior former diplomats who was then Governor of Bombay, G. S. Bajpai, who argued that India should tackle the question of the eastern sector of the border, as the Chinese had never accepted the McMahon Line as the frontier between India and Tibet, and this imperial legacy might store up future trouble between their two countries.[3]

In 1959 the President himself, Rajendra Prasad, took the Prime Minister to task in person at a Governors' Conference, and in two top secret letters, for leaving the country without adequate defence against China, given that Tibet had practically ceased to exist as a buffer state and India had a border with China running over

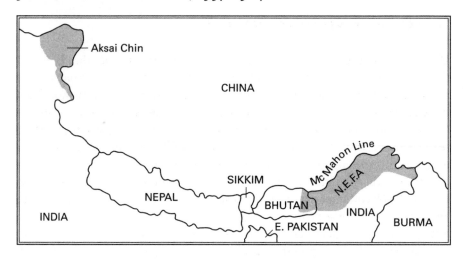

*5. Areas of dispute between India and China*

2,500 miles. He argued that additions would have to be made to the army, but that in the longer term they would also need to engage in road-building, communications and military posts to defend their frontier. Although he hoped the retrieval of Indian territory which now appeared to be subject to Chinese encroachment could be managed through negotiation he did not rule out the possible use of force. Sri Prakasa, looking back in 1962, remembered how irritated Nehru had been by Prasad's intervention at the Governors' Conference, and how he had spoken to the President 'in a manner that did not appear to me to be right and proper'. He also lamented that they had now learned the hard way how dangerous it was to leave all decisions to one man, however great and able.[4]

It is also evident that Nehru's dominance over foreign policy was made more problematic, and potentially dangerous, by the absence of adequate intelligence. Not only was there little perception of the nature of the Chinese state and the dynamics of its decision-making, leaving Nehru to take Chou's amiable front as an indication of Chinese Communism at work. There was no serious knowledge of what the Chinese were doing on the ground or how they were likely to react if they were challenged. For example, in 1956–7 the Chinese built a road to supply western Tibet through Aksai Chin, an area claimed by India. The first the Indian government knew of this was when its ambassador in Peking reported the news after reading about it in the Chinese press. It was then a full year before Indian reconnaissance confirmed that the road did indeed pass through what was considered Indian territory. There was little intelligence expertise within military circles, reflecting the fact that Indians had not had training in this under the British, and the civilian authorities were content not to encourage this aspect of the army's expertise, given their fear of a potential political role by the military, as in Pakistan. Moreover, the borders were until 1959 under the jurisdiction of the Home Ministry rather than the army, thus leaving intelligence to the civilian Intelligence Bureau under B. N. Mullik, a former police officer, who had considerable influence over policy because of his closeness to Nehru. He was convinced that China would not react forcefully to Indian attempts to man posts along the frontier, and this only confirmed Nehru's own view of China's peaceful intentions towards its Asian brother.

In his last letter to Chief Ministers of 1958 Nehru insisted that relations between India and China were still 'friendly' and that India intended to pursue a policy of 'friendship and co-operation wherever this is possible'.[5] However, 1959 turned out to be an *annus horribilis* in terms of Nehru's policy towards China, just as it proved to be one of unprecedented difficulty on the home front. Early in the year the Chinese made it plain that they did not accept India's contention that the border between them was settled; and simultaneously a rebellion in Tibet led to the flight of the Dalai Lama to India at the end of March. With considerable prescience the London-based *Economist* noted on 4 April that Nehru's India was emerging from 'the age of innocence. In later years, the republic of India may look back upon this month as its moment of truth.'[6]

The first half of 1959 was indeed the stage at which Nehru himself was forced to face doubts about his much-valued policy of *panchsheel*, though he did not repudiate it. By June he was writing to the president of the India–China Friendship Centre in Bengal, saying that he could not give a message on the anniversary of the declaration of the Five Principles because China was violating them.[7] Less publicly, within the Ministry of External Relations and in discussions with close colleagues, Nehru was expressing deep concern over the treatment of Indians in Tibet, and about the security of the border itself, when the Chinese claimed Indian troops were violating Chinese territory and India protested against what it saw as Chinese armed intrusion into its territory.[8]

Simultaneously sections of his compatriots began to doubt openly the wisdom of his leadership in foreign affairs. As Nehru's government trod an uneasy path, giving the Dalai Lama asylum yet refusing to recognise an alternative government of Tibet, he was subjected to vocal public criticism and a clamour for a firmer stand on Tibet. The *Indian Express* was one of the most critical English-language papers and accused Nehru of pusillanimity and of wanting to have his cake and eat it. If Nehru's government, it raged in early July, was 'now to equivocate in an attempt to regain a smile from Peking it will have made India a laughing stock in the eyes of independent minded people, invite the ridicule of the free world and the contempt of the Communists. And it will deserve it.' The *Hindustan Times* argued that India must allow the Dalai Lama to function politically, even if he did not have the status of an émigré government, otherwise India would not be acting according to the principles of anti-colonialism. The Chinese would not like this but India would be doing the cause of friendship with China a great disservice 'if we let them run away with the idea that a regard for their feelings is with us a directive principle of State policy'.[9] Nehru argued for realism and roundly told the critical editor of a Nagpur paper that he did not know what else India could have done about Tibet except shouting more loudly and making more verbal condemnations. 'Such shouting and condemnation does not seem to me to be the right basis of any policy. We have done everything we possibly could in this matter short of the shouting.'[10]

However, in the autumn, the tension over the border was so great, having led to armed clashes and the overwhelming of an Indian post at Longju, that Nehru at last placed matters before Parliament, including his most recent exchange with Chou En-Lai which made it plain that China's alignment of the border included about 40,000 square miles of what India assumed to be its territory. From now on Nehru's policies could not be insulated from the nation's major forum of educated public opinion. Inside his own party and among the opposition there was noisy insistence that there could be no negotiations with the Chinese while they presumed to be aggressors on Indian territory. The border was now not just a part of official assumptions discreetly maintained in the Ministry of External Affairs; it had become part of a national sense of identity, thus making any peaceful settlement of disputes infinitely more difficult.

A shift in Indian policy towards the border with China, the so-called Forward Policy, did not emerge until after one last meeting between Nehru and Chou in April 1960, billed as talks rather than negotiations to soothe Indian public opinion. Nehru probably still hoped that something might come of talking; and a public demonstration of a willingness to engage was undoubtedly helpful in strengthening international sympathy, not least from the USSR. He was already assured of considerable western sympathy. When President Eisenwhower paid a winter visit to Delhi in 1959 it was evident that the two leaders got on well together, as they had in America in 1956, while the public welcome for 'Ike' indicated how far Indian opinion had veered towards America in reaction to the Chinese danger – even taking into account the likely official encouragement of crowds to welcome the distinguished American guest. Even now Nehru could not really imagine that China would contemplate an attack in the north east, in such difficult terrain and at such an altitude. An American journalist in Ike's entourage reported what Nehru told him: 'Surely the Chinese knew this. And why should they attack to try to gain an almost uninhabited bit of territory?'[11]

However the visit from Chou was a chilly and unproductive occasion. There were no cheering crowds, as there had been for Ike, and no official receptions in the visitor's honour. Despite lengthy talks spanning several days the only constructive result was that officials from both sides should examine the material in their position on the alignment of the boundary. A British journalist later noted the frosty atmosphere, and also the hostility in political circles to anything resembling a deal with China. This put pressure on Nehru, as the parallel with Munich – Chamberlain's bid for peace with Hitler in 1938 – was frequently drawn, and any compromise would have been seen as appeasement. Moreover, the visit demonstrated hostility to Krishna Menon, even among officials close to Nehru in the Ministry of External Affairs, who felt that he did not recognise the Chinese threat and was a dangerous influence on Nehru in this context.[12]

Nehru was deeply affected by the way his cherished policy seemed to be unravelling round him. Not only did the Chinese stance undermine the intellectual and ideological approach to foreign policy which he had made peculiarly his own since 1947, in his pursuit of a new post-colonial world; it also baffled him intellectually. He admitted this in a speech on the opening day of a Commonwealth Prime Ministers' Conference in London in May, just after Chou's visit. Tellingly, he now admitted (echoing the warning Patel had given a decade earlier) that the Chinese were more driven by nationalism than Marxism, and were displaying aggressive and expansionist nationalist tendencies which were exacerbated by their international isolation.[13] It was also significant that he wrote nothing to his Chief Ministers between the beginning of January and the beginning of June 1960, except to forward some notes on making manure from fallen leaves, written by his brother-in-law, Dr K. N. Kaul, who was Director of the National Botanic Garden in Lucknow. When he did resume his letters the first one was largely a travelogue relating to the countries he had visited after his attendance at the Commonwealth Premiers' Conference. He apologised for his silence, and admitted that his failure to write was not so much because of the pressure of work but 'the real reason is that I could not tune my mind to the task of writing to you the kind of letters I would wish to write. All this indicates not a proper state of the mind; perhaps it means an unhealthy habit of worrying.'[14]

What came to be known as the Forward Policy towards China emerged after Chou's abortive visit to Delhi. It involved establishing Indian posts and sending patrols right to the boundary, though implementation of this policy was slow until late 1961, and nothing was done to retrieve the territory India thought China had usurped. It is understandable that Nehru's government had to take some new policy direction in a position of diplomatic stalemate when Indian public opinion was inflamed and vocal. But the policy hid some basic problems. One was the assumption that the Chinese would not attack Indian posts once they were established, and that therefore this policy was both a legitimate and sensible form of limited defence. A lack of serious intelligence about China's likely reactions to Indian moves, or what was basically driving its policy towards India, meant that when China invaded in October 1962 the government was caught totally by surprise. Mullick, Director of the Intelligence Bureau, was one of Nehru's most important advisers on this issue; and no one else in the military or the Ministries of Defence or External Affairs seems to have had the authority or expertise to challenge this perception. Krishna Menon, Minister of Defence, certainly seems to have shared the conviction that the Chinese problem was not a military one, and he even had to be pulled up by Nehru for prolonged absence in America in the critical winter of 1959, when issues of defence had to be tackled publicly.

A further and fundamental problem lay in the army itself. Given that India had not anticipated a possibility of serious military conflict, except with Pakistan, expenditure on the army had declined in recent budgets. Its manpower was adequate only for such limited defence of India's own territory, but it was already stretched by commitments to the UN in Gaza and the Congo (which absorbed a battalion each by 1961) and by its deployment within India against the Naga rebels. It was in purely numerical terms unprepared to respond additionally to a major land invasion. Nor was it by training and strategic expertise prepared for battle in the mountainous terrain of the borders with China. Its equipment was also totally inadequate for response to any major assault. In 1961–2 the military authorities were deeply concerned that they were being asked to expand the force but could not give the soldiers adequate or modern arms. Government policy had effectively emasculated them, placing non-alignment and development as the priorities, depriving the army of foreign assistance, and insisting that scarce foreign exchange should not be spent on buying equipment abroad. It was for India a tragic irony that the Chinese invasion should have occurred at the juncture when India's economic policy had run into profound difficulties, and before its own defence production was adequate for greater needs.

The ability of the army to respond to the new situation was also hampered by its role within the state and within the decision-making structures of government. Civilian officials and politicians distrusted military men and were determined that the Indian army should never achieve the influence now wielded by the army in Pakistan, where a military regime under Ayub Khan had been in place since a coup in October 1958. Thus military appeals for more resources were dismissed, as were military doubts about the Forward Policy decided on by civilians. For the army to make its voice heard effectively in the situation in which it now found itself it would have needed a strong and knowledgeable civilian Minister of Defence (the head of the armed forces as the post of Commander-in-Chief had been abolished), sensitive to the army's needs, who was prepared to argue the defence case in government against other ministers and even in the face of the Prime Minister himself. Instead it had Krishna Menon, who had been in post since 1957. His appointment to such a sensitive position was a sign of Nehru's growing isolation in politics as well as his conviction that Menon was one of the ablest Indians available in government. But here was a man who had no military experience or expertise, who craved the emotional security of Nehru's approval rather than being able to argue with him as an equal, and who was notorious for his incapacity to achieve good working relations with his colleagues. He was at loggerheads with the Finance Minister, Morarji Desai, which deepened the armed services' financial problems. He was also often in conflict with the officer corps, particularly on matters of promotion, which led to low morale at a critical time, and to the promotion to the highest rank of a man who had little or no field experience, who subsequently polarised the loyalty of officers for and against himself and, coming close to Nehru, gave him advice which more robust and experienced soldiers would not have done.

The Indian army was thus, for complex reasons outside its own control, inadequate for the task it would be asked to do. Even the Forward Policy was beyond its capabilities, and its most senior officers recognised that it would be unable to repel any major Chinese incursion. However, diplomatic initiatives had got nowhere in the aftermath of Chou's 1960 visit, and by mid-1962 the situation diplomatically and on the ground was increasingly tense. But even at this stage Nehru does not seem to have believed that conflict would break out, despite the violent domestic opposition to any talks. In September he flew to Britain for another Commonwealth Prime Ministers' Conference, accompanied by the Finance Minister. The Defence Minister was also scheduled to go abroad – hardly the stance of a government expecting invasion. In a working note on the world situation prepared for Nehru's use at the conference the Indian stance was still hopeful of a peaceful solution and indicated no inkling of the military gravity of the situation. Indian diplomats were clearly still struggling to understand why the Chinese were acting as they were.[15] Moreover, Nehru seems to have been totally convinced that the army was capable of dealing with any Chinese threat – indicating a lack of realism in the Ministry of Defence, and the fact that serious military opinion was no longer reaching the highest levels of government.

On 20 October China invaded India and for a month the Indian army battled to avoid being totally overwhelmed. By mid-November a series of humiliating reverses demonstrated the extent of Indian vulnerability to Chinese penetration deep into the heart of the northern states, and even into Uttar Pradesh, a state bordering Delhi. Not only was the terrain and altitude against the Indian soldiers. They were totally unprepared in terms of battle plans, equipment and logistical support. The neglect of the army in pursuit of other goals, and the political calculations of the government, now came home to roost.[16] Nehru himself admitted that the situation was desperate, and on 19 November asked President Kennedy for immediate American assistance in air defence; while on 21 November the American ambassador in Delhi noted that it was a day of ultimate panic in the city – 'the first time I have ever witnessed the disintegration of public morale'.[17] India was in fact saved not by American planes but by a unilateral Chinese cease-fire and withdrawal on 21 November – which was as inexplicable to Nehru as was the invasion itself.[18]

The man who had made friendship with China the cornerstone of his Asian policy for a large part of his political life, and since Indian independence had regarded it to an extent as the testing ground for a wider vision of peaceful co-existence, was nonplussed. However, from a historical distance the reasons for the Chinese invasion are clearer than they would have been at the time. There were several strands in Chinese thinking which made for a complex and unpredictable stance, in which force was deemed a legitimate and at times necessary *modus operandi*. This, and Chairman Mao's ultimate dominance in policy-making, was masked by the urbane presence of Chou in international gatherings and negotiations. One strand was a deep-rooted and persistent sense of historical humiliation feeding a xenophobic nationalism, which drove the Chinese leadership as powerfully after the Communist revolution as before. The leaders' sense of Chinese vulnerability was deepened in the early 1960s by the evidence of economic disaster and internal political disaffection which followed the abortive Great Leap Forward. In the light of this, Nehru's world repute and his claims for Indian leadership of post-colonial Asia were perceived as threatening and presumptuous; while Indian sympathy for Tibetan rebels only deepened Chinese suspicion of Indian collusion in subversion within territory China considered its own. The Forward Policy, particularly in the western sector, probably also appeared to threaten a critical line of what was seen as Chinese domestic communication through Aksai Chin. Ideology and theory also convinced the Chinese leadership by the end of the 1950s that Nehru's government was increasingly bourgeois, and aligned with the western powers, particularly through aid; and his stance on Tibet in 1959 only confirmed this.

Finally, and most dangerously for Nehru and India, was the way China's increasingly sensitive relations with India became entangled with the split between China and Soviet Russia by 1960. Relations with India became the symbol of the ideological divide between the policies of the two Communist powers towards non-Communist post-colonial regimes, and the attempt to humiliate India with a show of limited but effective violence became part of China's policy towards India as well as the USSR.[19] In retrospect Nehru's refusal to tackle the admittedly contentious problem of the joint border, in the belief that both countries had a mutual interest in peaceful neighbourliness, led India into a conflict in which a display of overwhelming force was in China's interests for a complex mixture of ideological and state-building reasons. The juxtaposition of the invasion with the

Cuban missile crisis made the danger even more dire for India; though ultimately the resolution of the Cuba issue meant that India's western sympathisers were in a position to help, while Russia was guardedly on its side.

The impact of the Chinese invasion on Nehru and his political life was profound. While the armed conflict was at its most threatening he seemed to observers to have become frail, old and deathly tired. (He was of course now seventy-three.) As he admitted to his old friend, Padmaja Naidu, 'We are passing through not only a national crisis, but a personal one also for many of us. Fortunately I do not have much time to think of it as work . . . keeps me fully occupied.'[20] This letter was written not just in the context of the failure of one of his key policies: he had also just had to accept the departure of his closest colleague in government, Krishna Menon. However, soon after the cease-fire he seemed to look much younger and more vigorous, and said that the tension of the crisis had agreed with him. He also drew comfort from the sense of unity he perceived in the country's response to the crisis and even said he thought that 'in the long run this will do good to our country and our people'.[21] Trying to capitalise on the opportunity, he urged that minority groups should be fully involved in the defence of India, whether as soldiers (in the case of the north-eastern tribal people) or in civil defence (as when he urged the Chief Minister of UP to recruit Muslims into provincial organisations of Home Guards and volunteers).[22]

Much of the work of responding to the crisis fell on him and a handful of close colleagues. As in normal times, he tended to bypass the full cabinet and took many of the decisions himself, or in conjunction with the Minister of Defence and an emergency committee of the cabinet, despite the anxiety of some cabinet members at being kept in the dark.[23] Keeping decision-making within such a close circle made Nehru more vulnerable than he might otherwise have been to the crescendo of public criticism of Krishna Menon. On 22 October even his long-standing colleague, Amrit Kaur, wrote him a personal letter saying that there was severe criticism of the government and particularly of the Defence Ministry for not having fortified India better, while already there were rumours of the inadequacy of the soldiers' equipment and clothing. She reported that Krishna Menon's words carried little weight and most people would be glad to see him gone.[24] By the next day it was clear that Congress as well as opposition Members of Parliament were concerting a move to get rid of Menon; and even from within his own government Nehru was receiving news of blistering opposition to his colleague. T. T. Krishnamachari told him roundly that the Defence Minister was incompetent and the defence organisation had been emasculated, while the true professionals, the soldiers, were not consulted as they should be. 'Whatever your views may be . . . the Defence Minister has demonstrably showed his utter incapacity to act.'[25] It was hardly surprising that opposition to Menon was growing within the army as well as outside it. Nehru's own correspondence with Krishna Menon indicated that even he was alarmed that his Defence Minister did not seem to be taking advantage of the various offers of help which were coming from abroad, particularly from Britain, the USA and Canada. In a secret and personal letter on this matter he also noted bluntly, 'I do not know how I shall explain to Parliament why we have been found lacking in equipment. It is not much good shifting about blame. The fact remains that we have been found lacking and there is an impression that we have approached these things in a somewhat amateurish way.'[26]

At the end of October Menon resigned and Nehru himself took over the defence portfolio as a temporary measure. But he kept Menon in the cabinet as Minister for Defence Production. Criticism persisted, most dangerously within the Congress parliamentary party, and from the former President of India, Rajendra Prasad, who told Nehru that not only was there strong public feeling that Menon was incompetent, but that within the army both officers and men were very discontented with him.[27] Nehru's own authority was now on the line in a way it had never been before, in the country and in the party. Nehru still felt the criticism of Menon was unjustified, as he told Prasad in his reply. But the feeling against Menon in the parliamentary party now endangered Nehru's own position, and its senior members told their Prime Minister on 7 November that Menon would have to go. He therefore accepted Menon's resignation from the government that day and forwarded it to the President. When he told Congress parliamentarians they cheered, while Menon sat hunched and silent. By his resignation he had effectively saved the political life of his friend, mentor and chief, resigning on the grounds that opposition to him within and outside the Congress Party was undermining national as well as party unity.[28]

Further, the departure of Menon obviously made it easier for India's western supporters, and America in particular, to render India assistance in this crisis. The *New York Times* noted a few days earlier when Menon had been removed from the Ministry of Defence that at least one good thing had come out of the Chinese attack (though it hoped he would be sacked completely from the cabinet): the man who had long been an irritant in India–US relations, and had made enemies for his country with his strident anti-western speeches in the UN, had been toppled from his key position, and this was a triumph for Washington.[29]

Nehru's burden of work was now extraordinarily heavy. His new Defence Minister, Y. B. Chavan only arrived in Delhi, on relinquishing his Chief Ministership as the invasion ended. As well as taking on defence he also had to undertake the work of explanation and attraction of support, within India and abroad. This included important secret letters to Chief Ministers, keeping them informed of the true gravity of the situation; speeches in Parliament and on the radio to keep up morale and plead for discipline and unity; and preparation of a statement from the Congress Working Committee. Much of his effort was also directed to influencing foreign governments to understand India's case against China. He engaged in a major ideological offensive aimed at the western world, the USSR and the non-aligned countries, with letters to government heads. For example, on 22 October he wrote a lengthy letter running to over six pages of typescript to Khrushchev, aware of the sensitivity of the Soviet position and eager to explain the Indian case and to portray it as a victim of aggression on the boundary issue.[30] It was deeply significant for him to have Russia at least benevolently neutral, and he could expect no more, given the Cuban missile crisis.[31]

It was perhaps the lack of comprehension of India's predicament among his non-aligned friends which was most disconcerting for Nehru. Only from the West did India receive material aid, particularly from Britain and America. (Despite western appreciation of the gravity of India's position, and the importance of sustaining its integrity and independence, there were voices which clearly echoed the tensions in Nehru's relations with the western world, and the ambiguities of non-alignment: some pleasure was derived from noting that at last he would have to realise the dangers of relying on the presumed good intentions of Communist governments.)[32] It was profoundly important for Nehru that the intervention of the UN Secretary-General helped to resolve the even more dire threat to world peace, focused on Cuba, which could have diverted the attention of his western sympathisers. But even in this time of desperate need, Indian requests for assistance were confused, indicating a persistent lack of coordination and direction at the heart of government.

Nehru survived the crisis of the Chinese war. But the departure of Krishna Menon did not end the erosion of his domestic authority. The opposition parties seized the chance to continue to criticise him and his government, and within Congress there was more private discontent. The main thrust of the opposition was against Nehru's policy of friendship towards China and the way that government was seen to have been both credulous and negligent in military preparation. The committed Gandhian, Vinoba Bhave, was a lonely voice calling for a conciliatory approach.[33] A veteran Congressman warned Nehru of the lobbying going on in Parliament to influence Congressmen against government policies, and urged that the party whips must organise a response to this. Or, as the American ambassador put it, China had driven a considerable wedge between Nehru and the Indian people, with many ordinary Indians now far to the right of the Prime Minister, anxious for alliance with America and disabused of the policy of non-alignment. Nonetheless, America still had to work with Nehru: there was no alternative.[34]

Although anger and resolve seemed to have given new energy to Nehru, the aftermath of the war indicates a government which had lost its creativity, and a Prime Minister who was still struggling to understand what had happened. By the end of the year he was more clearly aware of the complexity of drives within China's policy-making, and the way India had become central in the Sino-Soviet dispute, on the strength of information from various sources, including the United States and Yugoslavia. But he still could not accept the reality of India's military unpreparedness, placing the blame for defeat mainly on terrain and altitude, and defending even those senior officers who resigned, as competent and brave men who had no control over many of the factors which had led to defeat.[35] Given his age and his long-held convictions on foreign policy it was not surprising that he could see no new way forward; and on the diplomatic front there was little movement. A diplomatic initiative to achieve a peace settlement, the so-called Colombo Proposals, led by the Prime Minister of Ceylon and five other non-aligned powers, led only to stalemate on the logistical preliminaries to a possible discussion of peace terms. Nehru now accepted that there was little likelihood of an early end to the conflict with China, and India must build up its strength both for defence and as the basis for any meaningful talks.[36]

The possibility of a diplomatic breakthrough with Pakistan on Kashmir also evaporated. Nehru had been deeply concerned during the conflict that Pakistan might take advantage of India's predicament even to the extent of mounting an attack, even though he and Ayub Khan had, with the good offices of President Kennedy, exchanged letters which acknowledged the dangers of war on the subcontinent and noted the need for a peaceful settlement of the disputes between them.[37] After the immediate crisis was over the USA and Britain both used their leverage as sources of military aid to India to start talks between India and Pakistan on Kashmir, between them suggesting such devices as giving Pakistan some portion of the Valley, internationalising the Valley, or international mediation. However, the series of talks eventually broke down with no result, although Nehru maintained that the door to a settlement was not closed as India and Pakistan would eventually have to live in peace. But for the present, and from India's perspective, Pakistan was becoming increasingly close to China and was using this relationship and western anxiety to achieve peace on the subcontinent to put impossible demands to India. The status of the Valley was not negotiable, more particularly now that it was the major route to the defence of Ladakh, India's north-western border with China.[38]

Evidence also suggests that there was malaise and disarray deep within the heart of government, even on the critical matter of defence. This was understandable in the immediate crisis of conflict: but even after the Chinese withdrawal there was little understanding of what India would need to spend on defence and what this might imply for economic policy. As Pitambar Pant of the Planning Commission told Nehru briskly, there was even in the Planning Commission 'a general feeling of helpless inactivity, an inability to seize [the] initiative and give a lead'. He made a preliminary suggestion about military spending, the need to cut exports and the extra taxation which would have to be raised; but T. T. Krishnamachari thought that even this estimate underestimated what was really needed.[39] Krishnamachari had been given the new Ministry of Economic and Defence Coordination, but his papers suggest that his experience was initially something of a nightmare. Relations with the Defence Ministry were problematic, and he could get no serious idea of what defence needs were, or how they proposed to follow up American and British offers of help.[40] To his Prime Minister he was blunt. The country's defence had been neglected for years; leadership, strategic thinking and proper provisions of armaments had been lacking. He was appalled by what he saw from his new position – in relation to arms, vehicles, tanks, roads and the whole defence supplies organisation. It was no good just referring the problem to the new Minister of Defence. Nehru himself would have to be prepared to be ruthless with people and organisations in a way he had never been before. Nehru in an emollient reply said he did not think things were quite as bad as T. T. made out; but he brushed aside the hard issues of detail and the technicalities of defence.[41]

Ten days later T. T. returned to the fray, after a dispiriting meeting with Defence Minister Chavan and officers concerned with defence production. There was a complete air of unreality about it, and the officers, most of whom had been in post for a long time, seemed to have no idea of what would needed, what equipment they had or what state of repair it was in. The whole defence establishment needed overhauling in his view, though he recognised that this was difficult to admit as Nehru was still defending past policy and performance.[42] Through the early months of 1963 he sent letters and notes to Nehru telling him of the parlous state of defence preparation; the difficulties of his relationship with Chavan, who seemed to take no notice of him at all; and the extraordinarily inert state of the Secretariat in New Delhi. By August he was pleading with him again to be ruthless and to deal with the quality of the Planning Commission and to sort out the Defence Ministry.[43]

The main sources of long-term military assistance to India after the China war were the USA, Britain, Australia and Canada, and there was close consultation on India's needs and defensive strategy in the months after the Chinese withdrawal. Britain's Chief of Defence Staff was by this time Lord Mountbatten, anxious for the security of the India he loved, and for the welfare of his old friend Jawaharlal, whose declining strength he watched with concern and a feeling of helplessness.[44] In May 1963 he returned to India in person to assist with India's defence planning, and the confusion and incompetence at the heart of government were apparent.[45] Tactfully he addressed a meeting of the Military Affairs Committee, chaired by Nehru; trying to divest himself of anything suggesting a viceregal approach, he said that he was putting himself in the place of an Indian charged with defence against the Chinese. He ranged over the likely threat, appropriate tactics to combat this, Indian military requirements, intelligence and the Chiefs of Staff organisation. (Ironically at the same time he was central to the British reorganisation of its own defence.) Both then and at a later meeting at the office of the Defence Minister he noted the weakness of Indian intelligence and the vital importance of this before, during and after campaigns. Nearly six months after the war India still had no accurate knowledge of China's airfields, a vital precondition in planning its own air defence. Significantly, he had brought with him two intelligence experts, alongside a representative of each of the three armed services, who were available for more detailed discussion. Further, he urged his Indian colleagues to be realistic about their requests and to prioritise essentials, given that aid was limited. For example, if they persisted in wanting supersonic fighters, something else would have to be dropped from their 'shopping list', and he warned them against such high-tech armaments for which they did not have service facilities.

Evidence of the aftermath of the China war suggests that Nehru was unable to translate his own passion for the defence of India into professional planning against further attack, or to get to grips with problems at the heart of civil government or military administration. Moreover, some of the foundation stones of his foreign and domestic policy had been fatally undermined. Although he insisted that India stood by its policy of non-alignment, it was evident that when the defence of the country was at stake Nehru would accept help from wherever it was forthcoming. Moreover, the threat to India's integrity now demanded a reversal of spending policy, and a huge investment in the armed forces. The defence budget for 1963–4 was nearly 9 billion rupees, two and a half times the original budget for 1962–3, and three times the actual expenditure for 1961–2. By 1966 the armed forces were over double their size a decade earlier, and defence expenditure had more than trebled in the same decade.[46] This necessitated a serious increase in the tax burden.

The impact on domestic development and on public opinion had dangerous implications, and Nehru fought hard to defend the basics of the Third Five Year Plan. However, the American ambassador warned Nehru of tipping the balance too far away from economic development and social justice, given people's rising expectations. India's Five Year Defence Plan was calling for a massive military build-up and a large expenditure on defence that topped the combined defence spending of 'nationalist' China, Pakistan, Iran, Turkey and Greece. As a proportion of national income, defence spending would be 6.5 per cent, within range of that of European countries whose per capita incomes were far higher. Defence effectively had to have two strands – military and concomitant economic growth and greater social justice. Any deterioration in internal politics would in turn make effective defence impossible.[47] That Nehru should have received such a warning was a measure of how far the Chinese invasion had pushed him off the course he had set for himself and India with such passion since independence.

## THE END OF AN ERA

As Nehru resumed the reins of peacetime government in 1963 it seemed superficially as if little had changed. Despite his age and experience of debilitating illness early in 1962 he refused to countenance retirement or to appoint a deputy who might lighten his load. But it was evident that his pace and capacity for work had slowed, while those who were close to him worried at the obvious decline and the way the Chinese invasion had seemed to break his vitality. Krishna Menon, who was closer to him than almost anyone in Indian pubic life, later said that he believed that the Chinese invasion had affected Nehru deeply: 'it had a very bad effect on him. It demoralized him very much. Everything that he had built was threatened; India was to adopt a militaristic outlook which he did not like. And also he knew about the big economic burdens we were carrying.'[48] Marquis Childs, who had covered so much of Nehru's relations with America, and had come to know him well through private conversations, met him for the last time in London in 1963, when Nehru was attending a conference of Commonwealth Prime Ministers. He breakfasted with him at the residence of the Indian High Commissioner and found him a totally different man since the profound disillusion of the Chinese attack. He seemed physically to have shrunk, was withdrawn and spoke probably not more than a dozen words in the course of the meal, and Indira had to keep the conversation going. (Afterwards Mrs Childs actually asked her husband if the little old man they had met was really Nehru.)[49] T. T. later wrote to Indira Gandhi of 'the last two difficult years of your father's life', when he had been close to him and shared his worries. 'Even for you his daughter and his close companion, it would not be possible to imagine the intensity of it all.'[50]

The effect of the Prime Minister's decreasing capacity began to have its effect on government and on the political system itself, as people began reluctantly to realise that the end of an era was in sight, and that there was a new urgency about the question of who and what would succeed the man who had led India since independence, endowed with the legitimacy of an impeccable nationalist pedigree. A few were prepared to tell him to his face that urgent problems were not being dealt with. N. V. Gadgil, a left-wing opposition leader, wrote bluntly of the grave economic situation, which was even more problematic than the frontier: effective handling of inflation and food shortages was being prevented by 'let me frankly state, your hesitancy and your weakness'.[51] The comparatively small opposition parties on the left and right of the political spectrum were not alone in their criticism. The business community was horrified at rising taxes necessary to meet the higher defence expenditures, particularly those aimed at the wealthy and at business profits. The depth of opposition to Nehru and his government, expressed perfectly legitimately within the democratic system, was clear when in August 1963 he faced the first ever no-confidence motion in the Lok Sabha, launched on the issue of economic policy, on which conservative and left-wing opponents joined forces. The motion was defeated by a comfortable majority of 346 to 61, given Congress's dominance in the chamber: but it was a sign of the declining authority of the Prime Minister.

It was also becoming apparent that Congress itself was a weakening source of power and authority. In May 1963 Congress lost three crucial by-elections in what were considered safe seats – one in Gujarat and two in Nehru's own Uttar Pradesh. Three prominent opponents of Nehru, one Socialist, one Independent, and one representing the right-wing Swatantra Party, stood against equally prominent Congress candidates, including two members of Nehru's cabinet. The contests thus took on a national significance, and constituted a profound challenge to the Congress government's military and economic policies, as Nehru himself had recognised they would.[52] Even before this Nehru had been aware that in many regions Congress as a local party was rent by faction and that this was eroding public support. Eventually, when the Congress held its own post-mortem on its by-election defeats, this confirmed that internal dissension and decay of party organisation were important factors in its electoral failures. Nehru also believed that the absence of a clear ideological appeal had also damaged its public repute. In almost imperial tones of criticism of his colleagues, well before the crucial by-elections, he had noted to Chief Ministers that Congress strength in the past had been partly due 'to an appreciation by the general public of the moral fibre of Congressmen as a whole. I fear that appreciation is sadly lacking today and, without it, our message cannot go far or carry conviction . . . it is necessary for us to create the impression of a certain unselfish service of the nation.'[53]

With somewhat more realistic political analysis, T. T. told Nehru that Congress was immobilised and unable to lead the country because it was torn between the demands of its small but vocal left and right wings: its economic and fiscal policies were leading to a dead end, neither to social democracy nor to economic growth. He urged that Nehru needed to reorientate the party's policy, and also to deal with the tools for policy-making and implementation.[54] Beneath this plea there was the reality that even within his own party Nehru could no longer rely on loyalty. In May 1963 well over a hundred Congress Members of Parliament failed to turn up for a crucial debate on a constitutional amendment which would have safeguarded the legality of ceiling legislation, an integral part of Nehru's vision of a more equal rural society. The proposed bill was lost for lack of the necessary quorum to discuss constitutional amendments. The government was left humiliated, unable even to discipline its own members in the Lok Sabha. Moreover, Nehru found that his authority was challenged even within his own government on crucial policy matters, particularly by two ministers on the conservative wing of Congress. Morarji Desai, the Finance Minister, did not pursue the active policy of price control of essentials required by the Planning Commission in the post-war economic crisis. While the Minister of Food and Agriculture, S. K. Patil, similarly defied the Planning Commission's strategy for dealing with food shortages.[55]

The declining authority of the Prime Minister and his government in the country and problems of discipline and organisation in the Congress party itself lay behind a clever and unprecedented manoeuvre within Congress which became known as the Kamaraj Plan, after one of its authors, K. Kamaraj, the Congress Chief Minister of Madras. (The other was the Chief Minister of Orissa, Biju Patnaik.) It involved the resignation from office of senior Congressmen in government to free them to revitalise the Congress party organisation throughout the country. Nehru warmed to the idea when it was put to him in May, and he offered to resign himself, but this was unacceptable to the AICC. The CWC and AICC accepted the plan in August, and Nehru was left with the decision of which resignations to accept among his Chief Ministers and those in his own government. Eventually he accepted six resignations from central ministers (including Morarji Desai and S. K. Patil) and from six Chief Ministers, including Kamaraj himself and Patnaik, and those from Jammu and Kashmir, Bihar, UP and Madhya Pradesh.[56]

The plan was publicly presented as a device for strengthening the Congress organisation, and this was certainly a key element in the minds of the original authors. Kamaraj, for example, was well aware of the organisational challenge in his own Madras from the DMK, the Dravida Munnetra Kazhagam a regional party. The Congress's internal review of the reasons for its shocking electoral defeats similarly pointed to the urgent need to do something about the party organisation. Confirming this underlying motive was also the simultaneous decision by the CWC to set up an Organisational Affairs Committee. Morarji Desai later asserted that a further dimension of the Kamaraj Plan was to lessen his own chances of eventually succeeding Nehru. It is certainly true that Kamaraj and the group around him in the party, who became known as the Syndicate, were anxious to downgrade Morarji's position in Congress, and within the next six months they engineered the election of Kamaraj himself to the presidency of the party, and kept out of the newly elected CWC those who were not acceptable to them.[57]

For Nehru himself there were obvious advantages in accepting the Kamaraj Plan. Given his freedom to choose those who would leave office, he was able to rid himself of people who were a problem to him as well as releasing those who genuinely wanted to go. At the centre he removed Desai and Patil, both of whom were blocking policies which were essential to the continuation of the Third Five Year Plan. Patil himself was adamant that Nehru had used the opportunity to rid himself of those he considered right-wing and believed that the argument about strengthening the party organisation was 'camouflage'.[58] Among the departing Chief Ministers were those of Bihar and UP, both states where Congress factionalism was causing public scandal. He had written scoldingly to the UP Chief

Minister about this while the Kamaraj Plan was under discussion.[59] The administration of Kashmir and public opinion in the state had been causing him serious
concern at a time when Kashmiri loyalty was crucial for strategic reasons and in
the aftermath of the failed talks with Ayub Khan. The departure of the Chief
Minister allowed him eventually to secure the release of his old friend Sheikh
Abdullah, with whom he was able to mend fences and have a series of talks in the
spring of 1964.[60]

For Nehru there was also the chance offered by the Kamaraj Plan to tackle seriously the myriad internal problems which beset Congress. It is clear from evidence
in the summer of 1963 that he desperately wanted to purge the organisation of the
factionalism which seemed to be plaguing it, and to reinvent it as a party of
ideology and service. Again he seems to have been moved by a myth of the past,
a vision of the old Congress as a movement dedicated to national freedom rather
than a vehicle for office and personal aggrandisement.[61] Moreover, the whole ethos
behind the Kamaraj Plan echoed Gandhi's insistence on renunciation and service,
and probably reminded many of the times when Gandhi had himself walked away
from Congress when he felt it was in error. Sacrifice and service were powerful
themes for the Congress to underline, and the Congress General Secretaries
stressed them too in their report on the years 1962–3. But the ethos probably also
reflected the way in which Nehru himself increasingly turned to many of the
Mahatma's teachings when confronted with his own failure to transform party and
country as he had wished. As he had reminded Chief Ministers the previous year,
'Above all, we should always keep in mind that any real advance must have a moral
and spiritual foundation in the broadest sense of those terms.'[62]

However, for Nehru there was not the time left to try to press home these
initiatives to reinvigorate the party and to reassert his authority over policy. Late
in 1963 he became involved in the preparation of a resolution for the forthcoming
meeting of Congress at Bhubaneswar, Orissa, to be held in January and devoted
to Democracy and Socialism. It restated the party's social goals and supported the
economic strategy underlying the Five Year Plans. However at the Congress
meeting he suffered a slight stroke, just as he was rising to address the party. Indira
and then his aides caught him and escorted him out, and put him to bed in the
Governor's residence. Although he pulled through he was not well enough to
appear again and returned with his daughter to Delhi. His doctors tried to
persuade him to rest for a considerable time, but he made a bad patient and was
deeply reluctant to accept their advice. He was seriously unwell, and practically
confined to bed, for nearly a month, and he only began writing letters again early
in February.

Although he admitted that he was recovering more slowly than he hoped, he
refused to accept the idea of appointing a Deputy Prime Minister, and while he
was out of action his work as Prime Minister was shared between the Home

Minister and the new Finance Minister, his old and trusty colleague, T. T. Krishnamachari. He also consented to the return of Lal Bahadur Shastri, a central minister who had left under the Kamaraj Plan, but who now returned to assist Nehru as Minister without Portfolio. Shastri's appointment had the blessing of the Syndicate, but was opposed by both the left and right wings of the Congress, who saw that this appointment was bound to influence the eventual succession to the prime ministership. Shastri and Nehru then shared the work at the Ministry of External Affairs. But Mountbatten, passing through Delhi at the end of January, was dismayed at the way his friend's illness had deprived India of serious leadership, and he wrote to him, pleading with him to delegate responsibility for daily work and to cut out what was not vital. He was saddened to see that Nehru appeared to want to die in harness and to go on working at full stretch. 'That is what Edwina did to the great distress of all who loved her whom she left behind . . . But you owe it to India whose independence and greatness is due to you, the continuation of your overall leadership for as many more years as possible. So do please do what is best for India.'[63]

The pleas of one of his few close friends, and the invocation of Edwina's memory did not sway Nehru. By April he was gradually getting back to work, and feeling much better. To those around him it was clear that he was a changed man; his left leg and foot were obviously weak when he walked and he sometimes appeared sleepy. Senior Congressmen were increasingly convinced that he would not recover any further, and that such recovery as he had made was insufficient to permit him to continue. Nehru, however, insisted that he had no intention of retiring from public office, and was even planning a visit to London.[64] Indira was deeply involved in trying to look after her father, and was profoundly stressed by his obvious frailty as well as the sense of uncertainty and manoeuvre which prevailed in Delhi. However, she must have thought his recovery was well established because she left India for the last two weeks of April for a visit to Washington. On her return they both went to Bombay for an AICC meeting, and ten days later they went together to the relative cool of Dehra Dun for a three-day holiday. They returned to Teen Murti on 26 May. In the early hours of the next morning he woke in pain and his personal physician was called. He had suffered a ruptured aorta for which there was no possible medical help. Pain-killing injections eased him into unconsciousness and he died early in the afternoon. The cause of death, together with his earlier stroke, indicates that Nehru had been suffering from hypertension. Although his doctors would have known this, there was little they could advise except rest, as treatment for hypertension with drug therapy, particularly beta blockers, was in its infancy and still considered experimental. Prolonged rest was precisely what Nehru would not countenance. He thus in a sense killed himself rather than lay aside what he had felt was a vocation as well as his life's work.

Indira had rung her children and her aunts, who were all out of Delhi, when it was clear that Nehru's life was ebbing away. His sisters, his younger grandson, Sanjay, and his old friends Padmaja Naidu and Krishna Menon gathered to mourn with her. They were soon joined by senior Congressmen, and eventually by thousands of others – diplomats, politicians, and ordinary people. The privileged in the first hours after his death came to pay their respects in his bedroom, where he lay on his bed. In the evening his body was placed on a bier in the portico of Teen Murti, and the public were let into the grounds and permitted to see his body and to lay flowers around him. Delhi had seen nothing like this outpouring of emotion since the death of Gandhi in 1948, when Nehru had himself been central to the public mourning. The funeral took place the following afternoon, a little delayed to allow foreign dignatories to attend. Dean Rusk, the American Secretary of State, represented his country. Mountbatten, accompanied by his daughter Pamela, represented Queen Elizabeth, daughter of the last Emperor of India and now Head of the Commonwealth. Nehru's body was taken across the city to the banks of the Jumna, near the place where Gandhi had been cremated, and his cortège was followed by thousands of ordinary people. Although he had not desired a religious funeral ceremony, he was cremated according to Hindu rites, and his teenage grandson, Sanjay, lit the funeral pyre.[65] International press coverage noted the passing of this giant of a figure who had dominated the domestic stage of India and played a unique international role. Tributes to him were swift and often thoughtful and sensitive, even in America, where he had so often seemed enigmatic and at times hostile.[66]

Nehru had made a new will in 1954 in which he thanked his fellow Indians for their great affection. The *Rashtrapati* was determined in death, as in life, to be an icon to his people of the new India for which he had striven. Reflecting his devotion to India, he asked that his ashes be scattered from the air over the countryside to mingle with the soil of India, and that a small part of them should be thrown into the Ganges at Allahabad to link himself to India's cultural inheritance. He did not wish to cut himself off from the past even though he had discarded much tradition in his own life, and wanted his country to throw off those shackles of tradition which divided its people from each other and suppressed vast numbers of them. Accordingly Indira took some of the ashes to Allahabad, where they were submerged with some of Kamala's; and she scattered the rest from a plane over Kashmir, the region from which the family had originated, and which had given him such delight and such heartache. His passing was also marked by a peaceful political succession. The most senior member of the cabinet, G. L. Nanda, became acting Prime Minister until the Congress parliamentary party could elect its new leader. Kamaraj as Congress President worked with Radhakrishnan, President of India, to achieve an election by consensus, and after intensive consultation, Shastri was elected to succeed Nehru.[67] The question which had haunted political circles with increasing intensity, as Nehru's health had failed and his authority had been visibly eroded, was now answered within a week of his death, a remarkable tribute to the party he had led and the democracy whose foundation had been one of his life's aims.

# Conclusion

Jawaharlal Nehru was, in the mid-twentieth century, a towering and controversial figure, both in India and on an international stage. His was essentially a political life. He was born into a family which expected that its men would take a prominent professional role in public life, and this meant increasingly, in the circumstances of imperial rule, participation in new forms of politics. He was subsequently drawn into active political opposition to the British raj, inspired by Mahatma Gandhi, with his vision of an India reborn and his strategy of non-violent non-cooperation with the imperial rulers. From the age of about thirty Nehru's life was utterly dedicated to politics, at first to the politics of nationalism and then to the political work of constructing a free and democratic India as its first Prime Minister. His was a life of politics at the expense of normal family experience, of all but a few close friendships, and ultimately of his own health.

This portrait of his political life has had three main intentions and dimensions. Firstly, it has within a broad chronological framework 'told the story' of a life which was central to the creation of modern India. It has examined its dynamics, goals, achievements and limitations. To do this it has tried to understand the character and personality of the man – what drove him but also what sustained him, in terms of an inner vision, his intellectual and spiritual resources, and his significant relationships. It has asked what he hoped to do with his life, and the constraints on the fulfilment of those hopes, despite his apparently pre-eminent position in India after independence. Secondly, this portrait has been constructed as a window into India's rapidly changing political environment, and its division into parts has indicated how Nehru's own experience and concerns demonstrated different phases in India's broader political experience. Finally, the focus on Nehru and his many inner and external dilemmas illuminates some of the critical issues facing his generation, not only in India, but in other parts of Asia and

Africa, as thoughtful men and women grappled with the experience of imperialism and the deepening impact of western cultural, economic and political power on their own lives, their polities and societies, and worked for their independence and renewal. Mao in China, Nasser in Egypt, Nkrumah in Ghana, and Kenyatta in Kenya, for example, faced many problems similar to those which confronted Nehru. Nehru recognised this and it was in part for this reason that he found travels abroad so exhilarating, and was anxious to keep in personal touch with leaders in broadly parallel positions.

I

Nehru came from an unusual and distinctive background. The wealth and privilege which flowed from his father's success as a lawyer gave the young man education and experience which were the foundation of his political career within the Indian National Congress. They gave him a unique blend of skills which were irreplaceable within Congress, and helped to create his unusual position within it, although he was often out of sympathy with its ethos. However, he remained something of an outsider in the Indian political world – by virtue of his background in a small and successful migrant social group, his wide experience of the world outside India, and his cultural and intellectual orientation. He found his political vocation through association with Gandhi, though the relationship between the two men was never free of friction and deep ambiguity about ultimate ideals and goals. Of the many ironies in Nehru's life, one was the association of a young man fired by a left-wing and secular vision of a new India with a figure who was an icon of Hinduism, deeply rooted in Indian tradition and committed primarily to moral renewal. Another was the way Nehru was able to take the Gandhian road of self-denial in the service of the nation precisely because he had for much of his life the financial support of his father's wealth or his own income earned from his writing. This financial cushion reinforced and enabled Nehru's independence of stance in politics throughout his life.

As a personality Nehru had evolved by middle life into someone who was complex and sometimes at odds with himself as well as with those around him. He was cultivated, well-read and sometimes excellent company. He could be utterly charming and could arouse in others love and affection, and devotion from those who served him. But he was sometimes engulfed by anger, as his father had been; and his sense of cultured and intellectual superiority could make him supercilious and critical towards those whom he saw as stupid or vulgar. He thus generated dislike and hostility to himself as well as to his ideas, though comparatively few were prepared to voice their feelings, particularly given the need of the Congress party to achieve consensus and present unity to outsiders. He sometimes seemed like an ascetic as he adjusted to life in prison, or strove to live an iconic life of dedication to a new India. But he was meticulous about his personal appearance and physical well-being. He was also deeply sensual, and responded to physical beauty, whether in women or in his natural surroundings. Yet, as he recognised, he found it difficult to commit himself as a person even to those who were close to him, wrapping himself in a protective cocoon with his patrician style and his commitment to politics. He thus often lived in considerable personal and emotional isolation, and was happier responding to the somewhat impersonal affection of the crowds rather than forging close personal relationships.

The result was that after the death of Kamala his closest friends were those who could not challenge his position and who were in some sense removed from his political world. Some were foreigners, whose loyalty helped to keep him sane in prison, or who, while he was Prime Minister, sustained him with their letters and visits, but above all with their understanding of what he was trying to do. Supreme among these were Edwina Mountbatten and, in a different way, her husband. Within India his friends and those he trusted were few, and they were often in some sense also outsiders to the political world, whom he brought in to assist him, often with dangerous results. Krishna Menon was the most obvious example. His devotion to Nehru was unquestionable. But his unstable personality, his propensity to public tirades, his lack of experience in government as well as his view of the world made him a liability within and outside India, and this Nehru was deeply reluctant to acknowledge.

More sustaining for Nehru than almost any individual was his vibrant inner, intellectual world. The somewhat superficial young man at Cambridge developed into a serious thinker and an avid reader. As he once remarked, books were the only luxury on which he spent his money. Prison reading gave him the opportunity to enrich his mind, and to immerse himself in politics, history and science as well as literature; he never lost the habit and joy of reading, and was always eager to note new publications and acquire them for his collection at Teen Murti. By contrast the world of politics with its calculations and intrigues, its compromises and contradictions, held little appeal for him. Yet in the particular circumstances of India in the twentieth century, his intellectual convictions and his relationship with Gandhi drew him inexorably into politics and held him there until his death. Like a much earlier visionary and reformer, Martin Luther, he might have said, 'Here I stand. I can do no other.' A vision of a new and inclusive India, working to achieve national unity and the transformation of the lives of ordinary people, and leading the way to a more peaceful world of international relations, drove him on, regardless of the personal cost.

II

Nehru's vision of a new India was fashioned out of the urgent realities of Indian political experience and socio-economic conditions, as well as his own intellectual and moral commitments. His struggles to maintain that vision and the ways in which it was often frustrated, both before and after independence, also mean that his life is a window into Indian politics, through which later observers can see patterns of change. Focusing on his life with this intention does not impute to him in any simplistic way the power and position to dominate Indian politics, though it acknowledges what he did achieve, as well as what he did not, when his particular vision and skills were brought to bear in a particular political context.

Nehru's introduction to politics was the late nineteenth-century world of his father, when profound if slow-working changes in Indian society had generated a new kind of civil society and created a larger literate and articulate public, both of which were a potential challenge to the colonial rulers and the socio-economic order which sustained their rule. New forms of associational politics in relation to the structures of the colonial state gave men like Motilal Nehru the opportunity to further their own careers and enhance their public status, as well as new means of dealing with the constraints of British rule. But the young Nehru found these tamely conservative. His own deep commitment to political activism only came with the emergence of Gandhi in Indian politics, and the development both of a new era of larger-scale nationalism and of a deepening crisis for the imperial state, stemming from events in and outside the subcontinent.

The apparent success of the more radical politics of nationalism, and of Gandhi's strategies of broad-based and non-violent opposition to the British, masked deep issues of which Nehru was acutely aware and which made him profoundly uncomfortable within the Congress party. He saw that the nationalism of the Congress offered little to millions of India's people, particularly the most underprivileged, and that many of those who were influential in Congress, despite their lip-service to Gandhi's ideals of service to the poor and socio-economic transformation, were not intent on social and economic revolution, had little ideological vision and merely wanted to inherit the raj. Yet his sense of political realism kept him in alliance with the Congress as the one party and Gandhi as the one leader offering any chance of achieving independence and so opening the way to real change in public life.

Furthermore, Nehru saw with increasing dismay that as political participation deepened and widened, and as the message of the new Indian nation reached and was in turn received and passed on by thousands of people outside the elite represented by his father's generation, so the idea of India was often couched in cultural terms which often emphasised the Hindu foundations of the nation. Another fissure was opening up in public life which also limited the boundaries of the nation, and excluded millions of Indians, in ways he believed to be abhorrent and aberrant, rooted not in serious religious belief but in the interaction of class and old-fashioned superstition. The partition of the subcontinent did not resolve this problem, but deepened it, as India remained a nation with large minority religious groups, among them nearly as many Muslims as in the new country across the border founded in the name of Islam.

Nehru's years as Prime Minister were a time first of ebullient and hopeful creativity, and then of a growing realisation that much of the vision which had inspired and sustained him was being frustrated, often by the very forces which had led to independence. He had hoped that a democratic, independent India would be able to fashion a political system which would channel the demands of its diverse society and in turn deepen his compatriots' sense of belonging to a composite nation whose goal was a more equal as well as richer society. He spoke often of the great experiment in which India was engaged – of building a new social and economic order by democratic means, in contrast to the revolutionary and often violent experiments in communist states.

However, the constraints on his ability to implement his vision indicated how much remained of India's older political and social systems. India's new democracy was at one level a triumphant success: elections involving millions of new and often illiterate voters were held peacefully and working governments were elected in Delhi and in the states. But they tended not to deliver the goods expected by the underprivileged and intended by Nehru and his closest colleagues in Delhi. In part this was because the institutions and procedures of democratic politics had been captured by those who did not desire social revolution – many of them the people who had learned new modes of politics during the British raj, and with the assistance of Congress itself. Further, the administrative system was one inherited from the British, and often manned by those who had been schooled in the ways of an imperial raj whose priorities were order and revenue collection rather than social and economic reconstruction.

Perhaps only in foreign relations did Nehru have a more untrammelled arena in which to pursue a vision of a new post-colonial world order, where India would lead the way towards new patterns of peaceful coexistence. The Commonwealth was one of his enduring legacies, and for a time it seemed that he had helped to fashion a way of living peacefully within a divided world system. But the failure of his policy towards China effectively demolished this vision and helped to undermine Nehru's authority at home and abroad.

Nehru's record as Prime Minister, and his growing sense of frustration at his inability to achieve what he desired in so many areas of Indian life, indicate the nature of Indian politics as it emerged out of the experience of imperial rule. It is also important to consider how his fashioning of the prime ministerial role was in turn to affect Indian politics. Although he was an articulate and powerful advocate of democracy, and worked to sustain the practice of free and fair elections, to educate voters in the issues at stake in elections, and to nurture the institutions and practices of democratic government, his own style in office tended to be dictatorial and to bypass the norms of cabinet government and ministerial collegiality. This propensity had been clear to Mountbatten as Nehru prepared to take over the reins of power, and he tried to limit the institutional mechanisms by which Nehru might have acquired total dominance over his colleagues in government.

Even Nehru himself as a younger nationalist politician had recognised his own temptation to ride roughshod over democratic norms and to assert a dominance based on popular adulation. But in the highest political office in the country he developed a vast and unsustainable public role for himself. He proved incapable of delegating authority and effectively sharing power among colleagues; and he diverted much energy into attention to tiny details, such as the electricity bills of ministers or the standards of office cleanliness. The problems this caused were apparent in his own lifetime, as he wore himself out, and – more dangerously – as he failed to fashion policy in association with a number of colleagues who might have given him sound advice. He hung on to power, anxious to pursue his vision of a new nation, even when ill-health suggested that he should step aside or share his burden; and he did not nurture and encourage younger members of government, unlike his own mentor, Gandhi, who had groomed him for serious responsibility. Some of the problems this laid up for the country and for the party only became apparent well after his death, when his daughter took on his mantle after the unexpected death of L. B. Shastri. He had made the role virtually impossible except for one like himself, a personality driven by vision and a sense of personal vocation, and in a real sense an outsider to the grass-roots world of politics.

## III

If Nehru's life is a window into the changing world of Indian politics, it also provides insight into the inner world of men and women of his generation, who had to face similar issues in the context of the colonial experience and the spread of new assumptions about what was modern and desirable. Nehru was himself a fascinating figure in a deep and wide-ranging dialogue about tradition and modernity, about western and eastern, and he was articulate about the tensions this caused within himself and in his relations with other Indians. He had the best western education his father's money could buy, yet he lived in a home where Indian social and cultural traditions were as embedded as new ones accepted under the influence of British rule. His whole family were fiercely proud of their Indian inheritance and identity, and this brought them into alliance with Gandhi, himself a man who had been deeply influenced by his contacts with the western world, yet rejected much of its economic, cultural and political influence on India. Both men, in different ways and with different results, hammered out their own vision of what a new India should be like, and in what ideological and social soil it should be rooted, not by accepting western ideas and institutions or Indian ones in their entirety, but by drawing on both, and rejecting aspects of both.

Nehru's own experience of cultural dialogue continued throughout his life, and in some ways it seems to have drawn him closer to Gandhi's teaching as he himself aged. He wrestled with the place of tradition in the reinvention of India and the reconstruction of India's society and economy, for example as he confronted issues of caste and social status, as he questioned constructions of gender, and as he dealt with issues of domestic religious practice and of the authority of tradition in the intimacies of family life. It is an interesting vignette of change in his own family that he accepted an arranged marriage within his own caste for himself, but achieved a marital relationship which was in many ways both companionate and romantic; while in the next generation he permitted his daughter to choose her own husband, though he worried that his different community and social background might lead to her personal distress and social isolation. The legal difficulties experienced by his own sister when she was widowed and left with two daughters confirmed his determination to change the position of Hindu women in law. He himself abandoned any orthodox religious belief or practice, and was reluctantly prepared to attend Hindu rituals for the sake of his family. However, he retained a profound belief in a broad spirituality, which enriched and gave meaning to human life.

In the public sphere he grappled with a further range of issues common to so many of his generation. Among the most pressing in the particular context of India was the basis of national identity, and specifically the role, if any, of religion in the making of nations. Like his mentor he was resolute that India was a composite nation, whose strength lay in part in its diversity and the contribution multiple religious traditions and groups could bring to a tolerant and accommodating whole. Unlike Gandhi, he could only enunciate this in terms of modern secularism as opposed to communalism, and could find no other cultural idiom in which to expound it and commend it to Indians. During the years of nationalist opposition to imperial rule he confronted questions of political strategy, asking how best to confront the imperial ruler, while incorporating as many people as possible into the struggle. The answers to these questions given by Gandhi and the Congress party alike often failed to satisfy him, but pragmatically and for cultural reasons he preferred the way of Gandhian non-violence and believed that it had achieved independence, though he never pursued its potential as a political strategy after 1947.

After independence he struggled with the issues of the most appropriate means for social and economic reconstruction in a society marked by poverty and illiteracy, and, studying countries which seemed to be embarking on similar experiments, he led India down the route of state-sponsored and engineered change. Contemporaries and later observers have criticised his economic and social strategies, pointing to the crisis which his economic plans generated for his country, and noting the weaknesses in his legislative strategy for social change. But none can deny that he recognised some of the major issues confronting not only India but a whole generation of leaders in Asia and Africa, and was determined to grapple with them in ways the imperial rulers had never wished or had the authority to do.

Nehru was central to the making of modern India, with its strengths and weaknesses, its successes and failures. By the end of his century, India had the world's second largest population, and a much changed economy with huge further potential. It is still a culturally complex society, and questions of national identity which so disturbed him are still deeply contested, often violently. Despite the continuation of profound inequalities, it has witnessed incremental social change, often in ways to which Nehru aspired; and has exported millions of people to other parts of the world, where they have become significant and productive migrant groups. Moreover, India now stands geographically and culturally in a highly important strategic position, in a part of the world where instability threatens world peace in ways quite unpredictable to Nehru's generation. Unlike many of its neighbours, it has a strong democratic tradition, unbroken since independence, and a society where there is serious political discussion and space for dissent. At the start of the twenty-first century many of these aspects of India's position and experience have made people outside the subcontinent recognise its global importance in a new way. It is hoped that this study of the political life of one of its architects, with all its complexities, ambiguities, frustrations and failures, will help to illuminate how India has come to be what it is, and to demonstrate some of the resources with which it faces still critical domestic issues as well as those with major international dimensions.

# Appendix

# Elections in India, 1952–1962

The following tables are from R. L. Hardgrave, *India: Government and Politics in a Developing Nation*, 3rd edn (Harcourt Brace Jovanovich, New York, 1980), pp. 204, 206, 230.

Table A.1  The distribution of candidates, seats and votes in Lok Sabha elections, 1952–1962

| Parties | No. of candidates | No. of seats won | % of seats | % of votes |
|---------|------------------|------------------|-----------|-----------|
| **1952** | | | | |
| Congress | 472 | 364 | 74.4 | 45.0 |
| Communist Party of India | 49 | 16 | 3.3 | 3.30 |
| Socialist Party (SP) | 256 | 12 | 2.5 | 10.60 |
| Kisan Mazdoor Praja Party (KMPP) | 145 | 9 | 1.8 | 5.80 |
| Hindu Mahasabha | 31 | 4 | 0.8 | 0.95 |
| Jana Sangh | 93 | 3 | 0.6 | 3.10 |
| Ram Rajya Parishad | 55 | 3 | 0.6 | 2.03 |
| Republican Party | 27 | 2 | 0.4 | 2.36 |
| Other parties | 215 | 35 | 7.2 | 11.10 |
| Independents | 521 | 41 | 8.4 | 15.80 |
| Total | 1,864 | 489 | | |
| **1957** | | | | |
| Congress | 490 | 371 | 75.1 | 47.78 |
| Communist Party of India | 108 | 27 | 5.4 | 8.92 |
| Praja Socialist Party (SP and KMPP) | 189 | 19 | 3.8 | 10.41 |
| Jana Sangh | 130 | 4 | 0.8 | 5.93 |
| Republican Party | 19 | 4 | 0.8 | 1.50 |

Table A.1  (continued)

| Parties | No. of candidates | No. of seats won | % of seats | % of votes |
|---|---|---|---|---|
| Hindu Mahasabha | 19 | 1 | 0.2 | 0.86 |
| Ram Rajya Parishad | 15 | – | – | 0.38 |
| Other parties | 73 | 29 | 5.9 | 4.81 |
| Independents | 475 | 39 | 7.9 | 19.39 |
| Total | 1,518 | 494 | | |
| **1962** | | | | |
| Congress | 488 | 381 | 73.1 | 46.02 |
| Communist Party of India | 137 | 29 | 5.9 | 9.96 |
| Swatantra | 172 | 18 | 3.6 | 6.80 |
| Jana Sangh | 198 | 14 | 2.8 | 6.44 |
| Praja Socialist Party | 166 | 12 | 2.4 | 6.84 |
| Dravida Munnetra Kazhagam (Tamil Nadu only) | 18 | 7 | 1.4 | 2.02 |
| Socialist Party | 107 | 6 | 1.2 | 2.49 |
| Republican Party | 69 | 3 | 0.6 | 2.78 |
| Ram Rajya Parishad | 35 | 2 | 0.4 | 0.55 |
| Hindu Mahasabha | 32 | 1 | 0.2 | 0.44 |
| Other parties | 64 | 14 | 2.9 | 4.31 |
| Independents | 497 | 27 | 5.5 | 12.27 |
| Total | 1,983 | 494 | | |

Table A.2  The distribution of candidates, seats and votes in state assembly elections, 1952–1962

| Parties | No. of candidates | No. of seats won | % of seats | % of votes |
|---|---|---|---|---|
| **1952** | | | | |
| Congress | 3,153 | 2,246 | 68.4 | 42.20 |
| Socialist Party (SP) | 1,799 | 125 | 3.8 | 9.70 |
| Communist Party of India | 465 | 106 | 3.2 | 4.38 |
| Kisan Mazdoor Praja Party (KMPP) | 1,005 | 77 | 2.3 | 5.11 |
| Jana Sangh | 717 | 35 | 1.1 | 2.76 |
| Ram Rajya Parishad | 314 | 31 | 0.9 | 1.21 |
| Hindu Mahasabha | 194 | 14 | 0.4 | 0.82 |
| Republican Party | 171 | 3 | 0.1 | 1.68 |
| Other parties and independents | 7,492 | 635 | 19.3 | 32.14 |
| Total | 15,310 | 3,272 | | |

Table A.2 (continued)

| Parties | No. of candidates | No. of seats won | % of seats | % of votes |
|---|---|---|---|---|
| **1957** | | | | |
| Congress | 3,027 | 2,012 | 64.9 | 44.97 |
| Praja Socialist Party (SP and KMPP) | 1,154 | 208 | 6.7 | 9.75 |
| Communist Party of India | 812 | 176 | 5.7 | 9.36 |
| Jana Sangh | 584 | 46 | 1.5 | 3.60 |
| Ram Rajya Parishad | 146 | 22 | 0.7 | 0.69 |
| Republican Party | 99 | 21 | 0.7 | 1.31 |
| Hindu Mahasabha | 87 | 6 | 0.2 | 0.50 |
| Other parties and independents | 4,863 | 611 | 19.7 | 29.81 |
| Total | 10,772 | 3,102 | | |
| **1962** | | | | |
| Congress | 3,062 | 1,984 | 60.2 | 43.53 |
| Communist Party of India | 975 | 197 | 6.0 | 10.42 |
| Praja Socialist Party | 1,149 | 179 | 5.4 | 7.69 |
| Swatantra | 1,012 | 170 | 5.2 | 6.49 |
| Jana Sangh | 1,135 | 116 | 3.5 | 5.40 |
| Socialist Party | 632 | 64 | 1.9 | 2.38 |
| Dravida Mummetra Kazhagam (Tamil Nadu only) | 142 | 50 | 1.5 | 2.96 |
| Ram Rajya Parishad | 99 | 13 | 0.4 | 0.29 |
| Republican Party | 99 | 11 | 0.3 | 0.56 |
| Hindu Mahasabha | 75 | 8 | 0.2 | 0.24 |
| Other parties and independents | 5,313 | 555 | 15.4 | 20.04 |
| Total | 13,693 | 3,347 | | |

Table A.3  Election data, Indian parliamentary elections, 1952–1962

| Year | Seats | Candidates | Electorate (millions) | Polling stations | Votes polled (millions) | Turnout (%) |
|---|---|---|---|---|---|---|
| 1952 | 489 | 1,864 | 173.2 | 132,600 | 80.7 | 45.7 |
| 1957 | 494 | 1,519 | 193.7 | 220,500 | 91.3 | 47.8 |
| 1962 | 494 | 1,985 | 217.7 | 238,400 | 119.9 | 55.4 |

# Notes

## Introduction

1 The most important biographical study of Nehru based on access to the personal archive was the three-volume, semi-official one produced comparatively soon after his death: S. Gopal, *Jawaharlal Nehru* (Jonathan Cape, London, 1973–84). Others, which have not drawn on the Nehru papers post-1947, include S. Wolpert, *Nehru: A Tryst with Destiny* (OUP, New York, 1996) and my own previous small study in the Longman series, Profiles in Power, *Nehru* (Longman, London, 1999).

2 Nehru's *An Autobiography* was first published in 1936 (John Lane, London). Letters between Nehru and his daughter, Indira, were edited by Indira's daughter-in-law, Sonia Gandhi, and published as *Freedom's Daughter* covering 1922–39 (Hodder & Stoughton, London 1989) and *Two Alone, Two Together* covering 1940–64 (Hodder & Stoughton, London, 1992). Nehru's voluminous correspondence is collected and preserved in the Nehru Memorial Museum and Library, New Delhi (NMML); much of it is in process of publication under the title *Selected Works of Jawarhalal Nehru*. The 1st series was published by Orient Longman in New Delhi; the 2nd series is now being published by the Jawaharlal Nehru Memorial Fund in New Delhi. They will be cited as *SWJN(1) and SWJN(2)*. Examples of people who were close to Nehru in different ways and whose comments illuminate his personality are his sister, Vijaya-lakshmi Pandit, *The Scope of Happiness: A Personal Memoir* (Weidenfeld & Nicolson, London, 1979); and J. K. Galbraith, some time American ambassador to India, *Ambassador's Journal* (Hamish Hamilton, London, 1969).

## Chapter 1  India and the British Raj

1 M. K. Gandhi, *An Autobiography: The Story of my Experiments with Truth* (Jonathan Cape, London, 1966), p. 38. It was first published in 1927. For the ways British people struggled to make sense of India, see Thomas R. Metcalf, *Ideologies of the Raj* (CUP, Cambridge, 1994).

2   For demographic information see L. Visaria and P. Visaria, 'Population (1757–1947)', in D. Kumar and M. Desai (eds), *The Cambridge Economic History of India, Volume 2: c.1757–c.1970* (CUP, Cambridge, 1983).

3   On Allahabad see C. A. Bayly, *The Local Roots of Indian Politics: Allahabad 1880–1920* (Clarendon Press, Oxford, 1975).

4   An important modern work on caste is S. Bayly, *Caste, Society and Politics in India from the Eighteenth Century to the Modern Age* (CUP, Cambridge, 1999).

5   *Statement exhibiting the moral and material progress and condition of India during the year 1889–90* (HMSO, London, 1891), p. 17.

6   Ibid., p. 191.

7   An excellent introduction to this is B. R. Tomlinson, *The Economy of Modern India, 1860–1970* (CUP, Cambridge, 1993).

8   See J. Krishnamurty, 'The occupational structure', in Kumar and Desai, *Cambridge Economic History*.

9   For detailed studies see R. Chandarvarkar, *The Origins of Industrial Capitalism in India: Business Strategies and the Working Classes in Bombay, 1900–1940* (CUP, Cambridge, 1994); and M. Misra, *Business, Race, and Politics in British India c.1850–1960* (Clarendon Press, Oxford, 1999).

10  M. D. Morris, *The Emergence of an Industrial Labor Force in India: A Study of the Bombay Cotton Mills, 1854–1947* (OUP, Bombay, 1965), p. 63.

11  D. C. Potter, *India's Political Administrators 1919–1983* (Clarendon Press, Oxford, 1986), pp. 32–3. This is an excellent introduction to the elite administrative service throughout Nehru's own career.

12  This reached its peak in the 1876 Imperial Assemblage to mark the accession of Queen Victoria to the title of Empress of India. See B. S. Cohn, 'Representing authority in Victorian India', in E. Hobsbawm and T. Ranger (eds), *The Invention of Tradition* (CUP, Cambridge, 1983).

13  On the Talukdars of Oudh see T. R. Metcalf, 'From raja to landlord: the Oudh Talukdars, 1850–1870' and 'Social effects of British land policy in Oudh', in R. E. Frykenberg (ed.), *Land Control and Social Structure in Indian History* (University of Wisconsin Press, Madison, 1969), and P. Reeves, *Landlords and Governments in Uttar Pradesh: A Study of their Relations until Zamindari abolition* (OUP, Bombay, 1991).

14  Government of India Resolution, 18 May 1882, C. H. Philips (ed.), *The Evolution of India and Pakistan 1858 to 1947: Select Documents* (OUP, London, 1962), pp. 50–1.

15  *Census of India, 1931. Volume 1 India, Part 1 Report* (Government of India, Delhi, 1933), pp. 420–1, 424.

16  For an introduction to this see K. W. Jones, *Socio-religious reform movements in British India* (CUP, Cambridge, 1989).

17  See B. Parekh, *Colonialism, Tradition and Reform: An Analysis of Gandhi's Political Discourse* rev. edn (Sage, London, 1999); Judith M. Brown, *Gandhi: Prisoner of Hope* (Yale University Press, New Haven and London, 1989).

18  There is an immense literature on social reform in nineteenth-century India and on gender issues in particular. A good starting point is C. H. Heimsath, *Indian Nationalism and Hindu Social Reform* (Princeton University Press, Princeton, 1964); and G. Forbes, *Women in modern India* (CUP, Cambridge, 1996). An illuminating regional case study is M. Borthwick, *The Changing Role of Women in Bengal, 1845–1905* (Princeton University Press, Princeton, 1985). Muslim debates on women are examined in G. Minault, *Secluded Scholars: Women's Education and Muslim Social Reform in Colonial India* (OUP, Delhi, 1998).

19   Gandhi, *Autobiography*, pp. 10–11. See also T. Raychaudhuri, 'Love in a colonial climate: marriage, sex and romance in nineteenth-century Bengal', ch. 4 of T. Raychaudhuri, *Perceptions, Emotions, Sensibilities: Essays on India's Colonial and Post-colonial Experiences* (OUP, New Delhi, 1999).
20   V. S. S. Sastri to his brother, 10 Jan. 1915, *Letters of the Right Honourable V. S. Srinivasa Sastri*, ed. T. N. Jagadisan, (2nd edn, Asia Publishing House, Bombay, 1963), p. 41.
21   On the emergence and development of Congress see J. R. McLane, *Indian Nationalism and the Early Congress* (Princeton University Press, Princeton, 1977); also Judith M. Brown, *Modern India: The Origins of an Asian Democracy*, 2nd edn, (OUP, Oxford, 1994), pp. 183–9.

## Chapter 2   The Young Nehru

1    For details of the Nehru family background see B. R. Nanda, *The Nehrus: Motilal and Jawaharlal* (George Allen & Unwin, London, 1962); Nehru, *Autobiography*, pp. 1–11.
2    Nehru, *Autobiography*, p. 8.
3    J. Nehru to M. Saxena, 10 Apr. 1961, enclosing a brief note on his father for the celebration of the centenary of his birth: NMML, J. Nehru Papers post-1947, 2nd Instalment, File of Correspondence with M. Saxena, No. 251.
4    Nehru, *Autobiography*, p. 5.
5    Ibid., p. 12: a vivid picture of the privileged world of this home, Anand Bhavan, or 'Abode of happiness' is given in Pandit, *The Scope of Happiness*.
6    Nehru, *Autobiography*, p. 6.
7    Motilal to Jawaharlal, 20 Oct. 1905, *Selected Works of Motilal Nehru (SWMN)*, ed. R. Kumar and D. N. Panigrahi, vol. 1 (1899–1918) (Vikas, New Delhi, 1982), pp. 79–80.
8    Jawaharlal to Motilal, 1 Aug. 1907, *SWJN(1)*, vol. 1, p. 30; Nehru, *Autobiography*, p. 19.
9    Headmaster to M. Nehru, 19 May 1906, cited in Nanda, *The Nehrus*, p. 79.
10   Nehru to Syed Mahmud, 21 Mar. 1924, *SWJN(1)*, vol. 2, p. 217.
11   Nehru to Indira, 11 Mar. 1938, *SWJN(2)*, vol 3, p. 458; for Nehru's own account of his life at Cambridge, see Nehru, *Autobiography*, pp. 19ff.
12   Jawaharlal to Motilal, 30 Jan. and 20 Feb. 1908, *SWJN(1)*, vol. 1, pp. 44, 45–6.
13   Nehru, *Autobiography*, p. 21.
14   Jawaharlal to Motilal, 29 Oct. 1908, *SWJN(1)*, vol. 1, pp. 58–9.
15   Nehru, *Autobiography*, pp. 21–2.
16   Jawaharlal to Motilal, 2 Jan. 1908, *SWJN(1)*, vol. 1, pp. 41–2.
     On the split in Congress in 1907 see Brown, *Modern India*, pp. 189–90.
17   Motilal to Jawaharlal, 10 and 24 Jan. 1908, *SWMN*, vol. 1, pp. 136, 137. The episode closed with Jawaharlal's letter to his father of 10 Apr. 1908, *SWJN(1)*, vol. 1, p. 50.
18   Motilal to Jawaharlal, 24 June 1910, *SWMN*, vol. 1, pp. 148–9.
19   Nehru, *Autobiography*, pp. 24–5.
20   Jawaharlal to Motilal, 15 July and 19 Aug. 1910, *SWJN(1)*, vol. 1, pp. 76–7, 78–9.
21   Nehru, *Autobiography*, p. 25.
22   See letters from Jawaharlal to Motilal, 2 June and 29 Dec. 1911, 21 June 1912, *SWJN(1)*, vol. 1, pp. 88, 93, 97–9. Motilal's fierce letter of 30 May 1911 is cited in Nanda, *The Nehrus*, p. 121.
23   Motilal to Bansi Dhar Nehru, 22 June 1912, *SWMN*, vol. 1, p. 172.
24   Jawaharlal to his mother, 14 Mar. 1912, *SWJN(1)*, vol. 1, p. 97. For other letters on the question of his marriage see ibid., pp. 18–19, 67, 68, 92–3.

25    Cited in S. A. Wolpert, *Morley and India 1906–1910* (University of California Press, Berkeley, 1967), p. 139.

26    Nehru, *Autobiography*, p. 35.

27    Ibid., p. 28.

28    Jawaharlal to Motilal, 1 Sept. 1922, *SWJN(1)*, vol. 1, pp. 333–4.

29    J. Nehru to Gandhi, 24 July 1941, *SWJN(1)*, vol. 11, pp. 658–9.

30    There is evidence of Kamala's difficult adjustment to the Nehru household in Pandit, *The Scope of Happiness*; see also P. Kalhan, *Kamala Nehru* (1973; NIB Publishers, New Delhi, 1990).

31    Nehru, *Autobiography*, p. 34.

32    On the emergence of the Muslim League see P. Hardy, *The Muslims of British India* (CUP, Cambridge, 1972) and F. Robinson, *Separatism among Indian Muslims: The Politics of the United Provinces' Muslims 1860–1923* (CUP, Cambridge, 1974).

33    For Montagu's tour see E. S. Montagu, *An Indian Diary* (Heinemann, London, 1930): the meeting with Motilal is noted on p. 62. On the Montagu–Chelmsford Reforms of 1919 see Brown, *Modern India*, pp. 207–9.

34    Letter from Jawaharlal to the editor of *The Leader*, 21 June 1917, *SWJN(1)*, vol. 1, pp. 106–8.

35    *SWJN(1)*, vol. 1, pp. 140–4.

## Chapter 3   The Turning Point

1    Money caused tension between father and son because Motilal insisted that no child of his should depend for maintenance on any other person or on public funds, whereas Jawaharlal thought they should give away their capital. In 1921 when Motilal thought Jawaharlal had given away a considerable sum he wrote, 'You cannot have it both ways – insist on my having no money and yet expect me to pay you money.' Motilal to Jawaharlal, 27 June 1921, NMML, Nehru Papers.

2    There is a vast literature on Gandhi. Good starting-points are Parekh, *Colonialism, Tradition and Reform*; B. Parekh, *Gandhi's Political Philosophy: A Critical Examination* (Macmillan, London, 1989); Brown, *Gandhi: Prisoner of Hope*; and for the intricate details of his emergence into Indian politics Judith M. Brown, *Gandhi's Rise to Power: Indian Politics 1915–1922* (CUP, Cambridge, 1972).

3    Gandhi's own account of these processes is presented in graphic detail in his *Autobiography* which takes him to 1920 only, and of which the greater part is devoted to his life in South Africa. Tellingly he subtitled it *The Story of my Experiments with Truth*.

4    Ibid., p. 420.

5    The best edition of this pamphlet is *M. K. Gandhi. Hind Swaraj and Other Writings*, ed. A. J. Parel (CUP, Cambridge, 1997).

6    V. S. S. Sastri to his brother, V. S. R. Sastri, 10 Jan. 1915, and to H. S. Deva, 21 Jan. 1916, *Letters of V. S. Srinivasa Sastri*, pp. 41, 42.

7    Nehru, *Autobiography*, p. 35.

8    W. H. Lewis to W. B. Heycock, 29 Apr. 1917, Appendix D to Proceeding No. 323 of Home Political, A. July 1917, Nos 314–40, National Archives of India (NAI). Some warning of the problems that Gandhi could represent for a government had already been given to the Government of India: in 1914 the Secretary of State for the Colonies had expressed relief to the Viceroy that Gandhi would probably be returning to India.

'He is a quite astonishingly hopeless and impracticable person for any kind of deal, but with a sort of ardent, though restrained, honesty which becomes the most pig-headed obstinacy at the critical moment.' Lord Crewe to Lord Hardinge, 26 Mar. 1914, Cambridge University Library, Hardinge Papers (120).

9    E. S. Montagu to Chelmsford, 10 Oct. 1918, India Office Library and Records (IOLR), Chelmsford Papers, MSS EUR.E.264 (4).

10    One politician was amazed to find an illiterate Delhi *tonga* driver expressing his objections: 6 Mar. 1919, diary of G. S. Khaparde, NAI, Khaparde Papers.

11    Gandhi, *Autobiography*, pp. 391–2. The best examination of the campaign is R. Kumar (ed.), *Essays on Gandhian Politics: The Rowlatt Satyagraha of 1919* (Clarendon Press, Oxford, 1971).

12    *Young India,* 20 July 1920, *The Collected Works of Mahatma Gandhi* (Government of India, Delhi, 1958–84) (*CWMG*), vol. 18, p. 89.

13    Nehru, *Autobiography*, p. 46.

14    J. Nehru to M. Desai, Aug. 1923 (day not given), NMML, J. Nehru Papers pre-1947. See also Nehru, *Autobiography*, pp. 41–2.

15    J. Nehru to the Editor, *The Leader*, 4 Sept. 1920, *SWJN(1)*, vol. 1, p. 167.

16    M. Nehru to Sir Harcourt Butler, 19 May 1920, *SWMN*, vol. 2 (1919–22), pp. 144–6.

17    Presidential Speech, Amritsar Congress, Dec. 1919, *SWMN*, vol. 2, pp. 264–306.

18    Motilal to Jawaharlal, 27 July 1920, Nehru Papers.

19    Motilal to Jawaharlal, 27 and 29 Feb., 9 and 16 June 1920, Nehru Papers.

20    Motilal to Jawaharlal, 5 July 1920, Nehru Papers.

21    For a detailed analysis of the Calcutta session see Brown, *Gandhi's Rise to Power*, pp. 262–71.

22    Viceroy to Secretary of State, telegram, 9 Oct. 1920, Home Political, Dec. 1920, No. 84, Deposit.

23    Nehru, *Autobiography*, pp. 51–62. On the peasant movement see G. Pandey, 'Peasant revolt and Indian nationalism: the peasant movement in Awadh, 1919–22', in R. Guha (ed.), *Subaltern Studies 1: Writings on South Asian History and Society* (OUP, Delhi, 1982).

24    Nehru, *Autobiography*, pp. 52, 57.

# Chapter 4    The Making of a Politician

1    Nehru, *Autobiography*, p. 598.

2    Sir Frank Sly, Chief Commissioner of Central Provinces (where Nagpur was located), to Viceroy, 1 Jan. 1921, IOLR, MSS EUR.E.264 (26). For details on the Nagpur Congress see Brown, *Gandhi's Rise to Power*, pp. 289–304.

3    B. S. Moonje to M. R. Jayakar, 5 Jan. 1921, NAI, Jayakar Papers, Chronological Correspondence File No. 12, No. 2.

4    *Young India*, 9 Mar. 1921, *CWMG*, vol. 19, pp. 419–20. A summary of outbreaks of violence between July and Nov. 1921 is in a letter from the Secretary to the Government of India, S. P. O'Donnell, to all local governments, 24 Nov. 1921, Home Political, 1921, File No. 303. An official account of non-cooperation compiled for government use by the Deputy Director of the Intelligence Bureau of the Home Department, Government of India, is P. C. Bamford, *Histories of the Non-Co-operation and Khilafat Movements* (Government of India Press, Delhi, 1925).

5   Nehru to Indira, 15 May 1941, *SWJN(1)*, vol. 11, p. 594.

6   Nehru, *Autobiography*, p. 77.

7   Ibid., p. 76.

8   Speech at Jhansi, 13 June 1921, *SWJN(1)*, vol. 1, pp. 180–1.

9   Note by Nehru for Gandhi, Nov. 1921, *SWJN(1)*, vol. 1, p. 202.

10  Nehru, *Autobiography*, p. 73.

11  Ibid., p. 72.

12  Speech by Nehru, 4 Aug. 1954, *SWJN(2)*, vol. 26, p. 89.

13  Jawaharlal to Motilal, 13 July 1922, *SWJN(1)*, vol. 1, p. 324. Trial statement, 17 May 1922, ibid., pp. 252–7.

14  Gandhi to Jawaharlal, 19 Feb. 1922, *CWMG*, vol. 22, pp. 435–7.

15  *SWJN(1)* vol. 1, p. 295. Nehru's prison diary and attachments for the second imprisonment and a briefer diary for the first imprisonment are in this volume.

16  Nehru, *Autobiography*, p. 93.

17  Jawaharlal to Motilal, 1 Sept. 1922, *SWJN(1)*, vol. 1, pp. 333–4.

18  Motilal to Gandhi, 10 July 1924, Jayakar Papers, Correspondence File No. 403, No. 151; Motilal to Jawaharlal, n.d. but probably in April/May 1922 when Motilal was in prison and Jawaharlal was temporarily outside, Nehru Papers.

19  Gandhi to Jawaharlal, 19 Feb. 1922, *CWMG*, vol. 22, pp. 435–7. On the Chauri Chaura episode see S. Amin, *Event, Metaphor, Memory: Chauri Chaura, 1922–1992* (University of California Press, Berkeley, 1995).

20  Nehru, *Autobiography*, p. 86.

21  Viceroy to Secretary of State, telegrams 23 Aug. and 13 Sept. 1922, IOLR, Reading Papers, MSS EUR.E.238 (11).

22  See Home Political, 1922, File No. 900/IV and K.-W., for text of the report and government comments. The report is also the substance of *SWMN*, vol. 3.

23  27 Oct. 1922, handwritten note by Ajmal Khan, Jamia Millia Islamia, Ali Papers.

24  M. Nehru to M. R. Jayakar, 23 Jan. 1924, *SWMN*, vol. 4 (1923–5), pp. 35–7; the programme of the party adopted at Allahabad, 20–2 Feb. 1923 is in ibid., pp. 10–12.

25  Viceroy to Secretary of State, 3 July 1924, IOLR MSS EUR.E.238 (7) and telegram of 21 July 1924, MSS EUR.E.238 (13).

26  Presidential speech for a UP conference, 13 Oct. 1923, *SWJN(1)*, vol. 2, pp. 204–13.

27  Gandhi to M. Nehru, 2 Sept. 1924, *CWMG*, vol. 25, p. 65. Tensions between Motilal and his son did not only result from debates about a new strategy. Motilal was also deeply anxious in 1923 when his son was temporarily detained in the princely state of Nabha after going there to view a Sikh demonstration.

28  J. Nehru to M. Ali, 13 Jan. 1924, *SWJN(1)*, vol. 2, p. 89. Material relating to his work as general secretary is in ibid., pp. 81–199.

29  Note by Jawaharlal, 12 Sept. 1924, *SWJN(1)*, vol. 2, pp. 170–82.

30  Presidential speech for a UP conference, 13 Oct. 1923, *SWJN(1)*, vol. 2, p. 211.

31  Draft note for Delhi conference, Sept. 1924, *SWJN(1)*, vol. 2, pp. 184–5.

32  Nehru, *Autobiography*, ch. 19, 'Communalism rampant'.

33  In view of later relations between Jawaharlal and P. D. Tandon it is interesting that Tandon withdrew his own candidacy in favour of Jawaharlal when he saw that it might cause friction between Hindus and Muslims in the board: letter from J. Nehru to the editor of *The Leader*, 4 Apr. 1923, *SWJN(1)*, vol. 2. pp. 1–2. Material on Nehru's time as chairman is to be found in ibid., pp. 1–78, and in Nehru, *Autobiography*, ch. 20.

34  Circular to UP Congress office-holders, 5 Apr. 1923, *SWJN(1)*, vol. 2, pp. 3–5.

35  J. Nehru to B. M. Vyas, 26 Sept. 1923, *SWJN(1)*, vol. 2, pp. 31–2.

36  Note of 24 Apr. 1923, *SWJN(1)*, vol. 2, pp. 7–8.

37   In 1927 Nehru's sister, Vijayalakshmi, gave birth to a second daughter and reported to her brother, who was in Europe, that their mother was so distressed at the arrival of another female grandchild that she had been crying in the presence of callers who came to greet the family; V. Pandit to J. Nehru, NMML, Vijayalakshmi Pandit Papers.

38   Motilal to Jawaharlal, 6 Dec. 1925, *SWMN*, vol. 4 (1923–25), pp. 178–80.

39   Nehru, *Autobiography*, p. 147.

40   Jawaharlal to Padmaja Naidu, 29 Jan. 1926, *SWJN(1)*, vol. 2, p. 226.

## Chapter 5   A Radical Bound, 1926–1931

1    For Nehru's changing image in the eyes of government see the confidential report compiled from official records on the civil disobedience movement, for official use only: *The Civil Disobedience Movement 1930–34* (Government of India, New Delhi, 1936), e.g. pp. 22–3. This is available in IOLR, Hallett Papers, MSS EUR.E.251 (34). For Nehru's own growing popularity, somewhat to his surprise, see his *Autobiography*, pp. 204–7.

2    Motilal to Jawaharlal, 15 and 29 Apr. 1926, *SWMN*, vol. 5, pp. 33–4, 43–4.

3    Jawaharlal to Gandhi, 15 Mar. 1927, *SWJN(1)*, vol. 2, pp. 311–12. See also Jawaharlal to Motilal, 6 Oct. 1926, ibid., pp. 244–6.

4    *SWJN(1)*, vol. 2, pp. 259–70. Material on the European visit is in ibid., part 4, pp. 229ff., and in Nehru, *Autobiography*, pp. 148–65. A series of letters from Jawaharlal to his sister, Vijayalakshmi, describing the European visit in some detail is in Vijayalakshmi Pandit Papers. In these it is clear that their twenty-year old sister, 'Betty', was proving a handful and was very difficult to deal with.

5    Nehru, *Autobiography*, p. 163.

6    Reports by Nehru for the CWC on the Brussels Congress, 19 Feb. and 7 Mar. 1927, *SWJN(1)*, vol 2, pp. 278–97, 299–303.

7    *The Volunteer,* Apr. 1927, *SWJN(1)*, vol. 2, p. 327.

8    Jawaharlal to Rangaswami Iyengar, 16 Feb. 1927, *SWJN(1)*, vol. 2, p. 277.

9    Jawaharlal to Gandhi, 22 Apr. 1927, *SWJN(1)*, vol. 2, p. 326.

10   Jawaharlal to Vijayalakshmi, 10 and 12 Nov. 1927, *SWJN(1)*, vol. 2, pp. 369–70, 371–5.

11   J. Nehru, *Soviet Russia, Some Random Sketches and Impressions* (Allahabad, 1928), repr. in *SWJN(1)*, vol. 2, pp. 379–451.

12   Motilal to Jawaharlal, 14 Apr. 1927; see also his letter of 30 Mar. 1927, J. Nehru Papers, Part 1, vol. lxix.

13   Jawaharlal to Syed Mahmud, 24 May, 15 July, 11 Aug. and 12 Sept. 1926, in S. Mahmud, *A Nationalist Muslim and Indian Politics: Being the Selected Correspondence of the late Dr Syed Mahmud*, ed. V. N. Datta and B. E. Cleghorn (Macmillan, Delhi, 1974), pp. 58–60, 60–1, 62–3, 64–6.

14   Jawaharlal to Rangaswami Iyengar, 25 Jan. 1927, *SWJN(1)*, vol. 2, pp. 258–9.

15   Note of 13 Sept. 1927, *SWJN(1)*, vol. 2, pp. 348–64.

16   Jawaharlal to Syed Mahmud, 1 Dec. 1926, in Mahmud, *A Nationalist Muslim*, pp. 67–8.

17   Note published in India on 2 Mar. 1927, *SWJN(1)*, vol. 2, pp. 297–8.

18   On the 1927 Congress at Madras, see Nehru, *Autobiography*, pp. 167–8; Goschen, Governor of Madras to the Viceroy, Lord Irwin, 5 Jan. 1928, IOLR, Halifax Papers, MSS EUR.C.152 (22); Note by Publicity Officer enclosed in Viceroy to Secretary of State, 15 Nov. 1928, MSS EUR.C.152 (4).

19   Gandhi to Jawaharlal, 4 Jan. 1928, Jawaharlal to Gandhi, 11 Jan. 1928, *CWMG*, vol. 35, pp. 432–3, 540–4.

20    Gandhi to Jawaharlal, 17 Jan. 1928, *CWMG*, vol. 35, pp. 469–70.

21    Jawaharlal to Gandhi, 23 Jan. 1928, *SWJN(1)*, vol. 3, pp. 18–20.

22    Nehru, *Autobiography*, pp. 176–81.

23    Ibid., pp. 171–3.

24    Jawaharlal to V. Chattopadhyaya, 3 and 31 Oct. 1928, *SWJN(1)*, vol. 3, pp. 143–4, 150.

25    Jawaharlal to Motilal, 12 Jan. 1931, *SWJN(1)*, vol. 4, p. 452. (A hartal was a strike or voluntary cessation of work, sometimes used as a nationalist political strategy.)

26    For Gandhi's return to active politics see Judith M. Brown, *Gandhi and Civil Disobedience. The Mahatma in Indian Politics 1928–34* (CUP, Cambridge, 1977), esp. ch. 1.

27    Report by Sri Prakasa on UP to J. Nehru, 5 May 1929, NMML, AICC Papers, 1929, File No. P 24: other provincial reports are also in this file. J. Nehru to UP PCC, July 1929, *SWJN(1)*, vol. 4, pp. 115–6.

28    See letters in NMML, M. Nehru Papers, Subject File INC, e.g. G. B. Pant to M. Nehru, 5 June 1929.

29    Jawaharlal to Gandhi, 9 and 13 July 1929, *SWJN(1)*, vol. 4, pp. 155, 156–7.

30    Nehru, *Autobiography*, pp. 194–5.

31    Viceroy to Secretary of State, telegram, 26 Oct. 1929, IOLR, MSS EUR.C.152 (10). For a detailed discussion of the events leading up to the Irwin Declaration, see R. J. Moore, *The Crisis Of Indian Unity 1917–1940* (Clarendon Press, Oxford, 1974), pp. 51–94. Irwin's term of office is the subject of S. Gopal, *The Viceroyalty of Lord Irwin 1926–1931* (Clarendon Press, Oxford, 1957).

32    For details of the complex events of November–December 1929 see Brown, *Gandhi and Civil Disobedience*, pp. 64–74; also D.A. Low, *Britain and Indian Nationalism: The Imprint of Ambiguity 1929–1942* (CUP, Cambridge, 1997), ch. 3.

33    Jawaharlal to Gandhi, 4 Nov. 1929, J. Nehru Papers, part 1, vol. xxii.

34    For these two speeches see *SWJN(1)*, vol. 4, pp. 49–55, 184–98.

35    Nehru's prison diary with letters from 14 Apr. to 11 Oct. 1930 is in *SWJN(1)*, vol. 4, pp. 317–88. This comment, 14 Apr. 1930, is on p. 318.

36    27 Apr. 1930, ibid., p. 329.

37    24 Apr. 1930, ibid., p. 327.

38    23 Apr. 1930, ibid., p. 325.

39    31 May 1930, ibid., p. 357.

40    Minutes of Governors' conference, Simla, 23 July 1930, IOLR, MSS EUR.C.152 (25). For details of this episode see Brown, *Gandhi and Civil Disobedience*, pp. 158–67. Evidence is available in Nehru's jail diary and enclosures, *SWJN(1)*, vol. 4 and in his *Autobiography*, ch. xxxi; Jayakar Papers, Correspondence File Nos 770 and 771; IOLR, MSS EUR.C. 152 (6), (11), (25); IOLR, Sapru Papers, Series II; J. Nehru Papers, Subject file, Sapru–Jayakar Papers.

41    1 Aug. 1930, *SWJN(1)*, vol. 4, p. 373.

42    Statement on his release, *SWJN(1)*, vol. 4, p. 391.

43    For his jail diary with enclosures see *SWJN(1)*, vol. 4, pp. 413–62.

44    *SWJN(1)*, vol. 4, pp. 437–51.

45    Nehru to Padmaja Naidu, 24 Oct. 1931, *SWJN(1)*, vol. 12, p. 662.

46    Irwin to Wedgwood Benn, 26 Dec. 1930, IOLR, MSS EUR.C.152 (6); also telegram, 1 Jan. 1931, MSS. EUR.C.152 (11); Wedgwood Benn to Irwin, 15 Jan. 1931, Home Political, 1931, File No. 5/45.

47    Nehru, *Autobiography*, p. 247: also Nehru to his sister, Krishna, 21 Feb. 1931, *SWJN(1)*, vol. 4, p. 585, Nehru to Indira, 21 Apr. 1931, ibid., p. 519.

48    Jawaharlal to Motilal, *c.* 22 Jan. 1931, *SWJN(1)*, vol. 4, pp. 454–61.

49   V. S. S. Sastri to T. R. V. Sastri, 17 Feb. 1931, *Letters of V. S. Srinivasa Sastri*, p. 209.
     For the details of the negotiations see Brown, *Gandhi and Civil Disobedience*, pp. 177–91.
50   Nehru to Vijayalakshmi Pandit, 28 Feb. 1931, NMML, V. Pandit Papers.
51   Note for the CWC, probably 2 Mar. 1931, *SWJN(1)*, vol. 4, pp. 479–81.
52   For Bose's critique of Gandhi and his methods see ch. 11 of S. C. Bose, *The Indian Struggle 1920–1942* (Asia Publishing House, New York, 1964).
53   Jayakar to Sapru, 29 Mar. 1931, Sapru Papers, Series II.
54   Resolution on Fundamental Rights, *SWJN(1)*, vol. 4, pp. 511–13.
55   J. Nehru, *The Discovery of India* (1946; Asia Publishing House, 1960), p. 29.
56   Kamala Nehru to Syed Mahmud, 15 Mar., 1 Apr., 4 May 1927, in Mahmud, *A Nationalist Muslim*, pp. 69–70, 72, 73–4. See Nehru, *Autobiography*, p. 274, for the incident in Hyderabad in 1931.
57   See Low, *Britain and Indian Nationalism*, ch. 4; and Brown, *Gandhi and Civil Disobedience*, pp. 206–41.
58   Nehru's circular to PCCs, 31 Aug. 1931, *SWJN(1)*, vol. 5, pp. 27–8.
59   Nehru to Gandhi, 17 Sept. 1931, *SWJN(1)*, vol. 5, p. 43,
60   Speech at Christian Nationalist Party meeting, 13 June 1931, ibid., pp. 283–6. Also Nehru to Gandhi, 27 Sept. 1931, Nehru to Dr M. A. Ansari, 4 Oct. 1931, ibid., pp. 45–7, 48.
61   Lord Willingdon (now Viceroy) to Sir Samuel Hoare, Secretary of State for India, 13 and 26 Dec. 1923, IOLR Templewood Papers, MSS EUR.E.240 (5); Nehru to K. M. Munshi, 29 Apr. 1940, *SWJN(1)*, vol. 5, pp. 579–80. On the UP situation see Brown, *Gandhi and Civil Disobedience*, pp. 267–71.
62   Speech at Lucknow, 28 July 1931, *SWJN(1)*, vol. 5, p. 105; Nehru to Raja Rampal Singh, 5 Nov. 1931, ibid., pp. 170–2.

# Chapter 6    Whither India?

1   On Nehru's writing see B. R. Nanda, *Jawaharlal Nehru: Rebel and Statesman* (OUP, New Delhi, 1995), ch. 14, 'Nehru as a man of letters' and ch. 15, 'The Autobiography'. Nehru refused to write a biography of his father for personal reasons, and was reluctant that anyone should attempt it, because he felt the genre of biography was very poor in India compared with Europe. Nehru to Girdhari Lal, 20 Mar. 1933, *SWJN(1)*, vol. 5, pp. 466–7.
2   See table 8 in Brown, *Gandhi and Civil Disobedience*, pp. 284–6. On British policy towards civil disobedience, 1930–4, see D. A. Low (ed.), *Congress and the Raj: Facets of the Indian Struggle 1917–47* (Heinemann, London, 1977), ch. 4.
3   The compromise was known as the 'Poona Pact' and gave Untouchables a significantly larger number of reserved seats in the provincial legislatures than they would have had under British proposals, but they did not have separate electorates. The terms of the compromise were sent by the Bombay government to the Government of India on 24 Sept. 1932 and repeated to the Secretary of State: Home Political, 1932, File No. 31/113. Important insider accounts of the meetings which produced this compromise are the diaries of B. S. Moonje, a politician associated with the Hindu Mahasabha, 16–25 Sept. 1931, available on microfilm in the NMML; Sapru to H. Polak, 17 and 30 Sept. 1932, Sapru Papers, 2nd series.
4   Nehru to Vijayalakshmi, 4 Oct. 1932, *SWJN(1)*, vol. 5, p. 414.

5    Nehru to Indira, 26 May 1935, *SWJN(1)*, vol. 8, p. 784.

6    These with interleaved documents are available in *SWJN(1)*, vol. 5, pp. 343–501; vol. 6, pp. 227–73, 289–427.

7    25 Nov. 1932, *SWJN(1)*, vol. 5, p. 433.

8    5 Feb. 1933, *SWJN(1)*, vol. 5, p. 457.

9    15 Mar. 1932, *SWJN(1)*, vol. 5, p. 369.

10   10 July 1932, *SWJN(1)*, vol. 5, p. 488.

11   Nehru to Indira, 5 July 1935, *SWJN(1)*, vol. 6, p. 391.

12   Interview, 31 Aug. 1933, *SWJN(1)*, vol. 5, p. 507.

13   The list of books is in *SWJN(1)*, vol. 6, pp. 420–27.

14   Nehru to Betty, 13 June 1933, *SWJN(1)*, vol. 5, p. 483.

15   7 June 1933, *SWJN(1)*, vol. 5, p. 481.

16   Nehru, *Autobiography*, p. vii.

17   'Epilogue', in ibid., pp. 596–8.

18   Nehru to Syed Mahmud, 24 Nov. 1933, *SWJN(1)*, vol. 6, p. 211. The tensions in the family home and Kamala's problems are alluded to in Nehru to Vijayalakshmi Pandit, 12 September 1934 (Vijayalakshmi Pandit Papers). He acknowledged that his sister was one of the very, very few people dear to him, and he urged her to try to remove any discord which might have crept into family relations.

19   Their correspondence is available in S. Gandhi (ed.), *Freedom's Daughter*, pp. 50–219. (In *SWJN* there are only Nehru's letters interleaved with his jail diary, and not Indira's letters to him.)

20   Indira to Nehru, 28 May 1934, *Freedom's Daughter*, pp. 115–17; Nehru to Indira, 15 June 1934, ibid., pp. 119–22. Nehru poured out his worries about Indira to his sister, Vijayalakshmi, in a letter written from prison on 6 March 1933 (Vijayalakshmi Pandit Papers). He worried that Indira had become self-centred and selfish and a 'languid, languishing type of girl', and he wanted her to do something practical to bring her down to earth. He worried that she had not written to him for over a year despite his regular letters. It seems that the letters she wrote and which are available in *Freedom's Daughter* did not reach him.

21   Nehru to Indira, 19 July 1935, *Freedom's Daughter.*, pp. 191–6; Nehru to Madan Atal, 5 July 1935, *SWJN(1)*, vol. 6, pp. 384–5.

22   1 Feb. 1935, *SWJN(1)*, vol. 6, pp. 312–3.

23   19 Mar. 1935, *SWJN(1)*, vol. 6, p. 331.

24   5 Apr. 1935, *SWJN(1)*, vol. 6, p. 344.

25   Nehru to Kamala, 26 May, 19 July 1935, *SWJN(1)*, vol. 12, pp. 672–5, 682–7.

26   M. Desai to Nehru, 31 Aug. 1931, J. Nehru Papers, part I, vol. xvii.

27   22 Sept. 1932, *SWJN(1)*, vol. 5, pp. 407–8. Another politician who was disturbed by the 'awful experiment' of the fast as a form of moral coercion and called it 'whitemail' was V. S. S. Sastri; see his letter to P. K. Rao, 10 Oct. 1932, *Letters of V. S. Srinivasa Sastri*, pp. 237–9.

28   Nehru to Gandhi, telegram, 25 Sept. 1932, J. Nehru Papers, Part I, vol. xxii.

29   Nehru to Nan, 4 Oct. and 29 Nov. 1932, Vijayalakshmi Pandit Papers; Indira to Nehru, 27 Sept. 1932, *Freedom's Daughter*, pp. 68–9.

30   Gandhi to Nehru, 2 May 1933, and Nehru to Gandhi, 5 May 1933, J. Nehru Papers, Part I, vol. xxiii.

31   4 June 1933, *SWJN(1)*, vol. 5, pp. 478–9.

32   18 July 1933, *SWJN(1)*, vol. 5, pp. 488–9.

33    Nehru to Gandhi, 13 Sept. 1933, *SWJN(1)*, vol. 5, pp. 526–30; Gandhi to Nehru, 14 Sept. 1933, *CWMG*, vol. 55, pp. 426–30. See also Nehru, *Autobiography*, pp. 403–4.

34    Nehru's press statement, 14 Sept. 1933, *SWJN(1)*, vol. 5, pp. 531–2. For official views on this see Willingdon to Hoare, 24 Sept. 1933, IOLR, MSS EUR.E.240 (6); Bombay Special to Govt of India, Home Dept, telegram, 20 Oct. 1933, IOLR, Sykes Papers, MSS EUR.F.150 (5). See also Nehru to Subhas Bose, 2 Feb. 1939, *SWJN(1)*, vol. 9, p. 481.

35    Gandhi to Nehru, 21 Jan. 1934, J. Nehru Papers, Part I, vol. xxiv. See also Gandhi to V. Patel, 19 Aug. 1934, *CWMG*, vol. 58, p. 330; Gandhi to K. M. Munshi, 2 May 1935, *CWMG*, vol. 61, p. 28.

36    13 Apr., 12 May 1934, *SWJN(1)*, vol. 6, pp. 247–8, 251. For the complex reasoning behind Gandhi's decision, see Brown, *Gandhi and Civil Disobedience*, pp. 374–6

37    For Nehru's reflection on Gandhi's ideals and leadership see his *Autobiography*, pp. 504–52.

38    Nehru to Gandhi, 13 Aug. 1934, Gandhi to Nehru, 17 Aug. 1934, J. Nehru Papers, Part I, vol. xiv.

39    Nehru to Bhagavan Das, 23 Sept. 1933, *SWJN(1)*, vol. 5, p. 541.

40    *SWJN(1)*, vol. 6, pp. 1–16, 18–31.

41    *SWJN(1)*, vol. 6, p. 30; also Nehru to C. Mascarenhas, 10 Nov. 1933, ibid., p. 17.

42    20 June 1934, *SWJN(1)*, vol. 6, p. 259. See also his anguished draft note on Congress which seems to date from about this time, ibid., pp. 270–3.

43    Press statement, 12 Jan. 1934, and speech to students in Calcutta, 18 Jan. 1934, *SWJN(1)*, vol. 6, pp. 89, 106–7.

44    T.B. Sapru to M.R. Jayakar, 22 Feb. 1934, Jayakar Papers, Correspondence File No. 408.

45    See B. R. Nanda. 'Socialism in India, 1919–1939: a retrospect', in B. R. Nanda (ed.), *Socialism in India* (Vikas, Delhi, 1972).

46    Nehru to A. Rahim, 30 Oct. 1933, to M. R. Masani, 19 Dec. 1933, *SWJN(1)*, vol. 6, pp. 118, 135–6.

47    Nehru, *Autobiography*, p. 406.

48    S. C. Bose to Mrs K. Kurti, 23 Feb. 1934, *Ten Historic Netaji Documents* (Netaji Research Bureau Presentation, 1972), p. 6. See also, Bose, *The Indian Struggle*, pp. 263–4.

49    Nehru to S. A. Brelvi, 3 Dec. 1933, *SWJN(1)*, vol. 6, p. 172.

50    Nehru's article for the press, 27 Nov. 1933, *SWJN(1)*, vol. 6, pp. 161–71. See also Nehru to M. Alam, 29 Oct. 1933, ibid., p. 156; speech at Banares Hindu University, 12 Nov. 1933, ibid., pp. 157–8.

51    Nehru's article for the press, 27 Nov. 1933, *SWJN(1)*, vol. 6, p. 171.

52    Statement to press, 5 Jan. 1934, *SWJN(1)*, vol. 6, pp. 180–5.

53    28 Aug., 2 Sept. 1933, *SWJN(1)*, vol. 6, pp. 411, 416.

## Chapter 7   Isolation

1    For a detailed analysis of Congress politics during this period see B. R. Tomlinson, *The Indian National Congress and the Raj, 1929–1942: The Penultimate Phase* (Macmillan, London, 1976). See also essays in parts III and IV of R. Sisson and S. Wolpert (eds), *Congress and Indian Nationalism: The Pre-Independence Phase* (University of California Press, Berkeley, 1988).

2    Nehru to Agatha Harrison, 25 Sept. 1935, *SWJN(1)*, vol. 7, pp. 25–30. Recollections of his visits are in ibid., pp. 117–21; postscript to autobiography, *SWJN(1)*, vol. 11, pp. 759–64.

3    Nehru to Gandhi, 24 July 1941, *SWJN(1)*, vol. 11, pp. 658–9; Nehru, *The Discovery of India*, pp. 32–3. There is a deeply poignant run of letters from Nehru to Vijayalakshmi from 23 September 1935 to 26 February 1936, describing his time in Europe, the seriousness of Kamala's condition and the brief glimpses of hope as she seemed to improve, and then the final collapse just as he was preparing to return briefly to India; Vijayalakshmi Pandit Papers.

4    Nehru to Indira, 30 Sept. 1937, S. Gandhi (ed.), *Freedom's Daughter*, pp. 333–4; see also reminiscences in the Epilogue to the American edition of the autobiography entitled *Towards Freedom*, *SWJN(1)*, vol. 11, p. 163.

5    Nehru to Indira, 1 Nov. 1936, *SWJN(1)*, vol. 8, p. 800.

6    Nehru to Indira, 14 Jan. 1938, *Freedom's Daughter*, pp. 356–7.

7    Nehru to Indira, 15 Mar. 1938, ibid., pp. 386–7. Some insights into Indira's life at this time are in K. Frank, *Indira: The Life of Indira Nehru Gandhi* (HarperCollins, London, 2001).

8    Nehru to Indira, 23 Sept. 1937, *Freedom's Daughter*, p. 332; 11 May 1940, *SWJN(1)*, vol. 11, pp. 465–6.

9    Nehru's letters to Frances Gunther are gathered together in a file of correspondence included in his papers post–1947 although most of them date from before independence; NMML, J. Nehru Papers post-1947, 2nd Instalment, Correspondence File No. 105. Those from 1938 to 1942 are published in an appendix to *SWJN(1)*, vol. 14; others from 1945 and 1949 appear in the relevant chronological volume.

10   Nehru to Padmaja Naidu, 2 Mar. 1938, *SWJN(1)*, vol. 13, p. 695. The letters for these years from Nehru to Padmaja Naidu are in the appendix to ibid.

11   Nehru to Padmaja Naidu, 7 Apr. 1938, Nehru to Krishna Menon, 17 May 1939, *SWJN(1)*, vol. 13, pp. 698, 712–13.

12   Nehru to Indira, 22 Dec. 1938, *SWJN(2)*, vol. 3, p. 473; 3 July 1939, *SWJN(1)*, vol. 9, p. 626.

13   NMML, Bhulabhai Desai Papers, Diary 1935–6, entry for 12 Sept. 1935.

14   Ibid., entry for 7 Feb. 1936; J. B. Kripalani to R. Prasad, 15 Feb. 1936, NAI, Rajendra Prasad Papers, File No. III/36.Coll.1.

15   For Nehru's account of the way his mind was working see *Where Are We?*, articles published in Feb.–Mar. 1939, *SWJN(1)*, vol. 9, p. 495. Gandhi to Nehru, 12 and 22 Sept. 1935, J.Nehru Papers; R. Prasad to Nehru, 19 Dec. 1935, J. Nehru Papers.

16   Speech at Congress, 12 Apr. 1936, *SWJN(1)*, vol. 7, pp. 170–95.

17   G. D. Birla to P. Thakurdas, 20 Apr. 1936, NMML, P. Thakurdas Papers, File No. 177.

18   NMML AICC Papers, File No. G-31 (1936).

19   Sources for this episode include letters intercepted by the government in Home Political, File No. 32/12/1936, including one of 29 May 1936 from V. Patel to R. Prasad, Nehru to Gandhi, 25 May 1936, and Gandhi to Nehru, 29 May 1936. The resignations of R. Prasad, V. Patel, C. Rajagopalachariar, J. Kripalani, J. Doulatram, J. Bajaj, S. D. Dev, and B. Desai are in letter to Nehru, J. Nehru Papers. Prasad also wrote a long private letter to Nehru, 1 July 1936, explaining how they felt, but withdrawing the resignations after discussions with Gandhi, J. Nehru Papers.

20   Nehru to Sri Prakasa, 3 May 1936, *SWJN(1)*, vol. 7, pp. 622–3. The exchange with Gandhi (Nehru to Gandhi, 5 July 1936, and Gandhi to Nehru, 8 and 15 July 1936) is in J. Nehru Papers.

21  M. Desai to J. Nehru, 26 Aug. 1936, AICC Papers, File No. G-85 (1) (1936).

22  Gandhi to Nehru, 15 July 1936, J. Nehru Papers. See also Nehru to S. C. Bose, 3 Apr. 1939, *SWJN(1)*, vol. 9, pp. 535–6.

23  Nehru to Agatha Harrison, 3 Sept. 1936, *SWJN(1)*, vol. 7, p. 347. See also his account in *The Discovery of India*, pp. 50–5.

24  Congress Manifesto, 22 Aug. 1936, *SWJN(1)*, vol. 7, pp. 459–64.

25  'The Rashtrapati', 5 Oct. 1937, *SWJN(1)*, vol. 8, pp. 520–3. See also Nehru to Padmaja Naidu, 5 Oct. 1937, and to K. Kripalani, 2 June 1938, ibid., pp. 519, 525.

26  On the Khudai Khidmatgar or 'Red Shirt' movement on the Frontier see M. Banerjee, *The Pathan Unarmed: Opposition and Memory in the North West Frontier* (OUP, Oxford, 2000); S. Rittenberg, *Ethnicity, Nationalism and the Pakhtuns: The Independence Movement in Indian North-West Frontier Province* (Carolina Academic Press, Durham, N.C., 1988).

27  Nehru to R. Prasad, 21 July 1937, *SWJN(1)*, vol. 8, pp. 165–71.

28  On this change in the nature of Congress see Tomlinson, *The Indian National Congress*; for provincial and district case studies see C. J. Baker, *The Politics of South India 1920–1937* (CUP, Cambridge, 1976) and M. Weiner, *Party Building in a New Nation: The Indian National Congress* (University of Chicago Press, Chicago, 1967).

29  Nehru to Gandhi, 28 Apr. 1938, J. Nehru Papers. See also Nehru to Vijayalakshmi Pandit, 17 May 1939, Vijayalakshmi Pandit Papers.

30  J. Nehru to S. Mahmud, 12 Dec. 1939, NMML, Syed Mahmud Papers; press editorial, 31 Oct. 1939, *SWJN(1)*, vol. 10, pp. 215–17. Nehru's attitude to the various aspects of Congress's experience in 1936–9 are in the relevant chronological volumes of *SWJN(1)*. See also D. A. Low, 'The spider's web: Congress and provincial office 1937–1939', ch. 7 of his *Britain and Indian Nationalism*.

31  Nehru's views are to be found in the relevant sections of vols 8 and 9 of *SWJN(1)*; his 1938 letters to Jinnah are in sec. 3 of vol. 8. On Jinnah's life and his changing strategy see A. Jalal, *The Sole Spokesman: Jinnah, the Muslim League and the Demand for Pakistan* (CUP, Cambridge, 1985).

32  Nehru to J. B. Kripalani, 14 July 1938, and to S. C. Bose, 14 July 1938, *SWJN(1)*, vol. 9, pp. 57, 59.

33  Nehru's circular to PCCs, 31 Mar. 1937, *SWJN(1)*, vol. 8, pp. 122–4. See also M. Hasan, 'The Muslim mass contacts campaign: analysis of a strategy of political mobilization', ch. 10 of Sisson and Wolpert, *Congress and Indian Nationalism*.

34  Nehru to S. C. Bose, 4 Feb. 1939, *SWJN(1)*, vol. 9, pp. 480–5.

35  'Where are we?', *SWJN(1)*, vol. 9, pp. 488–520.

36  Nehru to Krishna Menon, 17 May 1939, *SWJN(1)*, vol. 13, pp. 712–13.

37  Nehru to Gandhi, 17 Apr. 1939, *SWJN(1)*, vol. 9, pp. 553–5; Nehru to R. Prasad, 17 Apr. 1939, J. Nehru Papers.

38  Nehru to Sri Prakasa, 15 Aug. 1939, J. Nehru Papers.

39  See Gandhi to Nehru, 25 Apr. 1938, Nehru to Gandhi, 28 Apr. 1938, ibid. Amrit Kaur, who was close to both Gandhi and Nehru, urged Nehru to have more time with Gandhi, and also assured him that Gandhi always welcomed Nehru's honest opposition: Amrit Kaur to Nehru, 24 May 1938, ibid.

40  These and other material relating to his European visit are in *SWJN(1)*, vol. 9, sec. 1.

41  See his lengthy report to Rajendra Prasad, President of Congress, 9 Aug. 1939, *SWJN(1)*, vol. 10, pp. 51–64,

42  For evidence relating to the China trip, see *SWJN(1)*, vol. 10, sec.2. His note on the need for contacts between China and India, 29 Aug. 1939, is on pp. 102–8.

43  On this work see Nehru, *The Discovery of India*, pp. 400ff.; *SWJN(1)*, vol. 9, sec. 5.

44  Nehru to Indira, 22 Dec. 1938, *SWJN(2)*, vol. 3, p. 473; Gandhi to Nehru, 11 Aug. 1939, *CWMG*, vol. 70, p. 86.

45  Nehru to K. T. Shah, 13 May 1939, *SWJN(1)*, vol. 9, pp. 373–4; for other broad-ranging surveys of his vision of planning for a free India as notes circulated to members of the National Planning Committee and its subcommittees, 4 and 19 June 1939, see ibid., pp. 375–80, 385–90.

## Chapter 8  The Experience of War, 1939–1945

1   For the intricacies of cabinet discussions over India during the war, see R. J. Moore, *Churchill, Cripps and India, 1939–1945* (Clarendon Press, Oxford, 1979), and Wm. Roger Louis, 'The Second World War, India, and the clash with Churchill 1940–1945', ch. 3 of Louis, *In The Name Of God, Go! Leo Amery and the British Empire in the Age of Churchill* (W. W. Norton, New York, 1992). The primary printed source for British policy towards India from 1942 to 1947 is the 12-volume *Constitutional Relations between Britain and India. The Transfer of Power, 1942–7*, published by HMSO, London, 1970–83 (henceforth referred to as *TOP*). Volumes 1–3 were edited by N. Mansergh and E. W. R. Lumby, and the subsequent ones by N. Mansergh and P. Moon. The Home Political files contain evidence of preparations during the first year of the war for effective action against any renewal of mass civil disobedience; a convenient summary is in the official compilation, 'History of the civil disobedience movement – 1940–41' in Home Political, File No. 3/6/42. India's contribution to the war is indicated in my entry on India in I. C. B. Dear and M. R. D. Foot (eds), *The Oxford Companion to the Second World War* (OUP, Oxford, 1995), pp. 557–65.

2   Gandhi to Dr B. C. Roy, 12 Oct. 1939, *CWMG*, vol. 70, pp. 248–9.

3   Nehru to Krishna Menon, 16 Sept. 1939, *SWJN(1)*, vol. 10, p. 140; CWC resolution, 14 Sept. 1939, and earlier drafts, ibid., pp. 122–38.

4   Nehru to G. Madgavkar, 6 Oct. 1939, *SWJN(1)*, vol. 10, pp. 173–4.

5   Nehru to Gandhi, 24 Jan. 1940, J. Nehru Papers. He reiterated this in a letter to Gandhi, 4 Feb. 1940, J. Nehru Papers.

6   Nehru to Indira, 16 Jan. and 4 Feb. 1940, *SWJN(1)*, vol. 10, pp. 646, 651.

7   For a very interesting assessment of Azad, by Nehru, see Nehru to Krishna Menon, 14 Mar. 1940, *SWJN(1)*, vol. 11, pp. 203–6. See also article on Azad by Nehru, 24 June 1942, *SWJN(1)*, vol. 12, pp. 610–12. Because Azad's command of literary English was limited, Nehru did the drafting of key documents for him at this time.

8   Nehru to Jinnah,14 Dec. 1939, *SWJN(1)*, vol. 10, pp. 399–401.

9   Nehru to Krishna Menon, 9 and 12 Apr. 1940, *SWJN(1)*, vol. 11, pp. 259, 16.

10  Nehru to R. Prasad, and to A. K. Azad, 16 May 1940, J. Nehru Papers.

11  Nehru was realistic about the impossibility of non-violent defence of India, but committed to working for world disarmament. See unfinished note, 25 Aug. 1940, *SWJN(1)*, vol. 11, pp. 123–7.

12  See G. D. Birla to P. Thakurdas, 11 Sept. 1940, in which Birla enclosed a letter of 28 Aug. he sent to the Viceroy's private secretary on the state of public opinion; P. Thakurdas Papers, File No. 239, Pt 1.

13  Gandhi to Nehru, 24 Oct. 1940, J.Nehru Papers. Verbatim notes on key discussions between Congress leaders, including a crucial one between Gandhi, Azad and Nehru

on 13 Oct. 1940 are in NMML, Papers of Raj Kumari Amrit Kaur (she was a Punjabi Christian of a princely family and was a very close adherent of Gandhi as well as a friend of Nehru). Azad noted his wish for a more extensive and active anti-war movement in his autobiographical work, *India Wins Freedom* (complete version, Sangam Books, London, 1988), pp. 35–6.

14   Nehru's prison diary and letters for this sentence, 31 Oct. 1940 to 4 Dec. 1941, are in *SWJN(1)*, vol. 11, pp. 485–597, 601–750.

15   23 Nov. 1940, *SWJN(1)*, vol. 11, pp. 503–4.

16   Nehru to Gandhi, 24 July 1941, diary entry for 3 Oct. 1941, *SWJN(1)*, vol. 11, pp. 659, 707.

17   Nehru to Indira, 9 July 1941, *SWJN(1)*, vol. 11, pp. 643–8.

18   Rajendra Prasad reported to Syed Mahmud in a letter of 11 Oct. 1941 that Gandhi was thoroughly satisfied and hopeful about the future; Syed Mahmud Papers.

19   Diary entry, 14 Aug. 1941, *SWJN(1)*, vol. 11, pp. 674–6; see also ibid., pp. 649–50.

20   Nehru to Padmaja Naidu, 16 Dec. 1941, *SWJN(1)*, vol. 12, p. 622.

21   Nehru to Sampurnanand, 14 Dec. 1941, *SWJN(1)*, vol. 12, pp. 15–16.

22   Two drafts and final version of the resolution passed at CWC, 30 Dec. 1941, *SWJN(1)*, vol. 12, pp. 45–55.

23   Sir M. Hallett to Linlithgow, 19 Jan. 1942, *TOP*, vol. 1, p. 39.

24   Nehru to C. Rajagoplachariar, 26 Jan. 1942, J. Nehru Papers.

25   Linlithgow to Sir M. Hallett, 4 Feb. 1942, *TOP*, vol. 1, pp. 236–7.

26   Prison diary, 14 July 1943, *SWJN(1)*, vol. 13, p. 186.

27   For very detailed discussion of the origins and course of the mission see Moore, *Churchill, Cripps, and India*, particularly chs 3–5; also P. Clarke, *The Cripps Version: The Life of Sir Stafford Cripps 1889–1952* (Penguin Press, London, 2002), pp. 276ff. Sources for the episode are in *TOP*, vol. 1; and *SWJN(1)*, vol. 12, sec. 2. Azad also makes some interesting observations in his *India Wins Freedom*, ch. 5.

28   Nehru to Stafford Cripps, 7 Apr. 1942, *SWJN(1)*, vol. 12, pp. 628–9; Cripps's 'personal and private' note, not dated, is in J. Nehru, *A Bunch of Old Letters* (Asia Publishing House, Bombay, 1958) p. 478, original in J. Nehru Papers.

29   Azad to Cripps, 10 Apr. 1942, J. Nehru Papers.

30   Nehru to E. Wood, 5 June 1942, *SWJN(1)*, vol. 12, pp. 241–2; Nehru to Krishna Menon, 3 Sept. 1945, *SWJN(1)*, vol. 14, pp. 80–1.

31   Discussions of CWC, 27 Apr.–1 May 1942, seized in a search of the AICC office in Allahabad and enclosed in Sir M. Hallett to Linlithgow, 31 May 1941, *TOP*, vol. 2, pp. 158–64.

32   Confidential note by Nehru on talks with Gandhi, 12–14 June 1942, *SWJN(1)*, vol. 12, pp. 359–62.

33   Nehru to Sampurnanand, 28 July 1942, *SWJN(1)*, vol. 12, p. 422. On the discussions over whether any compromise was still possible see reports of interviews, 16–17 July between Nehru and J. L. Berry, ibid., pp. 404–9.

34   Amery to Churchill, 13 July 1942, *TOP*, vol. 2, pp. 376–7. The main outlines of the planned policy towards Congress, designed 'to render movement abortive by removing its leaders', were communicated by telegram from the Govt of India, Home Dept, to Secretary of State, 3 Aug. 1942, ibid., pp. 534–7. The cabinet sanctioned this on 6 Aug. 1942, War Cabinet Minutes, ibid., pp. 586–8.

35   Nehru's prison diary from 9 Aug. 1942 to 15 June 1945 is in *SWJN(1)*, vol. 13, pp. 1–639.

36  Nehru to Gandhi, 24 July 1941, *SWJN(I)*, vol. 11, p. 659.

37  Nehru, *The Discovery of India*, p. 579.

38  Nehru to Indira, 15 Oct. 1942, *SWJN(I)*, vol. 13, p. 21.

39  Nehru to Indira, 11 Dec. 1943, *SWJN(I)*, vol. 13, p. 310. On Edward Thompson and his multiple connections with India see M. Lago, *'India's Prisoner': A Biography of Edward John Thompson, 1886–1946* (University of Missouri Press, Columbia, 2001).

40  21 Nov. 1943, diary entry, *SWJN(I)*, vol. 13, p. 297.

41  19 Mar. 1945, diary entry, *SWJN(I)*, vol. 13, pp. 582–7.

42  On the Quit India movement see F. G. Hutchins, *India's Revolution: Gandhi and the Quit India Movement* (Harvard University Press, Cambridge, Mass., 1973); and M. Harcourt, 'Kisan populism and revolution in rural India: the 1942 disturbances in Bihar and east United Provinces', ch. 10 of Low, *Congress and the Raj*. Two government sources are *Congress Responsibility for the Disturbances 1942–43* (New Delhi, 1943) and a further 1943 report on the disturbances compiled by T. Wickenden, ICS, and republished in 1976, P. N. Chopra (ed.), *Quit India Movement: British Secret Report* (Thompson Press (India), Faridabad).

43  5 Aug. 1944, diary entry, *SWJN(I)*, vol. 13, pp. 455–7.

44  Nehru to Indira, 12 Aug. 1944, *SWJN(I)*, vol. 13, pp. 459–61.

45  K. Hutheesing, 'My brother – Jawahar', *Asia*, 42, Vol. XLII, no. 1 (Jan. 1942). Nehru's comments on family tensions are in his diary entry, 8 Nov. 1943, *SWJN(I)*, vol. 13, pp. 272–4.

46  Nehru to Indira, 20 May 1944, *SWJN(I)*, vol. 13, pp. 414–5; V. Pandit, *The Scope of Happiness*, ch. 26, in which she also described the legal *cause célèbre* which ensued. Sapru appeared for her in court – an interesting reflection on his long connection with the family of his former legal colleague, despite their political differences. Eventually her brother-in-law released Ranjit Pandit's earned money, but gave them nothing from the joint estate. See also Vijayalakshmi Pandit to Nehru, 20 March 1944, Vijayalakshmi Pandit Papers.

47  Nehru to Indira, 7 Aug. 1943, *SWJN(I)*, vol. 13, p. 209; also diary entries, 13 Nov. 1942, 14 July 1943, ibid., pp. 28, 186.

48  *Wavell: The Viceroy's Journal*, ed. P. Moon (OUP, London, 1973), entries for 27 July and 29 Sept. 1943, pp. 12, 20.

49  Journal entry, 31 Aug. 1944, ibid., p. 88; Wavell to Churchill, 24 Oct. 1944, *TOP*, vol. 5, pp. 126–33.

## Chapter 9  The Experience of Independence, 1945–1948

1  Diary entry, 13 Nov. 1942, *SWJN(I)*, vol. 13, p. 28.

2  31 Dec. 1946, *Wavell*, p. 402. For detailed discussions of British policy see R. J. Moore, *Escape From Empire: The Attlee Government and the Indian Problem* (Clarendon Press, Oxford, 1983). Primary sources for 1945–7 are in *TOP*, vols 5–12.

3  See Jalal, *The Sole Spokesman*; also on the Pakistan movement, I. Talbot, *Provincial Politics and the Pakistan Movement. The Growth of the Muslim League in North-West and North-East India 1937–47* (OUP, Karachi, 1988). An important historiographical review article is A. Roy, 'The high politics of India's partition: the revisionist perspective', *Modern Asian Studies*, 24 (part 2) (May 1990), pp. 385–415, reprinted in the very useful collection, M. Hasan (ed.), *India's Partition: Process, Strategy and Mobilization* (OUP, New Delhi, 1993).

4  On the princes see I. Copland, *The Princes of India in the Endgame of Empire, 1917–1947* (CUP, Cambridge, 1997).

5  Nehru to Indira, 1 July 1945, *SWJN(1)*, vol. 14, pp. 569–70; Nehru to Vijayalakshmi Pandit, 26 July 1945, ibid., p. 60.

6  Instructions to Congress delegation, *SWJN(1)*, vol. 14, pp. 22–3. Sec. 1 of this volume contains evidence of the Simla Conference, as does *TOP*, vol. 5.

7  Wavell to HM King George VI, 19 July 1945, *TOP*, vol. 5, p. 1279.

8  Wavell's note on interview with Nehru, 14 July 1945, *TOP*, vol. 5, p. 1249.

9  Speech on 22 Dec. 1945, *SWJN(1)*, vol. 14, p. 503.

10  Casey to Wavell, 8 Dec. 1945, *TOP*, vol. 6, p. 623.

11  Election manifesto, Oct. 1945, *SWJN(1)*, vol. 14, pp. 105–9; on the reasoning behind the manifesto, Nehru to Patel, 10 Oct. 1945, ibid., pp. 104–5.

12  Patel to Nehru, 4–5 Nov. 1945, NMML, M. O. Mathai Papers, 2A, File of correspondence between Nehru and Patel.

13  Nehru to Cripps, 27 Jan. 1946, M.O.Mathai Papers, 2A, File of Correspondence between Cripps and Nehru. (In view of Nehru's opinion it is significant that Lord Pethick-Lawrence, Secretary of State for India, had produced in the India Office a memorandum on the viability of Pakistan, 13 Feb. 1946. It judged Pakistan a very unattractive proposition, agreed with Nehru on the question of defence and underlined the profound problems division would cause economically to both countries. *TOP*, vol. 6, pp. 951–63.)

14  Patel to Nehru, 20 Feb. 1946, M. O. Mathai Papers, 2A, File of Correspondence between Nehru and Patel.

15  Primary sources for the Cabinet Mission are to be found in *TOP*, vol. 7, and *SWJN(1)*, vol. 15, sec.5. *Wavell* is also helpful for the perspective of the harassed Viceroy. For the Mission through the experience of Cripps, see Clarke, *The Cripps Version*, pp. 393ff.

16  Wavell to HM King George VI, 8 July 1946, *TOP*, vol. 7, pp. 1091–5. A more private and robust assessment of why the Mission failed is in *Wavell*, pp. 309–15. He thought Gandhi was 'the real wrecker', and was shocked at the deference shown to him by Cripps and Pethick–Lawrence.

17  Nehru's letters to Wavell and to Pethick-Lawrence, 25 May 1946, *TOP*, vol. 7, pp. 692–6, 708.

18  For the accusation against Nehru, see Azad, *India Wins Freedom*, pp. 162–7. There is discussion of the internal Congress background in Moore, *Escape from Empire*, pp. 157–161; and in Nanda, *Jawaharlal Nehru*, pp. 155–7.

19  On the processes of this election see Nanda, *Jawaharlal Nehru*, pp. 178–80; also article by Gandhi, 10 July 1946, *CWMG*, vol. 84, p. 429. Nehru's reluctance to stand was expressed in a letter to Krishna Menon, 5 Feb. 1946, *SWJN(1)*, vol. 14, pp. 150–1.

20  Gandhi to Nehru, 3 Sept. 1946, *CWMG*, vol. 85, p. 252.

21  A secret official report of the visit is in *TOP*, vol. 7, pp. 134–6. Nehru's speeches and reports to the CWC are in *SWJN(1)*, vol. 15, sec. 3. Nehru was at this stage thinking towards the future morale and efficiency of the Indian army, and was grateful that the Government of India had diffused the problem of the INA by not starting any more trials of former members. See Nehru to Auchinleck, 30 Apr. and 2 May 1946, ibid., pp. 88–9, 90–2.

22  Nehru to Padmaja Naidu, 20 June 1946, *SWJN(1)*, vol. 15, pp. 385–6; Nehru to Vijaylakshmi Pandit, 25 June 1946, ibid., p. 393.

23  Minutes of governors' conference, 8 Aug. 1946, *TOP*, vol. 8, pp. 204–11.

24  Wavell to Pethick-Lawrence, telegram, 4 Aug. 1946, *TOP*, vol. 8, pp. 190–1.

25   Sir F. Burrows to Wavell, Nehru to Wavell, both 22 Aug. 1946, *TOP*, vol. 8, pp. 293–303, 265–6. A senior ICS man in Bengal, P. D. Martyn, called the violence in Calcutta 'civil war'. See his unpublished, typewritten memoirs in the Indian Institute Library, Oxford, pp. 27–8; to this MS he appended a diary prepared from rough notes kept during the disturbances of 16–20 Aug. 1946, when he was Chief Controller of Relief Operations in Calcutta.

26   Wavell to Pethick-Lawrence, 13 Nov. 1946, *TOP*, vol. 9, pp. 58–9; Nehru to Padmaja Naidu, 7 Oct. 1945, *SWJN(2)*, vol. 1, p. 606.

27   Wavell to H.M. King George VI, 22 Oct. 1946, describing the previous three months, *TOP*, vol. 8, pp. 769–76.

28   Note by Wavell on the Interim Government, undated but probably for the incoming Viceroy in Mar. 1947, *TOP*, vol. 9, pp. 1009–11.

29   Nehru to Wavell, 21 Nov. 1945, M. O. Mathai Papers, 2A, File of Correspondence between Nehru and Wavell; Nehru to Vijayalakshmi Pandit, 5 Dec. 1946, *SWJN(2)*, vol. 1, p. 133.

30   Wavell to Pethick-Lawrence, 30 Oct. 1946, and note by Nehru on his Frontier visit, 24 Oct. 1946, *TOP*, vol. 8, pp. 844, 816–25.

31   Nehru to G. S. Bajpai, 5 Dec. 1946; also note of 20 Dec. 1946, *SWJN(2)*, vol. 1, pp. 549–50, 553–6.

32   See *SWJN(2)*, vol. 2, sec.11, iii.

33   For this statement, 6 Dec. 1946, see *TOP*, vol. 9, pp. 295–6; the documents on the London conference are collected in ch. 2.

34   Record of meeting in the Secretary of State's room, India Office, 4 Dec. 1946, *TOP*, vol. 9, p. 257. Nehru reiterated his belief that Jinnah did not want either democracy or socio-economic change in an interview with an American diplomat in Delhi, 13 Dec. 1947, *SWJN(2)*, vol. 1, p. 144.

35   Wavell's reading of Congress politics was that Gandhi, 'that inveterate enemy of the British', was behind the refusal to accept the British statement without qualifications; and he told the King that Gandhi, working in eastern India for non-violence, reminded him of 'a submarine re-charging its batteries on the surface well away from any hostile craft'. Wavell to HM King George VI, 24 Feb. 1947, *TOP*, vol. 9, p. 802.

36   Nehru to Padmaja Naidu, 5 Nov. 1946, *SWJN(2)*, vol. 1, p. 65.

37   Nehru to V. Patel, 5 Nov. 1947, J. Nehru Papers.

38   Nehru to Gandhi, 30 Jan. 1947, *SWJN(2)*, vol. 1, p. 111; see also Nehru to Gandhi, 10 Feb. 1947, *SWJN(2)*, vol. 2, p. 36.

39   Nehru to Gandhi, 28 Feb. 1947, *SWJN(2)*, vol. 2, p. 621. For a discussion of this episode in Gandhi's life see Brown, *Gandhi: Prisoner of Hope*, pp. 376–8.

40   Annex to minutes of cabinet meeting, 10 Dec. 1946, *TOP*, vol. 9, pp. 319–20.

41   *Wavell*, p. 417.

42   Statement of 20 Feb. 1947, *TOP*, vol. 9, pp. 773–5.

43   Viceroy's Personal Report No. 3 (Apr. 1947), *TOP*, vol. 10, p. 303. On Mountbatten's personality and career generally see P. Ziegler, *Mountbatten: The Official Biography* (Collins, Glasgow, 1985).

44   Mountbatten to Sir E. Jenkins, 19 June 1947, *TOP*, vol. 11, p. 508.

45   Nehru to Mountbatten, 27 Aug. 1947, *SWJN(2)*, vol. 4, p. 649.

46   The best life of Edwina Mountbatten is Janet Morgan, *Edwina Mountbatten: A Life of her Own* (HarperCollins, London, 1991); see also Ziegler, *Mountbatten*, pp. 473–5. Chandralekha, Nehru's niece, told her mother in early 1949 how marvellous it was to have

Edwina visiting her uncle, as she brought excitement, fun and laughter into the house, and it was like being in New York; letters dated 19 and 23 February 1949, Vijayalakshmi Pandit Papers.

47  Nehru to Gandhi, 25 Mar. 1947, *SWJN(2)*, vol. 2, pp. 77–8.

48  For Nehru's reaction see his quick note and considered letter to Mountbatten, both 11 May 1947, *TOP*, vol. 10, pp. 756–7, 766–71.

49  There is a lengthy and detailed account of these weeks of negotiations and the differences between the Viceroy's original plan and the London revise in Moore, *Escape from Empire*, ch. 4.

50  Viceroy's Personal Report No. 8, 5 June 1947, *TOP*, vol. 11, pp. 160–3; minutes of meetings of 2 and 3 June 1947, ibid., pp. 39–47, 72–8. The paper on the administrative consequences of partition by 15 Aug. is in ibid., pp. 54–8.

51  Text of Nehru's 3 June broadcast, *TOP*, vol. 11, pp. 94–7.

52  Viceroy's Personal Report No. 10, 27 June 1947, *TOP*, vol. 11, p. 687. *TOP*, vols 11 and 12, provides considerable detail on the setting up of the States Department and subsequent negotiations. See also Copland, *The Princes of India*, ch. 7. The most significant civil servant involved in the negotiations to bring the states into this limited accession to either of the two Dominions was V. P. Menon, who had earlier been vital in discussions with Mountbatten over the nature of any successor states. He wrote his own account of this phase in his *The Story of the Integration of the Indian States* (1956: Orient Longmans, Madras, 1961).

53  Report of interview between Mountbatten and Krishna Menon, 22 Apr. 1947, *TOP*, vol. 10. p. 373.

54  Mountbatten to the Resident, Kashmir, 28 June 1947, *TOP*, vol. 11, p. 720.

55  Patel to Nehru, 3 Aug. 1947, M. O. Mathai Papers, 2A, File of Correspondence between Nehru and V. Patel. For Mountbatten's concerns see Viceroy's Personal Report No. 15, 1 Aug. 1947, *TOP*, vol. 12, pp. 451–2.

56  Nehru to Krishna Menon, 22 July 1947, *SWJN(2)*, vol. 3, pp. 343–4.

57  Nehru to R. Prasad, 7 Aug. 1947, *SWJN(2)*, vol. 3, pp. 189–92.

58  Speech in Constituent Assembly, *SWJN(2)*, vol. 3, pp. 135–6. On the celebration of independence day on the subcontinent see ch. 2 of T. Y. Tan and G. Kudaisya, *The Aftermath of Partition in South Asia* (Routledge, London, 2000). Mountbatten's account is in his Personal Report No. 17, 16 Aug. 1947, *TOP*, vol. 12, pp. 769–74.

59  There is a growing literature on many aspects of partition and its immediate and long-term consequences. See, for example, Tan and Kudaisya, *The Aftermath of Partition*; Hasan, *India's Partition*; G. Pandey, *Remembering Partition: Violence, Nationalism and History in India* (CUP, Cambridge, 2001); I. Talbot, *Freedom's Cry: The Popular Dimension in the Pakistan Movement and Partition in North-West India* (OUP, Karachi, 1996). On the Sikhs see I. Copland, 'The Master and the Maharajas: the Sikh princes and the East Punjab massacres of 1947', *Modern Asian Studies*, 36 (part 3) (July 2002), pp. 657–704. A powerful memoir by a British ICS man in the Punjab at the time is P. Moon, *Divide and Quit* (University of California Press, Berkeley, 1962).

60  Letter of 28 Sept. cited in Ziegler, *Mountbatten*, p. 436.

61  Nehru to Mountbatten 27 and 31 Aug. 1947, *SWJN(2)*, vol. 4, pp. 25–6, 44–5.

62  Nehru to R. Prasad, 17 Sept. 1947, J. Nehru Papers post-1947, 2nd Instalment, File No. 231, Correspondence with R. Prasad.

63  Top secret note by Nehru for cabinet, 12 Septeber 1947, M. O. Mathai Papers, Subject File No. 20, Disturbances in Delhi (1947).

64    Nehru to K. P. S. Menon, 12 Oct. 1947, *SWJN(2)*, vol. 4, p. 585.

65    Letter, 27 June 1948, cited in Ziegler, *Mountbatten*, p. 445.

66    Nehru to V.Patel, 27 Sept. 1947, M.O. Mathai Papers, 2A, File of Correspondence between Nehru and V. Patel.

67    Nehru to Attlee, telegram, 25 Oct. 1947, *SWJN(2)*, vol. 4, p. 275; Speech in Delhi, 6 Nov. 1947, ibid., p. 319.

68    Nehru to Sri Prakasa, 25 Nov. 1947, *SWJN(2)*, vol. 4, p. 347.

69    Government of India Cabinet Defence Committee Decision, 26 Oct. 1947, *SWJN(2)*, vol. 4, pp. 276–7.

70    On this and subsequent events many of the major Indian sources can be found in *SWJN(2)*, vol. 4, sec. 4. An account drawing mainly on British sources is R. J. Moore, *Making the New Commonwealth* (Clarendon Press, Oxford, 1987), pp. 45ff. See also A. Lamb, *Incomplete Partition: The Genesis of the Kashmir Dispute 1947–1948* (Roxford Books, Hertingfordbury, 1992) and *Birth of a Tragedy: Kashmir 1947* (Roxford Books, Hertingfordbury, 1994).

71    Nehru to Attlee, telegram, 28 Oct. 1947, Nehru to T. B.Sapru, 1 Nov. 1947, *SWJN(2)*, vol. 4, pp. 287,304–5.

72    Nehru to V.Patel, 30 Oct. 1947, *SWJN(2)*, vol. 4, pp. 290–1.

73    Nehru's commitment to a UN-supervised plebiscite/referendum is clear from a letter to Sheikh Abdullah, 31 Oct. 1947, and a broadcast on All-India Radio, 2 Nov. 1947, *SWJN(2)*, vol. 4, pp. 295, 310. He reiterated this in a telegram to the Pakistan Prime Minister, 21 Nov. 1947, ibid., pp. 332–5.

74    Nehru to Sheikh Abdullah, 21 Nov. 1947, *SWJN(2)*, vol. 4, pp. 336–7.

75    Nehru to Mountbatten, 26 Dec. 1947, telegram to Attlee, 28 Dec. 1947, *SWJN(2)*, vol. 4, pp. 399–403, 406–7.

76    Cabinet minutes, 14 Jan. 1948, *SWJN(2)*, vol. 5, pp. 6–7; Nehru to V. Pandit, telegram, 15 Jan. 1948, ibid., pp. 9–10.

77    The clearest sign of a crisis in their relationship came in a letter from Nehru to Patel, 23 Dec. 1947, in which he said that if he could not have the freedom to act as he thought fit he ought rather to resign; *SWJN(2)*, vol. 4, pp. 538–9. Both men subsequently sent notes to Gandhi, in anticipation of a meeting with him, in which they laid out their views: Nehru's note, 6 Jan. 1948, *SWJN(2)*, vol. 5, pp. 471–5, Patel's note, n.d. but pre-12 Jan. 1948, is in S. Patel, *Sardar Patel's Correspondence 1945–50*, ed. D. Das (10 vols, Navajivan, Ahmedabad, 1971–4), vol. 6, pp. 21–4.

78    Interview between Mountbatten and Nehru, 5 Feb. 1948, *SWJN(2)*, vol. 5, pp. 480–2.

79    A. Campbell-Johnson, *Mission with Mountbatten* (Robert Hale, London, 1951), p. 275.

80    Nehru's broadcast, 30 Jan. 1948, *SWJN(2)*, vol. 5, pp. 35–6.

81    Vijayalakshmi Pandit's youngest daughter wrote to her mother who was Ambassador in Moscow, on 1 February 1948, describing the funeral and said that Nehru was looking lost and dazed; they were trying to look after him but it was not an easy task as he had been so devoted to Bapu: Vijayalakshmi Pandit Papers.

## Chapter 10    Imagining the Nation

1    Speech on 11 July 1954, *SWJN(2)*, vol. 26, p. 38.

2    A broadly chronological approach within a thematic framework serves well to analyse Nehru's life while he was involved in the politics of nationalist opposition, when there was a clear chronological progression in his own development and his role in

Congress, as well as in the politics of nationalism. But with independence his life remained in a sense stable as Prime Minister until his death, and a thematic treatment of his life more vividly portrays the issues he considered vital. It also enables the author to make difficult choices among the huge weight of published evidence which was generated by his work after 1947. Only one of the serious biographical studies of Nehru (Gopal, *Jawaharlal Nehru*) gives adequate weight to his prime ministership; and by adopting a chronological approach it not only runs to considerable length (two volumes out of three) but tends to obscure the key issues facing Nehru.

3   There is a significant literature on the processes of imagining the self and the other within the imperial context in India. A good starting point for British imagining is Metcalf, *Ideologies of the Raj*, which has a good bibliographical essay. For Indian perceptions of the western world and the British in particular, see T. Raychaudhuri, *Europe Reconsidered: Perceptions of the West in Nineteenth Century Bengal* (OUP, Delhi, 1988) and ch. 2 of his *Perceptions, Emotions, Sensibilities*; also Parekh, *Colonialism, Tradition and Reform.*

4   Nehru to Chief Ministers, 2 May 1950, Jawaharlal Nehru, *Letters to Chief Ministers 1947–1964,* ed. G. Parthasarathi (J. Nehru Memorial Fund, New Delhi, 1985–9) (henceforth *LCM*), vol. 2, pp. 83–4.

5   Convocation address at Aligarh Muslim University, 24 Jan. 1948, *SWJN(2)*, vol. 5, p. 26.

6   Nehru to Chief Ministers, 28 Sept. 1953, *LCM*, vol. 3, pp. 390–1.

7   Nehru to Chief Ministers, 15 Aug. 1954, *LCM*, vol. 4, p. 21.

8   Press interview, 27 Feb. 1946, *SWJN(1)*, vol. 15, pp. 10–11.

9   Nehru to Chief Ministers, 16 June 1952, 28 Sept. 1953, *LCM*, vol. 3, pp. 18–19, 392–3. (In the June letter he noted with warmth and appreciation the experiment in social democracy attempted in Britain after the Second World War and was clearly deeply influenced by this attempt to find a 'middle path' between private enterprise and capitalism on the one hand, and socialism on the other.)

10   Convocation address at Aligarh Muslim University, 24 Jan. 1948, *SWJN(2)*, vol. 5, p. 26.

11   Nehru to Clare Boothe–Luce, 1 July 1948, *SWJN(2)*, vol. 7, p. 703; speech in Chicago, 27 Oct. 1949, *SWJN(2)*, vol. 13, p. 359.

12   On these arrangements see a confidential note by Nehru, 2 Dec. 1963 to rebut criticisms of Indira Gandhi's apparent use of official facilities, enclosed in G. L. Nanda to T. T. Krishnamachari, 10 Dec. 1963, NMML, T. T. Krishnamachari Papers, File of correspondence with G. L. Nanda. On Indira's domestic separation from her husband and the eventual breakdown of their relationship, see Frank, *Indira.* There had been some discussion on the fate of Birla's house, where Gandhi had died. There was public pressure for it to be turned into a memorial, and Birla offered it to Nehru as his official residence. Nehru disliked the idea of living in the house with all its memories, and Patel was adamant that it would be wrong to yield to public pressure and force Birla out. For correspondence on this see J. Nehru Papers post-1947, 1st Instalment, File of correspondence with G. D. Birla, No. 43; M. O. Mathai Papers, 2A, File of Correspondence between Nehru and Patel; V. Patel to R. Prasad, 14 May 1948 with encs, R. Prasad, *Dr Rajendra Prasad: Correspondence and Select Documents,* ed. V. Choudhary (21 vols, Allied, New Delhi, 1984–95), vol. 9, pp. 65–71.

13   Nehru to V. Pandit, 19 Mar. 1955, J. Nehru Papers post-1947, 1st Instalment, File No. 327, Part II; Note to the Home Minister, 11 Apr. 1955, *SWJN(2)*, vol. 28, pp. 599–601.

14   Nehru to N. Medhi, 19 Mar. 1954, *SWJN(2)*, vol. 25, p. 210.

15    M. O. Mathai to G. D. Birla, 13 Oct. 1956, J. Nehru Papers post-1947, 1st Instalment, File No. 479.

16    Between 1946 and 1950 Nehru earned the considerable sum of Rs 1,23,304 in royalties: see note on tax affairs from Mathai to Nehru, 26 July 1950, M. O. Mathai Papers, 2A, Subject Files, File No. 29. Evidence from later in the 1950s suggests that the royalty income continued to be very significant.

17    Top secret note on Nehru's attitude to the US, 2 Nov. 1950, in the Department of State, now declassified in the US National Archives. I owe this reference to Professor Wm. R. Louis.

18    Speech in Delhi, 6 Sept. 1951, *SWJN(2)*, vol. 16, ii, p. 71.

19    Nehru to G. B. Pant, 16 Sept. 1954, *SWJN(2)*, vol. 26, p. 609; Pant to Nehru, 22 Sept. 1954, G. B. Pant, *Selected Works of Govind Ballabh Pant*, ed. B. R. Nanda, vol. 15, (OUP, New Delhi, 2001), pp. 194–5.

20    Nehru to N. Chaudhuri, 21 Aug. 1953, *SWJN(2)*, vol. 23, pp. 260–1.

21    Sri Prakasa to Nehru, 14/16 Feb. 1952, J. Nehru Papers post-1947, 2nd Instalment, File of Correspondence with Sri Prakasa, No. 280.

22    Nehru to M. C. Khanna, 6 June 1949, *SWJN(2)*, vol. 11, p. 81.

23    Nehru to Chief Ministers, 1 Apr. 1950, *LCM*, vol. 2, p. 61.

24    Nehru to Rajagopalachariar, 25 July 1951, J. Nehru Papers post-1947, 2nd Instalment, File of Correspondence with C. Rajagopalachariar, No. 230.

25    Nehru to Patel, 26 Mar. 1950, Patel's reply, 28 Mar. 1950, *Sardar Patel's Correspondence*, vol. 10, pp. 9–14, 14–22.

26    Mountbatten to Patel, 16 Apr. 1950, ibid., pp. 89–91. Patel recounted his two-day visit to Calcutta in a letter of 18 Apr. 1950, ibid., pp. 117–19.

27    Nehru to Sri Prakasa, 16 Apr. 1950, *SWJN(2)*, vol. 14 ii, p. 52. Tandon believed that the Indian nation had to be rooted in a reinvigorated Hindu society, and, opposing Gandhian non-violence, he had been closely connected with local organisations in UP which pursued a strategy of cultivating physical fitness and organising volunteers for the defence of the national community. His career was one of many which demonstrated the range of interpretations of the 'nation' within the Congress, and the interpenetration of the Congress by those far more deeply rooted in Hindu society and thought than Nehru. See W. Gould, 'Congress radicals and Hindu militancy: Sampurnanand and Purushottam Das Tandon in the politics of the United Provinces, 1930–1947', *Modern Asian Studies*, 36 (part 3) (July 2002), pp. 619–55.

28    Nehru to Tandon, 8 Aug. 1950, to Patel, 9 Aug. 1950 and enc. draft statement of withdrawal from contest, *SWJN(2)*, vol. 15, i, pp. 90–2, 92–4, 94–5. These and other key documents are also in *Sardar Patel's Correspondence*, vol. 10, pp. 187–228. Many of the originals are in J. Nehru Papers post-1947, 2nd Instalment, Subject File No. 34, 3rd Instalment, File No. 42 (Congress Presidential elections 1950–2).

29    Details of this turbulent period are in S. A. Kochanek, *The Congress Party of India: The Dynamics of One-Party Democracy* (Princeton University Press, Princeton, 1968), ch. 2. Many of the key sources are in the relevant vols of *SWJN(2)*. Key files in the J. Nehru post-1947 papers are 2nd Instalment, Correspondence Files with P. Tandon (No. 287) and B. C. Roy (No. 248).

30    Nehru to B. C. Roy, 17 Aug. 1951, J. Nehru Papers post-1947, 2nd instalment, File of Correspondence with B. C. Roy, No. 248; Nehru to P. D. Tandon, 9 Aug. 1951, *SWJN(2)*, vol. 16, ii, pp. 157–9. (His formal resignation had been three days earlier.)

31 J. Kripalani to Nehru, 22 Dec. 1952, J. Nehru Papers post-1947, 2nd Instalment, File of Correspondence with J. B. Kripalani.

32 Nehru wrote to his Chief Ministers of his state of mind on 1 and 10 Oct. 1954, and in the latter enclosed a letter from him to PCC Presidents, 10 Oct. 1954, when he raised the idea of retirement; *LCM*, vol. 4, pp. 55, 63–4, 65–8. See also G. D. Birla to M. O. Mathai, 2 Oct. 1954, NMML, G. D. Birla Papers, correspondence with J. Nehru; Krishna Menon to Nehru, 29 Oct. 1954, Nehru's reply, 6 Nov. 1954, M. O. Mathai Papers, 2A, Subject Files, No. 35.

33 Speech in Constituent Assembly, 13 Dec. 1946, *SWJN(2)*, vol. 1, pp. 240–51.

34 For a detailed discussion of the making of the constitution, see G. Austin, *The Indian Constitution: Cornerstone of a Nation* (1966; OUP, Bombay, 1972).

35 Congress 1951 election manifesto, *SWJN(2)*, vol. 16, ii, pp. 3–13.

36 Nehru to C.D. Deshmukh, 14 Oct. 1951, *SWJN(2)*, vol. 16, p. 46.

37 Nehru to G.B. Pant, 25 Oct. 1951; also Nehru to Chief Ministers, 1 and 30 Nov. 1951, *LCM*, vol. 2, pp. 519, 530–1. Mohanlal Saxena a decade later reminded Nehru of the days and night spent scrutinising the lists of candidates sent in by PCCs, how even Nehru had had to give in to the wishes of Chief Ministers: Saxena to Nehru, 25 Oct. 1961, J. Nehru Papers post-1947, 2nd Instalment, File of Correspondence with M. Saxena, No. 251.

38 A selection of his speeches on tour is in *SWJN(2)*, vol. 17, pp. 47–90. For his personal sense of exhilaration see Nehru to Stafford Cripps, 6 Jan. 1952, J. Nehru Papers post-1947, 2nd Instalment, File of Correspondence with Stafford Cripps, No. 74.

39 He expounded the symbolism of the national flag, for example, in the press and in the Constituent Assembly in 1947, *SWJN(2)*, vol. 3, pp. 46–7, 66–73.

40 See the March 1955 correspondence in J. Nehru Papers post-1947, 1st Instalment, File No. 330, Pt. I.

41 Nehru to G. B. Pant, 26 May 1955, *SWJN(2)*, vol. 28, p. 519.

42 Nehru to Jagjivan Ram, 7 Oct. 1956, J. Nehru Papers post-1947, 1st Instalment, File No. 478.

43 Nehru to Chief Ministers, 19 Dec. 1949, *LCM*, vol. 1, pp. 507–9.

44 Note by Nehru to M. O. Mathai, 10 Apr. 1955, M. O. Mathai Papers, 2A, Subject File, No. 29.

45 On Ayodhya see *SWJN(2)*, vol. 14, ii, pp. 293–7. An important collection of historical essays on this issue, published just before the violence which broke out when Hindus tore down the mosque in 1992, is S. Gopal (ed.), *Anatomy of a Confrontation: The Babri Masjid-Ramjanmabhumi Issue* (Penguin, New Delhi, 1990).

46 For Prasad's stance see Prasad to Nehru, 10 Mar. 1951, to K. N. Katju, 25 Apr. 1951, *Dr Rajendra Prasad: Correspondence*, vol. 14, pp. 37–8,52–3; for Nehru's views see *SWJN(2)*, vol. 16, i, pp. 603–12.

47 Nehru to Chief Ministers, 20 Feb. and 15 Apr. 1948, *LCM*, vol. 1, pp. 71–2, 103–4.

48 Nehru to Chief Ministers, 15 Apr. 1948, *LCM*, vol. 1, pp. 104–5. (The architect was Otto Koenigsberger, a German town planner who was the Government of India's Director of Housing, 1948–51.)

49 There is an excellent discussion of Chandigarh and its meaning for Nehru in S. Khilnani, *The Idea of India* (1997; Farrar Straus Giroux, New York,1998), pp. 130–5.

50 For Nehru's concerns on this issue, see, for example, relating to early 1948, *SWJN(2)*, vol. 5, pp. 113–23. An important discussion of this issue is R. Menon and K. Bhasin, 'Recovery, rupture, resistance: the Indian state and the abduction of women during

Partition', ch. 10 of M. Hasan (ed.), *Inventing Boundaries: Gender, Politics and the Partition of India* (OUP, New Delhi, 2000). See also Pandey, *Remembering Partition*.

51   Congress election manifesto, 1951, *SWJN(2)*, vol. 16, ii, p. 12.

52   Nehru to Chief Ministers, 18 May 1952, *LCM*, vol. 2, p. 614.

53   See Attlee to Nehru (secret), 14 May 1948, M. O. Mathai Papers, 2A, File of Correspondence between Nehru and Attlee; Sri Prakasa to Nehru, 3 Feb. 1956, T. T. Krishnamachari Papers, File of Correspondence with Nehru (1956).

54   Speech in Chicago, 27 Oct. 1949, *SWJN(2)*, vol. 13, p. 359.

# Chapter 11   Structuring the Nation

1   See B. Parekh, 'Jawaharlal Nehru and the crisis of modernisation', ch. 2 of U. Baxi & B. Parekh (eds), *Crisis and Change in Contemporary India* (Sage, London, 1995).

2   The nature of the states in comparison with the former provinces of British India is dealt with in the second section of this chapter. On the constitution see Austin, *The Indian Constitution*, and (more succinctly) chs 3 and 4 of R. L. Hardgrave Jr, *India: Government and Politics in a Developing Nation*, 3rd edn (Harcourt Brace Jovanovich, New York, 1980).

3   K. M. Pannikkar to Nehru, 10 June 1953, and enc. undated note, J. Nehru Papers post-1947, 1st Instalment, File No. 483.

4   An important study of the shifts in the prime ministerial role is J. Manor (ed.), *Nehru to the Nineties: The Changing Office of Prime Minister in India* (Hurst, London, 1994).

5   Nehru's article in *Asia*, New York, June 1936, *SWJN(1)*, vol. 7, pp. 640–2; Nehru to L. K. Elmhirst, 21 Mar. 1939, *SWJN(1)*, vol. 9, p. 325.

6   Patel to Nehru, 27 Apr. 1948, original is in M. O. Mathai Papers, 2A, File of Correspondence between Patel and Nehru. See also Potter, *India's Political Administrators*, pp. 146–9. (Potter's study shows in detail the many similarities between the members of the ICS and their successors in independent India.)

7   Nehru to B. C. Roy, 7 May 1950, *SWJN(2)*, vol. 14 ii, p. 103; Nehru to Krishna Menon, 12 Aug. 1949, *SWJN(2)*, vol. 12, p. 465.

8   Nehru to Patel, 4 Mar. 1950, *SWJN(2)*, vol. 14, i, p. 462.

9   Sampurnanand to Nehru, 21 Apr. 1951, enclosing a forceful twenty-page note on the present situation, J. Nehru Papers post-1947, 3rd Instalment, File No. 43.

10   See the material in T. T. Krishnamachari Papers collected in files of correspondence with Nehru and G. B. Pant, and Subject File No. 9.

11   Nehru wrote to his Chief Ministers forcefully about Appleby's report in 1953; see letters of 19 Apr., 28 Sept., 17 Oct., 6 Nov. and enc., *LCM*, vol. 3, pp. 296–7, 392, 402–3, 413–4, 424–31.

12   Nehru note to Cabinet Ministers and others, 30 Sept. 1954, *SWJN(2)*, vol. 26, p. 114. In 1955 he wrote a note for the Cabinet Secretary, 11 Mar., expressing 'acute frustration' at the failure to make progress on budgetary and financial control despite months of discussion: J. Nehru Papers post-1947, 1st Instalment, File No. 325, Pt I.

13   On the discussions in the CWC which led to the creation of the Planning Commission, see Kochanek, *The Congress Party of India*, pp. 139–43.

14   Nehru to T. T. Krishnamachari, 29 and 30 Dec. 1953, *SWJN(2)*, vol. 24, pp. 136, 137–8.

15   Nehru to the Deputy Chairman of the Planning Commission, V. T. Krishnamachari, 6 Nov. 1953, *SWJN(2)*, vol. 24, pp. 128–9.

16  Nehru to Chief Ministers, 28 Sept. 1954, *LCM*, vol. 3, p. 394.

17  Message from Nehru on the creation of the new ministry, 20 Sept. 1956, J. Nehru Papers post-1947, 1st Instalment, File No. 475.

18  On the effectiveness of the new institutions of *panchayati raj*, see Hardgrave, *India*, pp. 105–9; A. H. Hanson and J. Douglas, *India's Democracy* (Weidenfeld & Nicolson, London, 1972), pp. 184–207.

19  Note by Nehru to N. R. Pillai, Secretary General of the Ministry of External Affairs, 11 June 1954, *SWJN(2)*, vol. 26, pp. 438–40.

20  Nehru to Morarji Desai, 12 Aug. 1954, *SWJN(2)*, vol. 26, pp. 449–50. There is important evidence on Nehru's discomfort over Goa, and his refusal to be pushed into action in J. Nehru Papers post–1947, 1st instalment, File Nos 329, Pt II, and 330, Pt I; and in NMML, AICC Papers post-1947, 2nd Instalment, Congress President's Correspondence File, 1955, No. 4307.

21  Nehru to Chief Ministers, 17 Mar. 1948, *LCM*, vol. 1, p. 88; Nehru to V. Pandit, 25 Mar. 1948, *SWJN(2)*, vol. 5, p. 575.

22  Nehru to Krishna Menon, 29 Aug. 1948, *SWJN(2)*, vol. 7, p. 223.

23  Speech in the Constituent Assembly, 7 Sept. 1948, *SWJN(2)*, vol. 7, pp. 228–33.

24  Moore, *Making the New Commonwealth*, pp. 85–7. (Conservative critics of Nehru included Churchill, Halifax – who as Lord Irwin had been Viceroy – and R. A. Butler, of a family with famous and long-standing connections to India and with the Nehru family itself.)

25  Nehru to Sri Prakasa, 24 Sept. 1948, *SWJN(2)*, vol. 7, pp. 267–8.

26  Primary sources showing Nehru's unfolding attitude to the resolution of the international aspect of the Kashmir issue are in the relevant volumes of *SWJN(2)*. Two useful accounts which take the conflict to the point of the cease-fire are chs 2 and 3 of Moore, *Making the New Commonwealth*, and C. Dasgupta, *War and Diplomacy in Kashmir 1947–48* (Sage, London, 2002). A recent work which puts the Kashmir problem in a broader context and a longer time frame is S. Das, *Kashmir And Sindh: Nation-Building, Ethnicity and Regional Politics in South Asia* (Anthem Press, London, 2001).

27  R. Prasad to Nehru, 14 July 1953, *Dr Rajendra Prasad: Correspondence*, vol. 16, pp. 90–5; Nehru to C. C. Desai, India's High Commissioner in Pakistan (1955–8), 27 Feb. 1955, J. Nehru Papers post-1947, 1st Instalment, File No. 321, Pt I.

28  Nehru to Cripps, 17 Dec. 1948, in reply to letter of 10 Dec. 1948, both in J. Nehru Papers, 2nd Instalment, File of Correspondence with Cripps, No. 74. See also Nehru to Vijayalakshmi Pandit, 25 June 1951, Vijayalakshmi Pandit Papers, in which he reiterated the importance of Kashmir and that it was not just 'a patch of territory'. He also indicated his anger at the attitudes of the UK and US governments.

29  For Nehru's despair at the collapse of his Kashmir strategy see his letters to Shaikh Abdullah, 27 Apr. and 28 June 1953, *SWJN(2)*, vol. 22, pp. 212–14, 193–9. Ibid., vol. 23 has a long section of important documents on the critical period in mid-summer before Abdullah was replaced. Evidence of Abdullah's deteriorating relations with the Government of India, and of internal Kashmiri politics is in J. Nehru Papers post-1947, 2nd Instalment, Subject File No. 27 – Kashmir.

30  Aide-memoire from Govt of Pakistan, 22 Nov. 1956, Nehru's note for the Ministry of External Affairs, 22 Nov. 1956, J. Nehru Papers post-1947, 1st Instalment, File No. 490.

31  For the modes of integration see table 1 in W. Richter, 'Traditional rulers in post-traditional societies: the princes of India and Pakistan', ch. 10 of R. Jeffrey (ed.), *People,*

*Princes and Paramount Power: Society and Politics in the Indian Princely States* (OUP, Delhi, 1978). See also Copland, *The Princes of India*, pp. 261–8.

32   See letters from Nehru to the princely governors, and from G. B. Pant as Home Minister, to them, both on 4 Oct. 1956, J. Nehru Papers post-1947, 1st Instalment, File No. 477.

33   Nehru wrote to the princes on 10 Sept. 1953 and 15 June 1954; these letters and reports on the replies are in J. Nehru Papers post-1947, 3rd Instalment, File Nos. 85 and 88.

34   Nehru to Bhopal, 25 May 1954, *SWJN(2)*, vol. 25, pp. 268–71.

35   Nehru to Nizam of Hyderabad, 6 Oct. 1956, J. Nehru Papers post-1947, 1st Instalment, File No. 478.

36   For a broad discussion of Nehru and many aspect of language see R. D. King, *Nehru and the Language Politics of India* (OUP, Delhi, 1997). The Constitution specified fourteen major vernacular languages in India. This did not include English, spoken by a great number of the educated, and the many dialects also spoken by thousands not exposed to the 'standard' modern vernaculars produced by education and print.

37   Nehru's reply to a question in the Constituent Assembly, 27 Nov. 1947, *SWJN(2)*, vol. 4, pp. 530–2.

38   Draft prepared by Nehru in Mar. 1949 and later adopted by the committee and by Congress, *SWJN(2)*, vol. 10, pp. 128–37,

39   Nehru to Chief Ministers, 14 May 1949, *LCM*, vol. 1, pp. 351–2.

40   Nehru to K. N. Katju, 8 Sept. 1953, *SWJN(2)*, vol. 23, pp. 198–200.

41   Gandhi's plan for Congress is in AICC Papers, File No. G-43, Pt 2 (1947–8). There is evidence of considerable discussion in Congress before this in File No. 34 (1946–7), No. G-11, Pt 1 (1947–8), No. 27 (1947); also in Rajendra Prasad Papers, File No. 16-P/45–46–47, Col. No. 1.

42   Two helpful discussions on Nehru and Congress are Parekh's discussion in Baxi and Parekh, *Crisis and Change*, and R. Jeffrey, 'The prime minister and the ruling party', ch. 9 of J. Manor, *Nehru to the Nineties*.

43   Remarks at conference of constructive workers, 13 Mar. 1948, *SWJN(2)*, vol. 5, p. 74.

44   Nehru to B. C. Roy, 22 June 1949, J. Nehru Papers post-1947, 2nd Instalment, File of Correspondence with B. C. Roy, No. 248.

45   Speech at Congress session, Kalyani, 23 Jan. 1954, *SWJN(2)*, vol. 24, p. 372; see also speech in Madras, 27 Nov. 1951, *SWJN(2)*, vol. 17, p. 50.

46   Nehru to Rajendra Prasad, 8 Dec. 1949, *Dr Rajendra Prasad: Correspondence*, vol. 11, pp. 185–8.

47   Nehru to Krishna Menon, 15 June 1949, *SWJN(2)*, vol. 11, pp. 153–4; Nehru to Lal Bahadur Sastri, 27 Dec. 1953, J. Nehru Papers post-1947, 2nd Instalment, File of Correspondence with L. B. Sastri, No. 143.

48   Nehru to Sri Krishna Sinha, 20 June 1954, *SWJN(2)*, vol. 26, pp. 243–6.

49   Speech to UP party workers, 21 May 1955, *SWJN(2)*, vol. 28, p. 91.

50   A useful guide to some of the literature on Congress as a party 'system' is in Hargrave, *India*, pp. 148–53. On Nehru and the Communists see Zoya Hasan, 'The prime minister and the left', ch. 10 of Manor, *Nehru to the Nineties*. For evidence of Nehru's private correspondence with former Congress colleagues who had now parted company with Congress to form separate Socialist parties, see J. Nehru Papers post-1947, 2nd Instalment, Files of Correspondence with J. P. Narayan (No. 127) and J. B. Kripalani (No. 141).

51   See part 3 of Kochanek, *The Congress Party of India*; and Weiner, *Party Building in a New Nation*.

## Chapter 12    Forging the Nation

1    Nehru to Chief Ministers, 4 Oct. 1948, *LCM*, vol. 1, p. 212.

2    See M. Hasan, *Legacy of a Divided Nation: India's Muslims since Independence* (OUP, New Delhi, 2001).

3    Nehru to Nawab of Bhopal, 9 July 1948, *SWJN(2)*, vol. 7, pp. 4–9; Nehru to Chief Ministers, 1 Mar. 1950, *LCM*, vol. 2, p. 41.

4    Nehru to M. Saxena, 19 Sept. 1949, J. Nehru Papers post-1947, 2nd Instalment, File of Correspondence with M. Saxena, No. 251.

5    Nehru to G. B. Pant, 19 Jan. 1952, *SWJN(2)*, vol. 17, p. 397; Nehru to Chief Ministers, special letter, 20 Nov. 1953, 26 Apr. 1954, *LCM*, vol. 3, pp. 451–2, 535–6.

6    Nehru to R. S. Shukla, 20 Mar. 1954, *SWJN(2)*, vol. 25, pp. 226–7; Nehru to Chief Ministers, 20 Sept. 1953, *LCM*, vol. 3, pp. 377–9.

7    Interview with the *Catholic Herald*, early 1946, *SWJN(1)*, vol. 15, p. 171.

8    Nehru to Chief Ministers, 20 Sept. 1953, *LCM*, vol. 3, pp. 376–7; also letter of 17 Oct. 1952, ibid., pp. 133–4.

9    On the Goa dimension to the treatment of Indian Christians see secret note by Nehru for the Ministry of External Affairs, 14 Mar. 1955, of meeting with the Cardinal Archbishop of Bombay and other Catholic bishops, J. Nehru Papers post-1947, 1st Instalment, File No. 326, Pt I; also Nehru to U. Dhebar, 27 May 1955, AICC Papers post-1947, 2nd Instalment, Congress President's Correspondence File, 1955, No. 4307.

10    For Nehru's attitude see an important policy note to the Ministry of Home Affairs, 25 Oct. 1953, *SWJN(2)*, vol. 24, pp. 322–5.

11    Nehru to R. Prasad, 10 Aug. 1953, *SWJN(2)*, vol. 23, pp. 245–7.

12    Letter from Cardinal Archbishop of Bombay to Nehru's Private Secretary, 10 Mar. 1955, J. Nehru Papers post-1947, 1st Instalment, File No. 325, Pt I; secret note by Nehru for Ministry of External Affairs, 14 Mar. 1955, of meeting with Cardinal Archbishop of Bombay and other Catholic bishops, ibid., File No. 326 Pt I.

13    Nehru to U. Dhebar, 27 May 1955, Dhebar to Nehru, 4 June 1955, AICC Papers post-1947, 2nd Instalment, Congress President's Correspondence File, 1955, No. 4307. In 1957 Dhebar also reported to Nehru (25–6 Aug. ) that in Bombay and Andhra Congress could not be persuaded to include Christians on their electoral slates, ibid, Congress President's Correspondence File, 1957, No. 4309.

14    Nehru's assurance to the Naga Hills National Council, printed in the *National Herald*, 6 Aug. 1946, *SWJN(1)*, vol. 15, pp. 278–80; letter to Phizo signed by Nehru's private secretary, *SWJN(2)*, vol. 16, ii, p. 434; Nehru, reporting on his meeting with Phizo, to B. N. Medhi, Chief Minister of Assam, 13 Mar. 1952, *SWJN(2)*, vol. 17, pp. 385–6.

15    Nehru to B. N. Medhi, 2 Feb. 1951, *SWJN(2)*,vol. 15, ii, pp. 182–7. (Interestingly he noted British policy in New Zealand towards Maoris.)

16    Enclosed detailed note on his recent tour of NEFA in Nehru to Chief Ministers, 30 Oct. 1952, *LCM*, vol. 3, pp. 147–65.

17    See R. Guha, *Savaging the Civilized: Verrier Elwin, his Tribals, and India* (OUP, New Delhi, 1999).

18    Nehru to B. N. Medhi, 9 Mar. 1955; note, 9 Mar. 1955, by Nehru for all cabinet ministers; both in J. Nehru Papers post-1947, 1st Instalment, File No. 324.

19    Speech on 19 Mar. 1955, *SWJN(2)*, vol. 28, pp. 33–4.

20　Nehru to Charan Singh (then a UP minister, who had suggested that government officers and legislators should be asked to marry outside their caste), 27 May 1954, *SWJN(2)*, vol. 25, pp. 153–4.

21　On Nehru and the Hindu Code Bill see L. Sarkar, 'Jawaharlal Nehru and the Hindu Code Bill', ch. 5 of B. R. Nanda (ed. ), *Indian Women: From Purdah to Modernity* (Sangam Books, London, 1990); R. Som, 'Jawaharlal Nehru and the Hindu Code: a victory of symbol over substance?', *Modern Asian Studies*, 28 (part 1) (Feb. 1994), pp. 165–94.

22　K. N. Katju to R. Prasad, 21 Aug. 1948, *Dr. Rajendra Prasad: Correspondence*, vol. 10, p. 56. The controversy between Nehru and Prasad is documented in ibid., vol. 9, pp. 220, 223, 240–1, 251, 265, 266–7.

23　For the imminent constitutional crisis see letters which passed between Nehru and Prasad between 15 and 21 Sept. 1951, ibid., vol. 14, pp. 104, 292–7, 104–6, 107–9, 110.

24　Nehru to Chief Ministers, 4 Oct. 1951, *LCM*, vol. 2, pp. 501–2.

25　Nehru to Chief Ministers, 15 June 1956, *LCM*, vol. 4, p. 384: his comment about the importance of these reforms is cited in Som, 'Jawaharlal Nehru and tthe Hindu Code', p. 189.

26　Nehru to R. Prasad, 22 July 1948, *SWJN(2)*, vol. 7, pp. 490–1.

27　Nehru to Chief Ministers, 15 July, 9 Sept. 1948, *LCM*, vol. 1, pp. 158, 205; Nehru to Patel, 27 Oct. 1948, *SWJN(2)*, vol. 8, p. 288.

28　Note to Home Minister, 25 July 1950, *SWJN(2)*, vol. 14, ii, p. 223.

29　Nehru to Chief Ministers, 16 June 1952, *LCM*, vol. 3, p. 21. On the first amendment to the constitution see ch. 3. of G. Austin, *Working a Democratic Constitution: The Indian Experience* (OUP, New Delhi, 1999).

30　P. Reeves, 'The Congress and the abolition of zamindari in Uttar Pradesh', in J. Masselos (ed. ), *Struggling And Ruling: The Indian National Congress 1885–1985* (Oriental University Press, London, 1987), pp. 154–67.

31　F. T. Jannuzi, *Agrarian Crisis in India: The Case of Bihar* (University of Texas Press, Austin, 1974).

32　Nehru to Chief Ministers, 5 July 1952, *LCM*, vol. 3, pp. 37–8.

33　See ch. 5 of Januzzi, *Agrarian Crisis in India*.

34　Nehru to G. Nanda, letter, 8 Sept. 1952, note, 22 Sept. 1952, *SWJN(2)*, vol. 19, pp. 102, 119–21.

35　Speech on Basic Education at Congress, 23 Jan. 1955, *SWJN(2)*, vol. 28, pp. 291–5.

36　J. P. Naik, 'Education', in S. C. Dube (ed. ), *India since Independence: Social Report on India 1947–1972* (Vikas, New Delhi, 1977), pp. 240–62.

37　Speech, 19 Mar. 1955, *SWJN(2)*, vol. 28, p. 33.

38　Message to conference on planned parenthood, 14 Oct. 1952, *SWJN(2)*, vol. 19, pp. 174–5; Nehru's lack of understanding of the significance of the growth rate was evident in a press conference in London, 8 June 1953, *SWJN(2)*, vol. 22, p. 174.

39　Nehru to Chief Ministers, 22 Dec. 1952, *LCM*, vol. 3, pp. 203–6.

40　Nehru to Chief Ministers, 3 Mar. 1953, *LCM*, vol. 3, pp. 252–5.

41　Nehru to Chief Ministers, 14 Apr. 1955, 16 Jan. 1956, *LCM*, vol. 4, pp. 155, 337.

42　Two good introductions to Nehru's vision of the role of planning are ch. 11 of Nanda, *Jawaharlal Nehru*; and B. R. Nayar, 'The economic policy of Jawaharlal Nehru', in M. Israel (ed.), *Nehru and the Twentieth Century*, South Asian Studies Papers 4 (University of Toronto, Toronto, 1991), pp. 142–72.

43　For documents relating to this controversy, in which the Planning Commission was a key issue, see *SWJN(2)*, vol. 14, ii, pp. 227–50.

44   An excellent introduction to economic policy from the end of the war through the Nehru years is ch. 4 of Tomlinson, *The Economy of Modern India*; more detailed on decision-making is F. R. Frankel, *India's Political Economy, 1947–1977: The Gradual Revolution* (Princeton University Press, Princeton, 1978).

45   Speech in the Constituent Assembly, 7 Apr. 1948, *SWJN(2)*, vol. 6, pp. 297–304.

46   Draft resolution for the CWC cited in Kochanek, *The Congress Party of India*, p. 141.

47   Frankel, *India's Political Economy*, p. 132.

48   Tarlok Singh had worked in a Punjab district suffering from famine before independence and wrote a book entitled *Poverty and Social Change: A Study in the Reorganization of Indian Rural Society* (1945) before becoming Nehru's personal secretary from Sept. 1946 to Sept. 1947. From then until the end of 1949 he supervised the resettlement of refugees from Pakistan in the Punjab, and in Mar. 1950 became Deputy Secretary of the Planning Commission. He only resigned from it in 1967. Subsequently he published a new edition of his earlier work with a reappraisal, and also *India's Development Experience* (Macmillan India, Delhi, 1974).

49   Nehru's draft resolutions for the Avadi Congress, *SWJN(2)*, vol. 27, pp. 255–61; nos. 1 and 5 were the key ones on the economy and the goal of policy.

50   Nehru to PCC Presidents, 9 Mar. 1955, *SWJN(2)*, vol. 28, pp. 539–43.

51   See J. S. Mehta, 'The Nehru we loved to serve: a personal nostalgia', in Israel, *Nehru and the Twentieth Century*, pp. 232–55.

# Chapter 13   Creating an International Identity

1   Speech at Agra, 7 July 1953, *SWJN(2)*, vol. 23, p. 28.

2   See S. Ganguly, 'The Prime Minister and foreign and defence policies', ch. 7 of Manor, *Nehru to the Nineties*. J. S. Mehta writes of the failure of higher civil servants to question Nehru, and their 'willing suspension of critical analysis' on crucial policy issues: 'Nehru's failure with China: intellectual naïveté or the wages of prophetic vision', in Israel, *Nehru and the Twentieth Century*.

3   Debate in Constituent Assembly, 4 Dec. 1947, *SWJN(2)*, vol. 4, pp. 594–603.

4   Some of the early statements of the emerging policy are Nehru's guidelines for the Indian position in the UN General Assembly, 12 Sept. 1948, *SWJN(2)*, vol. 7, pp. 609–14; note on foreign policy obviously for use by President of Congress, 2 Dec. 1948, *SWJN(2)*, vol. 8, pp. 325–8; speech in Constituent Assembly, 8 Mar. 1949, *SWJN(2)*, vol. 10, pp. 443–57. There is a helpful chapter (no. 12) on Nehru and nonalignment in Nanda, *Jawaharlal Nehru*.

5   M. W. Childs, *Witness to Power* (McGraw Hill, New York, 1975), p. 133, noting a long talk he had with Nehru in 1951.

6   Nehru's mature views are evident in important private letters to the industrialist G. D. Birla, who needed unofficial foreign policy briefings for his travels in Europe, UK and the USA. See Nehru to G. D. Birla, 21 May 1954, 6 June 1956, and a note by Nehru on Indo-US relations, 26 Feb. 1956, NMML, G. D. Birla Papers, Correspondence with J. Nehru.

7   Note from the Ministry of External Affairs, 16 Feb. 1955, describing how the new Foreign Service was put together, J. Nehru Papers post-1947, 1st Instalment, File No. 321, Pt I. For early difficulties with the Foreign Service see also G. S. Bajpai to Vijayalakshmi Pandit, 17 January 1948, 25 July 1951, Vijayalakshmi Pandit Papers.

8    Nehru to C. D. Deshmukh, 19 July 1951, J. Nehru Papers post-1947, 2nd Instalment, File of Correspondence with C. D. Deshmukh, No. 77.

9    Nehru to C. D. Deshmukh, 26 Jan. 1952, ibid.

10   See Amrit Kaur's reports to Nehru on Menon's 'collapsed' state, 31 May and 27 June 1951, J. Nehru Papers post-1947, 2nd Instalment, File of Correspondence with Amrit Kaur, No. 18. M. O. Mathai made similar reports, see Nehru to Mathai, 29 Sept. 1951, SWJN(2), vol. 16, ii, pp. 751–2. Nehru's exhortations to Menon to take six months' sick leave are 25 July, 25 Aug., 14 Oct. 1951 and telegram, 26 Oct. 1951, ibid., pp. 746–8, 748–51, 752–5, 756.

11   T. J. S. George, *Krishna Menon: A Biography* (Jonathan Cape, London, 1964) p. 167. Menon also made life difficult for his successors in London, including Nehru's sister, by maintaining his political contacts there and by-passing the Indian High Commissioner of the day. She claimed that Indian supporters of his in London also circulated rumours denigrating her, and urged her brother to see that there was another side to Menon than the one he saw. Vijayalakshmi to Nehru, note of 8 July 1955, letter of 4 February 1957, Vijayalakshmi Pandit Papers.

12   *New York Times*, 21 Dec. 1961; a report on Kennedy's frank talk with Nehru about Menon on 8 November is in ibid., 9 Nov. 1961. For considerable insight into Menon's views see M. Brecher, *India and World Politics: Krishna Menon's View of the World* (OUP, London, 1968). Much of this book consists of revealing dialogues between the author and Menon on a range of significant foreign policy issues; it also indicates the closeness of Menon to Nehru and the free hand Menon often had in implementing broad policy.

13   Nehru to Indira, 28 Oct. 1948, Gandhi, *Two Alone, Two Together*, pp. 560–1.

14   *New York Times*. 16 Dec. 1956.

15   V. Pandit, *The Scope of Happiness*, pp. 251–4.

16   CIA profile in 1948 in the papers of President Truman's Secretary, Harry Truman Library, cited in A. J. Rotter, *Comrades At Odds: The United States and India, 1947–1964* (Cornell University Press, Ithaca and London, 2000), p. 194. This study attempts to analyse and interpret Indo-US relations in terms of culture, particular the images each had of the other.

17   Dean Acheson, *Present at the Creation: My Years in the State Department* (W. W. Norton, New York, 1969), pp. 334–6; Childs, *Witness to Power*, 133–5.

18   The two notes on his 1955 visit to Russia and other countries are in J. Nehru Papers post-1947, 2nd Instalment, Subject File No. 62, and are reproduced in *LCM*, vol. 4, pp. 195–222, 227–49. The note on his 1956 tour is in ibid., pp. 406–19. Details of these tours are often to be found in subject files in J. Nehru Papers post–1947; M. O. Mathai's papers in NMML also contain valuable material on them, e.g. Subject File No. 42 (1956 visit to Paris, Yugoslavia, Beirut and Cairo), No. 44 (1956 visit to Germany).

19   Childs, *Witness to Power*, pp. 137–8.

20   Nehru to Chief Ministers, giving a detailed account of his talks with Chou En-lai, 1 July 1954, *LCM*, vol. 3, pp. 580–95.

21   Notes by Mathai for Nehru, 14 Mar. 1955, 20 Sept. 1956 J. Nehru Papers post-1947, 1st Instalment, File Nos 326 Pt I and 475.

22   Summary by R. K. Nehru of three pages of typed-up notes about Mrs Pandit's debt, M. O. Mathai Papers, 2A, Subject File No. 35.

23   Notes by Nehru, 21 Sept. 1956, J. Nehru Papers post-1947, 1st Instalment, File No. 475, 4 Oct. 1956, ibid., File No. 477.

24  A convenient introduction to this broad issue is the essay with bibliography by W. D. McIntyre, 'Commonwealth legacy', ch. 30 of Judith M. Brown and Wm. R. Louis (eds), *The Oxford History of the British Empire, Volume IV: The Twentieth Century* (OUP, Oxford and New York, 1999).

25  Nehru to Baldev Singh, 8 Apr. 1947, J. Nehru Papers post-1947, 2nd Instalment, File of Correspondence with Baldev Singh, No. 33.

26  See exchange of letters between Dr B. C. Roy, prominent Bengali Congressman who was in London, with Nehru: Roy to Nehru, 12 June 1947, Nehru to Roy, 20 June 1947, included in ibid., File of Correspondence with G. B. Pant, No. 208.

27  For Patel's attitude see Patel to Nehru, 14 May 1948, M. O. Mathai Papers, 2A, File of Correspondence between Nehru and Patel; Patel to Arthur Henderson, Under-Secretary of State for India and Burma in Attlee's government, 3 July 1948, *Sardar Patel's Correspondence*, vol. 6, p. 386.

28  The original of this letter from Attlee to Nehru, 11 Mar. 1948 is in M. O. Mathai Papers, 2A, File of Correspondence between Nehru and Attlee. On the intricate discussions in Britain, India and among the Dominions which went on behind the scenes in relation to India and the redefinition of the Commonwealth connection see Moore, *Making the New Commonwealth*, chs 4–7.

29  Nehru to Attlee, 18 Apr. 1948, to Krishna Menon, 16 Apr. 1948, *SWJN(2)*, vol. 6, pp. 470–2, 469.

30  See Nehru's speech in the Subjects' Committee at the Jaipur meeting of Congress, 16 Dec. 1949, pp. 333–4; Nehru to Chief Ministers, 16 Apr. 1949, *LCM*, 1, pp. 321–3. See also Nehru to V. Pandit, 8 June 1949, arguing that if India had isolated itself from the Commonwealth it would have had to 'slope' too much towards the USA: Vijayalakshmi Pandit Papers.

31  Official bound minutes, memoranda and final communiqué of this meeting are in J. Nehru Papers post-1947, 1st Instalment, Subject File No. 819. It is bound in blue and red with 'Prime Minister of India' on it in gold. Nehru was in telegraphic conversation with Vallabhbhai Patel during the conference and sent him accounts of the formal and private negotiations: J. Nehru Papers post-1947, 3rd Instalment, File No. 118. Patel's generous telegram of congratulation to Nehru on 27 Apr. is in this file.

32  Narayan to Nehru, 10 Apr. 1949, Nehru to Narayan, 14 Apr. 1949, J. Nehru Papers post-1947, 2nd Instalment, File of Correspondence with J. P. Narayan, No. 127.

33  See Nehru to MacKenzie King, 27 Apr. 1949, J. Nehru Papers post-1947, 3rd Instalment, File No. 118; Nehru to Indira Gandhi, 3 May 1949, Gandhi, *Two Alone, Two Together*, p. 564; Nehru to S. Cripps, 8 May 1949, J. Nehru Papers post-1947, 2nd Instalment, File of Correspondence with Stafford Cripps, No. 74.

34  Minutes of meeting of Commonwealth Prime Ministers, Oct. 1948, M. O. Mathai Papers, 2A, Subject File No. 25; file relating to this meeting, J. Nehru Papers post-1947, 3rd Instalment, File No. 78.

35  Note by Nehru, 8 Oct. 1950, on meeting with British High Commissioner that day, J. Nehru Papers post-1947, 2nd Instalment, File of Correspondence with C. Attlee, No. 27.

36  Official printed-up papers of the meeting in Jan. 1951, J. Nehru Papers post-1947, 3rd Instalment, File No. 120; note from Nehru to Attlee during conference, 10 Jan. 1951, J. Nehru Papers post-1947, 2nd Instalment, File of Correspondence with C. Attlee, No. 27.

37  Note by Nehru, 13 Nov. 1956, J. Nehru Papers post-1947, 1st Instalment, File No. 487; Nehru to Muriel Lester, 16 Nov. 1956, ibid. File No. 488.

38  Childs, *Witness to Power*, p. 133.

39  Secret and personal note for Churchill, 8 June 1953, J. Nehru Papers post-1947, 2nd Instalment, File of Correspondence with Winston Churchill, No. 70.

40  Address to the UN General Assembly, 3 Nov. 1948, *SWJN(2)*, vol. 8, pp. 290–5.

41  Nehru to N. Pasha, Prime Minister of Egypt, telegram, 26 June 1950, *SWJN(2)*, vol. 14 ii, pp. 364–5; Nehru to Chief Ministers, 3 Aug. 1950, *LCM*, vol. 2, pp. 156–7. (For the US Secretary of State's supercilious rejection of Nehru's reasoning see Acheson, *Present at the Creation*, pp. 419–20. )

42  *New York Times*, 13 Oct. 1949. Reporting covered the period 11–23 Oct.

43  Acheson, *Present at the Creation*, pp. 334–6. On Indo-US relations in this period, see Rotter, *Comrades at Odds*; and H. A. Gould and S. Ganguly (eds), *The Hope and the Reality: US–Indian Relations from Roosevelt to Reagan* (Westview Press, Boulder, 1992).

44  *New York Times*, 23 Oct. 1949; Nehru to S. Radhakrishnan, 6 Feb. 1950, quoted in Gopal, *Jawaharlal Nehru*, vol. 2, pp. 60–1.

45  Top secret note on Nehru, 2 Nov. 1950, declassified document in the US National Archives. (I owe this reference to Professor Wm. Roger Louis. )

46  See Nehru's correspondence in 1951 with Dorothy Norman, an American who edited a collection of his speeches and writings and became a close friend and firm advocate of Indian interests in America. Norman to Nehru, 1 June 1951, Nehru to Norman, 25 June 1951, J. Nehru Papers post-1947, 2nd Instalment, Subject File No. 37. Nehru's sister was Indian Ambassador to the USA at the time and his letters to her are full of the tension in India–USA relations: Vijayalakshmi Pandit Papers. On 11 April 1951 he wrote of the proposed conditions for food aid as likely to turn India into a semi-colonial country or an economic satellite of the US and he would not agree 'to this final humiliation'. On this episode see Rotter, *Comrades at Odds*, pp. 264–74; Gould and Ganguly, *The Hope and the Reality*, pp. 180–2.

47  *New York Times*, 28 Aug. 1951, cited in Nanda, *Jawaharlal Nehru*, p. 225.

48  Nehru's statement in the Lok Sabha, 1 Mar. 1954, including texts of letters exchanged with Eisenhower, *SWJN(2)*, vol. 25, pp. 335–43.

49  Nehru to Chief Ministers, 15 Mar., 26 Apr. 1954, *LCM*, vol. 3, pp. 502–7, 528–31.

50  Second note by Nehru on his visit to the Soviet Union, J. Nehru Papers post-1947, 2nd Instalment, Subject File No. 62.

51  Note for cabinet on background to the Bandung Conference, n.d. but probably 22 Mar. 1955, J. Nehru Papers post-1947, 1st Instalment, File No. 328.

52  Nehru to B. F. H. B. Tyabji, 20 Feb. 1955, ibid., File No. 328: also material in ibid., File No. 329 Pt II.

53  Secret note by Nehru on the conference, 28 Apr. 1955, enclosed in letter from Nehru to T. T. Krishnamachari, 29 Apr. 1955, T. T. Krishnamachari Papers, File of Correspondence with Nehru (1955). This note was also circulated to Chief Ministers.

54  Nehru to Edwina Mountbatten, 30 Apr. 1955, *SWJN(2)*, vol. 28, pp. 141–4.

55  Nehru's speeches are in *SWJN(2)*, vol. 28, pp. 100–28.

56  See Nehru to S. N. Haji, chairman of the All-India Manufacturers' Organisation, Bombay, 14 Nov. 1957, T. T. Krishnamachari Papers, File of Correspondence with J. Nehru (1957). Nehru to R. Singh, an MP, 26 June 1959 indicated even more strongly Nehru's fear that the Bandung nations might not even be able to agree on an agenda at a subsequent meeting and all the good of Bandung would be swept away: J. Nehru Papers post-1947, 1st Instalment, File No. 685.

57  The evidence for Nehru's role in the Suez and Hungarian crises, unless otherwise stated, is in J. Nehru Papers post-1947, 1st Instalment, in the chronological files for the months Sept. to Nov. 1956.

58  Nehru's speech to the Lok Sabha, 13 Sept. 1956, *Lok Sabha Debates, Volume VIII, 1956 (27 Aug.–13 Sept. 1956)*, cols 6963–7. Nehru to Chief Ministers, 20 Sept. 1956, *LCM*, 4, pp. 433–4.

59  *Hindustan Times*, 29 Sept. 1956, enclosed in J. Nehru Papers post-1947, 1st Instalment, File No. 477.

60  Philip Noel-Baker (who had been Labour Secretary of State for Commonwealth Relations) to Nehru, 26 Oct. 1956, ibid., File No. 482.

61  See for example Nehru's message to Eden via the British High Commission in Delhi, enc. in telegram, 1 Nov. 1956, from Indian Foreign Secretary to Indian High Commissioner in London, ibid., File No. 483. A similar message was conveyed to President Eisenhower, ibid.

62  Material on the visit is in J. Nehru Papers post-1947, 3rd Instalment, File No. 65. See also the coverage in the *New York Times* in mid-Dec., which was much fuller than for his 1949 visit. A mini profile on 17 Dec. was appreciative and perceptive, indicating considerable sensitivity towards Nehru's vision of an India finding its own identity and road to development

63  Secret telegram from the Ministry of External Affairs to the Indian embassy in Washington, 30 Oct. 1956, J. Nehru Papers post-1947, 1st Instalment, File No. 483.

64  Top secret note from Pillai to Nehru, 2 Nov. 1956, secret telegram from Indian ambassador in Washington, 3 Nov. 1956, ibid., File No. 484. Telegram, J. P. Narayan to Nehru, 5 Nov. 1956, ibid., File No. 485.

65  Telegrams from Nehru to K. P. S. Menon, Indian ambassador in Moscow, 2 and 3 Nov. 1956, ibid. File No. 484.

66  Eisenhower to Nehru, 5 Nov. 1956, ibid., File No. 485; Nehru to Eisenhower, 7 Nov. 1956, ibid., File No. 486.

67  The difficult exchange of telegrams between Nehru and Menon was on 11–12 Nov., ibid., File No. 487.

68  Mrs S. Lall to Nehru, 17 Nov. 1956, ibid., File No. 489.

69  Text of Nehru's statement in Parliament, 16 Nov. 1956, ibid., File No. 488; notes for Nehru's speech in Parliament on 19 Nov. 1956, ibid., File No. 489; note for M. O. Mathai from the Minister of Information and Broadcasting, 21 Nov. 1956, reporting Gerald Priestland's despatch from India on 20 Nov., ibid., File No. 490.

70  K. P. S. Menon to Nehru, 29 Nov. 1956, ibid., File No. 492.

71  V. Pandit to Nehru, 26 Nov. 1956, secret telegram, ibid, File No. 492. On the same day she reported to Nehru the anger in Britain over the Indian stand on Hungary and what was seen as India's double standard in relation to Hungary and Suez. India was accused of paving the way for its stand on Kashmir when the matter came up before the Security Council: V. Pandit's report for Nehru, 26 November 1956, Vijayalakshmi Pandit Papers.

72  For example, Nehru to Sheikh Abdullah, 10 Oct. 1947, *SWJN(2)*, vol. 4, p. 269.

73  Nehru to Chief Ministers, 20 Nov. 1952, *LCM*, vol. 3, p. 176.

74  Nehru to G. S. Bajpai, 30 July 1953, *SWJN(2)*, vol. 23, pp. 452–3.

75  For Nehru's Delhi meetings with Mohammed Ali see *SWJN(2)*, vol. 23, pp. 331–8, 343–6.

76  Statement by Nehru to the Lok Sabha, 1 Mar. 1954, *SWJN(2)*, vol. 25, pp. 335–43.

77  Note by Nehru to Foreign Secretary, 5 Dec. 1948, *SWJN(2)*, vol. 8, pp. 416–17; Nehru to V. Pandit, 1 July 1949, *SWJN(2)*, vol. 12, pp. 408–9.

78  Nehru to Thakin Nu, Prime Minister of Burma, 7 Jan. 1950, *SWJN(2)*, vol. 14, i, pp. 503–7; Nehru to K. M. Panikkar, 2 Sept. 1950, *SWJN(2)*, vol. 15 i, pp. 432–4.

79  Nehru to K. M. Panikkar, 25 Oct. 1950, *SWJN(2)*, vol. 15, i, pp. 438–43.

80   V. Patel to Nehru, 7 Nov. 1950, *Sardar Patel's Correspondence*, vol. 10, pp. 335–41.

81   Note, 18 Nov. 1950, *SWJN(2)*, vol. 15, ii, pp. 342–7.

82   Nehru to Chief Ministers, 2 Aug. 1952, *LCM*, vol. 3, pp. 73–5.

83   Statement in Parliament, 15 May 1954, *SWJN(2)*, vol. 25, pp. 398–400.

84   Records of these are in *SWJN(2)*, vol. 26, pp. 366–96, 398–406.

85   See M. O. Mathai Papers, 2A, Subject File No. 35 for papers relating to this visit, including the original signed report by Nehru, 14 Nov. 1954, on his visit which was later circulated to Chief Ministers and various diplomats. It is available in *LCM*, vol. 4, pp. 76–89. Details of the talks Nehru had are in *SWJN(2)*, vol. 27, pp. 6–40, 43–6.

86   Nehru to Edwina Mountbatten, 2 Nov. 1954, *SWJN(2)*, vol. 27, pp. 66–9.

87   Note for Minister of Defence Organisation and Defence Secretary, 6 Jan. 1951, *SWJN(2)*, vol. 27, pp. 494–5; secret note for Defence Minister, 3 Mar. 1955, J. Nehru Papers post-1947, 1st Instalment, File No. 322.

88   Minutes of meeting in Ministry of External Affairs, 3 Oct. 1956, J. Nehru Papers post-1947, 1st Instalment, File No. 478.

89   Winston Churchill to Nehru, 8 June 1953, 21 Feb. and 30 June 1955, J. Nehru Papers post-1947, 2nd Instalment, File of Correspondence with Churchill, No. 70; confidential letter of Eden to Nehru, 2 Feb. 1955, ibid., 1st Instalment, File No. 318.

## Chapter 14   The Realities of Democratic Leadership

1    Speech at Wardha at inauguration of a centre for Gandhian studies, 5 Jan. 1954, *SWJN(2)*, vol. 24, pp. 88–93.

2    Signed profile by James Reston, 'Magnetism of Nehru', *New York Times*, 20 Dec. 1956.

3    Sri Prakasa to Nehru, 3 Feb. 1956, copy in T. T. Krishnamachari Papers, File of Correspondence with Nehru (1956).

4    Eisenhower to Nehru, 1 May 1959, Khrushchev to Nehru, 8 May 1958, quoted in Gopal, *Jawaharlal Nehru*, vol. 3, p. 107; US Ambassador in Delhi to Secretary of State, 1 and 6 May 1958, Library of Congress, Microfiche collection of declassified State Department documents, Fiche No. 273.

5    Indira to Nehru, 1 May 1958, Gandhi, *Two Alone, Two Together*, p. 623; on this episode see also Nehru to Chief Ministers, 26 Mar., 18 May 1958, *LCM*, vol. 5, pp. 25–7, 40–2

6    On this phase see J. Nehru Papers post-1947, 1st Instalment, File No. 687. (It was typical of Nehru's human concerns that he was deeply shocked at the fatal accident which occurred to the doctor who had been regularly coming out from Simla to see him, sometimes twice a day, just after he had accompanied Nehru to Kalka.)

7    Sri Prakasa to Rajendra Prasad, 18 Oct. 1960, *Dr Rajendra Prasad: Correspondence*, vol. 8, p. 97; Nehru to P. G. Mavlankar, 30 Nov. 1961, Nehru to Jagadish Swarup, 14 Dec. 1961, J. Nehru Papers post-1947, 1st Instalment, File No. 728.

8    Dr B. C. Roy to Nehru, 30 April 1962, Nehru's reply, 3 May 1962, J. Nehru Papers post-1947, 2nd Instalment, File of Correspondence with B. C. Roy, No. 248.

9    Nehru to Chief Ministers, 10 July 1962, *LCM*, vol. 5, pp. 501–2.

10   See J. K. Galbraith's comments on Nehru's visit to America in Nov. 1961, *Ambassador's Journal*, pp. 245–53. Indira's comment was reported in the *New York Times*, 13 Nov. 1961.

11   Nehru to Mathai, 18 Jan. 1959, accepting his letter of resignation the same day, M. O. Mathai Papers, 2B, Correspondence with J. Nehru. Amrit Kaur, the Mountbattens and

'Nye' Bevan were deeply concerned at what they thought was the wrongful accusation and victimisation of Mathai. See Amrit Kaur's letters to Nehru of 23 Jan. and 15 July 1959, and Nehru's letter of 5 Mar. 1959, J. Nehru Papers post-1947, 2nd Instalment, File of Correspondence with A. Kaur, No. 18. Gopal asserts that Mathai was in the pay of the CIA, using as his authority records in the papers of his father, S. Radhakrishnan, who was at the time Vice-President of India; Gopal, *Jawaharlal Nehru*, vol. 3, p. 122. I can find no sources which shed light on this. A tendency to see 'the foreign hand' in difficult situations is common in India; but if it is true, then, as in the case of Krishna Menon, it underlines Nehru's unfortunate, and sometimes damaging, choice of close colleagues. Mathai published two accounts of his years in the Nehru household after Nehru's death which show great bitterness towards the family he had served: *My Days with Nehru* (Vikas, New Delhi, 1979) and *Reminiscences of the Nehru Age* (Vikas, New Delhi, 1978).

12   Kochanek, *The Congress Party of India*, pp. 66–8.

13   M. Brecher, *Nehru: A Political Biography* (OUP, London, 1959), p. 615. Indira Gandhi warned her father of the hostility in Congress, even in the CWC, to his reliance on a few men in relation to policy towards different regions of the country, 23 April 1956, Gandhi, *Two Alone, Two Together*, pp. 614–15.

14   Nehru to P. Chandra, 4 Sept. 1962, J. Nehru Papers post-1947,1st Instalment, File No. 737. See also Nehru to T. T. Krishnamachari, 15 July 1962, enclosing letter to the bank official, M. Singh, 15 July 1962, T. T. Krishnamachari Papers, File of Correspondence with J. Nehru (1962).

15   Nehru to N. E. Isaacs, American newspaper editor, 5 July 1959, J. Nehru Papers post-1947, 1st Instalment, File No. 686.

16   Nehru to Krishna Menon, secret telegram, 23 Nov. 1956, ibid., File No. 491.

17   Nehru to Chief Ministers, 1 Aug. 1957, *LCM*, vol. 4, p. 518.

18   Nehru to Chief Ministers, 24 Nov. 1957, *LCM*, vol. 4, p. 609.

19   Nehru to Chief Ministers, 25 Oct. 1957, *LCM*, vol. 4, pp. 584–5.

20   Nehru to Chief Ministers, 28 May 1959, *LCM*, vol. 4, pp. 258–60; Nehru to Minister of Health, 24 July 1959, J. Nehru Papers post-1947, 1st Instalment, File No. 687.

21   Note by Nehru, 23 July 1959, J. Nehru Papers post-1947, 1st Instalment, File No. 687; various notes on simplicity of governmental style written in July 1959 are in the same file.

22   S. Radhakrishnan to Nehru, 26 May 1957, J. Nehru Papers post-1947, 2nd Instalment, File of Correspondence with S. Radhakrishnan, No. 226.

23   22 June 1950, *SWJN(2)*, vol. 14 ii, pp. 417–8.

24   Nehru to Chief Minister of UP, secret and personal, 5 April 1957, AICC Papers post-1947, 1st Instalment, Congress President's Correspondence File, 1957, No. 4311.

25   Nehru to Chief Ministers, 27 June and 5 Aug. 1961, *LCM*, vol. 5, pp. 450–1, 493–4.

26   Nehru to G. B. Pant, 1 July 1948, J. Nehru Papers post-1947, 2nd Instalment, File of Correspondence with G. B. Pant, No. 208; speech, 26 July 1948, *SWJN(2)*, vol. 7, pp. 511–14. Nehru's distress at the fierce language debates in the Constituent Assembly were voiced in a letter to V. Pandit, 24 Aug. 1949, *SWJN(2)*, vol. 13, p. 287.

27   Nehru to Chief Ministers, 31 Dec. 1957, *LCM*, vol. 4, p. 625. See also Nehru to Mirza Ismail, 22 Feb. 1958, copied to U. Dhebar, AICC Papers post-1947, 2nd Instalment, Congress President's Correspondence Files, 1958, No. 4313.

28   Nehru to Chief Ministers, 18 Feb. 1963, *LCM*, vol. 5, pp. 577–80.

29   Nehru to Chief Ministers, 30 July 1960, 3 Sept. 1962, *LCM*, vol. 5, pp. 399–400, 523.

30  For the precise statistics of votes cast and seats won by each party see P. R. Brass, *The Politics of India since Independence* (CUP, Cambridge, 1990), pp. 70–2, 90. See also appendix above, pp. 346–8.

31  Nehru to T. T. Krishnamachari, 5 Jan. 1962, T. T. Krishnamachari Papers, File of Correspondence with J. Nehru (1962); Nehru to M. Bagdi, 19 Dec. 1961, J. Nehru Papers post-1947, 1st Instalment, File No. 728.

32  Nehru to Chief Ministers, 5 May 1957, *LCM*, vol. 4, pp. 484–5.

33  Nehru to Chief Ministers, 3 Sept. 1962, *LCM*, vol. 5, pp. 516–17.

34  Galbraith, *Ambassador's Journal*, p. 76.

35  Note by Nehru for Mathai, 3 May 1957, M. O. Mathai Papers, 2A Subject files, File No. 29; message from Nehru, 16 Oct. 1962, J. Nehru Papers post-1947, 1st Instalment, File No. 738.

36  Amrit Kaur to Nehru, marked personal for Nehru alone, 2 Aug. 1961, J. Nehru Papers post-1947, 2nd Instalment, File of Correspondence with Amrit Kaur, No. 18.

37  Nehru confidentially to N. Sanjiva Reddy, 27 Mar. 1960, AICC Papers post-1947, 2nd Instalment, File of Congress President's correspondence, No. 4321.

38  Cited in Kochanek, *The Congress Party of India*, p. 73. (This work is the best detailed discussion of the nature and working of Congress from 1946 to 1967.)

39  Nehru to K. N. Katju, 25 April 1959, AICC Papers post-1947, 2nd Instalment, Congress President's Correspondence Files, Nos 4313–20 (3).

40  Nehru to Sampurnanand, Chief Minister of UP, secret and personal, 5 April 1957, AICC Papers post-1947, 1st Instalment, Congress President's Correspondence File, No. 4311 (1957); Nehru to Charan Singh, Revenue Minister of UP, 21 Mar. 1959, to Sampurnanad, 25 April 1959, ibid., 2nd Instalment, Congress President's Correspondence Files, Nos 4313–20 (3). (An illuminating study of Congress in a state, which provides background to Nehru's concern for UP, is P. R. Brass, *Factional Politics in an Indian State: The Congress Party in Uttar Pradesh* (University of California Press, Berkeley, 1965).

41  For Lok Sabha figures see Brass, *The Politics of India*, pp. 70–1 and appendix above, pp. 346–7; for figures for the state elections, Hardgrave, *India*, p. 206. See also appendix above, p. 347–8.

42  Nehru to Sampurnanad, Chief Minister of UP, secret and personal, 5 April 1957, Nehru to U. Dhebar, confidential, 7 April 1957, Dhebar to Nehru, 30 April 1957, AICC Papers post-1947, 1st Instalment, Congress President's Correspondence File, No. 4311 (1957).

43  Nehru to U. Dhebar, 7 June 1957, J. Nehru Papers post-1947, 2nd Instalment, File of Correspondence with Dhebar, No. 81.

44  Message from Nehru for Mysore PCC, 21 July 1963, J. Nehru Papers post-1947, 1st Instalment, File No. 748.

45  B. Ramakrishna Rao to Nehru, 12 Oct. 1956, ibid., File No. 479; secret note by the Director of the Intelligence Bureau, sent by G. B. Pant to Dhebar, Congress President, AICC Papers post-1947, 2nd Instalment, Congress President's Correspondence File, 1956, No. 4302. The best background study on Kerala is T. J. Nossiter, *Communism In Kerala: A Study in Political Adaptation* (C. Hurst, London, 1982). On the 1959 crisis there is a brief article which depends largely on published reminiscences and press reports rather than the papers of the AICC or Nehru: R. Jeffrey, 'Jawaharlal Nehru and the smoking gun: who pulled the trigger on Kerala's Communist government in 1959?', *Journal of Commonwealth and Comparative Politics*, 29, no. 1 (Mar. 1991), pp. 72–85.

46  *Hindustan Times*, 11 June 1957, in J. Nehru Papers post-1947, 1st Instalment, File No. 792.

47  Press statement by Nehru, 6 June 1959, ibid., File No. 684; for evidence of Indira's attempts to steer the Kerala Congress away from an alliance with openly communal groups, in letters and at an AICC meeting in May, AICC Papers post-1947, 2nd Instalment, Congress President's Correspondence File, 1959, No. 4313–20 (5), Papers on Kerala.

48  Nehru to M. Padmanabhan, President of the so-called 'Liberation Committee', and to B. Ramakrishna Rao, and to R. Sankar, 15 June 1959, J. Nehru Papers post-1947, 1st Instalment, File No. 684. R. Sankar to Indira Gandhi, 15 June 1959, Indira's reply, 18 June 1959, AICC Papers post-1947, 2nd Instalment, Congress President's Correspondence File, 1959, No. 4313–20 (5), Papers on Kerala.

49  Nehru to Sri Prakasa, 23 June 1959, J. Nehru Papers post-1947, 1st Instalment, File No. 685.

50  *Indian Express*, 23, 24 and 26 June 1959, ibid., File No. 792.

51  Records of this meeting are in ibid., File No. 686. Also in AICC Papers post-1947, 2nd Instalment, Congress President's Correspondence File, 1959, No. 4313–20 (6).

52  Secret note of instructions for the Kerala PCC from the Central Parliamentary Board, 29 June 1959, in AICC Paprs, ibid., and J. Nehru Papers post-1947, 1st Instalment, File No. 685.

53  Nehru to E. Namboodiripad, 30 June 1959, J. Nehru Papers post-1947, 1st Instalment, File No. 685.

54  Note by Nehru on his talks with Namboodiripad that day, 11 July 1959, ibid., File No. 686.

55  *Tribune*, 7 July 1959, ibid., File No. 793.

56  E. Namboodiripad to Nehru, 17 July 1959, ibid., File No. 687.

57  Note to Indira as Congress President, 21 July 1959, Nehru to Kerala PCC President, 22 July 1959, confidential letter, Nehru to E. Namboodiripad, 26 July 1959, ibid.

58  Nehru to Governor of Kerala, top secret telegram and top secret letter, both on 30 July 1959, ibid.

59  Secret note by Nehru on non-violence for the committed Gandhian, Vinoba Bhave, n. d. but probably early May 1947, J. Nehru Papers post-1947, 2nd Instalment, File of Correspondence with Vinoba Bhave, No. 38. On Nehru's conviction that non-violence had forced British withdrawal, see Nehru to Chester Bowles, former US ambassador to India, 12 May 1955, ibid., File of Correspondence with Chester Bowles, No. 48.

60  See Rotter, *Comrades at Odds,* pp. 182–4.

61  Likely domestic pressures were underlined in the *New York Times*, 19 Dec. 1961.

62  Nehru to J. K. Galbraith, 12 Dec. 1959, to Harold Macmillan, Prime Minister of UK, 15 Dec., messages to U. Thant, 16 and 17 Dec. 1959, and message from Foreign Secretary in Delhi to Indian Ambassador in Washington, 17 Nov. 1959, J. Nehru Papers post-1947, 1st Instalment, File No. 728.

63  Mountbatten made this allegation in 1970 in an interview with S. Gopal: Gopal, *Jawaharlal Nehru,* vol. 3, p. 198. Michael Brecher also discussed Menon's role with him in his 1964–5 dialogues: Brecher, *India and World Politics.*

64  Reports in the *New York Times*, 19 Dec. 1961.

65  *New York Times*, 21 Dec. 1961.

66  Leader, 'India, the aggressor', and article by Arthur Krock, *New York Times*, 19 Dec. 1961.

67    Nehru to Cardinal Archibishop Gracias, 22 Dec. 1961, J. Nehru Papers post-1947, 1st Instalment, File No. 728. Further evidence of international outrage is in this file.
68    Nehru to President Kennedy, 29 Dec., ibid.


## Chapter 15    A New India?

1    Diary entry, 13 Nov. 1942, *SWJN(1)*, vol. 13, p. 28.
2    Tomlinson, *The Economy of Modern India 1860–1970* , p. 180; also Dube, *India since Independence*, chs on communications and economic development.
3    B. Kuppuswamy, *Population and Society in India* (Popular Prakashan, Bombay, 1975), p. 99.
4    Nehru to Chief Ministers, 13 Feb. 1959, *LCM*, vol. 5, p. 211; U. Dhebar to Nehru, 20 May 1961, enclosing note by Deputy Chairman of Planning Commission, J. Nehru Papers post-1947, 2nd Instalment, File of Correspondence with U. N. Dhebar, No. 81.
5    For statistics and discussion of population issues see Dube, *India since Independence*, ch. on India's demographic profile; and R. H. Cassen, *India: Population, Economy, Society* (Macmillan, London, 1978).
6    See discussion in Cassen, *India*, ch. 4.
7    Kuppuswamy, *Population and Society in India*, chs 5–7.
8    Undated note for cabinet from Minister of Finance, enclosed in letter from T. T. Krishnamachari to Nehru, 3 June 1957, T. T. Krishnamachari Papers, File of Correspondence with J. Nehru (1957); note by Nehru for cabinet, 8 June 1957, ibid.
9    Undated note enc. in letter from T. T. Krishnamachari to Nehru, 11 Jan. 1958, T. T. Krishnamachari Papers, File of Correspondence with J. Nehru (1958, 1959, 1960).
10    T. T. Krishnamachari to Nehru, 21 Aug. 1957, ibid., File of Correspondence with J. Nehru (1957).
11    Secret letter delivered in person to Nehru from Dhebar, 26 Oct. 1957, AICC Papers post-1947, 2nd Instalment, Congress President's Correspondence File, No. 4304 (1957). (Also in ibid., File No. 4311 (1957).
12    Secret letter from T. T. Krishnamachari to Nehru, 26 June 1962, J. Nehru Papers post-1947, 2nd Instalment, File of Correspondence with T. T. Krishnamachari, No. 142. Some of the problems with using the existing civil service and bureaucrats for important new roles had been noted by the notable Oxford economist Thomas Balogh, whose views were shown to Nehru and to U. Dhebar by Mathai as early as 1956; Balogh to Mathai 11 July 1956, AICC Papers post-1947, 2nd Instalment, Congress President's Correspondence Files, No. 4313 (1958).
13    Top secret note from T. T. Krishnamachari to Nehru, 31 May 1957, enclosing an undated note on state government overdrafts with the Reserve Bank, T. T. Krishnamachari Papers, File of Correspondence with J. Nehru (1957).
14    Table 13. 6, in A. Vaidyanathan, 'The Indian economy since independence (1947–70)', in Kumar and Desai, *The Cambridge Economic History*, vol. 2, p. 971. See also Nehru to Nasser, 28 June 1959, in which he gave him a brief analysis of India's planning policy: J. Nehru Papers post-1947, 1st Instalment, File No. 685.
15    *Hindustan Times*, 3 and 10 June 1959, J. Nehru Papers post-1947, 1st Instalment, File No. 792.
16    Nehru to Chief Ministers, 23–4 Jan., 30 July, 6 Sept. 1958, *LCM*, vol. 5, pp. 15–16, 106–10, 119–22.

17  Nehru to Chief Ministers, 13 Feb. 1959, *LCM*, vol. 5, p. 211.

18  Nehru to Chief Ministers, 25 Mar. 1959, *LCM*, vol. 5, pp. 223–6.

19  Sri Prakasa, then Governor of Bombay, to Nehru, 8 June 1957, J. Nehru Papers post-1947, 2nd Instalment, File of Correspondence with Sri Prakasa, No. 280.

20  Nehru to R. Prasad, 7 June 1959, in reply to Prasad's letter of same day, J. Nehru Papers post-1947, 1st Instalment, File No. 684; *Hindustan Times*, 18 and 25 June 1959, ibid., File No. 792. Prasad's letter to Nehru, 7 June 1959 is in *Dr Rajendra Prasad: Correspondence*, vol. 19, pp. 113–22.

21  See H. L. Erdman, *The Swatantra Party and Indian Conservatism* (CUP, Cambridge, 1967). On the organisation of business interests and their political influence more generally see ch. 5 of M. Weiner, *The Politics of Scarcity: Public Pressure and Political Response in India* (University of Chicago Press, Chicago, 1962).

22  Nehru to Chief Ministers, 14 Apr. 1963, *LCM*, vol. 5, p. 589. (This echoed a cogent letter Dhebar had written to him in 1957 when he urged Nehru not to forget the Gandhian principle of self-reliance, which was desperately important given that India's rural economy was so fragile. Secret letter from Dhebar to Nehru, 26 Oct. 1957, AICC Papers post-1947, 2nd Instalment, Congress President's Correspondence File No. 4304 (1957).

23  Nehru to T. T. Krishnamachari, 23 Mar. 1962, J. Nehru Papers post-1947, 2nd Instalment, File of Correspondence with T. T. Krishnamachari, No. 142; Krishnamachari to Nehru, 6 Sept. and 10 Oct. 1962, T. T. Krishnamachari Papers, File of Correspondence with J. Nehru (1962).

24  Frankel, *India's Political Economy*, pp. 190–5.

25  Tomlinson, *The Economy of Modern India*, p. 194.

26  Quoted in Jannuzi, *Agrarian Crisis in India*, pp. 53–4. The whole case study is on pp. 51–4, 196–9.

27  Frankel, *India's Political Economy*, p. 193.

28  M. Galanter, 'The abolition of disabilities – Untouchability and the law', ch. 10 of J. Michael Mahar (ed.), *The Untouchables in Contemporary India* (University of Arizona Press, Tucson, 1972).

29  *Status of Women in India: A Synopsis of the Report of the Naional Committee on the Status of Women (1971–74)* (Indian Council of Social Science Research, New Delhi, n.d.), p. 108.

30  Ibid., ch. 4 on 'Women and the law'. See also studies such as L. Sarkar, 'Reform of Hindu marriage and succession laws: still the unequal sex', ch. 6 of B. Ray and A. Basu (eds), *From Independence towards Freedom: Indian Women since 1947* (OUP, New Delhi, 1999); B. Agarwal, 'Widows versus daughters or widows as daughters? Property, land, and economic security in rural India', *Modern Asian Studies*, 32, (part 1) (Feb. 1998), pp. 1–48.

31  *Status of Women in India*, pp. 24–6.

32  Evidence on which these paragraphs are based is taken from text and tables in *Status of Women in India*.

33  Address in Calcutta, 14 Dec. 1957, G. D. Birla Papers, Correspondence between J. Nehru and G. Birla.

34  R. S. Newell, 'Ideology and realities: land redistribution in Uttar Pradesh', *Pacific Affairs*, 45, no. 2 (1972), pp. 220–39.

35  U. Dhebar to Nehru, 5 Sept. 1957, AICC Papers post-1947, 2nd Instalment, Congress President's Correspondence File, No. 4310 (1957). The increasing presence of people who had rural backgrounds and represented rural interests in Congress is shown well in Kochanek, *The Congress Party of India*, part 3.

36    Nehru to Chief Ministers, 29 Jan., 26 Mar. 1958, *LCM*, vol. 5, pp. 20–2, 31–2.

37    Nehru to Chief Ministers, 31 Dec. 1958, *LCM*, vol. 5, pp. 186–7.

38    Rajendra Prasad to Nehru, 7 June 1959, *Dr Rajendra Prasad, Correspondence*, vol. 19, pp. 113–22; *Hindustan Times*, 18 July 1959, J. Nehru Papers post-1947, 1st Instalment, File No. 573.

39    Enrolment figures are in Kuppuswamy, *Population and Society in India*, p. 90; government expenditure figures for various heads are in table 13.11 in Vaidyanathan, 'The Indian Economy since Independence', in Kumar and Desai (eds), *The Cambridge Economic History*, p. 975.

40    For an examination of this tiny group see G. Ostergaard and M. Currell, *The Gentle Anarchists: A Study of the Leaders of the Sarvodaya Movement for Non-violent Revolution in India* (Clarendon Press, Oxford, 1971). Considerable attention is devoted to the work of Vinoba Bhave, who had worked with Gandhi from the age of twenty-one and was heir to the Gandhian legacy of social reconstruction.

## Chapter 16   The Erosion of Authority

1    Undated note sent by Nehru to Vinoba Bhave, 4 May 1957, J. Nehru Papers post-1947, 2nd Instalment, File of Correspondence with V. Bhave, No. 38.

2    See above, chapter 13. Neville Maxwell, former foreign correspondent for *The Times*, in what became a deeply contentious book, argued that Nehru's stance was effectively a unilateral pronouncement of the boundary, and as such was deeply hostile to China: N. Maxwell, *India's China War* (1970), Pelican edn with postscript (Penguin Books, Harmondsworth, 1972). An opposing and important attempt to understand the roots of Nehru's understanding of China by someone who was in the Indian Foreign Service at the time, and a Deputy Secretary when relations with China deteriorated in 1959, is Jagat Singh Mehta, 'Nehru's failure with China: intellectual naïveté or the wages of a prophetic vision?' in M. Israel, *Nehru and the Twentieth Century*.

3    This episode is recounted in Maxwell, *India's China War*, pp. 70–1, and the source given is 'official unpublished papers'.

4    Sri Prakasa to R. Prasad, 15 Nov. 1959, *Dr Rajendra Prasad: Correspondence*, vol. 21, pp. 150–1. Prasad wrote a lengthy and critical letter to Nehru on security and defence of the northern border on 5 Dec. 1959, J. Nehru Papers post-1947, 2nd Instalment, File of Correspondence with R. Prasad, No. 231. (In this letter he referred to an earlier one he had written on 23 Sept. 1959, but this is not available in this file nor in *Dr Rajendra Prasad*.)

5    Nehru to Chief Ministers, 31 Dec. 1958, *LCM*, vol. 5, p. 192.

6    Cited in Gopal, *Jawaharlal Nehru*, vol. 3, p. 89, n. 83.

7    Nehru to President of India-China Friendship Centre, 15 June 1959, J. Nehru Papers post-1947, 1st Instalment, File No. 684.

8    Evidence of growing tension between India and China in June and July 1959 on both issues is in ibid., File Nos 685, 686, 687.

9    *Indian Express*, 1 July 1959, *Hindustan Times*, 2 July 1959, ibid., File No. 793.

10    Nehru to A. D. Mani, editor of *Hitavada*, 26 June 1959, ibid., File No. 685.

11    Childs, *Witness to Power*, p. 142. His account of the visit is on pp. 140–2.

12    Maxwell was correspondent for *The Times* in Delhi and gave a detailed account of Chou's visit in his later book, *India's China War*, pp. 159–76.

13    Speech by Nehru, 3 May 1960, at Commonwealth Prime Ministers' Conference, London, J. Nehru Papers post-1947, 3rd Instalment, File No. 121.

14    Nehru to Chief Ministers, 8 June 1960, *LCM*, vol. 5, p. 359.

15    J. Nehru Papers post-1947, 3rd Instalment, File No. 123. On the domestic opposition to any talks with China, see Galbraith, entry for 16 Aug. 1962, *Ambassador's Journal*, p. 404.

16    Blunt analyses of India's military and political failings by Hanson Baldwin are in the *New York Times*, 10 and 20 Nov. 1962.

17    Entry for 21 Nov. 1962, Galbraith, *Ambassador's Journal*, p. 487; two letters from Nehru to Kennedy, 19 Nov. 1962, cited in Gopal, *Jawaharlal Nehru*, vol. 3, pp. 228–9. (Gopal notes that Nehru made this request to America without consulting his cabinet colleagues, and only with the knowledge of the Foreign Secretary, M. J. Desai.)

18    In an exchange of letters with the retired president, Prasad, Nehru agreed that it was difficult to explain the Chinese cease-fire, but believed that it was part of Mao's theory of the uses of war, and also partly as a result of the dangers of extending operations into the plains, of Soviet pressure, and also of surprise at Indian resolve. Prasad to Nehru, 7 Dec. 1962, Nehru's reply, 10 Dec. 1962, *Dr Rajenda Prasad: Correspondence*, vol. 21, pp. 155–6, 157–8. Nehru was not alone in his confusion about Chinese intentions; western experts were also unsure and putting forward a range of suggestions, including the seizure of land as a negotiating weapon, demonstrating Chinese power in Asia and the superiority of the Chinese model of economic development, forcing India to divert resources from economic advance, and diverting Chinese people from domestic troubles by encouraging them to make sacrifices for the struggle against India. Article in *New York Times*, 21 Nov. 1962.

19    A good introduction to Chinese thinking, with valuable references, is ch. 6 of M. Yahuda, *The International Politics of the Asia-Pacific, 1945–1995* (Routledge, London, 1996). More detailed is the balanced academic analysis in the first five chapters of Allen S. Whiting, *The Chinese Calculus of Deterrence: India and Indonesia* (University of Michigan Press, Ann Arbor, 1975). Also valuable is the brief part 3, 'The view from Peking', of Maxwell, *India's China War*.

20    Nehru to P. Naidu, 12 Nov. 1962, J. Nehru Papers post-1947, 1st Instalment, File No. 739. For comments on Nehru's demeanour, see Galbraith, *Ambassador's Journal*, pp. 442, 466, 517.

21    Nehru to Jamal Khawaja, 15 Nov. 1962, J. Nehru Papers post-1947, 1st Instalment, File No. 739.

22    Nehru to Y. B. Chavan (now Minister of Defence), 25 Nov. 1962, Nehru to C. B. Gupta, 26 Nov., 1962, ibid.

23    Nehru to his Minister of Law, and Minister for Food and Agriculture, both 23 Nov. 1962, ibid.

24    Amrit Kaur to Nehru, 22 Oct. 1962, J. Nehru Papers post-1947, 2nd Instalment, File of Correspondence with Amrit Kaur, No. 18.

25    Note by T. T. Krishnamachari, Minister without Portfolio, for Nehru, 30 Oct. 1962, T. T. Krishnamachari Papers, File of Correspondence with Nehru (1962).

26    Nehru to Krishna Menon, 28 Oct. 1962, J. Nehru Papers post-1947, 1st Instalment, File No. 738.

27    Prasad to Nehru, 5 Nov. 1962, *Dr Rajendra Prasad: Correspondence*, vol. 21, pp. 144–5.

28    Nehru's reply to Prasad, 8 Nov. 1962, two letters from Krishna Menon to Nehru, 7 Nov. 1961, J. Nehru Papers post-1947, 1st Instalment, File No. 739; *New York Times*, 8

Nov. 1962. On 13 Nov. Nehru advised the President of the reorganisation of defence following Krishna Menon's resignation. Chavan, presently Chief Minister of Maharashtra, was to be Minister of Defence, and two other colleagues would be in charge of defence production and economic coordination.

29    *New York Times*, 1 Nov. 1962.

30    Nehru to Khrushchev, 22 Oct. 1962, J. Nehru Papers post-1947, 1st Instalment, File No. 738. Other letters to international leaders, such as President Kennedy and Harold Macmillan, are in the same file.

31    Nehru was deeply anxious to avoid any actions or speeches within India which would push the Soviet Union away from neutrality and towards China; for example, he rebuked his incoming Minister of Defence for saying that he did not believe the USSR would help in the crisis for India because of its policy of spreading communism by force. Nehru to Y. B. Chavan, 16 Nov. 1962, ibid., File No. 739. Khrushchev had in a letter to Nehru on 2 Nov. indicated that although his government was friendly towards India it would not alter its stance, and he urged Nehru to accept negotiation on Chinese terms; *New York Times*, 4 Nov. 1962.

32    For informed American voices, see *New York Times*, 23 and 30 Oct., 12 Nov. 1962. The Conservative government in Britain, led by Harold Macmillan, promised all necessary aid to India to a cheering House of Commons, and the official line was not to refer to past tensions. The veteran Labour politician Clement Attlee, however, said that Nehru was at last waking up to reality; he had had his head in the sand and must now realise that there was no such thing as neutrality. *New York Times*, 2 Nov. 1962.

33    Both types of criticism are clear in a file of correspondence between Nehru and Vinoba Bhave on the China war, No. 97 of J. Nehru Papers post-1947, 3rd Instalment. They included a printed pamphlet by Bhave, 'Sino-Indian conflict', 10 Dec. 1962, and an undated statement by the Socialist leader and ex-Congressman, J. B. Kripalani.

34    Galbraith, *Ambassador's Journal*, p. 512. The warning to Nehru about persistent opposition came from Jairamdas Doulatram in a letter of 26 Nov. 1962, J. Nehru Papers post-1947, 1st Instalment, File No. 739.

35    Nehru to Chief Ministers, 22 Dec. 1962, *LCM*, vol. 5, pp. 540–58.

36    Nehru to Chief Ministers, 21 May 1963, *LCM*, vol. 5, pp. 592–4.

37    Secret note, not to go into the office, from Nehru to the Foreign Secretary, 27 Nov. 1962, J. Nehru Papers post-1947, 1st Instalment, File No. 739. This followed an exchange of letters between Nehru and Ayub Khan on 6 and 11 Nov.: Nehru's letter of 11 Nov. is in this file.

38    Nehru to Chief Ministers, 21 May 1963, *LCM*, vol. 5, pp. 594–9; also copy of statement to be made by Nehru to Lok Sabha, Aug. 1963, J. Nehru Papers post-1947, 1st Instalment, File No. 749. See also in this file secret notes by Nehru for his senior officers in the Ministry of External Relations, 16 Aug. 1963, on his interviews with the UK High Commissioner and the US ambassador that day, when he had explained to them his position on Kashmir and the fruitlessness of talks with Pakistan at this juncture, although the door to a settlement was not closed.

39    Secret note for Nehru by P. Pant, 24 Nov. 1962, and Krishnamachari to Nehru, 28 Nov. 1962, commenting on the note, T. T. Krishnamachari Papers, File of Correspondence with Nehru (1962).

40    See evidence in ibid., Subject File No. 25.

41    T. T. Krishnamachari to Nehru, 16 Dec. 1962, and Nehru's reply the same day, ibid., File of Correspondence with Nehru (1962).

42   T. T. Krishnamachari to Nehru, 26 Dec. 1962, ibid.

43   Evidence in ibid., File of Correspondence with Nehru (1963). See particularly Krish-namachari's letter to Nehru of 4 Aug. 1963.

44   In June 1962 he responded to Vijayalakshmi Pandit's request to get Nehru to take things more easily by acknowledging that only Edwina could have done this, and he sympathised deeply with her having to watch her brother's physical and political decline. See Ziegler, *Mountbatten*, pp. 601–2.

45   Three top secret documents on Mountbatten's visit are available in T. T. Krishna-machari Papers, Subject File No. 27 (1963).

46   The defence budget for 1963–4 and other important evidence of the military build-up are in ibid.

47   Top secret memorandum from Chester Bowles to Nehru, 21 Apr. 1964, T. T. Krishna-machari Papers, File of Correspondence with Nehru (1964).

48   Menon in dialogue with M. Brecher some months after Nehru's death: Brecher, *India and World Politics*, p. 157.

49   Childs, *Witness to Power*, pp. 142–3.

50   T. T. Krishnamachari to Indira Gandhi, 2 Apr. 1969, ibid, File of Correspondence with Indira Gandhi.

51   N. V. Gadgil to Nehru, 12 Mar. 1964, J. Nehru Papers post-1947, 1st Instalment, File No. 753.

52   Nehru to C. B. Gupta, Chief Minister of UP, confidential letter of 3 Sept. 1962 and secret letter of 7 Sept. 1962 (in between which they had discussed the matter of one of the vacant UP seats in person), ibid., File No. 737.

53   Nehru to Chief Ministers, 3 Sept. 1962, *LCM*, vol. 5, pp. 517–18. An example of internal 'indiscipline' and factionalism was the Bihar Congress: see 28-page report on this by a seven-man Congress enquiry team in 1962 located (despite the date) in AICC Papers post-1947, 2nd Instalment, Congress President's Correspondence File, No. 4321 (1958). The AICC's report on the three by-elections is quoted at length in Frankel, *India's Political Economy*, pp. 222–3.

54   T. T. Krishnamachari to Nehru, 21 June 1963, T. T. Krishnamachari Papers, File of Correspondence with Nehru.

55   Frankel, *India's Political Economy*, pp. 224–7.

56   Nehru's note for the CWC, 24 Aug. 1963, detailing the history of the Kamaraj Plan and his suggestions for which resignations should be accepted, J. Nehru Papers post-1947, 3rd Instalment, File No. 52. File No. 104, ibid., also includes evidence of resig-nations, and letters from groups who asked that 'their man' should not go (e.g. the Depressed Classes League worried that Jagjivan Ram would leave central government), and from governors, whose views on their states' political situation Nehru had solicited. Another file, No. 749, 1st Instalment, contains letters dealing with the administrative arrangements in the central government following the implementation of the plan, including a confidential letter to the President, S. Radhakrishnan, detailing the outgoing and incoming ministers.

57   The details of this manoeuvring are outlined in Kochanek, *The Congress Party of India*, pp. 83–5.

58   Interview, 27 Aug. 1963, cited in Frankel, *India's Political Economy*, p. 229.

59   Nehru to C. B. Gupta, private and confidential letter, 29 July 1963, J. Nehru Papers post-1947, 1st Instalment, File No. 748.

60   Evidence of Nehru's invitation to Sheikh Abdullah to visit him in Delhi and their lengthy but inconclusive talks over 29 Apr.–1 May 1964, are in ibid., File No. 753.

61  See Nehru's message for the Mysore PCC for independence day, written 21 July 1963, ibid., File No. 748. He used this argument in his note for the CWC on the implementation of the Kamaraj Plan, 24 Aug. 1963, J. Nehru Papers post-1947, 3rd Instalment, File No. 52.

62  Nehru to Chief Ministers, 3 Septmber 1962, LCM, vol. 5, p. 518. The report of the Congress General Secretaries is cited in Kochanek, *The Congress Party of India*, p. 82.

63  Mountbatten to Nehru, 30 Jan. 1964, Ziegler, *Mountbatten*, p. 602.

64  For evidence of Nehru's sense of recovery and determination to continue in office, see letters from the last weeks of his life in J. Nehru Papers post-1947, 1st Instalment, File No. 753. On senior Congressmen's deepening concern, see *New York Times*, 27 May 1964.

65  Rajiv Gandhi was a student in England, or the task would have fallen to him as the older grandson. I am grateful to Granville Austin, who was working in Delhi, for having shared with me his eyewitness account of the hours after Nehru's death, which he wrote at the time.

66  See the leader in the *New York Times*, 28 May 1964, entitled 'The heart of a nation', and the signed appreciation by A. M. Rosenthal, metropolitan editor of the paper who had been its correspondent in India for four years.

67  The process of electing Nehru's successor is dealt with in detail in M. Brecher, *Succession In India: A Study in Decision-Making* (OUP, London, 1966), chs 2–4.

# Bibliography

Research for this book has involved numerous sources, but only those cited are listed here.

## 1  UNPUBLISHED PRIMARY SOURCES

*Nehru Memorial Museum and Library, New Delhi*
All India Congress Committee (AICC) Papers.
G. D. Birla Papers.
Bhulabhai Desai Papers.
Amrit Kaur Papers.
T. T. Krishnamachari Papers.
Syed Mahmud Papers.
M. O. Mathai Papers.
B. S. Moonje Papers.
Nehru Papers (being letters between M. and J. Nehru).
J. Nehru Papers pre-1947 (cited as J. Nehru Papers).
J. Nehru Papers post-1947 (three instalments).
M. Nehru Papers.
Vijayalakshmi Pandit Papers.
P. Thakurdas Papers.

*National Archives of India, New Delhi*
Home Political Records.
M. R. Jayakar Papers.
G. S. Khaparde Papers.
Rajendra Prasad Papers.

*Jamia Millia Islamia, Delhi*
M. Ali Papers.

*India Office Library and Records, British Library, London*
Lord Chelmsford Papers, MSS EUR. E. 264.
Lord Halifax Papers, MSS EUR. C. 152 (Halifax was Lord Irwin when he was Viceroy).
Sir M. Hallett papers, MSS EUR. E. 251.

Lord Reading Papers, MSS EUR. E. 238.

Sir T. B. Sapru Papers (these were actually consulted on microfilm in the Australian National University, Canberra).

Sir F. Sykes Papers, MSS EUR. F. 150.

Lord Templewood Papers, MSS Eur. E. 240 (Templewood was Sir Samuel Hoare when he was Secretary of State for India).

*Indian Institute Library, New Bodleian Library, Oxford*

Memoirs of P. D. Martyn, CIE, CBE, BA, ICS (Rtd). (Another copy of this typewritten MS is in the India Office Library and Records.)

*Cambridge University Library*

Lord Hardinge Papers.

*Library of Congress, Washington*

Microfiche collection of declassified State Department documents.


## 2  PUBLISHED PRIMARY SOURCES

*Newspapers*

*New York Times* (1949–64): on microfilm in the Library of Congress, Washington D.C.

Newspaper cuttings held in chronological files in the post-1947 J. Nehru Papers, Nehru Memorial Museum & Library, New Delhi.

*Published Documents, Autobiographies, Memoirs etc.*

Acheson, D., *Present at the Creation: My Years in the State Department*, W. W. Norton, New York, 1969.

Azad, A. K., *India Wins Freedom*, complete edn, Sangam Books, London, 1988.

Bamford, P. C., *Histories of the Non-co-operation and Khilafat Movements*, Government of India Press, Delhi, 1925.

Bose, S. C., *The Indian Struggle 1920–1942*, Asia Publishing House, New York, 1964.

[Bose, S. C., ] *Ten Historic Netaji Documents*, Netaji Research Bureau Presentation, 1972.

Campbell-Johnson, A., *Mission with Mountbatten*, Robert Hale, London, 1951.

*Census of India, 1931, Volume 1 India. Part 1 Report*, Government of India, Delhi, 1933.

Childs, M. W., *Witness to Power*, McGraw Hill, New York, 1975.

Chopra, P. N. (ed.), *Quit India Movement: British Secret Report*, Thompson Press (India), Faridabad, 1976.

*The Civil Disobedience Movement 1930–34*, Government of India, New Delhi, 1936.

*Congress Responsibility for the Disturbances 1942–43*, Government of India, New Delhi, 1943.

*Constitutional Relations between Britain and India. The Transfer of Power, 1942–7*, ed. N. Mansergh, E. W. R. Lumby and P. Moon, 12 vols, HMSO, London, 1970–83.

Galbraith, J. K., *Ambassador's Journal: A Personal Account of the Kennedy Years*, Hamish Hamilton, London, 1969.

Gandhi, M. K., *The Collected Works of Mahatma Gandhi*, Government of India, Delhi, 1958–84.

Gandhi, M. K., *An Autobiography. The Story of my Experiments with Truth* Jonathan Cape, London, 1966: 1st pub. 1927.

Gandhi, M. K., *M. K. Gandhi: Hind Swaraj and Other Writings*, ed. A. J. Parel, CUP, Cambridge, 1997.

Gandhi, S. (ed.) *Freedom's Daughter: Letters between Indira Gandhi and Jawaharlal Nehru 1922–39,* Hodder & Stoughton, London, 1989.

Gandhi, S. (ed.) *Two Alone, Two Together: Letters between Indira Gandhi and Jawaharlal Nehru 1940–1964,* Hodder & Stoughton, London, 1992.

Hutheesing, K., 'My brother – Jawahar', *Asia,* 42, no. 1 (Jan. 1942).

*Lok Sabha Debates.*

Mahmud, S., *A Nationalist Muslim and Indian Politics: Being the Selected Correspondence of the late Dr Syed Mahmud,* ed. V. N. Datta and B. F. Cleghorn, Macmillan, Delhi, 1974.

Mathai, M. O., *Reminiscences of the Nehru Age* Vikas, New Delhi, 1978.

Mathai, M. O., *My Days with Nehru,* Vikas, New Delhi, 1979.

Montagu, E. S., *An Indian Diary,* Heinemann, London, 1930.

Nehru, J., *An Autobiography,* John Lane, London, 1936.

Nehru, J., *A Bunch of Old Letters,* Asia Publishing House, Bombay, 1958.

Nehru, J., *The Discovery of India* (1946), Asia Publishing House, Bombay, 1960.

Nehru, J., *Letters to Chief Ministers 1947–1964,* ed. G. Parthasarathi, 5 vols, J. Nehru Memorial Fund, New Delhi, 1985–9.

Nehru, J., *Selected Works of Jawaharlal Nehru,* 1st series, ed. S. Gopal, Orient Longman, New Delhi, 1972–82

Nehru, J., *Selected Works of Jawaharlal Nehru,* 2nd Series, ed. S. Gopal, R. Kumar and H. Y. S. Prasad, Jawaharlal Nehru Memorial Fund, New Delhi, in process of publication, 1984–.

Nehru, M., *Selected Works of Motilal Nehru,* ed. R. Kumar and D. Panigrahi, 7 vols, Vikas, New Delhi, 1982–98.

Pandit, V. L., *The Scope of Happiness: A Personal Memoir,* Weidenfeld & Nicolson, London, 1979.

Pant, G. B., *Selected Works of Govind Ballabh Pant,* ed. B. R. Nanda, OUP, New Delhi, in process of publication, 1993–.

Patel, V., *Sardar Patel's Correspondence 1945–50,* ed. D. Das, Navajivan, Ahmedabad, 1971–4.

Philips, C. H., *The Evolution of India and Pakistan 1858 to 1947: Select Documents,* OUP, London, 1962.

Prasad, R., *Dr Rajendra Prasad: Correspondence and Select Documents,* ed. V. Choudhary, 21 vols, Allied Publishers, New Delhi, 1984–95.

Sastri, V. S. S., *Letters of the Right Honourable V. S. Srinivasa Sastri,* ed. T. N. Jagadisan, 2nd edn, Asia Publishing House, Bombay, 1963.

*Statement exhibiting the moral and material progress and condition of India during the year 1889–90,* HMSO, London, 1891.

*Status of Women in India: A Synopsis of the Report of the National Committee on the Status of Women (1971–74),* Indian Council of Social Science Research, New Delhi, n.d.

Wavell, Lord, *Wavell: The Viceroy's Journal,* ed. P. Moon, OUP, London, 1973.

## 3  SECONDARY SOURCES

Agarwal, B., 'Widows versus daughters or widows as daughters? Property, land, and economic security in rural India', *Modern Asian Studies,* 32 (part 1) (Feb. 1998), pp. 1–48.

Amin, S., *Event, Metaphor, Memory: Chauri Chaura, 1922–1992,* University of California Press, Berkeley, 1995.

Austin, G., *The Indian Constitution: Cornerstone of a Nation* (1966), OUP, Bombay, 1972.

Austin, G., *Working a Democratic Constitution: The Indian Experience,* OUP, New Delhi, 1999.

Baker, C. J., *The Politics of South India 1920–1937* CUP, Cambridge, 1976.

Banerjee, M., *The Pathan Unarmed: Opposition and Memory in the North West Frontier*, OUP, Oxford, 2000.

Bayly, C. A., *The Local Roots of Indian Politics: Allahabad 1880–1920*, Clarendon Press, Oxford, 1975.

Bayly, S., *Caste, Society and Politics in India from the Eighteenth Century to the Modern Age*, CUP, Cambridge, 1999.

Baxi, U. and Parekh, B. (eds), *Crisis and Change in Contemporary India*, Sage, London, 1995.

Borthwick M., *The Changing Role of Women in Bengal, 1845–1905*, Princeton University Press, Princeton, 1985.

Brass, P. R., *Factional Politics in an Indian State: The Congress Party in Uttar Pradesh*, University of California Press, Berkeley, 1965.

Brass, P. R, *The Politics of India since Independence*, CUP, Cambridge, 1990.

Brecher, M., *Nehru: A Political Biography*, OUP, London, 1959.

Brecher, M., *Succession in India: A Study in Decision-Making*, OUP, London, 1966.

Brecher, M., *India and World Politics: Krishna Menon's View of the World*, OUP, London, 1968.

Brown, Judith M. and Louis, Wm. Roger (eds), *The Oxford History of the British Empire, Volume IV: The Twentieth Century*, OUP, Oxford, 1999.

Brown, Judith M., *Gandhi's Rise to Power: Indian Politics 1915–1922*, CUP, Cambridge, 1972.

Brown, Judith M., *Gandhi and Civil Disobedience: The Mahatma in Indian Politics 1928–34*, CUP, Cambridge, 1977.

Brown, Judith M., *Gandhi: Prisoner of Hope*, Yale University Press, New Haven and London, 1989.

Brown, Judith M., *Modern India: The Origins of an Asian Democracy*, 2nd edn, OUP, Oxford, 1994.

Brown, Judith M., *Nehru*, Longman, London, 1999.

Cassen, R. H., *India: Population, Economy, Society*, Macmillan, London, 1978.

Chandarvarkar, R., *The Origins of Industrial Capitalism in India: Business Strategies and the Working Classes in Bombay, 1900–1940*, CUP, Cambridge, 1994.

Clarke, P., *The Cripps Version: The Life of Sir Stafford Cripps 1889–1952*, Penguin Press, London, 2002.

Copland, I., *The Princes of India in the Endgame of Empire, 1917–1947*, CUP, Cambridge, 1997.

Copland, I., 'The Master and the Maharajas: the Sikh princes and the East Punjab massacres of 1947', *Modern Asian Studies*, 36 (part 3) (July 2002), pp. 657–704.

Das, S., *Kashmir and Sindh: Nation-Building, Ethnicity and Regional Politics in South Asia*, Anthem Press, London, 2001.

Dasgupta, C., *War and Diplomacy in Kashmir 1947–48*, Sage, London, 2002.

Dear, I. C. B. and Foot, M. R. D. (eds), *The Oxford Companion to the Second World War*, OUP, Oxford, 1995.

Dube, S. C. (ed.), *India since Independence: Social Report on India 1947–1972*, Vikas, New Delhi, 1977.

Erdman, H. L., *The Swatantra Party and Indian Conservatism*, CUP, Cambridge, 1967.

Forbes, G., *Women in Modern India*, CUP, Cambridge, 1996.

Frank, K., *Indira: The Life of Indira Gandhi Nehru*, HarperCollins, London, 2001.

Frankel, F. R., *India's Political Economy, 1947–1977: The Gradual Revolution*, Princeton University Press, Princeton, 1978.

Frykenberg, R. E. (ed.), *Land Control and Social Structure in Indian History*, University of Wisconsin Press, Madison, 1969.

George, T. J. S., *Krishna Menon: A Biography*, Jonathan Cape, London, 1964.

Gopal, S., *The Viceroyalty of Lord Irwin 1926–1931*, Clarendon Press, Oxford, 1957.

Gopal, S., *Jawaharlal Nehru*, 3 vols, Jonathan Cape, London, 1973–84.

Gopal, S. (ed.), *Anatomy of a Confrontation: The Babri Masjid-Ramjanmabhumi Issue*, Penguin, New Delhi, 1990.

Gould, H. A. and Ganguly, S. (eds), *The Hope and the Reality: US–Indian Relations from Roosevelt to Reagan*, Westview Press, Boulder, 1992.

Gould, W., 'Congress radicals and Hindu militancy: Sampurnanand and Purushottam Das Tandon in the politics of the United Provinces, 1930–1947', *Modern Asian Studies*, 36 (part 3) (July 2002), pp. 619–55.

Guha, R., *Savaging the Civilized: Verrier Elwin, his Tribes, and India*, OUP, New Delhi, 1999.

Guha, R. (ed.), *Subaltern Studies 1: Writings on South Asian History and Society*, OUP, Delhi, 1982.

Hanson, A. H. and Douglas, J., *India's Democracy*, Weidenfeld & Nicolson, London, 1972.

Hardgrave Jr, R. L., *India: Government and Politics in a Developing Nation*, 3rd edn, Harcourt Brace Jovanovich, New York, 1980.

Hardy, P., *The Muslims of British India*, CUP, Cambridge, 1972.

Hasan, M. (ed.), *India's Partition: Process, Strategy and Mobilization*, OUP, New Delhi, 1993.

Hasan, M. (ed.), *Inventing Boundaries: Gender, Politics and the Partition of India*, OUP, New Delhi, 2000.

Hasan, M., *Legacy of a Divided Nation: India's Muslims since Independence*, OUP, New Delhi, 2001.

Heimsath, C. H., *Indian Nationalism and Hindu Social Reform*, Princeton University Press, Princeton, 1964.

Hobsbawm, E. and Ranger, T. (eds), *The Invention of Tradition*, CUP, Cambridge, 1983.

Hutchins, F. G., *India's Revolution: Gandhi and the Quit India Movement*, Harvard University Press, Cambridge, Mass., 1973.

Israel, M. (ed.), *Nehru and the Twentieth Century*, South Asian Studies Papers, 4, University of Toronto, Toronto, 1991.

Jalal, A., *The Sole Spokesman: Jinnah, the Muslim League and the Demand for Pakistan*, CUP, Cambridge, 1985.

Jannuzi, F. T., *Agrarian Crisis in India: The Case of Bihar*, University of Texas Press, Austin, 1974.

Jeffrey, R., 'Jawaharlal Nehru and the smoking gun: who pulled the trigger on Kerala's communist government in 1959?', *Journal of Commonwealth and Comparative Politics*, 29, no. 1 (Mar. 1991), pp. 72–85.

Jeffrey, R. (ed.), *People, Princes and Paramount Power: Society and Politics in the Indian Princely States*, OUP, Delhi, 1978.

Jones, K. W., *Socio-religious Reform Movements in British India*, CUP, Cambridge, 1989.

Kalhan, P., *Kamala Nehru* (1973), NIB Publishers, New Delhi, 1990.

Khilnani, S., *The Idea of India* (1997), Farrar Strauss Giroux, New York, 1998.

King, R. D., *Nehru and the Language Politics of India*, OUP, Delhi, 1997.

Kochanek, S. A., *The Congress Party of India: The Dynamics of One-Party Democracy*, Princeton University Press, Princeton, 1968.

Kumar, D. and Desai, M. (eds), *The Cambridge Economic History of India, Volume 2: c.1757–c. 1970*, CUP, Cambridge, 1983.

Kumar, R., *Essays on Gandhian Politics: The Rowlatt Satyagraha of 1919*, Clarendon Press, Oxford, 1971.

Kuppuswamy, B., *Population and Society in India*, Popular Prakashan, Bombay, 1975.

Lago, M., *"India's Prisoner": A Biography of Edward John Thompson, 1886–1946*, University of Missouri Press, Columbia, 2001.

Lamb, A., *Incomplete Partition: The Genesis of the Kashmir Dispute 1947–1948*, Roxford Books, Hertingfordbury, 1992.

Lamb, A., *Birth of a Tragedy: Kashmir 1947*, Roxford Books, Hertingfordbury, 1994.

Louis, Wm. R., *In the Name of God, Go! Leo Amery and the British Empire in the Age of Churchill*, W. W. Norton, New York, 1992.

Low, D. A., *Britain and Indian Nationalism. The Imprint of Ambiguity 1929–1942*, CUP, Cambridge, 1997.

Low, D. A. (ed.), *Congress and the Raj: Facets of the Indian Struggle 1917–47*, Heinemann, London, 1977.

McLane, J. R., *Indian Nationalism and the Early Congress*, Princeton University Press, Princeton, 1977.

Mahar, J. M. (ed.), *The Untouchables in Contemporary India*, University of Arizona Press, Tucson, 1972.

Manor, J. (ed.), *Nehru to the Nineties: The Changing Office of Prime Minister in India*, Hurst, London, 1994.

Masselos, J. (ed.), *Struggling and Ruling: The Indian National Congress 1885–1985*, Oriental University Press, London, 1987.

Maxwell, N., *India's China War* (1970), Pelican edn with postscript, Penguin, Harmondsworth, 1972.

Menon, V. P., *The Story of the Integration of the Indian States* (1956), Orient Longmans, Madras, 1961.

Metcalf, T. R., *Ideologies of the Raj*, CUP, Cambridge, 1994.

Minault, G., *Secluded Scholars: Women's Education and Muslim Social Reform in Colonial India*, OUP, Delhi, 1998.

Misra, M., *Business, Race, and Politics in British India c. 1850–1960*, Clarendon Press, Oxford, 1999.

Moon P., *Divide and Quit*, University of California Press, Berkeley, 1962.

Moore, R. J., *The Crisis Of Indian Unity 1917–1940*, Clarendon Press, Oxford, 1974.

Moore, R. J., *Churchill, Cripps and India, 1939–1945*, Clarendon Press, Oxford, 1979.

Moore, R. J., *Escape from Empire: The Attlee Government and the Indian Problem*, Clarendon Press, Oxford, 1983.

Moore, R. J., *Making the New Commonwealth*, Clarendon Press, Oxford, 1987.

Morgan, J., *Edwina Mountbatten: A Life of Her Own*, HarperCollins, London, 1991.

Morris, M. D., *The Emergence of an Industrial Labor Force in India: A Study of the Bombay Cotton Mills, 1854–1947*, OUP, Bombay, 1965.

Nanda, B. R., *The Nehrus: Motilal and Jawaharlal*, George Allen & Unwin, London, 1962.

Nanda, B. R., *Jawaharlal Nehru: Rebel and Statesman*, OUP, New Delhi, 1995.

Nanda, B. R. (ed.), *Socialism in India*, Vikas, Delhi, 1972.

Nanda, B. R. (ed.), *Indian Women: From Purdah to Modernity*, Sangam Books, London, 1990.

Newell, R. S., 'Ideology and realities: land redistribution in Uttar Pradesh', *Pacific Affairs*, 45, no. 2 (1972), pp. 220–39.

Nossiter, T. J., *Communism In Kerala: A Study in Political Adaptation*, C. Hurst, London, 1982.

Ostergaard, G. and Currell, M., *The Gentle Anarchists: A Study of the Leaders of the Sarvodaya Movement for Non-violent Revolution in India*, Clarendon Press, Oxford, 1971.

Pandey, G., *Remembering Partition: Violence, Nationalism and History in India*, CUP, Cambridge, 2001.

Parekh, B., *Gandhi's Political Philosophy: A Critical Examination*, Macmillan, London, 1989.

Parekh, B., *Colonialism, Tradition and Reform: An Analysis of Gandhi's Political Discourse*, rev. edn, Sage, London, 1999.

Potter, D. C., *India's Political Administrators 1919–1983*, Clarendon Press, Oxford, 1986.

Ray, B. and Basu, A. (eds), *From Independence towards Freedom: Indian Women since 1947*, OUP, New Delhi, 1999.

Raychaudhuri, T., *Europe Reconsidered: Perceptions of the West in Nineteenth Century Bengal*, OUP, Delhi, 1988.

Raychaudhuri, T., *Perceptions, Emotions, Sensibilities: Essays on India's Colonial and Post-colonial Experiences*, OUP, New Delhi, 1999.

Reeves, P., *Landlords and Governments in Uttar Pradesh: A Study of their Relations until Zamindari Abolition*, OUP, Bombay, 1991.

Rittenberg, S., *Ethnicity, Nationalism and the Pakhtuns: The Independence Movement in Indian North-West Frontier Province*, Carolina Academic Press, Durham, 1988.

Robinson, F., *Separatism among Indian Muslims: The Politics of the United Provinces' Muslims 1860–1923*, CUP, Cambridge, 1974.

Rotter, A. J., *Comrades at Odds: The United States and India, 1947–1964*, Cornell University Press, Ithaca, 2000.

Roy, A., 'The high politics of India's partition: the revisionist perspective', *Modern Asian Studies*, 24 (part 2) ( May 1990), pp. 385–415; repr. as ch. 6 of Hasan, *India's Partition*.

Singh, T., *India's Development Experience*, Macmillan India, Delhi, 1974.

Sisson, R. and Wolpert, S. (eds), *Congress and Indian Nationalism: The Pre-independence Phase*, University of California Press, Berkeley, 1988.

Som, R., 'Jawaharlal Nehru and the Hindu Code: a victory of symbol over substance?', *Modern Asian Studies*, 28 (part 1) (Feb. 1994), pp. 165–94.

Talbot, I., *Provincial Politics and the Pakistan Movement: The Growth of the Muslim League in North-West and North-East India 1937–47*, OUP, Karachi, 1988.

Talbot, I., *Freedom's Cry: The Popular Dimension in the Pakistan Movement and Partition Experience in North-West India*, OUP, Karachi, 1996.

Tan, T. Y. and Kudaisya, G., *The Aftermath of Partition in South Asia*, Routledge, London, 2000.

Tomlinson, B. R., *The Indian National Congress and the Raj, 1929–1942: The Penultimate Phase*, Macmillan, London, 1976.

Tomlinson, B. R., *The Economy of Modern India, 1860–1970*, CUP, Cambridge, 1993.

Weiner, M., *The Politics of Scarcity: Public Pressure and Political Response in India*, University of Chicago Press, Chicago, 1962.

Weiner, M., *Party Building in a New Nation: The Indian National Congress*, University of Chicago Press, Chicago, 1967.

Whiting, A. S., *The Chinese Calculus of Deterrence: India and Indonesia*, University of Michigan Press, Ann Arbor, 1975.

Wolpert, S., *Morley and India 1906–1910*, University of California Press, Berkeley, 1967.

Wolpert, S., *Nehru: A Tryst with Destiny*, OUP, New York, 1996.

Yahuda, M., *The International Politics of the Asia-Pacific, 1945–1995*, Routledge, London, 1996.

Ziegler, P., *Mountbatten: The Official Biography*, Collins, Glasgow, 1985.

# Index